Fodor's 99

Hawai'i

The complete guide, thoroughly up-to-date

Packed with details that will make your trip

The must-see sights, off and on the beaten path

What to see, what to skip

Mix-and-match vacation itineraries

City strolls, countryside adventures

Smart lodging and dining options

Essential local do's and taboos

Transportation tips and directions

Key contacts, savvy travel tips

When to go, what to pack

Clear, accurate, easy-to-use maps

Books to read, videos to watch, background essays

Fodor's Travel Publications, Inc.
New York • Toronto • London • Sydney • Auckland
www.fodors.com

Fodor's Hawai'i

EDITOR: Anastasia Redmond Mills

Editorial Contributors: Rob Andrews, David Brown, DeSoto Brown, Jennifer Crites, Gary Diedrichs, Audra Epstein, Betty Fullard-Leo, Pablo Madera, Heidi Sarna, Helayne Schiff, M. T. Schwartzman (Gold Guide editor), Dinah Spritzer, Marty Wentzel

Editorial Production: Linda K. Schmidt, Nicole Revere

Maps: David Lindroth, *cartographer*; Steven K. Amsterdam, *map editor*

Design: Fabrizio La Rocca, *creative director*; Guido Caroti, *associate art director*; Jolie Novak, *photo editor*

Production/Manufacturing: Mike Costa

Cover Photograph: Wayne Levin

Copyright

ISBN 0–679–00126–3

Grateful acknowledgment is made to the following for permission to reprint previously published material: "The Aloha Shirt: A Colorful Swatch of Island History" by DeSoto Brown reprinted from *ALOHA Magazine;* copyright © Davick Publications.

Special Sales

Fodor's Travel Publications are available at special discounts for bulk purchases for sales promotions or premiums. Special editions, including personalized covers, excerpts of existing guides, and corporate imprints, can be created in large quantities for special needs. For more information, contact your local bookseller or write to Special Markets, Fodor's Travel Publications, 201 East 50th Street, New York, NY 10022. Inquiries from Canada should be directed to your local Canadian bookseller or sent to Random House of Canada, Ltd., Marketing Department, 2775 Matheson Boulevard East, Mississauga, Ontario L4W 4P7. Inquiries from the United Kingdom should be sent to Fodor's Travel Publications, 20 Vauxhall Bridge Road, London SW1V 2SA, England.

PRINTED IN THE UNITED STATES OF AMERICA

10 9 8 7 6 5 4 3 2 1

CONTENTS

ON THE ROAD WITH FODOR'S

WHEN I PLAN A VACATION, the first thing I do is cast around among my friends and colleagues to find someone who's just been where I'm going. That's because there's no substitute for a recommendation from a good friend who knows your tastes, your budget, and your circumstances, someone who's just been there. Unfortunately, such friends are few and far between. So it's nice to know that there's Fodor's *Hawai'i '99*.

In the first place, this book won't stay home when you hit the road. It will accompany you every step of the way, steering you away from wrong turns and wrong choices and never expecting a thing in return. It includes a wonderful, full-color map from Rand McNally, the world's largest commercial mapmaker. Most important of all, it's written and assiduously updated by the kind of people you *would* hit up for travel tips if you knew them. They're as choosy as your pickiest friend, except they've probably seen a lot more of Hawai'i. In these pages, they don't send you chasing down every town and sight in the Islands but have instead selected the best ones, the ones that are worthy of your time and money. To make it easy for you to put it all together in the time you have, they've created short, medium, and long itineraries and, in cities, neighborhood walks that you can mix and match in a snap. Just tear out the map at the perforation, and join us on the road in Hawai'i.

About Our Writers

Our success in helping to make your trip the best of all possible vacations is a credit to the hard work of our extraordinary writers.

A 17-year resident of Honolulu, updater of the O'ahu (in which her Close-Up on Hawaiian music appears) and Lāna'i chapters, **Marty Wentzel** is a prolific freelance writer whose articles have appeared in publications around the world, including *American Way, Modern Bride,* and *ALOHA Magazine.* A specialist in the Hawai'i dining scene, she has coauthored cookbooks with two of the state's top chefs—Sam Choy and Roy Yamaguchi—but she's equally happy eating fresh mango on the beach at sunset. Her toddler daughter, who has already visited every Hawaiian island, is sure to lead the next generation of Fodor's writers.

Betty Fullard-Leo, a resident of the Islands since 1962, writes extensively about destinations, lifestyle, art, food, and culture in the Aloha State. Her work on Fodor's *Hawai'i* over the years has been invaluable; this year she was responsible for the Big Island (where her Close-Up on hula appears), Kaua'i, and Moloka'i chapters. She's a contributing food editor for *Hawai'i* magazine, and previously she was editor of *Pacific Art & Travel* and associate editor of *ALOHA Magazine.* Betty and her husband, Ainsley, are valued members of the Hawai'i community and are out and about the Islands frequently.

Pablo Madera, our Maui updater, is a freelance journalist, jazz drummer, and ethnobotanist who has made Maui his home base for 25 years. When he's not pursuing research projects on various Pacific islands, he tries to keep up with banana production on his small farm, which is off the road to Hāna.

Jennifer Crites, a freelance journalist who's lived in Honolulu for 23 years, applied her knowledge gained from being a *Hollywood Reporter* correspondent to writing about movies filmed in Hawai'i in the Books and Videos section in the Portraits chapter. Jennifer also wrote about the state's fascinating flora and fauna in a Close-Up for the Maui chapter and the native peoples' unique mythology for the Kaua'i chapter.

Editor **Anastasia Mills** had previously been to 49 of the United States, so her first trip to Hawai'i while researching this book was extra special for her, as she now has visited all of the states. Some say she saved the best for last, and Stasha is not going to put up a fight about that. She spent a week on Kaua'i and found it to be paradise; most striking to her were the miles and miles of beautiful, empty beaches. She would like to start a letter-writing campaign to convince Alan Wong (of Alan Wong's in Honolulu) to open a restaurant in New York City.

Fodor's wishes to extend a heartfelt mahalo to the wonderful writers who made this book the best it could be, and to Julie Applebaum at McNeil Wilson Communications, Hawaiian Hotels and Resorts, Princeville Hotel, Halekulani, and the many other people and organizations that have helped us gather information for this edition.

Connections

We're pleased that the American Society of Travel Agents continues to endorse Fodor's as its guidebook of choice. ASTA is the world's largest and most influential travel trade association, operating in more than 170 countries, with 27,000 members pledged to adhere to a strict code of ethics reflecting the Society's motto, "Integrity in Travel." ASTA shares Fodor's devotion to providing smart, honest travel information and advice to travelers, and we've long recommended that our readers—even those who have guidebooks and traveling friends—consult ASTA member agents for the experience and professionalism they bring to your vacation planning.

On Fodor's Web site (www.fodors.com), check out the new Resource Center, an online companion to the Gold Guide chapter of this book, complete with useful hot links to related sites. In our forums, you can also get lively advice from other travelers and more great tips from Fodor's experts worldwide.

How to Use This Book

Organization

Up front is the **Gold Guide,** an easy-to-use section arranged alphabetically by topic. Under each listing you'll find tips and information that will help you accomplish what you need to in Hawai'i. You'll also find addresses and telephone numbers of organizations and companies that offer destination-related services and detailed information and publications.

The first chapter in the guide, Destination: Hawai'i, helps get you in the mood for your trip. New and Noteworthy cues you in on trends and happenings, What's Where gets you oriented, Pleasures and Pastimes describes the activities and sights that

make Hawai'i unique, Great Itineraries lays out a selection of complete trips, Fodor's Choice showcases our top picks, and Festivals and Seasonal Events alerts you to special events you'll want to seek out.

Chapters in *Hawai'i '99* are arranged by island, with the most visited island (O'ahu) appearing first, the least (Lāna'i) last. Each chapter covers subjects in alphabetical order (exploring, beaches, dining, lodging, nightlife and the arts, outdoor activities and sports, and shopping) and ends with a section called A to Z, which covers getting there and getting around. It also provides helpful contacts and resources.

To help you decide what to visit in the time you have, all chapters begin with our recommended itineraries. The Exploring section is subdivided by city or region; each subsection recommends a walking or driving tour and lists sights alphabetically, including sights that are off the beaten path.

At the end of the book you'll find Portraits, wonderful essays about the Islands' fascinating geological history and the amusing origins of the aloha shirt. Following these is Hawaiian History at a Glance—a great way to take in the richness of these Islands' political and cultural development at one sitting. The Books and Videos section offers suggestions for pretrip research, from recommended reading and audiotapes to movies on tape with Hawai'i as a backdrop. A brief introduction to the Hawaiian language follows, along with a glossary of common terms and menu items—familiarity with this might brighten your waiter's day in Waikīkī or Waimea.

Icons and Symbols

★   Our special recommendations
✕   Restaurant
🏠   Lodging establishment
🐣   Good for kids (rubber duck)
☞   Sends you to another section of the guide for more information
✉   Address
☎   Telephone number
☉   Opening and closing times
💳   Admission prices (those we give apply to adults; substantially reduced fees are almost always available for children, students, and senior citizens)

Numbers in white and black circles ③ ❸ that appear on the maps, in the margins, and within the tours correspond to one another.

Dining and Lodging

The restaurants and lodgings we list are the cream of the crop in each price range. Price categories are as follows:

For restaurants:

CATEGORY	COST*
$$$$	over $60
$$$	$40–$60
$$	$20–$40
$	under $20

*per person for a three-course meal, excluding drinks, service, and 4.17% sales tax

For hotels:

CATEGORY	COST*
$$$$	over $200
$$$	$125–$200
$$	$75–$125
$	under $75

*All prices are for a standard double room, excluding 11.41% tax and service charges.

Hotel Facilities

We always list the facilities that are available—but we don't specify whether you'll be charged extra to use them: When pricing accommodations, always ask what's included. In addition, assume that all rooms have private baths unless noted otherwise. In addition, when you book a room, be sure to mention if you have a disability or are traveling with children, if you prefer a private bath or a certain type of bed, or if you have specific dietary needs or other concerns. The prevalent word lānai indicates a usually covered outdoor area that may be private or part of a public walkway.

Assume that hotels operate on the **European Plan** (EP, with no meals) unless we specify that they use the **Continental Plan** (CP, with a Continental breakfast daily), **Modified American Plan** (MAP, with breakfast and dinner daily), or the **Full American Plan** (FAP, with all meals). A full breakfast includes a hot entrée.

Restaurant Reservations and Dress Codes

Reservations are always a good idea; we mention them only when they're essential or are not accepted. Book as far ahead as you can, and reconfirm as soon as you arrive. Unless otherwise noted, the restaurants listed are open daily for lunch and dinner. We mention dress only when men are required to wear a jacket or a jacket and tie. Look for an overview of local dining-out habits in the Gold Guide.

Credit Cards

The following abbreviations are used: **AE,** American Express; **D,** Discover; **DC,** Diners Club; **MC,** MasterCard; and **V,** Visa.

Don't Forget to Write

You can use this book in the confidence that all prices and opening times are based on information supplied to us at press time; Fodor's cannot accept responsibility for any errors. Time inevitably brings changes, so always confirm information when it matters—especially if you're making a detour to visit a specific place.

Were the restaurants we recommended as described? Did our hotel picks exceed your expectations? Did you find a museum we recommended a waste of time? Keeping a travel guide fresh and up-to-date is a big job, and we welcome your feedback, positive *and* negative. If you have complaints, we'll look into them and revise our entries when the facts warrant it. If you've discovered a special place that we haven't included, we'll pass the information along to our correspondents and have them check it out. So send us your thoughts via e-mail at editors@fodors.com (specifying the name of the book on the subject line) or on paper in care of the Hawai'i editor at Fodor's, 201 East 50th Street, New York, New York 10022. In the meantime, have a wonderful trip!

Karen Cure

Karen Cure
Editorial Director

The Hawaiian Islands

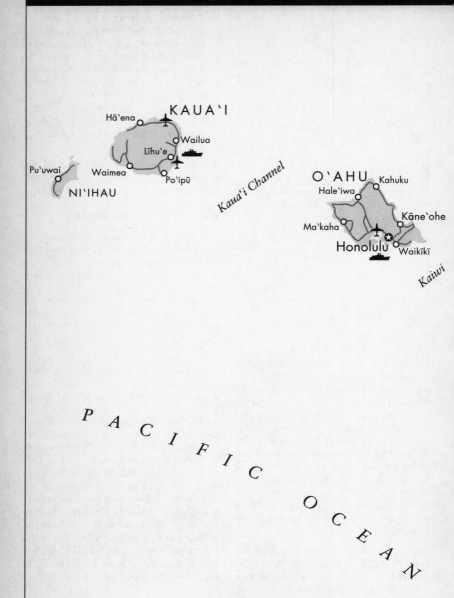

KAUA'I

Hā'ena

Wailua

Līhu'e

Waimea

Po'ipū

Pu'uwai

NI'IHAU

Kaua'i Channel

O'AHU

Kahuku

Hale'iwa

Kāne'ohe

Ma'kaha

Honolulu

Waikīkī

Kaiwi

PACIFIC OCEAN

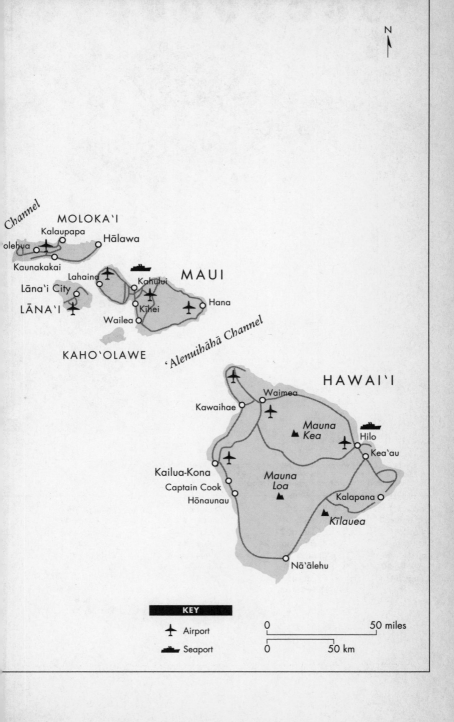

N

Channel

MOLOKA'I

Kalaupapa   Hālawa

olehua

Kaunakakai

Lahaina   Kahului   MAUI

Lāna'i City

LĀNA'I   Kīhei   Hana

Wailea

KAHO'OLAWE   _'Alenuihāhā Channel_

HAWAI'I

Waimea

Kawaihae   _Mauna Kea_   Hilo

Kea'au

Kailua-Kona   _Mauna Loa_

Captain Cook   Kalapana

Hōnaunau   _Kīlauea_

Nā'ālehu

KEY

✈ Airport

⛴ Seaport

0   50 miles

0   50 km

x

World Time Zones

Numbers below vertical bands relate each zone to Greenwich Mean Time (0 hrs.).
Local times frequently differ from these general indications,
as indicated by light-face numbers on map.

Algiers, **29**	Berlin, **34**	Delhi, **48**	Istanbul, **40**
Anchorage, **3**	Bogotá, **19**	Denver, **8**	Jerusalem, **42**
Athens, **41**	Budapest, **37**	Djakarta, **53**	Johannesburg, **44**
Auckland, **1**	Buenos Aires, **24**	Dublin, **26**	Lima, **20**
Baghdad, **46**	Caracas, **22**	Edmonton, **7**	Lisbon, **28**
Bangkok, **50**	Chicago, **9**	Hong Kong, **56**	London
Beijing, **54**	Copenhagen, **33**	Honolulu, **2**	(Greenwich), **27**
	Dallas, **10**		Los Angeles, **6**
			Madrid, **38**
			Manila, **57**

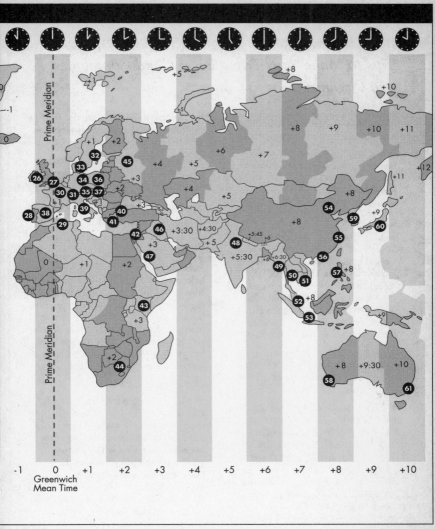

SMART TRAVEL TIPS A TO Z

Basic Information on Traveling in Hawai'i, Savvy Tips to Make Your Trip a Breeze, and Companies and Organizations to Contact

AIR TRAVEL

BOOKING YOUR FLIGHT

When you book, **look for nonstop flights** and **remember that "direct" flights stop at least once.** Try to **avoid connecting flights,** which require a change of plane.

CARRIERS

➤ MAJOR AIRLINES: **American** (☎ 800/433–7300) to Honolulu, Maui. **Continental** (☎ 800/525–0280) to Honolulu, Kaua'i. **Delta** (☎ 800/221–1212) to Honolulu, Maui. **Northwest** (☎ 800/225–2525) to Honolulu. **TWA** (☎ 800/221–2000) to Honolulu. **United** (☎ 800/241–6522) to Honolulu, Maui, Big Island, Kaua'i.

➤ SMALLER AIRLINES: **Hawaiian Airlines** (☎ 800/367–5320) to Honolulu and connecting flights to Neighbor Islands.

➤ FROM THE U.K.: **Air New Zealand** (☎ 0181/741–2299). **American** (☎ 0345/789–789). **Continental** (☎ 0800/776–464). **Delta** (☎ 0800/414–767). **United** (☎ 0800/888–555). All flights require a change of planes on the West Coast. **Trailfinders** (✉ 42–50 Earls Court Rd., Kensington, London, W8 6FT, ☎ 0171/937–5400) can arrange bargain flights.

➤ WITHIN HAWAI'I: The following carriers provide interisland service: **Aloha Airlines** (☎ 800/367–5250), **Hawaiian Airlines** (☎ 800/367–5320), **Island Air** (☎ 800/323–3345), **Trans Air** (☎ 800/634–2094).

CONSOLIDATORS

Consolidators buy tickets for scheduled international flights at reduced rates from the airlines, then sell them at prices that beat the best fare available directly from the airlines, usually without restrictions. Sometimes you can even get your money back if you need to return the ticket. Carefully read the fine print detailing penalties for changes and cancellations, and **confirm your consolidator reservation with the airline.**

➤ CONSOLIDATORS: **Cheap Tickets** (☎ 800/377–1000). **Up & Away Travel** (☎ 212/889–2345). **Discount Travel Network** (☎ 800/576–1600). **Unitravel** (☎ 800/325–2222). **World Travel Network** (☎ 800/409–6753).

COURIERS

When you fly as a courier, you trade your checked-luggage space for a ticket deeply subsidized by a courier service. It's all perfectly legitimate, but there are restrictions: You can usually book your flight only a week or two in advance, your length of stay may be set for a certain number of days, and you probably won't be able to book a companion on the same flight.

CUTTING COSTS

The least-expensive airfares to Hawai'i are priced for round-trip travel and usually must be purchased in advance. It's smart to **call a number of airlines, and when you are quoted a good price, reserve it or book it on the spot**—the same fare may not be available the next day. Airlines generally allow you to change your return date for a fee. If you don't use your ticket, you can apply the cost toward the purchase of a new ticket, again for a small charge. However, most low-fare tickets are nonrefundable. To get the lowest airfare, **check different routings.** Compare prices of flights to and from different airports if your destination or home city has more than one gateway. Also price off-peak flights, which may be significantly less expensive. If you're traveling a great distance, try pricing two round-trip tickets, say New York–LA and LA–Honolulu.

When flying within the U.S., **plan to stay over a Saturday night** and **travel**

during the middle of the week to get
the lowest fare. These low fares are
usually priced for round-trip travel
and are nonrefundable. You can,
however, change your return date for
a fee ($75 on most major airlines).

Travel agents, especially those who
specialize in finding the lowest fares
(☞ Discounts & Deals, *below*), can
be especially helpful when booking a
plane ticket. When you're quoted a
price, **ask your agent if the price is
likely to get any lower.** Good agents
know the seasonal fluctuations of
airfares and can usually anticipate a
sale or fare war. However, waiting
can be risky: The fare could go *up* as
seats become scarce, and you may
wait so long that your preferred flight
sells out. A wait-and-see strategy
works best if your plans are flexible.
If you must arrive and depart on
certain dates, don't delay.

CHECK IN & BOARDING

Airlines routinely overbook planes,
assuming that not everyone with a
ticket will show up, but sometimes
everyone does. When that happens,
airlines ask for volunteers to give up
their seats. In return these volunteers
usually get a certificate for a free
flight and are rebooked on the next
flight out. If there are not enough
volunteers, the airline must choose
who will be denied boarding. The
first to get bumped are passengers
who checked in late and those flying
on discounted tickets, so **get to the
gate and check in as early as possible,** especially during peak periods.

Although the trend on international
flights is to drop reconfirmation
requirements, many airlines still ask
you to reconfirm each leg of your
international itinerary. Failure to do
so may result in your reservation
being canceled.

Always **bring a government-issued
photo ID to the airport.** You may be
asked to show it before you are
allowed to check in.

ENJOYING THE FLIGHT

For better service, **fly smaller or
regional carriers,** which often have
higher passenger-satisfaction ratings.
Sometimes you'll find leather seats,
more legroom, and better food.

For more legroom, **request an emer-
gency-aisle seat.** Be aware that seats
in the row in front of the emergency
aisle or in front of a bulkhead may
not recline.

If you don't like airline food, **ask for
special meals when booking.** These
can be vegetarian, low-cholesterol, or
kosher, for example.

FLYING TIMES

Flying time is about 10 hours from
New York, 6 hours from Chicago,
and 3 hours from Los Angeles.

HOW TO COMPLAIN

If your baggage goes astray or your
flight goes awry, complain right away.
Most carriers require that you **file a
claim immediately.**

➤ AIRLINE COMPLAINTS: U.S. Depart-
ment of Transportation **Aviation
Consumer Protection Division** (✉
C-75, Room 4107, Washington, DC
20590, ☎ 202/366–2220). **Federal
Aviation Administration Consumer
Hotline** (☎ 800/322–7873).

AIRPORTS

Hawai'i's major airport is **Honolulu
International**, in O'ahu, about a 20-
minute drive from Waikīkī. If you're
flying from Honolulu to another
island, you'll need to locate one of the
two separate interisland terminals
(one for Aloha Airlines and Hawaiian
Airlines, and one for Island Air and
Trans Air) before reaching the main
terminal as you enter. A free Wiki
Wiki Shuttle will take you to and
from the interisland terminals.

Maui has two major airports: **Kahului
Airport,** in the island's central town of
Kahului, and **Kapalua-West Maui
Airport.** For visitors to West Maui, the
easiest arrival point is the Kapalua
facility; it saves about an hour's drive
from the Kahului airport. The tiny
town of **Hāna** in east Maui also has
an airstrip, but it is only serviced by
one commuter airline.

On Kaua'i, visitors fly into **Līhu'e
Airport,** on the east side of the island.
Princeville Airport, a landing strip
north of Līhu'e, is served by one
interisland carrier.

Those flying to the Big Island of
Hawai'i regularly land at one of two

fields. Kona's **Kona International Airport,** on the west side, best serves Kailua-Kona, Keauhou, and the Kohala Coast. **Hilo International Airport** is more appropriate for those going to the east side. One O'ahu-based airline has regular flights into **Waimea-Kohala Airport,** called Kamuela Airport by residents, who use it when commuting between islands.

Moloka'i's **Ho'olehua Airport** is small and centrally located, as is **Lāna'i Airport** on that island. Both rural airports handle a limited number of flights per day. Visitors to these islands must first stop in O'ahu and change to an interisland flight.

➤ AIRPORT INFORMATION: O'ahu: **Honolulu International** (☎ 808/836–6413). Maui: **Kahului Airport** (☎ 808/872–3830 or 808/872–3894), **Kapalua-West Maui Airport** (☎ 808/669–0623), **Hāna Airport** (☎ 808/248–8208). The Big Island of Hawai'i: **Kona International Airport** (☎ 808/329–2484; 808/329–3423 for visitor information), **Hilo International Airport** (☎ 808/934–5801), **Waimea-Kohala Airport** (☎ 808/885–4520). Kaua'i: **Līhu'e Airport** (☎ 808/246–1400), **Princeville Airport** (☎ 808/826–7969). Moloka'i: **Ho'olehua Airport** (☎ 808/567–6140). Lāna'i: **Lāna'i Airport** (☎ 808/565–6757).

CAMERAS & COMPUTERS

EQUIPMENT PRECAUTIONS

Always **keep your film, tape, and computer disks out of the sun.** Carry an extra supply of batteries, and **be prepared to turn on your camera, camcorder, or laptop** to prove to security personnel that the device is real. Always **ask for hand inspection of film,** which becomes clouded after successive exposure to airport X-ray machines, and **keep videotapes and computer disks away from metal detectors.**

TRAVEL PHOTOGRAPHY

➤ PHOTO HELP: Kodak Information Center (☎ 800/242–2424). *Kodak Guide to Shooting Great Travel Pictures,* available in bookstores or from Fodor's Travel Publications (☎ 800/533–6478; $16.50 plus $4 shipping).

CAR RENTAL

You can find yourself driving anything from a $26-a-day econobox to a $1,100-a-day Ferrari. It's wise to make reservations in advance. Rates in Honolulu begin at $28 a day and $144 a week for an economy car with air conditioning, an automatic transmission, and with unlimited mileage. Rates in Maui begin at $26 a day and $144 a week. This does not include tax on car rentals, which is 4.16%, or a $2-per-day road tax.

➤ MAJOR AGENCIES: **Alamo** (☎ 800/327–9633, 0800/272–2000 in the U.K.). **Avis** (☎ 800/331–1212, 800/879–2847 in Canada, 008/225–533 in Australia). **Budget** (☎ 800/527–0700, 0800/181181 in the U.K.). **Dollar** (☎ 800/800–4000; 0990/565656 in the U.K., where it is known as Eurodollar). **Hertz** (☎ 800/654–3131, 800/263–0600 in Canada, 0345/555888 in the U.K., 03/9222–2523 in Australia, 03/358–6777 in New Zealand). **National InterRent** (☎ 800/227–7368; 0345/222525 in the U.K., where it is known as Europcar InterRent).

➤ LOCAL AGENCIES: **Thrifty Car Rental** (☎ 808/973–5188) on O'ahu and Maui, and **VIP Car Rentals** (☎ 808/922–4605) on O'ahu.

CUTTING COSTS

To get the best deal, **book through a travel agent who is willing to shop around.** When pricing cars, **ask about the location of the rental lot.** Some off-airport locations offer lower rates, and their lots are only minutes from the terminal via complimentary shuttle. You also may want to **price local car-rental companies,** whose rates may be lower still, although their service and maintenance may not be as good as those of a name-brand agency. Remember to ask about required deposits and cancellation penalties.

Also **ask your travel agent about a company's customer-service record.** How has the company responded to late plane arrivals and vehicle mishaps? Are there often lines at the rental counter? If you're traveling during a holiday period, does a confirmed reservation guarantee you a car?

Be sure to **look into wholesalers,** companies that do not own fleets but rent in bulk from those that do and often offer better rates than traditional car-rental operations. Prices are best during off-peak periods.

➤ RENTAL WHOLESALERS: **Auto Europe** (☎ 207/842–2000 or 800/223–5555, FAX 800/235–6321). **Kemwel Holiday Autos** (☎ 914/835–5555 or 800/678–0678, FAX 914/835–5126).

INSURANCE

When driving a rented car you are generally responsible for any damage to or loss of the vehicle. You also are liable for any property damage or personal injury that you may cause while driving. Before you rent, **see what coverage you already have** under the terms of your personal auto-insurance policy and credit cards.

For about $15 to $20 per day, rental companies sell protection, known as a collision- or loss-damage waiver (CDW or LDW), that eliminates your liability for damage to the car; it's always optional and should never be automatically added to your bill.

In most states you don't need a CDW if you have personal auto insurance or other liability insurance. However, **make sure you have enough coverage to pay for the car.** If you do not have auto insurance or an umbrella policy that covers damage to third parties, purchasing liability insurance and a CDW or LDW is highly recommended.

REQUIREMENTS

In Hawai'i you must be 21 to rent a car, and rates may be higher if you're under 25. You'll pay extra for child seats (about $3 per day), which are compulsory for children under five, and for additional drivers (about $2 per day). Non-U.S. residents will need a reservation voucher, a passport, a driver's license, and a travel policy that covers each driver, in order to pick up a car.

In Hawai'i your unexpired mainland driver's license is valid for up to 90 days. If you plan to stay in the Islands for extended periods, apply for a Hawai'i driver's license (cost $18) at the State Department of Motor Vehicles office in Honolulu. You'll also have to take a $2 written exam.

CAR TRAVEL

Be sure to **buckle up.** Hawai'i has a strictly enforced seat-belt law for front-seat passengers. Children under three must be in a car seat (available from car-rental agencies). The highway speed limit is usually 55 mph; in-town traffic moves from 25 to 40 mph. Jaywalking is very common, so be particularly watchful for pedestrians, especially in congested areas such as Waikīkī. Unauthorized use of a parking space reserved for persons with disabilities can net you a $150 fine.

It's difficult to get lost in most of Hawai'i. Roads and streets, although they may challenge the visitor's tongue (Kalaniana'ole Highway, for example), are well marked. Keep an eye open for the Hawai'i Visitors and Convention Bureau's red-caped warrior signs that mark major visitor attractions and scenic spots. Ask for a map at the car rental counter; free visitor publications containing good-quality maps can be found on all islands, too.

Asking for directions will almost always produce a helpful explanation from the locals, but you should be prepared for an island term or two. Instead of using compass directions, Hawai'i residents refer to places as being either *mauka* (toward the mountains) or *makai* (toward the ocean) from one another. Other directions depend on your location: in Honolulu, for example, people say to "go Diamond Head," which means toward the famous landmark, or to "go ewa," meaning the opposite direction.

Technically, the Big Island of Hawai'i is the only island you can completely circle by car, but each island offers plenty of sightseeing from its miles of roadways. O'ahu can be circled except for the roadless west-shore area around Ka'ena Point. Elsewhere, major highways follow the shoreline and traverse the island at two points.

Rush-hour traffic (6:30–8:30 AM and 3:30–6 PM) can be frustrating around Honolulu and the outlying areas. Parking along many streets is curtailed during those times, and towing is strictly practiced. Read the curbside parking signs before leaving your vehicle, even at a meter.

Kaua'i has a well-maintained highway running south from Līhu'e to Barking Sands Beach; a spur at Waimea takes you along Waimea Canyon to Koke'e State Park. A northern route also winds its way from Līhu'e to end at Hā'ena, the beginning of the rugged and roadless Nā Pali Coast. Maui also has its share of impenetrable areas, although four-wheel-drive vehicles rarely run into problems on the island. Saddle roads run between the east and west land masses composing Maui; other highways follow the western coasts of East and West Maui. Although Moloka'i and Lāna'i have fewer roadways, car rental is still worthwhile and will allow plenty of interesting sightseeing. Opt for a four-wheel-drive vehicle if dirt-road exploration holds any appeal.

CHILDREN & TRAVEL

CHILDREN IN HAWAI'I

Be sure to plan ahead and **involve your youngsters** as you outline your trip. When packing, include things to keep them busy en route. On sightseeing days try to schedule activities of special interest to your children. If you are renting a car don't forget to **arrange for a car seat** when you reserve.

FLYING

If your children are two or older, **ask about children's airfares.** As a general rule, infants under two not occupying a seat fly at greatly reduced fares or even for free.

In general the adult baggage allowance applies to children paying half or more of the adult fare. When booking, **ask about carry-on allowances for those traveling with infants.** In general, for babies charged 10% of the adult fare you are allowed one carry-on bag and a collapsible stroller, which may have to be checked; you may be limited to less if the flight is full.

Experts agree that it's a good idea to use safety seats aloft for children weighing less than 40 pounds. Airlines, however, can set their own policies: U.S. carriers allow FAA-approved models but usually require that you buy a ticket, even if your child would otherwise ride free, since the seats must be strapped into regular seats. Airline rules vary, so it's important to **check your airline's policy about using safety seats during takeoff and landing.** Safety seats cannot obstruct the movement of other passengers in the row, so get an appropriate seat assignment as early as possible.

When making your reservation, **request children's meals or a freestanding bassinet** if you need them; the latter are available only to those seated at the bulkhead, where there's enough legroom. Remember, however, that bulkhead seats may not have their own overhead bins, and there's no storage space in front of you—a major inconvenience.

GROUP TRAVEL

When planning to take your kids on a tour, look for companies that specialize in family travel.

➤ FAMILY-FRIENDLY TOUR OPERATORS: **Families Welcome!** (✉ 92 N. Main St., Ashland, OR 97520, ☎ 541/482–6121 or 800/326–0724, ℻ 541/482–0660). **Rascals in Paradise** (✉ 650 5th St., Suite 505, San Francisco, CA 94107, ☎ 415/978–9800 or 800/872–7225, ℻ 415/442–0289).

HOTELS

Most hotels in Hawai'i allow children under a certain age to stay in their parents' room at no extra charge, but others charge them as extra adults; be sure to **ask about the cutoff age for children's discounts.**

CONSUMER PROTECTION

Whenever possible, **pay with a major credit card** so you can cancel payment or get reimbursed if there's a problem, provided that you can provide documentation. This is the best way to pay, whether you're buying travel arrangements before your trip or shopping at your destination.

If you're doing business with a particular company for the first time, contact your local **Better Business Bureau and the attorney general's offices** in your state and the company's home state, as well. Have any complaints been filed?

Finally, if you're buying a package or tour, always **consider travel insurance** that includes default coverage (☞ Insurance, *below*).

➤ LOCAL BBBs: **Council of Better Business Bureaus** (⌧ 4200 Wilson Blvd., Suite 800, Arlington, VA 22203, ☎ 703/276–0100, FAX 703/525–8277).

CRUISE TRAVEL

When Pan Am's amphibious *Hawaii Clipper* touched down on Pearl Harbor's waters in 1936, it marked the beginning of the end of regular passenger ship travel to the Islands. From that point on, the predominant means of transporting visitors would be by air, not by sea. Today, however, cruising to Hawai'i still holds a special appeal for those with the time and money to afford sailing, and with a bit of research, you can arrange passage aboard the luxury liners that call on Honolulu when traveling the seven seas.

No regularly scheduled American ships steam between the mainland and Hawai'i. Although foreign-owned vessels often ply the Pacific, the Jones Act of 1896 prohibits them from carrying passengers between two U.S. ports unless the ships first stop at an intervening foreign port or carry the passengers to a foreign destination. What that means to those wishing for the relaxing ways of ship travel is that they'll have to book with one of the major lines passing through Honolulu.

Cruises within the islands are available on the 1,021-passenger ship the SS *Independence,* under the direction of American Hawaii Cruises, which plans to add another passenger vessel by 2000. Seven-day cruises originate in Honolulu and visit the Big Island, Maui, and Kaua'i.

To get the best deal on a cruise, **consult a cruise-only travel agency.**

➤ CRUISE LINES: For details on cruises that pass through Honolulu: American Hawaii Cruises (☎ 800/765–7000). Cunard (☎ 800/221–4770). Holland America (☎ 800/426–0327), Princess (☎ 800/421–0522). Royal Caribbean Cruise Line (☎ 800/327–6700). Royal Cruise Line (☎ 415/956–7200).

CUSTOMS & DUTIES

When shopping, **keep receipts** for all of your purchases. Upon reentering the country, **be ready to show customs officials what you've bought.** If you feel a duty is incorrect, appeal the assessment. If you object to the way your clearance was handled, get the inspector's badge number. In either case, first ask to see a supervisor, then write to the appropriate authorities, beginning with the port director at your point of entry.

IN HAWAI'I

Plants and plant products are subject to regulation by the Department of Agriculture, both on entering and leaving Hawai'i. Pineapples and coconuts with the packer's agricultural inspection stamp pass freely; papayas must be treated, inspected, and stamped. All other fruits are banned for export to the U.S. mainland. Flowers pass except for gardenia, rose leaves, jade vine, and mauna loa. Also banned are insects, snails, soil, coffee, cotton, cacti, sugarcane, and all berry plants.

Leave dogs and other pets at home. A strict 30-day quarantine is imposed to keep out rabies, which is nonexistent in Hawai'i.

IN AUSTRALIA

Australia residents who are 18 or older may bring back A$400 worth of souvenirs and gifts (including jewelry), 250 cigarettes or 250 grams of tobacco, and 1,125 ml of alcohol (including wine, beer, and spirits). Residents under 18 may bring back A$200 worth of goods.

➤ INFORMATION: **Australian Customs Service** (Regional Director, ⌧ Box 8, Sydney, NSW 2001, ☎ 02/9213–2000, FAX 02/9213–4000).

IN CANADA

Canadian residents who have been out of Canada for at least 7 days may bring in C$500 worth of goods duty-free. If you've been away less than 7 days but more than 48 hours, the duty-free allowance drops to C$200; if your trip lasts 24–48 hours, the allowance is C$50. You may not pool allowances with family members. Goods claimed under the C$500 exemption may follow you by mail; those claimed under the lesser exemptions must accompany you. Alcohol and tobacco products may be included in the 7-day and 48-hour exemptions but not in the 24-hour exemption. If you meet the age requirements of the province or territory through which you reenter Canada, you may bring in, duty-free, 1.14 liters (40 imperial ounces) of wine or liquor *or* 24 12-ounce cans or bottles of beer or ale. If you are 16 or older you may bring in, duty-free, 200 cigarettes and 50 cigars.

You may send an unlimited number of gifts worth up to C$60 each duty-free to Canada. Label the package UNSOLICITED GIFT—VALUE UNDER $60. Alcohol and tobacco are excluded.

➤ INFORMATION: **Revenue Canada** (⊠ 2265 St. Laurent Blvd. S, Ottawa, Ontario K1G 4K3, ☎ 613/993–0534, 800/461–9999 in Canada).

IN NEW ZEALAND

If you're 17 or older, you may bring back $700 worth of souvenirs and gifts. Your duty-free allowance also includes 4.5 liters of wine or beer; one 1,125-ml bottle of spirits; and either 200 cigarettes, 250 grams of tobacco, 50 cigars, or a combo of all three up to 250 grams.

➤ INFORMATION: **New Zealand Customs** (⊠ Custom House, 50 Anzac Ave., Box 29, Auckland, New Zealand, ☎ 09/359–6655, ⊠ 09/309–2978).

IN THE U.K.

From countries outside the EU, including the United States, you may import, duty-free, 200 cigarettes or 50 cigars; 1 liter of spirits or 2 liters of fortified or sparkling wine or liqueurs; 2 liters of still table wine; 60 milliliters of perfume; 250 milliliters of toilet water; plus £136 worth of other goods, including gifts and souvenirs.

➤ INFORMATION: **HM Customs and Excise** (⊠ Dorset House, Stamford St., London SE1 9NG, ☎ 0171/202–4227).

IN THE U.S.

Non-U.S. residents ages 21 and older may import into the United States 200 cigarettes or 50 cigars or 2 kilograms of tobacco, 1 liter of alcohol, and gifts worth $100. Prohibited items include meat products, seeds, plants, and fruits.

➤ INFORMATION: **U.S. Customs Service** (Inquiries, ⊠ Box 7407, Washington, DC 20044, ☎ 202/927–6724; complaints, Office of Regulations and Rulings, ⊠ 1301 Constitution Ave. NW, Washington, DC 20229; registration of equipment, Resource Management, ⊠ 1301 Constitution Ave. NW, Washington DC 20229, ☎ 202/927–0540).

DISABILITIES & ACCESSIBILITY

ACCESS IN HAWAI'I

The Society for the Advancement of Travel for the Handicapped has named Hawai'i the most accessible vacation spot for people with disabilities. Ramped visitor areas and specially equipped lodgings are relatively common in the Islands.

➤ LOCAL RESOURCES: Contact the **Commission on Persons with Disabilities** (⊠ 919 Ala Moana Blvd., Room 101, Honolulu 96814, ☎ 808/586–8121). Its "Aloha Guide to Accessibility" lists addresses and telephone numbers for support-service organizations and rates the Islands' hotels, beaches, shopping and entertainment centers, and major visitor attractions for accessibility. The guide costs $15 but is available in sections for $3–$5 per section. Part I (general information) is free. For accessibility information on the Neighbor Islands, contact the commission office on Kaua'i (⊠ 3060 'Eiwa St., Room 207, Līhu'e 96766, ☎ 808/274–3308), or Maui (⊠ 54 High St., Wailuku 96793, ☎ 808/984–8219).

MAKING RESERVATIONS

When discussing accessibility with an operator or reservations agent, **ask hard questions.** Are there any stairs, inside *or* out? Are there grab bars next to the toilet *and* in the shower/tub? How wide is the doorway to the room? To the bathroom? For the most extensive facilities meeting the latest legal specifications, **opt for newer accommodations,** which are more likely to have been designed with access in mind. Older buildings or ships may have more limited facilities. Be sure to **discuss your needs before booking.**

TRANSPORTATION

Paratransit Services (HandiVan) (☏ 808/456–5555) will take you to a specific destination—not on sightseeing outings—in vans with lifts and lock-downs. With a HandiVan Pass, one-way trips cost $1.50. Passes are free and can be obtained from **the Department of Transportation Services** (✉ 711 Kapi'olani Blvd., Honolulu 96819, ☏ 808/523–4083; ⏱ weekdays 7:45-4:30); you'll need a doctor's written confirmation of your disability or a paratransit I.D. card. **Handi-Cabs of the Pacific** (☏ 808/524–3866) also operates ramp-equipped vans with lock-downs in Honolulu. Fares are $9 plus $2.25 per mile for curb-side service. Reservations at least one day in advance are required for all companies listed above.

Those who prefer to do their own driving may rent hand-controlled cars from **Avis** (☏ 800/331–1212; reserve 24 hrs ahead) and **Hertz** (☏ 800/654–3131; 24- to 72-hr notice required). You can use the windshield card from your own state to park in spaces reserved for people with disabilities.

➤ COMPLAINTS: **Disability Rights Section** (✉ U.S. Department of Justice, Civil Rights Division, Box 66738, Washington, DC 20035–6738, ☏ 202/514–0301 or 800/514–0301, TTY 202/514–0383 or 800/514–0383, FAX 202/307–1198) for general complaints. **Aviation Consumer Protection Division** (☞ Air Travel, *above*) for airline-related problems. **Civil Rights Office** (✉ U.S. Department of Transportation, Departmental Office of Civil Rights, S-30, 400 7th St. SW, Room 10215, Washington, DC 20590, ☏ 202/366–

4648, FAX 202/366–9371) for problems with surface transportation.

TRAVEL AGENCIES & TOUR OPERATORS

As a whole, the travel industry has become more aware of the needs of travelers with disabilities. In the U.S., the Americans with Disabilities Act requires that travel firms serve the needs of all travelers. Note, though, that some agencies and operators specialize in making travel arrangements for individuals and groups with disabilities.

➤ TRAVELERS WITH MOBILITY PROBLEMS: **Access Adventures** (✉ 206 Chestnut Ridge Rd., Rochester, NY 14624, ☏ 716/889–9096), run by a former physical-rehabilitation counselor. **Accessible Journeys** (✉ 35 W. Sellers Ave., Ridley Park, PA 19078, ☏ 610/521–0339 or 800/846–4537, FAX 610/521–6959), for escorted tours exclusively for travelers with mobility impairments. **Accessible Vans of Hawaii, Activity and Travel Agency** (✉ 186 Mehani Circle, Kihei, HI 96753, ☏ 808/879–5521 or 800/303–3750, FAX 808/879–0649). **Care-Vacations** (✉ 5019 49th Ave., Suite 102, Leduc, Alberta T9E 6T5, ☏ 403/986–6404, 800/648–1116 in Canada) has group tours and is especially helpful with cruise vacations. **Flying Wheels Travel** (✉ 143 W. Bridge St., Box 382, Owatonna, MN 55060, ☏ 507/451–5005 or 800/535–6790, FAX 507/451–1685), a travel agency specializing in customized tours and itineraries worldwide. **Hinsdale Travel Service** (✉ 201 E. Ogden Ave., Suite 100, Hinsdale, IL 60521, ☏ 630/325–1335), a travel agency that benefits from the advice of wheelchair traveler Janice Perkins.

➤ TRAVELERS WITH DEVELOPMENTAL DISABILITIES: **New Directions** (✉ 5276 Hollister Ave., Suite 207, Santa Barbara, CA 93111, ☏ 805/967–2841 or 888/967–2841, FAX 805/964–7344). **Sprout** (✉ 893 Amsterdam Ave., New York, NY 10025, ☏ 212/222–9575 or 888/222–9575, FAX 212/222–9768).

DISCOUNTS & DEALS

Be a smart shopper and **compare all your options.**

THE GOLD GUIDE / SMART TRAVEL TIPS

CLUBS & COUPONS

Many companies sell discounts in the form of travel clubs and coupon books. You must use participating advertisers, and only after you recoup the initial cost do you begin to save. If you plan to use the club or coupons frequently, you may save considerably.

➤ DISCOUNT CLUBS: **Entertainment Travel Editions** (✉ 2125 Butterfield Rd., Troy, MI 48084, ☎ 800/445–4137; $20–$51, depending on destination). **Great American Traveler** (✉ Box 27965, Salt Lake City, UT 84127, ☎ 801/974–3033 or 800/548–2812; $49.95 per year). **Moment's Notice Discount Travel Club** (✉ 7301 New Utrecht Ave., Brooklyn, NY 11204, ☎ 718/234–6295; $25 per year, single or family). **Privilege Card International** (✉ 237 E. Front St., Youngstown, OH 44503, ☎ 330/746–5211 or 800/236–9732; $74.95 per year). **Sears's Mature Outlook** (✉ Box 9390, Des Moines, IA 50306, ☎ 800/336–6330; $19.95 per year). **Travelers Advantage** (✉ CUC Travel Service, 3033 S. Parker Rd., Suite 1000, Aurora, CO 80014, ☎ 800/548–1116 or 800/648–4037; $59.95 per year, single or family). **Worldwide Discount Travel Club** (✉ 1674 Meridian Ave., Miami Beach, FL 33139, ☎ 305/534–2082; $50 per year family, $40 single).

CREDIT-CARD BENEFITS

When you use your credit card to make travel purchases you may get free travel-accident insurance, collision-damage insurance, and medical or legal assistance, depending on the card and the bank that issued it. American Express, MasterCard, and Visa provide one or more of these services, so **get a copy of your credit card's travel-benefits policy.** If you are a member of an auto club, always **ask hotel and car-rental reservations agents about auto-club discounts.** Some clubs offer additional discounts on tours, cruises, and admission to attractions.

DISCOUNT RESERVATIONS

To save money, **look into discount-reservations services** with toll-free numbers, which use their buying power to get a better price on hotels, airline tickets, even car rentals. When booking a room, always **call the hotel's local toll-free number** (if one is available) rather than the central reservations number—you'll often get a better price. Always ask about special packages or corporate rates.

➤ AIRLINE TICKETS: ☎ **800/FLY–4–LESS.** ☎ **800/FLY–ASAP.**

➤ HOTEL ROOMS: **Players Express Vacations** (☎ 800/458–6161). **RMC Travel** (☎ 800/245–5738). **Steigenberger Reservation Service** (☎ 800/223–5652).

PACKAGE DEALS

Packages and guided tours can save you money, but don't confuse the two. When you buy a package, your travel remains independent, just as though you had planned and booked the trip yourself. Fly/drive packages, which combine airfare and car rental, are often a good deal.

GAY & LESBIAN TRAVEL

➤ LOCAL RESOURCES: *Island Lifestyles,* put out by Island Publishing (✉ Box 11840, Honolulu 96828☎ 808/737–6400) is a monthly magazine ($3 per copy, $24 for 12 issues) covering news and entertainment in Hawai'i. For $4 an issue, Island Publishing also sells *The Pages,* a directory of gay and gay-supportive business organizations and services. **Pacific Ocean Holidays** (✉ Box 88245, Honolulu 96830, ☎ 808/923–2400 or 800/735–6600, www.gayhawaii.com) not only arranges independent travel in the Islands, but publishes the **Pocket Guide to Hawai'i,** distributed free in the state at gay-operated venues and available for $5 by mail.

A few small hotels and some bed-and-breakfasts in Hawai'i are favored by gay and lesbian visitors. A computerized Gay Community listing compiled by **GLEA** (Gay & Lesbian Education Advocacy Foundation, ☎ 808/532–9000) can be accessed by phone.

➤ GAY- AND LESBIAN-FRIENDLY TOUR OPERATORS: **Toto Tours** (✉ 1326 W. Albion Ave., Suite 3W, Chicago, IL 60626, ☎ 773/274–8686 or 800/565–1241, ℻ 773/274–8695), for groups.

➤ GAY- AND LESBIAN-FRIENDLY TRAVEL AGENCIES: **Corniche Travel** (✉ 8721

Sunset Blvd., Suite 200, West Holly-wood, CA 90069, ☎ 310/854–6000 or 800/429–8747, FAX 310/659–7441). **Islanders Kennedy Travel** (✉ 183 W. 10th St., New York, NY 10014, ☎ 212/242–3222 or 800/988–1181, FAX 212/929–8530). **Now Voyager** (✉ 4406 18th St., San Francisco, CA 94114, ☎ 415/626–1169 or 800/255–6951, FAX 415/626–8626). **Yellowbrick Road** (✉ 1500 W. Balmoral Ave., Chicago, IL 60640, ☎ 773/561–1800 or 800/642–2488, FAX 773/561–4497). **Skylink Travel and Tour** (✉ 3577 Moorland Ave., Santa Rosa, CA 95407, ☎ 707/585–8355 or 800/225–5759, FAX 707/584–5637), serving lesbian travelers.

HEALTH

From 1996 to 1998, reported cases of leptospirosis, a tropical disease spread by animal urine and carried in fresh-water streams and mud, were up 100% in Hawai'i, although the disease is still rare—there were only 60 cases reported in 1997. Initial symptoms include headaches, fever, nausea, and red eyes; if left untreated it can cause liver and kidney damage, respiratory failure, internal bleeding, and death.

DIVERS' ALERT

Do not fly within 24 hours after scuba diving.

MEDICAL PLANS

No one plans to get sick while traveling, but it happens, so **consider signing up with a medical-assistance company.** Members get doctor referrals, emergency evacuation or repatriation, 24-hour telephone hot lines for medical consultation, cash for emergencies, and other personal and legal assistance. Coverage varies by plan, so **review the benefits of each carefully.**

➤ MEDICAL-ASSISTANCE COMPANIES: **International SOS Assistance** (✉ 8 Neshaminy Interplex, Suite 207, Trevose, PA 19053, ☎ 215/245–4707 or 800/523–6586, FAX 215/244–9617; ✉ 12 Chemin Riant-bosson, 1217 Meyrin 1, Geneva, Switzerland, ☎ 4122/785–6464, FAX 4122/785–6424; ✉ 10 Anson Rd., 14-07/08 International Plaza, Singapore, 079903, ☎ 65/226–3936, FAX 65/226–3937).

HOLIDAYS

Major national holidays include: New Year's Day (Jan. 1); Martin Luther King, Jr. Day (third Mon. in Jan.); President's Day (third Mon. in Feb.); Memorial Day (last Mon. in May); Independence Day (July 4); Labor Day (first Mon. in Sept.); Thanksgiving Day (fourth Thurs. in Nov.); Christmas Eve and Day (Dec. 24–25); and New Year's Eve (Dec. 31).

INSURANCE

Travel insurance is the best way to **protect yourself against financial loss.** The most useful plan is a comprehensive policy that includes coverage for trip cancellation and interruption, default, trip delay, and medical expenses (with a waiver for preexisting conditions).

Without insurance, you will lose all or most of your money if you cancel your trip, regardless of the reason. Default insurance covers you if your tour operator, airline, or cruise line goes out of business. Trip-delay covers unforeseen expenses that you may incur due to bad weather or mechanical delays. It's important to compare the fine print regarding trip-delay coverage when comparing policies.

For overseas travel, one of the most important components of travel insurance is its medical coverage. Supplemental health insurance will pick up the cost of your medical bills should you get sick or injured while traveling. Residents of the United Kingdom can buy an annual travel-insurance policy valid for most vacations taken during the year in which the coverage is purchased. If you are pregnant or have a pre-existing condition, make sure you're covered. British citizens should buy extra medical coverage when traveling overseas, according to the Association of British Insurers. Australian travelers should buy travel insurance, including extra medical coverage, whenever they go abroad, according to the Insurance Council of Australia.

Always **buy travel insurance directly from the insurance company;** if you buy it from a cruise line, airline, or tour operator that goes out of business you probably will not be covered for the agency or operator's default, a major risk. Before you make any purchase, **review your existing health and home-owner's policies** to find out whether they cover expenses incurred while traveling.

➤ TRAVEL INSURERS: In the U.S., **Access America** (✉ 6600 W. Broad St., Richmond, VA 23230, ☎ 804/285–3300 or 800/284–8300). **Travel Guard International** (✉ 1145 Clark St., Stevens Point, WI 54481, ☎ 715/345–0505 or 800/826–1300). In Canada, **Mutual of Omaha** (✉ Travel Division, 500 University Ave., Toronto, Ontario M5G 1V8, ☎ 416/598–4083, 800/268–8825 in Canada).

➤ INSURANCE INFORMATION: In the U.K., **Association of British Insurers** (✉ 51 Gresham St., London EC2V 7HQ, ☎ 0171/600–3333). In Australia, the **Insurance Council of Australia** (☎ 613/9614–1077, ⅋ 613/9614–7924).

LEI GREETINGS

When you walk off a long flight, perhaps a bit groggy and stiff, nothing quite compares with a Hawaiian lei greeting. The casual ceremony ranks as one of the fastest ways to make the transition from the worries of home to the joys of your vacation. Though the tradition has created an expectation that everyone receives this flower garland on arrival, unfortunately, the state of Hawai'i cannot bedeck each of its nearly 7 million annual visitors. Still, it's possible to **arrange for a lei ceremony for yourself or your companions before you arrive.**

➤ LEI GREETERS: If you are traveling independently, you can arrange for a lei greeting from **Greeters of Hawai'i** (✉ Box 29638, Honolulu 96820, ☎ 808/836–0161; ☎ 808/834–7667 for airport desk, ⅋ 800/736–5665), the oldest greeting company in the Aloha State; 48 hours' notice is needed. Cost: $14.95 to $39.95 per person, add $10 for late notification. Also try **Aloha Lei Greeters** (☎ 808/951–9990 or 800/367–5255), which charges $10–$30 per person, depending on the kinds of flowers used.

Kama'aina Ali'i, Flowers & Greeters (✉ 3159-B Koapaka St., Honolulu, ☎ 808/836–3246 or 800/367–5183), which charges $10.95–$43 per greeting, will also put together fruit baskets, bouquets, and other special orders. They also cover Līhu'e Airport on Kaua'i, Kahului Airport on Maui, and Kona International Airport on the Big Island.

LODGING

APARTMENT & VILLA RENTALS

If you want a home base that's roomy enough for a family and comes with cooking facilities, **consider a furnished rental.** These can save you money, especially if you're traveling with a large group of people. Home-exchange directories list rentals (often second homes owned by prospective house swappers), and some services search for a house or apartment for you and handle the paperwork. Some send an illustrated catalog; others send photographs only of specific properties, sometimes at a charge. Up-front registration fees may apply.

➤ RENTAL AGENTS: **Europa-Let/Tropical Inn-Let** (✉ 92 N. Main St., Ashland, OR 97520, ☎ 541/482–5806 or 800/462–4486, ⅋ 541/482–0660). **Hometours International** (✉ Box 11503, Knoxville, TN 37939, ☎ 423/690–8484 or 800/367–4668). **Property Rentals International** (✉ 1008 Mansfield Crossing Rd., Richmond, VA 23236, ☎ 804/378–6054 or 800/220–3332, ⅋ 804/379–2073). **Rent-a-Home International** (✉ 7200 34th Ave. NW, Seattle, WA 98117, ☎ 206/789–9377 or 800/488–7368, ⅋ 206/789–9379). **Vacation Home Rentals Worldwide** (✉ 235 Kensington Ave., Norwood, NJ 07648, ☎ 201/767–9393 or 800/633–3284, ⅋ 201/767–5510). **Hideaways International** (✉ 767 Islington St., Portsmouth, NH 03801, ☎ 603/430–4433 or 800/843–4433, ⅋ 603/430–4444; membership $99) is a club for travelers who arrange rentals among themselves. **RDI World** (✉ Box 329, Wayne, PA 19087, ☎ 610/353–2335, ⅋ 610/353–7756) lists properties that can be rented directly from their owners.

B&BS

B&Bs have made heavy inroads into the Hawaiian market in the past several years.

➤ RESERVATION SERVICES: **Bed and Breakfast Hawai'i** (✉ Box 449, Kapa'a, Kaua'i, HI 96746, ☎ 800/733–1632, FAX 808/822–2723), **Pacific Hawai'i Bed and Breakfast** (✉ 99-1661 Aiea Heights Dr., Aiea, O'ahu, HI 96701, ☎ 808/486–8838, 800/262–6026, or 800/999–6026), **Bed and Breakfast Honolulu** (statewide) (✉ 3242 Kaohinani Dr., Honolulu, HI 96817, ☎ 808/595–3298, or 800/288–4666, FAX 808/595–2030), **Volcano Reservations–Select Statewide Accommodations** (✉ Box 998, Volcano Village, Hawai'i 96785, ☎ 808/967–7244, or 800/736–7140, FAX 808/967-8660), **Go Native . . . Hawaii** (2009 W. Holmes Rd. Suite #9, Lansing, Michigan 48910, ☎ 800/662–8483), and **Hawai'i's Best Bed and Breakfasts** (✉ Box 563, Kamuela, Hawai'i 96743, ☎ 808/885–4550 or 800/262–9912, FAX 808/885–0559), which specializes in upscale properties.

CAMPING

A variety of national, state, and county parks are available, some with bathroom and cooking facilities, others a bit more primitive. The National Park Service and Division of State Parks of the Hawai'i Department of Land and Natural Resources (☞ National and State Parks, *below*) can provide more information; details on local camping are available from the individual counties.

➤ CAMPING AND RV FACILITIES: The **City and County of Honolulu** (☎ 808/523–4525) can provide information about camping at county sites on O'ahu, and the **Hawai'i State Department of Parks and Recreation** (☎ 808/587–0300) handles the same questions for state camping sites. You can pack up your own sleeping bag and bring it along, or you can rent camping equipment at companies such as **Omar the Tent Man** (✉ 94-158 Leo'ole St., Waipahu, HI 96797, ☎ 808/677–8785), on O'ahu; **Pacific Rent-All** (✉ 1080 Kilauea Ave., Hilo, HI 96720, ☎ 808/935–2974), on the Big Island; and **Pedal 'n' Paddle**

(✉ Box 1413, Ching Young Village, Hānalei, HI 96714, ☎ 808/826–9069), on Kaua'i.

CONDOMINIUMS

Hawai'i is known for developing the resort condominium concept in the early 1970s and continues to maintain its status as a leader in the field. Besides large living areas and full kitchens, many condos now offer front-desk and daily maid services. Nearly 100 companies in Hawai'i and around the United States rent out condominium space in the islands. Your travel agent will be the most helpful in finding the condo you desire.

HOME EXCHANGES

If you would like to exchange your home for someone else's, **join a home-exchange organization,** which will send you its updated listings of available exchanges for a year and will include your own listing in at least one of them. It's up to you to make specific arrangements.

➤ EXCHANGE CLUBS: **HomeLink International** (✉ Box 650, Key West, FL 33041, ☎ 305/294–7766 or 800/638–3841, FAX 305/294–1148; $83 per year).

HOSTELS

No matter what your age, you can **save on lodging costs by staying at hostels.** In some 5,000 locations in more than 70 countries around the world, Hostelling International (HI), the umbrella group for a number of national youth hostel associations, offers single-sex, dorm-style beds and, at many hostels, "couples" rooms and family accommodations. Membership in any HI national hostel association, open to travelers of all ages, allows you to stay in HI-affiliated hostels at member rates (one-year membership is about $25 for adults; hostels run about $10–$25 per night). Members also have priority if the hostel is full; they're eligible for discounts around the world, even on rail and bus travel in some countries.

➤ HOSTEL ORGANIZATIONS: **Hostelling International—American Youth Hostels** (✉ 733 15th St. NW, Suite 840,

Washington, DC 20005, ☎ 202/783–6161, FAX 202/783–6171). **Hostelling International—Canada** (✉ 400-205 Catherine St., Ottawa, Ontario K2P 1C3, ☎ 613/237–7884, FAX 613/237–7868). **Youth Hostel Association of England and Wales** (✉ Trevelyan House, 8 St. Stephen's Hill, St. Albans, Hertfordshire AL1 2DY, ☎ 01727/855215 or 01727/845047, FAX 01727/844126); membership in the U.S. $25, in Canada C$26.75, in the U.K. £9.30).

HOTELS

You can find most major hotel brands in Hawai'i, plus large, locally based operators, such as Aston Hotels and Resorts and Outrigger Hotels Hawai'i, and a number of independents. The result is an extensive range of rooms, from rock-bottom economy units to luxurious suites.

NATIONAL & STATE PARKS

Look into discount passes to **save money on park entrance fees.** The Golden Eagle Pass ($50) gets you and your companions free admission to all parks for one year. (Camping and parking are extra.) Both the Golden Age Passport ($10), for those 62 and older, and the Golden Access Passport (free), for travelers with disabilities, entitle holders to free entry to all national parks, plus 50% off fees for the use of many park facilities and services. You must show proof of age and of U.S. citizenship or permanent residency (such as a U.S. passport, driver's license, or birth certificate) and, if requesting Golden Access, proof of disability. All three passes are available at all national park entrances where entrance fees are charged. Golden Eagle and Golden Access passes are also available by mail.

➤ PASSES BY MAIL: **National Park Service** (✉ National Capitol Area Office, 1100 Ohio Dr. SW, Washington, DC 20242).

➤ STATE PARKS: Details of state parks and historic areas come from the **District Office of the Hawai'i Department of Land and Natural Resources,** Division of State Parks (✉ 1151 Punchbowl St., Room 310, Honolulu, HI 96813, or Box 621, Honolulu, HI 96809, ☎ 808/587–0300).

OUTDOOR ACTIVITIES & SPORTS

DIVING

A comprehensive 24-page guide to dive spots also lists dive shops. To obtain the guide, send $2 to University of Hawai'i (✉ Seagrant Extension Service, MSB Room 226, 1000 Pope Rd., Honolulu, HI 96822).

PACKING

LUGGAGE

How many carry-on bags you can bring with you is up to the airline. Most allow two, but the limit is often reduced to one on certain flights. Gate agents will take excess baggage—including bags they deem oversize—from you as you board and add it to checked luggage. To avoid this situation, make sure that everything you carry aboard will fit under your seat. Also, get to the gate early, and request a seat at the back of the plane; you'll probably board first, while the overhead bins are still empty. Since big, bulky baggage attracts the attention of gate agents and flight attendants on a busy flight, make sure your carry-on is really a carry-on. Finally, a carry-on that's long and narrow is more likely to remain unnoticed than one that's wide and squarish.

If you are flying internationally, note that baggage allowances may be determined not by piece but by weight—generally 88 pounds (40 kilograms) in first class, 66 pounds (30 kilograms) in business class, and 44 pounds (20 kilograms) in economy.

Airline liability for baggage is limited to $1,250 per person on flights within the United States. On international flights it amounts to $9.07 per pound or $20 per kilogram for checked baggage (roughly $640 per 70-pound bag) and $400 per passenger for unchecked baggage. You can buy additional coverage at check-in for about $10 per $1,000 of coverage, but it excludes a rather extensive list of items, shown on your airline ticket.

Before departure, **itemize your bags' contents** and their worth, and label the bags with your name, address, and phone number. (If you use your home address, cover it so that potential thieves can't see it readily.) Inside each bag, **pack a copy of your itinerary.** At check-in, **make sure that each bag is correctly tagged** with the destination airport's three-letter code. If your bags arrive damaged or fail to arrive at all, file a written report with the airline before leaving the airport.

PACKING LIST

Hawai'i is casual: Sandals, bathing suits, and comfortable, informal clothing are the norm. In summer synthetic slacks and shirts, although easy to care for, can be uncomfortably warm. You'll easily find a bathing suit in Hawai'i if you forget your own, but bring a bathing cap with you: you can waste hours searching for one.

Probably the most important thing to tuck in your suitcase is sunscreen. This is the tropics, and the ultraviolet rays are much more powerful than those to which you are probably accustomed. Doctors advise putting on sunscreen when you get up in the morning. Don't forget to **reapply sunscreen periodically during the day,** since perspiration can wash it away. Consider using sunscreens with a sun protection factor (SPF) of 15 or higher. There are many tanning oils on the market in Hawai'i, including coconut and *kukui* (the nut from a local tree) oils, but doctors warn that they merely sauté your skin. Too many Hawaiian vacations have been spoiled by sunburn. Hats and sunglasses offer important sun protection, too. Both are easy to find in island shops, but if you already have a favorite packable hat or sun visor, bring it with you, and don't forget to wear it. All major hotels in Hawai'i provide beach towels.

As for clothing, in the Hawaiian Islands there's a saying that when a man wears a suit during the day, he's either going for a loan or he's a lawyer trying a case. Only a few upscale restaurants require a jacket for dinner, and none requires a tie. The aloha shirt is accepted dress in Hawai'i for business and most social occasions. Shorts are acceptable daytime attire, along with a T-shirt or polo shirt. Golfers should remember that many courses have dress codes

requiring a collared shirt; call courses you're interested in for details. If you're not prepared, you can pick up appropriate clothing at resort pro shops. If you're visiting in winter or planning to visit a volcano area, bring a sweater or light- to medium-weight jacket. Trade winds cool things off when the sun goes down, and things get chilly above 10,000 ft.

If you're a woman and don't own a *pareo,* buy one in Hawai'i. It's simply a length of light cotton (about 1½–2 yds long), usually in a tropical motif, that can be worn as a beach wrap, a skirt, or a dozen other wrap-up fashions. A pareo is useful wherever you go, regardless of the climate. It makes a good bathrobe, so you don't have to pack one. You can even tie it up as a handbag or sit on it at the beach.

In your carry-on luggage **bring an extra pair of eyeglasses or contact lenses** and **enough of any medication you take** to last the entire trip. You may also want your doctor to write a spare prescription using the drug's generic name, since brand names may vary from country to country. **Never put prescription drugs or valuables in luggage to be checked.** To avoid customs delays, carry medications in their original packaging. And don't forget to copy down and carry addresses of offices that handle refunds of lost traveler's checks.

PASSPORTS & VISAS

When traveling internationally, **carry a passport even if you don't need one** (it's always the best form of I.D.), and make **two photocopies of the data page** (one for someone at home and another for you, carried separately from your passport). If you lose your passport, promptly call the nearest embassy or consulate and the local police.

➤ U.K. CITIZENS: **U.S. Embassy Visa Information Line** (☎ 01891/200–290; calls cost 49p per minute, 39p per minute cheap rate), for U.S. visa information. **U.S. Embassy Visa Branch** (✉ 5 Upper Grosvenor St., London W1A 2JB), for U.S. visa information; send a self-addressed, stamped envelope. Write the **U.S.**

THE GOLD GUIDE / SMART TRAVEL TIPS

Consulate General (✉ Queen's House, Queen St., Belfast BTI 6EO) if you live in Northern Ireland.

PASSPORT OFFICES

The best time to apply for a passport or to renew is during the fall and winter. Before any trip, be sure to check your passport's expiration date and, if necessary, renew it as soon as possible. (Some countries won't allow you to enter on a passport that's due to expire in six months or less.)

➤ AUSTRALIAN CITIZENS: **Australian Passport Office** (☎ 131–232).

➤ NEW ZEALAND CITIZENS: **New Zealand Passport Office** (☎ 04/494–0700 for information on how to apply, 0800/727–776 for information on applications already submitted).

➤ U.K. CITIZENS: **London Passport Office** (☎ 0990/21010), for fees and documentation requirements and to request an emergency passport.

RADIO STATIONS

Most Hawaiians wake up with Perry and Price on **KSSK AM 59** or **FM 92**. The lively duo provides news, traffic updates, and weather reports between "easy listening music" and phone calls from listeners from 5 AM to 10 AM.

For contemporary hits, turn to **KIKI/HOT I-94 FM, KQMQ AM 690,** or **FM 93.1**; both stations also regularly report surf conditions. If it's new rock alternative you're after, tune into **97.5 The Edge, FM 97.5**. Listeners' votes choose the playlist "Radio Free Hawai'i" on **KDEO FM 102.7,** and contemporary Hawaiian music is on **KCCN AM 1420.**

Hawai'i's Public Radio stations on O'ahu are **KIFO AM 1380** (news); **KIPO FM 89.3** (news and information and jazz, classical and international music); **KHPR FM 88.1** (classical music, news, and informational programming); and on Maui, **KKUA FM 90.7** (classical music and news).

SENIOR-CITIZEN TRAVEL

To qualify for age-related discounts, **mention your senior-citizen status up front** when booking hotel reservations (not when checking out) and before

you're seated in restaurants (not when paying the bill). Note that discounts may be limited to certain menus, days, or hours. When renting a car, **ask about promotional car-rental discounts,** which can be cheaper than senior-citizen rates.

➤ EDUCATIONAL PROGRAMS: **Elderhostel** (✉ 75 Federal St., 3rd floor, Boston, MA 02110, ☎ 617/426–8056).

SHOPPING

On O'ahu, Ala Moana Center is one of the largest shopping spots; it's within easy walking distance of the west end of Waikīkī. The Royal Hawaiian Shopping Center is centrally located in Waikīkī itself. Farther away, you'll find Ward Warehouse, Aloha Tower Marketplace, the Kahala Mall, and Pearlridge Center.

The Neighbor Islands offer more in the way of smaller strips of shops. Still, it's possible to find larger stores grouped in areas such as Kaua'i's Kukui Grove Center in Līhu'e, Maui's Ka'ahumanu Shopping Center, and the Big Island's Prince Kūhiō Shopping Plaza in Hilo, and Keauhou Shopping Village and Lanihau Center in Kailua-Kona. Exclusive shops can often be found in the lobbies of luxury hotels on all the Islands.

STUDENT TRAVEL

➤ STUDENT I.D.s & SERVICES: **Council on International Educational Exchange** (✉ CIEE, 205 E. 42nd St., 14th floor, New York, NY 10017, ☎ 212/822–2600 or 888/268–6245, 🖷 212/822–2699), for mail orders only, in the United States. **Travel Cuts** (✉ 187 College St., Toronto, Ontario M5T 1P7, ☎ 416/979–2406 or 800/667–2887) in Canada.

➤ STUDENT TOURS: **Contiki Holidays** (✉ 300 Plaza Alicante, Suite 900, Garden Grove, CA 92840, ☎ 714/740–0808 or 800/266–8454, 🖷 714/740–2034).

TELEPHONES

COUNTRY CODES

The country code for the United States is 1.

DIRECTORY & OPERATOR INFORMATION

Dial 808/555–1212 for directory information and, within the state, 0 for an operator.

LOCAL CALLS

All Hawaiian island telephones have the area code 808; this area code must be used for interisland calls, as well as calls from other area codes. Many toll-free 800 numbers for hotels and other establishments may not be dialed from within the Islands. For facilities that have both an 808 phone number and an 800 number, use the 808 number once you arrive in Hawai'i. Include the area code when dialing if you are phoning to another island.

LONG-DISTANCE CALLS

Competitive long-distance carriers make calling within the United States relatively convenient and let you avoid hotel surcharges. By dialing an 800 number, you can get connected to a long-distance company.

➤ LONG-DISTANCE CARRIERS: **AT&T** (☎ 800/225–5288). **MCI** (☎ 800/888–8000). **Sprint** (☎ 800/366–2255).

TOUR OPERATORS

Buying a prepackaged tour or independent vacation can make your trip to Hawai'i less expensive and more hassle-free. Because everything is prearranged, you'll spend less time planning.

Operators that handle several hundred thousand travelers per year can use their purchasing power to give you a good price. Their high volume may also indicate financial stability. But some small companies provide more personalized service; because they tend to specialize, they may also be more knowledgeable about a given area.

BOOKING WITH AN AGENT

Travel agents are excellent resources. In fact, large operators accept bookings made only through travel agents. But it's a good idea to **collect brochures from several agencies,** because some agents' suggestions may be influenced by relationships with tour and package firms that reward

them for volume sales. If you have a special interest, **find an agent with expertise in that area**; ASTA (☞ Travel Agencies, *below*) has a database of specialists worldwide.

Make sure your travel agent knows the accommodations and other services. Ask about the hotel's location, room size, beds, and whether it has a pool, room service, or programs for children, if you care about these. Has your agent been there in person or sent others you can contact?

Do some homework on your own, too: Local tourism boards can provide information about lesser-known and small-niche operators, some of which may sell only direct.

BUYER BEWARE

Each year consumers are stranded or lose their money when tour operators—even very large ones with excellent reputations—go out of business. So **check out the operator.** Find out how long the company has been in business, and ask several travel agents about its reputation. If the package or tour you are considering is priced lower than in your wildest dreams, **be skeptical.** Try to **book with a company that has a consumer-protection program.** If the operator has such a program, you'll find information about it in the company's brochure. If the operator you are considering does not offer some kind of consumer protection, then ask for references from satisfied customers.

In the U.S., members of the National Tour Association and United States Tour Operators Association are required to set aside funds to cover your payments and travel arrangements in case the company defaults. It's also a good idea to choose a company that participates in the American Society of Travel Agent's Tour Operator Program (TOP). This gives you a forum if there are any disputes between you and your tour operator; ASTA will act as mediator.

➤ TOUR-OPERATOR RECOMMENDATIONS: **American Society of Travel Agents** (☞ Travel Agencies, *below*). **National Tour Association** (✉ NTA, 546 E. Main St., Lexington, KY 40508, ☎ 606/226–4444 or 800/

755–8687). **United States Tour Operators Association** (✉ USTOA, 342 Madison Ave., Suite 1522, New York, NY 10173, ☎ 212/599–6599 or 800/468–7862, FAX 212/599–6744).

COSTS

The more your package or tour includes, the better you can predict the ultimate cost of your vacation. Make sure you know exactly what is covered, and **beware of hidden costs.** Are taxes, tips, and service charges included? Transfers and baggage handling? Entertainment and excursions? These can add up.

Prices for packages and tours are usually quoted per person, based on two sharing a room. If traveling solo, you may be required to pay the full double-occupancy rate. Some operators eliminate this surcharge if you agree to be matched with a roommate of the same sex, even if one is not found by departure time.

GROUP TOURS

Among companies that sell tours to Hawai'i, the following have a proven reputation and offer plenty of options. The classifications used below represent different price categories, and you'll probably encounter these terms when talking to a travel agent or tour operator. The key difference is usually in accommodations, which run from budget to better, and better-yet to best.

➤ DELUXE: **Globus** (✉ 5301 S. Federal Circle, Littleton, CO 80123-2980, ☎ 800/221–0090 or 303/797–2800, FAX 303/795–0962). **Maupintour** (✉ 1515 St. Andrews Dr., Lawrence, KS 66047, ☎ 913/843–1211 or 800/255–4266, FAX 913/843–8351). **Tauck Tours** (✉ Box 5027, 276 Post Rd. W, Westport, CT 06881, ☎ 203/226–6911 or 800/468–2825, FAX 203/221–6866).

➤ FIRST-CLASS: **Caravan Tours** (✉ 401 N. Michigan Ave., Chicago, IL 60611, ☎ 312/321–9800 or 800/227–2826). **Collette Tours** (✉ 162 Middle St., Pawtucket, RI 02860, ☎ 401/728–3805 or 800/340–5158, FAX 401/728–4745). **Gadabout Tours** (✉ 700 E. Tahquitz Canyon Way, Palm Springs, CA 92262, ☎ 619/325–5556 or 800/952–5068). **Mayflower Tours** (✉ Box 490, 1225 Warren Ave., Downers Grove, IL 60515, ☎ 708/960–3430 or 800/323–7064).

➤ BUDGET: **Cosmos** (☞ Globus, *above*).

PACKAGES

Like group tours, independent vacation packages are available from major tour operators and airlines. The companies listed below offer vacation packages in a broad price range.

➤ AIR/HOTEL/CAR: **American Airlines Vacations** (☎ 800/321–2121). **Continental Vacations** (☎ 800/634–5555). **Delta Vacations** (☎ 800/872–7786). **Haddon Holidays** (✉ 1120 Executive Plaza, No. 400, Mt. Laurel, NJ 08054, ☎ 609/273–8778 or 800/257–7488). **Pleasant Hawaiian Holidays** (✉ 2404 Townsgate Rd., Westlake Village, CA 91361, ☎ 818/991–3390 or 800/242–9244). **TWA Getaway Vacations** (☎ 800/438–2929). **United Vacations** (☎ 800/328–6877).

➤ FLY/DRIVE: **Delta Vacations** (☎ 800/872–7786).

➤ FROM THE U.K.: **Hawaiian Travel Centre** (✉ Meridian House, 42 Upper Berkeley St., London W1H 8AB, ☎ 0171/304–5730, FAX 0171/224–9184). **Hawaiian Dream** (✉ 1–7 Station Chambers, High St. N, London E6 1JE, ☎ 0181/552–1201). **Jetsave** (✉ Sussex House, London Rd., East Grinstead, West Sussex RH19 1LD, ☎ 01342/327–711). **Kuoni Travel** (✉ Kuoni House, Dorking, Surrey RH5 4AZ, ☎ 01306/740–500). Many Hawai'i packages include stopovers in California or other mainland destinations.

THEME TRIPS

➤ ADVENTURE: **American Wilderness Experience** (✉ Box 1486, Boulder, CO 80306, ☎ 303/444–2622 or 800/444–0099, FAX 303/444–3999). **TrekAmerica** (✉ Box 189, Rockaway, NJ 07866, ☎ 201/983–1144 or 800/221-0596, FAX 201/983–8551).

➤ BICYCLING: **Backroads** (✉ 801 Cedar St., Berkeley, CA 94710-1800, ☎ 510/527–1555 or 800/462–2848, FAX 510/527–1444). **Bicycle Adventures** (✉ Box 11219, Olympia, WA 98508, ☎ 360/786–0989 or 800/443–6060, FAX 360/786–9661). **Rocky Mountain Worldwide Cycle Tours** (✉

333 Baker St., Nelson, BC0, Canada
V1L 4H6, ☎ 250/354–1241 or 800/
661–2453, FAX 250/354–2058).

➤ FISHING: **Fishing International**
(✉ Box 2132, Santa Rosa, CA
95405, ☎ 800/950–4242). **Rod &
Reel Adventures** (✉ 566 Thomson
Ln., Copperopolis, CA 95228, ☎
209/785–0444, FAX 209/785–0447).

➤ HIKING/WALKING: **American Wilderness Experience** (☞ Adventure,
above). **Backroads** (☞ Bicycling,
above). **Country Walkers** (✉ Box 180,
Waterbury, VT 05676-0180, ☎ 802/
244–1387 or 800/464–9255, FAX 802/
244–5661). **New England Hiking
Holidays** (Box 1648, North Conway,
NH 03860, ☎ 603/356–9696 or 800/
869–0949). **Walking the World** (✉
Box 1186, Fort Collins, CO 80522,
☎ 970/498–0500 or 800/340–9255,
FAX 970/498–9100) specializes in tours
for ages 50 and older.

➤ HORTICULTURE: **Expo Garden Tours**
(70 Great Oak, Redding, CT 06896,
☎ 203/938–0410 or 800/448–2685,
FAX 203/938–0427).

➤ LEARNING: **Earthwatch** (✉ Box
9104, 680 Mount Auburn St., Watertown, MA 02272, ☎ 617/926–8200
or 800/776–0188, FAX 617/926–8532)
for research expeditions. **National
Audubon Society** (✉ 700 Broadway,
New York, NY 10003, ☎ 212/979–
3066, FAX 212/353–0190). **Nature
Expeditions International** (6400 E. El
Dorado Cir. #210, Tucson, AZ 85715,
☎ 520/721–6712 or 800/869–0639),
☎ 415/441–1106 or 800/326–7491,
FAX 415/474–3395). **Victor Emanuel
Nature Tours** (✉ Box 33008, Austin,
TX 78764, ☎ 512/328–5221 or 800/
328–8368, FAX 512/328–2919).

➤ SPAS: **Spa-Finders** (✉ 91 Fifth Ave.,
Suite 301, New York, NY 10003-
3039, ☎ 212/924–6800 or 800/255–
7727).

➤ SINGLES AND YOUNG ADULTS: **Contiki Holidays** (✉ 300 Plaza Alicante,
Suite 900, Garden Grove, CA 92840,
☎ 714/740–0808 or 800/266–8454,
FAX 714/740–0818).

➤ YACHT CHARTERS: **Ocean Voyages**
(✉ 1709 Bridgeway, Sausalito, CA
94965, ☎ 415/332–4681, FAX 415/
332–7460).

TRAVEL AGENCIES

A good travel agent puts your needs
first. Look for an agency that has
been in business at least five years,
emphasizes customer service, and has
someone on staff who specializes in
your destination. In addition, **make
sure the agency belongs to a professional trade organization,** such as
ASTA in the United States. If your
travel agency is also acting as your
tour operator, *see* Buyer Beware *in*
Tour Operators, *above*.

➤ LOCAL AGENT REFERRALS: **American Society of Travel Agents** (ASTA,
☎ 800/965–2782 24-hr hot line,
FAX 703/684–8319). **Association of
Canadian Travel Agents** (✉ Suite
201, 1729 Bank St., Ottawa, Ontario
K1V 7Z5, ☎ 613/521–0474, FAX 613/
521–0805). **Association of British
Travel Agents** (✉ 55–57 Newman
St., London W1P 4AH, ☎ 0171/
637–2444, FAX 0171/637–0713).
**Australian Federation of Travel
Agents** (☎ 02/9264–3299). **Travel
Agents' Association of New Zealand**
(☎ 04/499–0104).

TRAVEL GEAR

Travel catalogs specialize in useful
items, such as compact alarm clocks
and travel irons, that can **save space
when packing.**

➤ CATALOGS: **Magellan's** (☎ 800/
962–4943, FAX 805/568–5406). **Orvis
Travel** (☎ 800/541–3541, FAX 540/
343–7053). **TravelSmith** (☎ 800/
950–1600, FAX 800/950–1656).

VISITOR INFORMATION

TOURIST INFORMATION

Before you go, contact the Hawai'i
Visitors & Convention Bureau for
general information on each island, an
accommodations and car rental guide
(which includes everything from a
property's distance from the beach to
its amenities), and an entertainment
and dining listing containing one-line
descriptions of bureau members.

➤ CONTACT: **Hawai'i Visitors &
Convention Bureau** (✉ 2270
Kalakaua Ave., Suite 801, Honolulu,
HI 96817, ☎ 808/923–1811). For
brochures on the Islands call 800/
464–2924. In the United Kingdom
contact the **Hawai'i Visitors & Con-**

THE GOLD GUIDE / SMART TRAVEL TIPS

vention Bureau (✉ Box 208, Sunbury, Middlesex, TW16 5RJ, ☎ 0181/941–4009). Send a £2 check or postal order for an information pack.

U.S. GOVERNMENT

Government agencies can be an excellent source of inexpensive travel information. When planning your trip, **find out what government materials are available.**

➤ PAMPHLETS: **Consumer Information Center** (✉ Consumer Information Catalogue, Pueblo, CO 81009, ☎ 719/948–3334 or 888/878–3256) for a free catalog that includes travel titles.

WEB SITES

Do **check out the World Wide Web** when you're planning. You'll find everything from up-to-date weather forecasts to virtual tours of famous cities. Fodor's Web site, www.fodors .com, is a great place to start your on-line travels. For more information specifically on Hawaii, visit:

www.visit.hawaii.org is the official Web site of the Hawai'i Convention and Visitors Bureau.

www.hawaiian-index.com reports that "If it's about Hawai'i, it's here."

www.starbulletin.com is the site of Honolulu's daily paper, the *Honolulu Star-Bulletin.*

www.hawaii.net has links to more than 100 Hawaiian sites (click on Visitor Center).

www.search-hawaii.com has an engine that can search all linked Hawaiian Web pages by topic or word.

WHEN TO GO

Hawai'i's long days of sunshine and fairly mild year-round temperatures

make it a year-round destination. In resort areas near sea level, the average afternoon temperature during the coldest winter months of December and January is 75 °F; during the hottest months of August and September the temperature often reaches 92°F. Cold weather (30°F) can occur in Hawai'i in winter, but only near the summit of the Big Island's Mauna Ke'a crater, where skiing is possible.

Slight differences exist when it comes to monthly rainfall, high-and low-season travel rates, and the number of fellow travelers you'll find upon arrival. Winter is the season when most travelers prefer to head for the islands. From mid-December through mid-April, visitors from the mainland and other areas covered with snow find Hawai'i's sun-splashed beaches and balmy trade winds particularly appealing. Not surprisingly, this high season also means that fewer travel bargains are available; room rates average 10%–15% higher during this season than the rest of the year.

The only weather change most areas experience during the December–February span is a few more days of rainfall, though the sun is rarely hidden behind the clouds for a solid 24-hour period. Visitors should remember that regardless of the season, the northern shores of each island usually receive more rain than those on the south. Kaua'i and the Big Island's northern sections get more annual rainfall than the rest of Hawai'i.

CLIMATE

The following are average maximum and minimum temperatures for Honolulu; the temperatures throughout the Hawaiian Islands are similar.

HONOLULU, O'AHU

Jan.	80F	27C	May	85F	29C	Sept.	88F	31C
	65	18		70	21		73	23
Feb.	80F	27C	June	86F	30C	Oct.	87F	31C
	65	18		72	22		72	22
Mar.	81F	27C	July	87F	31C	Nov.	84F	29C
	69	21		73	23		69	21
Apr.	83F	28C	Aug.	88F	31C	Dec.	81F	27C
	69	21		74	23		67	19

➤ FORECASTS: **Weather Channel Connection** (☎ 900/932–8437), 95¢ per minute from a Touch-Tone phone.

1 Destination: Hawai`i

COMING TO PARADISE

THE FIRST TIME I TRAVELED from California to Hawai'i, I wondered if I would ever touch ground again—the flight seemed endless. Then, 5½ hours and 2,390 mi later, a landscape new to me came into view. I could see the green spires of the Ko'olau Mountains, the glimmering high-rises of Waikīkī, the aqua intensity of the water, the fleets of white sails dotting the sea, and the network of crisscrossing freeways, pineapple plantations, and sugarcane fields.

A trip to Hawai'i from anywhere else in the world makes you aware of its remoteness—it waits in the middle of the Pacific Ocean like a crossroads as well as a cloister. This island group is the most isolated archipelago in the world, more than 2,000 mi from the closest major land mass. The Hawaiian Islands are at the northernmost reaches of Polynesia (meaning "many islands"), within an area referred to as the Polynesian Triangle; New Zealand and Easter Island form the triangle's other points. Yet, while it is influenced by its distant Polynesian, Asian, and American neighbors, Hawai'i remains very much its own destination. As a state, it often seems as exotic as a foreign land.

Visitors often arrive with the sort of dazed, uncertain look that comes from spending hours cooped up inside a jumbo jet. Gradually their quizzical expressions will change to ones of delight, as the scent of tropical flowers carried aloft cool trade winds surrounds them and refreshes their weary lungs and limbs. Within hours they're blissed out: Paradise has enveloped their hearts, and they become determined to stay forever.

That is how many folks discover Hawai'i: They come on vacation and then realize this is where they really want to live. Yet Hawai'i's true nature is much more far-reaching and complex than one's first few deliciously seductive impressions. Relocating to the Islands is a big step—you must learn a whole new way of life.

People here operate on Hawaiian (or Island) time, which means that if you're late for a party, an appointment, a meeting, a dinner, or any other social function, you just don't worry about it. On Hawaiian time people take a much more laid-back approach to everything. This may be why residents here live longer than those in other states.

Living in Hawai'i teaches respect for nature. You stay out of the water when the huge winter waves come up on the north shores. You don't plan hiking trips in the valleys during rainy days when flash floods are possible. Windows get taped up before hurricanes as a precaution against strong, damaging winds. And when the sun starts to make its descent to the horizon, you stop what you're doing to enjoy the splendor of a Hawaiian sunset: It's a guaranteed spectacle almost every day of the year.

Natural Beauty

Hawai'i is America's most enticingly exotic and tropical state, with 132 islands and atolls stretching across some 1,600 mi of the South Seas. It is blessed with a uniform climate of predictably warm temperatures and cool trade winds; except for the occasional squalls of December, January, and February, the rains pass quickly. They say that clean de-ionized air comes all the way from the Arctic—with no pollutants to interrupt its path—and bathes these fragrant shores.

It's hard to believe that such a gentle place sprang from tremendously violent beginnings; the Islands emerged from the ocean as a result of continual volcanic eruptions. For centuries Hawai'i's fiery heights scorched the clouds; then for centuries more, wind and water erosion—crashing surf, mighty sea winds, and powerful rivers—carved and chiseled the great mountains and lush valleys visible today.

Each year almost 7 million visitors arrive to experience the beauty of nature's handiwork. While most head straight for Waikīkī, many bypass O'ahu altogether and make the Neighbor Islands (as the rest of Hawai'i is called) their final destination. What they find on any island is a combination of the wild and the tame, the serene and the slick.

Sun worshipers can't go wrong on Hawai'i. On O'ahu alone there are more than 50 mi of beaches. Pāpōhaku Beach, on Moloka'i, measures a whopping 3 mi in length. The Big Island's shores, a photographer's delight, include black-sand beaches and an unusual green-olivine beach, created long ago when a cinder cone of the mineral collapsed into a bay.

Throughout Hawai'i, nature lovers find countless delights to satisfy their senses. On an easy hike in the Tantalus hills above Waikīkī, you pass by tropical plants with leaves 10 times the size of those of ordinary house plants. Birds with bright yellow wings and unusual names, such as 'ō'ō, flit in the highlands of Kaua'i. Perhaps most miraculously of all, as you walk along the bleak, steaming floor of Kīlauea Iki Crater on the Big Island, you can see new life growing up from cracks in the lava: ferns, grasses, and 'ohi'a trees with scarlet blossoms.

Hawai'i's lands have been generous to its people; millions of acres have produced abundant pineapple and sugarcane crops. Historically, products from these crops make up the Islands' two most famous exports, but faced with global competition Hawaiian farmers have had to become more diversified. First came macadamia nut farms and coffee plantations, then orchid and anthurium nurseries, and now a diverse range of such fruits and vegetables as guava, mango, bananas, and sweet onions are grown. Kaua'i's farmers grow baby vegetables for use in Hawai'i's upscale restaurants, which rely more and more on local produce for their unique cuisine. On the Big Island, dairies are making their own butter from the milk of local herds and creating a fresher, more flavorful product. And Maui is becoming well known for its Upcountry farms, which cultivate such fresh herbs as fennel, basil, and thyme.

This rich natural environment now needs special protection. The people of Hawai'i are aware of their fragile surroundings, and they have joined forces in order to take care of it. In the forefront of this movement is the Nature Conservancy of Hawai'i, a group that manages lands on most every island. It oversees programs to ensure the protection of endangered birds as well as Pēpē'ōpae, Hawai'i's most ancient bog, and Moloka'i's Mo'omomi Dunes, one of the few remaining coastal dune areas in Hawai'i.

Local painters, potters, sculptors, weavers, photographers, and others respond to their tropical surroundings in innovative ways. With deft fingers and the flick of a wrist, craftspeople handily turn *lau hala*—the leaves of the hala or pandanus tree—into a basket, or plumeria blossoms into a fresh, fragrant lei. One group of artists thrives near a volcano's edge on the Big Island. On Maui, world-famous poet W. S. Merwin finds inspiration in the wonder and majesty of his delicate Island home. On O'ahu, photographer Kim Taylor Reece has spent much of his time capturing the elegance of the hula. These and many other Islanders share their vision of Hawai'i in a heartfelt outpouring of creativity, acting as nature's own voice.

Hawai'i is one of the world's great sports destinations. Sports are the Island's number-one pastime. A veritable regatta takes to the sea each day, from snorkeling-cruise boats to ocean liners. People hit the tennis courts, the golf courses, the running routes, the bridle paths, and the bike trails. Most of the major hotels offer some sort of fitness opportunities, be they aerobics classes, nature walks, weight-lifting rooms, or guided hikes to nearby outdoor attractions.

The Past in the Present

The natural physical charms of the Islands allow for a variety of accommodations, from the countrified to the chic. You might find yourself on Kaua'i, staying at a bed-and-breakfast and hearing stories about the Garden Isle. Or you might wind up on the Big Island in a posh Kohala Coast hotel decorated with fishponds, waterfalls, tropical gardens, gondolas, and a multimillion-dollar collection of international art. Some development has emphasized a more luxurious, upscale, and cosmopolitan Hawai'i, making backcountry options harder to track down.

But with the Islands' cultural traditions paramount—and gaining importance—the old will never completely disappear. To this day the locals have a custom of blessing all things that are new by paying tribute to the past, with a dance, a chant, a lei, or even just a few words spoken by a minister. They respect the legends of their ancestors and honor the gods accordingly. Dancers return reverently to the huge hula pavilion on the north shore of Kaua'i, a site that is dedicated to Laka, the goddess of the dance. Hikers leave rocks wrapped in ti leaves to thank the gods for their smooth passage. On the Big Island those who visit the steaming Halema'uma'u pit toss in flowers and gifts to the volcano goddess, Pele, to appease her unpredictable wrath.

Many Island customs can be learned and enjoyed by guests. One, of course, is the widely familiar, traditional lei greeting. Centuries ago, garlands of leaves, nuts, or flowers were offered to the gods; today they are a customary gift for family or friends on special occasions. Lei greetings can also be arranged for incoming visitors. It is said that the idea of bestowing a kiss along with a lei dates from World War II, when during a show a female entertainer smooched a soldier after draping him with a flower lei. Then she justified it by saying, "It's tradition in Hawai'i." It has been so ever since.

The past endures thanks to several concerned organizations that have been fighting to save the visible remnants of days gone by. For instance, a nonprofit group called the Historic Hawai'i Foundation works to preserve the state's unique, decades-old structures despite the new high-rises springing up around them.

The results are within plain view. In downtown Honolulu you can see the historic gem that is the 'Iolani Palace, dating from 1882. King Kalākaua commissioned this colonial-style building for his short but dynamic reign. The only official royal residence built on American soil, it has slowly but carefully been put back together inside and out, complete with many restored furnishings from its original days.

The Neighbor Islands offer further examples of architectural preservation. In Kona, on the Big Island, you can visit the charming Moku'aikaua Church, constructed in 1837 of coral and lava rock; on Kaua'i, one of the most popular visitor attractions is Kilohana, a gracious sugar plantation dating from 1835. Maui's Wānanalua Church in Hana was built in 1838 out of native lava rock, timber from local hills, and coral from the surround-

ing seas. Moloka'i has 19th-century churches built by the priest Father Damien. On Lāna'i, during construction of the Lodge at Kō'ele in the late '80s, the developers actually took time to relocate historic Kalokahi O Ka Mālamalama Church and the former homes of two old cowboys in order to preserve them.

As crucial to the restoration and preservation of Hawaiiana is the upkeep of its *heiau,* or ancient outdoor temples. On the Big Island you can visit Mo'okini Heiau, the birthplace of King Kamehameha the Great and now a National Historic Landmark. 'Ili'ili'ōpae, as big as a football field and the largest outdoor shrine in the Islands, awaits you on Moloka'i. In Pūpūkea on O'ahu is Pu'uomahuka, a "hill of escape" where Hawaiians still leave offerings, while on Lāna'i is another time-honored gathering place called Halulu Heiau, near the summer home of that great king.

Cultural Potpourri

Not the least of Hawai'i's treasures are its people, who are open, fun-loving, and welcoming. From earliest times the Islands have beckoned to races from around the globe, beginning back when Polynesian kings and queens ruled these lands. Along the way, both Russia and France tried to claim Hawai'i as their own, as did Great Britain. Many modern residents are descended from people brought here to work on the Islands' sugar and pineapple plantations. They came from Japan, China, the Philippines, Korea, Vietnam, Samoa, Thailand, and Portugal, bringing with them their cultural traditions and turning Hawai'i into a Pacific melting pot.

You can taste the local color in Hawai'i's foods, a wonderful stew of flavors from around the world. On any given night you can dine on Japanese sashimi, Indian curry, Hawaiian lomilomi salmon, or Chinese roast duck, not to mention French, German, Korean, American, Mexican, Thai, Italian, Moroccan, and Greek dishes.

There are, of course, tastes that are uniquely tropical, especially when it comes to fruit. Hawai'i's trademark bananas, papayas, and pineapple grow throughout the year, while the prized mangos, watermelons, and litchis appear only in the summer. Island seafood is equally splashy, with Pacific delicacies as exotic as their names: mahimahi

5

What's Where

5

(dolphin fish), ʻōpakapaka (pink snapper), *ulua* (crevalle), and ʻahi (yellowfin tuna), to name a few.

Hawaiʻi has made a dent in the international dining scene, thanks to an influx of talented chefs from around the world and the delicious attractions of Hawaiʻi Regional cuisine, which showcases fresh local products.

Hawaiʻi's ethnic mix is also evident on the cultural calendar, which is a wonderful hodgepodge of events that includes Japanese *bon* dances, Filipino festivals, Samoan shindigs, Chinese New Year celebrations, Scottish Highland flings, Greek galas, and the yearly Aloha Festivals.

Hawaiian customs still stand out in this cross-cultural mix. Highly cherished are the hula and chants, which have their roots in ancient Island history and have been handed down for centuries—in fact, the chants *are* the Islands' history, preserved in oral rather than written form. Today chants and hula are practiced almost religiously; in fact, children can learn hula in school. Each year enthusiastic audiences turn out to greet performers at hula festivals on the Big Island, Oʻahu, and Maui.

Along with the swaying hips of the hula, the strumming sound of the ʻukulele has become innately associated with Hawaiʻi. The ʻukulele (the name means "jumping flea") was brought from Portugal by sugar-plantation workers. Today most every musical group that plays old-time Hawaiian songs includes a ʻukulele.

The Aloha Spirit

Hospitality is not a new feature of the Hawaiian lifestyle. Even in ancient times, community members who failed to welcome incoming guests were shunned by the rest of society. Since then it has been a revered Island custom that when people come to call, they are not treated like anonymous tourists but embraced as cherished guests or long-lost friends. In this very special way Hawaiʻi becomes everyone's home—each visitor is a new and welcome member of the family.

Hawaiians go out of their way to help one another. On the freeway, even during rush hour, drivers often smile and wave you into their lane of traffic when you signal. At your hotel, the bellman carries your bag

as if it's an honor, and your waitress seems genuinely excited that you're about to taste your first mai tai. People in the tourist industry aren't taught such friendliness, kindness, and goodwill; it's in their nature.

Visitors to Hawaiʻi find this friendly spirit as intoxicating as the fragrance of the air—a blend of plumeria, ginger, mock-orange blossoms, freshly clipped hedges, newly mowed lawns, and the salt air from the Pacific surf. This alluring essence can turn the most jaded traveler into a giddy aficionado of the Islands. Its name? The aloha spirit, of course!

Aloha spirit pervades each island so strongly that it is impossible to ignore. It makes people stay in Hawaiʻi for much longer than they originally planned, and it's also the best reason to pay a visit to the 50th state. Enjoy your trip, and remember that you are invited to stay as long as you like.

— Marty Wentzel

WHAT'S WHERE

Oʻahu

Third-largest of the Hawaiian Islands, Oʻahu is home to 75% of the state's population. On the south side of the island, in the shadow of Diamond Head, Waikīkī is a 2½-mi hot spot with more than 31,000 hotel rooms and condominiums, scores of restaurants, and seemingly endless shopping. Waikīkī is part of Honolulu, the state's capital. Surfers who want a totally tubular experience head to the north shore.

Maui

The lush island of Maui, second-largest of the Hawaiian chain, takes its nickname, Valley Isle, from its topographic profile—an arc slung between the peaks of two volcanoes. Hāna, on Maui's eastern shore, is a sleepy little town where you might still be able to get a sense of what Hawaiʻi was like before T-shirt tourism. West Maui, "the Golf Coast," has resort after resort. Haleakalā, a 10,023-ft dormant volcano, towers in the distance. The former whaling town of Lahaina livens up the west coast with shops and eateries.

The Big Island of Hawai'i

The Big Island is almost twice the size of all the other Hawaiian Islands combined, and can be divided into six sightseeing areas: Hilo on the eastern side; Hamakua, the northern seacoast; Kohala, the northern mountainous region with the northwest coastline; Kona, the western seaside village of Kailua-Kona together with the upcountry coffee region; Ka'u and the vast stretches of lava and desert to the south; and Puna, east of Kīlauea volcano.

Kaua'i

The oldest of the Hawaiian Islands, Kaua'i's 550 square mi are rich in natural and cultural history. The banks of Kaua'i's bubbling Wailua River on the eastern shoreline attracted the first Polynesian settlers. Visitors now populate the beaches of its Coconut Coast or head south to the sunny resort of Po'ipū. The cooler, damper north shore is verdant and lush, a startling contrast to Kaua'i's western side with its Waimea Canyon, called the "Grand Canyon of the Pacific."

Moloka'i

Ten miles wide and 38 mi long, Moloka'i is made up of two volcanic mountains connected by a plain. Visitors readily embrace the down-to-earth charm of the "Friendly Isle." In the island's highest reaches you can explore Kamakou Preserve, a 2,774-acre wildlife refuge. There are also plenty of opportunities to enjoy snorkeling, swimming, and sunbathing.

Lāna'i

Lāna'i's only population center is Lāna'i City, smack in the middle of the island. The town is surrounded by natural wonders: Garden of the Gods, an eerie hilltop strewn with colorful boulders to the northwest; breathtaking Hulopo'e Beach to the south; and Lāna'ihale, the highest point on the island, to the east.

PLEASURES AND PASTIMES

Beaches

Ask people why they vacation here and most of them will tell you it's for the sun, sand, and surf—the secret beach bum in all of us hungers for Hawai'i's shores. It's true that some of the most beautiful beaches in the world are here in the 50th state; easy to get to and just a stone's throw from each other, they ring these tropic isles like garlands of plumeria flowers. All beaches, even those fronting hotels, are open to the public. Just follow the blue beach-access signs posted along the highways.

O'ahu's Waikīkī Beach *means* Hawai'i to most visitors. This hotel-studded strip of sand at the foot of Diamond Head sees its share of sun worshipers along what is actually a collection of smaller sections known as Ft. De Russy, Gray's, and Queen's Surf beaches. It's tough to beat for convenience to hotels, restaurants, and shopping.

Also on O'ahu and synonymous with surfing the big waves are the North Shore's Sunset Beach and Waimea Bay; Kailua Beach Park is the site of international windsurfing competitions; its neighbor, Lanikai Beach, is often referred to as the most beautiful beach in the world; and Makapu'u Beach, near Sea Life Park, has some of the best bodysurfing in the state.

The sun arcs slowly over Maui's beaches, according to legend, because the demigod Maui caught the swift culprit in his lasso and demanded longer daylight hours. Catching old Sol's rays on the Valley Isle can mean seclusion on the sands of Mākena, admiring windsurfing skills at Ho'okipa, or people-watching extraordinaire at luxury resort-lined Kā'anapali Beach.

Kaua'i's ideal beaches and dramatic cliffs have found fame as movie sets. And white, black, and green-sand beaches are attractions in their own right on the Big Island, where Kīlauea Volcano is actively adding to the island's future sandy shores by sending rivers of hot lava steaming into the ocean.

Even diminutive Moloka'i and Lāna'i can claim their share of exceptional sandy retreats, such as Moloka'i's 3-mi-long Pāpōhaku Beach, the largest white-sand beach in the state; and Lāna'i's Hulopo'e Beach, where snorkeling in a marine preserve is, well, pretty fishy.

Facilities vary at each location; many beaches have at least outside showers and restrooms. Picnic tables, however, are few and far between. Visitors are asked to do their part in keeping beaches clean and litter-free.

Safety deserves a mention here. Ocean waves and currents are often unpredictable, so prudence dictates caution whenever you enter unknown waters, even if you're an experienced swimmer. Watch for signs warning of dangerous undertows or occasional invasions of stinging jellyfish; and check to see if the beach you have chosen comes equipped with a lifeguard—many do not. You should also exercise appropriate caution if you rent equipment for windsurfing, snorkeling, sailing, or parasailing.

Bicycling

Hawai'i's near-perfect climate makes for ideal cycling conditions. Match that with the well-maintained coast-hugging roadways, and you'll discover an exciting place for a cycling vacation. No doubt you've heard of the Ironman Triathlon, where, among other sweaty endeavors, contestants bike 112 mi over the Big Island's wide-open, volcanic roadways, which are ideal at any time for long-distance touring.

Biking is a wonderful way to appreciate Kaua'i's scenic beauty, and Maui county workers have recently been busy painting hundreds of miles of white bikeway lines on many major highways, adding another biking option for those who have already coasted down the slopes of Haleakalā. O'ahu has a cycle-friendly mayor who bikes with his constituents. Once every couple of months, a scenic area of the island is closed to traffic while hundreds of enthusiasts join the mayor on his designated "Sunday on Wheels" trek. O'ahu also has an extensive system of bikeways including a dozen or so bike paths that meander along coastal areas and are ideal for a family outing.

Dining

Hawai'i's melting-pot population accounts for its great variety of epicurean delights. In addition to American and Continental cuisines, you can choose from Hawaiian, Thai, Korean, Japanese, Chinese, Philippine, Vietnamese, and other kinds of cooking. Hawaiian food, of course, has a loyal following among visitors. Many rate their experience of a lū'au among the highlights of their stay. Delicacies you're likely to find at one of these outdoor feasts include the traditional *kālua* pig—roasted underground in an *imu* (oven); poi, the starchy, bland paste made from the taro root; and *laulau*—fish, meat, and other ingredients wrapped and steamed in ti leaves. Many hotels and visitor attractions around the state offer a lū'au, or you can ask most any local for directions to a favorite Hawaiian-style feast.

You'll also find plenty in the way of Continental offerings. Nearly every European country is represented—from Austria to Spain, Italy to Switzerland. Almost all luxury hotels have at least one gourmet dining spot for Continental cuisine, and a healthy number of independent operations can be found as well. Currently, chefs and fine restaurants are emphasizing Hawai'i Regional cuisine, with beautifully presented fresh-caught Island fish and the best of locally grown produce.

Diving

Hawai'i is among the most popular scuba diving destinations in the world due to its water clarity, marine life, underwater scenery, diving facilities, and accommodations. Thousands of certified divers visit the Islands each year, and many more experience their first dive here. Snorkeling, too, is extremely popular.

With its splendid aquatic resources, Hawai'i supports plenty of experienced dive operators. Before signing on with any of these outfitters, however, it's a good idea to ask a few pointed questions: What is the dive operator's safety record? How often is the rental equipment updated and maintained? Are the dive boats custom built for divers? Do they have secure areas for diving gear and personal belongings, an extra wide boarding ladder, easy entry into the water, a canopy for protection from the sun, and how many passengers do they carry? Is there oxygen on board and someone who knows how to use it? How long is the trip to the dive site? How deep are the dives, and what are dive conditions (visibility, currents, water temperature)? Are the dives guided? How many dives are included in the package price? Are interesting shore diving spots available nearby, and is there an extra charge for tanks for shore dives? How well staffed is the dive operation, and what level of training, including rescue, do staff members have? What certification courses are offered? Are advanced and specialty courses available? Is there a recompression chamber in the area? Does the shop offer gear repair, and are tanks and weights included in the dive package price?

You might also check to see if they rent underwater cameras and video equipment so you can capture on film some of the spectacular underwater scenery. As the Islands emerged millions of years ago, molten lava spilling into the sea cooled to form huge cavernous rooms, mammoth archways, tall pinnacles needling skyward, and networks of tunnels called lava tubes. The colorful coral reefs are home to nearly 600 species of tropical fish, almost a third of which are found only in Hawai'i.

In addition to brightly hued wrasses and parrot fish, yellow butterfly fish, and the official state fish, the aggressive humuhumunukunukuāpua'a with its distinctive chevrons, Hawai'i's waters are full of friendly green sea turtles, acrobatic spinner dolphins, graceful manta rays and spotted eagle rays, and cruising white-tip, black-tip, hammerhead, sandbar, and tiger sharks. Even whales come to dive in Hawai'i. Between November and May, lucky divers may catch a distant glimpse of a humpback on its annual migration from Alaska.

A number of areas, such as Molokini Crater off the coast of Maui, are protected marine preserves where no fishing or shell collecting is allowed. The fish here are so tame and plentiful that they readily approach visitors for a handout. Don't feed them though. Hawai'i's marine environments are delicate, and endemic fish do poorly on a diet of white bread. Other great diving spots—where you may occasionally happen upon a scuba wedding ceremony—include the wrecks of sunken ships, aircraft, and World War II tanks. Just a note on surf conditions for divers: surf's up on the north and east shores of each island during the winter months, making beach entry dangerous. The most popular dive sites are on the south and west shores—the lee sides—protected from the trade winds. Wherever you dive in the Islands, you can usually count on visibility of more than 100 ft, and a comfortable, year-round water temperature of 75°F–80°F.

Fishing

In the late 1700s, when King Kamehameha the Great ruled all the Islands, Hawaiians built underwater lava rock enclosures with wooden sluice gates, called mākāhā, at each entrance. Small fish were lured through gaps in the gate, then well fed and fattened so they couldn't return the way they came. Often these fishponds were the exclusive preserve of the ruling ali'i (chiefs), but commoners skilled in the art of fishing developed equally effective ways of putting their catch on the table. Hollow bamboo shafts filled with burning, oily kukui nuts (from the candlenut tree) provided a light for spear-wielding fishermen at night when big-eyed soldierfish emerged from crevices to feed. After each fishing expedition, part of the catch was laid on a fishing stone or shrine as an offering to the god who had made that harvest possible.

Today, Hawai'i residents still know how to take advantage of the waters surrounding their state, and they'll pass on their fishing secrets to anyone with an interest in hooks, lines, and sinkers.

A big lure for visiting fishing enthusiasts is deep-sea trolling for marlin, especially off the shores of the Big Island. Each morning an entire fleet of sportfishing boats leaves Kona in search of the elusive game fish. If the marlin aren't biting, reels are often whining with catches of local 'ahi or 'ōpakapaka.

Golf

Without a doubt, Hawai'i is a golfer's paradise. It seems like every square foot of available land has a golf course on it, and many of these challenging and beautiful links have been designed by such golfing legends as Arnold Palmer, Ben Crenshaw, and Robert Trent Jones, Sr.

Maui's fairways and greens get the most press due to several nationally televised professional tournaments, especially the EMC Ka'anapali Classic in October, where top SENIOR PGA players compete for $1 million in prize money, and Mercedes Championships (formerly the Lincoln-Mercury Kapalua International) held in January on Kapalua's Plantation Course. Maui can also claim Wailea's stunning trio of 18-holers clinging to the slopes of Haleakalā. Wailea's Gold Course features prehistoric lava rock walls and gardens of indigenous grasses along with stunning ocean vistas guaranteed to take your mind off the game.

Not to be outdone when it comes to scenery, many of the Big Island's courses are emerald oases in the midst of black, barren lava fields. Towering over this picture is snow-capped, 13,796-ft Mauna Kea, home of Poli'ahu, the Hawaiian snow goddess. On Kaua'i and O'ahu, golf enthusiasts have the enviable task of choosing between fairways that tumble down the sides of mountains, leapfrog across rocky crevices beside the ocean, glide over gently rolling terrain, or serve as nesting areas and playgrounds for black swans. Even Lāna'i has two championship courses, and you can play the game on Moloka'i on 160 manicured acres designed by Ted Robinson.

Hiking

The ancient Hawaiians blazed a wide variety of trails across their archipelago domains, and many of these paths can still be hiked today. Part of the King's Trail at 'Anaeho'omalu on the Big Island winds through a field of lava rocks covered with prehistoric carvings meant to communicate stories of births, deaths, marriages, and similar family events. Another option on the Big Island is hiking atop an active volcano at Hawai'i Volcanoes National Park. Kaua'i offers rain forests and the Kalalau Trail, which traverses rugged, oceanside cliffs. Maui's Haleakalā Crater hike leads through a surreal moonscape. On O'ahu, Ka'ena Point Natural Area Reserve is a storehouse of fossilized shells, a nesting area for such seabirds as wedgetail shearwaters, and, according to Hawaiian lore, a jumping off point for souls leaping into the afterlife. At the island's opposite end, the trek up the slopes of Diamond Head rewards hikers with a breathtaking view of the brilliant blue Pacific, Honolulu's skyline, and the populous island beyond. For a preview of the lay of the land, the Hawai'i Trail and Mountain Club, Sierra Club, and Hawai'i Nature Center offer group and guided hikes for a small fee.

Horseback Riding

Riders may saddle up on all the major Islands for guided horseback trips through a range of unique tropical terrain. Two recommended rides explore Maui's Haleakalā Crater and Kaua'i's south shore.

Lū'au

Just about everyone who comes to Hawai'i goes to at least one lū'au. Traditionally, the lū'au would last for days, with feasting, sporting events, hula, and song. But at today's scaled-down and, for the most part, inauthentic version, you're as likely to find macaroni salad on the buffet as poi and big heaps of fried chicken beside the platter of kālua pig. Traditional dishes that visitors actually enjoy include laulau, lomilomi salmon, and haupia. As for the notorious poi, the clean, bland taste goes nicely with something salty, like bacon or kālua pig.

If you want authenticity, look in the newspaper to see if a church or civic club is holding a lū'au fund-raiser. You'll not only be welcome, you'll experience some down-home Hawaiiana.

National and State Parks

Like many other states, Hawai'i has sought to protect some of its natural beauty by designating portions of its property national and state parkland. The Islands have a total of seven national parks, national historic parks, and national memorials, along with more than 75 state parks and historic sites.

Hawai'i's two national parks are the Big Island's Hawai'i Volcanoes National Park, with 207,643 acres, and Maui's 27,284-acre Haleakalā National Park. Both offer excellent views and opportunities to learn about volcanoes and their role in the formation of the Islands. Kīlauea volcano in Hawai'i Volcanoes National Park has been in a state of constant eruption since 1982, and at times, you can catch a glimpse of molten lava hissing into the ocean by looking through high-powered binoculars set up by the park service. Helicopter tours over the active volcano represent the best way to see the action; in the past, environmentalists and hikers have complained about helicopter noise, but the two sides have worked out some federally mandated compromises that will probably ensure the future of Hawai'i's flight-seeing industry. Maui's Haleakalā, which means "house of the sun," draws a large number of tours and individuals who make the two-hour drive to the summit to see the sun rise each morning. Any time of day, however, will find plenty of sights on, in, and around the dormant volcano.

The Big Island encompasses three other national areas: Kaloko-Honokōhau National Historical Park, a royal fishpond area; Pu'uhonua o Hōnaunau National Historical Park, better known as the City of Refuge; and Pu'ukoholā Heiau National Historic Site, an ancient place of worship. Moloka'i's Kalaupapa National Historical Park, site of Father Damien's leper colony, and the Arizona Memorial at Pearl Harbor on O'ahu round out the national selection.

State parks range in size from the 2½-acre wayside stop at O'ahu's Nu'uanu Pali Lookout to the 6,175-acre Nā Pali Coast State Park on Kaua'i. Falling somewhere in between are other popular spots, including Maui's haunting 'Iao Valley State Monument, Kaua'i's Kōke'e State Park and Wailua River State Park, and the Big Island's Hāpuna Beach State Recreation Area—at what is often claimed to be the prettiest beach on that island.

Shopping

Hawai'i is not only an international hot spot for beaches, bathing, and dining; it's a premier place to shop. You'll be astonished at the variety of its offerings. Where else in the world, for example, could you find a convenience store selling sundries, rare black-coral jewelry, University of Hawai'i T-shirts, and intricately etched scrimshaw—right next to the tony boutiques of Ferragamo, Cartier, and Armani?

ALOHA AND RESORT WEAR➤ Aloha shirts and Hawaiian dresses (especially mu'umu'u and the less familiar holokū) are standard dress on Fridays each work week. Hilo Hattie, Liberty House, and JCPenney department stores all offer a wide selection. Original designs can be found in Waikīkī, Lahaina, and other spots, or in boutiques at resort hotels.

KONA COFFEE➤ The nation's only commercial coffee plantations are found on the western slopes of the Big Island and on Kaua'i, Maui, and Moloka'i. If you want the strongest java, go for pure Kona coffee; blends of Kona coffees with other types are not always marked as such. Kaua'i's Island Coffee has a milder flavor.

MACADAMIA NUTS➤ Also grown on the Big Island, these nuts are among the richest and most delicious foodstuffs in Hawai'i. You'll find them everywhere and treated in every way—from chocolate-covered to chopped for cookie filling.

PINEAPPLES➤ Nothing evokes the real Hawai'i like the taste of a locally grown pineapple. Taking the fruit of the Islands home with you is simple: you may either purchase the fruit in a shop or grocery store, or buy it boxed, for a slightly higher price, from the vendors at Honolulu International Airport.

T-SHIRTS➤ Hawai'i may be the T-shirt capital of the Pacific. You'll find stores devoted solely to these ubiquitous symbols of American style; prices vary widely, the least expensive shirts often can be found in convenience stores.

WOOD PRODUCTS➤ Attractive trays, bowls, furniture, and other products are wrought from unusually beautiful or rare native woods. Rich koa (the wood favored for outrigger canoes), mango, milo, and monkeypod are the favorites of local craftspeople. Because the great koa forests are dwindling, visitors might consider buying only antique koa products.

Surfing

Such Hawai'i names as the Banzai Pipeline and Sunset Beach are to surfers what the Super Bowl and the Astrodome are to football players. Little surprise, then, that surf enthusiasts from around the world come to Hawai'i to ride the waves. Waikīkī Beach and Lahaina on Maui are probably the two best spots for first-time surfers to pick up the basics, and there are plenty of surfing concessions and schools staffed by experienced local surfers who will be happy to show you the ropes; O'ahu's North Shore is an excellent place to view the veterans, especially during high-surf period in December and January.

Tennis

The court sport is popular at island hotels and condominiums, many of which have courts that are lighted for night play. Forget your racket? No problem. The adjoining pro shops and retail centers will be happy to rent the latest to you and will even offer a brush-up lesson or find you a partner if you need one.

Waterskiing

Skimming across the water's surface in Hawai'i usually translates into surfing, but waterskiing also has its fans in the state. O'ahu and Maui offer ocean skiing; companies on Kaua'i offer ski trips up and down the Wailua River near Līhu'e.

Windsurfing

Hawai'i's steady winds, seaside bluffs, and surf conditions make it one of the premier windsurfing spots on the planet. O'ahu and Maui attract the sport's most ardent devotees—athletes and onlookers alike. Beginning, intermediate, and advanced equipment can be rented from a variety of shops, and lessons are easily arranged.

GREAT ITINERARIES

If You Have 6 Days

Start with a short early-morning hike to the top of Diamond Head Crater on **O'ahu** for a great island and ocean view, then head out to Pearl Harbor for a tour of the *Arizona* Memorial. In the afternoon, explore Waikīkī and spend your evening enjoying some of the city's eclectic nightlife. On day two, visit the Waikīkī Aquarium in the morning then take a bus tour to the Polynesian Cultural Center and stay for the evening lū'au and Polynesian show.

Next morning, fly to **Moloka'i** to visit the historic settlement of Kalaupapa; you can either fly directly to the settlement (advance reservations are required) or take a mule trip down the highest sea cliffs in the world. Fly back to Honolulu either that night or the next morning.

Fly to **Maui** on day four and book a van tour to Hāna (if you have to concentrate on navigating the twists and turns of the winding highway, you won't see much of the spectacular scenery). Explore Lahaina in the late afternoon and evening and overnight either there or in nearby Kā'anapali. Begin your fifth day before dawn at the chilly summit of Haleakalā and watch the sun come up over the moonscape crater. On the way down the mountain, stop at Kula Botanical Gardens to see exotic protea and other tropical blooms before flying to Hilo on the **Big Island** and spending the rest of the day at Hawai'i Volcanoes National Park. On your last day, hop a flight to **Kaua'i** and take a flight-seeing tour of the painted-desert gorges of Waimea Canyon and the deeply fluted cliffs of the rugged Nā Pali Coast. A boat

trip up Wailua River to Fern Grotto is a great way to end your trip.

If You Have 9 Days

Start in **O'ahu**: Hike the Diamond Head Crater and visit the Waikīkī Aquarium, *Arizona* Memorial, USS *Blowfin,* and Bishop Museum before taking in the shops, restaurants, and other attractions of Waikīkī. On day two, drive around Diamond Head to see the windsurfers then follow the coast to Hanauma Bay and the windward town of Kailua. Take side trips to the Nu'uanu Pali Lookout and Byodo-In Temple en route to the Polynesian Cultural Center. It's a long, dark drive back to Waikīkī after the show, so you might want to stay at a B&B in the area. On your third day, continue along the North Shore, stopping at Waimea Bay and Waimea Valley and Adventure Park on the way back to Waikīkī. Once you're in Honolulu, take a walk through Chinatown, stop for lunch, take a guided tour of 'Iolani Palace, and stroll around Mission Houses Museum and Kawaiha'o Church.

Spend day four on **Moloka'i** at Kalaupapa, and on your fifth day, head to **Maui.** Wander through 'Iao Valley State Park and Bailey House Museum in Wailuku before setting out on the Road to Hāna. Overnight in Hāna and on day six, visit 'Ohe'o Gulch and Lindbergh's grave before backtracking on the Hāna Highway and exploring Lahaina. Plan to be at the chilly summit crater of Haleakalā before dawn on your seventh day to watch the sun rise then fly to Kailua-Kona on the **Big Island,** where you can visit Hulihe'e Palace and wander around town. In the afternoon, drive north to explore the Kohala Coast resorts and nearby petroglyph carvings and to get a look at snowcapped Mauna Ke'a. On day eight you'll be heading south through Hōlualoa, Kealakekua, and Captain Cook. Be sure to spend some time at Pu'uhonua o Hōnaunau National Historic Park before continuing on to Hawai'i Volcanoes National Park. Hilo is the best place to spend the night before flying to **Kauai** for your final day. On the Garden Isle, see the spectacular Waimea Canyon, Nā Pali Coast from a helicopter and take the Wailua River boat trip to Fern Grotto.

If You Have 12 Days

Start in **O'ahu** with the Diamond Head Crater hike and snorkeling in Hanauma

Bay, then head for the windward side of O'ahu and lunch in Kailua. Take in Byodo-In Temple and the view from Nu'uanu Pali Lookout before continuing to Lā'ie and the Polynesian Cultural Center. Spend the night in Lā'ie, and the morning of your second day, see Waimea Valley and Adventure Park and the surfing spots on the North Shore as well as the surfing town of Hale'iwa. Visit the *Arizona* Memorial and enjoy the restaurants, shops, and nightlife in Waikīkī. On your third day, check out Waikīkī Beach, the Waikīkī Aquarium, 'Iolani Palace Mission Houses Museum, Kawaiha'o Church, Honolulu Academy of Arts, Chinatown, Bishop Museum, and Queen Emma's Summer Palace.

Spend day four on **Moloka'i** at Kalaupapa, and start day five on **Maui** with 'Iao Valley State Park, Bailey House Museum, and Maui Tropical Plantation in the Wailuku area; Alexander and Baldwin Sugar Museum in Kahului; and the windsurfing mecca of Pāi'ia. Take an afternoon drive on the Road to Hāna and stay overnight in Hāna. The morning of day six, visit 'Ohe'o Gulch and Lindbergh's grave. If you've rented a four-wheel drive, you can continue around remote East Maui and explore Upcountry, with stops at Tedeschi Winery and Makawao. Overnight in Kā'anapali, then get up early on your seventh day for a sailing/snorkeling cruise out of Lahaina to **Lana'i**. Lahaina's shops, walking tours, art galleries, and nightlife should round out the day.

On day eight, see the sun rise at Haleakalā and fly to Hilo on the **Big Island.** Don't miss Rainbow Falls, Hawai'i Tropical Botanical Garden, and 'Akaka Falls State Park, then leave the rest of the day to investigate Hawai'i Volcanoes National Park. Begin day nine with a drive up the Hāmākua Coast to Waimea, home of Kamuela Museum and the Parker Ranch Visitor Center as well as some great souvenir shops. On your way to the Kohala Coast resorts, look for the snowcapped top of Mauna Ke'a. Day 10 should include Hōlualoa, Kealakekua, Captain Cook, and Pu'uhonua o Hōnaunau National Historic Park; then turn around and visit the Astronaut Ellison S. Onizuka Space Center at Ke'āhole-Kona Airport. There's plenty to do in Kailua-Kona before you fly to **Kauai** the next morning. Begin your tour of the Garden Isle with spectacular Waimea Canyon, then return along the south shore and visit one of the tropical botanical gardens and the eclectic shops at Kilohana. Spend the evening at Po'ipū Beach. On your last day, cruise up Wailua River to the Fern Grotto, take a flightseeing tour, stop at Kīlauea Lighthouse and Hanalei Valley Overlook, and spend your final evening watching the sun set at Hanalei Bay.

NEW AND NOTEWORTHY

American Hawaii Cruises is adding three ships that will quadruple its passenger capacity. At present, its one ship, which cruises at near capacity year-round, has a seven-day Hawaiian Islands itinerary.

O'ahu

Good news for east coast travelers: At press time Continental Airlines was scheduled to begin nonstop flights from Newark to Honolulu in summer 1998.

The state-of-the-art Hawai'i Convention Center (HCC) in Waikīkī opened summer 1998 on a 10-acre site. Its design mixes modern and Hawaiian architectural elements, with courtyards, terraces, indoor palm groves, and a 70-ft lobby waterfall. The HCC's 200,000-sq-ft exhibition space is expected to broaden the state's appeal as a business destination.

Honolulu's gone retail crazy! In Waikīkī, the 81,000-sq-ft Kalākaua Plaza opened in 1998 with such stores as Niketown and Banana Republic. Neiman Marcus and Nordstrom will add new luster to Ala Moana Shopping Center with their respective 1998 and 2000 openings. Also in the works is an enormous retail and entertainment complex anchored by Saks Fifth Avenue, opening on the current site of Ward Warehouse in 2001.

The USS *Missouri* was towed from Bremerton, Washington to Pearl Harbor in mid-1998. The famed battleship will open as a museum and interactive educational center in January 1999, about 1,000 ft from the *Arizona* Memorial.

A new highway, which connects the windward side of the island with Pearl Harbor, opened Dec. 12, 1997. The four-lane H-3 is reached from Honolulu via the Halawa Interchange, near Aloha Stadium.

Maui

The island's biggest news—and a must-see for all visitors—is the new Maui Ocean Center, a world-class aquarium focusing on the marine life and ocean ecology of the Pacific. Its main attraction is a 2.5-million-liter open-ocean tank with a walk-through acrylic tunnel. The Reef Building simulates a walk down into a reef, level by level, from the shoreline to the seafloor.

The famous Road to Hāna has been spruced up, but the State Highways Division is still scratching its head over a bad stretch of cliffside road that has crumbled to one lane in the Ke'anae area. Some officials have proposed the unthinkable—closing the road entirely for up to nine months. It's not clear yet what action will be taken. Till then, drivers can count on a good road not only into Hāna but all the way around East Maui on the belt road. There's still one rather irritating 4-mi rocky stretch in Kaupo, but passenger cars will experience no trouble on this spectacular "back side" two-lane route.

While in Hāna, the thoughtful visitor will want to take a two-hour guided tour of Kahanu Garden and Pi'ilanihale Heiau, the largest pre-discovery monument in the state. The temple dates to the 16th century; it's surrounded by a federally funded botanic research facility specializing in the ethnobotany of the Pacific. For years this remarkable place was closed to the public, in part because the Hawaiian guardians preferred it that way. They've opened it now to visitors who respect the site's sacred significance—and who call ahead for an appointment.

The old Courthouse in Lahaina is slated to emerge in January 1999 from a one-year restoration to its 1925 configuration. Besides government offices, the renewed Courthouse will have changing displays on Lahaina and Maui history as well as the (probable) return of its former tenant, the Lahaina Arts Society. The Lahaina Visitors Center, formerly in the Courthouse, will relocate to a new building on Front Street just mauka of the town library.

After 23 years of planning and development, Maui now has its version of Cen-tral Park—Keōpūolani Park in Kahului. The park comprises seven ball fields, a picnic area, a walking trail, a botanical garden, and a children's petting zoo—all wheelchair-accessible and landscaped largely with native plants.

The Big Island of Hawai'i

The Big Island has seen a steady increase in visitors since Kona International Airport lengthened its runway and improved its facilities in 1995. As a consequence, Kailua-Kona has experienced exceptional growth. Shopping centers have expanded, as new merchants continue to open their doors. Latest in this march to progress was the opening of the Crossroads Center, which houses Wal-Mart and Safeway.

New visitor attractions are eco-sensitive and culturally aware. For example, the Orchid at Mauna Lani has found enthusiastic acceptance for its "beach boy" program of free activities—educational walks along the coast, sessions in weaving baskets, handling throw nets, and paddling outrigger canoes—conducted by Islanders. At the Four Seasons Resort Hualālai, a beautifully appointed Cultural Center draws not only hotel guests but local people to learn about Hawaiian culture.

Brochures that designate trails for mountain biking and self-guided driving tours of Kona coffee country are available at Hawai'i Visitor Bureau outlets. New visitor attractions include a tour of Uchida Coffee Farm, a renovated farm and mill that is a living museum illustrating the way early Japanese coffee farmers lived and worked their own small coffee businesses.

Another new attraction is the Kohala Mountain Kayak Cruise, a guided excursion through the dark tunnels of the Kohala irrigation ditch, an amazing engineering feat when it was completed in 1906.

Kaua'i

United's new nonstop flights between Los Angeles and Lihu'e will put smiles on a lot of weary faces. With $30 million allotted for a 2,000-ft extension of the runway at Līhu'e Airport so larger aircraft can land and take off, visitor traffic is expected to rise from direct flights in the coming years. Sightseers traveling by car to Kaua'i's northern reaches may find traffic flow improved near Hanalei, as new two-lane bridges are planned to replace the historic single-lane Waipā and Waikoko bridges.

The reopening of the Sheraton Kaua'i Resort's 413 rooms and suites, following a $40 million reconstruction project in the wake of the hotel's destruction by Hurricane 'Iniki in 1992, had the island rejoicing. Eight hundred new jobs were created, and nearly 90% of the employees were returnees.

On Kaua'i's eastern shoreline, the former Wailua Bay Resort was renovated to the tune of $3 million and opened as the first Holiday Inn SunSpree Resort in all the islands. SunSpree aims to appeal to families with a KidSpree Vacation Club program that provides free organized activities for youngsters. Adults can also take advantage of free snorkeling, beach volleyball, and tennis.

The new Grove Farm Golf course in Līhue opened to widespread raves from resident and visiting golfers alike.

Hollywood continues to spotlight Kaua'i's white sand beaches and jungle terrain with *Six Days, Seven Nights,* starring Harrison Ford and Anne Heche, and *Mighty Joe Young,* a remake of a giant ape saga.

Moloka'i

Moloka'i suffered an economic setback when the closure of Mahalo Airlines caused the cancellation of seven flights to the island's peaceful shores, creating a shortage of airline seats. Island Air and Hawaiian Airlines continue daily service to Moloka'i, but travelers should make reservations well in advance.

Moloka'i Ranch Wildlife Conservation Park has closed, but the Ranch has opened Kolo Camp, with yurt tents perched high on a bluff over the ocean, and Koloa Camp, with canvas tents near the sea, to supplement the Ranch's original Paniolo Camp near Maunaloa. The Ranch has also continued to develop Maunaloa Town. The island's first triplex cinema now shows first-run movies, and Jojo's Café was remodeled and opened as the Village Grill.

Lāna'i

Lāna'i's Lodge at Kō'ele now has a poolside fitness center with workout equipment and massage services. Red Rover, specializing in off-road vehicle rentals, opened right across the street from Lāna'i City Service, which previously monopolized the island's car-rental scene. And Pele's Other Garden, a combination juice bar/deli/pizza place opened in Lāna'i City.

FODOR'S CHOICE

Beaches

★ **O'ahu: Kahaloa and Ulukou Beaches.** Fronting the Royal Hawaiian and Sheraton Moana Surfrider hotels in Waikīkī, these two beaches offer great swimming.

★ **Maui: Nāpili Beach.** This sparkling white beach forms a secluded cove tailor-made for honeymooners.

★ **The Big Island: Hāpuna Beach.** In summer, this clean, wide white-sand beach is a perfect snorkeling and scuba-diving spot. At the north end, there's a cove with tidal pools where children can romp.

★ **Kaua'i: Polihale Beach.** Come here for the breathtaking views of the rugged sea cliffs, not for swimming—the surf and currents are dangerous.

★ **Moloka'i: Pāpōhaku Beach.** You can always find a private section of glorious white sand on Hawai'i's longest beach.

★ **Lāna'i: Hulopo'e Beach.** The only swimming beach on the island, this beach offers ideal snorkeling.

Dining

★ **O'ahu: A Pacific Cafe O'ahu, at Ward Centre.** Chef Jean-Marie Josselin's award-winning menu is served up in an interior that's both whimsical and modern. $$

★ **Maui: Trattoria Ha'ikū.** A country-style Italian dinner house brings white linens to the jungle and serves locally produced foods in a 1920s house, formerly a lunchroom for pineapple cannery workers. $$–$$$

★ **The Big Island: Pahu i'a at Four Seasons Resort Huālalai.** Meals are imaginative and beautifully presented, especially at night, with the surf spotlighted just a breath away from your table. $$–$$$$

★ **Kaua'i: Hamura Saimin, Līhu'e.** Do as approximately 999 other diners do each day: Order a steaming bowl of *saimin* (broth and noodle soup with varying other ingredients, such as pork, fish cake, and wonton). $

★ **Molokaʻi: Kanemitsu Bakery and Restaurant, Kaunakakai.** The round Molokaʻi bread baked here is delicious. $

★ **Lānaʻi: Formal Dining Room, Lodge at Kōʻele.** Fresh local ingredients and gourmet cuisine are served in an elegant up-country atmosphere. $$$–$$$$

Lodging

★ **Oʻahu: Kāhala Mandarin Oriental.** For luxurious privacy, great food, and elegant accommodations, while near enough to Waikīkī shopping and attractions, this hotel fits the bill . . . beautifully. $$$$

★ **Maui: Ritz-Carlton, Kapalua.** A magnificent setting, beautifully appointed rooms (most with ocean views toward Molokaʻi over landscaped golf courses), terraced swimming pools, fine dining, and exemplary service guarantee an Island idyll. $$$$

★ **The Big Island: Four Seasons Resort Huālalai.** This is a resort movie moguls only dream of, with accommodations in two-story bungalows arranged around swimming pools by the ocean's edge and connected by torch-lit paths. $$$$

★ **Kauaʻi: Princeville Hotel.** Kauaʻi's most romantic retreat is a spectacular cliffside property with breathtaking views across Hanalei Bay and the wide Pacific, framed by mountain peaks. The service and facilities are unrivaled, and the golf course world-class. $$$$

★ **Molokaʻi: Molokaʻai Ranch.** The rates at Molokaʻi Ranch's three upscale camps include meals, an enormous variety of activities, and evening musical and "talk story" entertainment by the local *paniolo*: "City Slickers" never had it this good. $$$$

★ **Lānaʻi: Lodge at Kōʻele, Lānaʻi City.** This sprawling mountain retreat in the cool highlands has fireplaces, local artwork, and rare Pacific artifacts. $$$$

Quintessential Hawaiʻi

★ **Attraction: *Arizona* Memorial, Oʻahu.** With its gleaming white memorial and powerful presentation, it remains a must-see destination for practically every visitor to the Islands.

★ **Flightseeing: Maui and Kauaʻi.** Gaze down on the moonscape craters of Maui's Haleakalā volcano or zoom over rain forests, waterfalls, wide beaches, and emerald-green carpeted canyons. See the cliffs of the Nā Pali Coast on Kauaʻi from the awe-inspiring heights you only reach by riding in a whirlybird.

★ **Sunsets: Big Island.** On the Kohala Coast, the sun consistently sets as a blazing red orb, casting fiery orange and magenta hues across an ocean view broken only by a few palm trees at the ocean's edge or an occasional billowing sail on the horizon.

★ **Whale-Watching: Maui.** See humpback whales breach and blow right offshore during the peak of the season, between November and May.

FESTIVALS AND SEASONAL EVENTS

WINTER

Dec.➤ **Triple Crown of Surfing** (O'ahu; ☎ 808/638–7266): The world's top pro surfers gather on the North Shore during November and December for the big winter waves and some tough competition. **Nā Mele O Maui** (Maui; ☎ 808/661–3271): The first week of December, this Hawaiiana festival at Ka'anapali features arts and crafts, and schoolchildren competing in Hawaiian song and hula performances. **Honolulu Marathon** (O'ahu; ☎ 808/734–7200): Watch or run in one of the country's most popular marathons. **Bodhi Day** (all Islands; ☎ 808/522–9200): The traditional Buddhist Day of Enlightenment is celebrated at temples statewide; visitors are welcome. **Jeep Aloha Bowl** (O'ahu; ☎ 808/947–4141): Two top college football squads meet in this annual contest held at Aloha Stadium on Christmas Day. **Christmas** (all Islands): Hotels outdo each other in such extravagant exhibits and events as Santa arriving by outrigger canoe. **Rainbow Classic** (O'ahu; ☎ 808/956–7523): The UH Rainbows and seven top-ranked college basketball teams from the mainland compete at the University of Hawai'i between Christmas and New Year's Day. **First Night Honolulu** (O'ahu; ☎ 808/532–3131): An alcohol-free New Year's Eve street festival of arts and entertainment at dozens of downtown locations.

Jan.➤ **Hula Bowl Game** (Maui; ☎ 808/947–4141): This annual college all-star football classic is followed by a Hawaiian-style concert. **Morey Boogie World Body Board Championships** (O'ahu; ☎ 808/396–2326): Competition days for the world's best body boarders are determined by the wave action at Banzai Pipeline. **Cherry Blossom Festival** (O'ahu; ☎ 808/949–2255): This popular celebration of all things Japanese includes a run, cultural displays, cooking demonstrations, music, and crafts. It runs through the end of March. **Celebration of Whales** (Maui; ☎ 808/874–8000): Scientists and conservationists convene at the Four Seasons Resort Wailea for a week of lectures, videos, and whale-watch outings. Visitors are welcome.

Jan.–Feb.➤ **Narcissus Festival** (O'ahu; ☎ 808/533–3181): The Chinese New Year is welcomed with a pageant, coronation ball, cooking demonstrations, fireworks, and Lion dances.

Feb.➤ **NFL Pro Bowl** (O'ahu; ☎ 808/486–9300): This annual pro football all-star game is played at Aloha Stadium a week after the Super Bowl. **Hilo Mardi Gras** (Big Island; ☎ 808/935–8850): Hilo celebrates New Orleans style with an elegant ball, Cajun cook-off, festival, and parade. **Hawaiian Open Golf Tournament** (O'ahu; ☎ 808/831–5400): Top golf pros tee off at the Wai'alae Country Club. **Punahou Carnival** (O'ahu; ☎ 808/944–5752): Hawai'i's most prestigious private school stages an annual fund-raiser with rides, arts and crafts, local food, and a great white-elephant tent. **Sand-Castle Building Contest** (O'ahu; ☎ 808/956–7225): Students of the University of Hawai'i School of Architecture take on Hawai'i's professional architects in a friendly competition; the result is some amazing and unusual sand sculpture at Kailua Beach Park.

Feb.–Mar.➤ **Buffalo's Annual Big Board Surfing Classic** (O'ahu; ☎ 808/695–8935): The event features surfing as it used to be, on old-fashioned 12- to 16-ft boards, plus food and entertainment.

SPRING

Mar.➤ **Opening Day of Polo Season** (O'ahu; ☎ 808/637–6688): Games are held every Sunday through August at 2 PM at Mokule'ia and Waimānalo. **Hawai'i Challenge International Sportkite Championships** (O'ahu; ☎ 808/735–9059): Spectacular kite-flying demonstrations, workshops, and competitions at Kapi'olani Park. **Art Maui** (Maui; ☎ 808/874–1319): This prestigious annual event is held at the Maui Arts & Cultural Center in Kahului. **Prince Kuhio Day** (all Islands; ☎ 808/822–5521): March 26, a local holiday, honors Prince Kuhio, a member of Congress who might have become king if Hawai'i had not become a U.S. territory and later a state. **Celebration of the Arts** (Maui; ☎ 808/669–6200): For three days the Ritz-Carlton Kapalua pays tribute to Hawai'i's culture with hula and chanting demonstrations, art workshops, a lu'au, and Hawaiian music and dance concerts—most activities are free.

APR.➤ **Merrie Monarch Festival** (Big Island; ☎ 808/935–9168): A full week of ancient and modern hula competition begins with a parade the Saturday morning following Easter Sunday. Tickets must be purchased (and hotel rooms reserved) months in advance; the competition is held at the Edith Kanaka'ole Auditorium in Hilo. **Buddha Day** (all Islands; ☎ 808/536–7044): Flower pageants are staged at Island Buddhist temples to celebrate Buddha's birth. **Honolulu International Bed Race and Parade** (O'ahu; ☎ 808/735–6092): Big names in town turn out for this wild event centered in Waikīkī. The race and after-dark electric light parade are part of a charity fund-raiser.

MAY➤ **Lei Day** (all Islands; ☎ 808/547–7393): This annual flower-filled celebration on May 1 includes music, hula, food, and lei-making competitions, with lots of exquisite leis on exhibit and for sale. **Prince Lot Music Festival** (Kaua'i; ☎ 808/826–9644): Princeville's signature event attracts local musicians and distinguished American composers,

plus there are hula performances and art and cultural exhibits. **Ka Hula Piko** (Moloka'i; ☎ 800/800–6367): A community celebration of the birth of hula marked by performances, storytelling, Hawaiian food, crafts, and lectures.

MAY–JUNE➤ **50th State Fair** (O'ahu; ☎ 808/845–8845): Produce exhibits, food stands, amusement rides, and live entertainment occur at Aloha Stadium over several weekends.

MAY–AUG.➤ **The Wildest Show in Town** (O'ahu; ☎ 808/531–0101): Popular local entertainers perform free early-evening concerts Wednesday at the Honolulu Zoo.

SUMMER

JUNE➤ **King Kamehameha Day** (all Islands; ☎ 808/586–0333): Kamehameha united all the Islands and became Hawai'i's first king. Parades and fairs abound, and twin statues of the king—in Honolulu, O'ahu, and Hāwī on the Big Island—are draped in giant leis. **Kapalua Wine and Food Symposium** (Maui; ☎ 800/527–2582): Wine and food experts and enthusiasts gather for tastings, discussions, and gourmet dinners at the Kapalua Bay Resort.

JULY➤ **Pu'uhonua O Hōnunau Festival** (Big Island; ☎ 808/328–2288): Ancient Hawaiian games, hula performances, food tasting, and lau hala and coconut-frond weaving demonstrations take place at the historic City

of Refuge. **Makawao Statewide Rodeo** (Maui; ☎ 808/572–2076): This old-time Upcountry rodeo, held at the Oskie Rice Arena in Makawao on the July 4 weekend, includes a parade and three days of festivities. **Independence Day** (all Islands): The national holiday on July 4 is celebrated with fairs, parades, and, of course, fireworks. Special events include an outrigger canoe regatta featuring 30 events held on and off Waikīkī Beach. **Prince Lot Hula Festival** (O'ahu; ☎ 808/839–5334): A whole day of hula unfolds beneath the towering trees of O'ahu's Moanalua Gardens. **International Festival of the Pacific** (Big Island; ☎ 808/934–0177): This event features music, dance, a lantern parade, floats, sporting events, and food from Japan, China, Korea, Portugal, Tahiti, New Zealand, and the Philippines. **Kīlauea Volcano Wilderness Marathon and Rim Runs** (Big Island; ☎ 808/967–8222): More than 1,000 athletes from Hawai'i, the mainland, and Japan run 26.2 mi across Ka'ū desert, 5 mi around the Kīlauea Caldera rim, and 5.5 mi into Kīlauea Iki Crater. The event takes place in Hawai'i Volcanoes National Park. **Cuisines of the Sun** (Big Island; ☎ 808/885–6622): Well-known guest chefs present imaginative cuisine paired with fine wines at cooking classes and evening galas during a five-day celebration of food at the Mauna Lani Bay Hotel & Bungalows. **Kane'ohe BayFest** (O'ahu; ☎ 808/254–7679):This event is the largest military festival of its kind in Hawai'i—with rides, contests, food and entertainment.

JULY–AUG.➤ **Bon Odori Season** (all Islands; ☎ 808/661–4304): Buddhist temples invite everyone to festivals that honor ancestors and feature Japanese Bon dancing.

AUG.➤ **Hawai'i State Farm Fair** (O'ahu; ☎ 808/848–2074): Farm products, agricultural exhibits, arts and crafts, a petting zoo, contests, and a country market are featured on the grounds of Aloha Stadium.
Hawaiian International Billfish Tournament (Big Island; ☎ 808/329–6155): This international marlin fishing tournament, held in Kailua-Kona includes a parade with amusing entries.
Queen Lili'uokalani Keiki Hula Competition (O'ahu; ☎ 808/521–6905): Tickets for this popular children's hula competition, held over three days, are usually available at the end of June and sell out soon after. **Admission Day** (all Islands): The state holiday, on August 18, recognizes Hawai'i's attainment of statehood.

AUTUMN

SEPT.➤ **Maui Music Festival** (Maui; ☎ 800/245–9229): On Labor Day weekend, well-known contemporary jazz, Hawaiian, and other musicians converge on the Ka'anapali Beach Resort for two days of nonstop music on several outdoor stages. **Big Island Bounty**

Festival (Big Island; ☎ 800/845–9905): Hawai'i's top chefs celebrate Hawai'i Regional cuisine with cooking demonstrations, wine tastings, an outdoor market, dinners, and receptions at The Orchid at Mauna Lani on Labor Day weekend. **Maui Writers Conference** (Maui; ☎ 808/879–0061): Bestselling authors and powerhouse agents and publishers offer advice—and a few contracts—to aspiring authors and screenwriters at this Labor Day Weekend gathering. **Taste of Lahaina** (Maui; ☎ 808/667–9175): Maui's best chefs compete for top cooking honors, and samples of their entries are sold at a lively open-air party featuring live entertainment.

SEPT.–OCT.➤ **Aloha Festivals** (all Islands; ☎ 808/545–1771): This traditional celebration, started in 1946, preserves Hawaiian native culture. Crafts, music, dance, pageantry, street parties, and canoe races are all part of the festival. **Bankoh Moloka'i Hoe** (Moloka'i and O'ahu; ☎ 808/261–6615): Two annual canoe races from Moloka'i to O'ahu finish in Waikīkī. The women's race is in September; the men's is in October.

OCT.➤ **Talking Island Festival** (O'ahu; ☎ 808/592–7029): Storytellers share legends and myths of Polynesia at Ala Moana Park's McCoy Pavilion. **Ironman Triathlon World Championships** (Big Island; ☎ 808/329–0063):

This popular annual sporting event is limited to 1,250 competitors who swim, run, and bicycle.

OCT.–DEC.➤ **Hawai'i Winter Baseball** (O'ahu, Maui, Kaua'i, Big Island; ☎ 808/973–7247): Teams include promising minor leaguers from the mainland and Japan.

NOV.➤ **King Kalakaua Kupuna and Keiki Hula Festival** (Big Island; ☎ 808/329–1532): This big, popular hula contest features both a children's competition and one for *kupuna*—adults 55 years and older. **Kona Coffee Cultural Festival** (Big Island; ☎ 808/326–7820): A weeklong celebration, including two parades and a family day with ethnic foods and entertainment at Hale Halawai Recreation Pavilion, follows the coffee harvest. **Winter Wine Escape** (Big Island; ☎ 800/882–6060): Three days of food and wine pairings, cooking demonstrations, receptions, dinners, and a farmers' market showcase Hawai'i Regional cuisine at the Hāpuna Beach Prince Hotel. **Mission Houses Museum Annual Christmas Fair** (O'ahu; ☎ 808/531–0481): Artists and craftspeople sell their creations in an open market.
Hawai'i International Film Festival (O'ahu and Neighbor Islands; ☎ 808/528–3456): The visual feast showcases films from the United States, Asia, and the Pacific and includes seminars with filmmakers and critics.

2 O'ahu

Hawai'i's most populated island offers an eclectic blend of people, customs, and cuisines. Here's all the tropical splendor you've dreamed of, plus the urbanity of Honolulu. Sparkling Waikīkī Beach graces the bay near fabled Diamond Head, and generates the kind of buzz befitting an international hot spot.

MORE AND MORE HAWAI'I RESIDENTS CLAIM that O'ahu is their favorite island, with the most spectacular scenery in all of Hawai'i. Part of its dramatic appearance lies in its majestic highlands: the western Wai'anae Mountains, which rise 4,000 ft above sea level, and the verdant Ko'olau Mountains, which cross the island's midsection at elevations of more than 3,000 ft. Eons of erosion by wind and weather have carved these ranges' sculptured, jagged peaks, deep valleys, sheer green cliffs, and dynamic vistas. At the base of these mountains more than 50 beach parks lie draped like a beautiful lei, each one known for a different ocean activity: snorkeling, bodysurfing, swimming, or windsurfing.

Updated by
Marty Wentzel

Third largest of the Hawaiian Islands and covering 608 square mi, O'ahu was formed by two volcanoes that erupted 4–6 million years ago and, over time, created the peaceable kingdom we see today. Honolulu is on the island of O'ahu, and though 75% of Hawai'i's 1.1 million residents live on O'ahu, somehow there is also enough room for wide-open spaces and a pace that allows you sufficient time to take a deep breath and relax.

Hawai'i's last kings and queens ruled from Honolulu's 'Iolani Palace, near the present downtown. It was at 'Iolani that the American flag first flew over the Islands. Even in those days of royalty, the virtues of Waikīkī as a vacation destination were recognized. Long processions of *ali'i* (nobility) made their way across streams and swamps, past the duck ponds, to the coconut groves and the beach.

By the 1880s, guest houses were scattered along the beach like seashells. The first hotel, the Moana (now the Sheraton Moana Surfrider), was built at the turn of the century. At that time Waikīkī was connected to the rest of Honolulu by tram, which brought townspeople to the shore. In 1927 the "Pink Palace of the Pacific," the Royal Hawaiian Hotel, was built by the Matson Navigation Company to accommodate travelers arriving on luxury liners. It was opened with a grand ball, and Waikīkī was launched as a first-class tourist destination: duck ponds, taro patches, and all. The rich and famous came from around the world. December 7, 1941, brought that era to a close, with the bombing of Pearl Harbor and America's entry into the war in the Pacific. The Royal Hawaiian was turned over to American forces and provided hundreds of war-weary soldiers and sailors with a warm welcome in Waikīkī.

With victory came the post-war boom. By 1952, Waikīkī had 2,000 hotel rooms. In 1969 there were 15,000. Today that figure has more than doubled. Hundreds of thousands of visitors now sleep in the more than 31,000 rooms of Waikīkī's nearly 120 hotels and condominiums. To this 1½-sq-mi Pacific playground come sun bunnies, honeymooners, marines on holiday, Europeans and Canadians with a lot of time to spend, Japanese, and every other type of tourist imaginable. With Waikīkī leading the way, O'ahu maintains its status as an exciting destination, with more things to see and do, and more places to eat than all the other Hawaiian Islands combined.

Pleasures and Pastimes

Dining

The strength of Hawai'i's tourist industry has allowed O'ahu's hotels to attract and pay for some of the best culinary talent in the world. However, more and more former hotel chefs have started their own restaurants, which is good news for diners who want fine food, but don't want to pay the generally high hotel restaurant prices.

O'ahu's cuisines are as complex as its population, with Asian, European, and Pacific flavors most prevalent. So pervasive is the Eastern influence that even the McDonald's menu is posted in both English and *kanji*, the universal script of the Orient. In addition to its regular fare, McDonald's serves saimin, a Japanese noodle soup that ranks as the local favorite snack. Thai and Vietnamese cuisines are also local mainstays.

In addition you'll find influences from such far-flung destinations as Mexico and Turkey as well as the staples of the Hawaiian diet. Honolulu is much, but not all, of the O'ahu dining scene. As you head ⸻ town there are a handful of culinary gems, which are often ⸻sive than the city restaurants.

⸻s, many of Honolulu's successful restaurants are serving ⸻rary fare. Some chefs call it Hawai'i Regional, others Euro⸻ still others Pacific Rim, but by any name, this cutting-edge ⸻cuses on the use of Hawai'i's products to keep flavors fresh ⸻-inspired.

⸻n the sand at sunset may epitomize the romance of Hawai'i, ⸻e around the island brings you face-to-face with O'ahu's sheer ⸻eauty. Roll along the wave-dashed coastline of the eastern shore, ⸻hotogenic beaches, islands, and cliffs. Drive through the cen⸻s past acres of red soil, once rich in pineapple and now sup⸻diversified crops, such as coffee. Head to the North Shore, ⸻ of old O'ahu with its rickety storefronts and trees hanging ⸻ith bananas and papaya. Roll down the windows and smell ⸻ir of the windward coast, dominated by mountains chiseled ⸻ries of winds, rains, and waterfalls. A drive through Waikīkī ⸻ its own unparalleled scenery, from high-fashion boutiques and ⸻get souvenir stands to the throngs of tourists wandering up ⸻ down the avenues.

Lodging

O'ahu's diverse lodgings play to bigwigs, backpackers, and everyone in between. Waikīkī has the island's largest selection, from high-rise hotels to beachfront condos to four-story walk-ups away from the beach. Waikīkī is small enough that you don't have to pay a premium for a hotel *near* the beach. You can rent a little room three blocks from the ocean and still spend your days on the sand rubbing elbows with the rich and famous. First-time guests do well by this South Shore tourist mecca, since shopping, restaurants, nightlife, and the beach are all just a stroll away. Business travelers like to stay on the eastern edge of Waikīkī, near the new Hawai'i Convention Center, or in downtown Honolulu's sole hotel. Windward and North Shore digs are casual, including hostels and bed-and-breakfasts. Except for the peak months of January, ʾebruary, and August, you'll have no trouble getting a room if you call ⸺ead of time. When making your reservations, either on your own or through a travel agent, ask about packages and extras. Some hotels have special tennis, golf, honeymoon, or room-and-car deals.

Shopping

Honolulu is experiencing a retail boom, from the expansion of existing shopping centers to the construction of new ones. Many of the big mainland chains are here now, like Nieman Marcus, Nordstrom, and Nike Town, and a complex of outlet stores west of Honolulu draws shoppers with big-name bargains. What makes shopping on O'ahu additionally interesting is the rich cultural diversity of its products and the many items unique to Hawai'i, such as bowls made of koa wood

20 Third Avenue, New ⸻rk, NY 10021; 212-517-⸻0. "Lola" round scrub ⸻ush, $2.80, from Dean & ⸻Luca, 560 Broadway, New ⸻rk, NY 10012; 212-431-⸻1 or 800-221-7714. Catalog **Wooden toothbrush,** ⸻5, *from Cambridge* ⸻emists, 21 East 65th Street, ⸻w York, NY 10021; 212-⸻5678 or 800-241-1447.* ⸻e 110 ⸻e-shine brush,* $5.95,* ⸻ suede brush,* $2.99,* ⸻ Gracious Home, see above.* **sting paintbrush** ⸻107), $10.95, *from Jeff* and jewelry fashioned from rare shells from the island of Ni'ihau. Waikīkī, Honolulu proper, and Hale'iwa on the North Shore are particularly good places to find handmade Hawaiian souvenirs.

Water Sports

Whether you soar above them, sail on them, or dive into them, the waters surrounding O'ahu are teeming with activity. The seas off Waikīkī call to tourists looking for a surfing lesson and outrigger canoe ride, while the North Shore is the headquarters for accomplished wave riders. Snorkeling and scuba diving at Hanauma Bay, on the island's eastern tip, bring you face to face with a rainbow of sea creatures. Honolulu's Kewalo Basin is the starting point for most fishing charters. Windsurfers and ocean kayakers head to the beaches of the windward side, Lanikai in particular, for equipment rentals and lessons in near-perfect conditions. Year-round and island-wide, the water temperature is conducive to a dip, but don't so much as wade if the waves and currents are threatening.

EXPLORING O'AHU

O'ahu is a mixed bag, with enough sightseeing attractions and adventures to fill an entire vacation. Waikīkī is the center of the island's visitor industry, with its beachside strip of accommodations, stores, restaurants, nightclubs, and activities. Dominated by Diamond Head crater, Waikīkī's less populated eastern end includes a zoo and aquarium, and it encourages urban hiking and jogging. West of Waikīkī awaits Hawai'i's capital city of Honolulu, a bustling blend of history and modern-day commerce. The photogenic East O'ahu coast is fringed with white-sand beaches and turquoise seas, and it has a drive right over the top of the Ko'olau Mountains. Finally, a circle-island tour takes you to central, northern, and windward O'ahu, where shoes and cell phones give way to sandy toes and Hawaiian time.

Most of the time it's just too warm and sunny to spend all day exploring in the car or on a walking tour. So take it easy, see only what you are interested in, and relax the rest of the time. Whether you're driving, taking a tour, or riding the bus, this section will give you an idea of what you want to see.

Directions on O'ahu are often given as *mauka*—toward the mountains, or *makai*—toward the ocean. In Honolulu and Waikīkī, you may also hear people referring to "Diamond Head"—toward that landmark; and *'ewa*—away from Diamond Head. You'll find these terms used throughout this section.

Numbers in the text correspond to numbers in the margin and on the Honolulu Including Waikīkī, Waikīkī, Downtown Honolulu, and O'ahu maps.

Great Itineraries

IF YOU HAVE 1 DAY

If you have a short layover on your way to another island or if you can only tear yourself away from a convention (or a honeymoon resort) for just one day of sightseeing, the first thing you should do is treat yourself to a dawn hike up **Diamond Head** ㉑, then have breakfast at one of Waikīkī's beachfront restaurants. Next, take the bus or drive to nearby **Ala Moana Shopping Center** (☞ Shopping, *below*), which has stores to satisfy all souvenir needs. Buy a carry-out lunch from its food court, cross Ala Moana Boulevard, and spend a little time picnicking, sunning, and swimming at **Ala Moana Beach Park** (☞ Beaches, *below*). Go on a late-afternoon outrigger canoe ride with one of

Waikīkī's beachboys, followed by mai tais at sunset at the **Halekūlani** ⑦ or **Royal Hawaiian Hotel** ⑧.

IF YOU HAVE 3 DAYS

On your first day, get your bearings by following the Waikīkī and/or Kapiʻolani Park tours described below. Start the second day at the **Hawaiʻi Maritime Center** ㉒ in downtown Honolulu, followed by shopping and lunch at the adjacent **Aloha Tower Marketplace** ㉓. Don't miss the ride up to the top of the tower! Spend the afternoon prowling around downtown Honolulu before heading back to Waikīkī for sunset and dinner. On day three, get an early start so you arrive at **Hanauma Bay** ㊶ by 7:30 AM. Take your time snorkeling in this pristine marine preserve, then drive north along the coastal highway to **Sea Life Park** ㊳ for lunch and some splashy marine shows. From here, follow the East Oʻahu Ring tour in reverse, back to Waikīkī.

IF YOU HAVE 5 DAYS

Devote the first day to Waikīkī, the second to downtown Honolulu, and the third to east Oʻahu. On day four, get an early start in order to see the **Arizona Memorial** ㊺, since the waiting lines lengthen throughout the morning. Or, take the 7:30 AM boat tour to Pearl Harbor courtesy of Dream Cruises (☞ Guided Tours, *below*). From there, drive to the **Bishop Museum** ㊸ and spend some time immersed in Hawaiiana. Keep the rest of the day low-key until evening, when you can take in a cocktail or dinner show followed by dancing. Devote day five to the North Shore. Drive to **Haleʻiwa** ㊽ for breakfast and shopping, then tour **Waimea Valley** ㊾. Have a picnic lunch on the beach, followed by an afternoon visit to the **Polynesian Cultural Center** ㉛. Avoid the late-afternoon rush-hour traffic by spending the night at **Backpackers Vacation Inn** (☞ Lodging, *below*), a lodge imbued with the mellow North Shore spirit.

WHEN TO TOUR OʻAHU

The ideal seasons to visit Oʻahu are spring and fall, when fewer tourists are around and the weather is warm—but not too warm. Fall is additionally fun thanks to the Aloha Festivals, two weeks of free Hawaiian-style celebrations and special events. Festival highlights on Oʻahu include a floral parade and evening block parties in downtown and Waikīkī. Since many families travel in the summer, most every Oʻahu hotel offers children's programs from June through August. Come December, downtown Honolulu is a veritable wonderland during the holiday festival of lights.

Waikīkī

If Hawaiʻi is America's most exotic, most unusual state, then Waikīkī is its generator, keeping everything humming. On the dry, sunny side of Oʻahu, it incorporates all the natural splendors of the Islands and synthesizes them with elegance and daring into an international resort city in the middle of the vast blue Pacific.

A tropical playground since the days of Hawaiʻi's kings and queens, Waikīkī sparkles along 2½ mi of spangled sea from the famous Diamond Head crater on the east to the Ala Wai Yacht Harbor on the west. Separated on its northern boundary from the sprawling city of Honolulu by the broad Ala Wai Canal, Waikīkī is 3½ mi from downtown Honolulu and worlds apart from any other city in the world. Nowhere else is there such a salad of cultures so artfully tossed, each one retaining its distinct flavor and texture. Even McDonald's is multi-ethnic, with burgers next to *saimin* (noodle soup). You'll find

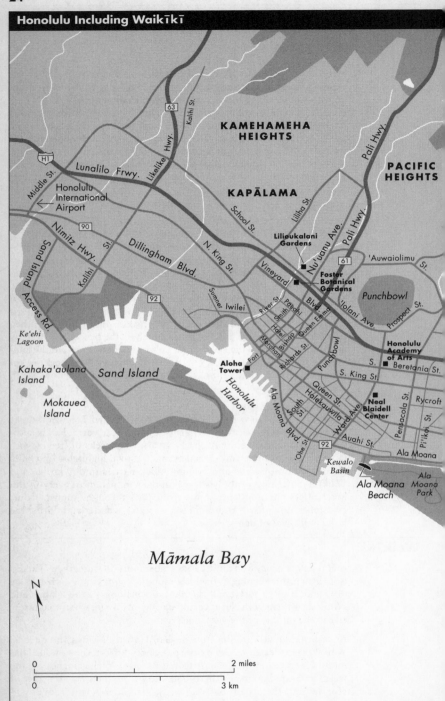

KAMEHAMEHA
HEIGHTS

PACIFIC
HEIGHTS

KAPĀLAMA

63

Kalihi St.

Likelike Hwy.

Pali Hwy.

H1

Lunalilo Frwy.

Middle St.

Honolulu
International
Airport

School St.

Liliha St.

Nu'uanu Ave.

Pali Hwy.

'Auwaiolimu St.

90

Nimitz Hwy.

Kalihi St.

Dillingham Blvd.

N. King St.

Vineyard

Lilioukalani
Gardens

61

Sand Island Access Rd.

92

Sumner

Iwilei

River St.

Pauahi

Smith

Hotel

Beretania St.

Foster
Botanical
Gardens

'Iolani Ave.

Punchbowl

Prospect St.

Ke'ehi
Lagoon

Kahaka'aulana
Island

Sand Island

Mokauea
Island

Aloha
Tower

Fort

Honolulu
Harbor

Meridian

Bishop

Richards St.

Queen Emma

Punchbowl

S. King St.

Honolulu
Academy
of Arts

S.

Beretania St.

Rycroft

Queen St.

Holekauwila

Ala Moana Blvd.

South St.

'Ohe St.

92

Auahi St.

Ward Ave.

Neal
Blaidell
Center

Pensacola St.

Pi'ikoi St.

Ala Moana

Kewalo
Basin

Ala Moana
Beach

Ala
Moana
Park

Māmala Bay

N

0   2 miles

0   3 km

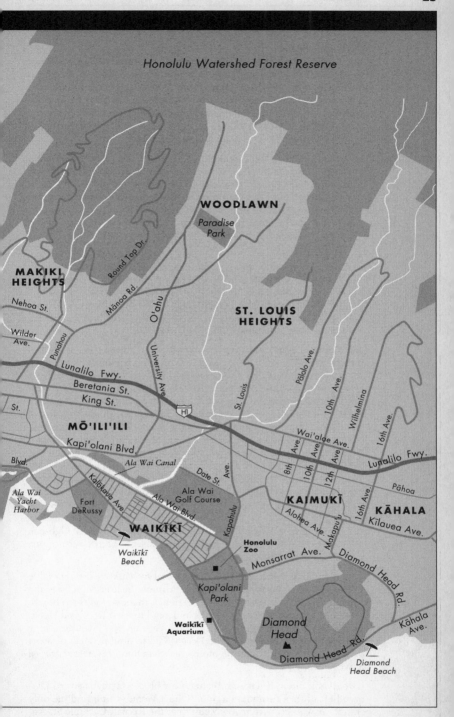

Honolulu Watershed Forest Reserve

WOODLAWN

Paradise Park

MAKIKI HEIGHTS

Round Top Dr.

Nehoa St.

Mānoa Rd.

O'ahu

Wilder Ave.

Punahou

University Ave.

ST. LOUIS HEIGHTS

Pālolo Ave.

Lunalilo Fwy.

Beretania St.

King St.

St. Louis

10th Ave.

Wilhelmina

16th Ave.

St.

H1

MŌ'ILI'ILI

Kapi'olani Blvd.

Wai'alae Ave.

Ala Wai Canal

Blvd.

Date St.

Ave.

8th Ave.

10th Ave.

12th Ave.

Lunalilo Fwy.

Ala Wai Yacht Harbor

Kalākaua Ave.

Fort DeRussy

Ala Wai Blvd.

Ala Wai Golf Course

Kapahulu

KAIMUKĪ

16th Ave.

Pāhoa

KĀHALA

WAIKĪKĪ

Kapahulu

Alohea Ave.

Makapuu

Kīlauea Ave.

Waikīkī Beach

Honolulu Zoo

Monsarrat Ave.

Diamond Head Rd.

Kapi'olani Park

Waikīkī Aquarium

Diamond Head

Diamond Head Rd.

Kāhala Ave.

Diamond Head Rd.

Diamond Head Beach

yourself saying things like aloha and *mahalo* (thank you), and you'll encounter almost as many sushi bars as ice-cream stands.

A Good Walk

A good place to start a Waikīkī walking tour is from the **Ala Wai Yacht Harbor** ①, home to an armada of pleasure boats and two members-only yacht clubs. It's just makai of the 'Ilikai Hotel Nikko Waikīkī at 1777 Ala Moana Boulevard. From here head toward the main intersection of Ala Moana Boulevard and Kālia Road, turn right at the big sign to **Hilton Hawaiian Village** ②, and wander through this lush, 20-acre resort complex past gardens and waterfalls.

Continue makai on Kālia Road to Ft. DeRussy, home of the **U.S. Army Museum** ③ and its display of wartime artifacts. Across the street, on Saratoga Road, nestled snugly amid the commerce of Waikīkī, is an oasis of tranquillity: the **Tea House of the Urasenke Foundation** ④, an offshoot of a centuries-old institution based in Kyoto, Japan. Take part in an authentic Japanese tea ceremony; you'll be served tea and sweets by kimono-clad ladies.

With a little zip from the tea and some Zen for the road, head mauka until you reach Kalākaua Avenue, then turn toward Diamond Head. At the intersection with Lewers Street, stop and peer into the lobby of the **First Hawaiian Bank** ⑤; you'll spy six massive murals portraying the indigenous peoples of Hawai'i and their cultural history. Diagonally across Kalākaua Avenue is one of Waikīkī's architectural landmarks, the **Gump Building** ⑥.

Walk down Lewers Street toward the ocean. It dead-ends at the impressive **Halekūlani** ⑦, one of Waikīkī's most prestigious hotels, famed for its elegant hospitality. From the Halekūlani stroll toward Diamond Head along the paved oceanside walkway. It leads past the Sheraton Waikīkī to the gracious, historic, and very pink **Royal Hawaiian Hotel** ⑧. It is hidden from Kalākaua Avenue by the three-story Royal Hawaiian Shopping Center. Back on the mauka side of Kalākaua Avenue, walk two blocks 'ewa and one block mauka to the **Hawai'i IMAX Theater** ⑨, home of continuous huge-screen films, including a great one about Hawai'i. Return to Kalākaua and walk toward Diamond Head. Your next stop on the mauka side of the street is the **International Market Place** ⑩, a tropical tangle of 200 shops under a spreading banyan complete with its own Swiss Family Robinson–style tree house—shopping is part of the adventure in Waikīkī. Continue heading toward Diamond Head to reach the Hyatt Regency Waikīkī. This sleek high-rise hotel is notable for its small second-floor museum of artifacts, quilts, and crafts called **Hyatt's Hawai'i** ⑪.

Across Kalākaua Avenue is the oldest hotel in Waikīkī, the venerable **Sheraton Moana Surfrider** ⑫. Wander through the breezy lobby to the wide back porch, called the Banyan Veranda, that overlooks the beach. From here, walk down to the beach and head toward Diamond Head. At the beach showers next to Kalakaua Avenue you'll find the four **Kahuna (Wizard) Stones of Waikīkī** ⑬. Said to hold magical powers, they are often overlooked and, more often than not, irreverently draped in wet towels.

If you walk along Kalakaua Avenue four blocks farther toward Diamond Head then turn mauka onto 'Ōhua Avenue you'll find the only church in Waikīkī with its own building, the Roman Catholic St. Augustine's. In the back of the church is the **Damien Museum** ⑭, a small but fascinating two-room exhibit centering on the life and work of the Belgian priest Father Joseph Damien de Veuster. Father Damien came to Hawai'i and labored and died while ministering to victims of Hansen's disease (leprosy) on the island of Moloka'i.

TIMING

A world unto itself, Waikīkī can take days to explore. If you're looking for T-shirts or souvenirs, you can spend several hours at the Royal Hawaiian Shopping Center alone. Perusing the Damien Museum will take a half hour and the U.S. Army Museum an hour, if you're so inclined. To fully appreciate the Tea House of the Urasenke Foundation, allow yourself an hour.

Many shops and attractions are open every day of the year from sunup to way past sundown, to cater to the body clocks and pocketbooks of tourists from around the world. Still, Waikīkī is most inviting in the cool of the early morning. Until 9:30 or 10 AM there's less traffic to contend with, fewer people on the sidewalks, and more room on the beach. The weather is sunny and pleasant almost every day of the year, so you'll rarely need a jacket or umbrella.

Allow yourself at least one full day for this walk, and time it so that you'll wind up on Waikīkī Beach at sunset.

Sights to See

❶ Ala Wai Yacht Harbor. Every other summer the Trans-Pacific yacht race from Los Angeles makes its colorful finish here, complete with flags and on-board parties; it will next arrive July 1999. Stroll around the docks and check out the variety of craft, from houseboats to luxury cruisers. ✉ *1777 Ala Moana Blvd., ocean side across from 'Ilikai Hotel Nikko Waikīkī.*

⑭ Damien Museum. Browse the low-key exhibits about Father Damien, the priest who worked with the lepers of Moloka'i during the late 1800s, and ask to see the museum's 20-minute videotape. It is low-budget, but well-done and emotionally gripping. ✉ *130 'Ōhua Ave.,* ☎ *808/923–2690.* ⊡ *Free.* ⊙ *Weekdays 9–3.*

❺ First Hawaiian Bank. Art, not commerce, may seem to take precedence at this bank: Half a dozen murals depict the evolution of Hawaiian culture, from Hawaiian arts before contact with the Western world to the introduction of the first printing press to the Islands in 1872. The impressive panels were painted between 1951 and '52 by Jean Charlot (1898–1979), whose work is represented in Florence at the Uffizi Gallery and in New York at both the Metropolitan Museum and the Museum of Modern Art. The murals are beautifully lit at night, with some panels visible from the street. ✉ *2181 Kalākaua Ave,* ☎ *808/943–4670.* ⊡ *Free.* ⊙ *Mon.–Thurs. 8:30–3, Fri. 8:30–6.*

❻ Gump Building. Built in 1929 in Hawaiian-colonial style, with Asian architectural motifs and a blue-tile roof, the structure that once housed Hawai'i's premier store, Gump's (known for high-quality Asian and Hawaiian objects), has been replaced by a branch of Louis Vuitton. ✉ *2200 Kalākaua Ave.*

❼ Halekūlani. Incorporated into this relatively new hotel is a portion of its old (1917) structure, which was the setting for the first of the Charlie Chan detective novels, *The House Without a Key.* Today one of the most appealing things about the hotel, aside from its famed restaurants, is the gigantic floral arrangement in the lobby. Take a peek at the swimming pool with its huge orchid mosaic on the bottom. ✉ *2199 Kālia Rd.,* ☎ *808/923–2311.*

Waikīkī

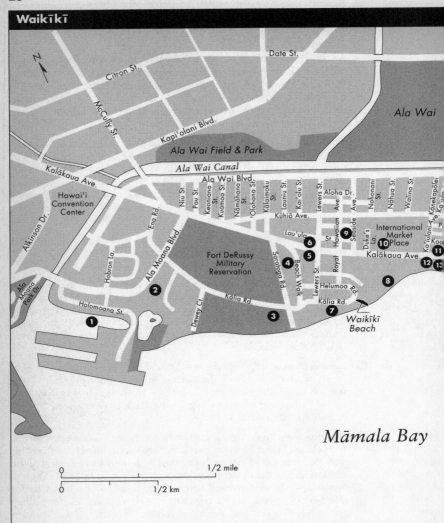

Ala Wai

Date St.

Citron St.

McCully St.

Kapiʻolani Blvd.

Kalākaua Ave.

Ala Wai Field & Park

Ala Wai Canal

Hawaiʻi Convention Center

Ala Wai Blvd.

Niu St. Pau St. Keoniana St. Kuamoʻo St. Nāmāhana St. ʻOlohana St. Kālaimoku St. Launiu St. Kaiʻolu St. Lewers St. Aloha Dr. Nohonani St. Nāhua St. Walina St.

Kūhiō Ave.

Lauʻula

St. Hawaiian Ave. Seaside Duke's La. International Market Place

Kalākaua Ave.

Royal Hawaiian Ave.

Ena Rd.

Atkinson Dr.

Hobron La.

Ala Moana Blvd.

Fort DeRussy Military Reservation

Saratoga Rd.

Beach Walk

Lewers St.

Helumoa Rd.

Ala Moana Park Dr.

Holomoana St.

Dewey Cir.

Kālia Rd.

Kālia Rd.

Waikīkī Beach

Māmala Bay

0 ——— 1/2 mile
0 ——— 1/2 km

Ala Wai Yacht Harbor, **1**
Damien Museum, **14**
Diamond Head, **21**
First Hawaiian Bank, **5**
Gump Building, **6**
Halekūlani, **7**
Hawaiʻi IMAX Theater, **9**
Hilton Hawaiian Village, **2**

Honolulu Zoo, **15**
Hyatt's Hawaiʻi, **11**
International Market Place, **10**
Kahuna (Wizard) Stones of Waikīkī, **13**
Kapiʻolani Bandstand, **18**
Kodak Hula Show, **17**
Royal Hawaiian Hotel, **8**

Sheraton Moana Surfrider, **12**
Tea House of the Urasenke Foundation, **4**
U.S. Army Museum, **3**
Waikīkī Aquarium, **19**
Waikīkī Shell, **16**
Waikīkī War Memorial Natatorium, **20**

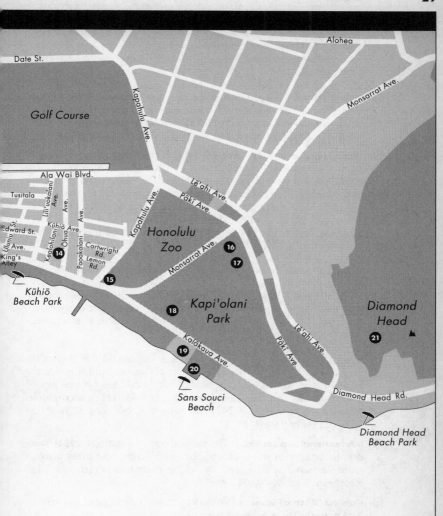

Alohea

Date St.

Monsarrat Ave.

Golf Course

Kapahulu Ave.

Ala Wai Blvd.

Lēʻahi Ave.

Tusitala

Pāki Ave.

Liliʻuokalani Ave.

Kealohilani Ave.

ʻŌhua Ave.

Kūhiō Ave.

Edward St.

Uluniu Ave.

Paoakalani Ave.

Cartwright Rd.

Honolulu Zoo

King's Alley

14

Lemon Rd.

Monsarrat Ave.

16

17

Diamond Head

15

Kūhiō Beach Park

18

Kapiʻolani Park

Lēʻahi Ave.

Pāki Ave.

21

Kalākaua Ave.

19

20

Diamond Head Rd.

Sans Souci Beach

Diamond Head Beach Park

NEED A
BREAK?

If it's lunchtime or close to sunset, get a table at **House Without a Key,** an alfresco gathering place at the Halekūlani (☞ Dining, *above*). Offering a view of Diamond Head from most every table, it has a light lunch menu and serves wonderful tropical drinks and *pūpū* (hors d'oeuvres) before dinner.

🍴 ➒ **Hawai'i IMAX Theater.** Immerse yourself in what's on a screen five stories high and 70 ft wide while surrounding you with digital stereo sound. Show subjects and times vary. ⊠ *325 Seaside Ave.,* ☎ *808/923–4629.* 🎫 *$7.50, 2 films on same day $10, 3 films $12.* ⊙ *Daily 9–9.*

➋ **Hilton Hawaiian Village.** For sure, this is the picture of a quintessential tropical getaway, complete with a little island in Kahanamoku Lagoon and palm trees all around. Look for the penguin pond in the back of the main lobby. The village is a hodgepodge of Asian architecture, with a Chinese moon gate, a pagoda, and a Japanese farmhouse with a waterwheel, all dominated by a tall mosaic mural of the hotel's Rainbow Tower. The **Rainbow Bazaar** here is a good place to browse for souvenirs. ⊠ *2005 Kālia Rd.,* ☎ *808/949–4321.*

NEED A
BREAK?

Hawaiian Village Mini Golf, open daily at the Hilton Hawaiian Village (☞ *above* and in Lodging, *below*), is the only miniature golf course in Waikīkī. Choose between two 18-hole challenges: a rain forest course with lush foliage, waterfalls, and tiki torches; or a beach course with sand, seashells, and surfboards. Play all 36 holes and you get a break on the rates.

⓫ **Hyatt's Hawai'i.** To help visitors become acquainted with Hawaiian arts and crafts, Aunty Malia, resident Hawaiian authority for the Hyatt Regency Waikīkī, has assembled what she calls her "sharing place." It's a charming collection, and she's a one-of-a-kind Hawai'i resource. ⊠ *Hyatt Regency Waikīkī, 2424 Kalākaua Ave., 2nd floor,* ☎ *808/923–1234.* ⊙ *Daily 9AM–11PM.*

❿ **International Market Place.** The tropical open-air setting is fun to wander through, with wood-carvers, basket-weavers, and other artisans from various Pacific islands hawking their handicrafts. ⊠ *2330 Kalākaua Ave.,* ☎ *808/923–9871.*

⓭ **Kahuna (Wizard) Stones of Waikīkī.** According to legend, these boulders preserve the magnetic legacy of four sorcerers—Kapaemahu, Kinohi, Kapuni, and Kahaloa—who came here from Tahiti sometime before the 16th century. Before leaving the Islands they transferred their mystic knowledge and healing powers to these rock-solid totems. Just to the west of these revered rocks is the **Duke Kahanamoku Statue,** erected in honor of Hawai'i's celebrated surfer and swimmer. Known as the "father of modern surfing," Duke won a gold medal for the 100-m freestyle at the 1912 Olympics. ⊠ *Waikīkī Beach, Diamond Head side of Sheraton Moana Surfrider.*

➑ **Royal Hawaiian Hotel.** Affectionately nicknamed the Pink Palace, the Royal Hawaiian was built in 1927. The lobby, with its pink decor, is reminiscent of another era when visitors to the Islands arrived on luxury liners. A stroll through the old gardens with their tall, swaying coconut palms is like a walk through a time when Waikīkī was a sleepy, tropical paradise with only two luxury hotels. ⊠ *2259 Kalākaua Ave.,* ☎ *808/923–7311.*

NEED A
BREAK?

The kiosk **Island Snow** (⊠ Royal Hawaiian Shopping Center, 2201 Kalākaua Ave., ☎ 808/922–0588 for information on free hula lessons, crafts demonstrations, and other special events) serves shave ice—a local favorite and the Hawaiian version of a snow cone. It comes in such exotic fruit flavors as litchi and mango. Have it with ice cream and adzuki beans.

⑫ Sheraton Moana Surfrider. This renovated landmark dates from 1901; it has period furnishings, historical exhibits, and plenty of nostalgia. They've done a beautiful job on this Beaux Arts–style hotel, which has been placed on the National Register of Historic Places. Visit the **Historical Room** in the rotunda above the main entrance to enjoy a collection of old photographs and memorabilia dating from the opening of the hotel. Then have a drink on the back **Banyan Veranda.** ⊠ *2365 Kalākaua Ave.,* ☎ *808/922–3111.*

❹ Tea House of the Urasenke Foundation. This teahouse was the first of its kind to be built outside Japan and provides an excellent introduction to Japanese culture. Wear something comfortable enough for sitting on the floor (but no shorts, please). ⊠ *245 Saratoga Rd.,* ☎ *808/ 923–3059.* ⚏ *Minimum donation $2.* ⊙ *Wed. and Fri. 10 AM–noon.*

✋ ❸ U.S. Army Museum. This museum at Ft. DeRussy houses an intimidating collection of war paraphernalia. The major focus is on World War II memorabilia, but exhibits range from ancient Hawaiian weaponry to displays relating to the Vietnam War. It's within Battery Randolf (Building 32), a bunker built in 1911 as a key to the defense of Pearl Harbor and Honolulu. Some of its walls are 22 ft thick. Guided group tours can be arranged. ⊠ *Ft. DeRussy, Bldg. 32, Kālia Rd.,* ☎ *808/438–2821.* ⚏ *Free.* ⊙ *Tues.–Sun. 10–4:30.*

Kapi'olani Park and Diamond Head

Established during the late 1800s by King Kalākaua and named after his queen, Kapi'olani Park is a 500-acre expanse where you can play all sorts of sports, enjoy a picnic, see wild animals, or hear live music. It lies in the shadow of Diamond Head, Hawai'i's most famous natural landmark. Diamond Head got its name from sailors who thought they had found precious gems on its slopes; the diamonds proved to be volcanic refuse.

A Good Walk

The 'ewa end of Kapi'olani Park is occupied by the **Honolulu Zoo** ⑮, on the corner of Kalākaua and Kapahulu avenues. Its 40 acres are home to 2,000 furry and finned creatures. On weekends look for the Zoo Fence Art Mart, on Monsarrat Avenue outside the zoo, on the Diamond Head side. You might find some affordable works by contemporary artists and craftspeople that make better Hawai'i keepsakes than the ashtrays and monkeypod bowls carved in the Philippines.

Across Monsarrat Avenue, between Kalākaua Avenue and Pākī Street in Kapi'olani Park, is the **Waikīkī Shell** ⑯, Honolulu's outdoor concert arena. Next to the Shell is the site of the **Kodak Hula Show** ⑰, a free presentation of Hawaiian song and dance. Cut across the park to the **Kapi'olani Bandstand** ⑱, where you'll hear more free island tunes.

Cross Kalākaua Avenue to the **Waikīkī Aquarium** ⑲. Next door is the **Waikīkī War Memorial Natatorium** ⑳, an open-air swimming stadium-by-the-sea built in 1927 to commemorate lives lost in World War I.

As it leaves Kapi'olani Park, Kalākaua Avenue forks into Diamond Head Road, a scenic 2-mi stretch popular with walkers and joggers. The road climbs a steep hill and passes handsome Diamond Head Lighthouse (not open to the public). Lookout areas along the top of the hill offer views of the surfers and windsurfers below.

For those willing to undertake more strenuous walking, the hike to the summit of **Diamond Head** ㉑ offers a marvelous view. To save time and energy, drive, don't walk, along Diamond Head Road, turn left at Monsarrat Avenue, head a mile up the hill, and look for a sign on the left to the entrance to the crater. Drive through the tunnel to the inside of the crater. The trail begins at the parking lot.

TIMING

Budget a full day to see Kapi'olani Park and Diamond Head. The park is particularly nice in the early morning when only a few joggers and walkers are around; walking around the rim of the park is easiest before 9 AM. If you want to hike up to the crater's summit, do it before breakfast. That way you beat not only the heat but the crowds. Hiking Diamond Head takes an hour round-trip, but factor in some extra time to enjoy the views from the top. Keep an eye on your watch if you're there at day's end, because the gates close promptly at 6 PM. If you want to see the Honolulu Zoo, it's best to go there right when it opens, since the animals are livelier in the cool of the morning. Give the aquarium an hour, including 10 minutes in its Sea Vision Theater. For the best seats at the 10 AM Kodak Hula Show, get there by 9. Unless you're visiting around the Thanksgiving or Christmas holidays, you'll have no trouble getting into all of the following sights, with the exception of the Kodak Hula Show, which runs Tuesday through Thursday only.

Sights to See

㉑ **Diamond Head.** Once a military fortification, this 760-ft extinct volcanic peak provides the ideal perspective for first-time O'ahu visitors. From its height, panoramas sweep across Waikīkī and Honolulu in one direction and out to Koko Head in the other, with surfers and windsurfers scattered like confetti on the cresting waves below. Most guidebooks say there are 99 steps on the trail to the top. That's true of one flight, but there are four flights altogether. Bring a flashlight to see your way through a narrow tunnel and up a very dark flight of winding stairs. ✉ *Monsarrat Ave.* 🎫 *Free.* ☉ *Daily 6–6.*

☝ ⑮ **Honolulu Zoo.** There are bigger and better zoos, but this one is pretty, and on Wednesday evenings in summer, the zoo puts on "The Wildest Show in Town," a free program of singing, dancing, and island entertainment; check the local newspaper. The best part of the zoo is its 7½-acre African savanna, where animals roam freely on the other side of hidden rails and moats. ✉ *151 Kapahulu Ave.,* ☎ *808/971–7171.* 🎫 *$6.* ☉ *Daily 9–4:30.*

⑱ **Kapi'olani Bandstand.** There's usually a free show of some kind at this open-air stage; on Sunday at 2, for instance, it's the Royal Hawaiian Band. Check the newspaper for particulars. Some excellent hula dances are performed here by local groups that don't frequent the hotels. ✉ *'Ewa end of Kapi'olani Park, mauka side of Kalākaua Ave.*

⑰ **Kodak Hula Show.** This one-hour show, in the bleachers adjacent to the Waikīkī Shell, is colorful, lively, and fun; it's been wowing crowds for more than 50 years. Naturally, it's a great opportunity to take photographs. ✉ *2805 Monsarrat Ave.,* ☎ *808/627–3379.* 🎫 *Free.* ☉ *Tues.–Thurs. at 10 AM.*

☝ ⑲ **Waikīkī Aquarium.** This amazing little attraction harbors more than 300 species of Hawaiian and South Pacific marine life, including the giant clam, the chambered nautilus, and sharks. Check out the Sea Visions Theater, whose 10-minute films enhance the current exhibits. ✉ *2777 Kalākaua Ave.,* ☎ *808/923–9741.* 🎫 *$6.* ☉ *Daily 9–5.*

⓰ **Waikīkī Shell.** Local people bring a picnic and get "grass seats" (lawn seating). Here's a chance to have a magical night listening to some of Hawaiʻi's best musicians and visiting pop stars, while lying on a blanket with the moon shining over Diamond Head. Most concerts are held between May 1 and Labor Day. Check the newspapers to see what's playing. ✉ *2805 Monsarrat Ave.,* ☎ *808/924–8934.*

⓴ **Waikīkī War Memorial Natatorium.** Although it has fallen into disrepair and is no longer open to the public, this World War I monument stands proudly, its outer wall lighted at night, showing off what's left of the pair of eagle statues that sits atop the entrance. Built in 1927, the natatorium narrowly escaped the wrecker's ball but continues to await restoration. ✉ *2777 Kalākaua Ave., Diamond Head side of Waikīkī Aquarium.*

NEED A BREAK?

Next to the Natatorium, you can snack outdoors in the shade of a *hau* tree at the New Otani Kaimana Beach Hotel. Dubbed the **Hau Tree Lānai** (✉ 2863 Kalākaua Ave., ☎ 808/921–7066), it's one of the island's most pleasant options for oceanfront refreshments.

Downtown Honolulu

Honolulu's past and present play a delightful counterpoint throughout the downtown sector. Modern skyscrapers stand directly across from the Aloha Tower, which was built in 1926. Old structures have found new meaning here. For instance, today's governor's mansion, built in 1846, was the home of Queen Liliʻuokalani until her death in 1917.

To reach downtown Honolulu from Waikīkī by car, take Ala Moana Boulevard to Alakea Street. There are public parking lots (50¢ per half hour) in buildings along Alakea Street and Bethel Street, two blocks ʻewa. Keep in mind that parking in most downtown lots is expensive ($2 per half hour).

If you travel by public transportation, take Bus 19 or 20 from Kuhio Avenue in Waikīkī. After about 15 minutes, get off at Alakea Street and walk makai to Ala Moana Boulevard. Most of the historic sites are clustered within easy walking distance.

A Good Walk

Begin at the **Hawaiʻi Maritime Center** ㉒, which is across Ala Moana Boulevard from Alakea Street in downtown Honolulu. The lively oceanfront museum traces the history of Hawaiʻi's love affair with the sea.

Just ʻewa of the Hawaiʻi Maritime Center is **Aloha Tower Marketplace** ㉓, a complex of harborside shops and restaurants where you can shop 'til you drop, have a drink and a bite to eat, and listen to live music.

Cross Ala Moana Boulevard, walk a block ʻewa, and turn mauka on Ft. Street Mall, a pedestrian walkway that passes buildings old and new. Sit on a bench for a few minutes and watch the fascinating passing parade, from businesspeople to street preachers. Turn left on King Street, and in a few blocks you'll reach **Chinatown** ㉔, the old section of downtown Honolulu, which is crammed with mom-and-pop shops, art galleries, ethnic restaurants, and a big open market.

Walk back toward Diamond Head along King Street until it intersects with Bishop Street. On the mauka side is lovely **Tamarind Park** ㉕, a popular lunchtime picnic spot for Honolulu's workforce, which gathers under its shady plumeria, *kukui,* and monkeypod trees—and one tamarind.

34

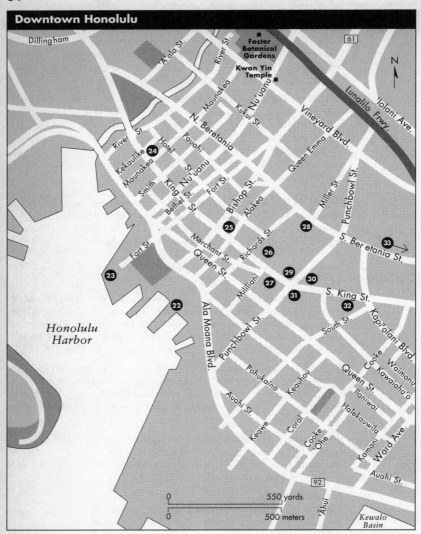

Downtown Honolulu

Dillingham
A'ala St.
River St.
Foster Botanical Gardens
Kwan Yin Temple
61
Lunalilo Frwy.
'Iolani Ave.
Maunakea
Kukui St.
Nu'uanu
Vineyard Blvd.
N. Beretania
River St.
Queen Emma
Kekaulike
Hotel
Pauahi
Maunakea
King St.
S. Nu'uanu
Fort St.
Bishop St.
Miller St.
Punchbowl St.
Smith
Bethel St.
Fort St.
Alakea
S. Beretania St.
24
25
28
33
Merchant St.
Richards St.
26
Fort St.
Queen St.
29
30
23
Mililani
27
31
S. King St.
22
Ala Moana Blvd.
Punchbowl St.
32
Kapi'olani Blvd.
Honolulu Harbor
South St.
Cooke
Waimanu
Kawaiaha'o
Pohukaina
Keouhou
Queen St.
Ilaniwai
Auahi St.
Halekauwila
Kamani
Ward Ave.
Keawe
Coral
Cooke
'Ohe
92
Auahi St.
'Āhui
Kewalo Basin

0 .... 550 yards
0 .... 500 meters

Continue along King Street until you reach **'Iolani Palace** ㉖, on the mauka side. This graceful Victorian structure was built by King David Kalākaua in 1882. Take a guided tour of the restored interior, then stop at the 'Iolani Barracks. Also on the palace grounds is the Kalākaua Coronation Bandstand, where the Royal Hawaiian Band performs at noon most Fridays.

Across King Street from 'Iolani Palace is Ali'iōlani Hale, the old judiciary building that served as the parliament hall during the kingship era. In front of it is the gilded **Kamehameha I Statue** ㉗, which honors Hawai'i's greatest monarch.

Walk one block mauka up Richards Street to tour the **Hawai'i State Capitol** ㉘, where Hawai'i's legislators spend their days. Almost across the street from the state capitol is Washington Place, a graceful old mansion and currently the home of Hawai'i's governor. You can only peer through the wrought-iron gates, since the residence is not open to the public.

Return to King Street, stay on the mauka side, and proceed in a Diamond Head direction. Past the palace is the massive stone **Hawai'i State Library** ㉙, built in 1913 and renovated in 1992, a showcase of architectural restoration.

On the mauka side of South King Street, at Punchbowl Street, is **Honolulu Hale** ㉚, or City Hall. Across the street, on another corner of King and Punchbowl streets, is the **Kawaiaha'o Church** ㉛, Hawai'i's most famous religious structure. On the Diamond Head side of the Kawaiaha'o Church is the **Mission Houses Museum** ㉜, where the first American missionaries in Hawai'i lived.

From here it's three long blocks toward Diamond Head to Ward Avenue and one block mauka to Beretania Street, but the **Honolulu Academy of Arts** ㉝ is worth the extra mileage (you might choose to drive there instead); it houses a world-class collection of Western and Asian art.

TIMING

Downtown Honolulu merits a full day of your time, especially if you set aside a half day for Aloha Tower Marketplace. Be sure to stop by the palace Tuesday through Saturday, the only days tours are offered. Remember that the Mission Houses Museum and Honolulu Academy of Arts are closed Monday. Touring the State Capitol can take up to two hours and is only possible during the week. Saturday morning is the best time to walk through Chinatown; that's when the open-air markets do their biggest business with local families. A walk through Chinatown can take an hour, as do tours of the Mission Houses and 'Iolani Palace.

Wrap up your day at sunset with refreshments or dinner back at the Aloha Tower Marketplace, which stays open late into the evening, with live entertainment on the docks.

Sights to See

🐚 ㉓ **Aloha Tower Marketplace.** This is a two-story conglomeration of shops, kiosks, indoor and outdoor restaurants, and live entertainment next to Honolulu Harbor, with Aloha Tower as its anchor. For a bird's-eye view of this working harbor, take the free ride up to the tower's observation deck. ✉ *101 Ala Moana Blvd., at Piers 8, 9, and 10,* ☎ *808/528–5700 or 800/378–6937.*

㉔ **Chinatown.** Slightly on the tawdry side, this historic neighborhood has everything from art galleries in renovated structures to lei stands, herb shops, acupuncture studios, noodle factories, and Chinese and Thai restaurants. A major highlight is the colorful O'ahu Market, an open-air emporium with hanging pig heads, display cases of fresh fish, row after row of exotic fruits and vegetables, and vendors of all ethnic backgrounds. ⊠ *King St., between Smith and River Sts.*

NEED A
BREAK?
There are Chinese, Thai, Japanese, Korean, and Italian food stalls at **Maunakea Marketplace** (⊠ 1120 Maunakea St., ☎ 808/524–3409), one block mauka of King Street. A courtyard has some seating.

🖐 ㉒ **Hawai'i Maritime Center.** The main exhibits (some of which are interactive) are in the **Kalākaua Boat House,** where you learn about such topics as Hawai'i's whaling days, the history of Honolulu Harbor, the Clipper seaplane, and surfing and windsurfing in Hawai'i. Also at the Center are the *Falls of Clyde,* a century-old, four-masted, square-rigged ship now used as a museum, and the *Hōkūle'a,* a reproduction of an ancient double-hull voyaging canoe. *Hōkūle'a* has completed several journeys throughout the Pacific, during which the crew used only the stars and the sea as their guide. ⊠ *Pier 7, Ala Moana Blvd.,* ☎ *808/536–6373.* ☞ *$7.50.* ☉ *Daily 8:30–5.*

㉘ **Hawai'i State Capitol.** The capitol's architecture is richly symbolic: the columns look like palm trees, the legislative chambers are shaped like volcanic cinder cones, and the central court is open to the sky, representing Hawai'i's open society. The building is surrounded by reflecting pools, just as the Islands are embraced by water. ⊠ *215 S. Beretania St.,* ☎ *808/586–0178.* ☞ *Free. 1- to 2-hr guided tour weekdays at 1:30.*

㉙ **Hawai'i State Library.** This beautifully renovated main library is wonderful to explore. Its "Asia and the Pacific" room has a fascinating collection of books old and new about Hawai'i. ⊠ *478 King St.,* ☎ *808/586–3500.* ☞ *Free.* ☉ *Mon., Fri., and Sat. 9–5; Tues. and Thurs. 9–8; Wed. 10–5.*

㉝ **Honolulu Academy of Arts.** Dating to 1927, the Academy has an impressive permanent collection including Japanese prints, Italian Renaissance paintings, and American and European art. Six open-air courtyards provide a casual counterpart to the more formal interior galleries. Call about special exhibits, concerts, and films. ⊠ *900 S. Beretania St.,* ☎ *808/532–8700.* ☞ *$5.* ☉ *Tues.–Sat. 10–4:30; Sun. 1–5.*

㉚ **Honolulu Hale.** Center of city government, this Mediterranean/Renaissance-style building was constructed in 1929. Stroll through the cool, open-ceiling lobby with exhibits of local artists, and time your visit to coincide with one of the free live concerts sometimes offered in the evening, when the building stays open later. ⊠ *530 S. King St.,* ☎ *808/527–5666.* ☞ *Free.* ☉ *Weekdays 8–4:30.*

㉖ **'Iolani Palace.** Built in 1882 on the site of an earlier palace and beautifully restored today, this is America's only royal residence. It contains the thrones of King Kalākaua and his successor (and sister) Queen Lili'uokalani. The palace is open for guided tours only; reservations are essential. Take a look at the gift shop, formerly the 'Iolani Barracks, built to house the Royal Guard. ⊠ *King and Richards Sts.,* ☎ *808/522–0832.* ☞ *$8.* ☉ *Tues.–Sat. 9–2:15.*

NEED A
BREAK?
For a quick pick-me-up, stop by **Lion Coffee** (⊠ 222 Merchant St., between Alakea and Richards Sts.) for an espresso, cappuccino, latte, or plain ol' cuppa joe along with a fresh-baked muffin, scone, or cookie. Lion Coffee shares space with **Native Books & Beautiful Things,** a lovely shop selling Hawaiian crafts and publications.

㉗ Kamehameha I Statue. This downtown landmark pays tribute to the Big Island chieftain who united all the warring Hawaiian Islands into one kingdom. He stands with one arm outstretched in welcome. The original version is in Kapa'au, on the Big Island, near the king's birthplace. Each year on June 11, his birthday, the statue is draped in leis. ⊠ *417 S. King St., outside Ali'iōlani Hale.*

㉛ Kawaiaha'o Church. Fancifully called Hawai'i's Westminster Abbey, this coral-block house of worship witnessed the coronations, weddings, and funerals of generations of Hawaiian royalty. The graves of missionaries and of King Lunalilo are in the yard. The upper gallery has an exhibit of paintings of the royal families. Services in English and Hawaiian are given each Sunday. While there are no guided tours, you can look around the church at no cost. ⊠ *957 Punchbowl St., at King St.,* ☎ *808/522–1333.* ▨ . ☉ *Service Sun. at 8 and 10:30, Wed. at 6* PM.

㉜ Mission Houses Museum. The stalwart Hawai'i missionaries arrived in 1820, gaining royal favor and influencing every aspect of Island life. Their descendants have become leaders in government and business. You can walk through their original dwellings, including a white-frame house that was prefabricated in New England and shipped around the Horn. ⊠ *553 S. King St.,* ☎ *808/531–0481.* ▨ *$5.* ☉ *Tues.–Sat. 9–4, Sun. 12:30–4; certain areas of museum may be seen only on 1-hr guided tour, Tues.– Sat. at 9:30, 10:30, 11:30, 1, 2, and 3 and Sun. at 1, 2, and 3.*

㉕ Tamarind Park. From jazz and Hawaiian tunes to the U.S. Marine Band, music fills this pretty park at noon on Friday. Check the newspaper to find out the schedule. Do as the locals do: Pick up lunch at one of the many carry-out restaurants bordering the park and find a bench or patch of grass and enjoy. ⊠ *S. King St., between Bishop and Alakea Sts.* ▨ *Free.*

The East O'ahu Ring

At once historic and contemporary, serene and active, the east end of O'ahu holds remarkable variety within its relatively small area, and its scenery includes wind-swept cliffs and wave-dashed shores. For this drive, don't forget the camera!

A Good Drive

From Waikīkī there are two routes to Lunalilo Freeway (H-1). On the Diamond Head end, go mauka on Kapahulu Avenue and follow the signs to the freeway. On the 'ewa end, take Ala Wai Boulevard and turn mauka at Kalākaua Avenue, staying on it until it ends at Beretania Street, which is one-way going left. Turn right off Beretania Street at Pi'ikoi Street, and the signs will direct you onto the freeway heading west.

Take the freeway exit marked Pali Highway (Hwy. 61), one of two roads that cut through the Ko'olau Mountains. On the right is the **Queen Emma Summer Palace** ㉞. The colonial-style white mansion, which once served as the summer retreat of King Kamehameha IV and his wife, Queen Emma, is now a museum maintained by the Daughters of Hawai'i.

As you drive toward the summit of the highway, the road is lined with sweet ginger in summer and red poinsettias in winter. If it has been raining, waterfalls will be tumbling down the sheer, chiseled cliffs of the Ko'olau, creating a veritable wonderland in green.

Watch for the turn to the **Nu'uanu Pali Lookout** ㉟. There is a small parking lot and a lookout wall from which you can see all the way up and down the windward coast—a view that Mark Twain called the most beautiful in the world.

Kawela Bay

Waiale'e

Turtle Bay
Hilton

83

Sunset Beach

'Ehukai Beach
Banzai Pipeline

Pu'uomahuka
Heiau

50

Waimea Bay

49 Waimea
Valley

← TO KAUA'I

Hale'iwa Beach Park

Waialua
Bay

48 Hale'iwa

Ka'ena Pt.

Mokulē'ia

930

Farrington Hwy.

Kamehameha Hwy.

99

Yokohama
Bay

803

Dole
Pineapple
Pavilion

47

80 Wahiawā

Schofield Barracks

Wahiawā
Botanical
Gardens

Mākaha Beach
Park

Wheeler
Air Force
Base

H2

Mākaha

99

Wai'anae

750

Mā'ili

Hawai'i's
Plantation
Village

46

93

Waipahu

Nānākuli

Pearl
Harbo

H1

Arizon
Memorie

'Ewa

N

0   5 miles

0   5 km

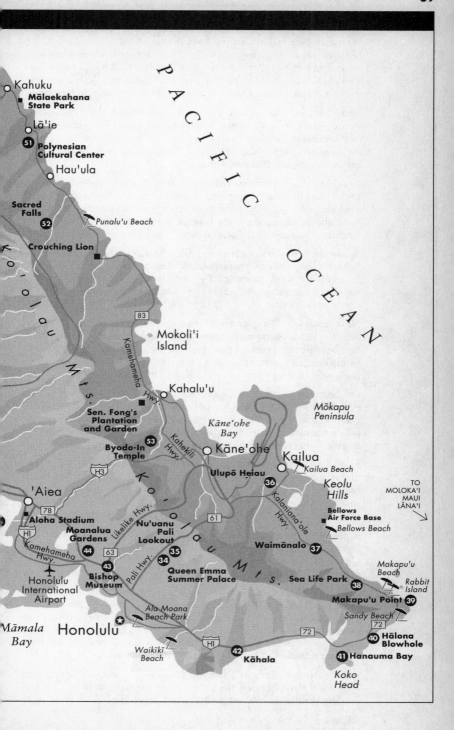

PACIFIC OCEAN

Kahuku
Mālaekahana State Park
Lā'ie
51 Polynesian Cultural Center
Hau'ula
Sacred Falls
52
Punalu'u Beach
Crouching Lion

Ko'olau Mts.

83
Mokoli'i Island
Kahalu'u
Sen. Fong's Plantation and Garden
Kāne'ohe Bay
Mōkapu Peninsula
53 Byodo-In Temple
Kāne'ohe
Kailua
Ulupō Heiau
Kailua Beach
36
Keolu Hills
H3
'Aiea
78
Aloha Stadium
Moanalua Gardens
Nu'uanu Pali Lookout
Bellows Air Force Base
Bellows Beach
61
Waimānalo
37
H1
Kamehameha Hwy.
44 63
43
34 35
Queen Emma Summer Palace
Sea Life Park
38
Makapu'u Beach
Rabbit Island
Bishop Museum
Makapu'u Point
39
Honolulu International Airport
Ala Moana Beach Park
Sandy Beach
Honolulu
Māmala Bay
Waikīkī Beach
H1
72
40 Hālona Blowhole
42 Kāhala
41 Hanauma Bay
Koko Head

TO MOLOKA'I MAUI LĀNA'I

Kamehameha Hwy.
Kohekili Hwy.
Likelike Hwy.
Pali Hwy.
Kalaniana'ole Hwy.
Ko'olau Mts.

As you follow the highway down the other side of the mountain, continue straight along what becomes Kailua Road. If you are interested in Hawaiian history, look for the YMCA at the Castle Hospital junction of Kalaniana'ole Highway and Kailua Road. Behind it is **Ulupō Heiau** ㊱, an ancient outdoor shrine. Ready for a detour? Head straight on Kailua Road to Kailua Beach (☞ Beaches, *below*), which many people consider the best on the island. The road twists and turns, so watch the signs.

Retracing your route back to Castle Junction, turn left at the intersection onto Kalaniana'ole Highway. Soon you will come to the simple town of **Waimānalo** ㊲. Waimānalo's two beaches are Bellows Beach, great for swimming and bodysurfing, and Waimānalo Beach Park, also safe for swimming (☞ Beaches, *below*).

Another mile along the highway, on the right, is **Sea Life Park** ㊳, home to the world's only "wholphin," the offspring of a romance between a whale and a dolphin. From the cliffs above Sea Life Park, colorful hang gliders often soar in the breezes. It takes a lot of daring to leap from these imposing heights, and there have been several fatalities here.

Across the highway from Sea Life Park is Makapu'u Beach (☞ Beaches, *below*), a beautiful cove that is great for seasoned bodysurfers but treacherous for the weak swimmer. The road winds up a hill, at the top of which is a turnoff on the makai side to **Makapu'u Point** ㊴, a fabulous photo opportunity.

Next you'll see a long stretch of inviting sand called Sandy Beach (☞ Beaches, *below*). Tempting as this beach looks, it is not advisable to swim here because the waves are powerful and tricky. The steady winds make Sandy Beach a popular place to fly kites. From here the road twists and turns next to steep cliffs along the Koko Head shoreline.

Offshore, the islands of Moloka'i and Lāna'i call like distant sirens, and every once in a while, Maui is visible in blue silhouette. For the best photos, pull into the parking lot at **Hālona Blowhole** ㊵. At the top of the hill on the makai side of the road is the entrance to **Hanauma Bay** ㊶, a marine conservation district and the island's premier snorkeling spot.

From here back to Waikīkī the highway passes several residential communities called Hawai'i Kai, Niu Valley, and 'Āina Haina, each of which has a small shopping center with a food store if you need a soda or a snack. Best to keep driving, however, because during rush hour Kalaniana'ole Highway becomes choked with commuter traffic.

Right before you turn off from Kalaniana'ole Highway you'll notice a long stretch of green on the makai side. This is the private Wai'alae Country Club, scene of the televised annual Hawaiian Open golf tournament (☞ Outdoor Activities and Sports, *below*).

Take the Kāhala exit. Turn left at the stoplight onto Kīlauea Avenue. Here you'll see Kāhala Mall (☞ Shopping, *below*), an upscale shopping complex with yuppie eateries, high-fashion stores, and eight movie theaters. A few blocks past the mall, take a left on Hunakai Street and follow it until it dead-ends at Kāhala Avenue. Turn right and drive through **Kāhala** ㊷, O'ahu's wealthiest neighborhood.

Kāhala Avenue becomes Diamond Head Road; follow it straight to Kapi'olani Park. Stay on the right side of the park until you hit Kapahulu Avenue. Take a left, and you're back in Waikīkī.

TIMING

If Hanauma Bay is your main focus, avoid Wednesday, when hours are limited. Also note that the bay is best in the early hours before the waters are churned up. You could reverse the above directions and get there first thing in the morning, before the crowds. Allow two hours for Hanauma Bay, two hours for Sea Life Park, and one for Queen Emma Summer Palace. Another tip: Look up to the top of the mountains and, if it's clear, head directly to the Pali Lookout; it's a shame to get there only to find the view obscured by clouds or fog. Bring a jacket along; temperatures at the summit are several degrees cooler than in warm Waikīkī.

Take your time, take all day, and enjoy a few beaches along the way. The weather is sunny and warm year-round, and the scenery of Oʻahu's east side is too miraculous to rush through.

Sights to See

40 **Hālona Blowhole.** Below a scenic turnout along the Koko Head shore-line, this well-photographed lava tube that sucks the ocean in and spits it out in lofty plumes may or may not perform, depending on the currents. Nearby is the tiny beach used to film the wave-washed love scene in *From Here to Eternity*. As you face the blowhole and the ocean, look down to your right to see the beach. A rough, steep trail leads to the beach, which is pretty but not recommended for swimming or even wading. Lock your car, because the spot is frequented by thieves. ⊠ *Kalanianaʻole Hwy., 1 mi east of Hanauma Bay.*

41 **Hanauma Bay.** If you make only one stop during your drive, this should be it. Even from the overlook, the horseshoe-shape bay is a beauty, and you can easily see the reefs through the clear aqua waters. You can also see the crowds of people snorkeling and sunbathing, but it's still worth a visit to this marine conservation district. ⊠ *7455 Kalanianaʻole Hwy.,* ☎ *808/396–4229.* ☞ *Donation $3; parking $1; mask, fins, and snorkel rental $6.* ☉ *Thurs.–Tues. 6 AM–7 PM, Wed. noon–7.*

42 **Kāhala.** Oʻahu's wealthiest neighborhood has streets lined with multimillion-dollar homes, and the classy **Kāhala Mandarin Oriental Hotel** attracts a prestigious clientele. At intervals along tree-lined Kāhala Avenue are narrow lanes that provide public access to **Kāhala Beach.** ⊠ *East of Diamond Head.*

39 **Makapuʻu Point.** This spot has breathtaking views of the ocean, mountains, and the windward islands. The peninsula jutting out in the distance is **Mōkapu,** site of a U.S. Marine base. The spired mountain peak is **Mt. Olomana.** In front of you on the long pier is part of the **Makai Undersea Test Range,** a research facility that is closed to the public. Offshore is **Rabbit Island,** a picturesque cay so named because some think it looks like a swimming bunny.

Nestled in the cliff face is the **Makapuʻu Lighthouse,** which is closed to the public. Near the Makapuʻu Point turnout, however, you'll find the start of a mile-long paved road (closed to traffic). Hike up it to the top of the 647-ft bluff for a closer view of the lighthouse. ⊠ *Kalanianaʻole Hwy., turnout above Makapuʻu Beach.*

35 **Nuʻuanu Pali Lookout.** This panoramic perch looks out to windward Oʻahu. It was in this region that King Kamehameha I drove defending forces over the edges of the 1,000-ft-high cliffs, thus winning the decisive battle for control of Oʻahu. Lock your car if you get out, because break-ins have occurred here. ⊠ *Top of Pali Hwy.*

34 **Queen Emma Summer Palace.** Built in 1848, this stately white home was used by Queen Emma and her family as a retreat from the rigors of court life in hot and dusty Honolulu during the mid-1800s. It contains many excellent examples of Hawaiian quilts and koa furniture of the period, as well as the queen's wedding dress and shoes. ⊠ *2913 Pali Hwy.,* ☎ *808/595–3167.* ☞ *$5.* ☉ *Guided tour daily 9–4.*

🖐 ❸❽ **Sea Life Park.** Dolphins leap and spin, penguins frolic, and a killer whale performs impressive tricks at the shows in this marine life attraction. There's also a 300,000-gallon Hawaiian reef tank where you can come nose-to-nose with hundreds of marine creatures. The Pacific Whaling Museum teaches you about the fascinating history of whaling in Hawai'i. Even if you've seen trained cetaceans at other marine parks, the distinctively Hawaiian flavor makes this place special. The setting alone, right across from the ocean, is worth the price of admission. ✉ *Kalaniana'ole Hwy., Waimānalo,* ☎ *808/259–7933.* 🎫 *$19.95.* ☉ *Daily 9:30–5.*

❸❻ **Ulupō Heiau.** Though they may look like piles of rocks to the uninitiated, *heiau* are sacred stone platforms for the worship of the gods and date to ancient times. *Ulupō* means "night inspiration," referring to the legendary *menehune,* a mythical race of diminutive people, who supposedly built the heiau under the cloak of darkness. ✉ *Behind YMCA at Kalaniana'ole Hwy. and Kailua Rd.*

NEED A BREAK?   Generations of children have purchased their beach snacks and sodas at **Kalapawai Market** (✉ 306 S. Kalāheo Ave.), near Kailua Beach. A windward landmark since 1932, the green-and-white market has distinctive charm. It's a good source for your carry-out lunch, since there's no concession stand at the beach.

❸❼ **Waimānalo.** This modest little seaside town flanked by chiseled cliffs is worth a visit. Its biggest draw is its beautiful beach, offering glorious views to the windward side. Down the side roads, heading mauka, are little farms that grow a variety of fruits and flowers. Toward the back of the valley are small ranches with grazing horses. If you see any trucks selling corn and you're staying at a place where you can cook it, be sure to get some in Waimānalo. It may be the sweetest you'll ever eat, and the price is the lowest on O'ahu. ✉ *Kalaniana'ole Hwy.*

Around the Island

After visiting three historic attractions in populated West Honolulu, you'll find that the O'ahu landscape turns increasingly rural as you head north. The center of the island is carpeted in pineapple and sugarcane plantations, which are slowly being phased out in favor of diversified agriculture. On the North Shore there are ranches, banana farms, and fields of exotic flowers grown for export. The plantation towns are small; some have become cute with boutiques and little art galleries. Others are just themselves—old, wooden, and picturesque—the small homes surrounded by a riot of flowers and trees heavy with mango, pomelo, and litchi.

A Good Drive

Follow H-1 Freeway heading west. Take the exit for Likelike Highway. Stay in the right lane and look for signs to the **Bishop Museum** ㊸, a center of Polynesian archaeology, ethnology, and history. The building alone, with its huge Victorian turrets and immense stone walls, is a sight worth seeing.

Back on the freeway heading west, the road merges into the Moanalua Freeway (Rte. 78). Stay on this past the Pu'uloa Road–Tripler Hospital exit for **Moanalua Gardens** ㊹, a lovely park with huge, spreading monkeypod trees.

On your left you'll pass Aloha Stadium, a 50,000-seat arena that hosts football and baseball games and big-name rock concerts. On weekends the Aloha Flea Market (☞ Shopping, *below*) is held here.

As you approach the stadium on the freeway, bear right at the sign to ʻAiea, then merge left onto Kamehameha Highway (Rte. 99) going south to Pearl Harbor. Turn right at the Hālawa Gate for a tour of the **Arizona Memorial** ㊺, part of Pearl Harbor, and the adjacent USS *Bowfin,* a vintage submarine.

Follow H-1 west to Waipahu (exit 8B) and onto Farrington Highway. Turn right at Waipahu Depot Road and left onto Waipahu Street to reach **Hawaiʻi's Plantation Village** ㊻, a collection of restored original and replicated homes from a 19th-century plantation town.

Take H-1 to H-2 to Highway 80 (Kamehameha Hwy.), heading to Wahiawā, home of the U.S. Army base at Schofield Barracks. Head north until Highway 80 meets Highway 99, where you'll see a scrubby-looking patch called the Del Monte Pineapple Variety Garden. Unpromising as it looks, it's actually quite interesting, with varieties of the ubiquitous fruit ranging from thumb-size pink ones to big golden ones.

Merge left on Kamehameha Highway and you'll see the **Dole Pineapple Pavilion** ㊼, a big hit with Oʻahu sightseers since 1951. From here, Kamehameha Highway cuts through pineapple and sugarcane fields. Close to the bottom of the hill, a traffic-light intersection invites you to take the Haleʻiwa bypass road to save time. Don't. Turn left instead and drive to the traffic circle. Go around the circle and continue 7 mi to Mokulēʻia on Route 930. Soon you'll come to Dillingham Airfield, where you can fly in a glider.

Back at the traffic circle, follow the signs to **Haleʻiwa** ㊽, a sleepy plantation town that has come of age with fashion boutiques, surf shops, restaurants, souvenir stands, and the best grilled mahimahi sandwich on the North Shore, at Kua ʻAina Sandwich (☞ Dining, *below*). Leaving Haleʻiwa and continuing along Kamehameha Highway (Rte. 83), you'll pass the famous North Shore beaches, where the winter surf comes in size large. The first of these is Waimea Bay (☞ Beaches, *below*), a popular family picnic spot with a big, broad beach and fine facilities. Across the street, on the mauka side of the road, is **Waimea Valley** ㊾, home of an ancient Hawaiian community and now a popular attraction. If you're interested in seeing a fine example of an ancient Hawaiian heiau, turn mauka at the Foodland store and take Pūpūkea Road up the steep climb, not quite a mile, to the dirt road on the right, leading to the **Puʻuomahuka Heiau** ㊿.

Continue along the coastal road past more famous surfing beaches, including ʻEhukai and Sunset (☞ Beaches, *below*). If it's wintertime, keep clear of those waves, which sometimes rise as high as 30 ft. Leave the sea to the daring (some say crazy) surfers who ride the towering waves with astounding grace.

The only hotel of any consequence in these parts is your next landmark: the Turtle Bay Hilton (☞ Lodging, *below*). If it's Sunday between 9 AM and 2 PM, you might want to stop for its incredibly extensive champagne brunch, served in a pretty oceanside dining room. Along this stretch of Kamehameha Highway, there is often a small lean-to set up with Kahuku watermelons for sale. By all means, buy one. They're the juiciest, sweetest melons you'll find in the Islands.

As you approach the town of Lāʻie, there is a long stretch of pine trees on the makai side. Look for the entrance to Mālaekahana State Park (☞ Beaches, *below*). Coming up on the mauka side is the sprawling **Polynesian Cultural Center** ⑤. A visit to the center isn't cheap, but it's worth the money to see the 40 acres of lagoons and seven re-created South Pacific villages.

About 4 mi down the highway on the mauka side of the road, look for the Hawaiʻi Visitors and Convention Bureau's (HVCB) distinctive red-warrior sign for **Sacred Falls** ㉒, a state park with a pretty hiking trail.

The next thing to look for, although it's not spectacular, is the Crouching Lion mountain formation on the ridge line behind an inn of the same name. If someone tells you it has a deeply significant Hawaiian legend attached to it, don't believe them. The lion was an idea thought up by modern-day promoters. As you continue driving along the shoreline, notice the picturesque little island of Mokoliʻi ("little lizard"), a 208-ft-high sea stack. According to Hawaiian legend, the island was created when the goddess Hiʻiaka, sister of Pele, slew the dragon Mokoliʻi and flung its tail into the sea, forming the distinct islet. Other dragon body parts—in the form of rocks, of course—were scattered along the base of nearby Kualoa Ridge.

Continue straight on Kahekili Highway (Rte. 83) and look on your right for **Senator Fong's Plantation and Gardens,** an agricultural attraction showcasing the splendors of Hawaiʻi's rich soil and climate. Two miles farther on the right is the Valley of the Temples and its lovely **Byodo-In Temple** ㉓, a replica of a 900-year-old temple in Kyoto, Japan.

Follow Kahekili Highway to Likelike Highway (Hwy. 63), where you turn mauka and head back toward Honolulu through the Wilson Tunnel. The highway leads to Lunalilo Freeway going east. Exit at Pali Highway and go south through downtown Honolulu on Bishop Street, then turn left on Ala Moana Boulevard, which leads to Kalākaua Avenue in Waikīkī.

TIMING

Unless you don't plan on stopping at any of the sights, allot nothing less than a day to circle the island. Try to factor in two or three different excursions north, so that you can appreciate all it has to offer without wearing yourself out. Don't rush through the Polynesian Cultural Center, because you'll miss much of what makes it so well done. Instead, devote an afternoon and evening to the center, perhaps stopping first for a morning at Waimea Valley. Note that the center is closed Sunday.

On another day, allow a full afternoon for the Bishop Museum. Afternoons, you may have to wait as long as two hours to see the *Arizona* Memorial; the best bet is to head out there early in the day.

Haleʻiwa deserves two hours: factor in some extra North Shore time for hiking, relaxing on a beach, going kayaking, taking a glider ride, and having a snack. Wear your flip-flops but bring a pair of walking shoes or sneakers as well.

The weather is mercurial on the North Shore. It can be sunny and clear in Waikīkī and cloudy in the country. Carry along a light jacket, a hat, and sunscreen: then you're ready for anything.

Sights to See

㊺ *Arizona* **Memorial.** A simple, gleaming white structure shields the hulk of the USS *Arizona*, which sank with 1,102 men aboard when the Japanese attacked Pearl Harbor on December 7, 1941. The tour includes a 20-minute documentary and a shuttle-boat ride to the memorial. Appropriate dress is required (no bathing suits or bare feet). Nearby is the USS *Bowfin* (☞ *below*).

At press time, the USS *Missouri* was scheduled to arrive in Pearl Harbor in the spring of 1998, and open as a memorial museum in the first quarter of 1999. The public will have access to the historic battleship and an adjoining visitor center with educational exhibits. The admission fee will probably be $9. ⊠ *USS Arizona Memorial and Visitor Center, National Park Service, Pearl Harbor,* ☎ *808/422–0561.* 🎟 *Free. Tour tickets distributed on a first-come first-served basis, with 1- to 3-hr waits common.* ◔ *Daily 8–3.*

43 **Bishop Museum.** Founded in 1889 by Charles R. Bishop as a memorial to his wife, Princess Bernice Pauahi, the museum began as a repository for the royal possessions of this last direct descendant of King Kamehameha the Great. It is world famous for its displays of the best of Polynesia: lustrous feather capes, the skeleton of a giant sperm whale, an authentic, well-preserved grass house, and changing photography and craft displays. At press time, the old **planetarium** was scheduled to close in the fall of 1998 to make way for a new, high-tech facility that will open during the second half of 1999. ⊠ *1525 Bernice St.,* ☎ *808/848–4129.* 🎟 *$14.95.* ◔ *Daily 9–5.*

53 **Byodo-In Temple.** A 2-ton statue of the Buddha presides over a re-created Japanese temple set dramatically against the sheer, green cliffs of the Ko'olau Mountains, on the windward side. ⊠ *47-200 Kahekili Hwy., Kāne'ohe,* ☎ *808/239–8811.* 🎟 *$2.* ◔ *Daily 9–4:30.*

47 **Dole Pineapple Pavilion.** Celebrate Hawai'i's famous golden fruit at this promotional, tourist-oriented center with exhibits, a 10,000-sq-ft plantation gift shop, restaurant, and tram tours of an agricultural field. ⊠ *64-1550 Kamehameha Hwy.,* ☎ *808/621–8408.* 🎟 *Free.* ◔ *Daily 9–6.*

48 **Hale'iwa.** During the 1920s this seaside hamlet was a trendy retreat at the end of a railroad line. During the '60s hippies gathered here, followed by surfers. Now, Hale'iwa is a fun mix of yesterday and today. Old general stores peacefully coexist with contemporary boutiques, galleries, and eateries. Be sure to stop in **Lili'uokalani Protestant Church,** founded by missionaries in the 1830s. It's fronted by a large, stone archway built in 1910 and covered with night-blooming cereus. ⊠ *Follow H-1 west from Honolulu to H-2 north, exit at Wahiawā and follow Kamehameha Hwy. 6 mi, turn left at signaled intersection then right into Hale'iwa.*

NEED A BREAK?

For a real slice of Hale'iwa life, stop at **Matsumoto's,** a family-run business on the main road through town. In a building dating to 1910, it sells shave ice, a tropical snow cone that costs about $1. They shave the ice right before your eyes and offer every flavor imaginable, including banana, mango, papaya, coconut, and strawberry. If you want to do it right, get it with vanilla ice cream and sweet adzuki beans.

46 **Hawai'i's Plantation Village.** Displays and authentically furnished buildings, both original and replicated, re-create Hawai'i's plantation era. Tour a Chinese social hall, a Japanese shrine, a sumo ring, a saimin stand, an old-time garage and dental office, and historic homes at this "living museum," which is 30 minutes from downtown Honolulu.⊠ *94-695 Waipahu St., Waipahu,* ☎ *808/677–0110.* 🎟 *$5.* ◔ *Guided tour hourly Mon.–Sat. 9–3, Sun. 10–3.*

44 **Moanalua Gardens.** This lovely park is the site of a major hula festival on the third weekend in July. Throughout the year hikes leave from here to Moanalua Valley; call for specific times. ⊠ *1401 Mahiole St., Honolulu,* ☎ *808/833–1944.* 🎟 *Free.* ◔ *Weekdays 8–4.*

☜ **51** **Polynesian Cultural Center.** Re-created villages represent Hawai'i, Tahiti, Samoa, Fiji, the Marquesas, New Zealand, and Tonga. Shows and demonstrations enliven the area, and there's a spectacular IMAX film about the sea. Its expansive open-air shopping village features Polynesian handicrafts that are good for souvenirs. If you're staying in Honolulu, it's better to see the center as part of a van tour, so you won't have to drive home after the overwhelming two-hour evening show. Various packages are available, from basic admission with no transportation to an all-inclusive deal. ⊠ 55-370 Kamehameha Hwy., Lā'ie, ☎ 808/293–3333 or 808/923–1861. ☞ $27–$95. ☉ Mon.–Sat. 12:30–9.

㊿ Pu'uomahuka Heiau. Worth a stop for its spectacular views from a bluff high above the ocean, this sacred spot was once the site of human sacrifices; it's now on the National Register of Historic Places. ⊠ ½ mi north of Waimea Bay on Rte. 83, turn right on Pūpūkea Rd. and drive 1 mi uphill.

㉒ Sacred Falls. This wild state park, with a strenuous 2-mi hike to an 80-ft-high waterfall, is Hawaiian country as you dreamed it would be. A swim in the pool beneath the falls is a welcome refresher at trail's end. Be sure to go with someone else, and don't attempt the hike if there has been rain; the valley is subject to flash flooding, and the trail can be slippery. ⊠ Kamehameha Hwy., Hau'ula. ☞ Free. ☉ Oct.–Mar., daily 7–6:45; Apr.–Sept., daily 7 AM–7:45 PM.

OFF THE
BEATEN PATH

SENATOR FONG'S PLANTATION AND GARDENS – Hiram Fong, the first Asian-American to be elected to Congress, hasn't been a senator for many years, but this enterprising elder statesman still watches over his estate. At his 700-acre O'ahu plantation, there's a 45-minute guided tram tour of the landscaped grounds, including human-made ponds fed by natural springs. The visitor center has a snack bar, rest rooms, and a gift shop. ⊠ 47-285 Pūlama Rd., off Kahekili Hwy., 2 mi north of Byodo-In Temple, Kahalu'u, ☎ 808/239–6775. ☞ $8.85. ☉ Tram tours daily 10:30–3.

USS *Bowfin.* This World War II submarine is moored near the *Arizona Memorial* visitor center (☞ above). Children under 4 are not admitted. ⊠ 11 Arizona Memorial Dr. at Pearl Harbor, ☎ 808/423–1341. ☞ $8. ☉ Daily 8–5.

Wahiawā Botanical Gardens. These gardens are a peaceful retreat from the town of Wahiawā, which means "place of noise" in Hawaiian. Free and open daily, the gardens comprise 27 acres of exotic plants and flowers in which to bathe your senses. Wahiawā is just south of the **Dole Pineapple Pavillion** (☞ above). ⊠ 1396 California Ave., Wahiawā, ☎ 808/621–7321. ☞ Free. ☉ Daily 9–4.

㊾ Waimea Valley. At this 1,800-acre attraction, remnants of an early Hawaiian civilization are surrounded by more than 2,500 species of flora from around the world. The garden trails are well marked, and the plants are labeled. You might spot a Hawaiian nēnē, the state bird. There's a spectacular show of cliff-diving from 45-ft-high falls, and you can take part in Hawaiian games and dances. Check out the park's free "moonwalks," held two nights at the time of each full moon. There are picnic areas and a restaurant on the grounds. ⊠ 59-864 Kamehameha Hwy., Hale'iwa, ☎ 808/638–8511. ☞ $19.95. ☉ Daily 10–5:30.

BEACHES

For South Seas sun, fun, and surf, Hawai'i is a dream destination, but first some words of caution: When approaching any Hawaiian beach, take notice of the signs! If they warn of dangerous surf conditions or currents, pay attention. Before you stretch out beneath a swaying palm, check it for coconuts: The trade winds can bring them tumbling down on top of you with enough force to cause serious injury. Don't forget to use sunscreen and reapply it often, especially after swimming. Waikīkī is only 21 degrees north of the equator, and the ultraviolet rays are much more potent than they are at home. No alcoholic beverages are allowed on the beaches here, and no matter which beach you choose, it's best to lock your car.

Waikīkī Beaches

The 2½-mi strand called Waikīkī Beach actually extends from Hilton Hawaiian Village on one end to Kapiʻolani Park and Diamond Head on the other. Areas along this sandy strip have separate names but subtle differences. The Waikīkī Beach Center, opposite the Hyatt Regency Waikīkī, is where you can find restrooms, showers, a police station, and surfboard lockers. Beach areas are listed here from west to east.

Kahanamoku Beach and Lagoon. The lagoon's calm waters are safe for small children, and you can lazily paddle around it in a little boat. The beach has decent snorkeling and swimming and a gentle surf; its sandy bottom slopes gradually. Named for Hawaiʻi's famous Olympic swimming champion, Duke Kahanamoku, the area has a snack concession, showers, a beach-gear and surfboard rental shop, catamaran cruises, and a sand volleyball court. ✉ *In front of Hilton Hawaiian Village.*

Ft. DeRussy Beach. Sunbathers, swimmers, and windsurfers enjoy this beach, the widest in Waikīkī. It trails off to a coral ocean bottom with fairly good snorkeling sights. The beach is frequented by military personnel but is open to everyone. There are volleyball courts, food stands, picnic tables, dressing rooms, and showers. ✉ *In front of Ft. DeRussy and Hale Koa Hotel.*

Gray's Beach. Named for a little lodging house called Gray's-by-the-Sea that stood here in the 1920's, this beach is best known for the two good surfing spots called Paradise and Number Threes just beyond its reef. High tides often cover the narrow beach. The Hawaiians used to consider this a place for spiritual healing and baptism and called it *Kawehewehe* (the removal). You'll find food stands, surfboard and beach-gear rental shops, and canoe and catamaran rides. ✉ *In front of Halekūlani Hotel.*

Kahaloa and Ulukou Beaches. A lot of activities and possibly the best swimming are available along this little stretch of Waikīkī Beach. Try a catamaran or outrigger canoe ride out into the bay, unless you're ready to sign up for a surfing lesson at the Waikīkī Beach Center nearby. The Royal Hawaiian Hotel cordons off a small section of sand for its guests, bringing to mind a rich kid's sandbox. Facilities include public rest rooms, changing rooms, showers, and a snack stand. The police station is here as well. ✉ *In front of Royal Hawaiian Hotel and Sheraton Moana Surfrider.*

Kūhiō Beach Park. Prince Jonah Kūhiō Kalanianaʻole, a distinguished native statesman, had his home here on Waikīkī's shore earlier in this century. The residence was torn down in 1950, 14 years after his death, to enlarge the beach. There's a breakwater seawall that runs out about 1,300 ft parallel to the beach from Kapahulu Groin, a cemented-over storm drain jutting out from shore at the Diamond Head end of the beach. This seawall, built to stem beach erosion, created two semi-enclosed pools, with water fairly deep out near the breakwater. Though the water appears calm, swimming here has its dangers: unpredictably deep holes can form in the sandy bottom as a result of swirling currents, and children should be watched closely. Beyond the Groin's cement wall, boogie boarders and bodysurfers enthusiastically ride the waves. The Groin is a great place to watch a Hawaiian sunset, but be sure of your footing: It's slippery when wet. ⊠ *Waikīkī Beach Center to Kapahulu Groin.*

Queen's Surf. A great place for a sunset picnic, this beach is beyond the seawall, toward Diamond Head, at what's known as the "other end of Waikīkī." It was once the site of Queen Lili'uokalani's beach house, hence the name. A mix of families and gays gathers here, and it seems as if someone is always playing a bongo drum. There are good shade trees, picnic tables, and a changing house with showers. ⊠ *Across from entrance to Honolulu Zoo.*

Sans Souci. Nicknamed "Dig-Me Beach" because of its outlandish display of skimpy bathing suits, this small rectangle of sand is nonetheless a good sunning spot for all ages. Children enjoy its shallow, safe waters, and the shore draws many ocean kayakers and outrigger canoers. Serious swimmers and triathletes also swim in the channel here, beyond the reef. There's no food concession, but near one end is the Hau Tree Lānai, an open-air eatery that is part of the New Otani Kaimana Beach Hotel. A grassy area is popular with picnickers and volleyball buffs, and there's an outdoor shower. ⊠ *Makai side of Kapi'olani Park, between New Otani Kaimana Beach Hotel and Waikīkī War Memorial Natatorium.*

Beaches Around O'ahu

Here are O'ahu's finer beaches, listed in alphabetical order.

Ala Moana Beach Park. Ala Moana has a protective reef, which keeps the waters calm and perfect for swimming. After Waikīkī, this is the most popular beach among visitors. To the Waikīkī side is a peninsula called Magic Island, with picnic tables, shady trees, and paved sidewalks ideal for jogging. Ala Moana also has playing fields, changing houses, indoor and outdoor showers, lifeguards, concession stands, and tennis courts—a beach for everyone, but only in the daytime; crimes have occurred here after dark. ⊠ *Honolulu, makai side of Ala Moana Shopping Center and Ala Moana Blvd., from Waikīkī take Bus 8 to shopping center and cross Ala Moana Blvd.*

Bellows Beach. The waves here are great for bodysurfing, and the sand is soft for sunbathing. Locals come here for the fine swimming on weekends (and holidays), when the Air Force opens the beach to civilians. There are showers, abundant parking, and plenty of spots for picnicking underneath shady ironwood trees. There is no food concession, but McDonald's and other take-out fare is available right outside the entrance gate. ⊠ *Entrance on Kalaniana'ole Hwy. near Waimānalo town center, signs on makai side of road.*

'Ehukai Beach Park. 'Ehukai is part of a series of beaches running for many miles along the North Shore. What sets it apart is the view of the famous Banzai Pipeline, site of international surfing competitions. The winter waves are fierce, and the lifeguards are constantly shooing people away from the shore break. There's a grassy area above the beach and a steep dune dropping down to it. The long, wide, and generally uncrowded beach has a changing house with showers and an outdoor shower and water fountain. Bring along a cooler with sodas, because there is virtually no shade here, and the nearest store is a mile away. ⊠ *North Shore, 1 mi north of Foodland store at Pūpūkea, turn makai off Kamehameha Hwy. directly into the small 'Ehukai parking lot, which borders highway.*

Hale'iwa Beach Park. The winter waves are impressive here, but in summer the ocean is like a lake, ideal for family swimming. The beach itself is big and often full of locals; its broad lawns off the highway invite volleyball and Frisbee games and groups of barbecuers. There is a changing house with showers but no food concessions. Hale'iwa has everything you need for provisions. ⊠ *North Shore, makai side of Kamehameha Hwy., north of Hale'iwa town center and past harbor.*

Hanauma Bay. The main attraction here is snorkeling. The coral reefs are clearly visible through the turquoise waters of this sunken crater, a designated marine preserve. Crowds flock to its palm-fringed shores and fill the water and the narrow crescent of packed sand. Beyond the reef is a popular site for scuba-diving classes. The bay is best early in the morning (7 AM), before the crowds arrive; it can be difficult to park later in the day. There is a busy food and snorkel equipment rental concession on the beach, plus changing rooms and showers. No smoking is allowed on the beach. **Hanauma Bay Snorkeling Excursions** (☎ 808/951–1111) run to and from Waikīkī. ⊠ *7455 Kalaniana'ole Hwy.,* ☎ *808/396–4229.* 🎫 *Donation $3; parking $1; mask, snorkel, and fins rental $6.* ⊙ *Thurs.–Tues. 6 AM–7 PM, Wed. noon–7.*

Kahana Bay Beach Park. Local parents often bring their children to wade in safety at this pretty beach cove with very shallow, protected waters. A grove of tall ironwood and pandanus trees keeps the area cool, shady, and ideal for a picnic. An ancient Hawaiian fishpond, which was in use until the '20s, is visible nearby. There are changing houses, showers, and picnic tables. Across the highway is Kahana Valley, burgeoning with banana, breadfruit, and mango trees. ⊠ *Windward side of island, makai of Kamehameha Hwy., north of Kualoa Park.*

Kailua Beach Park. Steady breezes attract windsurfers by the dozens to this long, palm-fringed beach with gently sloping sands. You can rent equipment in Kailua and try it yourself. Young athletes and members of the military enjoy this beach, as do local families, so it gets pretty crowded on weekends. There are showers, changing rooms, picnic areas, and a concession stand. Buy your picnic provisions at the Kalapawai Market nearby. ⊠ *Windward side, makai of Kailua town, turn right on Kailua Rd. at market, cross bridge, then turn left into beach parking lot.*

Kualoa Regional Park. This is one of the island's most beautiful picnic, camping, and beach areas. Grassy expanses border a long, narrow stretch of beach with spectacular views of Kāne'ohe Bay and the Ko'olau Mountains. Dominating the view is an islet called Mokoli'i, which rises 206 ft above the water. At low tide you can wade out to the island on the reef, but be sure to wear sneakers. The one drawback is that it's usually windy. Bring a cooler; no refreshments are sold here. There are places to shower, change, and picnic in the shade of palm trees. ⊠ *Windward side, makai of Kamehameha Hwy., north of Waiāhole.*

Mākaha Beach Park. Because it's off the beaten tourist path this beach provides a slice of local life most visitors don't see. Families string up tarps for the day, fire up hibachis, set up lawn chairs, get out the fishing gear, and strum 'ukulele while they "talk story" (chat). The swimming is generally decent in the summer, but avoid the big winter waves. The ¼-mi beach has a changing house and showers and is the site of a yearly big-board surf meet. ⊠ *Wai'anae Coast, 1½ hrs west of Honolulu on H-1 Fwy. and Farrington Hwy., makai side of highway.*

Makapu'u Beach. Swimming at Makapu'u should be attempted only by strong strokers and bodysurfers, because the swells can be overwhelmingly big and powerful. Instead, consider this tiny crescent cove—popular with the locals—as a prime sunbathing spot. The beach lies at the base of high cliffs: look up, and you just might see a hang glider being launched from the bluffs overhead. With its small lot, parking can be tricky here. In a pinch, try parking on the narrow shoulder and walking down to the beach. There is a changing house with indoor and outdoor showers. ⊠ *Makai of Kalaniana'ole Hwy., across from Sea Life Park, 2 mi south of Waimānalo.*

Mālaekahana Beach Park. The big attraction here is tiny Goat Island, a bird sanctuary just offshore. At low tide the water is shallow enough—never more than waist high—that you can wade out to it, but be sure to wear sneakers so you don't cut yourself on the coral. Families love to camp in the groves of ironwood trees at Mālaekahana State Park; the shade provides a welcome respite from the heat of the day. The beach itself is fairly narrow, but long enough for a 20-minute stroll, one way. The waves are never too big and sometimes they're just right for the beginning bodysurfer. There are several changing houses, indoor and outdoor showers, and picnic tables. Note that the entrance gates are easy to miss, because you can't see the beach from the road. ⊠ *Windward side, entrance gates are makai of Kamehameha Hwy., ½ mi north of Lā'ie.*

Sandy Beach. Strong, steady winds make "Sandy's" a kite-flyer's paradise. But the shore break is vicious here, and there's generally a rescue truck parked on the road, which means that people are swimming where they shouldn't and getting hurt. Do not swim here. Sandy's is a popular spot for the high school and college crowd. There's a changing house with indoor and outdoor showers, but no food concessions. ⊠ *Makai of Kalaniana'ole Hwy., 2 mi east of Hanauma Bay.*

Sunset Beach. This is another link in the chain of North Shore beaches, which extends for miles. It is popular for its gentle summer waves and crashing winter surf. The beach is broad, and the sand is soft. Lining the adjacent highway there are usually carry-out truck stands selling shave ice, plate lunches, and sodas. A new comfort station with showers, restrooms, and a paved parking lot was expected to open on the mauka side of the highway in late 1998. ⊠ *North shore, 1 mi north of 'Ehukai Beach Park, on makai side of Kamehameha Hwy.*

Waimānalo Beach Park. Boogie-boarders and bodysurfers enjoy the predictably gentle waves of this beach. The lawn at Waimānalo attracts hundreds of local people who set up minicamps for the weekend, complete with hibachis, radios, lawn chairs, coolers, and shade tarps. Sometimes these folks are not very friendly to tourists, but the beach itself is more welcoming, and from here you can walk a mile along the shore for fantastic windward and mountain views. The grassy, shady grounds have picnic tables and shower houses. ⊠ *Windward side, look for signs makai of Kalaniana'ole Hwy., south of Waimānalo town.*

Waimea Bay. Made popular in that old Beach Boys song, "Surfin' USA," Waimea Bay is a slice of hang-ten heaven. Winter is when you should stand well away from the shore break and leave the 25-ft-high waves to the hot doggers. Summer is the time to swim and snorkel in the calm waters. The beach is a broad crescent of soft sand, backed by a shady area with tables, a changing house, and showers. Parking is almost impossible in the lot on weekends, so folks just park along the road and walk down. ⊠ *North shore, across from Waimea Valley, 3 mi north of Hale'iwa, on makai side of Kamehameha Hwy.*

Yokohama Bay. You'll be one of the few tourists at this Wai'anae Coast beach at the very end of the road. It feels and looks remote and untouched, which may explain its lack of crowds. Locals come here to fish and swim in waters that are calm enough for children in summer. The beach is narrow and rocky in places. Bring provisions, because the nearest town is a 15-minute drive away. There's a changing house and showers, plus a small parking lot, but most folks just pull over and park on the side of the bumpy road. ⊠ *Wai'anae Coast, northern end of Farrington Hwy., about 7 mi north of Mākaha.*

DINING

For snacks and fast food around the island, look for the *manapua* wagons, the food trucks usually parked at beaches, and *okazuya* stores, the local version of delis, which dispense tempura, sushi, and plate lunch, Hawai'i's unofficial state dish. A standard plate lunch has macaroni salad, "two scoop rice," and an entrée that might be curry stew, *kālua* (roasted) pork and cabbage, or sweet-and-sour spareribs.

One of the trendiest places to dine in downtown Honolulu is at Aloha Tower Marketplace, in one of the numerous restaurants right on the water (a rarity on O'ahu). A trolley runs regularly between the marketplace and Waikīkī. For an explanation of price categories, *see* On the Road with Fodor's in the beginning of the book.

Waikīkī

Chinese

$$–$$$ ★ ✕ **Golden Dragon.** A tasty bill of fare focuses primarily on Cantonese and unconventional nouvelle-Chinese cuisine, prepared and served by chef Steve Chiang to his rigorously maintained high standards of excellence. The restaurant has a stunning red-and-black color scheme, and there are big lazy Susans on each table for easy sampling of your companion's menu choices. Signature dishes include stir-fried lobster, and Szechuan beef. Peking duck and beggar's chicken (whole chicken wrapped in lotus leaves and baked in a clay pot) must be ordered 24 hours in advance. ⊠ *Hilton Hawaiian Village, 2005 Kālia Rd.,* ☎ *808/ 946–5336. Reservations essential. AE, D, DC, MC, V.* ⊘ *No lunch.*

Contemporary

$$$–$$$$ ★ ✕ **Orchids.** Flavors from the East and West intermingle on the Orchids menu. Dubbed Indo-Pacific cuisine, the dishes here focus on combinations of Asian spices and herbs in Western-style preparations. For instance, the Peking chive poi crepe is filled with spiny Hawaiian lobster, Chinese greens, and spicy tomato coulis. The duck leg confit with Asian spices comes with sautéed spinach and wild mushrooms. You can't beat the setting right beside the sea, with Diamond Head in the distance and fresh orchids everywhere. Outdoor and indoor seating is available, with the best views from the lānai. The popular Sunday brunch has table after table of all-you-can-eat delights. ⊠ *Halekūlani, 2199 Kālia Rd.,* ☎ *808/923–2311. Reservations essential. AE, MC, V.*

$$$ ★ ✕ **Bali by the Sea.** Like the island it's named for, this restaurant is breeze-swept and pretty, with an oceanside setting offering glorious views of Waikīkī Beach. But don't be fooled by the name. This is not a Polynesian eatery but an internationally acclaimed restaurant featuring such entrées as roast duck with black currant and litchi glaze. Another favorite is the *kiawe 'ōpakapaka* (mesquite-broiled red snapper) with shiitake and asparagus risotto. American pastry chef Gale O'Malley is so talented that he has been decorated by the French government, and the sommelier is one of the wisest and wittiest in Waikīkī. ⊠ *Hilton Hawaiian Village, 2005 Kālia Rd.,* ☎ *808/941–2254. Reservations essential. AE, D, DC, MC, V. No dinner Sun.*

$$–$$$ ✕ **Cascada.** This Waikīkī gem is surprisingly serene, considering it's right next to the lobby of its host hotel. The dining room has warm yellow walls, a hand-painted trompe l'oeil ceiling, and ceramic wall

panels. Tables spill out onto an outer marble terrace with tropical gardens and a cascading waterfall. Cuisines of France, Italy, and California are all in evidence in such entrées as scallops topped with an orange-pomegranate butter sauce, roast duck with sweet-sour cherry sauce, and sautéed veal with a compote of Maui onions and tamarind and port wine sauce. ⊠ *Royal Garden at Waikīkī, 440 'Olohana St.,* ☎ *808/943–0202. AE, D, DC, MC, V.*

$$–$$$ ✕ **Hau Tree Lānai.** This restaurant right beside the sand at Kaimana Beach is often overlooked, but it shouldn't be. At breakfast, lunch, or dinner, you can dine under graceful hau trees and hear the whisper of the waves. Breakfast offerings include a huge helping of eggs Benedict, a fluffy Belgian waffle with your choice of toppings (strawberries, bananas, or macadamia nuts), and a tasty fresh salmon omelet. Two standout dinner entrées are the jumbo shrimp with mushrooms, tomatoes, Maui onions, and white wine over fettuccine, and a blue cheese–and–herb crusted New York steak. Romantic torchlight makes this a great place to toast your love. ⊠ *New Otani Kaimana Beach Hotel, 2863 Kalākaua Ave.,* ☎ *808/921–7066. Reservations essential. AE, D, DC, MC, V.*

$$–$$$ ✕ **House Without a Key.** One of the jewels of Waikīkī, this casual seaside spot serves salads, sandwiches, and hearty meals. Special meat, fish, pasta, and chicken entrées are available for lunch or dinner. Favorites include Joy's Sandwich (crabmeat salad, bacon, and avocado on whole-wheat bread) and the beef burger on a kaiser roll. With the ocean and Diamond Head in view, this is a mesmerizing place at sunset, when there's wonderful live entertainment. A breakfast buffet is served daily 7–10:30. ⊠ *Halekūlani, 2199 Kālia Rd.,* ☎ *808/923–2311. Reservations not accepted. AE, MC, V.*

French

$$$–$$$$ ✕ **La Mer.** In the exotic, oceanfront atmosphere of a Mandalay man-
★   sion, you'll be served neoclassic French cuisine that many consider to be the finest dining in Hawai'i. Portions are beautifully presented. A standout among the entrées is *onaga* (snapper) fillet cooked skin-side crisp with confit of tomato, truffle juice, and fried basil. A favorite sweet is the symphony of four desserts. Each evening there are two complete dinner menus: four courses for $89 and six courses for $105. Highly recommended is the cheese and port course, offered in lieu of dessert. ⊠ *Halekūlani, 2199 Kālia Rd.,* ☎ *808/923–2311. Reservations essential. Jacket required. AE, MC, V. No lunch.*

Italian

$$–$$$$ ✕ **Sergio's.** Started in 1976 by the late Sergio Battistetti, this popular dining room offers a tantalizing taste of Italy in the heart of Waikīkī. The atmosphere is sophisticated and romantic, with dark leather booths providing plenty of intimacy. Watch out: Appetizers like baby artichokes dipped in marinara sauce are so good they can ruin your appetite for dinner. Among the pasta dishes is the *bugili puttanesca,* whose wide noodles swim in a tomato sauce spiced by anchovies and capers. Other fine entrées include fettuccine *fruitti di mare* with shrimp, scallops, mussels, and calamari. The wine list is extensive and well thought out. ⊠ *'Ilima Hotel, 445 Nohonani St.,* ☎ *808/926–3388. MC, V.*

$$$ ✕ **Caffelatte Italian Restaurant.** There are only three restaurants in Honolulu run by native Italians, and this is one of them. A family from Milan operates this tiny trattoria with limited seating inside and a few tables outside on the narrow lānai. Every dish is worth ordering, from the gnocchi in a thick, rich sauce of Gorgonzola cheese, to the veal scallopini in a light white wine sauce sprinkled with parsley. For dessert, the tiramisu (an airy mocha-and-mascarpone trifle) is the best in town. Be aware that each person must order three courses (appetizer, main course, and dessert), a rule that keeps the tab on the high side. The

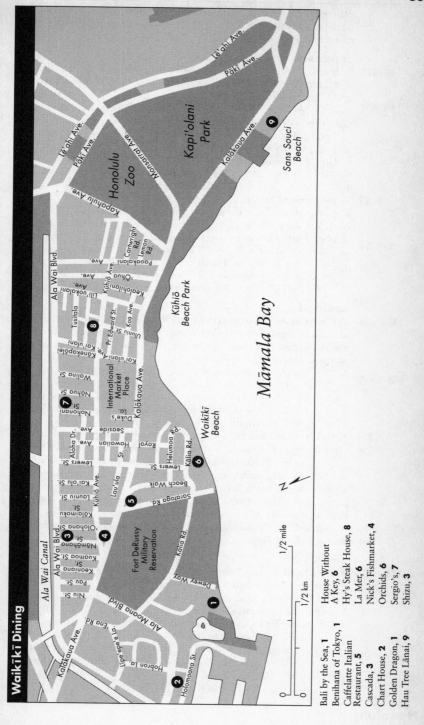

Waikīkī Dining

Bali by the Sea, **1**
Benihana of Tokyo, **1**
Caffelatte Italian
Restaurant, **5**
Cascada, **3**
Chart House, **2**
Golden Dragon, **1**
Hau Tree Lānai, **9**

House Without
A Key, **6**
Hy's Steak House, **8**
La Mer, **6**
Nick's Fishmarket, **4**
Orchids, **6**
Sergio's, **7**
Shizu, **3**

chef will prepare a special mystery dinner for two for $60. There's no parking, so walk here if you can. ⊠ *339 Saratoga Rd., 2nd level,* ☎ *808/924–1414. AE, DC, MC, V. Closed Tues.*

Japanese

$$–$$$ ✕ **Shizu.** Looking out to an extensive Japanese rock garden, this 40-seat dining room has marble floors and walls, beige and black-lacquer tables and chairs, and etched-glass partitions. The two teppanyaki rooms, which seat 8 and 10 people respectively, have spectacular stained-glass windows with vibrant irises. Teppanyaki diners sit around a massive iron grill on which a dexterous chef slices and cooks sizzling meats and vegetables, served with rice. Traditional Japanese cuisine ranges from sashimi, sushi, and tempura to an elaborate 10-course teppanyaki dinner. Try green-tea cheesecake for dessert. ⊠ *Royal Garden at Waikīkī, 440 'Olohana St., 4th floor,* ☎ *808/943–0202. AE, D, DC, MC, V.*

$–$$ ✕ **Benihana of Tokyo.** These restaurants are as famous for their cutting-board theatrics at the *teppan* (iron grill) tables as they are for their food. You are seated at a long table with other diners, to watch as steak, chicken, seafood, and a variety of vegetables are sliced, diced, tossed, and sautéed before your eyes. There's not much variety to the menu, but it's still a lot of fun. Finish off the meal with some green-tea ice cream, a Benihana tradition. ⊠ *Hilton Hawaiian Village, 2005 Kālia Rd.,* ☎ *808/955–5955. Reservations essential. AE, D, DC, MC, V.*

Seafood

$$–$$$$ ✕ **Chart House.** You can overlook Ala Wai Yacht Harbor from this popular cocktail spot's second-floor location. (Salty dogs may want to visit Yacht Harbor Pub first, just to the right and below Chart House, where sailors of all sorts gather to quaff a few and swap tales.) The decor ranges from varnished wood to saltwater aquariums, glass fishing floats to racing sailboat photos. Dinner specialties include Hawaiian lobster and other seafood, as well as steak. The Dungeness crab is quite good. ⊠ *'Ilikai Waikīkī Hotel, Marina Bldg., 1765 Ala Moana Blvd.,* ☎ *808/941–6669. AE, D, DC, MC, V.*

$$–$$$$ ✕ **Nick's Fishmarket.** It's a little old-fashioned, perhaps—black booths, ★ candlelight, and formal table settings—but for seafood, it's hard to beat Nick's. The bouillabaisse is an outstanding combination of lobster, crab, prawns, mussels, clams, and fish. Nick's is one of the few places with abalone on the menu; here it's sautéed and served with lobster risotto. Leave room for vanbana pie, a decadent combination of bananas, vanilla Swiss almond ice cream, and hot caramel sauce. ⊠ *Waikīkī Gateway Hotel, 2070 Kalākaua Ave.,* ☎ *808/955–6333. Reservations essential. AE, D, DC, MC, V.*

Steak

$$–$$$$ ✕ **Hy's Steak House.** Things always seem to go well at Hy's, from the filet mignon tartare and oysters Rockefeller right through to the flaming desserts, such as cherries jubilee. The atmosphere is snug and librarylike, and you can watch the chef perform behind glass. Tuxedoed waiters, catering to your every need, make helpful suggestions about the menu. Hy's is famous for its *kiawe*-broiled New York strip steak (kiawe is a mesquite-type wood), peppercorn steak, and rack of lamb. The Caesar salad is excellent, as are the panfried O'Brien potatoes. ⊠ *Waikīkī Park Heights Hotel, 2440 Kūhiō Ave.,* ☎ *808/922–5555. Reservations essential. AE, DC, MC, V. No lunch.*

Honolulu

American/Casual

$–$$ ✕ **California Pizza Kitchen.** This pair of dining and watering holes for young fast-trackers is worth the more-than-likely wait for a table. At the Kāhala site, a glass atrium with tiled and mirrored walls and one side open to the shopping mall creates a sidewalk-café effect. The pizzas have toppings you'd never expect, such as Thai chicken, Peking duck, and Caribbean shrimp. The pastas, made fresh daily on the premises, include angel hair, fettuccine, rigatoni, fusilli, and linguine. ⊠ *Kāhala Mall, 4211 Wai'alae Ave.,* ☎ *808/737–9446;* ⊠ *1910 Ala Moana Blvd., Waikīkī,* ☎ *808/955–5161. Reservations not accepted. AE, D, DC, MC, V.*

$–$$ ✕ **Hard Rock Cafe.** The Honolulu branch of this international chain has rock-and-roll memorabilia along with surfboards and aloha shirts for local color. The Hard Rock has always sold more T-shirts than T-bones, so don't expect any culinary surprises on its formula menu. The portion-controlled quarter-pound burgers hold sway, but don't overlook the 'ahi steak sandwiches or baby back ribs as alternatives. French fries are, of course, a must with any choice. The decibel level of the oldies playing over the sound system is set at "too loud," and you'll probably have to wait for a table. ⊠ *1837 Kapi'olani Blvd.,* ☎ *808/ 955–7583. Reservations not accepted. AE, MC, V.*

Barbecue

$–$$ ✕ **Dixie Grill.** This Southern-inspired eatery emphasizes just how much fun food can be. Why, there's even an outdoor sandbox for the kids! Dixie Grill specializes in baby back ribs, smoked barbecue chicken, whole Dungeness crab, campfire steak, and fried catfish. Recipes for the barbecue sauces come from Memphis, the Carolinas, Georgia, and Texas. Sandwiches, salads, and comfort foods like meatloaf round out the dinner menu. Save room for the Georgia peach cobbler. ⊠ *404 Ward Ave.,* ☎ *808/596–8359. AE, D, DC, MC, V.*

Chinese

$–$$ ✕ **Maple Garden.** The fine reputation of Maple Garden is founded on spicy Mandarin cuisine, not on decor. There are some booths, some tables, an Oriental screen or two, and lights that are a little too bright at times. It's comfortable, however, and that's all that matters, because the food is delicious. A consistent favorite is the eggplant in a tantalizing hot garlic sauce. ⊠ *909 Isenberg St.,* ☎ *808/941–6641. MC, V.*

Contemporary

$$–$$$ ✕ **Alan Wong's.** Wong focuses heavily on Hawaiian-grown products
★ to keep the flavors super-fresh, and he's utterly creative, turning local "grinds" into gourmet treats. For starters, get "Da Bag," a puffed-up foil bag that's punctured at the table, revealing steamed clams, *kālua* pork, spinach, and shiitake mushrooms. Garlic-mashed potatoes come with a black bean salsa, grilled pork chops with a coconut-ginger sweet potato puree. The low-key dining room has a display kitchen, while the enclosed lānai serves up views of the Ko'olau Mountains. Don't miss the coconut sorbet served in a chocolate–and–macadamia nut shell, surrounded by exotic fruits. Finding the restaurant can be difficult: Look for a white apartment building and a small sign after a parking garage, where your car can be valet parked. ⊠ *McCully Court, 1857 S. King St., 3rd floor,* ☎ *808/949–2526. AE, MC, V. No lunch.*

$$–$$$ ✕ **Hoku's.** Wall-to-wall ocean views, a gleaming kitchen visible to diners, and an oyster and sushi bar vie for attention at this multilevel restaurant, the Kāhala Mandarin's signature dining room. Asian, Mediterranean, and French cuisines command the menu. You might choose an appetizer of Peking duck spring rolls with mango, sunflower sprouts, and hoisin sauce. Entrées range from roast chicken with bok choy to bouillabaisse with lobster, prawns, scallops, and clams. Be sure to sample naan bread from the tandoori oven. ⊠ *Kāhala Mandarin Oriental Hawai'i, 5000 Kāhala Ave.,* ☎ *808/739–8888. AE, DC, MC, V.*

$$-$$$ ✕ **Kāhala Moon.** Koa furnishings, brocade upholstery, and local art
★ set the tone at this pretty restaurant in one of Honolulu's most upscale
neighborhoods. Local ingredients pervade the menu, from Waimānalo
greens to kukui nut salad dressing. Start with the meaty portobello mushrooms on French bread in a demi-glace. As a main dish, try the fillet
of snapper on a bed of julienned zucchini and carrots. When banana
soufflé with chocolate sauce is offered, don't hesitate to order it. ⊠
4614 Kīlauea Ave., ☎ *808/732–7777. AE, DC, MC, V.*

$$-$$$ ✕ **Sam Choy's.** His motto is "Never trust a skinny chef," and indeed,
★ Choy's broad girth and even broader smile let you know you'll be well
taken care of here. The theme is upscale local, as the Hawai'i-born chef
contemporizes the foods he grew up with. The result? Brie-stuffed
wontons with pineapple marmalade, fresh fish and vegetables wrapped
in ti leaves, seared 'ahi seasoned with ginger, and roasted duck with a
Big Island orange sauce. Portions are huge; two people can easily split
an entrée. ⊠ *449 Kapahulu Ave., 2nd level,* ☎ *808/732–8645. AE,
MC, V. No lunch.*

$$-$$$ ✕ **Sunset Grill.** The sweet smell of wood smoke greets you as you enter
the Sunset Grill, which specializes in *kiawe*-broiled foods. The place
is supposed to feel unfinished, with the marble bar top and white
tablecloths contrasting nicely with the concrete floors. The *salade
niçoise,* big enough for a whole dinner, includes red-top lettuce, beans,
tomato, egg, potatoes, and olives, with marinated grilled 'ahi. The trout
and scallops, cooked in a wood oven, are both very good, and the daily
specials, especially the pastas, are always worth a try. ⊠ *Restaurant
Row, 500 Ala Moana Blvd.,* ☎ *808/521–4409. AE, DC, MC, V.*

$$-$$$ ✕ **3660 On The Rise.** This stellar eatery is a 10-minute drive from
★ Waikīkī, in the up-and-coming culinary mecca of Kaimukī. Light hard-
woods, frosted glass, green marble, and black granite mix in a leisurely
fashion here, and there's almost always a full house in the 90-seat dining room (with room for 20 on a street-side lānai outside). Homegrown
ingredients are combined with European flavors: Dungeness crab cakes
are prepared in a nest of angel hair and served with a ginger-cilantro
aioli, and fettuccine is topped with assorted sautéed shellfish and
grilled shiitake mushrooms. For dessert, try the warm chocolate soufflé cake with espresso sauce and vanilla ice cream. ⊠ *3660 Wai'alae
Ave.,* ☎ *808/737–1177. AE, DC, MC, V.*

$$ ✕ **Indigo.** Local boy Glenn Chu turned Honolulu on its ear by dar-
★ ing to open a trendy restaurant in a seedy downtown neighbor-
hood—and succeeding. The decor emphasizes wicker and track
lighting, with a charming back lānai that shields you from the down-
town hubbub. Marrying East with West, Chu's variations on foods
from his Chinese heritage include crispy wontons stuffed with hot
goat cheese, Szechuan peppered beef loin in black bean sauce, and
prawns with hot chili-garlic sauce. ⊠ *1121 Nu'uanu Ave.,* ☎ *808/
521–2900. AE, D, DC, MC, V.*

$$ ✕ **A Pacific Café O'ahu.** Take Asian, Mediterranean, and Indian cusines
★ and combine them with a love of Hawai'i's homegrown products. The
result: Chef Jean-Marie Josselin's award-winning menu, a true O'ahu
standout. Lunch highlights include a mixed green salad with grilled Japanese eggplant, goat cheese, and chili vinaigrette; and a shiitake mush-
room sandwich with mozzarella. At dinner the wok-charred mahimahi
with a garlic, sesame crust, and lime-ginger beurre blanc is superb. The
interior—designed by Josselin's wife, Sophronia—is at once whimsical, sophisticated, and modern. ⊠ *Ward Centre, 1200 Ala Moana Blvd.,*
☎ *808/593–0035. AE, DC, MC, V.*

$-$$$ ✕ **Palomino.** At the top of a grand staircase, lavish Palomino has
★ handblown glass chandeliers, hand-painted roses, American and African
woods, and a 50-ft marble and mahogany bar. Entrées from the wood-

Honolulu Dining

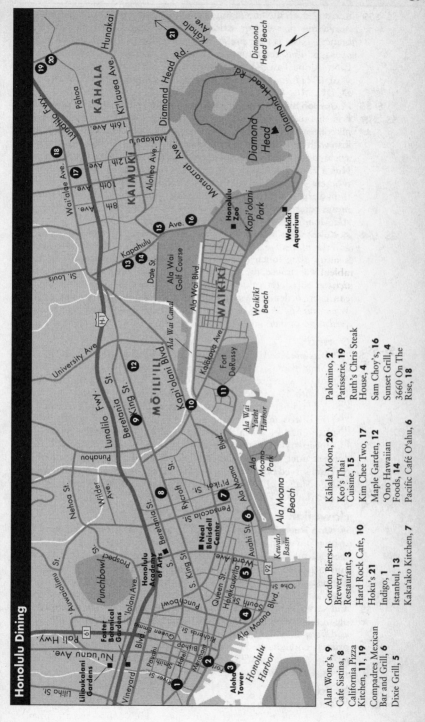

Alan Wong's, **9**
Cafe Sistina, **8**
California Pizza Kitchen, **11, 19**
Compadres Mexican Bar and Grill, **6**
Dixie Grill, **5**

Gordon Biersch Brewery Restaurant, **3**
Hard Rock Cafe, **10**
Hoku's **21**
Indigo, **1**
Istanbul, **13**
Kaka'ako Kitchen, **7**

Kāhala Moon, **20**
Keo's Thai Cuisine, **15**
Kim Chee Two, **17**
Maple Garden, **12**
'Ono Hawaiian Foods, **14**
Pacific Café O'ahu, **6**

Palomino, **2**
Patisserie, **19**
Ruth's Chris Steak House, **4**
Sam Choy's, **16**
Sunset Grill, **4**
3660 On The Rise, **18**

burning oven include mahimahi with creamy polenta, fig-caper-olive relish, and mussels. For seafood, order the crab cakes with pesto buerre blanc; if pasta is your preference, go for the fusilli with hot Portuguese sausage. This restaurant is close to downtown's Hawai'i Theatre. From Aloha Tower Marketplace, look for it across Ala Moana Boulevard. ⊠ *Harbor Court, 66 Queen St., 3rd floor,* ☎ *808/528–2400. AE, D, DC, MC, V.*

$–$$ ✕ **Gordon Biersch Brewery Restaurant.** Snuggling up to Honolulu Har-
   ★   bor, this indoor-outdoor eatery, part of a West Coast–based chain of microbreweries, is Aloha Tower Marketplace's busiest. The menu is American with an Island twist, from chicken skewers in a hot peanut-coconut sauce to fresh-seared *'ahi* in a *sansho* (tuna in a Japanese pepper) crust, plus a variety of pastas and pizzas. You can smell the garlic fries the moment you walk in. All that spicy food goes well with the beer, which is made on the premises. Ask for tastes of the dark, medium, and light brews before choosing your favorite. ⊠ *Aloha Tower Marketplace, 101 Ala Moana Blvd.,* ☎ *808/599–4877. AE, D, DC, MC, V.*

$ ✕ **Kaka'ako Kitchen.** The floors are concrete, the furniture is plastic, and the plates are Styrofoam. Never mind; this is the place to go for a healthy plate lunch (previously a contradiction in terms). In a converted warehouse, the kitchen turns out local favorites like pan-seared chicken salad, teriyaki chicken sandwich, and sautéed mahimahi. You can even order brown rice and a side of mesclun greens. ⊠ *1216 Waimanu St.,* ☎ *808/594–3663. Reservations not accepted. No credit cards. No dinner Sat.–Tues.*

German

$ ✕ **Patisserie.** By day, this bakery is dominated by fluorescent lights and a shining display case, but five nights a week it turns into a 24-seat restaurant with great German food, a rarity in Hawai'i. The menu is small, with 10 entrées, but any choice is a good choice. The Wiener schnitzel is juicy within its crispy crust, and veal ribs are garnished with a sprig of rosemary. Try the potato pancakes, crisp outside and soft inside, joined by a healthy spoonful of applesauce. Tossed salad and European-style breads are included in the price. The single dessert is apple strudel, standing high and full of rum-soaked raisins and tart apples and served on a rich sauce of cream, egg yolks, and vanilla beans.⊠ *Kāhala Mall, 4211 Wai'alae Ave.,* ☎ *808/735–4402. Reservations not accepted. MC, V. BYOB. Closed Sun.–Mon.*

Hawaiian

$ ✕ **'Ono Hawaiian Foods.** Locals frequent this no-frills hangout for a regular hit of their favorite foods. You can tell it's good, because there's usually a line outside after about 5 PM. In a plain storefront site and furnished simply with tables and booths, this small (it seats about 40) restaurant is a good place to do some taste testing of such Island innovations as poi, *lomilomi* salmon (salmon massaged until tender and served with minced onions and tomatoes), *laulau* (steamed bundle of ti leaves containing pork, butterfish, and taro tops), *kālua* pork, and *haupia* (a light, gelatinlike dessert made from coconut). Appropriately enough, the Hawaiian word *'ono* means delicious. ⊠ *726 Kapahulu Ave.,* ☎ *808/737–2275. Reservations not accepted. No credit cards. Closed Sun.*

Italian

$–$$ ✕ **Cafe Sistina.** Sergio Mitrotti has gained quite a following with his inventive Italian-Mediterranean cuisine. He's concocted an appetizer of goat cheese, chili peppers, garlic, prosciutto, and Greek olives, and he fills ravioli with such delights as Gorgonzola, porcini mushrooms, red peppers, and pancetta cream. Linguine *alla puttanesca* comes alive with tomatoes, onions, capers, and kalamata olives. Fresh chewy bread comes with a pesto butter to die for. A graphic artist by training, Mitrotti has painted the café's walls with Italianesque scenes. ⊠ *1314 S. King St.*, ☎ *808/596–0061. AE, MC, V.*

Korean

$ ✕ **Kim Chee Two.** Here's an unassuming little carry-out and sit-down restaurant featuring Korean food. The prices are low and the portions are big, and you get little side dishes of spicy *kimchi* (a fiery pickled Korean condiment) with your meal. This is a fun place to try such specialties as *bi bim kook soo* (noodles with meat and vegetables), meat *jun* (barbecued beef coated with egg and highly seasoned), *chop chae* (fried vegetables and noodles), and fried *man doo* (plump meat-filled dumplings). ⊠ *3569 Wai'alae Ave.*, ☎ *808/737–0006. Reservations not accepted. No credit cards. BYOB.*

Mediterranean

$–$$ ✕ **Istanbul.** Surrounded by tourist posters and serenaded by recorded Turkish music, diners here can encounter the lively flavors of the sunny Mediterranean. Rolled, deep-fried *mezeler* (appetizers) contain combinations of such fillings as feta cheese with parsley and fried eggplant with yogurt. Kebab plates come with beef, lamb, or chicken accompanied by rice and a zesty cucumber-onion-tomato salad with lemon. Depending on your mood, you may or may not want to time your visit with the nightly belly dancing (7:30–8:30). ⊠ *740 Kapahulu Ave.*, ☎ *808/735–6667. AE, MC, V. No lunch.*

Mexican

$–$$ ✕ **Compadres Mexican Bar and Grill.** The after-work crowd gathers here for frosty pitchers of potent margaritas and yummy pūpū. An outdoor terrace with patio-style furnishings is best for cocktails and chips. Inside, the wooden floors, colorful photographs, and lively paintings create a festive setting for imaginative Mexican specialties. Fajitas, baby back ribs, and grilled shrimp are just a few of the many offerings. ⊠ *Ward Centre, 1200 Ala Moana Blvd.*, ☎ *808/591–8307. Reservations not accepted. D, MC, V.*

Steak

$$–$$$ ✕ **Ruth's Chris Steak House.** At last, a steak joint that doesn't look like one. This pastel-hued dining room on Restaurant Row caters to meat lovers by serving mouthwatering top-of-the-line steak cuts. The portions are large, so bring an appetite. Side orders include generous salads and an ultra-creamy spinach au gratin. Charbroiled fish, veal, and lamb chops provide tasty alternatives to the steaks. For dessert, try the house special, a bread pudding happily soaked in whisky sauce. ⊠ *Restaurant Row, 500 Ala Moana Ave.*, ☎ *808/599–3860. AE, DC, MC, V.*

Thai

$$ ✕ **Keo's Thai Cuisine.** Hollywood celebrities have discovered this twin-
★   kling nook with tables set amid lighted trees, big paper umbrellas, and sprays of orchids everywhere. In fact, photos of Keo with different star patrons are displayed on one wall. Favorite dishes include Evil Jungle Prince (shrimp, vegetables, or chicken in a sauce flavored with fresh basil, coconut milk, and red chili) and *chiang mai* salad (chicken salad seasoned with lemongrass, red chili, mint, and fish sauce). Ask for your food mild or medium; it'll still be hot, but not as hot as it *could* be. For dessert, the apple bananas (small, tart bananas grown in Hawai'i) in coconut milk are wonderful. ⊠ *625 Kapahulu Ave.*, ☎ *808/737–8240. Reservations essential. AE, D, DC, MC, V. No lunch.*

Around the Island

Haleʻiwa

AMERICAN/CASUAL

$ ✕ **Kua ʻAina Sandwich.** A must-stop spot during a drive around the island, this tiny eatery has a few tables inside and a few more on the lānai, next to the road. Burgers are heaped with bacon, cheese, salsa, or pineapple, and the grilled mahimahi sandwich has fresh white meat and a homemade tartar sauce. Check out the pictures of old Haleʻiwa on the walls. ✉ *66-214 Kamehameha Hwy., ☎ 808/637–6067. Reservations not accepted. No credit cards.*

Hawaiʻi Kai

CONTEMPORARY

$$ ✕ **Roy's.** Two walls of windows offer views of Maunalua Bay and Diamond Head in the distance, and a glassed-in kitchen affords views of what's cooking at Roy Yamaguchi's Hawaiʻi Kai venture. This is a noisy two-story restaurant with a devoted following; Roy also has branches on the Big Island, Maui, and Kauaʻi. The menu matches Hawaiʻi flavors with Euro-Asian accents. It's hard to find a better blackened ʻahi in a hot, soy-mustard butter sauce. Of the individual pizzas, the best is topped with vine-ripened tomatoes, goat cheese, and roasted garlic. ✉ *Hawaiʻi Kai Corporate Plaza, 6600 Kalanianaʻole Hwy., ☎ 808/ 396–7697. AE, D, DC, MC, V.*

Kailua

MEXICAN

$ ✕ **Bueno Nalo.** Long a Waimānalo landmark, this family-run eatery moved to the windward side of the island in 1998. It's still run by the same owners, who are dedicated to healthy Mexican cuisine. Velvet paintings and piñatas add a fun, funky flavor to the setting. The food is reliably good. *Topopo* salad is a heap of greens, tomatoes, onions, tuna, olives, cheese, and beans on top of a tortilla. Combination plates with tacos, enchiladas, and tamales are bargains, and the chili rellenos are expertly seasoned. Families will appreciate the eight-piece Mexican pizzas and the keiki menu for children 10 and under. ✉ *20 Kainehe St., ☎ 808/263–1999. Reservations not accepted for parties of fewer than 6. AE, MC, V.*

Niu Valley

FRENCH

$$–$$$ ✕ **Cliquo.** Contemporary French cuisine using healthy sauces and organic vegetables: That's the unique selling point of this semi-sophisticated neighborhood restaurant. Chef Yves Menoret's fillet of ʻōpakapaka (snapper) with watercress has a Maui onion compote in ginger beurre blanc, and his roasted chicken breast comes with a corn cake and julienne of celery in cabernet sauce. ✉ *Niu Valley Shopping Center, 5730 Kalanianaʻole Hwy., ☎ 808/377–8854. AE, MC, V. No lunch.*

SWISS

$–$$ ✕ **Swiss Inn.** With waitresses in dirndls and color photos of Alpine villages adding to the scene, you're primed to yodel for this Old World setting and feast on the talents of Swiss-born chef Martin Wyss. Appetizers include *Bundnerfleisch* (thinly sliced air-dried beef) and *croûte emmental* (creamed mushrooms on toast with ham and Swiss cheese). Dinners come complete with soup, salad, vegetables, and coffee or tea. Veal medallions Florentine, served on a bed of spinach and covered with sliced bacon and Swiss cheese, is an outstanding entrée. With her sparkling aloha spirit, Martin's wife, Jeanie, does an excellent job of keeping things running smoothly. ✉ *Niu Valley Shopping Center, 5730 Kalanianaʻole Hwy., ☎ 808/377–5447. AE, D, DC, MC, V.*

Bueno Nalo, **2**
Cliquo, **4**
Hoku's, **5**
Kua 'Aina
Sandwich, **1**
Roy's, **3**
Swiss Inn, **4**

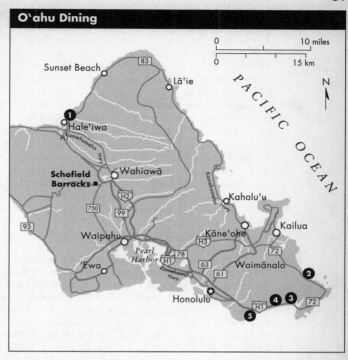

O'ahu Dining

LODGING

O'ahu has a wide range of accommodations, so it pays to plan ahead to find your perfect vacation home-away-from-home. First consider whether your South Seas dream vacation includes getting away from the usual hustle and bustle. If so, look at the listings in the "Around the Island" category. If you prefer proximity to the action, go for a hotel or condominium in or near Waikīkī, where most of the island's lodgings are.

Below is a selective list of lodging choices in each price category; for a complete list of every hotel and condominium on the island, write or call the Hawai'i Visitors and Convention Bureau for a free *Accommodation Guide* (☞ Visitor Information *in* O'ahu A to Z, *below*). It details amenities and gives each hotel's proximity to the beach. For price category explanations, *see* On the Road with Fodor's at the beginning of the book.

Waikīkī

$$$$ 🏨 **Aston Waikīkī Beach Tower.** Elegance oozes out of this 39-story luxury condominium resort overlooking Waikīkī Beach. It has stylish one- and two-bedroom suites fitted with microwaves, dishwashers, wet bars, washer/dryers, and private lānai. ⊠ *2470 Kalākaua Ave., Honolulu 96815,* ☎ *808/926–6400 or 800/922–7866,* 🆎 *808/922–8785. 140 suites. Kitchenettes, pool, sauna, paddle tennis, shuffleboard. AE, D, DC, MC, V.*

$$$$ 🏨 **Halekūlani.** Today's sleek, modern, and luxurious Halekūlani was
★ built around the garden lānai and 1931 building of the gracious old Halekūlani Hotel. Throughout its colorful history it has attracted visitors looking for an elegant oceanside retreat. The tidy marble-and-wood

rooms have accents of white, beige, blue, and gray. All have lānai, sitting areas, bathrobes, many terrific toiletries, and dozens of little touches that are sure to please. The hotel has two of the finest restaurants in Honolulu and an oceanside pool with a giant orchid mosaic. ⊠ *2199 Kālia Rd., Honolulu 96815,* ☎ *808/923–2311 or 800/367–2343,* FAX *808/926–8004. 412 rooms, 44 suites. 3 restaurants, 3 bars, refrigerators, pool, exercise room, beach, meeting rooms. AE, DC, MC, V.*

$$$$ 🏨 **Hawai'i Prince Hotel Waikīkī.** In a departure from the traditional Hawaiian motif, the Prince is a sleek high-rise with the sort of sophisticated interior design generally reserved for a city hotel. You know you're in Waikīkī, however, when you look out your window at the Ala Wai Yacht Harbor. Harbor views can also be had from the elegant Prince Court restaurant, while Hakone serves some of the best authentic Japanese food on the island, including a tantalizing 10-course *kaiseki* dinner (a traditional meal of small, artful, bite-size portions). There's a free shuttle to the beach and downtown. ⊠ *100 Holomoana St., Honolulu 96815,* ☎ *808/956–1111 or 800/321–6248,* FAX *808/946–0811. 467 rooms, 54 suites. 3 restaurants, lobby lounge, pool, meeting rooms. AE, DC, MC, V.*

$$$$ 🏨 **Hilton Hawaiian Village.** Each year Hilton spends a bundle to main-
★ tain this lavishly landscaped resort, the largest in Waikīkī. Surrounding its four towers are cascading waterfalls, colorful fish and birds, and even a botanical garden with labeled flora. Rooms are decorated in attractive raspberry or aqua shades, with rattan and bamboo furnishings. The hotel has a dock for its catamaran and a fine stretch of beach. ⊠ *2005 Kālia Rd., Honolulu 96815,* ☎ *808/949–4321 or 800/445–8667,* FAX *808/947–7898. 2,180 rooms, 365 suites. 6 restaurants, 5 lounges, 3 pools, beach. AE, D, DC, MC, V.*

$$$$ 🏨 **Hyatt Regency Waikīkī.** A 10-story atrium with a two-story waterfall and mammoth metal sculpture, shops, live music, and Harry's Bar make this one of the liveliest lobbies anywhere, though you may get lost in it. The Ciao Mein restaurant serves both Italian and Chinese food. Since the hotel has two towers, there are two Regency Clubs and eight penthouses. Each guest room has a private lānai. The hotel is across from the beach and a short walk from Kapi'olani Park. ⊠ *2424 Kalākaua Ave., Honolulu 96815,* ☎ *808/923–1234 or 800/233–1234,* FAX *808/923–7839. 1,212 rooms, 18 suites. 4 restaurants, 2 lobby lounges, pool, shops. AE, D, DC, MC, V.*

$$$$ 🏨 **'Ilikai Hotel Nikko Waikīkī.** It's not on the beach, but it's one of the closest hotels to Ala Moana Shopping Center and Ala Moana Beach Park. It's also the acknowledged tennis hotel of Waikīkī (courts are on the rooftops). There are three towers and a huge esplanade, which is always busy, and crowds gather at sunset for the torch lighting, hula dancing, and live Hawaiian music. ⊠ *1777 Ala Moana Blvd., Honolulu 96815,* ☎ *808/949–3811 or 800/367–8434,* FAX *808/947–0892. 728 rooms, 51 suites. 4 restaurants, 2 lobby lounges, 2 pools, 7 tennis courts, meeting rooms. AE, D, DC, MC, V.*

$$$$ 🏨 **Royal Hawaiian Hotel.** This "Pink Palace of the Pacific" was built
★ in 1927, an age of gracious and leisurely travel when people sailed here on luxury liners and spent months in Waikīkī. As befits its era, the hotel has high ceilings, period furniture, and flowered wallpaper. Pink telephones in each room and corridors of pink carpeting add a dreamy quality. The modern wing is more expensive, but for charm—and the tinkle of massive crystal chandeliers—the original building can't be beat. For a magical introduction to the Islands sip a tropical drink at the beachside Mai Tai Bar with its views of Diamond Head. ⊠ *2259 Kalākaua Ave., Honolulu 96815,* ☎ *808/923–7311 or 800/325–3535,* FAX *808/924–7098. 472 rooms, 53 suites. 3 restaurants, bar, pool, meeting rooms. AE, DC, MC, V.*

Waikīkī Lodging

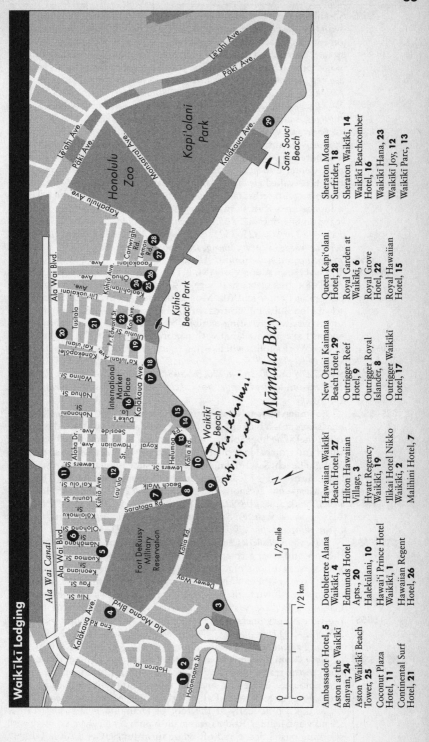

Ambassador Hotel, **5**
Aston at the Waikiki
Banyan, **24**
Aston Waikiki Beach
Tower, **25**
Coconut Plaza
Hotel, **11**
Continental Surf
Hotel, **21**

Doubletree Alana
Waikiki, **4**
Edmunds Hotel
Apts., **20**
Halekūlani, **10**
Hawai'i Prince Hotel
Waikiki, **1**
Hawaiian Regent
Hotel, **26**

Hawaiian Waikiki
Beach Hotel, **27**
Hilton Hawaiian
Village, **3**
Hyatt Regency
Waikiki, **19**
'Ilikai Hotel Nikko
Waikiki, **2**
Malihini Hotel, **7**

New Otani Kaimana
Beach Hotel, **29**
Outrigger Reef
Hotel, **9**
Outrigger Royal
Islander, **8**
Outrigger Waikiki
Hotel, **17**

Queen Kapi'olani
Hotel, **28**
Royal Garden at
Waikiki, **6**
Royal Grove
Hotel, **22**
Royal Hawaiian
Hotel, **15**

Sheraton Moana
Surfrider, **18**
Sheraton Waikiki, **14**
Waikiki Beachcomber
Hotel, **16**
Waikiki Hana, **23**
Waikiki Joy, **12**
Waikiki Parc, **13**

$$$$ 🏨 **Sheraton Moana Surfrider.** The Moana Hotel, built in 1901, merged with the newer Surfrider next door. As in the old days, the furnishings on each floor are made of a different kind of wood: mahogany, oak, maple, cherry, and rare Hawaiian koa. The Banyan Court is the focal point for beachfront activity, and you can relax on the gracious veranda, sip tea, and tune yourself in to turn-of-the-century living. ☒ *2365 Kalākaua Ave., Honolulu 96815,* ☎ *808/922–3111 or 800/325–3535,* FAX *808/923–0308. 750 rooms, 41 suites. 3 restaurants, bar, 3 lobby lounges, snack bar, pool, beach, meeting rooms. AE, DC, MC, V.*

$$$$ 🏨 **Sheraton Waikīkī.** Towering over its neighbors, the Sheraton has spacious rooms, many of which have grand views of Diamond Head. The hotel is just steps away from the multilevel Royal Hawaiian Shopping Center and next to the Royal Hawaiian Hotel. Be sure to take the glass-walled elevator up to the Hanohano Room, an elegant dining room with breathtaking panoramas of the sea and Waikīkī. There's a lounge area with showers for guests who arrive on early flights or leave on late ones. ☒ *2255 Kalākaua Ave., Honolulu 96815,* ☎ *808/ 922–4422 or 800/325–3535,* FAX *808/922–7708. 1,588 rooms, 131 suites. 5 restaurants, 3 lobby lounges, 2 pools, health club, beach, children's programs, meeting rooms. AE, DC, MC, V.*

$$$–$$$$ 🏨 **Doubletree Alana Waikīkī.** Leisure and business travelers like this hotel's location on the west edge of Waikīkī, two blocks from Ala Moana Shopping Center and Ala Moana Beach Park and 4 mi from downtown Honolulu. Public areas of the 19-story high-rise are modern and attractive, with rotating exhibits of local works in the lobby. Guest rooms have private lānai with panoramic views of the mountains or ocean. Workaholics will like the 'round-the-clock services of the business center. ☒ *1956 Ala Moana Blvd., Honolulu 96815,* ☎ *808/ 941–7275 or 800/367–6070,* FAX *808/949–0996. 268 rooms, 45 suites. Restaurant, lobby lounge, pool, exercise room, business services. AE, D, MC, V.*

$$$–$$$$ 🏨 **Hawaiian Regent Hotel.** With two towers and two lobbies, this property's layout is a bit confusing, but if you can get past that, this is a decent hotel. The huge lobbies and courtyards open to ocean breezes are sunlit and tropical in feeling. Better yet, it's right across the street from Waikīkī Beach. Several dining choices include two Japanese restaurants and a cutting-edge Mediterranean dining room called Acqua. The shopping arcade has 20 shops and boutiques. ☒ *2552 Kalākaua Ave., Honolulu 96815,* ☎ *808/922–6611 or 800/367–5370,* FAX *808/921–5222. 1,337 rooms, 9 suites. 5 restaurants, 2 lobby lounges, 2 pools, tennis court, shops, dance club, meeting rooms. AE, D, MC, V.*

$$$–$$$$ 🏨 **Hawaiian Waikīkī Beach Hotel.** The site—close to Kapiʻolani Park, the zoo, and other attractions and across from the beach—is excellent, and the seawall in front of the hotel offers the best sunset views. The mauka tower offers mainly ocean views. The rooms have rattan furniture, right down to the headboards, and each has a private lānai. The Captain's Table serves meals in surroundings modeled after those of old-time luxury liners. ☒ *2570 Kalākaua Ave., Honolulu 96815,* ☎ *808/922–2511 or 800/877–7666,* FAX *808/923–3656. 673 rooms, 40 suites. 2 restaurants, 3 lobby lounges, pool. AE, D, DC, MC, V.*

$$$–$$$$ 🏨 **New Otani Kaimana Beach Hotel.** Polished to a shine, this hotel is
   ★   open to the trade winds and furnished with big, comfortable chairs. The ambience is cheerful and charming, and the lobby has a happy, unpretentious feel. Best of all, it's right on the beach at the quiet end of Waikīkī, practically at the foot of Diamond Head. The staff is friendly and helpful. Rooms are smallish but very nicely appointed, with soothing pastel decor and off-white furnishings. Get a room with an ocean view and dine at least once at the Hau Tree Lānai. ☒ *2863 Kalākaua Ave., Honolulu 96815,* ☎ *808/923–1555 or 800/356–8264,*

FAX 808/922–9404. 119 rooms, 6 suites. 2 restaurants, lobby lounge, meeting rooms. AE, D, DC, MC, V.

$$$–$$$$ 🏨 **Queen Kapi'olani Hotel.** Built in 1969, this 19-story hotel is at the east edge of Waikīkī, right across from the Honolulu Zoo and Kapi'olani Park and a half-block from the beach. It appeals to those in search of clean, basic accommodations within walking distance of Waikīkī's main attractions. Rooms have refrigerators, and there's a large fresh-water swimming pool and sundeck on the third floor. ⊠ 150 Kapahulu Ave., Honolulu 96815, ☎ 808/922–1941 or 800/367–5004, FAX 808/922–2694. 308 rooms, 7 suites. Refrigerators, 2 restaurants, bar, pool, meeting rooms. AE, D, DC, MC, V.

$$$–$$$$ 🏨 **Waikīkī Joy.** This boutique hotel is a lesser-known gem. One tower has all suites, and another has standard hotel rooms. Units have either ocean or partial ocean views; each has a lānai, a whirlpool bath, a deluxe stereo system with Bose speakers, and a control panel by the bed. The location is great, tucked away on a quiet side street yet still close to Waikīkī's dining, shopping, and entertainment. ⊠ 320 Lewers St., Honolulu 96815, ☎ 808/923–2300 or 800/922–7866, FAX 808/924–4010. 50 rooms, 44 suites. Restaurant, lobby lounge, kitchenettes, pool, sauna. AE, D, DC, MC, V.

$$$–$$$$ 🏨 **Waikīkī Parc.** Billed as offering affordable luxury, this hotel lives
★ up to its promise in all essentials except its main entrance (down a nar-row side street) and location (not on the beach). The lobby is light and airy, with mirrors and pastel tones. Guest rooms are done in cool blues and whites, with lots of rattan. The hotel has a fine Japanese restaurant called Kacho and the lovely Parc Café, known for its reasonably priced all-you-can-eat buffets. ⊠ 2233 Helumoa Rd., Honolulu 96815, ☎ 808/921–7272 or 800/422–0450, FAX 808/923–1336. 298 rooms. 2 restaurants, in-room safes, refrigerators, pool. AE, D, DC, MC, V.

$$$ 🏨 **Aston at the Waikīkī Banyan.** Families enjoy this high-rise condo-minium resort near Diamond Head, one block from Waikīkī Beach and two blocks from the Honolulu Zoo. One-bedroom suites have daily maid service and private lānai. Look for the fishpond in the lobby area. ⊠ 201 'Ōhua Ave., Honolulu 96815, ☎ 808/922–0555 or 800/922–7866, FAX 808/922–8785. 876 suites. Snack bar, kitchenettes, pool, sauna, tennis court. AE, D, DC, MC, V.

$$$ 🏨 **Outrigger Reef Hotel.** The big advantage here is a location right on the beach, just steps away from any room in the building. There are fashion and souvenir boutiques in the lobby and the rooms are done in soft mauves and pinks, many with lānai. Ask for an ocean view; the other rooms have decidedly less delightful views. ⊠ 2169 Kālia Rd., Honolulu 96815, ☎ 808/923–3111 or 800/688–7444, FAX 808/924–4957. 846 rooms, 39 suites. 2 restaurants, 4 bars, no-smoking rooms, pool, beach, nightclub, meeting rooms. AE, D, DC, MC, V.

$$$ 🏨 **Outrigger Waikīkī Hotel.** Outrigger Hotels & Resorts' star prop-erty, on Kalākaua Avenue in the heart of the best shopping and din-ing action, stands next to some of the nicest sands in Waikīkī. Rooms have a Polynesian motif, and each has a lānai. For more than 25 years, the main ballroom has been home to the sizzling Society of Seven and the group's Las Vegas–style production. ⊠ 2335 Kalākaua Ave., Honolulu 96815, ☎ 808/923–0711 or 800/688–7444, FAX 800/622–4852. 500 rooms, 30 suites. 6 restaurants, 5 bars, lobby lounge, kitchenettes, pool. AE, D, DC, MC, V.

$$$ 🏨 **Royal Garden at Waikīkī.** From the outside, this 25-story hotel looks like your average Waikīkī high-rise. But step inside and it whispers el-egance, from the marble and etched glass in the lobby to the genuine graciousness of the staff. Guest rooms have sitting areas, private lānai, and marble and brass baths.There's a free shuttle service to and from Kapi'olani Park, Ala Moana Shopping Center, Royal Hawaiian Shopping Center, and duty-free shops. ⊠ *440 'Olohana St., Honolulu 96815,* ☎ *808/943–0202 or 800/367–5666,* FAX *808/946–8777. 202 rooms, 18 suites. 2 restaurants, lobby lounge, kitchenettes, in-room safes, 2 pools, meeting rooms. CP. AE, D, DC, MC, V.*

$$$ 🏨 **Waikīkī Beachcomber Hotel.** With an excellent location right across ★ the street from Waikīkī Beach, it's also a short walk from the Royal Hawaiian Shopping Center and the International Market Place. Rooms have simple Island-style rattan furnishings, with a rose, beige, and off-white color scheme and prints by local artists. Rooms have private lānai. Two evening shows are presented here: the venerable Don Ho and talented ventriloquist Freddie Morris. ⊠ *2300 Kalākaua Ave., Honolulu 96815,* ☎ *808/922–4646 or 800/622–4646,* FAX *808/923–4889. 487 rooms, 7 suites. Restaurant, lobby lounge, snack bar, no-smoking rooms, pool. AE, DC, MC, V.*

$$–$$$ 🏨 **Ambassador Hotel.** The Ambassador's west-Waikīkī location puts guests in a good position. It's within walking distance of the beach and all that Waikīkī has to offer while close to the new convention center, the Ala Wai Canal, and Ala Moana Shopping Center. There's nothing glamorous about the exterior of this high-rise hotel; the rooms' carpeting, curtains, fixtures, lighting, and furnishings look fresh. All rooms have private lānai, and superior units come with a stove and oven. Keo's Thai restaurant opened here in 1998. ⊠ *2040 Kūhiō Ave., Honolulu 96815,* ☎ *808/941–7777 or 800/923–2620,* FAX *808/941–4717. 187 rooms, 34 suites. Restaurant, in-room safes, kitchenettes, refrigerators, 1 pool. AE, D, DC, MC, V.*

$$–$$$ 🏨 **Coconut Plaza Hotel.** With its intimate size and service, Coconut Plaza is a true boutique hotel. On the Ala Wai Canal, three blocks from the beach, its tropical plantation decor features rattan furnishings and floral bedspreads. Guest rooms have private lānai, and all except standard view rooms come with kitchenettes. Free Continental breakfast is served daily on the lobby veranda. ⊠ *450 Lewers St., Honolulu 96815,* ☎ *808/923–8828 or 800/882–9696,* FAX *808/923–3473. 70 rooms, 11 suites. Kitchenettes, pool, meeting rooms. AE, D, DC, MC, V.*

$$ 🏨 **Continental Surf Hotel.** One of the better budget hotels of Waikīkī, this appealing high-rise is along the Kūhiō Avenue strip, two blocks from the ocean and convenient to many shops and restaurants. The lobby is large and breezy, and the comfortable rooms are decorated in Polynesian hues of browns and golds. The units have limited views and no lānai. Guests may use the facilities of its sister hotel, the Miramar, 1½ blocks away. ⊠ *2426 Kūhiō Ave., Honolulu 96815,* ☎ *808/922–2232,* FAX *808/923–9487. 141 rooms. Kitchenettes. No credit cards.*

$$ 🏨 **Outrigger Royal Islander.** This inexpensive link in the Outrigger hotel chain boasts a great location—just a two-minute walk from a very nice section of Waikīkī Beach. The rooms have tapa-print bedspreads and ceramic lamps with matching patterns, and there are Island-inspired pictures on the walls. Each room also has a private lānai. Choose between studios, one-bedroom apartments, or suites. The staff is helpful in arranging activities, such as golf and scuba packages and sightseeing tours. Guests have access to pools at other Outrigger hotels. ⊠ *2164 Kālia Rd., Honolulu 96815,* ☎ *808/922–1961 or 800/688–7444,* FAX *808/923–4632. 94 rooms, 7 suites. In-room safes, coin laundry. AE, D, DC, MC, V.*

$–$$ 🏨 **Waikīkī Hana.** Smack dab in the middle of Waikīkī and a block away from the beach, this eight-story hotel is convenient for exploring just about every shop, restaurant, and activity in O'ahu's tourist hub. Accommodations are clean and plain; many have their own lānai. Pay a little extra per day and you can rent a refrigerator. ⊠ *2424 Koa Ave., Honolulu 96815,* ☎ *808/926–8841 or 800/367–5004,* FAX *808/*

924–3770. 70 rooms, 2 suites. Restaurant, lobby lounge, kitchenettes, in-room safes, coin laundry. AE, DC, MC, V.

$ ⊞ **Edmunds Hotel Apartments.** On the Ala Wai Canal, four blocks from the ocean, this has been a budget alternative for decades. Long lānai wrap around the building, so each room has its own view of the pretty canal and glorious Manoa Valley beyond—views that look especially lovely at night, when lights are twinkling up the mountain ridges. If you can put up with the constant sounds of traffic on the boulevard, this is a real bargain. ⊠ *2411 Ala Wai Blvd., Honolulu 96815,* ☎ *808/ 923–8381 or 808/732–5169. 12 rooms. Kitchenettes. No credit cards.*

$ ⊞ **Malihini Hotel.** There's no pool, it's not on the beach, none of the units has a TV or air-conditioning, and the rooms are spartan. Still, the atmosphere of this low-rise complex is cool and pleasant, and the gardens are well maintained. All rooms are either studios or one-bedrooms, and all have kitchenettes and daily maid service. The low prices and good location make this a popular place, so be sure to book well in advance. ⊠ *217 Saratoga Rd., Honolulu 96815,* ☎ *808/923–9644. 21 rooms, 9 suites. Kitchenettes. No credit cards.*

$ ⊞ **Royal Grove Hotel.** You won't go wrong with this flamingo-pink family-oriented hotel, reminiscent of Miami. With just six floors, it is one of Waikīkī's smaller hotels. The lobby is comfortable; the rooms, though agreeably furnished, have no theme and no views. The pool area is bright with tropical flowers (the hotel is not on the beach). ⊠ *15 Uluniu Ave., Honolulu 96815,* ☎ *808/923–7691, FAX 808/922–7508. 78 rooms, 7 suites. Kitchenettes, pool. AE, D, DC, MC, V.*

Honolulu

$$$$ ⊞ **Kāhala Mandarin Oriental Hawai'i.** Minutes away from Waikīkī,
★ on the quiet side of Diamond Head, this elegant oceanfront hotel is hidden in the wealthy neighborhood of Kāhala. Formerly the Kāhala Hilton, it reopened in 1996 after a $75 million renovation. The room decor combines touches of Asia and old Hawai'i, with mahogany furniture, teak parquet floors, hand-loomed area rugs, local art, and grass-cloth wall coverings. The popular dolphin pool has been expanded; it's now easier to see these friendly creatures. ⊠ *5000 Kāhala Ave., 96816,* ☎ *808/734–2211 or 800/367–2525, FAX 808/737–2478. 341 rooms, 29 suites. 3 restaurants, 2 lobby lounges, pool, outdoor hot tub, sauna, steam room, exercise room, beach, dive shop, snorkeling, business services, meeting rooms. AE, D, DC, MC, V.*

$$$ ⊞ **Aston Executive Centre Hotel.** Here's a great option for the corporate traveler who wants to avoid Waikīkī. Downtown Honolulu's only hotel is an all-suite high-rise in the center of the business district and 10 minutes from Honolulu International Airport. Suites are on the top 10 floors of a 40-story glass-walled tower, providing views of downtown and Honolulu Harbor. Each unit has a separate living area and kitchenette stocked with cold beverages. ⊠ *1088 Bishop St., 96813,* ☎ *808/539–3000 or 800/949–3932, FAX 808/523–1088. 116 suites. Restaurant, in-room safes, kitchenettes, pool, exercise room, business services, meeting rooms. CP. AE, DC, MC, V.*

$$–$$$ ⊞ **Ala Moana Hotel.** This longstanding landmark has an excellent location, right next to the popular Ala Moana Shopping Center (they're connected by a pedestrian ramp) and one block from Ala Moana Beach Park. Each room in this 36-story high-rise has a lānai with a view of either the ocean, the Ko'olau Mountains, or Diamond Head. Amenities are modern; for instance, you can order room service at the touch of a remote control button. Concierge floor rooms on the 29th to 35th floors provide such upgraded services as in-room whirlpool baths and free use of the conference room. ⊠ *410 Atkinson Dr.,*

96814, ☎ *808/955–4811 or 800/367–6025,* FAX *808/944–2974. 1,102 rooms, 67 suites. 4 restaurants, bar, 2 lobby lounges, in-room safes, pool, dance club, nightclub, meeting room. AE, DC, MC, V.*

$$–$$$ 🏨 **Mānoa Valley Inn.** Here's an intimate surprise tucked away in Mānoa Valley, just 2 mi from Waikīkī. Built in 1919, this stately hotel serves a complimentary Continental breakfast buffet on a shady lānai and fresh tropical fruit and cheese in the afternoon. Rooms are furnished in country-inn style, with antique four-poster beds, marble-top dressers, patterned wallpaper, and fresh flowers; there's a reading room with a TV and VCR. ✉ *2001 Vancouver Dr., Honolulu 96822,* ☎ *808/947–6019 or 800/535–0085,* FAX *800/633–5085. 8 rooms, 4 with private bath; 1 cottage. CP. AE, DC, MC, V.*

$$–$$$ 🏨 **Pagoda Hotel.** Minutes away from Ala Moana Shopping Center and Ala Moana Beach Park, the Pagoda is well placed. A free shuttle bus makes the trip between the hotel and its sister property, the Pacific Beach in Waikīkī. The location, along with the moderate rates, makes this a good choice if you're simply looking for a place to sleep and to catch a couple of meals. Studio rooms include a full-size refrigerator, a stove, and cooking utensils. There are no memorable views, since the hotel is surrounded by high-rises. The Pagoda floating restaurant is notable for its Japanese gardens and carp-filled waterways. ✉ *1525 Rycroft St., Honolulu 96814,* ☎ *808/941–6611 or 800/472–4632,* FAX *808/955–5067. 364 rooms. 2 restaurants, refrigerators, pool. AE, D, DC, MC, V.*

Around the Island

$$$$ 🏨 **'Ihilani Resort & Spa.** On O'ahu's western shore, 'Ihilani is a 25-minute
★   drive from Honolulu International Airport. Providing a Neighbor Island atmosphere, the resort has a sleek 15-story hotel illuminated by a glass-dome atrium. Guest rooms have marble bathrooms with deep soaking tubs, private lānai with teak furnishings, in-room CD players and a selection of CDs, and a high-tech control system (lights, temperature controls, and more) built into the telephones. Most rooms have ocean views. The 35,000-sq-ft 'Ihilani Spa offers everything from seaweed baths to stair-climbers, and there's a championship golf course and a wonderful brunch. The resort joined Nikko Hotels International in 1998. ✉ *92–1001 'Ōlani St., Kapolei 96707,* ☎ *808/679–0079 or 800/626–4446,* FAX *808/679–0295. 333 rooms, 54 suites. 4 restaurants, 2 pools, spa, 18-hole golf course, 6 tennis courts, baby-sitting. AE, DC, MC, V.*

$$$$ 🏨 **Turtle Bay Hilton.** Though it needs renovation, this oceanside retreat has everything it takes for a relaxing stay away from town. The rooms, in three wings, have private lānai and are furnished in wicker, brass, pastels, and light woods, with pastel prints on the walls. Check out the hotel's mammoth Sunday champagne brunch ($26.95), and dine next to huge windows with views of the crashing surf. Adjacent to the hotel are studio cabanas that have two double beds; they are pricier but offer more privacy. ✉ *57-091 Kamehameha Hwy. (Box 187), Kahuku 96731,* ☎ *808/293–8811 or 800/445–8667,* FAX *808/293–9147. 450 rooms, 30 suites, 86 cabanas. 2 restaurants, lobby lounge, pool, 2 18-hole golf courses, 10 tennis courts, horseback riding, beach, shops. AE, D, DC, MC, V.*

$–$$$ 🏨 **Schrader's Windward Marine Resort.** Here is another rural resort with fewer luxuries than you would find in Waikīkī but with perhaps a little more personalized attention. Some rooms open onto Kāne'ohe Bay, which is so close that people have been known to fish right off their lānai. Other rooms face the Ko'olau Mountains. One- to three-bedroom accommodations are available. On a peninsula, this is a popular spot for water activities. ✉ *47-039 Lihikai Dr., Kāne'ohe 96744,* ☎ *808/239–5711 or 800/735–5711,* FAX *808/239–6658. 22 rooms. Kitchenettes, pool. AE, D, DC, MC, V.*

O'ahu Lodging

$–$$ 🏨 **Backpackers Vacation Inn and Plantation Village.** In spirit as well as location, Backpackers is far, far removed from the hustle and bustle of Waikīkī. Near Waimea Bay on the North Shore, Backpackers provides double rooms (some with a double bed, others with two single beds), hostel accommodations, and cottages. Guests can use free snorkel equipment, boogie boards, and tennis racquets. It's a three-minute walk to the supermarket. This is a great place for budget travelers. ⊠ 59-788 Kamehameha Hwy., Hale'iwa 96712, ☎ 808/638–7838, 𝔽𝔸𝕏 808/638–7515. 25 rooms. Kitchens. MC, V.

NIGHTLIFE AND THE ARTS

Nightlife on O'ahu can be as simple as a barefoot stroll in the sand or as elaborate as a dinner show with all the glitter of a Las Vegas production. You can view the vibrant hues of a Honolulu sunset during a cocktail cruise, or hear the melodies of ancient chants at a lū'au on a remote west-shore beach.

Waikīkī is where nearly all O'ahu's night action takes place, and what action there is! Kalākaua and Kūhiō avenues come to life when the sun goes down and the lights go on. Outside Honolulu, offerings are slimmer but equally diverse. You can dance the two-step at a waterfront café one night and then boogie to live bands in a tiny second-story windward bar the next. The North Shore is more conducive to settling back to the music of a slack-key guitar and lilting falsetto voice, while the ranch country of Waimānalo lends itself to country tunes and fiddle playing.

Wafting through the night air of O'ahu is the sound of music of every kind—from classical to contemporary. Music has been the language of Hawai'i from the beginning, and O'ahu has the best selection.

Meanwhile, hula dancers wear sequin skirts in Waikīkī and authentic ti-leaf skirts at Paradise Cove; they are accompanied by everything from *ipu* drums to electric guitars, mercifully not on the same stage in most cases. The latest high-tech, multimedia video discos may also be found on Oʻahu, but then, so are acoustic ʻukulele trios.

The arts thrive right alongside the tourist industry in Oʻahu's balmy climate. The island has an established symphony, a thriving opera company, chamber music groups, and community theaters. Major Broadway shows, dance companies, and rock stars also make their way to Honolulu. Check the local newspapers—the morning *Honolulu Advertiser* or the afternoon *Honolulu Star-Bulletin*—for the latest happenings.

Bars, Cabarets, and Clubs

Drinking age is 21 on Oʻahu and throughout Hawaiʻi. Many bars will admit younger people but will not serve them alcohol. By law, all establishments that serve alcoholic beverages must close at 2 AM. The only exceptions are those with a cabaret license, which have a 4 AM curfew. Though billed as discotheques, they are required to have live music. Most places have a cover charge of $2–$5.

Waikīkī

Banyan Veranda has such Hawaiian entertainers as Jerry Santos and Pumehana Davis, who perform on the open-air lānai. ⊠ *Sheraton Moana Surfrider, 2365 Kalākaua Ave.,* ☎ *808/922–3111.* ☉ *Daily breakfast–11 PM.*

Blue Zebra Café is a mirrored, split-level disco that plays live and recorded contemporary music for dancing. ⊠ *Restaurant Row, 500 Ala Moana Blvd.,* ☎ *808/538–0409.* ☉ *Nightly 8–4.*

Club 1739. Punk and funk find their home at this dance club, where live bands take turns with DJs keeping twentysomethings up all night. Honolulu's weekly alternative newspaper voted this the best place to dance in Waikīkī. ⊠ *1739 Kalākaua Ave.,* ☎ *808/949–1739.* ☉ *Sun.–Thurs 9–2, Fri.–Sat. 9 PM–8 AM, live music Thurs. and Sat. 9–midnight.*

Coconuts Nightclub. Blues, jazz, and soul are alive and well at this small nightclub by the Ala Wai Yacht Harbor. ⊠ *ʻIlikai Hotel Nikko Waikīkī, 1777 Ala Moana Blvd.,* ☎ *808/949–3811.* ☉ *Live music nightly 8–midnight.*

Cupid's Lobby Bar. A variety of musicians take to the stage in this hotel lounge. Mellow Friday night gigs by local pianist/singer/composer Jay Larrin appeal to a mature crowd. ⊠ *Prince Kūhiō Hotel, 2500 Kūhiō Ave.,* ☎ *808/922–0811.* ☉ *Daily 11–11, live music Tues.–Sat. 7–11.*

Duke's Canoe Club. It's smack dab on Waikīkī Beach, in an old-Hawaiʻi open-air atmosphere of bamboo, tiki torches, palm-thatch roofs, and luscious koa wood. What better setting in which to sip a mai tai, watch the sunset, and hear some of Hawaiʻi's most popular musicians? ⊠ *Outrigger Waikīkī Hotel, 2335 Kalākaua Ave.,* ☎ *808/922–2268.* ☉ *Nightly 4–6 and 10–midnight.*

Esprit. Honolulu, an all-male octet, performs music from the big band era of the 1930s up through current pop hits, with Broadway numbers, too. Each band member plays no less than three instruments in this high-energy show. ⊠ *Sheraton Waikīkī Hotel, 2255 Kalākaua Ave.,* ☎ *808/922–4422.* ☉ *Mon.–Tues. 8:30 PM–2 AM.*

Hanohano Room. Late-night jazz prevails during weekly jam sessions by some of Hawaiʻi's best musicians. They get into everything from jazz to swing to bebop. ⊠ *Sheraton Waikīkī Hotel, 2255 Kalākaua Ave., 30th floor,* ☎ *808/922–4422.* ⊙ *Sat. 11 PM–1 AM.*

Lewers Lounge. Singer Loretta Ables performs contemporary jazz and standards here Tuesday through Saturday evenings. A vocalist/pianist sits in Sunday and Monday. A dessert menu is offered. ⊠ *Halekūlani, 2199 Kālia Rd.,* ☎ *808/923–2311.* ⊙ *Nightly 9–12:30.*

Mai Tai Bar. Keith and Carmen Haugen sing island duets at this open-air Waikīkī Beach bar. Carmen's hula is a thing of beauty. Catch them Tuesday and Wednesday; entertainers vary on other nights. ⊠ *Royal Hawaiian Hotel, 2259 Kalākaua Ave.,* ☎ *808/923–7311.* ⊙ *Nightly 5:30–7:30.*

Moose McGillycuddy's Pub and Cafe. Loud bands play for the beach-and-beer gang in a blue-jeans-and-T-shirt setting. ⊠ *310 Lewers St.,* ☎ *808/923–0751.* ⊙ *Nightly 9–1:30.*

Nicholas Nickolas. A splendid view, good music, and a well-dressed crowd somehow come together here as a bit stiff and stuffy. But, hey! Who says you can't make your own fun if the mood and the music click? ⊠ *Ala Moana Hotel, 410 Atkinson Dr.,* ☎ *808/955–4466.* ⊙ *Dancing Sun.–Thurs. 9:30 PM–2 AM, Fri. and Sat. 10 PM–3 AM.*

Nick's Fishmarket. This is probably the most comfortable of Waikīkī's upscale dance lounges, with an elegant crowd, smooth music, and an intimate, dark atmosphere. There's some singles action here. ⊠ *Waikīkī Gateway Hotel, 2070 Kalākaua Ave.,* ☎ *808/955–6333.* ⊙ *Nightly 9–1:30.*

Paradise Lounge. A variety of acts, including the longtime band Olomana, perform in this pretty outdoor club. ⊠ *Hilton Hawaiian Village, 2005 Kālia Rd.,* ☎ *808/949–4321.* ⊙ *Fri. and Sat. 8 PM–midnight.*

Pool Stage. Throughout the week, by the hotel's oceanfront pool, various local performers present outstanding Hawaiian song and dance. One of the most popular mainstays is 'ukulele wizard Moe Keale, familiar to TV viewers from his roles on *Hawai'i Five-O.* ⊠ *Sheraton Waikīkī Hotel, 2255 Kalākaua Ave.,* ☎ *808/922–4422.* ⊙ *Nightly 6–8:30.*

Royal Garden at Waikīkī. Some of O'ahu's top jazz stylists like singing in the elegant, intimate lobby lounge of this side-street hotel. ⊠ *Royal Garden at Waikīkī, 444 'Olohana St.,* ☎ *808/943–0202.* ⊙ *Tues.–Sun. 8–11.*

Rumours. The after-work crowd loves this spot, which has dance videos, disco, and throbbing lights. On Big Chill nights each Friday the club plays oldies from the '60s and '70s and serves free pūpū. There's ballroom dancing Sunday evening from 5 to 9. ⊠ *Ala Moana Hotel, 410 Atkinson St.,* ☎ *808/955–4811.* ⊙ *Wed.–Fri. 5 PM–2 AM, Sat. 8 PM–4 AM.*

Scruples. There's disco dancing to Top 40 tunes, with a young-adult, mostly local crowd. The Thursday night bikini contest packs 'em in. ⊠ *Waikīkī Market Place, 2310 Kūhiō Ave.,* ☎ *808/923–9530.* ⊙ *Nightly 8–4.*

Shore Bird Beach Broiler. This beachfront disco spills right out onto the sand; it features a large dance floor and 10-ft video screen. Karaoke sing-alongs are held nightly. ⊠ *Outrigger Reef Hotel, 2169 Kālia Rd.,* ☎ *808/922–2887.* ⊙ *Nightly 9–2.*

Wave Waikīkī. Dance to live rock and roll until 1:30 AM, recorded music after that. It can be a rough scene, but the bands are tops. ⊠ *1877 Kalākaua Ave.,* ☎ *808/941–0424.* ⊙ *Nightly 9–4.*

Honolulu

Anna Bannana's. At this two-story, smoky dive, the live music is fresh, loud, and sometimes experimental. Different local favorites deliver ultracreative dancing music, and the likes of blues singer Taj Mahal have been known to slip in for a set or two. ⊠ *2440 S. Beretania St.,* ☎ *808/946–5190.* ⊗ *Nightly 11:30–2, live music Thurs.–Sat. 9–2.*

Gordon Biersch Brewery Restaurant. Live duos and trios serenade patrons of the outside bar that flanks Honolulu Harbor. While there's no dancing, this is the place in Honolulu to see and be seen. ⊠ *Aloha Tower Marketplace, 101 Ala Moana Blvd.,* ☎ *808/599–4877.* ⊗ *Wed.–Sat. 7 PM–1 AM.*

Pier Bar. Here's one of the few places in Honolulu to hear live music outdoors. The Pier Bar attracts a grab bag of groups; call ahead to find out who's playing. ⊠ *Aloha Tower Marketplace, 101 Ala Moana Blvd.,* ☎ *808/536–2166,* ⊗ *Nightly 6:30–4.*

Row Bar. Restaurant Row's outdoor gathering place mixes it up each weekend with live reggae, rock, and rhythm 'n' blues. Single professionals meet here *pau hana* (after work). ⊠ *Restaurant Row, 500 Ala Moana Blvd.,* ☎ *808/528–2345,* ⊗ *Fri.–Sat. 8–11:45, Sun. jazz 5:30–8:30.*

Sand Island Rhythm & Blues. When red-hot blues acts from the mainland come to town, they often play in this small bar near downtown Honolulu. A high-tech sound system does them justice. Opening hours vary; check local papers or call ahead. ⊠ *197 Sand Island Access Rd.,* ☎ *808/847–4274.*

World Cafe. Honolulu's only upscale billiards nightclub also has a sports bar and dancing to Top 40 tunes. ⊠ *Restaurant Row, 500 Ala Moana Blvd.,* ☎ *808/599–4450.* ⊗ *Mon.–Thurs. 11:30 AM–2 AM, Fri. and Sat. 11:30 AM–4 AM, Sun. 3 PM–2 AM.*

'Aiea

Pecos River Cafe. Billing itself as Hawai'i's premier country-and-western nightclub, this easygoing establishment has live music nightly. ⊠ *99–016 Kamehameha Hwy.,* ☎ *808/487–7980.* ⊗ *Nightly 9–2.*

Kahuku

Bayview Lounge. A beautiful place to watch the sun set over the North Shore water, this lounge hosts a variety of local bands that play contemporary Hawaiian tunes. ⊠ *Turtle Bay Hilton,* ☎ *808/293–8811.* ⊗ *Nightly 6–9.*

Kailua

Fast Eddie's (⊠ 52 Oneawa St., ☎ 808/261–8561). If you want to boogie, visit this hot spot for live local and national bands playing everything from rock to Top 40 songs. Attention, ladies: The Fast Eddie's Male Revue is a longstanding tradition not to be missed. Live band and revue schedules vary.

Cocktail and Dinner Cruises

Most of the following boats set sail daily from Fisherman's Wharf at Kewalo Basin, just 'ewa of Ala Moana Beach Park, and head along the coast toward Diamond Head. There's usually dinner, dancing, drinks, and a sensational sunset. Except as noted, dinner cruises cost approximately $50–$60, cocktail cruises $20–$30. Most major credit cards are accepted.

Ali'i Kai Catamaran. Patterned after an ancient Polynesian vessel, this huge catamaran casts off from historic Aloha Tower with 1,000 passengers. The deluxe dinner cruise has two open bars, a huge dinner, and an authentic Polynesian show with colorful hula music. The food is good, the after-dinner show loud and fun, and everyone dances on the way back to shore. ✉ *Pier 5, street level, Honolulu,* ☎ *808/539–9400.* ☉ *Nightly at 5:30.*

Dream Cruises. The 100-ft motor yacht *American Dream* handles up to 225 guests for evening cruises off the shores of Waikīkī. Decks have plenty of outdoor space for views of the twinkling city lights. The dinner cruise includes one mai tai, buffet, and soft drinks; you pay for extra booze. After a hula demonstration with audience participation, a disc jockey spins dancing tunes from the '50s through the '70s. ✉ *1085 Ala Moana Blvd., Suite 103, Honolulu* ☎ *808/592–5200.*

Paradise Cruises. Prices vary depending on which deck you choose on the 1,600-passenger, four-deck *Star of Honolulu.* For instance, a seven-course French dinner on the top costs $199, while a steak and crab feast on level two costs $72. Evening excursions also take place on the 340-passenger *Starlet I* and 230-passenger *Starlet II.* ✉ *1540 S. King St., Honolulu* ☎ *808/593–2493.*

Royal Hawaiian Cruises. The sleek *Navatek* is a revolutionary craft designed to sail smoothly in rough waters. That allows it to power farther along Waikīkī's coastline than its competitors. During the cocktail cruise, there's sizzling entertainment by such local singers as Nohelani Cypriano, and the dinner cruise includes gourmet food by acclaimed Maui chef George Mavrothalassitis. ✉ *Honolulu Harbor,* ☎ *808/848–6360.* ☉ *Dinner cruise nightly 5:30–8.*

Tradewind Charters. This is a real sailing experience, a little more expensive and a lot more intimate than the other cruises mentioned. The three-hour sunset sail carries no more than six people. Champagne and hors d'oeuvres are extra. ✉ *1833 Kalākaua Ave., Suite 612, Honolulu,* ☎ *808/973–0311.*

Windjammer Cruises. The pride of the fleet is the 1,000-passenger *Kulamanu,* done up like a clipper ship. Formerly the *Rella Mae,* it was once a Hudson River excursion boat in New York. Cocktails, dinner, a Polynesian revue, and dancing to a live band are all part of the package. Prices vary from $49 for a dinner buffet to $100 for the deluxe steak and lobster spread. ✉ *Pier 7, Honolulu Harbor, Honolulu,* ☎ *808/537–1122.* ☉ *Nightly at sunset.*

Cocktail and Dinner Shows

Some Oʻahu entertainers have been around for years, and others have just arrived on the scene. Either way, the dinner-show food is usually acceptable, but certainly not the main reason for coming. If you want to dine on your own and then take in a show, sign up for a cocktail show. Dinner shows are all in the $45–$60 range; cocktail shows run $30–$35. The prices usually include one cocktail, tax, and gratuity. In all cases, reservations are essential, and most major credit cards are accepted. Be sure to call in advance; you never know when an artist may have switched venues.

Charo. The "coochie-coochie" girl's latest show takes place in one of Waikīkī's most popular showrooms, one block from the beach. Latin rhythms, flamenco dancing, songs of the Islands, and international music add up to a fiery evening with this explosive performer. ✉ *Polynesian Palace, Outrigger Reef Towers Hotel, 227 Lewers St.,* ☎ *808/923–7469.* ☉ *Tues.–Sat. at 7.*

Don Ho. Waikīkī's old pro still packs them in for his Polynesian revue (with a cast of young and attractive Hawaiian performers), which has found the perfect home in an intimate club. ⊠ *Waikīkī Beachcomber Hotel, 2300 Kalākaua Ave.,* ☎ *808/931–3009.* ⊘ *Candlelight dinner show Tues.–Fri. and Sun. at 7, cocktail show Tues.–Fri. and Sun. at 9.*

Frank DeLima. Local funny man Frank DeLima places a heavy accent on the ethnic humor of the Islands and does some pretty outrageous impressions. By the end of the evening he's poked fun at everyone in the audience—and folks eat it up. A word of caution: Reserve a stage-side table only if you're up for a personal ribbing. ⊠ *Hula Hut, 286 Beach Walk,* ☎ *808/923–8411.* ⊘ *Fri.–Sat. at 8:45.*

Kalo's Polynesian South Seas Revue. This musical excursion features songs and dances from Tahiti, Tonga, and the Hawaiian Islands. Two shows nightly include an all-you-can-eat prime-rib buffet. ⊠ *Hawaiian Hut Theater Restaurant, Ala Moana Hotel, 410 Atkinson Dr.,* ☎ *808/941–5205.* ⊘ *Dinner seating nightly at 5:30, show nightly at 6:30.*

Legends in Concert. Elvis Presley, Madonna, and Michael Jackson look- and sound-alikes take to the stage at this glitzy extravaganza. The setting is an elaborate 1,000-seat showroom with a million-dollar sound and light system. Featuring backup singers and dancers and special effects, it's patterned after a Las Vegas show of the same name. ⊠ *Aloha Showroom, Royal Hawaiian Shopping Center,* ☎ *808/971–1400.* ⊘ *Nightly at 6:30 and 9.*

Magic of Polynesia. Magician John Hirokawa displays mystifying sleight-of-hand in this highly entertaining show, which also includes the requisite hula dancers and Island music. ⊠ *Hilton Hawaiian Village Dome, 2005 Kālia Rd.,* ☎ *808/949–4321.* ⊘ *Nightly at 6:30 and 8:45.*

Polynesian Cultural Center. Easily one of the best shows on the Islands, it has soaring moments and an "erupting volcano." The actors are students from Brigham Young University's Hawai'i campus. ⊠ *55–370 Kamehameha Hwy., Lā'ie,* ☎ *808/293–3333.* ⊘ *Dinner seating Mon.–Sat. at 4:30; show Apr., May, and Sept.–Christmas, Mon.–Sat. at 7:30, and Christmas–Mar. and June–Aug., Mon.–Sat. at 6 and 7:45.*

Sheraton's Spectacular Polynesian Revue. From drumbeats of the ancient Hawaiians to Fijian war dances and Samoan slap dances, this show takes audiences on a musical tour of Polynesia. The highlight is a daring Samoan fire knife dancer. A fashion show precedes the evening entertainment. ⊠ *'Āinahau Showroom, Sheraton Princess Ka'iulani Hotel, 120 Ka'iulani Ave.,* ☎ *808/922–5811.* ⊘ *Dinner seatings nightly at 5:15 and 8, cocktail seatings nightly at 5:45 and 8:15, shows nightly at 6 and 8:30.*

Society of Seven. This lively, popular septet has great staying power and, after more than 25 years, continues to put on one of the best shows in Waikīkī. They sing, dance, do impersonations, play instruments, and above all, entertain with their contemporary sound. ⊠ *Outrigger Waikīkī Hotel, 2335 Kalākaua Ave.,* ☎ *808/923–0711.* ⊘ *Mon.–Sat. at 9; extra show Wed., Fri., and Sat. at 7.*

Dance

Every year, at least one of mainland America's finer ballet troupes makes the trip to Honolulu for a series of dance performances at the **Neal Blaisdell Center Concert Hall** (⊠ Ward Ave. at King St., Honolulu, ☎ 808/591–2211). A local company, **Ballet Hawai'i** (☎ 808/988–7578), is active during the holiday season with its annual production of *The Nutcracker,* which is usually held at the Mamiya Theater (⊠ 3142 Wai'alae Ave., Chaminade University, Honolulu).

HAWAIIAN MUSIC

ASK MOST VISITORS ABOUT Hawaiian music and they'll likely break into a lighthearted rendition of "Little Grass Shack." When they're done, lead them directly to a stereo.

First, play them a recording of singer Kekuhi Kanahele, whose compositions combine ancient Hawaiian chants with modern melodies. Then ask them to listen to a CD by guitarist Keola Beamer, who loosens his strings and plays slack-key tunings dating back to the 1830s.

Share a recording by falsetto virtuoso Amy Hanaiali'i Gilliom, one of the very few singers perpetuating the upper-register vocal style. Then take them to a concert by Henry Kapono, who writes and sings of the pride—and pain—of being pure Hawaiian.

These artists, like many, are proving just how multifaceted Hawaiian music has become. They're unearthing their Island roots in the form of revered songs and chants, and they're reinterpreting them for today's audiences. It's "chicken-skin" (goosebumps) stuff, to be sure, and it's made only in Hawai'i.

Granted, "Little Grass Shack" does have its place in the history books. After Hawai'i became a U.S. territory in 1900, the world discovered its music thanks to touring ensembles who turned heads with swaying hips, steel guitars, and pseudo-Hawaiian lyrics. Once radio and movies got into the act, dreams of Hawai'i came with a saccharine Hollywood sound track.

But Hawaiian music is far more complex. It harkens back to the sounds of the ancient Islanders who beat rough-hewn drums, blew haunting calls on conch shells, and intoned repetitive chants for their gods. It recalls the voices of 19th-century Christian missionaries who taught Islanders how to sing in four-part harmony, a style that's still popular today.

The music takes on international overtones thanks to gifts from foreign immigrants: the 'ukulele from Portuguese laborers, for instance, and the guitar from Mexican traders. And it's enlivened by a million renderings of "Tiny Bubbles," as mainstream entertainers like Don Ho croon Hawaiian-pop hits for Waikīkī tourists.

Island music came full circle in the late 1960s and '70s, a time termed the Hawaiian Renaissance. While the rest of the world was rocking 'n' rolling, a few dedicated artists began giving voice to a resurgence of interest in Hawaiian culture, history, and traditions.

Today's artistic trailblazers are digging deep to explore their heritage, and their music reflects that thoughtful search. They go one step further by incorporating such time-honored instruments as nose flutes and gourds, helping them keep pace with the past.

Why is Hawaiian music such a well-kept secret? Simply put, it's rarely played outside of the Islands. A handful of local performers are making their mark on the mainland and in Japan. But if you want to experience the true essence of Hawaiian music, you must come to Hawai'i. Check ads and listings in local papers for information on concerts, which take place in indoor and outdoor theaters, hotel ballrooms, and cozy nightclubs. When you hear the sound, you'll know it's Hawaiian because it'll make you feel right at home.

Film

Art, international, classic, and silent films are screened at the little theater at the **Honolulu Academy of Arts.** ⊠ *900 S. Beretania St., Honolulu,* ☎ *808/532–8768.* ⊡ *$4.*

The **Hawai'i International Film Festival** (⊠ 700 Bishop St., Suite 400, Honolulu, ☎ 808/528–3456) may not be Cannes, but it is unique and exciting. During the weeklong festival, held from the end of November to early December, top films from the United States, Asia, and the Pacific are screened day and night at several theaters on O'ahu.

Varsity Theater (⊠ 1106 University Ave., Honolulu, ☎ 808/973–5834) is a two-theater art house that brings internationally acclaimed motion pictures to Honolulu.

Waikīkī generally gets the first-run films at its trio of theaters dubbed, appropriately, the **Waikīkī 1, Waikīkī 2, and Waikīkī 3** (☎ 808/971–5033). Check newspapers for what's playing.

Kāhala Mall (⊠ 4211 Wai'alae Ave., Honolulu, ☎ 808/733–6233) has eight movie theaters showing a diverse range of films. It's a 10-minute drive from Waikīkī.

Lū'au

Here are some good lū'au that emphasize fun over strict adherence to tradition. They generally cost $40–$75. Reservations are essential, and most major credit cards are accepted.

Germaine's Lū'au. You and a herd of about 1,000 other people are bused to a private beach near the industrial area, 35 minutes from Waikīkī. The bus ride is actually a lot of fun, and the beach and the sunset are pleasant. The service is brisk in order to feed everyone on time, and the food is so-so, but the show is warm and friendly. The bus collects passengers from 13 Waikīkī hotels; lū'au start at 6. ☎ 808/941–3338. ⊙ *Tues.–Sun.*

Paradise Cove Lū'au. This is another mass-produced event for 1,000 or so. Once again, a bus takes you from one of six Waikīkī hotel pickup points to a remote beach beside a picturesque cove on the western side of the island, 27 mi from Waikīkī. There are palms and a glorious sunset, and the pageantry is fun, even informative. The food—well, you didn't come for the food, did you? ☎ 808/973–5828. ⊙ *Lū'au begin daily at 5:30, doors open at 5.*

Polynesian Cultural Center Lū'au. An hour's drive from Honolulu, this North Shore O'ahu attraction takes place amid seven re-created villages of Polynesia. Dinner is all-you-can-eat, followed by a world-class revue. ☎ 808/923–1861. ⊙ *Mon.–Sat. at 5:30.*

Royal Hawaiian Lū'au. This is a notch above the rest of the commercial lū'au on O'ahu, perhaps because it takes place at the wonderful Pink Palace. With the setting sun, Diamond Head, the Pacific Ocean, and the enjoyable entertainment, who cares if the lū'au isn't totally authentic? ☎ 808/923–7311. ⊙ *Mon. at 6.*

Music

Chamber Music Hawai'i (☎ 808/947–1975) gives 25 concerts a year at the Honolulu Lutheran Church (⊠ 1730 Punahou St., Honolulu), Honolulu Academy of Arts (⊠ 900 S. Beretania St., Honolulu), and other locations around the island.

Hawai'i Opera Theater's season spans January through March, and includes such works as *Romeo and Juliet, Don Giovanni,* and *Mac-*

beth. All are performed in their original language with projected English translation. ⊠ *Neal Blaisdell Concert Hall, Ward Ave. and King St., Honolulu,* ☎ *808/596–7858.* ⊞ *$20–$65 at box office.*

Honolulu Symphony Orchestra, led by a young and dynamic conductor named Samuel Wong, is a top-notch ensemble whether it's playing by itself or backing up a guest artist. International performers are headlined from time to time, and pops programs are also offered. Write or call for a complete schedule. Shows take place at the Blaisdell Center and Hawai'i Theatre Center. ⊠ *677 Ala Moana Blvd., Honolulu,* ☎ *808/524–0815.* ⊞ *$10–$50.*

During the school year, the faculty of the **University of Hawai'i Music Department** (☎ 808/956–8742) gives concerts at Orvis Auditorium on the Manoa campus.

Rock concerts are usually performed at the cavernous **Neal Blaisdell Center Arena** (☎ 808/591–2211).

Internationally famous performers pack them in at **Aloha Stadium** (☎ 808/486–9300). Check newspapers for upcoming events.

Theater

Because the Islands are so expensive to get to and stay on, major touring companies seldom come to Hawai'i. As a result, O'ahu has developed several excellent local theater troupes, which present first-rate entertainment on an amateur and semiprofessional level all year long.

Army Community Theatre is a favorite for its revivals of musical theater classics, presented in an 800-seat house. The casts are talented and the fare is great for families. ⊠ *Richardson Theater, Fort Shafter, Honolulu,* ☎ *808/438–4480.* ⊞ *$12–$15.*

ASATAD, short for All Singing! All Talking! All Dancing!, is as versatile as its name implies. There are special works for hearing-impaired audiences. The campus theater is a 30-minute drive from Waikīkī. ⊠ *Windward Community College, 45-720 Kea'ahala Rd., Kāne'ohe,* ☎ *808/247–6939.* ⊞ *$17.*

Diamond Head Theater is in residence five minutes away from Waikīkī, right next to Diamond Head. Its repertoire includes a little of everything: musicals, dramas, experimental, contemporary, and classics. ⊠ *520 Makapu'u Ave., Honolulu,* ☎ *808/734–0274.* ⊞ *$10–$40.*

The beautiful **Hawai'i Theatre Center** in downtown Honolulu, built in the 1920s, hosts a wide range of events, including theatrical productions. ⊠ *1130 Bethel St., Honolulu,* ☎ *808/528–0506.* ⊞ *Prices vary.*

☺ **Honolulu Theater for Youth** stages delightful productions for children around the Islands from July to May. Write or call for a schedule. ⊠ *2846 Ualena St., Honolulu,* ☎ *808/839–9885.* ⊞ *$10.*

John F. Kennedy Theater at the University of Hawai'i's Manoa campus is the setting for eclectic dramatic offerings—everything from musical theater to Kabuki, Noh, and Chinese opera. ⊠ *1770 East–West Rd., Honolulu,* ☎ *808/956–7655.* ⊞ *$7–$12.*

Kumu Kahua is the only troupe presenting shows and plays written on and about the Islands. It stages five or six productions a year. ⊠ *46 Merchant St., Honolulu,* ☎ *808/536–4441.* ⊞ *$12–$15.*

Manoa Valley Theater gives wonderful nonprofessional performances in an intimate theater in Manoa Valley from September to July. ⊠ *2833 E. Manoa Rd., Honolulu,* ☎ *808/988–6131.* ⊞ *$23–$25.*

OUTDOOR ACTIVITIES AND SPORTS

Participant Sports

Biking

The good news is that the coastal roads are flat and well paved. On the downside, they're also awash in vehicular traffic. Frankly, biking is no fun in either Waikīkī or Honolulu, but things are a bit better outside the city. Be sure to take along a nylon jacket for the frequent showers on the windward side and remember that Hawai'i is Paradise after the Fall: Lock up your bike.

Mountain bikes are available for rent at **Blue Sky Rentals & Sports Center** (⊠ 1920 Ala Moana Blvd., across from the Hilton Hawaiian Village, ☎ 808/947–0101). Rates are $15 a day (8–6) or $20 for 24 hours plus a $25 deposit; this includes a bike, a helmet, a lock, and a water bottle.

You buy a bike or, if you brought your own, you can get it repaired at **Eki Cyclery Shop** (⊠ 1603 Dillingham Blvd., Honolulu, ☎ 808/847–2005). If you want to find some biking buddies, write ahead to the **Hawai'i Bicycling League** (⊠ Box 4403, Honolulu 96813, ☎ 808/735–5756), which can tell you about upcoming races (frequent on all the Islands).

Fitness Centers

Clark Hatch Physical Fitness Center has weight-training facilities, an indoor pool, a racquetball court, aerobics classes, treadmills, and indoor-running apparatus. ⊠ 745 Fort St., Honolulu, ☎ 808/536–7205. *About $10 per day.* ☉ *Weekdays 6 AM–8 PM, Sat. 7:30–5:30.*

'Ihilani Resort & Spa (⊠ Ko Olina Resort, Kapolei, ☎ 808/679–0079), about 30 minutes from the airport, has O'ahu's largest health and fitness center, with 35,000 square ft of space for classes, weight rooms, relaxation programs, hydrotherapies—you name it. Call to arrange nonguest privileges.

24-Hour Fitness is Waikīkī's most accessible fitness center. There are weight-training machines, cardiovascular equipment, free weights, and a pro shop. ⊠ *Pacific Beach Hotel, 2nd floor, 2490 Kalākaua Ave.,* ☎ 808/971–4653. *$10 per day for guests of many Waikīkī hotels (call for list), $20 nonguests.* ☉ *Daily.*

Golf

O'ahu has more golf courses than any other Hawaiian island. One of the most popular facilities is the **Ala Wai Golf Course** on Waikīkī's mauka end, across the Ala Wai Canal. It's par 70 on 6,424 yards and has a pro shop and a restaurant. The waiting list is long, so if you plan to play, call the minute you land. ⊠ *404 Kapahulu Ave.,* ☎ 808/733–7387. *Greens fee: $40; cart $14.*

Advance reservations are recommended at the 18-hole, 6,222-yard **Hawai'i Kai Championship Course** and the neighboring 18-hole, 2,386-yard **Hawai'i Kai Executive Course.** ⊠ *8902 Kalaniana'ole Hwy., Honolulu,* ☎ 808/395–2358. *Greens fee: weekdays $85 and $37, respectively; weekends and holidays $95 and $42. Cart included.*

The 27-hole **Hawai'i Prince Golf Club** welcomes visiting players. ⊠ *91-1200 Ft. Weaver Rd., 'Ewa Beach,* ☎ 808/944–4567. *Greens fee: $90 guests, $135 nonguests; cart included.*

The nine-hole walking-only **Kahuku Golf Course** is played more by locals than by visitors. ⊠ *Kahuku,* ☎ 808/293–5842. *Greens fee: $20 visitors.*

Ko Olina Golf Club is affiliated with the Ihilani Resort on Oahu's west side. Its 18 holes are beautifully landscaped with waterfalls and ponds where black and white swans serve as your gallery. ⊠ *Ko Olina Resort, 92-1220 Ali'inui Dr., Kapolei,* ☎ *808/676–5300* ☜ *Greens fee: $95 guests, $145 nonguests.*

The 18-hole **Links at Kuilima** were designed by Arnold Palmer. ⊠ *Turtle Bay Hilton, 57-091 Kamehameha Hwy., Kahuku,* ☎ *808/293–8574.* ☜ *Greens fee: $75 guests, $125 nonguests; a separate 9-hole course costs $25; cart included.*

The **Sheraton Mākaha Country Club** has two exceptional 18-hole courses in a beautiful valley setting. ⊠ *84-626 Mākaha Valley Rd., Wai'anae,* ☎ *808/695–9544.* ☜ *Greens fee: $160 until noon, $90 noon–2:30, $50 2:30–closing; cart included.*

Horseback Riding

Kualoa Ranch (⊠ 49-560 Kamehameha Hwy., Ka'a'awa, ☎ 808/237–8515 or 808/538–7636 in Honolulu), on the windward side, across from Kualoa Beach Park, leads trail rides in Ka'a'awa, one of the most beautiful valleys in all Hawai'i. Kualoa has other activities as well, like windsurfing and jet skiing. Try one of their all-inclusive packages, starting at $79, with transportation from Waikīkī and a choice of activities.

Turtle Bay Hilton (⊠ 57-091 Kamehameha Hwy., Kahuku, ☎ 808/293–8811) has 75 acres of hotel property—including a private beach—for exploring on horseback at a cost of $35 (guests and nonguests) for 45 minutes.

Jogging

In Honolulu, the most popular places are the two parks, **Kapi'olani** and **Ala Moana,** at either end of Waikīkī. In both cases, the loop around the park is just under 2 mi. You can run a 4½-mi ring around **Diamond Head crater,** past scenic views, luxurious homes, and herds of other joggers.

If you jog along the 1½-mi **Ala Wai Canal,** you'll probably glimpse outrigger-canoe teams practicing on the canal. If you're looking for jogging companions, show up for the free **Honolulu Marathon Clinic** that starts at the Kapi'olani Park Bandstand (Mar.–Nov., Sun. 7:30 AM).

Once you leave Honolulu, it gets trickier to find places to jog that are scenic as well as safe. Best to stick to the well-traveled routes, or ask the experienced folks at the **Running Room** (⊠ 819 Kapahulu Ave., Honolulu, ☎ 808/737–2422) for advice.

Rock Climbing

The Mokulē'ia Wall on the North Shore is one of the world's best venues for rock climbing. This 900-ft vertical trail is as challenging as any in the world. Those skilled enough to make it to the top get glorious views of the coastline. From Farrington Highway (Hwy. 930), west of Haleiwa, there is a trail leading to the base of the Mokulē'ia Wall, but the trailhead is poorly marked and easy to miss. For help in finding it, call or visit the experts at **Climbers Paradise** (⊠ 214 Sand Island Rd., Honolulu ☎ 808/842–7625), an indoor climbing center that also rents gear and offers lessons.

Tennis

In the Waikīkī area, there are four free public courts at **Kapi'olani Tennis Courts** (⊠ 2748 Kalākaua Ave., ☎ 808/971–2525); nine at the **Diamond Head Tennis Center** (⊠ 3908 Pākī Ave., ☎ 808/971–7150); and 10 at **Ala Moana Park** (⊠ Makai side of Ala Moana Blvd., ☎ 808/522–7031).

Several Waikīkī hotels have tennis facilities open to nonguests, but guests have first priority. The **'Ilikai Hotel Nikko Waikīkī** (⌧ 1777 Ala Moana Blvd., ☎ 808/949–3811) has seven courts, one lighted for night play, plus a pro shop, tennis clinics, and a ball machine. The hotel also offers special tennis packages. There's one championship tennis court at the **Hawaiian Regent Hotel** (⌧ 2552 Kalākaua Ave., ☎ 808/922–6611). There are two courts at the **Pacific Beach Hotel** (⌧ 2490 Kalākaua Ave., ☎ 808/922–1233); instruction is available. The **Hawai'i Prince Golf Club** (⌧ 91-1200 Ft. Weaver Rd., 'Ewa Beach, ☎ 808/944–4567) has two tennis courts.

Water Sports

The seemingly endless ocean options can be arranged through any hotel travel desk or beach concession. Try the **Waikīkī Beach Center,** next to the Sheraton Moana Surfrider, or the **C & K Beach Service** by the Hilton Hawaiian Village (no telephones).

DEEP-SEA FISHING

For fun on the high seas try **Coreene-C Sport Fishing Charters** (☎ 808/226–8421), **Island Charters** (☎ 808/593–9455), **Tradewind Charters** (☎ 808/973–0311), or **ELO-1 Sport Fishing** (☎ 808/947–5208). All are berthed in Honolulu's Kewalo Basin. On the North Shore call **Ku'uloa Kai Charters** (☎ 808/637–5783).

Plan to spend from $100 to $115 per person to share a boat for a full day (6:30–3). Half-day (five-hour) rates are $90. Boat charters start at about $550 for a full day and $450 for a half day. Some companies have a six-hour private charter rate of $500. All fishing gear is included, but lunch is not. The captain usually expects to keep the fish. Tipping is customary, and $20 to the captain is not excessive, especially if you keep the fish you caught.

OCEAN KAYAKING

This dynamic sport is catching on fast in the Islands. You sit on top of a board and paddle on both sides; it's great fun for catching waves or just exploring the coastline. Bob Twogood, a name that is synonymous with O'ahu kayaking, runs a shop called **Twogood Kayaks Hawai'i** (⌧ 345 Hahani St., Kailua, ☎ 808/262–5656), which makes, rents, and sells the fiberglass craft. Twogood rents solo kayaks for $22 a half day, and $28 for a full day; tandems are $29 a half day and $39 for a full day, including kayak delivery and pickup across from Kailua Beach.

SAILING

Lessons may be arranged through **Tradewind Charters** (⌧ 1833 Kalākaua Ave., Honolulu, ☎ 808/973–0311). Instruction follows American Sailing Association standards. The cost for a one-hour private sailing lesson is $65 per person. Transportation from Waikīkī is available. Tradewind specializes in intimate three-hour sunset sails for a maximum of six people at $75 per person, including hors d'oeuvres, champagne, and other beverages. Moonlight sails can be scheduled on an exclusive basis. Ready to take the plunge? Ask about their shipboard weddings.

SCUBA DIVING AND SNORKELING

For scuba diving, **South Seas Aquatics** (⌧ 2155 Kalākaua Ave., Suite 112, Honolulu, ☎ 808/922–0852) offers two-tank boat dives for $75. Several certification courses are available; call for rates. **Captain Bruce's Scuba Charters** (☎ 808/373–3590) focuses on trips for experienced divers. Led by a naturalist guide, charters run out of O'ahu's west coast, known for its great scuba sites. A two-tank boat dive costs $104 per person including transportation from Waikīkī, equipment, and refreshments.

The most famous snorkeling spot in Hawai'i is Hanauma Bay. **Hanauma Bay Snorkeling Excursions** (☎ 808/373–5060) runs to and from Waikīkī and costs $21 round-trip, including park admission, snorkeling gear, and lessons. **Hanauma Bay Snorkeling Tours & Rentals** (☎ 808/944–8828) has a half-day Hanauma Bay excursion for the same price.

DIVE SITES

Area dive sites include: **Maunalua Bay,** east of Diamond Head, has several sites, including Turtle Canyon, with lava flow ridges and sandy canyons teeming with green sea turtles of all sizes; *Kāhala Barge,* a penetrable, 200-ft sunken vessel; Big Eel Reef, with many varieties of moray eels; and Fantasy Reef, a series of lava ledges and archways populated with barracuda and eels.

Mahi Wai`anae is a 165-ft minesweeper sunk in 1982 to create an artificial reef. It's intact and penetrable. Goatfish, tame lemon butterfly fish, blue-striped snapper, and a 6-ft moray eel can be seen hanging about. Depths are from 50 ft to 90 ft.

Hanauma Bay, east of Koko Head, is an underwater state park and a popular dive site. The shallow inner reef gradually drops from 10 ft to 70 ft at the outer reef. Among the tame, colorful tropical fish you'll see here are butterfly fish, goatfish, parrot fish, and surgeon fish; there are also sea turtles.

Shark's Cove, on the North Shore, is diveable in the summer months only, and should be explored only by experienced divers. There are large, roomy caverns where sunlight from above creates a stained-glass effect. Easily accessible from shore, the cove's depths range from 15 ft to 45 ft. This is the most popular cavern dive on the island.

Three Tables, on the North Shore, is named for the trio of flat rocks that break the surface near the beach. Beneath the waves are large rock formations, caverns, and ledges. Diveable only in the summer months, the site has easy access from shore.

SURFING

To rent a board in Waikīkī, contact **C & K Beach Service,** on the beach fronting the Hilton Hawaiian Village (☎ no phone). Rentals cost $8–$10 per hour, depending on the size of the board, and $12 for two hours. Lessons are $30 per hour with board, and they promise to have you riding the waves by lesson's end.

On the North Shore, rent a short board for $5 an hour or a long board for $7 from a shop called **Surf 'N' Sea** (☎ 808/637–9887). Their two-hour surfing lessons cost $65 and start daily at 1 PM.

WATERSKIING

Suyderhoud Water Ski Center (✉ Koko Marina Shopping Center, 7192 Kalaniana'ole Hwy., Hawai'i Kai, ☎ 808/395–3773) has a package with round-trip transportation from Waikīkī and a half-day of water skiing in Hawai'i Kai Marina for $99 per person. A 30-minute lesson costs $490; four-passenger ski boat rental is $98 per hour.

WINDSURFING

This sport was born in Hawai'i, and O'ahu's Kailua Beach is its cradle. World champion Robby Naish and his family build and sell boards, rent equipment, run "windsurfari" tours, and offer instruction out of **Naish Hawai'i** (✉ 155A Hāmākua Dr., Kailua, ☎ 808/261–6067). A four-hour package, including 90 minutes of instruction, costs $55.

Windsurfing Hawai'i (✉ 155A Hāmākua Dr., Kailua, ☎ 808/261–3539) carries a complete line of boardsailing equipment and accessories. **Kailua Sailboard Company** (✉ 130 Kailua Rd., Kailua, ☎ 808/262–

2555) rents equipment and transports it to the waterfront five minutes away. On the North Shore **Surf 'N' Sea** (Hale'iwa, ☎ 808/637–
9887) rents windsurfing gear for $12 per hour; a two-hour windsurf-
ing lesson costs $58.

Spectator Sports

Football

The nationally-televised **Jeep Aloha Bowl Football Classic,** held on
Christmas Day at Aloha Stadium in Honolulu (☎ 808/486–9300), is
a sports tradition bringing together powerhouse college teams from the
PAC-10 and BIG-12 conferences. For local action the **University of
Hawai'i Rainbows** take to the field at Aloha Stadium in season, with
a big local following. There are often express buses from Kapi'olani
Park (☎ 808/956–6508 for details).

Golf

The giants of the greens return to Hawai'i every January or February
(depending on the TV scheduling) to compete in the **Hawaiian Open
Golf Tournament** (☎ 808/526–1232), a PGA tour regular with a $1
million purse. It is held at the exclusive Wai'alae Country Club near
Waikīkī, and it's always mobbed.

Mountain Biking

Professional mountain bikers come to O'ahu each year for the **Outrigger
Hotels Hawaiian Mountain Tour,** a four-day, five-stage race across the
most rugged terrain of the windward coast.

Running

The **Honolulu Marathon** is a thrilling event to watch as well as to participate in. Join the throngs who cheer at the finish line at Kapi'olani
Park as internationally famous and local runners tackle the 26.2-mi
challenge. It's held on a Sunday in early December and is sponsored
by the Honolulu Marathon Association (☎ 808/734–7200).

Surfing

For two weekends each March, **Buffalo's Annual Big-Board Surfing Classic** fills Mākaha Beach with Hawaiian entertainment, food booths, and
the best in big-board surfing (☎ 808/696–3878 or consult the newspaper).

In winter be sure to head out to the North Shore to watch the best surfers
in the world hang ten during the **Triple Crown Hawaiian Pro Surfing
Championships.** This two-day event, scheduled according to wave conditions, is generally held at the Banzai Pipeline and Sunset Beach during November and December. Watch newspapers for details.

Triathlon

Swim-bike-run events are gaining in popularity and number in Hawai'i.
Most fun to watch (or enter) is the **Tinman Triathlon** (☎ 808/732–7311),
held in mid-July in Waikīkī.

Volleyball

This is an extremely popular sport in the Islands, and no wonder. Both
the men's and women's teams of the **University of Hawai'i** have blasted
to a number-one league ranking in years past. Crowded, noisy, and very
exciting home games are played from September–December (women's)
and January–April (men's) in the university's 10,000-seat special-events
arena. ⊠ *Lower Campus Rd., Honolulu,* ☎ *808/956–4481.* ☎ *$8.*

Windsurfing

Watch the pros jump and spin on the waves during July's **Pan Am Hawaiian Windsurfing World Cup** off Kailua Beach. There are also windsurfing

competitions off Diamond Head point, including August's **Wahine Classic,** featuring the world's best female boardsailors. Consult the sports section of the daily newspaper for details on these events.

SHOPPING

As the capital of the 50th state, Honolulu is the number-one shopping town in the Islands and an international crossroads of the shopping scene. It has sprawling shopping malls, spiffy boutiques, hotel stores, family-run businesses, and a variety of other enterprises selling brand-new merchandise as well as priceless antiques and one-of-a-kind souvenirs and gifts. As you drive around the island, you'll find souvenir stands and what appear to be discount stores for local products; merchandise here is often tacky and expensive.

Major shopping malls are generally open daily from 10 to 9, although some shops may close at 4 or 5.

Shopping Centers

In Waikīkī

The fashionable new **King Kalākaua Plaza** (⊠ 2080 Kalākaua Ave.) opened its flagship store **Banana Republic** in late 1997, with **Nike Town, All Star Cafe,** and other high-profile tenants opening throughout 1998.

Royal Hawaiian Shopping Center (⊠ 2201 Kalākaua Ave., ☎ 808/922–0588 for information on free hula lessons, crafts demonstrations, and other special events), fronting the Royal Hawaiian and Sheraton Waikīkī hotels, is three blocks long and contains 120 stores on three levels. There are such upscale establishments as **Chanel** and **Cartier,** as well as local arts and crafts from the **Little Hawaiian Craft Shop,** which features Bishop Museum reproductions, Niʻihau shell leis (those super-expensive leis from the island of Niʻihau), feather hatbands, and South Pacific art. **Bijoux Jewelers** has a fun collection of baubles, bangles, and beads for your perusal. **Royal Hawaiian Gems** fashions gold bracelets, necklaces, and rings with Hawaiian names engraved in them. You can get a refreshing shave ice at **Island Snow Hawaiʻi** and buy a whimsical T-shirt at **Crazy Shirts Hawaiʻi.**

Waikīkī Shopping Plaza (⊠ 2270 Kalākaua Ave.) is across the street from the Royal Hawaiian Shopping Center. Its landmark is a 75-ft-high water-sculpture gizmo, which looks great when it's working. **Sawada Pro Golf Shop** sells accessories to improve your game.

Waikīkī Trade Center (⊠ At the corner of Kūhiō and Seaside Aves.) is slightly out of the action and has shops only on the first floor. **Bebe Sport,** which leans to the leather look, is for the slim and affluent. **C. June Shoes** offers European designer shoes, clothing, handbags, belts, and accessories. Need some water sportswear? Stop by the **Town & Country Surf Shop.**

Waikīkī has three theme-park-style shopping centers. Right in the heart of the area is the **International Market Place** (⊠ 2330 Kalākaua Ave.), a tangle of 200 souvenir shops and stalls under a giant banyan tree. **Waikīkī Town Center** (⊠ 2301 Kūhiō Ave.) has plenty of touristy beads, beach towels, and shirts. **King's Village** (⊠ 131 Kaʻiulani Ave., ☎ 808/944–6855 for special-event information) looks like a Hollywood stage set of monarchy-era Honolulu, complete with a changing-of-the-guard ceremony every evening at 6:15.

Around Honolulu

Ala Moana Shopping Center (✉ 1450 Ala Moana Blvd., ☎ 808/946–2811 for special-event information) is a gigantic open-air mall just five minutes from Waikīkī by bus. The 50-acre, 200-shop center is on the corner of Atkinson and Ala Moana boulevards. All of Hawai'i's major department stores are here, including **Neiman Marcus, Nordstrom, Sears,** and **JCPenney. Liberty House** is highly recommended for its selection of stylish Hawaiian wear. Upscale fashions are available at **Gucci, Ann Taylor, Chanel, Louis Vuitton,** and **Emporio Armani.** For stunning Hawaiian prints, try the **Art Board,** and buy your local footwear at the **Slipper House.**

Ala Moana also has a huge assortment of local-style souvenir shops, such as **Hawaiian Island Creations, Irene's Hawaiian Gifts,** and **Products of Hawai'i.** Its **Makai Market** is a large international food bazaar. Stores at Ala Moana open their doors daily at 9:30 AM. The shopping center closes Monday through Saturday at 9 PM and Sunday at 5, with longer hours during the Christmas holidays.

Heading west from Waikīkī, toward downtown Honolulu, you'll run into **Ward Warehouse** (✉ 1050 Ala Moana Blvd.), a two-story mall with 65 shops and restaurants. **Ward Centre** (✉ 1200 Ala Moana Blvd.) has 30 upscale boutiques and eateries, including **R. Field Wine Co.** and **Compadres** (Mexican food).

Restaurant Row (✉ 500 Ala Moana Blvd. between South and Punchbowl Sts., ☎ 808/538–1441 for special-event information) is a trendy conglomeration of fun retailers and eateries. Stop by **Honolulu Chocolate Company** for the best sweets this side of Paradise.

Aloha Tower Marketplace (✉ 101 Ala Moana Blvd., at Piers 8, 9, and 10, ☎ 808/528–5700 for special-event information) cozies up to Honolulu Harbor and bills itself as a festival marketplace. Along with restaurants and entertainment venues, it has shops and kiosks selling mostly visitor-oriented merchandise, from expensive sunglasses to souvenir refrigerator magnets.

Aloha Flea Market is a thrice-weekly outdoor bazaar that attracts hundreds of merchants and thousands of bargain hunters. Operations range from slick tents with rows of neatly stacked, new wares to blankets spread on the pavement, covered with rusty tools and cracked china. You'll find gold trinkets, antique furniture, digital watches, Japanese fishing floats, T-shirts, mu'umu'u, and palm-frond hats. Price haggling—in moderation—is the order of the day. ✉ 99-500 Salt Lake Blvd., ☎ 808/732–9611. 🎟 $6, including round-trip shuttle from Waikīkī. ☉ Wed. and weekends 6–3.

Kāhala Mall (✉ 4211 Wai'alae Ave.) is 10 minutes by car from Waikīkī in the chic residential neighborhood of Kāhala, near the slopes of Diamond Head. This mall features such clothing stores as **Liberty House** and **The Gap. Reyn's** is the acknowledged place to go for men's resort wear; its aloha shirts have muted colors and button-down collars, suitable for most social occasions. **Banana Republic** has outdoor wear. Along with an assortment of gift shops, Kāhala Mall also has **eight movie theaters** (☎ 808/733–6233) for post-shopping entertainment.

The **Waikele Shopping Plaza** (✉ H-1 Fwy., 10 min. west of downtown Honolulu) reflects Hawai'i's latest craze: warehouse shopping at discount prices. Among its occupants is the **Sports Authority.**

Specialty Stores

Clothing

HIGH FASHION

Chocolates for Breakfast (⊠ Ala Moana Shopping Center, ☎ 808/947–3434) is the trendy end of the high-fashion scene. For the latest in shoes and bags, **C. June Shoes** (⊠ Waikīkī Trade Center, ☎ 808/926–1574) displays an elegant array of pricey styles. Top-of-the-line international fashions for men and women are available at **Mandalay Imports** (⊠ Halekūlani, 2199 Kālia Rd., ☎ 808/922–7766), home of Star of Siam silks and cottons, Anne Namba couture, and designs by Choisy, who works out of Bangkok. **Pzazz** (⊠ 1419 Kalākaua Ave., ☎ 808/955–5800), which sells high fashion at low prices, is nicknamed the Ann Taylor of consignment shops.

RESORT WEAR

For stylish Hawaiian wear, the kind worn by local men and women, look in one of the **Liberty House** branches at Ala Moana Shopping Center, Kāhala Mall (☞ Shopping Centers, *above*), or in downtown Honolulu (⊠ 2314 Kalākaua Ave., Waikīkī, ☎ 808/941–2345 for all stores). **Carol & Mary** (⊠ Halekūlani, ☎ 808/971–4269; ⊠ Hilton Hawaiian Village, ☎ 808/973–5395; ⊠ Royal Hawaiian Hotel, ☎ 808/971–4262) sells high-end resort wear for women. Moderately priced muʻumuʻu may be found at **Andrade** (⊠ Sheraton Princess Kaʻiulani Hotel, ☎ 808/971–4266; ⊠ Sheraton Waikīkī Hotel, ☎ 808/971–4264). For menswear, try **Reyn's** (⊠ Ala Moana Shopping Center, ☎ 808/949–5929; ⊠ Kāhala Mall, ☎ 808/737–8313; ⊠ Sheraton Waikīkī Hotel, ☎ 808/923–0331).

If you want something bright, bold, and cheap, try **Hilo Hattie** (⊠ 700 N. Nimitz Hwy., ☎ 808/544–3500), the world's largest manufacturer of Hawaiian and tropical fashions. For convenience, they offer free shuttle service from Waikīkī. For vintage aloha shirts, try **Bailey's Antique Clothing and Thrift Shop** (⊠ 517 Kapahulu Ave., ☎ 808/734–7628), on the edge of Waikīkī.

McInerny has several locations (⊠ Ala Moana Shopping Center, ☎ 808/973–5380; ⊠ Hilton Hawaiian Village, ☎ 808/973–5392; ⊠ Royal Hawaiian Hotel, ☎ 808/971–4263; ⊠ Royal Hawaiian Shopping Center, ☎ 808/971–4275) where you can find a wide selection of colorful resort wear for men and women, with styles for day and evening.

Food

Bring home some fresh pineapple, papaya, or coconut to savor or share with your friends and family. Jam comes in flavors like pohā, passion fruit, and guava. Kona coffee has an international following. There are such dried-food products as saimin, *haupia* (a firm coconut pudding), and teriyaki barbecue sauce. All kinds of cookies are available, as well as exotic teas, drink mixes, and pancake syrups. And don't forget the macadamia nuts, from plain to chocolate-covered and brittled. By law, all fresh-fruit products must be inspected by the Department of Agriculture. The stores listed below carry only inspected fruit, ready for shipment. For cheap prices on local delicacies, try one of the many **Long's Drugs** stores (⊠ Ala Moana Shopping Center, 1450 Ala Moana Blvd., 2nd level, ☎ 808/941–4433; Kāhala Mall, ☎ 808/732–0784; ⊠ 1088 Bishop Street Mall, downtown, ☎ 808/536–4551). **Tropical Fruits Distributors of Hawaiʻi** (⊠ 64-1551 Kamehameha Hwy., Honolulu, ☎ 808/621–7062) specializes in packing inspected pineapple and papaya; they will deliver to your hotel and to the airport baggage check-in counter or ship to the mainland United States and Canada.

Gifts

Robyn Buntin Galleries (✉ 848 S. Beretania St., Honolulu, ☎ 808/523–5913) presents Chinese nephrite jade carvings, Japanese lacquer and screens, Buddhist sculptures, and other international pieces. **Takenoya Arts** (✉ Halekūlani, 2199 Kālia Rd., ☎ 808/926–1939) specializes in intricately carved *netsuke* (toggles used to fasten containers to kimonos), both antique and contemporary, and one-of-a-kind necklaces. **Following Sea** (✉ Kāhala Mall, ☎ 808/734–4425) sells beautiful handmade jewelry and pottery.

Hawaiian Art and Crafts

One of the nicest gifts is something handcrafted of native Hawaiian wood. Some species of trees grow only in Hawai'i. Koa and milo each have a beautiful color and grain. The great koa forests are disappearing because of environmental factors, so the wood is becoming valuable.

The best selection of Hawaiian arts and crafts in Waikīkī is at the **Little Hawaiian Craft Shop** (✉ Royal Hawaiian Shopping Center, ☎ 808/926–2662). Some items are Bishop Museum reproductions, with a portion of the profits going to the museum. The shop also has a good selection of Ni'ihau shell leis, feather hatbands, and South Pacific arts.

For hula costumes and instruments, try **Hula Supply Center** (✉ 2346 S. King St., ☎ 808/941–5379). For comforters stitched with traditional Island designs, try **Quilts Hawai'i** (✉ 2338 S. King St., ☎ 808/942–3195). For high-end collector's items, head to **Martin & MacArthur** (✉ Aloha Tower Marketplace, ☎ 808/524–6066), specialists in koa furniture.

Jewelry

You can buy gold chains by the inch on the street corner, and jade and coral trinkets by the dozen. **Bernard Hurtig's** (✉ Hilton Hawaiian Village Ali'i Tower, ☎ 808/947–9399; ✉ Tapa Tower, ☎ 808/955–3559) has fine jewelry with an emphasis on 18-karat gold and antique jade. Hawaiian heirloom jewelry is popular with Island residents. Bracelets, earrings, and necklaces are imprinted with distinctive black letters that spell out your name in Hawaiian. In Waikīkī, try **Royal Hawaiian Heritage Jewelry** (✉ 4325 Seaside Ave., ☎ 808/922–9699; ✉ 1525 Kalākaua Ave., ☎ 808/942–7474).

Haimoff & Haimoff Creations in Gold (✉ Halekūlani, 2199 Kālia Rd., ☎ 808/923–8777) sells the original work of award-winning jewelry designer Harry Haimoff.

O'AHU A TO Z

Arriving and Departing

By Plane

FROM THE MAINLAND UNITED STATES

Honolulu International Airport (☎ 808/836–6413) is one of the busiest in the nation. It is only a 20-minute drive from Waikīkī. Most flights originate in Los Angeles or San Francisco, which, of course, means they are nonstop. Flying time from the West Coast is 4½–5 hours.

American carriers coming into Honolulu include **American** (☎ 808/833–7600 or 800/433–7300), **Continental** (☎ 800/525–0280), **Delta** (☎ 800/221–1212), **Hawaiian** (☎ 808/838–1555 or 800/367–5320), **Northwest** (☎ 808/955–2255 or 800/225–2525), **TWA** (☎ 800/221–2000), and **United** (☎ 800/241–6522).

FROM THE UNITED KINGDOM
Air New Zealand (☎ 800/262–1234), **American** (☎ 808/833–7600 or 800/433–7300), **Continental** (☎ 800/523–3273), **Delta** (☎ 800/221–1212), and **United** (☎ 800/241–6522)are among the airlines that fly to Honolulu from the United Kingdom. An APEX ticket costs about £559 for a midweek flight, plus taxes. Check around for the best offer.

DISCOUNT FLIGHTS
Charter flights are the least expensive and the least reliable—with chronically late departures and occasional cancellations. They also tend to depart less frequently (usually once a week) than do regularly scheduled flights. If the savings are worth the potential annoyance, charter flights serving Honolulu International Airport include **American Trans Air** (☎ 800/225–9920) and **Hawaiian Airlines** (☎ 808/838–1555 or 800/367–5320). Consult your local travel agent for further information.

BETWEEN THE AIRPORT AND WAIKĪKĪ
There are taxis right at the airport baggage claim exit. At $1.50 start-up plus $1.50 for each mile, the fare to Waikīkī will run approximately $20, plus tip. Drivers are also allowed to charge 30¢ per suitcase. **TransHawaiian Services** (☎ 808/566–7333) runs an airport shuttle service to Waikīkī (🖃 $8 one-way, $14 round-trip). The municipal bus is only $1, but you are allowed only one bag that must fit on your lap. Some hotels have their own pickup service. Check when you book your reservations.

If you do find yourself waiting at the airport with extra time on your hands, be sure to visit the **Pacific Aerospace Museum** in the central waiting lobby of the main terminal. It includes a 1,700-sq-ft, three-dimensional, multimedia theater presenting the history of flight in Hawai'i, and a full-scale space shuttle flight deck. Hands-on exhibits include a mission control computer program tracing flights in the Pacific. ☎ *808/839–0777.* 🖃 *$3.* ☉ *Daily 9–6.*

By Ship
Boat Day used to be the biggest day of the week. Jet travel has almost obscured that custom, and it's too bad, because arriving in Hawai'i by ship is a great experience. If you have the time, it is one sure way to unwind. Many cruises are planned a year or more in advance and fill up fast. Most cruise-ship companies offer a fare that includes round-trip air travel to the point of embarkation.

Cunard/N.A.C. Line, Royal Cruises, P & O/Princess Cruises, and **Royal Viking** have cruise ships passing through Honolulu once or twice a year. The S.S. *Independence* stops in Honolulu each Saturday morning and departs each Saturday night on its week-long interisland cruises. You can also book three- and four-day packages on the Hawai'i-based luxury liner. ⊠ *American Hawai'i Cruises, 1380 Port of New Orleans Pl., Robin St. Wharf, New Orleans 70130,* ☎ *504/586–0631 or 800/543–7637.*

Getting Around

Waikīkī is only 2½ mi long and ½ mi wide, which means you can usually walk to where you are going and there are plenty of places to stop and rest.

By Bus
You can go all around the island or just down Kalākaua Avenue for $1 on Honolulu's municipal transportation system, affectionately known as **The Bus** (☎ 808/848–5555). You are also entitled to one free transfer per fare if you ask for it when boarding. Board at the front of the bus. Exact change is required, and dollar bills are accepted. A four-

day pass for visitors costs $10 and is sold at the more than 30 ABC Stores (Hawaiian chain stores that sell sundries and are geared to tourists) in Waikīkī. Monthly passes cost $25.

There are no official bus-route maps, but you can find privately published booklets at most drugstores and other convenience outlets. The important route numbers for Waikīkī are 2, 4, 8, 19, 20, and 58. If you venture afield, you can always get back on one of these.

There are also a number of brightly painted private buses, many free, that will take you to such commercial attractions as dinner cruises, garment factories, and the like.

By Car

Hawai'i's drivers are generally courteous, and you rarely hear a horn. People will slow down and let you into traffic with a wave of the hand. A friendly wave back is customary. If a driver sticks a hand out the window in a fist with the thumb and pinky sticking straight out, this is a good thing: The Hawaiian symbol for "hang loose," it's called the chakra and is often used to say "thanks," as well. Hawai'i has a seatbelt law for front-seat passengers and children under age three must be in a car seat, available from your car-rental agency.

It's hard to get lost in Hawai'i. Roads and streets, although they may be unpronounceable to the visitor (Kalaniana'ole Highway, for example), are at least well marked. Major attractions and scenic spots are marked by the distinctive HVCB sign with its red-caped warrior. Although it's hard to get lost, driving in Honolulu can be frustrating, as many streets are one-way and there are many traffic lights.

Driving in rush-hour traffic (6:30 AM–8:30 AM and 3:30 PM–5:30 PM) can be frustrating, not only because of the sheer volume of traffic but because left turns are forbidden at many intersections. Parking along many streets is curtailed during these hours, and towing is strictly enforced. Read the curbside parking signs before leaving your vehicle, even at a meter.

Remember not to leave valuables in your car. Tourists are targets for thieves, because they probably won't be here by the time the case comes to trial, even if the crooks are caught.

By Limousine

Cloud Nine Limousine Service (☎ 808/524–7999) will provide red-carpet treatment in its chauffeur-driven Rolls-Royce limousines. Riding in such style costs $60 an hour, plus tax and tip, with a two-hour minimum service required. Another reliable company is **Lowy Limousine Service** (☎ 808/455–2444), which specializes in Lincoln stretch limos starting at $60 per hour, with a two-hour minimum.

By Moped, Motorcycle, and Bicycle

Aloha Funway Rentals (☎ 808/973–5188) rents a variety of motorcycles for $50–$200 a day. **Blue Sky Rentals & Sports Center** (✉ 1920 Ala Moana Blvd., across from Hilton Hawaiian Village, ☎ 808/947–0101) rents mopeds for $20 a day (8–6) and $25 for 24 hours. Mountain bikes cost $15 a day and $20 for 24 hours plus a $25 deposit, including helmet, lock, and water bottle.

By Pedicab

You may have heard about them, but they have been banned, and they no longer operate on the main streets. You may still find some cruising the side streets. Be sure to settle on the fare ahead of time, and don't buy anything else from the operator.

By Taxi

You can usually get one right outside your hotel. Most restaurants will call a taxi for you. Rates are $1.50 at the drop of the flag, plus $1.50 per mile. Drivers are generally courteous, and the cars are in good condition, many of them air-conditioned. The two biggest taxicab companies are **Charley's** (☎ 808/531–1333), a fleet of company-owned cabs; and **SIDA of Hawai'i, Inc.** (☎ 808/836–0011), an association of individually-owned cabs.

By Trolley

An **open trolley** (☎ 808/596–2199) cruises Waikīkī, the Ala Moana area, and downtown, making 20 stops along a two-hour route. The trolley ride provides a good orientation. The conductor narrates, pointing out sights and shopping, dining, and entertainment opportunities along the way. The trolley departs from the Royal Hawaiian Shopping Center every 15 minutes daily 8–4:30. Buy an all-day pass from the conductor for $18.

Contacts and Resources

Car Rentals

If you plan to tour O'ahu itself, and not just restrict your visit to Waikīkī, renting a car is essential. During peak seasons—summer, Christmas vacations, and February—car-rental reservations are necessary.

Rental agencies abound in and around the Honolulu International Airport and in Waikīkī. Often it is cheaper to rent in Waikīkī than at the airport. **Avis** (☎ 800/321–3712), **Budget** (☎ 800/350–0540), **Dollar** (☎ 800/367–7006), **Hertz** (☎ 800/654–3011), and **National** (☎ 800/227–7368) have airport and downtown offices. Local budget and used rental-car companies include **Courtesy Car and Truck Rentals** (☎ 808/831–2277), which rents Jeeps, convertibles, and luxury cars, has three offices on O'ahu; **Classic Car Rentals** (☎ 808/923–6446), with a line of restored oldies; **VIP** (☎ 808/922–4605), at the airport and in Waikīkī; and **Thrifty** (☎ 808/833–0046).

Doctors

At **Doctors on Call** a doctor, laboratory/radiology technician, and nurses are always on duty. Appointments are recommended but not necessary. Services include diagnosis and treatment of illness and injury, laboratory testing, and X-ray on site, and referral, when necessary. Dozens of kinds of medical insurance are accepted, including Medicare, Medicaid, and most kinds of travel insurance. ⊠ *Bank of Hawai'i Bldg., 2222 Kalākaua Ave., 2nd floor,* ☎ *808/971–6000.*

Doctors Who Care (⊠ Pacific Beach Hotel, 2490 Kalākaua Ave., ☎ 808/926–7776) offers quick service for such minor ailments as sunburn.

HOSPITALS

Castle Medical Center (⊠ 640 Ulukahiki, Kailua, ☎ 808/263–5500). **Kapiolani Medical Center for Women and Children** (⊠ 1319 Punahou St., Honolulu, ☎ 808/973–8511). **Queen's Medical Center** (⊠ 1301 Punchbowl St., Honolulu, ☎ 808/538–9011). **Straub Clinic** (⊠ 888 S. King St., Honolulu, ☎ 808/522–4000).

Emergencies

Police, fire department, ambulance, and **suicide center** (☎ 911).

Coast Guard Rescue (☎ 800/552–6458).

Guided Tours

AERIAL TOURS

Biplane Rides. After suiting up with goggles and leather helmets, you can climb into an open cockpit of a restored Stearman biplane for loops, rolls, hammer heads, and other aerobatic maneuvers above O'ahu's North Shore. Only one person can go up at a time.✉ *Dillingham Airfield, Mokulē'ia,* ☎ *808/637–4461.* 🎫 *20 min $125, 40 min $175.* 🕐 *Daily 10:30–5:30.*

Glider Rides. Through the bubble top of a sleek sail plane you get aerial views of O'ahu's North Shore with its coral pools, sugarcane fields, windsurfers, and in winter, humpback whales. On-board live videotaping is available. Reservations are not accepted. ✉ *Dillingham Airfield, Mokulē'ia,* ☎ *808/677–3404.* 🎫 *1 passenger $100, 2 passengers $120.* 🕐 *Daily 10:30–5, 20-min flights every 20 min.*

EXCURSIONS

Circle Island Tour. There are several variations on this theme; read Exploring (☞ *above*) to decide what's important to you, then choose a tour package that comes the closest to matching your desires. Some of these all-day tours include lunch. Transport is either bus or minibus, the latter being slightly more expensive. 🎫 *$45–$65.*

Little Circle Tour. These tours cover the territory discussed in The East O'ahu Ring, (☞ Exploring, *above*). Most of these are the same, no matter what the company. This is a half-day tour. 🎫 *$25–$40.*

Pearl Harbor and City. This comprehensive tour includes the boat tour to Pearl Harbor run by the National Park Service. (☞ Exploring, *above,* for particulars on Pearl Harbor.) 🎫 *$25–$40.*

Polynesian Cultural Center. The only advantage of the tour is that you don't have to drive yourself back to Waikīkī after dark if you take in the evening show. (☞ Exploring, *above,* for details on the center.) 🎫 *$70–$80.*

SEA TOURS

Dream Cruises presents tours of Pearl Harbor aboard the 100-ft motor yacht *American Dream.* The trip takes place in the early morning to coincide with the time that Pearl Harbor was attacked on Dec. 7, 1941. It includes a stop near the USS *Arizona* Memorial, where the captain conducts a brief memorial service and lei placement ceremony. Narration and videos help describe the sights. In winter, this cruise is paired with a whale watch. ✉ *1085 Ala Moana Blvd., Suite 103, Honolulu 96814,* ☎ *808/592–5200.* 🎫 *$19.95.* 🕐 *Daily 7:30 AM–10:15 AM.*

TOUR COMPANIES

Many ground tour companies handle these excursions. Some herd you onto an air-conditioned bus and others use smaller vans. Vans are recommended because less time is spent picking up passengers, and you get to know your fellow passengers and your tour guide. Whether you go by bus or van, you'll probably be touring in top-of-the-line equipment, as the competition among these companies is fierce, and everyone has to keep up. If you're booking through your hotel travel desk, ask whether you'll be on a bus or a van and exactly what the tour includes in the way of actual "get-off-the-bus" stops and "window sights."

Most of the tour guides have been in the business for years. Many have taken special Hawaiiana classes to learn their history and lore. Tipping ($2 per person at least) is customary. **American Express** (☎ 808/947–2607) books through several tour companies and can help you choose which tour best suits your needs. **E Noa Tours** (☎ 808/591–2561) uses minibuses exclusively and likes to get you into the great outdoors. **Polynesian Adventure Tours** (☎ 808/833–3000) has motorcoaches, vans, and minicoaches. **Polynesian Hospitality** (☎ 808/593–9890) provides narrated tours. **Roberts Hawai'i** (☎ 808/539–9400) has equipment ranging from vans to presidential limousines. **Trans-Hawaiian Services** (☎ 808/566–7000) offers multilingual tours.

UNDERWATER TOURS

Atlantis **Submarines** operates two vessels off Waikīkī: a 65-ft, 80-ton sub carrying up to 48 passengers, and a newer 102-ft, 64-passenger craft. Rides are popular with the children; a trip includes a catamaran ride to the dive site, providing great views of the Waikīkī and Diamond Head shoreline. The subs dive up to 100 ft to see a sunken Navy yard oiler and an artificial reef populated by brilliant fish. While the human-made concrete reef looks more like a fish tenement, it is drawing reef fish back to the area. You get a two-hour cruise with informative narration. The dive itself lasts about one hour. Children must be at least 3′ tall to board. Note: Flash photography will not work; use film speed ASA 200 or above without flash. ✉ *1600 Kapi'olani Blvd., Suite 1630, Honolulu 96814,* ☎ *808/973–9811.* ✑ *$89 –$105, depending on which sub (48- or 64-ft) you go on.*

WALKING TOURS

Aunty Malia's Walking Tours. Aunty Malia, the Hyatt Regency's resident Hawaiiana expert, leads free three-hour strolls through the streets of Waikīkī, pointing out historic and cultural sites of interest along the way. Tours begin and end at the hotel. There is a minimum of six people per tour, and reservations are required. ✉ *Hyatt Regency Waikīkī, 2424 Kalākaua Ave.,* ☎ *808/923–1234.* ☉ *Tours summer, daily at 10, weather permitting.*

Chinatown Walking Tour. Meet at the Chinese Chamber of Commerce (✉ 42 N. King St.) for a fascinating peek into herbal shops, an acupuncturist's office, open-air markets, and specialty stores. The 2-½ hour tour is sponsored by the Chinese Chamber of Commerce. Reservations are required. ☎ *808/533–3181.* ✑ *$5.* ☉ *Tues. at 9:30.*

Historic Downtown Walking Tour. Volunteers from the Mission Houses Museum (✉ 553 S. King St.) take you on a two-hour walk through Honolulu, where historic sites stand side by side with modern business towers. During the first hour, you get a tour of the Mission Houses themselves. Reservations are required. ☎ *808/531–0481.* ✑ *$7.* ☉ *Thurs. 9:30 AM–12:30 PM.*

Honolulu Time Walks. History springs to life for young and old alike during these fun jaunts, which come with appropriately costumed narrators. Tours include "Haunted Honolulu," "Honolulu's Crime Beat," "Mysteries of Mō'ili'ili," "Mark Twain's Honolulu," and the "Old Hawai'i Saloon Walk." The company also presents theater shows and films about the Islands. ☎ *808/943–0371.* ✑ *$7–$45.*

Late-Night Pharmacies
Kuhio Pharmacy (✉ Outrigger West Hotel, 2330 Kuhio Ave., ☎ 808/923–4466). **Long's Drugs Store** (✉ Ala Moana Shopping Center, 1450 Ala Moana Blvd., 2nd level, ☎ 808/949–4010).

Visitor Information
Hawai'i Visitors & Convention Bureau (✉ Royal Hawaiian Shopping Center, 2201 Kalākaua Ave., Suite A-401-A, Honolulu 96815, ☎ 808/923–1811 or 800/464–2924. **O'ahu Visitor Bureau** (☎ 888/464–6665), www.visit-oahu.com). **Surf Report** (☎ 808/596–7873). **Weather:** (☎ 808/973–4381) for O'ahu weather.

3 Maui

Lush Maui's tropical sun, surf, and sports activities have gained it an international reputation. In laid-back Hāna, on the eastern shore, you can get a taste of what Hawai'i was like before T-shirt tourism. West Maui's gorgeous "Golf Coast" resorts draw eager putters, while shoppers head for the old whaling town of Lahaina.

Updated by
Pablo Madera

MAUI NŌ KA ʻOI IS WHAT THE LOCALS SAY—it's the best, the most, the top of the heap. To those who know Maui well, there's good reason for the superlatives. The second-largest island in the Hawaiian chain, Maui has made an international name for itself with its tropical allure, heady nightlife, and miles of perfect-tan beaches. Maui magically weaves a spell over the 2 million people who visit its shores each year—and leaves them wanting more. Many visitors decide to return for good.

In many ways Maui comes by its admirable reputation honestly. The island's 729 square mi contain Haleakalā, a 10,023-ft dormant volcano whose misty summit beckons the adventurous; several villages where Hawaiian is still spoken; more millionaires per capita than nearly anywhere else in the world; four major resort destinations that have set new standards for luxury; Lahaina, an old whaling port that still serves as one of the island's commercial crossroads; and more than 80,000 residents who work, play, and live on what they fondly call the Valley Isle.

Maui residents have quite a bit to do with their island's successful tourism story. In the mid-'70s, savvy marketers on Maui saw a way to increase their sleepy island's economy by positioning it as an island apart. Maui was tired of settling for its meager 50,000 or so visitors each year and decided it didn't want to be one of the gang anymore. So community leaders started advertising and promoting their Valley Isle separately from the rest of the state. They nicknamed West Maui "the Golf Coast," luring in heavyweight tournaments that, in turn, would bring more visitors. They renovated their finest hotels to accommodate a more upscale clientele that would pay more for the best. And they became the state's condominium experts, emphasizing the luxurious privacy these accommodations can provide. Maui's visitor count swelled, putting it far ahead of that of the other Neighbor Islands.

That quick growth has led to its share of problems. During the busy seasons—from Christmas to Easter and then again during the summer—West Maui can be overly crowded. Although the county of Maui has widened the road that connects Lahaina and Kāʻanapali, the occasional traffic congestion here is not what you bargained for.

But then consider Maui's natural resources. The island is made up of two volcanoes, one now extinct and the other dormant, that both erupted long ago and joined into one island. The resulting depression between the two is what gives Maui its nickname, the Valley Isle. West Maui's 5,788-ft Puʻu Kukui was the first volcano to form, a distinction that gives that area's mountainous topography a more weathered look. Rainbows seem to grow wild over this terrain as gentle mists move quietly from one end of the long mountain chain to the other. Sugarcane gives the rocky region its life, with tall green stalks moving in the trade winds.

The Valley Isle's second volcano is the 10,023-ft Haleakalā, a mountain so enormous that its lava filled in the gap between the two volcanoes. To the Hawaiians, Haleakalā is holy, and it's easy to see why. It's a mammoth mountain, and if you hike its slopes or peer into its enormous crater you'll witness an impressive variety of nature, with desertlike terrain butted up against tropical forests.

The island's volcanic history gives Maui much of its beauty. The roads around the island are lined with rich red soil, the fertile foothold for sugarcane that has covered the hills here for years. As the deep blue of ocean and sky mingle with the red and green of Maui's topography, it looks as if an artist had been busy painting the landscape. Indeed, visual artists love Maui. Maybe it's the natural inspiration; maybe it's the slower pace, so conducive to creativity.

Farmers also appreciate the Valley Isle. On the slopes of Haleakalā, the volcanic richness of the soil has yielded lush results. Sweetly scented flowers bloom large and healthy; grapes cultivated on Haleakalā's slopes ripen evenly and deliciously, and are then squeezed for wine and champagne. Horses graze languidly on rolling meadows of the best Up-country grasses, while jacaranda trees dot the hillsides with spurts of luscious lavender. As the big brute of a volcano slides east and becomes the town of Hāna, the rains that lavishly fall there turn the soil into a jungle. Ferns take over the forest, waterfalls cascade down the crags, and moss becomes the island's carpeting.

Maui is full of people ready to share the friendly aloha spirit. If you take the drive to Hāna, around dozens of hairpin curves, across bridges, and past waterfalls, you'll find a gentle folk who still speak the Hawaiian language. On a stroll through the streets of Wailuku, you'll meet elderly Filipino men who can remember their parents' stories of the old country. Or if you relax on the wharf in historic Lahaina, you can watch transplanted Californians have a great time surfing—most of them find West Maui the best place in the world to work and live. All these residents love their island and will gladly help you have a good time.

Although a fantastic time can be had simply by bronzing on the silky-soft, white-sand beaches, the wonder of Maui is that much, much more awaits your discovery. Don't be surprised if quite a few of your fantasies are actually fulfilled. The Valley Isle hates to let anyone down.

Pleasures and Pastimes

Beaching

Maui's beaches win awards for being the best in the world. (Yes, there are awards for beaches.) Those of Wailea and Kapalua lead the pack. Maui residents particularly revere Mākena Beach, beyond Wailea—so much so that they launched a successful grassroots campaign to have it preserved as a state park. Don't expect to find the island ringed with sand; in fact, most of the coastline is dramatically craggy. Beaches tend to be pockets, each one with a personality of its own and that can be completely explored in half a day. The thin, clean strand of Kā'anapali, though, goes on for 7 mi, past resort after resort. Offshore here—in what's called the Lahaina Roadstead, a protected stretch of sea between Maui and her small sister islands—yachts, catamarans, and parasail riders drift across brilliant porcelain-blue water. Many of Maui's beaches are a little difficult to spot from the road, especially where homes and hotels have taken up shoreline property. Just remember that you can go to any beach you want. Access to the sea is a sacred trust in Hawai'i, preserved from ancient times. Sometimes you have to poke around to find the beach—then again, maybe those are the ones you want. A word to the wise, though: sunscreen.

Culture

Maui people like the arts—like them enough to build the $32 million Maui Arts & Cultural Center, with its well-designed 1,200-seat Castle Theater and its Kazuma Art Gallery. The island also has one of the oldest community theater groups in the country and one of the highest per capita populations of painters anywhere. Friday night is Art Night in Lahaina, and commercial galleries line Front Street. But many artists have retreated to the Upcountry region, making Makawao their hub.

Up here, Hui No'eau Visual Arts Center has been providing classes, studios, and exhibits since the 1930s. The resorts, too, are lined with splendid art collections. Some of these are like museums—particularly the Grand Wailea and the Hyatt Regency (in Kā'anapali). The hotels also perpetuate Hawaiian culture; the best at this are the Ritz-Carlton Kapalua and the Kā'anapali Beach Hotel. Maui's curious history and mixed cultures are also interesting; the best way to explore this subject is to tour the small museums—Baldwin House in Lahaina, Bailey House in Wailuku, the Alexander & Baldwin (A&B) Sugar Museum in Pu'nēnē, the Hana Cultural Center, and the 'Ulupalakua Ranch History Room, to name a handful. Or go to the local events, the festivals and benefit concerts, a Japanese *o-bon* dance or a Portuguese church bazaar. There's always something going on—check *The Maui News* on Thursday ("The Scene") and Sunday ("Currents").

Dining

On Maui you can eat a great meal every night for two months without ever dining twice in the same place. The resorts set very high standards, and restaurants that surround them—in Lahaina particularly, the Kīhei/Wailea area, and even Upcountry—have risen to the challenge. Chefs seem to be competing to create a Hawai'i Regional or Pacific Rim cuisine, or at least figuring out how to adapt classic cooking styles to the fresh-caught fish, the produce and meats, and the traditional eating styles of Maui. If you're a food explorer, take advantage of the fact that Maui is a cultural mixing bowl. Check out the *saimin* (noodle soup) shops and the local markets, especially in Wailuku.

Maui continues to attract fine chefs, several of whom are known for their trendsetting Hawai'i Regional cuisine. This growing movement uses fruits and vegetables unique to Hawai'i in classic European or Asian ways—spawning such dishes as *'ahi* (yellowfin tuna) carpaccio, breadfruit soufflé, and papaya cheesecake. Sometimes a touch of California or Mexico is added as well.

Of course, you can find plain old local-style cooking on the Valley Isle—particularly if you wander into the less touristy areas of Wailuku or Kahului, for example. Greasy spoons abound; though they are not for the overly fastidious, some of them offer the most authentic local food, or what residents call "plate lunches," for very low prices. A good plate lunch will fulfill your daily requirement of carbohydrates: macaroni salad, two scoops of rice, and an entrée of, say, curry stew, teriyaki beef, or *kālua* (roasted) pig and cabbage.

Driving

Maui is blessed with bad roads in beautiful places. Lots of visitors take a break from the beach and just go driving—usually taking day trips from their lodgings around Lahaina or Kīhei. Maui's landscape is extraordinarily diverse for such a small island; your sense of place (and the weather) will seem to change every few miles. If you drive to the top of Haleakalā, the giant that forms East Maui, you rise from coconut-lined beaches to the rare world inhabited by airplanes in only an hour and a half. And East Maui is compact enough that you can drive all the way around it in a day, first testing your reflexes on the rain-gouged windward side (the road to Hāna and "Seven Pools"), then if you can spare the extra hour and not turn back, keep going all the way around the rugged leeward side. "Upcountry," as they say— around Makawao and Ha'ikū—you can literally drive into and out of the rain, with rainbows that seem to land on the hood of your car. Older, smaller West Maui has its own moods. 'Īao Valley in Wailuku captures the spirit of these mountains best. You can completely encircle West

Maui, too. You'll be astonished how quickly civilization vanishes north of Kapalua, and further astonished by the rugged but spectacular drive from there to Kahului.

If you see a bad road, take it (but be aware of possible liability issues with your rental car company). They're actually quite well-surfaced, for the most part. And there aren't very many, so it's hard to get lost.

Lodging
Maui's three planned resort communities offer self-contained environments of such luxury and beauty that the effect is almost surreal. Whatever is beautiful about Maui, these resorts re-create it on the premises, doing their best to improve on nature. And their best is pretty amazing—opulent gardens, fantasy swimming pools with slide-down waterfalls and hidden grottoes (sometimes with swim-up bars in them), spas, cultural events, championship golf courses, priceless art collections, tennis clubs. . . They make it hard to work up the will power to leave the resort and go see the real thing. Kāʻanapali, the grand dame, sits at the heart of Lahaina's action. Kapalua, farther north, is more private and serene—and catches a bit more wind and rain. Sprawling Wailea on the South Shore has excellent beaches and three designer golf courses, each with its distinct personality. Of course, resort prices are not for everyone. Many visitors compromise on the luxury and find condominium apartments in Nāpili and Kahana (for West Maui) or in Kīhei (East Maui). With a few exceptions, you'll find that accommodations are all clustered along these leeward shores. If you want to stay elsewhere on the island—say, Upcountry or in Hāna (without using the Hotel Hāna-Maui)—seek out a bed-and-breakfast.

Water Sports
For anything that anyone can possibly do that involves water, this is the place. The West Maui vacation coast (from Lahaina to Kapalua) centers on Lahaina Harbor, where you can find boats for snorkeling, scuba diving, deep-sea fishing, whale-watching, sea-kayaking, wind-surfing, parasailing, and sunset cocktail-partying. At the harbor, you can learn to surf or you can ride a submarine; catch a ferry ride to Lānaʻi or catch a seat on a fast inflatable and explore all the way around it. The East Maui vacation coast has Māalaea Harbor and the great snorkeling beaches of Kīhei and Wailea. If you want to walk through the ocean without getting wet, visit the top-notch new aquarium in Maʻalaea. If you'd rather watch, drive to Hoʻokipa, near Pāʻia, for surfers and windsurfers.

Whale-Watching
One of the best signs of the high intelligence of humpback whales is that they return to Maui every year. Having fattened themselves in sub-arctic waters all summer, they migrate south in the winter to breed, and thousands of them cruise the Lahaina Roadstead in particular. The Pacific Whale Foundation in Kīhei is your best resource for discovering these creatures. From December 15–May 1 the Pacific Whale Foundation has naturalists stationed in two places (on the rooftop of their headquarters and at the scenic viewpoint on the *pali,* or cliffside stretch, of the highway into Lahaina); they also have whale-watch boats that depart every hour of the day. In fact, every boat on the island will go out of its way to watch humpbacks when the opportunity arises—which it does often, as the whales themselves seem to have a penchant for people-watching. For in-depth information about the big cetaceans, check out the Whale Center of the Pacific, an excellent free museum, at Whaler's Village in Kāʻanapali.

EXPLORING MAUI

There is plenty to see and do on the Valley Isle besides spending time on the beach. To help you organize your time, this guide divides the island into four areas to explore—West Maui, Central Maui, Haleakalā and Upcountry, and the Road to Hāna (East Maui). You can spend half a day to a full day or more in each area depending on how long you have to visit. The best way to see the whole island is by car, but there are opportunities for good walking tours.

To get yourself oriented, first look at a map of the island. You will notice two distinct circular landmasses volcanic in origin and dominated by mountains. The smaller landmass, on the western part of the island, consists of 5,788-ft Pu'u Kukui and the West Maui Mountains, some of whose reaches now grow sugarcane and pineapple. The interior of these mountains is one of the earth's wettest spots; 400 inches of rain each year have sliced the land into impassable gorges and razor-sharp ridges. Oddly enough, the area's leeward, western shore—what most people mean when they say "West Maui"—is sunny and warm year-round. Most of the island's visitor industry is centered here.

The large landmass in the eastern portion of Maui was created by Haleakalā, the cloud-wreathed volcanic peak at its center. One of the best-known mountains in the world, Haleakalā is popular with hikers and sightseers. This larger region of the island is called East Maui, with the resorts, condominiums, and beaches of Wailea, Kīhei, and Mākena flanking its leeward shore; Hāna and its wilder environs—past where the pavement stops—sit on the eastern shore.

Between the two mountain areas is Central Maui, which was once the ocean until Haleakalā spewed lava into the channel that separated East from West. Central Maui is the location of the county seat of Wailuku, from which the islands of Maui, Lāna'i, Moloka'i, and Kaho'olawe are governed. It's also the base for much of the island's commerce and industry.

In the Islands, the directions *mauka* (toward the mountains) and *makai* (toward the ocean) are often used. We've included them in the text here as well.

Numbers in the text correspond to numbers in the margin and on the Maui, Lahaina, and Kahului-Wailuku maps.

Great Itineraries

Maui is designed for day trips. Many visitors never get over the spell of the sea, and never go inland to explore the island and its people. Those who do, though, launch out early from their beachside hotel or condo, loop through a district, then wind up back "home" for sunsets and mai tais. When you live on an island, you get used to going in circles. Don't be too goal-oriented as you travel around. If you rush to "get there," you might find you've missed the point of going—which is to encounter one of the most beautiful islands in the world, still mostly wilderness and largely unpopulated.

IF YOU HAVE 1 DAY

This is a tough choice. But how can you miss the opportunity to see **Haleakalā National Park** ㉝ and the volcano's enormous, other-worldly crater? Sunrise at the summit has become the thing to do. It's quite dramatic (and chilly), but there are drawbacks. Namely, you miss seeing the landscape and views on the way up in the dark; also, you have to get up early. How early? You'll need an hour and a half from the bottom of **Haleakalā Highway** (Highway 37) ㉜ to the summit. Add to that the time of travel to the highway—at least 45 minutes from Lahaina or Kīhei. *The Maui News* posts the hour of sunrise every day. The best experience of the crater takes all day and good legs. Hike in. Start at the summit, hike down Sliding Sands trail, cross the crater floor, and come back up the Halemau'u switchbacks. (This works out best if you leave your car at the Halemau'u trailhead parking lot and get a lift for the last 20-minute drive to the mountaintop.) All you need is a packed lunch, water, and decent walking shoes. If you don't hike, leave the mountain early enough to go explore **'Iao Valley State Park** ㉛ above Wailuku. This will show you the island's leafy, freshwater, jungle landscape and will compensate for the fact that you're missing the drive to Hāna.

IF YOU HAVE 3 DAYS

Give yourself the volcano experience one day, then rest up a little with a beach-snorkel-exploring jaunt on either East or West Maui. The East Maui trip would have to include the **Maui Ocean Center** ⑱ (the new aquarium at Ma'alaea), a sampling of the little beaches in Wailea, then a good dose of big golden Mākena Beach. Be sure to drive on past Mākena into the rough lava fields, the site of Maui's last (about 200 years ago) lava flows that formed rugged La Pérouse Bay. The 'Āhihi-Kina'u Marine Preserve has no beach, but it's a rich spot for snorkeling.

Or take the West Maui trip over the *pali* through Olowalu, **Lahaina** ④–⑰, **Kā'anapali** ③, and dodge off the highway to find small beaches in Nāpili, Kahana, **Kapalua** ①, and beyond. The road gets narrow and sensational around **Kahakuloa** ②; if you're enjoying it, keep circling West Maui and return through the Central Valley. For your third day, do **Hāna** ㊺. Be sure not to rush, and be sure to pull over to let residents pass. Stop in **Pā'ia** ㊴ for food, pause at **Ho'okipa** ㊵ for the surf action, and stop and drink in the sight of the taro fields of **Ke'anae Arboretum** ㊻ and **Wailua Lookout** ㊽. Nearly everyone keeps going past Hāna town to **'Ohe'o Gulch** ㊻, the "seven pools."

IF YOU HAVE 5 DAYS

Explore Upcountry. Get to **Makawao** ㊲ and use that as your pivot point. Head north at the town's crossroads and drive around **Ha'ikū** ㊶ by turning left at the first street (Kokomo Road), right at Ha'ikū Road, then come back uphill on any of those leafy, twisting, gulch-country roads. After you've explored Makawao town, drive out to Kula on the Kula Highway. This is farmland, with fields of flowers and vegetables and small ranches with well-nourished cattle. Stop in little Kēōkea for coffee, and keep driving on Highway 37 to the 'Ulupalakua Ranch at the **Tedeschi Vineyards and Winery** ㉟. You can't be a Maui aficionado unless you've spent some time Upcountry. Add some time in Central Maui to really get to the heart of things, especially **Wailuku** ⑲–㉘ with its old buildings and curious shops. From here you can loop out to **Pā'ia** ㊴ and spend some time there enjoying beaches in the Spreckelsville area and poking around in the boutiques and shops of this old plantation town.

When To Tour Maui

Although Maui has the usual temperate-zone shift of seasons—a bit rainier in the winter, hotter and drier in the summer—these seasonal changes are negligible on the leeward coasts where most visitors stay. The only season worth mentioning is tourist season, when the roads around Lahaina and Kīhei get crowded. Peak visitor activity occurs from Christmas to March, then picks up again in summer. If traffic is bothering you, just remember that Maui is mostly unpopulated. Get out of town and explore the countryside. During high season, the road to Hāna tends to clog—well, not clog exactly but develop little choo-choo trains of cars, with everyone in a line of six or a dozen driving as slowly as the first car. The solution: leave early (dawn) and return late (dusk). And if you find yourself playing the role of locomotive, pull over. Maui has a variety of community festivals, but they're spread throughout the year. Look in the local paper or ask the Maui Visitors Bureau (☞ Visitor Information *in* Maui A to Z, *below*). If something's going on, check it out.

West Maui

West Maui, anchored by the amusing old whaling town of Lahaina, was the focus of development when Maui set out to become a premier tourist destination. The condo-filled beach towns of Nāpili, Kahana, and Honokōwai are arrayed between the stunning resorts of Kapalua and Kā'anapali, north of Lahaina.

A Good Drive

Begin this tour in **Kapalua** ①; even if you're not staying there, you'll want to have a look around the renowned Kapalua Bay Hotel and enjoy a meal or snack before you begin exploring. From Kapalua drive north on the Honoapi'ilani Highway (Hwy. 30). This used to be the route to Wailuku. It has been paved, but storms now and then make it partly impassable, especially on the winding, 8-mi stretch that is only one lane wide, with no shoulder and a sheer drop off into the ocean. However, you'll discover some gorgeous photo opportunities along the road, and if you go far enough, you'll come to **Kahakuloa** ②, a sleepy fishing village tucked into a cleft in the mountain. You've now come about as far as you can on this "highway." The road pushes on to Wailuku, but you may be tired of the narrow and precipitously winding course you have to take.

From Kahakuloa turn around and go back in the direction from which you came—south toward Kā'anapali and Lahaina, past the beach towns of Nāpili, Kahana, and Honokōwai. If you wish to explore these towns, get off the Upper Honoapi'ilani Highway and drive closer to the water. If you're not staying there, you may want to visit the planned resort community of **Kā'anapali** ③, especially the Hyatt Regency Maui and the Westin Maui. To reach them, take the third Kā'anapali exit from Honoapi'ilani Highway (the one closest to Lahaina), then turn left on Kā'anapali Parkway. Next, head for Lahaina. Before you start your Lahaina trek, take a short detour by turning left from Honoapi'ilani Highway onto Lahainaluna Road, and stop at the **Printing House** ④, built by Protestant missionaries in 1831. Return the way you came on Honoapi'ilani Highway, and turn left on Kēnui Street, then left on Front Street.

Lahaina is best explored on foot, so use the drive along Front Street to get oriented, then park at or near **505 Front Street** ⑤, at the south end of the town's historic and colorful commercial area. Heading back into town, turn on Prison Street and you'll come to the **Old Prison** ⑥, which was built from coral blocks. Then return to Front Street where it's a short stroll to the **Banyan Tree** ⑦, one of the town's best-known landmarks, and behind it, the old **Court House** ⑧. Next door, also in Banyan Park, stand the reconstructed remains of the waterfront **Fort** ⑨. About a half block northwest, you'll find the site of Kamehameha's **Brick Palace** ⑩. **Brig Carthaginian II** ⑪ is anchored at the dock nearby and is open to visitors. If you walk from the brig to the corner of Front and Dickenson streets, you'll find the **Baldwin Home** ⑫, restored to reflect the decor of the early 19th century. Next door is the **Master's Reading Room** ⑬, Maui's oldest building and now home to the Lahaina Restoration Foundation.

Maui

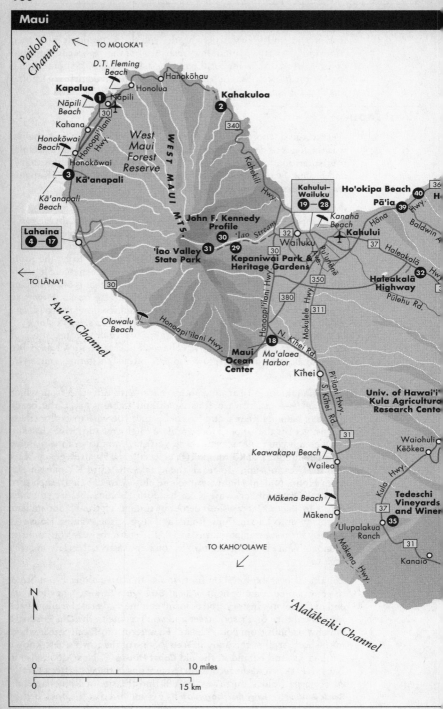

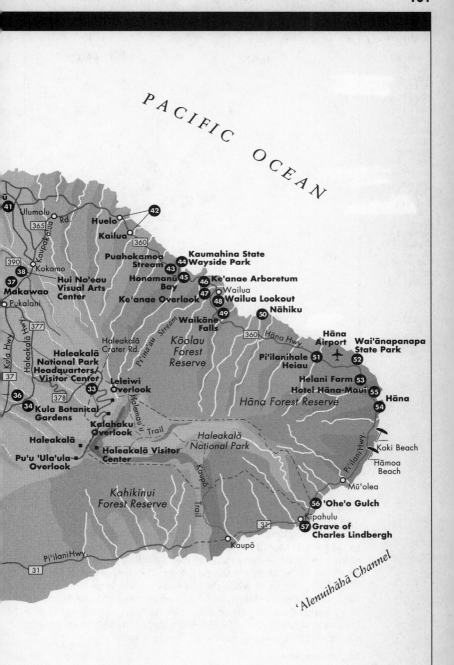

PACIFIC OCEAN

41 Ū
Ulumalu
365 Rd
42
Huelo
Kailua
360
Puahokamoa
Stream
390
38 Kokomo
37
Makawao
Pukalani
377
Kula Hwy
Haleakalā Hwy
Haleakalā
National Park
Headquarters/
Visitor Center
37
36
378
33
34 **Kula Botanical**
Gardens
Haleakalā
Pu'u 'Ula'ula
Overlook

Hui No'eau
Visual Arts
Center
Honomanū
Bay
Ke'anae Overlook

43
44 **Kaumahina State**
Wayside Park
45
46 **Ke'anae Arboretum**
47
Wailua
48 **Wailua Lookout**
49
50 **Nāhiku**

Haleakalā
Crater Rd.
Leleiwi
Overlook
Kalahaku
Overlook
Haleakalā Visitor
Center

Pi'ina au Stream
Kōolau
Forest
Reserve
Waikāne
Falls

360 Hāna Hwy

Hāna
Airport
Wai'ānapanapa
State Park
Pi'ilanihale
Heiau
51
52

Helani Farm **53**
Hotel Hāna-Maui **55**
54 **Hāna**

Hāna Forest Reserve

Pi'ilani Hwy

Koki Beach
Hāmoa
Beach

Mū'olea

Haleakalā u Trail
Haleakalā
National Park
Kaupō Trail

Kahikinui
Forest Reserve

56 **'Ohe'o Gulch**
Kipahulu
57 **Grave of**
Charles Lindbergh

Pi'ilani Hwy
31
Kaupō
31

'Alenuihāhā Channel

TO THE BIG ISLAND OF HAWAI'I ↓

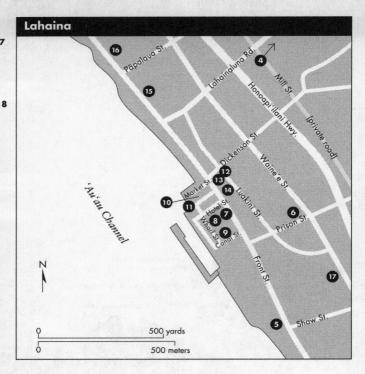

Lahaina

Wander north or south on Front Street to explore Lahaina's commercial side. At the Wharf Cinema Center, you can see the **Spring House** ⑭, built over a freshwater spring. If you continue north on Front Street, you'll come to **Wo Hing Temple** ⑮; another two blocks north and you'll find the **Seamen's Hospital** ⑯. If you're finished walking before dusk and have a hankering for just one more stop, try the **Waiola Church and Cemetery** ⑰. Walk south down Front Street, make a left onto Dickenson Street, then make a right onto Waine'e Street and walk another few blocks.

TIMING

You can walk the length of Lahaina's Front Street in fewer than 30 minutes if you don't stop along the way; just *try* not to be intrigued by the town's colorful shops and historic sites. Realistically, you'll need at least half a day—and can easily spend a full day—to check out the area's coastal beaches, towns, and resorts. The Banyan Tree in Lahaina is a terrific spot to be when the sun sets—mynah birds settle in here for a screeching symphony, which can be an event in itself. If you arrange to spend a Friday afternoon exploring Front Street, you can dine in town and hang around for Art Night, when the galleries stay open into the evening and entertainment fills the streets.

Sights to See

★ ⑫ **Baldwin Home.** An early missionary to Lahaina, Ephraim Spaulding finished building this plaster-and-whitewash coral stone home in 1835; in 1836 Dr. Dwight Baldwin—also a missionary—moved in with his family. The home is now run by the Lahaina Restoration Foundation and has been restored and furnished to reflect the period. You can view the living room with the family's grand piano, the dining room, and Dr. Baldwin's dispensary. ⊠ *696 Front St., Lahaina,* ☎ *808/661–3262.* ⊡ *$3.* ☉ *Daily 10–4.*

⑦ Banyan Tree. This massive tree, a popular and hard-to-miss meeting place if your party splits up for independent exploring, was planted in 1873. It is the largest of its kind in the state and provides a welcome retreat for the weary who come to sit under its awesome branches. ⊠ *Front St., between Hotel and Canal Sts., Lahaina.*

⑩ Brick Palace. All that's left of the palace built by King Kamehameha I around 1802 to welcome the captains of visiting ships are the excavated cornerstones and foundation in front of the Pioneer Inn. Hawai'i's first king lived only one year in the palace because his favorite wife, Ka'ahumanu, refused to stay there. It was then used as a warehouse, storeroom, and meeting house for 70 years until it collapsed. ⊠ *Makai end of Market St., Lahaina.*

★ **⑪ Brig *Carthaginian II*.** This vessel's sailing days are over, but it makes an interesting museum. It was built in Germany in the 1920s and is a replica of the type of ship that brought the New England missionaries around Cape Horn to Hawai'i in the early 1800s. A small museum below deck features the "World of the Whale," a colorful multimedia exhibit about whaling and local sea life. ⊠ *At dock opposite north end of Wharf St., Lahaina,* ☎ *808/661–3262.* ☜ *$3.* ☼ *Daily 10–4.*

⑧ Court House. This old civic building was erected in 1859, rebuilt in 1925, and restored to its 1925 condition in 1998. At one time or another it served as a customs house, a post office, a vault and collector's office, a governor's office, a police court, and a courtroom. Until restoration began, it housed the Lahaina Visitors Center and the Lahaina Art Society with its exhibits and educational programs. At the time of this writing it was not clear who would next occupy this all-purpose relic. The Visitor Center has been relocated two blocks northwest on Front Street. ⊠ *649 Wharf St., Lahaina,* ☎ *808/661–0111.*

⑤ 505 Front Street. Quaint New England–style architecture characterizes this mall, which houses small shops and restaurants connected by a wooden sidewalk. It isn't as crowded as some other areas in Lahaina, probably because between here and the nearby Banyan Tree the town turns into a sleepy residential neighborhood and some people, walking from the more bustling center of Front Street, give up before they reach the mall. Still, the casual eateries lure their share of fun-lovers. ⊠ *South end of Front St. near Shaw St., Lahaina.*

⑨ Fort. Used mostly as a prison, this fortress was positioned so that it could police the whaling ships that crowded the harbor. It was built after sailors, angered by a law forbidding local women from swimming out to ships, lobbed cannonballs at the town. Cannons raised from the wreck of a warship in Honolulu Harbor were brought to Lahaina and placed in front of the fort, where they still sit today. The building itself is an eloquent ruin. ⊠ *Canal and Wharf Sts., Lahaina.*

③ Kā'anapali. The theatrical look of Hawai'i tourism—planned resort communities where luxury homes mix with high-rise hotels, fantasy swimming pools, and a Disneyesque landscape—all began right here in the 1960s. Three miles of uninterrupted white beach and playground-placid water form the front yard for this artificial utopia, with its 40 tennis courts and its two championship golf courses (Kā'anapali North and South). The six major hotels are all worth visiting just for the look around, especially the Hyatt Regency Maui, with its multimillion dollar art collection. One of Maui's best attractions sits here in the Whalers Village shopping complex, the **Whale Center of the Pacific**. This small but excellent museum uses ingenious displays to teach all about the big cetaceans—and there's no charge for admission. ⊠ *2435 Kā'anapali Pkwy., Suite H16,* ☎ *808/661–5992.* ☜ *Donation.* ☼ *Daily 9:30 AM–10 PM.*

❷ **Kahakuloa.** This tiny fishing village seems lost in time. Untouched by progress, it's a relic of pre–jet travel Maui. Many remote villages similar to Kahakuloa used to be tucked away in the valleys of this area. This is the wild side of West Maui; true adventurers will find terrific snorkeling and swimming along this coast, as well as some good hiking trails. ✉ *North end of Honoapi'ilani Hwy.*

❶ **Kapalua.** This resort, set in a beautifully secluded spot surrounded by pineapple fields, got its first big boost in 1978, when the Maui Land & Pineapple Company built the luxurious Kapalua Bay Hotel. It was joined in 1992 by a dazzling Ritz-Carlton. The hotels host dedicated golfers, celebrities who want to be left alone, and some of the world's richest folks. Kapalua's shops and restaurants are some of Maui's finest, but expect to pay big bucks for whatever you purchase. ✉ *Bay Dr., Kapalua.*

★ **Lahaina.** This little whaling town has a notorious past; there are stories of lusty whalers who met head-on with missionaries bent on saving souls. Both groups journeyed to Lahaina from New England in the early 1800s. At first, Lahaina might look touristy, but there's a lot that's genuine here as well. The town has renovated most of its old buildings, which date from the time when it was Hawai'i's capital. Much of the town has been designated a National Historic Landmark, and any new buildings must conform in style to those dating before 1920. ✉ *Honoapi'ilani Hwy., about 3 mi south of Kā'anapali.*

☾ **Lahaina–Kā'anapali & Pacific Railroad.** Affectionately called the Sugarcane Train, this is Maui's only passenger train; it's an 1890s-vintage railway that once shuttled sugar but now moves sightseers between Kā'anapali and Lahaina. This quaint little attraction is a big deal for Hawai'i but probably not much of a thrill for those more accustomed to trains. The kids will like it. You can also get a package that combines a ride and lunch in Lahaina or a historic Lahaina tour. ✉ *1½ blocks north of the Lahainaluna Rd. stoplight on Honoapi'ilani Hwy., Lahaina,* ☎ *808/661–0089.* 🎟 *$13.50.* ☉ *Daily 9–5:30.*

⓭ **Master's Reading Room.** This is Maui's oldest residential building, constructed in 1834. In those days the ground floor was a mission's storeroom, and the reading room upstairs was for sailors. Now the **Lahaina Restoration Foundation** occupies the building, and its knowledgeable staff is here 8–4 to answer almost any question about historic sites in town. Ask for their walking-tour brochure. ✉ *Front and Dickenson Sts., Lahaina,* ☎ *808/661–3262.*

❻ **Old Prison.** Known as Hale Pa'ahao (stuck-in-irons-house), because of its wall shackles and ball-and-chain restraints, this compound was built in the 1850s by convict laborers out of blocks of coral that had been salvaged from the demolished waterfront **Fort**(☞ *above*). Most prisoners were there for desertion, drunkenness, or reckless horse riding. Today, the building is rented for community use. ✉ *Waine'e and Prison Sts., Lahaina.* ☉ *Daily 8–5.*

❹ **Printing House.** Part of Lahainaluna Seminary, founded by Protestant missionaries in 1831, the print shop turned out many of the first Hawaiian-language textbooks and other teaching aids. An exhibit features a replica of the original Rampage press and facsimiles of early printing. The oldest U.S. educational institution west of the Rockies, the seminary now serves as Lahaina's public high school. ✉ *980 Lahainaluna Rd., Lahaina.* 🎟 *Donation.* ☉ *Weekdays 10–3.*

⓰ **Seamen's Hospital.** Built in the 1830s to house King Kamehameha III's royal court, this property was later turned over to the U.S. government, which used it as a hospital for whalers. Next door is a typical **sugar plantation camp residence**, circa 1900. ⊠ *1024 Front St., Lahaina,* ☎ *808/661–3262.*

⓮ **Spring House.** Built by missionaries to shelter a freshwater spring, this historic structure is now home to a huge Fresnel lens, once used in a local lighthouse that guided ships to Lahaina. ⊠ *Wharf Cinema Center, 658 Front St., Lahaina.*

NEED A BREAK?

Has all this fresh air given you a yen for a big beefy burger? Head for **Cheeseburger in Paradise** (⊠ Front St. at Lahainaluna Rd., Lahaina, ☎ 808/661–4855). Upcountry locals, who raise their own beef, travel to Lahaina for these $5 behemoths topped with cheddar, mozzarella, or Swiss cheese.

⓱ **Waiola Church and Cemetery.** The Waiola Cemetery is actually older than the neighboring church, dating from the time when Kamehameha's sacred wife Queen Keōpūolani died and was buried there in 1823. The first church here was erected in 1832 by Hawaiian chiefs, and was originally named Ebenezer by the queen's second husband and widower, Governor Hoapili. It was later named Waine'e, after the district in which it is located. Aptly immortalized in James Michener's *Hawai'i* as the church that wouldn't stand, it was burned down twice and demolished in two windstorms. The present structure was put up in 1953 and named Waiola (water of life). ⊠ *535 Waine'e St., Lahaina,* ☎ *808/661–4349.*

⓯ **Wo Hing Temple.** Built by the Wo Hing Society in 1912 as a social center for Chinese residents, this eye-catching building now contains Chinese artifacts and a historic theater that features Thomas Edison's films of Hawai'i, circa 1898. Upstairs is the only public Taoist altar on Maui. ⊠ *858 Front St., Lahaina,* ☎ *808/661–3262.* ▨ *Donation.* ☉ *Daily 10–4.*

Central Maui

Kahului, an industrial and commercial town in the center of the island, is home to many of Maui's permanent residents, who find their jobs close by. The area was developed in the early '50s to meet the housing needs of workers for the large sugarcane interests here, specifically those of Alexander & Baldwin. The large company was tired of playing landlord to its many plantation workers and sold land to a developer who promised to create affordable housing. The scheme worked, and Kahului became the first planned city in Hawai'i. Ka'ahumanu Avenue (Hwy. 32), Kahului's main street, runs from the harbor to the hills. It's the logical place to begin your exploration of Central Maui.

A Good Tour

Begin at the south end of the central valley by visiting the **Maui Ocean Center** ⑱, easily spotted and accessed from the Honoapíilani Highway (Hwy. 30) at Mā'alaea. When you've had your fill of ogling sealife in this world-class aquarium and exploring Mā'alaea Boat Harbor, get back on the highway and take the second right turn, the Kūihelani Highway (Hwy. 380) to Kahului. Five miles later turn right at the traffic light, Pu'unēnē Avenue (Hwy. 350), and watch for the **Alexander & Baldwin Sugar Museum** ⑲ on the left, just before the still-operating sugar mill. The museum was opened in 1988 by "A&B," Maui's largest landowner and linchpin of its sugar industry, to detail the historic influence of sugarcane in the Islands. It's a fascinating exhibit well worth your time.

From here, explore **Kahului,** the commercial center of Maui, which looks nothing like the lush tropical paradise most people envision as Hawai'i.

106

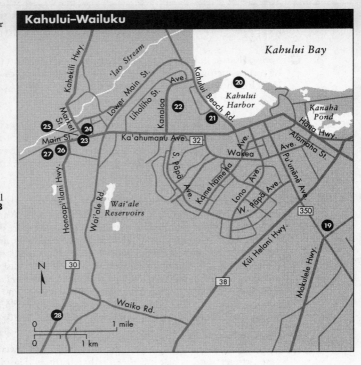

Head back on Pu'unēnē Avenue all the way to its end at Ka'ahumanu Avenue, and turn left. Three blocks ahead you'll see the sputnik-looking canvas domes of Ka'ahumanu Center, Maui's largest shopping center. If you turn right at the signal just before that, you'll follow the curve of Kahului Beach Road and see any ships in port at **Kahului Harbor** ⑳. On your left are the cream-and-brown buildings of **Maui Arts & Cultural Center** ㉑; continue on the beach road until you reach Kanaloa Avenue. Make a left here and return to Ka'ahumanu Avenue passing the new **Keōpūolani Park** ㉒ and the War Memorial Stadium, site of the annual Hooters Hula Bowl. Turn right to reach Wailuku (Ka'ahumanu eventually becomes Wailuku's Main Street). To get a closer look at **Wailuku's Historic District** ㉓, turn right from Main Street onto Market Street, where you can park for free within view of the landmark **'Iao Theater** ㉔. The theater is a good place to begin your walking tour. Next door to the theater is Traders of the Lost Art, the first of many amusing shops that line **Market Street** ㉕ between Vineyard and Main streets. Then it's a short walk along Main Street to **Ka'ahumanu Church** ㉖ on High Street, just around the corner from Main and across the way from the County Court House. Retrieve your car and return to Main Street, where you'll turn right. After a few blocks, on your left, you'll see **Bailey House** ㉗. Follow Highway 30 south a couple of miles to the **Maui Tropical Plantation** ㉘.

From the plantation drive toward the mountains. Main Street turns into 'Iao Valley Road, the air cools, and the hilly terrain gets more lush. Soon you'll come to **Kepaniwai Park & Heritage Gardens** ㉙. As you drive on you'll pass a less imposing landmark called **John F. Kennedy Profile** ㉚. 'Iao Valley Road ends at **'Iao Valley State Park** ㉛, home of the erosion-formed gray and moss-green rock called 'Iao Needle. If you still have the stamina, you can end your touring with a good hike.

TIMING

The complete itinerary will take a full day. But you can explore Central Maui comfortably in little more than half a day if you whiz through the Maui Ocean Center and the Maui Tropical Plantation, or save them for another day. If you want to combine sightseeing with shopping, this is a good itinerary for it, but you'll need more time. Hikers may want to expand their outing to a full day to explore ʻIao Valley State Park, especially in spring, when any plant that can blossom does.

Sights to See

★ ⑲ **Alexander & Baldwin Sugar Museum.** "A&B," Maui's largest landowner, was one of five companies known collectively as the Big Five that spearheaded the planting, harvesting, and processing of the valuable agricultural product sugarcane. Although Hawaiian cane sugar has now been supplanted by cheaper foreign versions—as well as by sugar derived from less costly sugar beets—the crop was for many years the mainstay of the Hawaiian economy. You'll find the museum in a small, restored plantation manager's house next to the post office and the still-operating sugar refinery (black smoke billows up when cane is burning). Historic photos, artifacts, and documents explain the introduction of sugarcane to Hawaiʻi and how plantation managers brought in laborers from other countries, thereby changing the Islands' ethnic mix. Exhibits also describe the sugar-making process. ⊠ *3957 Hansen Rd., Puʻunēnē,* ☎ *808/871–8058.* ☒ *$4.* ♡ *Mon.–Sat. 9:30–4:30.*

㉗ **Bailey House.** This was the home of Edward and Caroline Bailey, two prominent missionaries who came to Wailuku to run the first Hawaiian girls' school on the island, the Wailuku Female Seminary; the school's main function was to train the girls in the "feminine arts." It once stood next door to the Baileys' home, which they called **Halehōʻikeʻike** (House of Display), but locals always called it the Bailey House, and the sign painters eventually gave in.

Construction of the house, between 1833 and 1850, was supervised by Edward Bailey himself. The **Maui Historical Society** runs a museum in the plastered stone house, with a small collection of artifacts from before and after the missionaries' arrival and with Mr. Bailey's paintings of Wailuku. Some rooms have missionary-period furniture. The Hawaiian Room has exhibits on the making of tapa cloth, as well as samples of pre–Captain Cook weaponry. ⊠ *2375A Main St., Wailuku,* ☎ *808/244–3326.* ☒ *$4.* ♡ *Mon.–Sat. 10–4.*

㉔ **ʻIao Theater.** One of Wailuku's most photographed landmarks, this charming movie house went up in Wailuku in 1927 and served as a community gathering spot. When restoration work was completed in 1996, the Maui Community Theatre returned to its Wailuku headquarters, though it still performs at Maui Arts & Cultural Center's Castle Theater, as well. The Art Deco building is now the showpiece of Wailuku's Main Street. The front of the building is now a theater-theme café offering light breakfasts, lunches, and showtime refreshments. ⊠ *68 N. Market St., Wailuku,* ☎ *808/242–6969.*

NEED A
BREAK?

Maui Bake Shop & Deli Ltd. (⊠ 2092 Vineyard St., Wailuku, ☎ 808/242–0064) serves salads, sandwiches, and a daily changing variety of light entrées, but what you're really going to crave here are the pastries—a feast for the eyes as well as the palate. The pastel-frosted frogs, chicks, rabbits, and mice, made of orange butter-cream cookie dough, are simply irresistible.

★ ㉛ **ʻIao Valley State Park.** When Mark Twain saw this park, he dubbed it the Yosemite of the Pacific. Yosemite it's not, but it is a lovely, deep valley with the curious ʻIao Needle, a spire that rises more than 2,000 ft from the valley floor. You can take one of several easy hikes from the parking lot across ʻIao Stream and explore the junglelike area. This park offers a beautiful network of well-maintained walks, where you can stop and meditate by the edge of a stream or marvel at the native plants and flowers. Mist occasionally rises if there has been a rain, which makes being here even more magical. ✉ *Western end of Hwy. 32.* ☎ *Free.* ☉ *Daily 7–7.*

❸⓿ John F. Kennedy Profile. Hawaiians, it seems, can recognize something in almost every rock formation throughout the Islands. Still, this one does uncannily resemble the profile of the late president. ✉ *Hwy. 32, about 1 mi east of ʻIao Valley State Park.*

❷❻ Kaʻahumanu Church. It's said that Queen Kaʻahumanu attended services on this site in 1832 and requested that a permanent structure be erected. Builders first tried adobe, which dissolved in the rain, then stone. The present wooden structure, built in 1876, is classic New England style, with white exterior walls and striking green trim. You won't be able to see the interior, however, unless you attend Sunday services. The church conducts a service entirely in the Hawaiian language each Sunday at 9:30 AM. ✉ *Main and High Sts., Wailuku,* ☎ *808/244–5189.*

Kahului. The town of Kahului is the industrial and commercial center for Maui's year-round residents, as close to a bustling urban center as Maui gets. Most visitors arrive at the airport here and see all they will see of the town as they drive on to their hotels, unless they stop to explore Maui's largest mall, the Kaʻahumanu Center.

❷⓿ Kahului Harbor. This is Maui's chief port, since it's the island's only deep-draft harbor. American-Hawaiʻi's 800-passenger SS *Independence* and SS *Constitution* each stop here once a week, as do cargo ships and smaller vessels, including the occasional yacht. Surfers sometimes use this spot to catch some good waves, but it's not a good swimming beach. ✉ *Kahului Beach Rd., Kahului.*

❷❷ Keōpūolani Park. Maui's new "Central Park" covers 101 acres and—reflecting Maui residents' traditional love of sports—it has seven playing fields. Named for the great Maui queen who was born near here and is buried in Lahaina's Waiola Church cemetery, the park is planted with native species that will take a few years to reach their potential. The park also includes a children's petting zoo, a native plant botanical garden, a picnic area, and a 3 mi walking path.✉ *Kanaloa Ave., next to the YMCA.*

☞ ❷❾ Kepaniwai Park & Heritage Gardens. This county park is a memorial to Maui's cultural roots, with picnic facilities and ethnic displays dotting the landscape. There's an early Hawaiian shack, a New England–style saltbox, a Portuguese-style villa with gardens, and dwellings from such other cultures as China and the Philippines. Next door the **Hawaiʻi Nature Center** has an interactive exhibit and offers hikes that are good for children.

The peacefulness here belies the history of the area. During his quest for domination, King Kamehameha I brought his troops from the Big Island of Hawaiʻi to the Valley Isle in 1790 and engaged in a particularly bloody battle against the son of Maui's chief, Kahekili, near Kepaniwai Park. An earlier battle at the site had pitted Kahekili himself against an older Big Island chief, Kalaniʻōpuʻu. Kahekili prevailed, but the carnage was so great that the nearby stream became known as Wailuku (water of destruction) and the place where fallen warriors choked the stream's flow was called Kepaniwai (the water dam). ⊠ *Valley Rd., Wailuku.* ⬛ *Free.* ⊘ *Daily 7–7.*

㉕ Market Street. An idiosyncratic assortment of shops—with proprietors to match—makes Wailuku's Market Street a delightful place for a stroll. Merchants are happy to chat with visitors, recommend a restaurant, and offer advice or directions.

㉑ Maui Arts & Cultural Center. This $32 million facility opened in 1994 after an epic fund drive led by the citizens of Maui. The top-of-the-line Castle Theater seats 1,200 people on orchestra, mezzanine, and balcony levels. Rock stars play the A& B Amphitheater. The Center (as it's called) also includes a small black box theater, an art gallery with interesting exhibits, and classrooms. The building itself is worth the visit. It incorporates work by Maui artists, and its signature lava-rock wall pays tribute to the skills of the Hawaiians. ⊠ *Just above the harbor on Kahului Beach Rd., Kahului,* ☎ *808/242–2787, box office 808/242–7469.* ⊘ *Weekdays 9–5.*

⑱ Maui Ocean Center. This new aquarium that focuses on Hawaii and the Pacific will make you feel as though you're walking from the seashore down to the bottom of the reef, and then through an acrylic tunnel in the middle of the sea. Special tanks get you close up with turtles, rays, and the bizarre creatures of the tide pools. ⊠ *Enter from Honoapi'ilani Hwy. (Hwy. 30) as it curves past Mā'alaea Harbor, Mā'alaea,* ☎ *808/244–3337.* ⬛ *$17.50.* ⊘ *Daily 9–5.*

🐥 ㉘ Maui Tropical Plantation. This visitor attraction used to be a huge sugarcane field, but when Maui's once-paramount crop declined severely in importance, a group of visionaries decided to open an agricultural theme park. The 120-acre preserve, on Highway 30 just outside Wailuku, offers a 30-minute tram ride through its fields with an informative narration covering growing processes and plant types.

Children will also probably enjoy a historical characters exhibit, as well as fruit-testing, coconut-husking, and lei-making demonstrations and bird shows. There's a restaurant on the property and a souvenir shop that sells fruits and vegetables. On Tuesday and Thursday nights, the Maui Tropical Plantation stages a country-western show and barbecue (☞ *Nightlife, below*). ⊠ *Honoapi'ilani Hwy. (Hwy. 30), Waikapu,* ☎ *808/244–7643.* ⬛ *Free; tram ride with narrated tour $8.50.* ⊘ *Daily 9–5.*

㉓ Wailuku's Historic District. The National Register of Historic Places lists many of this district's old buildings, preserved with their wooden facades intact. Overall, the little town is sleepy and one would not know that it is Maui's county seat. The mayor sits at the top floor of the tallest building in town, on the corner of Main and High streets.

In ancient times Wailuku was a favored place for the inhabitants of Maui, who maintained two *heiau* (temples) on the hills above. It was easy to spot intruders from the hills, and villages grew up around the temples. The first missionaries chose this as a principal station in the 1820s. ⊠ *High, Vineyard, and Market Sts., Wailuku.*

Haleakalā and Upcountry

The fertile western slopes leading up to majestic Haleakalā are called Upcountry. This region is responsible for much of Hawai'i's produce—lettuce, tomatoes, and sweet Maui onions—but the area is also a big flower producer. As you drive along you'll notice plenty of natural vegetation, as clumps of cacti mingle with purple jacaranda, wild hibiscus, and towering eucalyptus trees.

Upcountry is also fertile ranch land, with such spreads as the 20,000-acre 'Ulupalakua Ranch, long famous for raising cattle, and the 20,000-acre Haleakalā Ranch, which throws its well-attended rodeo in Makawao each July 4th. Tedeschi Vineyards and Winery, with just a few acres of 'Ulupalakua land, is the island's only wine producer.

A Good Drive

Start in Kahului fairly early in the morning, since the clouds move over the top of the mountain as early as 11 AM. Make sure you have a full gas tank; there are no service stations on the mountain. Drive on **Haleakalā Highway** ㉜ (Hwy. 37) toward **Haleakalā National Park** ㉝ and the mountain's breathtaking summit. Try to make the drive without stopping since you'll want the best views possible.

Watch the signs: Haleakalā Highway divides. If you go straight it becomes Kula Highway, which is still Highway 37; if you veer to the left it becomes Highway 377, the road you want. After about 6 mi, make a left onto Highway 378; the switchbacks begin here. Near the top of the mountain is the Park Headquarters/Visitor Center—a good spot to stop and stretch your legs.

Continuing up the mountain, you'll come to several overlooks, including Leleiwi Overlook and Kalahaku Overlook, both with views into the crater. Not far from Kalahaku Overlook you'll find the Haleakalā Visitor Center. Eventually you'll reach the highest point on Maui, the Pu'u 'Ula'ula Overlook.

Now head back down the way you came, taking time to see and explore the lower nooks and crannies of Haleakalā. When you reach Highway 377 again, make a left. Go about 2 mi, and you'll come to **Kula Botanical Gardens** ㉞ on your left. It's worth a stop here to admire a beautiful abundance of tropical flora. Continue on Highway 377, away from Kahului, and you'll soon join Highway 37 again. Turn left and, about 8 mi farther on, you'll reach 'Ulupalakua Ranch headquarters and **Tedeschi Vineyards and Winery** ㉟, where you can sample Hawai'i's only homegrown wines.

Returning the way you came, head north toward Kahului on Highway 37. When you get to the Highway 37/377 fork, bear to the left to stay on Highway 37. This is Kula Highway; another name change will make it Haleakalā Highway again (this isn't as confusing as it sounds). About 2 mi past the fork, you'll see a turnoff to the right called Copp Road. About ½ mi later, turn left onto Mauna Place to visit the **University of Hawai'i's Kula Agricultural Research Center** ㊱ and view its extraordinary collection of protea.

Retrace your way to Kula Highway and again head toward Kahului. In about 4 mi you'll come to the bedroom community of Pukalani. If you're pressed for time you can take Highway 37 from here back to Kahului. Otherwise, head north on Highway 365 toward the *paniolo* (Hawaiian cowboy) village of **Makawao** ㊲, formerly a Portuguese settlement. **Hui No'eau Visual Arts Center** ㊳ is about mile from the Makawao crossroads as you head down Baldwin Avenue. From here it's a short drive down toward the ocean to the Hāna Highway. Make a left on the Hāna Highway to return to Kahului.

This can be an all-day outing even without the detours to Tedeschi Vineyards and Makawao. If you start early enough to catch the sunrise from Haleakalā's summit, you'll have plenty of time to enjoy a short hike on the mountain, have lunch in Kula, and end your day with dinner in Makawao or Ha'iku.

Sights to See

③② **Haleakalā Highway.** On this road, you'll travel from sea level to an elevation of 10,023 ft in only 38 mi—a feat you won't be able to repeat on any other car route in the world. It's not a quick drive, however; it'll take you about two hours—longer if you can't resist the temptation to stop and enjoy the spectacular views. ⊠ *Hwy. 37.*

★ **③③** **Haleakalā National Park.** A trip to Maui would not be complete without a visit here. **Haleakalā** is the centerpiece of this 27,284-acre national park, which was dedicated in 1961 to preserving the area. The 10,023-ft dormant volcano is the font from which all of East Maui flowed. It is now home to a wide variety of sights, sounds, and smells; its terrain, climate, flora, and fauna—not to mention its views—are often strange, and always memorable. The crater is actually an "erosional valley," created by centuries of wind and rain chipping away at the mountain's summit (where there may have once been a small crater), sculpting the dramatic landscape you see today. The small hills within the valley are volcanic cinder cones, each with a small crater at its top, and each the site of an eruption. The mountain has terrific camping and hiking opportunities, including a trail that loops through the crater.

Before you head up Haleakalā, call (☎ 808/871–5054) for the latest park weather conditions. Extreme gusty winds, heavy rain, and even snow in winter are not uncommon—even if it is paradise as usual down at beach level. Because of the high altitude, the mountaintop temperature is often as much as 30 degrees cooler than that at sea level. Be sure to pack an extra jacket.

You can stop and learn something of the volcano's origins and eruption history at the **Park Headquarters/Visitor Center,** at 7,000-ft elevation on Haleakalā Highway. Maps, posters, and other memorabilia are available at the gift shop here.

Leleiwi Overlook, at about an 8,800-ft elevation on Haleakalā, is one of several lookout areas in the park. If you're here in the late afternoon, it's possible you'll experience a phenomenon called the Brocken Specter. Named after a similar occurrence in East Germany's Harz Mountains, the "specter" allows you to see yourself reflected on the clouds and encircled by a rainbow. Don't wait all day for this, because it's not a daily occurrence.

The famous silversword plant grows amid the desertlike surroundings at **Kalahaku Overlook,** at the 9,000-ft level on Haleakalā. This endangered flowering plant grows only here in the crater at the summit of this mountain. The silversword looks like a member of the yucca family and produces a stalk 3 ft–8 ft tall with several hundred purple sunflowers. At this lookout the silversword is kept in an enclosure to protect it from souvenir hunters and nibbling wildlife.

Haleakalā Visitor Center, at 9,740-ft elevation on Haleakalā, has exhibits inside and a trail from here leads to White Hill, a small crater nearby. This is a short, easy walk that will give you an even better view of the valley. Hosmer Grove, just off the highway before you get to the visitor center, has camp sites and interpretive trails. Park rangers maintain a changing schedule of talks and hikes both here and at the top of the mountain; check the center's bulletin board for details.

Just before the summit, the **Crater Observatory** offers warmth and shelter, informative displays, and an eye-popping view of the cinder-cone-studded, 7-mi by 3-mi crater. The highest point on Maui is the **Puʻu ʻUlaʻula Overlook,** at the 10,023-ft summit of Haleakalā. Here you'll find a glass-enclosed lookout with a 360-degree view. The building is open 24 hours a day, and this is where visitors gather for the best sunrise view. Dawn generally begins between 5:45 and 7, depending on the time of year. On a clear day, you can see the islands of Molokaʻi, Lānaʻi, Kahoʻolawe, and Hawaiʻi. On a *really* clear day, you can even spot Oʻahu glimmering in the distance.

On a small hill nearby, you'll see **Science City,** a research and communications center that looks like it's straight out of an espionage thriller. The University of Hawaiʻi and the Department of Defense don't allow visitors to enter the facility, however. The university maintains an observatory here, while the Department of Defense tracks satellites. ☒ *Haleakalā Crater Rd. (Hwy. 378), Makawao,* ☎ *808/572–9306.* ☒ *$10 per car.* ☉ *Park headquarters and visitor center, daily 7:30–4; Haleakalā visitor center, daily sunrise–3.*

NEED A
BREAK?

Kula Lodge (☒ Haleakalā Hwy., Kula, ☎ 808/878–2517) serves hearty breakfasts from 6:30 to 11:15—a favorite with visitors coming down from a sunrise visit to Haleakalā's summit as well as those on their way up for a later morning tramp in the crater. Spectacular ocean views fill the windows of this mountainside lodge (☞ Lodging, *below*).

38 **Hui Noʻeau Visual Arts Center.** This nonprofit cultural center is on the old Baldwin estate, just outside the town of Makawao. The main house, an elegant two-story Mediterranean-style villa designed in the 1920s by the defining Hawaiʻi architect C. W. Dickey, shines from the efforts of renovations. "The Hui," more than 60 years old, is the grand dame of Maui's well-known art scene. The acreage seems like a botanical garden, and the nonstop exhibits are always satisfying. The Hui also offers classes and maintains working artists' studios. ☒ *2841 Baldwin Ave., Makawao,* ☎ *808/572–6560.* ☒ *Free.* ☉ *Tues.–Sun. 10–4.*

34 **Kula Botanical Gardens.** Specimens grow somewhat naturally here, and you'll see all kinds of flora that may be unfamiliar. There are *koa* trees, the wood from which is often made into finely turned bowls and handcrafted furniture, and *kukui* trees (ancient Hawaiians used the tree's nuts, which are filled with oil, for lighting). In addition the gardens have Maui's hallmark protea, several varieties of ginger, and stands of bamboo orchid. ☒ *RR 2, Upper Kula Rd., Kula,* ☎ *808/878–1715.* ☒ *$4.* ☉ *Daily 9–4.*

37 **Makawao.** This once-tiny town has managed to hang onto its country charm (and eccentricity) as it has grown in popularity. The district was settled originally by Portuguese and Japanese immigrants, who came to Maui to work the sugar plantations and then moved "Upcountry" to establish small farms, ranches, and stores. Descendants now work the neighboring Haleakalā and ʻUlupalakua ranches. Every Fourth of July the paniolo set comes out in force for the Makawao Rodeo. The crossroads of town, lined with places to shop, see art, and get food, reflects a growing population of people who came here just because they like it. ☒ *Hwy. 365, East Maui.*

HAWAIʻI'S FLORA AND FAUNA

HAWAIʻI HAS THE DUBIOUS distinction of claiming more extinct and endangered animal species than the rest of the North American continent. The Hawaiian crow, or ʻalalā, for example, has been reduced to a population of only 15 birds, and most of these have been raised in captivity on the Big Island. The ʻalalā is now facing a serious threat from another endangered bird—the ʻio, or Hawaiian hawk. Still "protected" although making a comeback from its former endangered status, the nēnē goose, Hawaiʻi's state bird, roams freely in parts of Maui, Kauaʻi, and the Big Island, where mating pairs are often spotted ambling across roads in Hawaiʻi Volcanoes National Park.

The mongoose is not endangered, although some residents wish it were. Alert drivers can catch a glimpse of the ferretlike mongoose darting across country roads. The mongoose was brought to Hawaiʻi in 1883 in an attempt to control the rat population, but the plan had only limited success since the hunter and hunted rarely met: Mongooses are active during the day, rats at night. Another creature, the rock wallaby, arrived in Honolulu in 1916 after being purchased from the Sydney Zoological Garden. Two escaped, and today about 50 of the small, reclusive marsupials live in remote areas of Kalihi Valley.

At the Kīlauea Point National Wildlife Refuge on Kauaiʻi, hundreds of Laysan albatross, wedge-tail shearwaters, red-footed boobies, and other marine birds glide and soar within photo-op distance of visitors to Kīlauea Lighthouse. Boobie chicks hatch in the fall and emerge from nests burrowed into cliffside dirt banks and even under stairs—

any launching pad from which the fledgling flyer can catch the nearest air current.

Hawaiʻi has only two native mammals. Threatened with extinction, the rare Hawaiian bat hangs out primarily at Kealakekua Bay on the Big Island. On the endangered species list, doe-eyed Hawaiian monk seals breed in northwestern Islands. With only 1,500 left in the wild, you won't catch many lounging on the beaches of Hawaiʻi's populated islands, but you can see rescued pups and adults along with "threatened" Hawaiian green sea turtles at Sea Life Park and the Waikīkī Aquarium on Oahu.

Tropical flowers such as plumeria, orchids, hibiscus, red ginger, heliconia, and anthuriums grow wild on all islands. Pīkake blossoms make the most fragrant leis, and fragile orange ʻilima (once reserved only for royalty), the most elegant leis. The lovely wood rose is actually the dried seed pod of a species of morning glory. Mountain apple, Hawaiian raspberry, thimbleberry, and strawberry guava provide refreshing snacks for hikers; and giant banyan trees, hundreds of years old, spread their canopies over families picnicking in parks, inviting youngsters to swing from their hanging vines.

Sprouting ruby, pompomlike lehua blossoms—thought to be the favorite flower of Pele, the volcano goddess—ʻōhiʻa trees bury their roots in fields of once-molten lava. Also growing on the Big Island as well as the outer slopes of Maui's Haleakalā, exotic protea flourish only at an elevation of 4,000 ft; while within Haleakalā's moonscape crater, the rare and otherworldly silversword—a 7-ft stalk with a single white spike and pale yellow flower found nowhere else on earth—blooms once and then dies.

NEED A
BREAK?

One of Makawao's most famous landmarks is **Komoda Store & Bakery** (✉ 3674 Baldwin Ave., ☎ 808/572–7261)—a classic mom-and-pop store little changed over 70-odd years—where you can get a delicious cream puff if you arrive early enough in the day. They make hundreds—but sell out each day. Cream puffs or not, Komoda's is a nifty little stop, with plenty of tasty snacks as well as all the other trappings of an old-fashioned general store.

★ ㉟ **Tedeschi Vineyards and Winery.** You can take a tour of the winery and its historic grounds, the former Rose Ranch, and sample the island's only wines: a pleasant Maui Blush, the Maui Brut-Blanc de Noirs Hawaiian Champagne, and Tedeschi's annual Maui Nouveau. The most unusual wine, Maui Blanc, is made from pineapples; you'll want to taste it before you buy—it's not appreciated by everyone. The tasting room is a cottage built in the late 1800s for the frequent visits of King Kalākaua. The cottage also contains the 'Ulupalakua Ranch History Room, which tells colorful stories of the ranch's owners, the paniolo tradition that developed here, and Maui's polo teams. The old General Store may look like a museum; in fact it's an excellent pit stop. The ranch and winery are not too out of the way when you're returning from a visit to Haleakalā, and it's definitely worth a stop. ✉ *Kula Hwy., 'Ulupalakua Ranch,* ☎ *808/878–6058.* 🎟 *Free.* ☉ *Daily 9–5, tours daily 9–2:30.*

㊱ **University of Hawai'i's Kula Agricultural Research Center.** The first protea was planted here in the mid-'60s and since then the station has become the world's foremost protea research and development facility. Within its gates you'll see as many as 300 varieties of the exotic blooms, most with names to match: Rickrack Banksia, Veldfire Sunburst, Pink Mink, and Safari Sunset, to name just a few. You can talk to the growers to find out more about the plants, which were brought to Maui from Australia in 1965 by Dr. Philip Parvin, a University of Hawai'i horticulture professor. You must first stop at the office and sign a sheet releasing the station from any liability; they'll provide you with a map to help you find your way.

Now that you have your botanical education, proceed to one of Upcountry Maui's many commercial outlets and buy your favorite blooms. Fresh-cut or dried (protea dry beautifully), these unusual-looking blossoms make great send-home gifts, but fresh flowers leaving Hawai'i must bear an inspection stamp. Most sellers will inspect, pack, and express-ship them for you. ✉ *Mauna Pl., Kula,* ☎ *808/878–1213.* 🎟 *Free.* ☉ *Mon.–Thurs. 7–3:30.*

The Road to Hāna

Don't let anyone tell you the Hāna Highway is impassable, frightening, or otherwise unadvisable. Because of all the hype, you're bound to be a little nervous approaching it for the first time. But once you try it, you'll wonder if maybe there's somebody out there making it sound tough just to keep out the hordes. The 55-mi road begins in Kahului, where it is a well-paved highway. The eastern half of the road is challenging, as it is riddled with turns and bridges, and you'll want to stop often so the driver can enjoy the view, too. But it's not a grueling, all-day drive. The challenging part of the road takes only an hour and a half. By and large the road is well maintained. Still, you might check ahead when you're in Maui to find out about possible delays; the Hana police station (☎ 808/248–8311) always knows the latest.

A Good Drive

Start your trip to Hāna in the little town of **Pā'ia** ㊲, where the main street in town is Hāna Highway. You'll want to begin with a full tank of gas—there are no gas stations along the Hāna Highway, and the stations in Hāna close by 6 PM. You can also pick up a picnic lunch here and really make a delicious day of it. Lunch and snack choices along the way are limited to local fare from extremely rustic fruit stands and truck markets. Once the road gets twisty remember that many people—mostly those who live in Hāna—make this trip frequently. You'll recognize them because they're the ones who'll be zipping around every curve; they've seen this so many times before that they don't care to linger. Pull over or slow down to let them pass.

Two miles east of Pā'ia, you'll see **Ho'okipa Beach** ㊵, arguably the windsurfing capital of the world. Two mi later the bottom of Ha'ikū Road offers a right-turn side-trip to **Ha'ikū** ㊶, Maui's verdant gulch country. About 6 mi later, at the bottom of Kaupakalua Road, the roadside mileposts begin measuring the 36 mi to Hana town. The road's trademark noodling starts about 3 mi after that. All along this stretch of road, waterfalls are abundant. Turn off the radio and open the windows to enjoy the sounds and smells. There are plenty of places to pull off and park; all are ideal spots to stop and take pictures. You'll want to plan on doing this a few times, as the road's curves make driving without a break difficult. When it's raining (which is often), the drive is particularly beautiful.

As you drive on you'll pass the sleepy country villages of **Huelo** ㊷ and Kailua. At about Mile Marker 11 you can stop at the bridge over **Puahokamoa Stream** ㊸, where there are more pools and waterfalls. If you'd rather stretch your legs and use a flush toilet, continue on another mile to the **Kaumahina State Wayside Park** ㊹. Near Mile Marker 13 you can see the vast **Honomanū Bay** ㊺. Another 4 mi brings you to the **Ke'anae Arboretum** ㊻, where you can add to your botanical education or enjoy a challenging hike into a forest. Nearby you'll find the **Ke'anae Overlook** ㊼. Coming up is the halfway mark to Hāna. If you've had enough scenery, this is as good a time as any to turn around and head back to civilization.

Don't expect a booming city when you get to Hāna. It's the road that's the draw. Continue on from Mile Marker 20 for about ¾ mi to **Wailua Lookout** ㊽. After another ½ mi, you'll hit the best falls on the entire drive to Hāna, **Waikāne Falls** ㊾. At about Mile Marker 25, you'll see a road that heads down toward the ocean and the village of **Nāhiku** ㊿, once a popular native settlement. Just after Mile Marker 31, the left turn at 'Ula'ino Road doubles back for a mile, loses its pavement, and even crosses a streambed just before Kahanu Garden and **Pi'ilanihale Heiau** (51), the largest in the state. Back on the road and less than ½ mi farther is the turnoff for **Hāna Airport.** Just beyond Mile Marker 32 you'll pass **Wai'ānapanapa State Park** (52); stop here for a swim at its black-sand beach. Closer to Hāna you'll come to a private 60-acre tropical enclave, **Helani Farm** (53). **Hāna** (54) is just minutes away from here; its fabled **Hotel Hāna-Maui** (55), with its surrounding ranch, is the mainstay of Hāna's economy.

Once you've seen Hāna, you might want to drive 10 mi past the town to the pools at **'Ohe'o Gulch** (56). Now called Pi'ilani Highway, the drivable road continues, though not always gracefully, all the way around the leeward side of Haleakalā. The trip adds an hour to your return time, but you won't see this kind of huge rugged landscape anywhere else on Maui. Many people travel the mile past 'Ohe'o Gulch to see the **Grave of Charles Lindbergh** (57). The world-renowned aviator is buried next to Palapala Ho'omau Congregational Church. Past Seven Pools, past the scattered houses of Kipahulu, past tiny St. Paul's Church, on the right is the nearly hidden massive chimney of a ruined sugar mill. Just past the mill on the left side of the road is a pasture and then a galvanized-steel gate swung permanently open on a rutted track that heads toward the sea. The road goes to the Palapala Hoʻomau Congregational Church, a few hundred yards away, mostly hidden behind thick vegetation. The simple, one-room church sits on a bluff over the sea, with a small graveyard on the ocean side.

TIMING

With stops, the drive from Pāʻia to Hāna should take you between two and three hours. Lunch in Hāna, hiking, and swimming can easily turn the round-trip into a full-day outing. Since there's so much lush scenery to take in, try and plan your Road to Hāna drive for a day that promises fair, sunny weather. And be prepared for car trains that form spontaneously during the busier tourist seasons in winter and midsummer. (If you find one forming behind you, pull over). If you make this trip in winter, when the north shore waves are the highest, you may have the chance to watch astonishing windsurfing feats at Hoʻokipa Beach, but sometimes the winter conditions are too dangerous even for daredevils.

Sights to See

57 Grave of Charles Lindbergh. The world-renowned aviator chose to be buried here because he and his wife, writer Anne Morrow Lindbergh, spent a lot of time living in the area in a home they built. He was buried here in 1974, next to Palapala Hoʻomau Congregational Church. Remember, this is a churchyard, so be considerate and leave everything exactly as you found it. ⊠ *Palapala Hoʻomau Congregational Church, Kīpahulu.*

OFF THE
BEATEN PATH

KAUPŌ ROAD – This stretch of road beyond Kīpahulu has rough stretches, most notably a 4-mi unpaved portion in Kaupo; bad storms will occasionally cause temporary washouts and closures. It's a beautiful drive, however, and people travel it every day in two-wheel-drive cars. The pay-off is the chance to see the leeward "back side" of Haleakalā—rugged, grand, and unpopulated. In pre-discovery days, this whole part of the island was heavily populated. You can still see the old rock walls and house platforms that were abandoned 150 years ago. Along the way, the little Kaupō Store, about 15 mi past Hāna, sells a variety of essential items, such as groceries, fishing tackle, and hardware; it's also a good place to stop for a cold drink. You'll also pass the renovated Hui Aloha Church, a tiny, wood-frame structure surrounded by an old Hawaiian graveyard. In Kanaio, you'll pass through the zone of Haleakalā's last eruption, 200 years ago. You'll eventually wind up at ʻUlupalakua.

41 Haʻikū. At one time, this town vibrated around a couple of enormous pineapple canneries; now the place is reawakening to itself as a self-reliant community. At the town center, the old cannery has turned into a rustic mall; nearby warehouses are following suit. Continue 2 mi up Kokomo Road to see a large *puʻu* (cinder cone) capped with a grove of columnar pines, and the 4th Marine Division Memorial Park. During World War II American GIs trained here for battles on Iwo Jima and Saipan. Locals have nicknamed the cinder cone "Giggle Hill," because it was a popular place for Maui girls to entertain their favorite servicemen. You might want to return to Hāna Highway by following Haʻikū Road east. This is one of Maui's prettiest drives, and it passes West Kuiaha Road, where a left turn will bring you to a second renovated cannery. ⊠ *Intersection of Haʻikū and Kokomo Rds.*

★ **54 Hāna.** For many years, the fabled Hotel Hāna-Maui was the only attraction for diners and shoppers determined to spend some time and money in Hāna after their long drive. The **Hāna Cultural Center Museum** (☎ 808/248–8622), on Ukea Street, helps to meet that need. Besides operating a well-stocked gift shop, it displays artifacts, quilts, a replica of an authentic *kauhale* (an ancient Hawaiian living complex, with thatched huts and food gardens, and other Hawaiiana). The knowledgeable staff can explain it all to you.

As you wander around Hāna, keep in mind that this is a company town. Although sugar was once the mainstay of Hāna's economy, the last plantation shut down in the '40s. In 1946 rancher Paul Fagan built the Hotel Hāna-Maui and stocked the surrounding pastureland with cattle. Suddenly, it was the ranch and its hotel that were putting food on most tables.

The cross you'll see on the hill above the hotel was put there in memory of Fagan. After his death in the mid-'60s, ownership of the ranch and town passed to 37 shareholders, most of whom didn't care about their property. Then the Rosewood Corporation purchased most of Hāna's valuable land and put megamillions into restoring the Hotel Hāna-Maui. In 1989 Rosewood sold its Hāna holdings to a Japanese company, which appointed Sheraton as manager. Sheraton renovated the old hotel and added the plantation-look Sea Ranch health spa across the road, and the isolated resort became a favorite hideaway for health-conscious celebrities. The property was sold again in 1995 to the New York–based Manolis Company, which promptly announced plans to build a golf course on part of the land; many local residents just as promptly announced their opposition to the proposal. The golf-course permit lapses in fall 1998; at press time the property was up for sale.

Because the town is so small, most of the people you'll see are the hands-on suppliers of the services and amenities that make hotel guests happy. Moreover, many locals have worked at the hotel for years; a fascinating family tree that hangs near the lobby shows the relationships among all the employees. If you're at all curious, be sure to talk to some of the townspeople. They're candid, friendly, and mostly native Hawaiian— or at least born and raised in Hāna. ⊠ *Hāna Hwy., Mile Marker 35.*

Hāna Airport. Think of Amelia Earhart. Think of Waldo Pepper. If these picket-fence runways don't turn your thoughts to the derring-do of barnstorming pilots, you haven't seen enough old movies. Only the smallest planes can land and depart here, and when none of them happen to be around, the lonely wind sock is the only evidence that this is a working airfield. ⊠ *Hāna Hwy., past Mile Marker 30,* ☎ *808/ 248–8208.*

㊾ Helani Farm. Known as the birthplace of tropical flowers on Maui, this 60-acre enclave with its signature tree house used to be open to the public on a drop-in basis. Now, 20-minute guided tours are by appointment only and reserved for truly serious horticulture enthusiasts. The place is still worth an unscheduled stop, though, because the flower shop at the entrance sells bouquets of 10 tropicals for only $2 and also has gift boxes. ⊠ *Helani Farm, Hāna,* ☎ *808/248–8274 or 800/385–5241.* ☜ *$10.*

㊺ Honomanū Bay. At Mile Marker 14 the Hāna Highway drops into and out of this enormous valley, with its rocky black-sand beach. The Honomanū Valley was carved by erosion during Haleakalā's first dormant period. At the canyon's head, there are 3,000-ft cliffs and a 1,000-ft waterfall, but don't try to reach them. There's not much of a trail, and what does exist is practically impassable. ⊠ *Hāna Hwy. before Keʻanae.*

★ ④⓪ **Ho'okipa Beach.** There is no better place on this or any other island to watch the world's best windsurfers in action. The surfers know five different surf breaks here by name. Unless it's a rare day without wind or waves, you're sure to get a show here. It's not safe to park on the shoulder; use the ample parking lot at the county park entrance. ⊠ 2 *mi past Pā'ia on Hwy. 36.*

⑤⑤ **Hotel Hāna-Maui.** This fabled hotel, a favorite of privacy-seeking celebrities, is one of the best in the state. The newer Sea Ranch cottages across the road are also part of the Hāna-Maui; the cottages were built to look like authentic plantation housing, but only from the outside. ⊠ *Hāna Hwy., Hāna,* ☎ *808/248–8211.*

④② **Huelo.** This sleepy little farm town has two quaint and lovely churches but little else of interest to tourists. Yet it's a good place to meet local residents and learn about a rural lifestyle you might not have expected to find in the Islands. The same could be said, minus the churches, for nearby **Kailua** (Mile Marker 6), home to Alexander & Baldwin's irrigation employees. ⊠ *Hāna Hwy., near Mile Marker 5.*

④④ **Kaumahina State Wayside Park.** The park has a picnic area, rest rooms, and a lovely overlook to the Ke'anae Peninsula. Hardier souls can camp here—with a permit (☎ 808/984–8109 weekdays 8–4). ⊠ *Hāna Hwy., Mile Marker 12, Kailua.* 🆓 *Free.*

④⑥ **Ke'anae Arboretum.** Here's a place to learn the names of the many plants and trees now considered native to Hawai'i. The meandering Pi'ina'au Stream adds a graceful touch to the arboretum and provides a swimming pond besides. You can take a fairly rigorous hike from the arboretum, if you can find the trail at one side of the large taro patch. Be careful not to lose the trail once you're on it. A lovely forest waits at the end of the hike. ⊠ *Hāna Hwy., Mile Marker 17, Ke'anae.* 🆓 *Free.*

④⑦ **Ke'anae Overlook.** From this observation point, you'll notice the patchwork-quilt effect the taro farms create below. The ocean provides a dramatic backdrop for the farms; in the other direction there are awesome views of Haleakalā through the foliage. This is a great spot for photos. ⊠ *Hāna Hwy. near Mile Marker 17, Ke'anae.*

....

NEED A
BREAK?

Just past Ke'anae on Hāna Highway pull over at **Uncle Harry's** (☎ 808/ 248–7019), a refreshment stand run by the family of fondly remembered Harry Mitchell, a Hawaiian elder and social activist who held no official title. A little shop has souvenirs and Hawaiian crafts for sale, and the family has restored a grass house to demonstrate how their ancestors lived. The Mitchells have some Hawaiian food available, as well as fruit, home-baked breads, and beverages. Just don't expect the stainless steel and Formica slickness of, say, Denny's.

....

⑤⓪ **Nāhiku.** This was a popular settlement in ancient times, with hundreds of residents. Now only about 80 people live in Nāhiku, mostly native Hawaiians and some back-to-the-land types. A rubber grower planted trees here in the early 1900s. The experiment didn't work out, so Nāhiku was essentially abandoned. The road ends at the sea in a pretty landing. This is the rainiest, densest part of the East Maui rain forest. ⊠ *Makai side of Hāna Hwy., Mile Marker 25.*

⑤⑥ **'Ohe'o Gulch.** Meg Ryan's rhapsody in the 1994 film *I.Q.*, about Maui's "seven sacred pools," may have ruined this spot forever, filling visitors with wrong-headed expectations. Here's the straight scoop: Maui residents call this place 'Ohe'o Gulch; there are many waterfalls well over 100 ft high, but there is no 100-ft-high waterfall that anyone could safely slide down; there are more than seven pools (the actual number depends on rainfall and what you consider a "pool"); and sunbathing and hiking are both popular activities, but swimming here can be hazardous, and there are no lifeguards. From the paved parking lot, you can walk a short way to the first of the pools. Rocks are available for sunbathing, and caves may be explored. In spring and summer it can get quite crowded here, and it doesn't even thin out when it rains. The best way to escape the crowd is to hike upstream. The 2-mi trail to dynamic **Waimoku Falls** passes two thrilling footbridges and a boardwalk through a bamboo forest. ✉ *Pi'ilani Hwy., 10 mi south of Hāna.*

★ ㊴ **Pā'ia.** This little town on Maui's north shore was once a sugarcane enclave, with a mill and plantation camps. Shrewd immigrants quickly opened shops to serve the workers, who probably found it easier to buy supplies near home. The town boomed during World War II when the Marines set up camp in nearby Ha'ikū. After the war, however, sugar producer Alexander & Baldwin closed its Pā'ia operation, many workers moved on, and the town's population began to dwindle.

In the '70s Pā'ia became a hippie town as dropouts headed for Maui to open boutiques, galleries, and unusual eateries. In the '80s windsurfers discovered nearby Ho'okipa Beach, and brought an international flavor to Pā'ia. You can see this in the youth of the town and in the budget inns that have cropped up to offer accommodations to those who windsurf for a living. Pā'ia is certainly a fun place.

Apart from windsurfing, what keeps Pā'ia in business these days is feeding Hāna-bound visitors. If you are setting out on the road to Hāna and *not* hankering to sample the local fare at the extremely rustic fruit stands and truck markets that will be your only choices along the Hāna Highway, you might also want to purchase a picnic lunch in Pā'ia. Nearly any restaurant in town will pack up whatever you need. **Picnics** (✉ 30 Baldwin Ave., ☎ 808/579–8021) specializes in food for the road.

If you want to do some shopping as well, Pā'ia is a friendly little town. You can find clothing and handcrafted keepsakes or snacks and sweets in abundance. Pā'ia is also home to Lama Tenzin, a Tibetan monk who lives and teaches at a small open temple called **Karma Rimay O Sal Ling**, on Baldwin Avenue half a mile from the traffic light. ✉ *Hwys. 390 and 36, north shore.*

(51) **Pi'ilanihale Heiau.** The largest prehistoric monument in Hawai'i, this temple platform was built for a great 16th-century Maui king named Pi'ilani. This king also supervised the construction of a 10-ft wide road that completely encircled the island. (That's why his name is part of most of Maui's difficult-to-pronounce highway titles.) Hawaiian families continue to maintain and protect the sacred site as they have for centuries, and they have not been eager to turn it into a tourist attraction. In 1998, however, two-hour appointment-only guided tours became available. Tours include 122-acre **Kahanu Garden**, a federally funded research center focusing on the ethnobotany of the Pacific. ✉ *Left on 'Ula'ino Rd. at Mile Marker 31,* ☎ *808/248–8912.* 🎫 *Donation.* ⏲ *By appointment.*

㊸ **Puahokamoa Stream.** The bridge over Puahokamoa Stream is the first of many you'll cross en route from Pā'ia to Hāna. It spans pools and waterfalls. Picnic tables are available, so many people favor this as a stopping point, but there are no rest rooms. ✉ *Hāna Hwy. near Mile Marker 11.*

(52) **Wai'ānapanapa State Park.** With a permit you can stay in state-run cabins here for less than $30 a night—the price varies depending on the number of people—but reserve early; they often book up a year in

advance. The park is right on the ocean, and it's a lovely spot to picnic, hike, or swim. An ancient burial site is nearby, as well as a heiau.
Wai'ānapanapa also has one of Maui's only black-sand beaches and
some freshwater caves for adventurous swimmers to explore. ⊠ *Hāna
Hwy. near Mile Marker 32, Hāna,* ☎ *808/248–8061.* 🄳 *Free.*

49 **Waikāne Falls.** Though not necessarily bigger or taller than the other
falls, these are the most dramatic—some say the best—falls you'll find
on the Road to Hāna. That's partly because the water is not diverted
for sugar irrigation; the taro farmers in Wailua need all the runoff. This
is another good spot for photos. ⊠ *Hāna Hwy. past Mile Marker 21,
Wailua.*

48 **Wailua Lookout.** From the parking lot, you can see Wailua Canyon,
but you'll have to walk up steps to get a view of Wailua Village. The
landmark in Wailua Village is a church made of coral, built in 1860.
Once called St. Gabriel's Catholic Church, the current Our Lady of
Fatima Shrine has an interesting legend surrounding it; as the story goes,
a storm washed just enough coral up onto the shore to build the
church, but then took any extra coral back to sea. ⊠ *Hāna Hwy. near
Mile Marker 21, Wailua.*

BEACHES

Maui has about 120 mi of coastline. Not all of this is beach, of course,
but Maui's striking white crescents do seem to be around every bend.
All of Hawai'i's beaches are free and open to the public—even those
that grace the front yards of fancy hotels—so you can feel free to make
yourself at home on any one of them. Blue beach-access signs indicate
right-of-ways through condominium and resort properties.

Although they don't appear often, be sure to pay attention to any signs
or warning flags on the beaches. Warnings of high surf or rough currents should be taken seriously. Before you seek shade under a swaying palm tree, watch for careening coconuts; though the trade winds
seem gentle, they are strong enough to knock the fruit off the trees and
onto your head. Also be sure to apply that sunscreen diligently. Maui
is closer to the equator than the beaches to which you're probably accustomed, so although you may think you're safe, take it from those
who've gotten a beet-red burn in 30 minutes or less—you're not.
Drinking alcoholic beverages on beaches in Hawai'i isn't allowed.

West Maui offers quite a few beach choices. If you start at the northern end of West Maui and work your way down the coast, you'll find
the beaches described below.

D. T. Fleming Beach is one of West Maui's most popular beaches. This
charming, mile-long sandy cove is better for sunbathing than for swimming, because the current can be quite strong. There are rest room facilities, including showers, picnic tables and grills, and paved parking.
⊠ *Hwy. 30 about 1 mi north of Kapalua Resort.*

On the northern side of Nāpili Bay is the smaller and even more pristine **Kapalua Beach.** You may have to share sand space with a number of other beachgoers, however, because the area is quite popular for
lazing, swimming, and snorkeling. There are showers, rest rooms, and
a paved parking lot. ⊠ *Past Bay Club restaurant off Lower Honoapi'ilani
Hwy., before Kapalua Bay Hotel.*

The lovely **Nāpili Beach** is right outside the Nāpili Kai Beach Club, a
popular little resort for honeymooners. This sparkling white crescent
makes a perfect cove for strolling and sunbathing. Despite condo-

miniums and other development around the bay, the only facilities available here are showers at the far right end of the beach, and a low tap by the beach-access entrance where you can wash the sand off your feet, but you're only a few miles south of Kapalua. ⊠ *5900 Lower Honoapiʻilani Hwy., from upper highway follow cutoff road closest to Kapalua Resort and look for Nāpili Pl. or Hui Dr.*

Honokōwai Beach is a bust if you're looking for that classic Hawaiian stretch of sand. Still, children will enjoy the lawn area and rocks that have formed a pool. This beach, in the midst of condominium row, does have rest rooms, showers, picnic tables, and paved parking. ⊠ *3636 Lower Honoapiʻilani Rd., across from Honokōwai Superette.*

Fronting the big hotels at Kāʻanapali is one of Maui's best people-watching spots, **Kāʻanapali Beach.** This is not the beach if you're looking for peace and quiet, but if you want lots of action, lay out your towel here. Cruises, windsurfers, and parasailers head out from this beach while the beautiful people take in the scenery. Although no facilities are available, the nearby hotels have rest rooms and some, like the Marriott, have outdoor showers. You're also close to plenty of shops and concessions. ⊠ *Follow any of 3 Kāʻanapali exits from Honoapiʻilani Hwy., and park at any of the hotels.*

South of Lahaina at Mile Marker 14 are the narrow stretches of white sand known as **Olowalu Beaches,** a swimming and snorkeling haven. There's no parking here—people just pull off the road—and there are no facilities except a small general store nearby where you can get a soda, but it's one of Maui's best sandy spots. With mask and fins, you'll see yellow tangs, parrot fish, and sometimes the state fish, the *humuhumunukunukuāpuaʻa.* You can call it a humu, if you like. ⊠ *Hwy. 30, Mile Marker 14, south of Lahaina.*

Farther south of Olowalu, you'll find **Wailea's five crescent beaches,** which stretch for nearly 2 mi with relatively little interruption by civilization. Several hotels call Wailea home, and more condominiums are under construction. So far, the buildings haven't infringed on the beaches in a noticeable way. With any luck, the population boom won't affect this area either. Swimming is good here; the crescents protect the shoreline from rough surf. Few people populate these beaches—mostly hotel guests who have briefly forsaken the pools of the nearby lodgings—which makes Wailea a peaceful haven. Rest rooms and showers are available. ⊠ *Drive south of Kilei, along western shore of East Maui.*

Just south of Wailea is the town of **Mākena,** with two good beaches. **Big Beach** is 3,000 ft long and 100 ft wide. The water off Big Beach is fine for swimming and snorkeling, and you'll find showers, rest rooms, and paved parking here. If you walk over the cinder cone at Big Beach, you'll reach **Little Beach,** which is used for nude sunbathing. Officially, nude sunbathing is illegal in Hawaiʻi, but several bathers who've pushed their arrests through the courts have found their cases dismissed. Understand, though, that you take your chances if you decide to indulge in this favorite local practice at Little Mākena.

If you're staying in the Central Maui area, try **Kanahā Beach** in Kahului. A long, golden strip of sand bordered by a wide grassy area, this is a popular spot for windsurfers, joggers, and picnicking Maui families. Kanahā Beach has toilets, showers, picnic tables, and grills. ⊠ *Drive through the airport and back out to the car-rental road (Koeheke), turn right, and keep going.*

If you want to see some of the world's finest windsurfers, stop at **Hoʻokipa Beach** on the Hāna Highway. The sport has become an art—

and a career, to some—and its popularity was largely developed right at Hoʻokipa. This is also one of Maui's hottest surfing spots. Waves get as high as 15 ft. This is not a good swimming beach, nor the place to learn windsurfing yourself, but plenty of picnic tables and barbecue grills are available for hanging out. ⊠ *Hwy. 36, 1 mi past Pāʻia.*

In Hāna, **Kōkī Beach** offers unusully good bodysurfing because the sandy bottom stays shallow for a long way out. There are no facilities here, but the spot is rich in Hawaiian lore. It sits beneath a prominent cinder cone called Ka Iwi O Pele ("Pele's Bone"), and the small island off shore, ʻĀlau Island, is the place where the demigod Mauī fished the Hawaiian islands out of the sea. Watch conditions; the riptide here can be mean. Just down the road is the beach James Michener called the best in the Pacific—crescent-shape **Hāmoa Beach.** Park on the roadside and walk down either one of the steep paths. Hotel Hāna-Maui keeps facilities here for its guests but has politely included a shower and rest room for the public. ⊠ *Haneoʻo Loop Rd., 2 mi east of Hāna town.*

DINING

Some, but not all, of the island's best restaurants are in hotels—not surprising, considering that tourism is the island's number-one industry. In the resorts you'll find some of Maui's finest Continental restaurants and some good coffee shops as well. In addition, because many of the upscale hotels sit right on the beach, you'll often have the benefit of an oceanfront ambience.

Except as noted, reservations are not required at Maui restaurants, but it's never a bad idea to phone ahead to book a table. Restaurants are open daily unless otherwise noted.

Few restaurants on Maui require jackets. An aloha shirt and pants for men and a simple dress or pants for women are acceptable in all but the fanciest establishments. For price category explanations, *see* On the Road with Fodor's at the beginning of the book.

West Maui

American

$$–$$$ ✕ **Longhi's.** This Lahaina establishment has been around since 1976,
    ★   serving great Italian pasta as well as sandwiches, seafood, beef, and chicken dishes. All the pasta is homemade and the in-house bakery is constantly busy preparing breakfast pastries, desserts, and hot-out-of-the-oven bread. Longhi's is the only restaurant on Maui to win *Wine Spectator*'s prestigious Best Award of Excellence. Even on a warm day, you won't need air-conditioning here with two spacious, breezy, open-air levels to choose from. The black-and-white tile floors are a nice touch. ⊠ *888 Front St., Lahaina,* ☎ *808/667–2288. AE, D, DC, MC, V.*

$–$$ ✕ **Lahaina Coolers.** This breezy little café with a surfboard hanging
   ★   from its ceiling serves up such tantalizing fare as shrimp pesto linguine with prawns, basil, garlic, and cream; and Evil Jungle Pasta (grilled chicken in spicy Thai peanut sauce), as well as pizzas, steaks, burgers, and such desserts as a chocolate taco filled with tropical fruit and berry salsa. Pastas are made fresh in-house. Don't be surprised to see a local fisherman walk through the dining area with a freshly caught snapper, or a harbor captain reeling in a hearty breakfast. ⊠ *180 Dickenson St., Lahaina,* ☎ *808/661–7082. AE, MC, V.*

Continental

$$$–$$$$ ✕ **Swan Court.** You enter this elegant eatery via a grand staircase and
     ★   what seems like a tropical, cathedral-ceiling ballroom, where black and

white swans glide across a waterfall-fed lagoon. The menu applies European and Pacific Rim flavors to fresh, locally grown vegetables, seafood, and meats. Try the crispy scallop dim sum (a type of wonton) in plum sauce; creamy lobster coconut bisque brimming with chunks of fish, lobster, shrimp, and button mushrooms; or charbroiled lamb chops in macadamia satay sauce. Arrive early and ask for a table on the left side, where the swans linger in the evening. The restaurant is also open for a breakfast buffet. ⊠ *Hyatt Regency Maui, Kā'anapali Beach Resort, 200 Nohea Kai Dr., Lahaina,* ☎ *808/661–1234. AE, D, DC, MC, V.*

$$–$$$$ ✕ **Bay Club.** A candle-lit dinner at this lovely spot on a rocky promon-
★ tory overlooking the ocean is a romantic way to cap off a fun-filled day in the sun, especially if you've been swimming at crescent-shape Kapalua beach just a few yards from the door. However, you won't want to bring sandy feet into the richly paneled, casually elegant interior. Anything on the menu is recommended, especially the fresh catch of the day. For a truly relaxing evening with a view, lean back, sip a glass of cabernet or Riesling from the excellent wine list, and watch the sun slip gloriously past the Maui horizon. ⊠ *Kapalua Bay Hotel, 1 Bay Dr., Kapalua,* ☎ *808/669–5656. AE, D, DC, MC, V.*

French

$$$–$$$$ ✕ **Gerard's.** The French are famous for their exquisite food prepara-
★ tion and savory sauces. This charming establishment has honored that tradition since it opened in 1982. Owner and celebrated chef Gerard Reversade started cooking at the age of 10, and at 12 was baking croissants from scratch. Now he prepares rack of lamb with poached garlic; medallions of venison with pepper sauce, and fish so fresh it's almost wriggling. The menu changes once a year, but many favorites—such as the sinfully good crème brûlée—remain. If you should see Michael Jordan or Robert Redford dining at a nearby table, pretend not to notice. ⊠ *Plantation Inn, 174 Lahainaluna Rd., Lahaina,* ☎ *808/661–8939. AE, D, DC, MC, V.* ☉ *No lunch.*

$$–$$$$ ✕ **Chez Paul.** Since 1975 this tiny roadside restaurant between Lahaina
★ and Ma'alaea in Olowalu has been serving excellent classical French cuisine, such as fresh island fish poached in white wine with shallots, cream, and capers, to a packed house of repeat customers. The nondescript building belies the fine art, 14 linen-draped tables, the 22-seat private dinng room, the wine cellar, and charming atmosphere inside. Don't blink or you'll miss this small group of buildings huddled in the middle of nowhere. ⊠ *Hwy. 30, 4 mi south of Lahaina,* ☎ *808/661–3843. Reservations essential. AE, D, MC, V.* ☉ *No lunch.*

Hawai'i Regional/Pacific Rim

$$$–$$$$ ✕ **'Ānuenue Room.** In Hawaiian, ānuenue means "rainbow." It's an apt name for the Ritz-Carlton's signature restaurant where you may be lucky enough to catch a rainbow arcing over the ocean. In the meantime, you can enjoy a rainbow of such menu choices as caramelized salmon in orange shoyu glaze, seared veal filet mignon with black truffle risotto, or Dungeness crab cakes. Service is excellent, as you might expect at the Ritz. ⊠ *Ritz-Carlton, Kapalua, 1 Ritz-Carlton Dr., Kapalua,* ☎ *808/669–1665. AE, D, DC, MC, V.*

$$–$$$$ ✕ **David Paul's Lahaina Grill.** When Crazy Shirts magnate Rick Ralston was looking for a chef to open a new restaurant in Lahaina in 1990, David Paul wasn't interested—until he saw the location in the romantic, Victorian-era Lahaina Hotel, which Ralston had restored. Since then, the popular restaurant has expanded twice, and offers a well stocked wine cellar, in-house bakery, wine and cheese tastings on weekdays from 5 to 6, piano stylings on a baby grand in the lounge, and free "Fear of Cooking" classes. The award-winning menu is re-

124

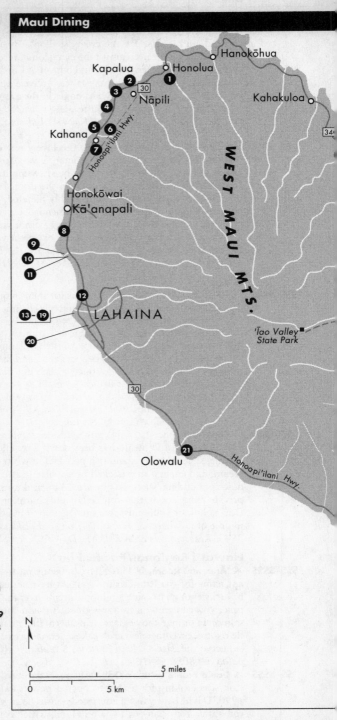

Maui Dining

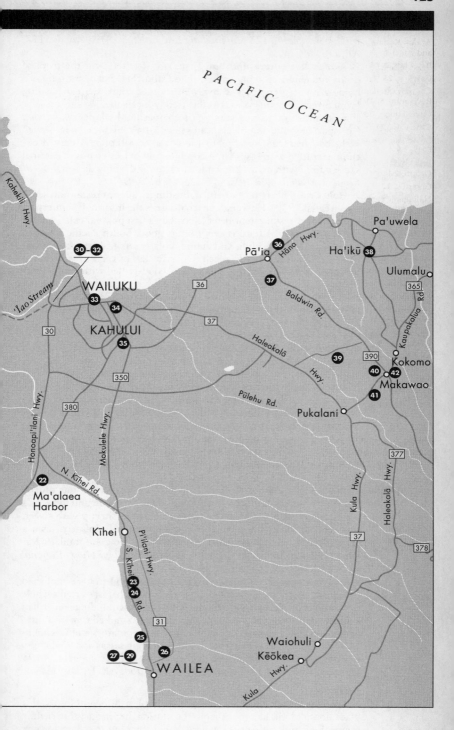

PACIFIC OCEAN

Kahekili Hwy.

Pa'uwela

30 – 32

Pā'ia 36

Hana Hwy.

Ha'ikū 38

Ulumalu

'Iao Stream

WAILUKU

36

37

Baldwin Rd.

365

Kaupakalua Rd.

33

34

37

Haleakalā

390

Kokomo

30

KAHULUI

35

39

40 42

Makawao

350

Hwy.

41

Pūlehu Rd.

Pukalani

380

Honoapi'ilani Hwy.

Mokulele Hwy.

377

N. Kīhei Rd.

22

Kula Hwy.

Haleakalā Hwy.

Ma'alaea
Harbor

Kīhei

Pi'ilani Hwy.

37

378

S. Kīhei Rd.

23
24

31

25

Waiohuli

27 29

26

Kēōkea

WAILEA

Kula Hwy.

Kula

vised seasonally, but you can count on finding the signature tequila shrimp and firecracker rice along with such scrumptious desserts as triple-berry pie. ✉ *127 Lahainaluna Rd., Lahaina,* ☎ *808/667–5117. AE, DC, MC, V.*

$$–$$$ ✕ **Avalon Restaurant and Bar.** Ferns and fronds form the tropical
★   decor and lend a relaxing ambiance to California chef Mark Ellman's home-grown eatery, tucked away in a quiet courtyard off bustling Front Street. Signature items at this trendy locale include shrimp with shiitake mushrooms and sundried tomatoes; and whole *'ōpakapaka* (snapper) in garlic and black bean sauce. Don't miss the "new wave" sushi bar, featuring such innovations as the lollipop: A carved cucumber stuffed with raw fish. A combination of fresh fruits in caramel sauce paired with macadamia nut ice cream is the only dessert. ✉ *844 Front St., Lahaina,* ☎ *808/667–5559. AE, D, DC, MC, V.*

$$–$$$ ✕ **Hula Grill.** This family-oriented, bustling, 300-seat restaurant set in a re-created 1930's Hawaiian beach house is the informal counterpart to genial chef-restaurateur Peter Merriman's first popular eatery on the Big Island, and the food is every bit as good. South Pacific snapper, baked with tomato, chili, and cumin aioli, is served with black bean, Maui onion, and avocado relish. Or try a slab of spare ribs, steamed imu-style in banana leaves, then kiawe wood-grilled with mango barbecue sauce. Every table has an ocean-beach view, or you can actually dine on the beach, toes in the sand, at the Barefoot Bar where Hawaiian entertainment is presented every evening. ✉ *Whalers Village, 2435 Kā'anapali Pkwy., Kā'anapali,* ☎ *808/667–6636. AE, DC, MC, V.*

$$–$$$ ✕ **Plantation House Restaurant.** It's hard to decide which is best here, the food or the view. Rolling hills, grassy volcanic ridges lined with pine trees, and fairways that appear to drop off into the ocean provide an idyllic setting for such entrées as duck breast "under the influence" of cabernet-port reduction sauce, roasted Moloka'i pork chops with mushroom-mashed potatoes and caramelized Maui onion sauce, and fresh fish charbroiled on soba noodles and vegetable stir-fry with ginger-sesame broth. This high up in the West Maui mountains, the breeze through the restaurant's large shuttered windows can be cool, so you may want to bring a sweater, or sit by the fireplace. ✉ *Plantation Course Clubhouse, 2000 Plantation Club Dr., past Kapalua,* ☎ *808/669–6299. AE, MC, V.*

$$–$$$ ✕ **Roy's Kahana Bar & Grill.** Anyone who's ever eaten at one of Roy Yamaguchi's restaurants knows how good the cuisine is, and this Roy's is no exception. Such Asian-Pacific specialties as shrimp with sweet, spicy chili sauce keep regulars returning for more. Locals say this is a great place to get together with friends for fun and good food. ✉ *Kahana Gateway Shopping Center, 4405 Honoapi'ilani Hwy., Kahana,* ☎ *808/669–6999. AE, D, DC, MC, V.*

$$ ✕ **Roy Yamaguchi's Nicolina.** Instead of adding on to his established restaurant next door, innovative chef Roy Yamaguchi just started a whole new restaurant that caters to the spice-loving crowd. Indulge on grilled southwestern-style chicken with chili hash and smoked tomato sauce, or smoked and peppered duck with ginger sweet potatoes and Szechuan-Mandarin sauce. You may even find some zippy salsas and a jalapeño pepper or two. ✉ *Kahana Gateway Shopping Center, 4405 Honoapi'ilani Hwy., Kahana,* ☎ *808/669–5000. AE, D, DC, MC, V.*

Italian

$–$$ ✕ **Scaroles Ristorante.** A longtime favorite of visitors and locals, this place doesn't look like much from the outside, but inside, the friendly atmosphere and authentic northern Italian cooking make up for any lack of chic and draw plenty of loyal fans. In fact, some customers have complained that the bustling place is too small and that squeezing in like a sardine, Italian-style, is no fun. The pasta, chicken, veal, and seafood dishes are all worthy choices, as is the ricotta cheesecake for dessert. They'll even allow you to bring your own libations. ✉ *930 Waine'e St., Lahaina*, ☎ *808/661–4466. Reservations essential. D, DC, MC, V.*

Japanese

$–$$ ✕ **Nikko.** Fourteen table-top grills are the performing stages for knife-wielding chefs demonstrating the ancient art of Teppanyaki cooking. Meat and seafood are their tasty targets, and outstanding fare is your reward for watching the show at this oceanview restaurant. "Samurai Sunset" early dinner specials are served from 6 to 6:30. ✉ *Maui Marriott Hotel, Ka̅'anapali Beach Resort, 100 Nohea Kai Dr., Ka̅'anapali*, ☎ *808/667–1200. AE, D, DC, MC, V.*

Mexican-American

$–$$ ✕ **Aloha Cantina.** Masses of Mexican-theme posters and artifacts hang on the walls while simulated palm tree trunks hold up a fake leafy ceiling sparkling with hot-pepper-shape tree lights. On your first breakfast visit try a stack of macadamia nut pancakes covered with coconut syrup. For lunch, order the grilled snapper paired with white wine sauce and coleslaw and wrapped in a flour tortilla—in other words, a fish taco. It's a hit. Also on the varied Maui Mex-American menu you'll find a Mexican pizza, a jalapeño garden burger, a chicken Caesar taco, Thai Cobb salad, and tortilla soup. Worth several visits. ✉ *839 Front St., Lahaina*, ☎ *808/661–8788. AE, MC, V.*

Seafood

$$–$$$ ✕ **Erik's Seafood Grotto.** This seafood diner is so proud of its large selection of fresh fish, it displays the whole offering nightly as a photo opportunity. Additional house specialties include bouillabaisse chock full of clams, scallops, lobster, shrimp, and fish and served with toasted garlic bread; and *cioppino*, a seafood stew served over homemade fettuccine. A stop at the oyster bar is a worthwhile detour: Try half-shells topped with horseradish mayonnaise and baked with Gruyère cheese. Come to this nautical spot between 5 and 6 and catch the $12.95–$13.95 early-bird specials. ✉ *Kahana Villas, 4242 Lower Honoapi'ilani Hwy., Kahana*, ☎ *808/669–4806. AE, D, DC, MC, V.*

$$–$$$ ✕ **Pacific'O.** You can sit outdoors at umbrella-shaded tables a few feet from the water's edge, or find a spot inside Pacific'O's light and breezy interior. With protective reefs to keep the swelling seas nearby at bay, it's easy to see why this spot was chosen by King Kamehameha the Great as his personal playground. He would have enjoyed the cuisine, too, which includes the Asian, Polynesian, and European flavors of such delectables as shrimp and basil wonton, banana imu-style fish with vanilla bean sauce, 'ahi parfait with passion fruit dressing, and marinated scallops and shrimps seared with red Thai curry and coconut milk sauce. Live jazz is also on the menu Thursday through Saturday nights from 9 to midnight. ✉ *505 Front St., Lahaina*, ☎ *808/667–4341. AE, D, DC, MC, V.*

$$ ✕ **Lokelani.** Here you'll find elegant dining with attentive service in a
★ relaxed garden-style atmosphere. The chefs do a standout job melding traditional preparations with Asian and Polynesian flavors. The result includes such appetizers as Asian shrimp stuffed with spicy crab meat in sweet Thai sauce and banana salsa; 'ahi tempura with ginger shiitake mushrooms; and grilled Muscovy duck summer rolls filled with papaya, basil, and kaiware sprouts in sweet Thai chili sauce. The menu suggests the perfect wine for each dish, including such desserts as chocolate macadamia nut–cream cheese pie and coffee crème brûlée. ✉ *Maui Marriott, 100 Nohea Kai Dr., Ka̅'anapali*, ☎ *808/667–1200, ext. 51. AE, D, DC, MC, V.*

$–$$ ✕ **Kimo's.** Outstanding seafood is just one of the options here. Also good are Hawaiian-style chicken and pork dishes, burgers, sandwiches, vegetarian pasta, and sashimi. The smoked marlin appetizer is especially tasty. On a warm Lahaina summer day, it's a treat to relax at an umbrella-shaded table on the open-air lānai, sip a pineapple-passion-guava fruit drink, and watch sailboats and parasailers glide in and out of the harbor. Try the signature dessert, Hula Pie: vanilla macadamia nut ice cream topped with chocolate fudge and whipped cream in an Oreo-cookie crust. ✉ *845 Front St., Lahaina,* ☎ *808/661–4811. AE, DC, MC, V.*

Thai

$–$$ ✕ **Orient Express.** Have your Thai food and enjoy it too—hot, medium, or mild—at this decidedly Asian locale with red lacquer and yellow flowers evident everywhere. Eating Thai is always an adventure with such menu choices as beef strips marinated in coconut milk and spices, skewered on bamboo sticks and grilled, or shrimp cooked with bamboo shoots, water chestnuts, and dried chilies. ✉ *Nāpili Shores Resort, 5316 Lower Honoapi'ilani Hwy., Nāpili,* ☎ *808/669–8077.* ◷ *No lunch. AE, MC, V.*

Central Maui

Italian

$$ ✕ **Marco's Grill & Deli.** This convenient eatery outside the Kahului airport is home to some of the best-priced and best-tasting Italian fare on Maui. Fettuccine alfredo, linguine with sausage, and vodka rigatoni are all on the extensive menu, along with an unforgettably good Reuben sandwich and the best Greek salad you'll ever find. The local business crowd fills the place for breakfast, lunch, and dinner; it's become so popular that a second Marco's will open in Kīhei by press time. Look for the green awning. ✉ *444 Hāna Hwy., Kahului,* ☎ *808/877-4446. AE, D, DC, MC, V.*

Japanese

$ ✕ **Restaurant Matsu.** The Maui Mall can appear pretty deserted with so many folks opting for the multilevel Ka'ahumanu Shopping Center a few blocks away, but that doesn't mean there aren't some gems here. This tiny, nondescript kitchen and lunchroom is one of them. Its authentic Japanese fare is well-known to local residents who come for the sushi, noodles, soup, tempura vegetables, and fish entrées served over the counter daily. ✉ *Maui Mall, Ka'ahumanu Ave., Kahului,* ☎ *808/871-0822. No credit cards.*

Steak

$$–$$$ ✕ **Chart House.** Of the three Chart House locations, this one gets the best reviews from locals. Overlooking Kahului Harbor and decorated with the model ships, boat hulls, and surf prints expected of a harborside steak house, this branch offers big lunch portions and hearty fish, steaks, and prime rib dinners—along with their famous mud pie dessert. ✉ *500 N. Pu'unēnē Ave., Kahului,* ☎ *808/877-2476. AE, D, MC, V.*

Thai

$-$$ ✕ **Saeng's Thai Cuisine.** Making a choice from the six-page menu here requires determination, but the food is worth the effort, and most dishes can be tailored to your taste buds: hot, medium, or mild. Begin with spring rolls and a dipping sauce; move on to such entrées as Evil Prince Chicken (cooked in coconut sauce with Thai herbs) or red curry shrimp, and finish up with tea and tapioca pudding. The dining room is decorated with Asian artifacts, flowers, and a waterfall, and tables on a veranda will satisfy outdoor lovers. ⊠ *2119 Vineyard, Wailuku,* ☎ *808/244–1567. AE, MC, V.*

$-$$ ✕ **Siam Thai.** Behind a somewhat weathered storefront you'll find some of the best Thai food on Maui. This local favorite serves traditional chicken-coconut soup, beef and chicken sautéed with ginger and bamboo shoots, curries, and vegetarian dishes—about 60 selections in all. The food tends to be spicy, the portions small, and huge crowds arrive at lunchtime. Some patrons opt for takeout because there's not much in the way of decor. ⊠ *123 Market St., Wailuku,* ☎ *808/244–3817. AE, D, DC, MC, V.*

Vietnamese

$-$$ ✕ **A Saigon Café.** The only storefront sign announcing this small, delightful hideaway is one reading OPEN. Once you find it, treat yourself to *banh hoi chao tom,* more commonly called shrimp pops burritos (ground marinated shrimp, steamed and grilled on a stick of sugarcane). It's fun and messy. You might also be in the mood for vegetarian fare. They have that, too. The interior is decorated in white with Vietnamese carvings and other interesting artwork. ⊠ *1792 Main St., Wailuku,* ☎ *808/243–9560. D, MC, V.*

East Maui

American

$$-$$$ ✕ **Joe's Bar & Grill.** With friendly service, a great view of Lāna'i and such dishes as New York steak with caramelized onions, wild mushrooms, and Gorgonzola cheese crumble, there are lots of reasons to stop in at this spacious, breezy spot. Owners Joe and Bev Gannon, who run the immensely popular Hāli'imaile General Store, have brought their flair for food home to roost in this treetop-level restaurant at the Wailea Tennis Club, where you can dine in comfort while watching exciting court action from a front-row balcony seat. ⊠ *131 Wailea Ike Pl., Wailea,* ☎ *808/875–7767. AE, MC, V.*

$-$$ ✕ **Hapa's Brewhaus & Restaurant.** Maui's newest microbrewery has such lagers as Maui Moonset, Paradise Pale, and Black Lava on tap; a comprehensive selection of wines; and an assortment of great eats that includes pizza, calzones, pastas, chicken-teriyaki burgers, vegetarian stir-fry, sashimi, and lobster bisque. The roomy facility also has a game room with one pool table and some dart boards, and live entertainment from 9:30 to 1 Monday through Saturday. ⊠ *Lipoa Center, 41 E. Lipoa St., Kīhei,* ☎ *808/879–9001. D, DC, MC, V.*

$-$$ ✕ **Sandcastle at Wailea.** Tucked away in the middle of the Wailea Shopping Village, this convenient eatery serves tasty burgers and fries, creative salads, and hefty sandwiches in an indoor garden-style setting that is surprisingly secluded considering the bustling shopping activity outside. ⊠ *3750 Wailea Alanui, Wailea,* ☎ *808/879–0606. D, MC, V.*

Continental/Tropical

$$$$ ✕ **Seasons.** Acclaimed executive chef George Mavrothalassitis prepares standout dishes that marry fresh Island ingredients with flavors from Provence (Chef Mavro's homeland), China, Japan, Thailand, and the Pacific islands. Sensational ocean vistas add to the delicious ambience.

✉ *Four Seasons Resort Maui, 3900 Wailea Alanui, Wailea,* ☎ *808/ 874–8000. AE, D, DC, MC, V.* ⊘ *No lunch.*

Hawai'i Regional/Pacific Rim

$$–$$$ ✕ **Hāli'imaile General Store.** What do you do with a lofty wooden build-
★ ing that used to be a camp store in the 1920s and is surrounded by a
tiny town in the middle of sugarcane and pineapple fields? If you're
Bev Gannon, you turn it into a legendary Island fine-dining tradition.
The Szechuan barbecued salmon and rack of lamb Hunan-style are classics. For a filling and innovative appetizer, try a sashimi napoleon, a
tower of crispy wonton layered with smoked salmon. The outstanding house salad is topped with Maui onions, mandarin oranges, wal-
nuts, and crumbled blue cheese on request. ✉ *900 Hāli'imaile Rd., left
at the exit off Hwy. 37, 5 mi from the Hānā Hwy., Hali'imaile,* ☎ *808/
572–2666. MC, V.*

$$–$$$ ✕ **Hula Moons.** This delightful oceanside spot is full of memorabilia
chronicling the Island life of Don Blanding, a writer, artist, and poet
who became Hawai'i's unofficial ambassador of aloha. The outstanding
menu blends fresh, locally grown produce with Pacific Rim and European preparations. Try the scallops with Chinese black bean sauce,
charbroiled T-bone steak with pineapple compote and Moloka'i sweet
potatoes, or a just-off-the-boat fresh catch of the day. You can dine inside, poolside, or outside on the terrace while you choose your vintage
from an extensive wine list. ✉ *Aston Wailea Resort, 3700 Wailea
Alanui, Wailea,* ☎ *808/879–1922. AE, D, DC, MC, V.*

$$–$$$ ✕ **A Pacific Cafe.** Hawai'i Regional cuisine, the culinary edge in the
★ Islands these days, began with a few innovative Island chefs, such as
Jean-Marie Josselin, whose creations are now served by four establishments. Such flavor combinations as pan-seared mahimahi with
garlic, a sesame crust, and lime-ginger sauce; roasted duck with garlic-mashed potatoes and sundried-cherry and star anise sauce; and
seared scallops in crisp polenta crust with caramel sauce and seared
corn and avocado salsa are just some of the mouthwatering choices.
The restaurant's tropical, whimsical decor has been described as "the
Flintstones meet the Jetsons." ✉ *Azeka Place II Shopping Center,
1279 S. Kīhei Rd., Kīhei,* ☎ *808/879–0069. AE, D, DC, MC, V.* ⊘
No lunch.

Italian

$$$–$$$$ ✕ **Carelli's.** Dine beachside with the sound of gentle waves washing
the shore, while sampling steamed clams in white wine, butter, and gar-
lic; pasta stuffed with lobster in lemon-basil cream sauce; or chicken
breast stuffed with ricotta cheese and organic spinach. Carelli's is a
gourmet's delight, but if you'd like to know how good the cuisine here
really is, just ask some of the customers: Jack Nicholson, Goldie Hawn,
and Joe Montana, to name a few. ✉ *2980 S. Kīhei Rd., Keawakapu,*
☎ *808/875–0001. Reservations essential. AE, MC, V.*

$$–$$$ ✕ **Casanova Italian Restaurant & Deli.** In true Italian style, congenial
co-owner Steven Burgelin is on hand most evenings to greet and chat
up guests at this neighborhood spot on the slopes of Haleakalā. If you're
pining for pasta, imagine chicken and porcini mushrooms stuffed into
bite-size ravioli and topped with a sage butter sauce, or ricotta and
spinach dumplings languishing in a creamy Gorgonzola sauce. Another
savory flavor here is pizza cooked in a brick, wood-burning oven im-

ported from Italy. Don't even try to resist such desserts as flourless chocolate mousse cake with raspberry sauce. Casanova is also known for
it's extra-large dance floor and entertainment by well-known Island
and mainland musicians(☞ Nightlife, *below*). ⊠ *1188 Makawao Ave.,
Makawao,* ☎ *808/572–0220. D, DC, MC, V.*

$$–$$$ ✕ **Trattoria Ha'ikū.** The rural hills of Tuscany and the leafy gulches of
Ha'ikū not only look alike but, with the opening of this classy little
country dinner house, they now taste alike, too. The understated theater of this jungle discovery—with its white linens, splashing fountains,
and graceful tuxedo-shirted waiters—does a wonderful job of inter-
preting the classic Italian *trattoria,* or family-operated inn. Ingredients
are regional (vegetables from local contract gardens, fresh-catch Maui
fish, herbs from the restaurant's own garden). The preparation is simple and delicious (as odd as it sounds, the spaghetti-and-meatballs is
unforgettable). And the portions are generous (their special cut for steak
Florentine would please two lumberjacks). House wines, a good Chi-
anti and Pinot Grigio, are served the Italian way—in 5-ounce juice glasses.
The house itself is actually a renovated mess hall, built in the 1920s,
for workers at the adjacent pineapple cannery. ⊠ *Olde Ha'ikū Cannery, corner of Ha'ikū and Kokomo Rds.,* ☎ *808/575–2820. MC, V.*

Mexican

$–$$ ✕ **Polli's.** This Mexican restaurant in the paniolo town of Makawao
★ not only has a wide selection of such delicious taste treats as seafood
enchiladas, chimichangas, quesadillas, and fajitas, but also offers to
prepare any item on the menu with seasoned tofu or vegetarian taco
mix instead of meat—and the meatless dishes are just as good. A special treat are the *bunuelos*—light pastries topped with cinnamon,
maple syrup, and a scoop of ice cream. The intimate interior plastered
with colorful sombreros and other knickknacks will make you think
you've wandered into a south-of-the-border cantina. ⊠ *1202 Makawao
Ave., Makawao,* ☎ *808/572–7808. AE, D, DC, MC, V.*

Seafood

$$–$$$$ ✕ **Ma'alaea Waterfront Restaurant.** At this harborside establishment
★ fresh fish is prepared in a host of sumptuous ways: Baked in buttered
parchment paper; imprisoned in ribbons of angel hair potato; or topped
with tomato salsa, smoked chili pepper, and avocado. Tourists come
early to dine at sunset on the outdoor patio. The varied menu also of-
fers outstanding rack of lamb and veal scallopini. Pass the Maui Ocean
Center and veer left into Ma'alaea Village, then follow the blue WA-
TERFRONT RESTAURANT signs to the third condominium. ⊠ *50 Hau'oli
St., Ma'alaea,* ☎ *808/244–9028. AE, D, DC, MC, V.*

$$–$$$ ✕ **Mama's Fish House.** As you enjoy the landscaped grounds and
★ ocean views at this cliff-top restaurant, check out the stone path en-
graved with whimsical Hawaiian geckos. But the real treat here is the
fish, prepared in seven mouthwatering ways—baked in a creamy herb
sauce, sautéed with macadamia nuts, or grilled with spicy wasabi but-
ter, for example. That's why this thatched-hut restaurant with a Hawai-
ian nautical theme is packed every evening. The chicken, steak, and
kālua pig dishes are worth trying, as well. About 1½ mi east of Pa'ia
on the Hāna Highway, look for Mama's classic '40s-era Ford trucks
parked on grassy knolls at both entrances; self parking and valet. ⊠

799 Poho Pl., Kū'au, ☎ 808/579–8488. Reservations essential. AE, D, DC, MC, V.

Steak
$$ ✕ **Makawao Steak House.** Where better to go for great steaks than ranch country. This paniolo restaurant, nestled in a restored house that was built in 1927 on the slopes of Haleakalā, serves downright good prime rib, rack of lamb, and fresh fish with consistency you can count on and friendly service. Three fireplaces and an intimate lounge create a cozy, welcoming atmosphere. ✉ *3612 Baldwin Ave., Makawao,* ☎ *808/572–8711. D, DC, MC, V.* ⊘ *No lunch.*

Picnics

On Maui you'll find plenty of secluded spots for a laptop lunch for two. Also, if you're on your way to Haleakalā or Hāna, you might want to take a picnic along. Many hotels will prepare the essentials for you, or try one of these Maui delis:

Casanova Italian Restaurant & Deli (✉ 1188 Makawao Ave., Makawao, ☎ 808/572–0220) packs Italian specialties for the road, for the beach, or for back at the condo, from 8:30 AM to 6:30 PM.

Picnics (✉ 30 Baldwin Ave., Pā'ia, ☎ 808/579–8021) has experience and style when preparing lunch for the road. Their carry-out meals start at $8 per person. A $50 extravaganza for two–four people comes in a basket with cooler, tablecloth, and a "Road to Hāna" cassette.

LODGING

Maui has the highest percentage of upscale hotel rooms in the state, and the island has the highest average accommodation cost of any Hawaiian island—the average lodging rate on Maui can run as much as $70 more per night than on the other Islands. Maui also has the state's highest concentration of condominium units. Many are oceanfront and offer the ambience of a hotel suite without the cost. Most lodgings have outdoor swimming pools.

The county hasn't officially sanctioned B&Bs, not wanting to siphon business from the hotels. However, they exist, and they exist now in such numbers that county officials have begun to struggle, a bit too late, to define, organize, and regulate them. Many have their units in separate guest houses, which allow privacy while still giving you a chance to get to know your hosts, and many offer a secluded retreat on the cool, Upcountry slopes of Haleakalā. Rates for most B&Bs range from $35 a night to as much as $150. For more information about Maui B&Bs and condos, *see* Bed and Breakfasts *or* Rental Agencies *in* Maui A to Z.

What you'll pay depends in part on where you want to stay. West Maui is the center of tourism, with more rooms available here than elsewhere on the island; most are high-quality and expensive. Two major resort areas anchor West Maui: the Kā'anapali Beach Resort, with its six hotels and seven condominiums, and the Kapalua Bay Resort, with two hotels and several condo complexes.

East Maui is a mixed bag when it comes to accommodations. You can find just about any rate and just about any degree of comfort. That's partly because the area is so huge, encompassing the Wailea and Mākena resorts along the southwestern shore; Kīhei, a hodgepodge strip running north from Wailea (Kīhei is especially popular with families vacationing from other islands, it's easy for children to find playmates by the pool); Upcountry Maui, the area that rises into the clouds of Haleakalā; and Hāna, secluded in the easternmost part of Maui. For price category explanations, *see* On the Road with Fodor's at the beginning of the book.

West Maui

$$$$ ★ 🏨 **Embassy Vacation Resort.** This all-suite hotel with spacious one- and two-bedroom suites may be Maui's best-kept secret. Rooms are decorated in olive and tan. Inviting touches include an oversize bathroom with large soaking tub and glass-enclosed shower, a minikitchen, an entertainment center, and wicker chaise longues. Guest privileges to a nearby 18-hole golf course and tennis courts are also included, and the hotel has a rooftop 18-hole miniature golf course. ✉ *104 Kā'anapali Shores Pl., Lahaina 96761,* ☎ *808/661–2000 or 800/462–6284,* ℻ *808/667–5821. 413 suites. 3 restaurants, fans, in-room modem lines, in-room VCRs, pool, hot tub, exercise room, beach, shops, video games, children's program (ages 4–10), coin laundry, airport shuttle (West Maui airport only). AE, D, DC, MC, V.*

$$$$ 🏨 **Hyatt Regency Maui.** A recent $16 million face-lift upgraded public spaces and guest rooms, improved access for people with disabilities, and added some new facilities—an outdoor Jacuzzi, a wedding gazebo, and a beachfront bar—to this renowned Maui fantasyland filled with art, waterfalls, and a collection of exotic animals, including penguins. ✉ *Kā'anapali Beach Resort, 200 Nohea Kai Dr., Lahaina 96761,* ☎ *808/661–1234 or 800/233–1234,* ℻ *808/667–4499. 815 rooms. 4 restaurants, 6 bars, in-room safes, 12 no-smoking floors, pool, 2 golf courses, 6 tennis courts, health club, beach, shops, library, children's program (ages 3–12), chapel. AE, D, DC, MC, V.*

⚹ $$$$ 🏨 **Kā'anapali Ali'i.** Yes, this is a condominium, but you'd never know it; the four 11-story buildings are put together so well you still have the feeling of seclusion. Instead of tiny rooms, you can choose between one- and two-bedroom apartments. Each features lovely amenities: a chaise in an alcove, a bidet, a sunken living room, a whirlpool, oak kitchen cabinets, and a separate dining room. Run by a company called Classic Resorts, the Kā'anapali Ali'i is maintained like a hotel—with daily maid service, an activities desk, and a 24-hour front desk. ✉ *50 Nohea Kai Dr., Lahaina 96761,* ☎ *808/667–1400 or 800/642–6284,* ℻ *808/661–1025. 264 units. 2 pools, sauna, 18-hole golf course, 6 tennis courts, beach. AE, D, DC, MC, V.*

⚹ $$$$ 🏨 **Kapalua Bay Hotel.** Built in 1978 fronting what was once voted America's best beach, at lovely Kapalua Bay, this hotel has a real Maui feel to it: The exterior is understated white and natural wood. The open lobby, filled with flowering vanda and dendrobium orchids, has a view of the ocean. The plantation-style rooms are decorated in earth tones with green accents, and all have views of Lāna'i and Moloka'i. A shopping plaza outside the main hotel entrance has some fine restaurants and boutiques. Guests receive preferred rates and tee times at three 18-hole golf courses in Kapalua. ✉ *1 Bay Dr., Kapalua 96761,* ☎ *808/ 669–5656 or 800/367–8000,* ℻ *808/669–4694. 209 rooms. 3 restaurants, 2 pools, 6 tennis courts, beach. AE, DC, MC, V.*

$$$$ 🏨 **Kapalua Bay Villas.** Privately owned and individually decorated one- and two-bedroom units may be rented through the Kapalua Bay Hotel. Condos are assigned to one of five luxury categories and regularly inspected to ensure that standards are maintained. Renters enjoy a free shuttle to the hotel and guest rates for golf, tennis, and other hotel amenities. ✉ *1 Bay Dr., Kapalua 96761,* ☎ *808/669–5656 or 800/367–8000,* ℻ *808/669–4694. 125 units. AE, D, DC, MC, V.*

Maui Lodging

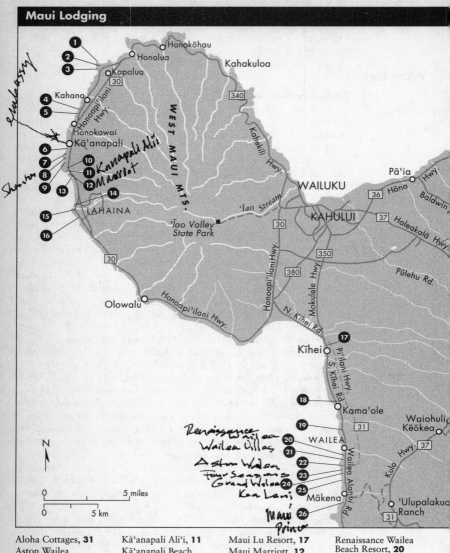

Aloha Cottages, **31**

Aston Wailea
Resort, **22**

Embassy Vacation
Resort, **6**

Four Seasons
Resort, **23**

Grand Wailea, **24**

Heavenly Hāna
Inn, **30**

Hotel Hāna-Maui, **32**

Hyatt Regency
Maui, **13**

Kāʻanapali Aliʻi, **11**

Kāʻanapali Beach
Hotel, **9**

Kamaʻole Sands, **18**

Kapalua Bay Hotel, **2**

Kapalua Bay Villas, **3**

Kea Lani Hotel Suites
& Villas, **25**

Kula Lodge, **29**

Lahaina Hotel, **14**

Mana Kai Maui, **19**

Maui Lu Resort, **17**

Maui Marriott, **12**

Maui Prince, **26**

Nāpili Kai Beach
Club, **4**

Olinda Country
Cottage & Inn, **28**

Papakea Beach
Resort, **5**

Pheasant Run, **27**

Pioneer Inn, **16**

Plantation Inn, **15**

Renaissance Wailea
Beach Resort, **20**

Ritz-Carlton,
Kapalua, **1**

Royal Lahaina
Resort, **7**

Sheraton Maui, **8**

Wailea Villas, **21**

Westin Maui, **10**

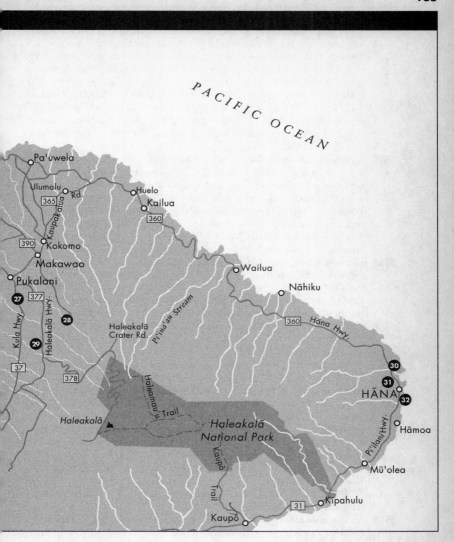

PACIFIC OCEAN

Pa'uwela

Ulumalu

365

Kaupakalua Rd.

Huelo

Kailua

360

390

Kokomo

Makawao

Pukalani

Wailua

Nāhiku

27

377

28

Kula Hwy.

Haleakalā Hwy.

29

Haleakalā
Crater Rd.

Pi'ina'au Stream

360

Hāna Hwy.

37

378

30

31

HĀNA

32

Haleakalā

Haleamau'u Trail

Haleakalā
National Park

Hāmoa

Kaupō Trail

Pi'ilani Hwy.

Mū'olea

31

Kīpahulu

Kaupō

$$$$ 🏨 **Maui Marriott.** Rooms here are large and tastefully done in pastel tones and bamboo furnishings, and nearly 90% have ocean views. Besides enjoying access to a beachside massage tent and privileges at two 18-hole golf courses in Kāʻanapali, guests can join classes featuring aerobics; hula; Hawaiian arts, crafts, and language; food preparation; and a number of sports. The best thing here, however, is the service: The staff is genuinely friendly and helpful. ⊠ *100 Nohea Kai Dr., Lahaina 96761,* ☎ *808/667–1200 or 800/228–9290,* ℻ *808/667–8300. 720 rooms. 4 restaurants, 2 lobby lounges, 2 pools, 2 hot tubs, 5 tennis courts, health club, beach, bicycles, shops, children's program (ages 5–12). AE, D, DC, MC, V.*

$$$$ 🏨 **Nāpili Kai Beach Club.** These lodgings on 10 beautiful beachfront acres appeal to a loyal following. Hawaiian-style rooms are done in seafoam green, mauve, and rattan; shoji doors open onto your lānai, with the beach and ocean right outside. Packages that include a car, breakfast, and other extras are available to guests who stay five nights or longer. ⊠ *5900 Lower Honoapiʻilani Rd., Nāpili Bay 96761,* ☎ *808/669–6271 or 800/367–5030,* ℻ *808/669–5740. 162 rooms. Kitchenettes, 4 pools, hot tub, 2 putting greens, beach. AE, MC, V.*

$$$$ 🏨 **Ritz-Carlton, Kapalua.** This beachfront hotel features spacious, com-
★   fortable rooms with oversize marble bathrooms, lānai overlooking the three-level pool, and all the grace, elegance, and service that this classy hotel chain is known for. Most rooms have ocean views. Guests on the Club floors have a private lounge with complimentary snack and beverage service all day long. All guests have golf privileges at three 18-hole courses in Kapalua. ⊠ *1 Ritz-Carlton Dr., Kapalua 96761,* ☎ *808/669–6200 or 800/262–8440,* ℻ *808/665–0026. 548 rooms. 4 restaurants, 5 lobby lounges, pool, beauty salon, 10 tennis courts, health club, beach, shops, children's programs. AE, D, DC, MC, V.*

$$$$ 🏨 **Royal Lahaina Resort.** The lānai at this Outrigger Hotels property afford stunning ocean or golf-course views. What distinguishes the Royal Lahaina are the two-story cottages, each divided into four units; the bedrooms open to the trade winds on two sides. The upstairs units each have a private lānai, and downstairs units share. The walkway to the courtyard wedding gazebo is lined with stepping stones engraved with the names of past brides and grooms and their wedding dates. ⊠ *2780 Kekaʻa Dr., Lahaina 96761,* ☎ *808/661–3611 or 800/447–6925,* ℻ *808/661–3538. 592 rooms. 3 restaurants, 3 pools, 18-hole golf course, tennis courts, beach. AE, D, DC, MC, V.*

$$$$ 🏨 **Sheraton Maui.** Gold and rust tones accent custom-made wicker furnishings in each room, most with direct ocean views, at this spectacular property. In the lush gardens you'll find an enormous freshwater swimming lagoon and the famous Puʻu Kekaʻa sunset cliff-diving ceremony. The Sheraton's 53-ft catamaran takes off regularly for snorkel, champagne sunset, and seasonal whale-watch sailings; there are guest privileges at two 18-hole golf courses nearby. ⊠ *2605 Kāʻanapali Pkwy., Lahaina 97671,* ☎ *808/661–0031 or 800/782–9488,* ℻ *808/ 661–0458. 510 rooms. 3 restaurants, 3 lobby lounges, in-room safes, refrigerator, pool, 3 tennis courts, fitness center, beach, summer children's programs. AE, D, DC, MC, V.*

$$$$ 🏨 **Westin Maui.** This is a hotel for active people who like to be out and about and won't spend all their time in their rooms, which are rather small for the price. But compensations are provided—an "aquatic playground" with five heated swimming pools, privileges at two 18-hole golf courses in Kāʻanapali, and the centralmost position on Kāʻanapali Beach. The landscaping is lush; there are abundant waterfalls—15 at last count—and lagoons. A valuable Asian and Pacific art collection is displayed throughout the property. ⊠ *2365 Kāʻanapali Pkwy., Lahaina 96761,* ☎ *808/667–2525 or 800/228–3000,* ℻ *808/661–5831.*

761 rooms. 3 restaurants, 4 lobby lounges, 5 pools, beauty salon, hot tub, health club, beach, children's programs. AE, D, DC, MC, V.

$$$–$$$$ ⊞ **Plantation Inn.** Charm and luxury set apart this inn reminiscent of
★ a Southern plantation home. Filled with Victorian and Far East fur-
nishings, it's set on a quiet street in the heart of Lahaina. Secluded lānai
draped with hanging plants face a central courtyard, pool, and garden
pavilion perfect for morning coffee. Each guest room or suite is deco-
rated differently, with hardwood floors, French doors, antiques, four-
poster beds, and ceiling fans. Some have kitchenettes and whirlpool
baths. Breakfast served poolside is included in the room rate, and
downstairs one of Hawai'i's best French restaurants, Gerard's, adds
to the allure. ⊠ *174 Lahainaluna Rd., Lahaina 96761,* ☎ *808/667–
9225 or 800/433–6815,* FAX *808/667–9293. 18 rooms. Restaurant, re-
frigerators, pool, hot tub, free parking. AE, MC, V.*

$$$ ⊞ **Kā'anapali Beach Hotel.** This property is right in the middle of all
the Kā'anapali action and has much more reasonable rates than its neigh-
bors. Instead of glitz and flash, you'll find a comfortable hotel with a
friendly Hawaiian staff. There are complimentary classes in hula, lei
making, and 'ukulele playing, and guests have privileges at the two 18-
hole Kā'anapali golf courses. ⊠ *2525 Kā'anapali Pkwy., Lahaina
96761,* ☎ *808/661–0011 or 800/262–8450,* FAX *808/667–5978. 430
rooms. 2 restaurants, lobby lounge, pool, beach. AE, D, DC, MC, V.*

$$$ ⊞ **Papakea Beach Resort.** This resort is an active place to stay if you
consider all the classes held here, such as swimming, snorkeling, and
pineapple cutting. In Honokōwai, Papakea has built-in privacy because
its units are spread out among 11 low-rise buildings on some 13 acres
of land. You aren't really aware that you're sharing the property with
363 other units. Bamboo-lined walkways between buildings and fish-
stocked ponds create a serene mood. There's a two-day minimum stay.
Despite its name, there is no beach on the premises, although there are
several nearby. ⊠ *3543 Honoapi'ilani Hwy., Lahaina 96761,* ☎ *808/
669–9680 or 800/367–5637,* FAX *808/669–0751. 36 studios; 224 1-bed-
room and 224 2-bedroom units. 2 pools, hot tub, saunas, putting
green, 4 tennis courts. AE, MC, V.*

$$$ ⊞ **Pioneer Inn.** Known officially as the Best Western Pioneer Inn–
Maui, this historic building has occupied its ringside seat on Lahaina's
action since 1901. Its dockside ambience capitalizes on Lahaina's 19th-
century whaling days. All rooms are air-conditioned, and New England–
style mahogany furnishings recapture Lahaina's missionary era. It's often
possible to stay in one of the small rooms for under $100 a night. You
might not want to spend your entire vacation here, as the area can be
a bit noisy in the evenings, but for a night or two of bargain-price historic atmosphere, the place can't be beat. ⊠ *658 Wharf St., Lahaina
96761,* ☎ *808/661–3636 or 800/457–5457,* FAX *808/667–5708. 34
rooms. 3 restaurants. AE, D, DC, MC, V.*

$$ ⊞ **Lahaina Hotel.** Honolulu businessman Rick Ralston, also respon-
sible for the rebirth of the Mānoa Valley Inn on O'ahu, has stocked
this 12-room Maui property with antique beds, wardrobes, and chests,
as well as delightful country-print curtains and spreads. Downstairs,
the trendy David Paul's Lahaina Grill, near the lively corner of Front
Street and Lahainaluna Road, attracts diners. ⊠ *127 Lahainaluna
Rd., Lahaina 96761,* ☎ *808/661–0577 or 800/669–3444,* FAX *808/667–
9480. 12 rooms. Restaurant. AE, D, MC, V.*

East Maui

$$$$ ⊞ **Aston Wailea Resort.** The tropical lobby and interior spaces show-
case a remarkable collection of Hawaiian and Pacific Rim artifacts. All
the spacious rooms have private lānai and are styled with a tropical

theme in wicker and beige. The grounds are beautiful, with walks along paths accented with palm, banana, and torch ginger. There are golf privileges at three nearby courses, as well as tennis privileges at the Wailea Tennis Club. ⊠ *3700 Wailea Alanui Dr., Wailea 96753,* ☎ *808/879–1922 or 800/922–7866,* 𝔽𝔸𝕏 *808/874–8331. 516 rooms. 2 restaurants, 3 pools, hot tub, beach. AE, D, DC, MC, V.*

$$$$ 🏨 **Four Seasons Resort.** This is a Maui favorite, partially because of
★ its location, on one of the Valley Isle's finest beaches with all the amenities of the well-groomed Wailea Resort, including access to three 18-hole golf courses and a "Wimbledon West," with 11 championship tennis courts. The property itself has great appeal, with terraces, courtyards, gardens, waterfalls, and fountains. Nearly all the rooms have an ocean view and combine traditional style with tropical touches. You'll find terry-cloth robes and whole-bean coffee grinders in each room. ⊠ *3900 Wailea Alanui, Wailea 96753,* ☎ *808/874–8000 or 800/334–6284,* 𝔽𝔸𝕏 *808/874–6449. 380 rooms. 3 restaurants, 2 bars, pool, health club, 2 tennis courts, beach. AE, D, DC, MC, V.*

$$$$ 🏨 **Grand Wailea.** Sunny opulence is everywhere at this 42-acre resort.
★ Elaborate water features include a 2,000-ft multilevel "canyon riverpool" with slides and grottoes. The Spa Grande cossets guests with rejuvenating offerings, from aerobics classes to exotic water-and-massage therapies. Luxury pervades the spacious ocean-view rooms, beautifully outfitted with such amenities as an overstuffed chaise longue, a comfortable writing desk, and an oversize tub and separate shower. Guests have access to three 18-hole golf courses, and tennis privileges are available. ⊠ *3850 Wailea Alanui Dr., Wailea 96753,* ☎ *808/875–1234 or 800/888–6100,* 𝔽𝔸𝕏 *808/874–2442. 761 rooms. 5 restaurants, 6 bars, 3 pools, health club, beach, children's programs, chapel. AE, D, DC, MC, V.*

$$$$ 🏨 **Hotel Hāna-Maui.** One of the best places to stay in Hawai'i is this
★ small, secluded hotel in Hāna surrounded by a 7,000-acre ranch. The original hotel buildings have white plaster walls and trellised verandas, while inside, the spacious rooms have bleached wood floors, furniture upholstered in natural fabrics, and such decorator touches as fine art and orchids. The newer Sea Ranch Cottages across the road surround a state-of-the-art fitness center. A shuttle carries guests to a secluded beach nearby. ⊠ *Box 9, Hāna 96713,* ☎ *808/248–8211 or 800/321–4262,* 𝔽𝔸𝕏 *808/248–7264. 96 units. Restaurant, bar, 2 pools, massage, tennis courts, exercise room, horseback riding, jogging, beach, library. AE, D, DC, MC, V.*

$$$$ 🏨 **Kamaʻole Sands.** This is a huge property for Kīhei—11 four-story buildings wrap around a grassy slope on which are clustered swimming and wading pools, a small waterfall, whirlpool baths, and barbecues. All units have kitchens, laundry facilities, and private lānai. Managed by Castle Resorts & Hotels, this condominium property has a 24-hour front desk and an activities desk and is across the road from Kīhei Beach. ⊠ *2695 S. Kīhei Rd., Kīhei 96753,* ☎ *808/874–8700 or 800/367–5004,* 𝔽𝔸𝕏 *808/879–3273. 11 studios; 211 1-bedroom, 83 2-bedroom, and 4 3-bedroom condo units. Restaurant, pool, wading pool, 4 tennis courts. AE, D, DC, MC, V.*

$$$$ 🏨 **Kea Lani Hotel Suites & Villas.** This Moorish-domed, all-suite resort offers seclusion and privacy at oceanside two- and three-bedroom villas, each with its own small pool and within easy reach of attractions in Wailea and West Maui. Accommodations in the main hotel are spacious one-bedroom suites with dining lānai and marble bathrooms. Guests have access to three 18-hole golf courses, and tennis privileges are available. ⊠ *4100 Wailea Alanui, Wailea 96753,* ☎ *808/875–4100 or 800/882–4100,* 𝔽𝔸𝕏 *808/875–1200. 413 suites, 37 villas. 3 restaurants, 2 lobby lounges, deli, in-room VCRs, refrigerators, 3 pools, beauty* *salon, 2 hot tubs, health club, beach, shops, children's programs. AE, D, DC, MC, V.*

$$$$ 🏨 **Maui Prince.** The attention to service, style, and presentation are apparent from the minute you walk into the delightful open-air lobby of the hotel. Rooms on three levels surround the courtyard, which is home to a Japanese garden with a bubbling stream. Each evening a small ensemble performs chamber music in the courtyard. Room decoration is understated, in tones of mauve and beige. Unfortunately, there's an earth berm between the hotel and the beach—part of the agreement the hotel had to make with the zoning commission and local residents—so an ocean view isn't possible from the first floor. ✉ *5400 Mākena Alanui Rd., Mākena 96753,* ☎ *808/874–1111 or 800/321–6284,* 📠 *808/879–8763. 290 rooms. 4 restaurants, pool, 2 18-hole golf courses, 6 tennis courts, beach. AE, DC, MC, V.*

$$$–$$$$ 🏨 **Renaissance Wailea Beach Resort.** On fantastic Mōkapu Beach, most of the hotel's rooms are contained in a seven-story, T-shape building. Tapestries and gorgeous carpets enhance the public areas; outside, you'll find exotic gardens, waterfalls, and reflecting ponds. The VIP Mōkapu Beach Club building houses 26 luxury accommodations and has its own concierge, pool, and beach cabanas. Guest rooms are decorated in shades of cream and each has a lānai. Guests have access to the nearby golf and tennis facilities. ✉ *3550 Wailea Alanui Dr., Wailea 96753,* ☎ *808/879–4900 or 800/992–4532,* 📠 *808/874–6128. 345 rooms. 4 restaurants, lobby lounge, refrigerators, 2 pools, hot tub, basketball, health club, Ping-Pong, shuffleboard, beach, children's programs. AE, D, DC, MC, V.*

$$$–$$$$ 🏨 **Wailea Villas.** The Wailea Resort opened with three fine condominiums, calling them, appropriately, Wailea 'Ekahi, Wailea 'Elua, and Wailea 'Ekolu (Wailea One, Two, and Three). Since then, Wailea has added the Grand Champions Villas, and the adjoining Mākena Resort has built Mākena Surf and Polo Beach Club. All have beautifully landscaped grounds, large units with exceptional views, and access to five of the island's best beaches. Wailea 'Elua Village, Polo Beach Club, and Mākena Surf are the more luxurious properties, with rates to match. The three original villas are an expansive property, with all the amenities of the fine Wailea Resort, including daily maid service and a concierge. ✉ *3750 Wailea Alanui Dr., Wailea 96753,* ☎ *808/879–1595 or 800/367–5246,* 📠 *808/874–3554. 9 studios; 94 1-bedroom, 157 2-bedroom, and 10 3-bedroom apartments. 6 pools. AE, MC, V.*

$$–$$$ 🏨 **Kula Lodge.** This venue isn't typically Hawaiian: The lodge resembles a chalet in the Swiss Alps, and two of its five units have a gas fireplace. Charming and cozy, in spite of the nontropical ambience, this is a perfect spot for a romantic interlude. Units are in two wooden cabins; four have lofts in addition to the ample bed space downstairs. On 3 wooded acres, the lodge has views of the valley and ocean enhanced by the surrounding forest and tropical gardens. The property has a restaurant and lounge, as well as a gift shop and a protea store that will pack flowers for you to take home; units do not have phones or TVs. ✉ *RR 1, Box 475, Kula 96790,* ☎ *808/878–2517 or 800/233–1535,* 📠 *808/878–2518. 5 units. Restaurant. MC, V.*

$$–$$$ 🏨 **Mana Kai Maui.** This lodging is a real find in Kīhei, partly because
★ of the property itself and partly because it sits on the end of one of the nicest beaches in the state, just down the strip from the Renaissance Wailea. Here you can get a studio without a kitchen, or a one- or two-bedroom unit with a kitchen. The decor is modest—what people in the Islands might call typical tropical—but recently renovated, and the view of the ocean right beyond the lānai steals your attention anyway. The Mana Kai has a very good beachfront restaurant, open for all meals. There's daily maid service and no minumum-stay requirement.✉ *2960*

S. Kīhei Rd., Kīhei 96753, ☎ 808/879–1561; for reservations and information, contact Condominium Rentals Hawai'i:✉ 362 Huku Li'i Pl., Suite 204, Kihei 96753, ☎ 808/879–2778 or 800/367–5242, FAX 808/879–7825. 98 units. Restaurant, lobby lounge, air-conditioning, refrigerators, pool, beach, shops, beauty salon. AE, MC, V.

$$–$$$ 🏨 **Olinda Country Cottage & Inn** The restored Tudor home and adjacent cottage are so far up Olinda Road above Makawao you'll keep thinking you must have passed it, but keep driving to reach the inn, which sits amid a 8.6-acre protea farm surrounded by forest and some wonderful hiking trails. There are three delightful accommodations in the Inn: two upstairs bedrooms with private baths, and the downstairs Pineapple Sweet with its French doors; but best of all is the ultraromantic cottage, which looks like a dollhouse from the outside. It would be easy to settle in for a long winter here, but bring slippers and warm clothes—the mountain air can be chilly. ✉ *536 Olinda Rd., Makawao 96768, ☎ FAX 808/572–1453 or ☎ 800/932–3435. 2 rooms with bath, 1 room shares bath, 2 cottages. Hiking, laundry. CP. No credit cards.*

$$ 🏨 **Aloha Cottages.** If you want to meet the people in little Hāna town, check into one of these cottages, run by Fusae Nakamura. Tourism is Mrs. Nakamura's way of earning extra money for her family now that she's retired, and she takes her vocation seriously. The one three-bedroom and three two-bedroom units and one studio all have kitchens or kitchenettes. The rooms are sparsely furnished but clean and adequate. The carefully tended fruit trees on the neighboring property provide a special touch—Mrs. Nakamura often supplies her guests with the harvest, which includes papaya, bananas, and avocados. ✉ *Hāna 96713, ☎ 808/248–8420. 5 cottages. No credit cards.*

$$ 🏨 **Heavenly Hāna Inn.** An impressive Japanese gate marks the entrance at this upscale inn. The three suites, one a two-bedroom unit, all have TVs. Decor is spare, with Japanese overtones; the furniture was built by Hāna residents. ✉ *Box 790, Hāna 96713, ☎ 808/248–8442. 3 suites. No credit cards.*

$$ 🏨 **Maui Lu Resort.** The first hotel in Kīhei and now operated by Aston Resorts, this place is reminiscent of a rustic lodge. The main lobby was the summer home of the original owner—a Canadian logger—and over the years, the Maui Lu has added numerous wooden buildings and cottages to its 28 acres. Of the 120 rooms, 50 are right on the beach, and some have their own private coves. The rest are across Kīhei Road, on the main property. The decor isn't fancy, but it isn't motel-tacky either. ✉ *575 S. Kīhei Rd., Kīhei 96753, ☎ 808/879–5881 or 800/922–7866, FAX 808/879–4627. 120 rooms. Restaurant, lounge, refrigerators, in-room safes, pool, 2 tennis courts, beach. AE, D, DC, MC, V.*

$ 🏨 **Pheasant Run.** For that warm-sky Upcountry ranch feeling, head for Pheasant Run, in pasture with a magnetic panorama of the entire island. The owner is a master builder, and this sprawling house has obviously been his labor of love. There are bonuses for animal-lovers—the company of a Dr. Dolittle–inspired assortment of animals, including Ollie, a surfing dog. The beautifully designed rental, one bedroom and two stories, is separated from the main house by a breezeway. ✉ *692 Naele Rd., Kula 96790, ☎ 808/878–6739, FAX 808/572–2265. 1 room. Laundry. No credit cards.*

NIGHTLIFE AND THE ARTS

Nightlife on Maui can be of the make-your-own-fun variety. As on all the Neighbor Islands, the pace is a bit slower than what you'll find in Waikīkī. Dancing, lū'au shows, dinner cruises, and so on are found mainly in the resort areas. Kā'anapali in particular can really get hopping, with myriad activities for visitors of all ages. The old whaling port of Lahaina also parties with the best of them—its Halloween observances are legendary—and attracts a younger, often towheaded crowd who all seem to be visiting from towns on the West Coast.

Most of Maui's cultural activities are community efforts, with theater, film, and symphony productions held in the island's central towns of Kahului and Wailuku. Since it opened in 1994, the **Maui Arts & Cultural Center** (✉ Maui Central Park, Kahului, ☎ 808/242–2787) has become the venue for more and more of the island's best live entertainment. The complex includes the 1,200-seat Castle Theater, which hosts classical, country, and world-beat concerts by touring musicians; a 4,000-seat amphitheater for large outdoor concerts; and the 350-seat McCoy Theater for plays and recitals. Art, crafts, and hula lessons are offered regularly in the center's workshops and studios. For information on current programs, check the Events Box Office (☎ 808/242–7469) or the daily newspaper, *The Maui News*. Most major credit cards are accepted at the venues listed below.

For nightlife of a different sort, children and astronomy buffs will enjoy stargazing at **Tour of the Stars,** a unique nightly one-hour program on the roof of the Hyatt Regency Maui in Kāʻanapali. You can look through giant binoculars and a deep-space telescope. The program is run by a real astronomer. ✉ *Hyatt Regency Maui's Lahaina Tower, 200 Nohea Kai Dr., Kāʻanapali,* ☎ *808/661–1234, ext. 4727.* 🎟 *$12.* ⊙ *Nightly at 8, 9, and 10; meet in hotel lobby.*

Bars and Clubs

Contemporary Music

Makai Bar (✉ Maui Marriott, Kāʻanapali Beach Resort, ☎ 808/667–1200). Live Hawaiian and contemporary music nightly, awesome sunset views, and the best pūpū on Maui according to a Maui News readers' poll, are at this comfortable spot on the Kāʻanapali coast.

Molokini Lounge (✉ Maui Prince Hotel, Mākena Resort, ☎ 808/874–1111). This is a pleasant bar with an ocean view, and you can even see Molokini Island before the sun goes down. Live music is presented, often Hawaiian in theme. There's a dance floor for late-night revelry.

Country and Western

Lone Star Cookhouse (✉ 1234 Lower Main St., Wailuku, ☎ 808/242–6616; ✉ 1913 S. Kīhei Rd., Kīhei, ☎ 808/975–2838). When you find yourself hankerin' for strummin' and twang, move 'em out to this country-western hangout and two-step to the latest tunes. Tables are moved to make way for a dance floor when a live band takes the stage. The cookhouse serves burgers and fries as well as authentic Texas barbecue, smoked brisket, and ribs; there's an all-you-can-eat soup and salad bar. Reggae, rock-and-roll, and alternative sounds might find their way into the audio mix here, too.

Maui Paniolo Posse (☎ 808/669–4946). Appreciated by those who are hooked on country-western dancing but aren't fond of smoky bars, Ron, Micki, and their friends teach fun and fast-paced line dancing at various venues around Maui: Lahaina Civic Center, Pukalani Civic Center, and Kīhei Civic Center. Call for a current schedule. They usually have snacks to share, but everyone adds to the pot.

Jazz

Pacific'O (✉ 505 Front St., Lahaina, ☎ 808/667–4341). There's only one place to hear live jazz on the beach. It's a mellow, pacific sort of jazz—naturally—and it plays from 9 till midnight on Thursday through

Saturday nights. A little something to accompany the cocktails and jazz? The shrimp wontons with Hawaiian salsa is a winner.

Rock Music

Casanova (✉ 1188 Makawao Ave., Makawao, ☎ 808/572–0220), voted "Best Late Night on Maui" in a *Maui News* reader survey, claims to be the best place for singles to meet and the largest dance floor on Maui. When a DJ is not spinning hits, contemporary musicians rock on with blues, country-western, rock-and-roll, and reggae. Past favorites have included Kool and the Gang, Los Lobos, and Taj Mahal. Expect a cover charge on nights featuring entertainment.

Cheeseburger in Paradise (✉ 811 Front St., Lahaina, ☎ 808/661–4855) is known for, what else, big beefy cheeseburgers. Locals also know it as a great place to tune in to live bands playing rock-and-roll, Top 40, and oldies sounds from 4:30 PM to closing. There's no dance floor, but the second-floor balcony is a good place to watch Lahaina's Front Street action.

Hapa's Brewhaus & Restaurant (✉ Lipoa Center, 41 E. Lipoa St., Kīhei, ☎ 808/879–9001 or, for the entertainment hot line, 808/875–1990). Good food and some fine homemade brews are on the menu here along with sports TV, rock and funk bands, disco, hula shows, comedy, and a game room. These folks have gone all out to create a first-rate club with a large stage, roomy dance floor, state-of-the-art lighting and sound systems, and tier seating so that everyone gets a good view. Even non-smokers will find the club comfortable: The air-conditioning system removes secondhand smoke.

Hard Rock Cafe (✉ Lahaina Center, 900 Front St., Lahaina, ☎ 808/667–7400). Maui's version of the Hard Rock is popular with young locals as well as visitors who like their music *loud*.

Luigi's Pasta & Pizzeria (✉ Maui Mall, 70 E. Kaʻahumanu Ave., Kahului, ☎ 808/877–3761). Nightlife is limited in Kahului, but this inviting little Italian restaurant provides a fun evening out. The after-9 PM action alternates between karaoke and dancing to Top 40 recorded hits.

Moose McGillycuddy's (✉ 844 Front St., Lahaina, ☎ 808/667–7758). The Moose offers no-cover live music on Tuesday and Thursday; otherwise, it's recorded music, but it's played so loud you'd swear it's live. This entertaining place tends to draw a young crowd, who come for the burgers and beer, to dance, and to meet one another. Specials include all-you-can-eat king crab and, on other nights, a 22-ounce porterhouse.

Planet Hollywood (✉ 744 Front St., Lahaina, ☎ 808/667–7877). There's no live music, but making the scene here is popular entertainment. Movie and television memorabilia, a celebrity handprint wall, and movie preview trailers make this place more than just another place to eat. The Maui edition of this chain adds island touches to its basic pasta, burgers, and rock-music fare—such local specialties as Maui potato chips and Hawaiian pizza. (Pineapple is a better pizza topping than you might imagine.)

Radio Cairo Maui (✉ 2439 S. Kīhei Rd., Kīhei, ☎ 808/879–4404) is proof that the late-night music and dance action in the condo town of Kīhei is in full swing. Sunday and Monday nights, jazz is on the agenda. The rest of the week, take your pick of oldies, Top 40, or well-known contemporary Hawaiian artists. Also on view is a unique collection of African art.

Tsunami (✉ Grand Wailea, 3850 Wailea Alanui Dr., ☎ 875–1234). You can dance to recorded Top 40 hits in high-tech disco where laser beams zigzag high above floor. The music plays from 9 PM to 3 AM. Thursday Friday is "Flashback Fever," and Saturday focuses on contemporary dance. On other nights, the room is used for private parties. Expect a $5 cover charge (this is a bar), except on Ladies' Night, when it's free. Don't wear beach clothes.

World Cafe (✉ 900 Front St., Lahaina, ☎ 808/661–1515). Combine a variety of tasty food, a video game room, lots of pool tables, televised sports, two dance floors on two levels, and a mix of recorded and live music that includes contemporary Hawaiian, old-time rock-and-roll, and reggae, and you have the hottest 15,000 square ft of night-club space in West Maui. Just to make sure the action never stops, the management has added country-western dance lessons, a grass-roots comedy club, and a female impersonation show, all of which necessitate a cover charge. This is a great place for people-watching.

Dinner and Sunset Cruises

America II **Sunset Sail.** The star of this two-hour cruise is the craft itself—a 1987 America's Cup 12-m class contender that is exceptionally smooth and steady, thanks to its renowned winged-keel design. ✉ *Lahaina Harbor, Slip 5, Lahaina,* ☎ *808/667–2195.* 🖃 *$25.*

Kaulana **Cocktail Cruise.** This two-hour sunset cruise (with a bit of whale-watching thrown in, in season) features a *pūpū* menu (hot and cold hors d'oeuvres), open bar, and live music. ✉ *Lahaina Harbor, Lahaina,* ☎ *808/871–1144.* 🖃 *$39.*

Pride **Charters.** A 65-ft catamaran built specifically for Maui's waters, the *Pride of Maui* features a large cabin, a large upper sundeck for unobstructed viewing, and a stable, comfortable ride. Morning and afternoon cruises; breakfast, lunch, and beverages are provided. ✉ *Ma'alaea Harbor, Ma'alaea,* ☎ *808/242–0955.* 🖃 *$30.*

Scotch Mist **Charters.** A two-hour champagne sunset sail is offered on the 25-passenger Santa Cruz 50 sloop *Scotch Mist II.* ☎ *808/661–0386.* 🖃 *$35.*

Windjammer Cruises. This cruise includes a prime rib and Alaskan salmon dinner, and live entertainment on the 70-ft, 93-passenger *Spirit of Windjammer,* a three-mast schooner. ✉ *283 Wili Ko Pl., Suite 1, Lahaina,* ☎ *808/661–8600.* 🖃 *$69.*

Film

Hawai'i International Film Festival. This acclaimed salute to celluloid used to be restricted to Honolulu, but now festival films are also presented on the Neighbor Islands, including Maui. Each November, the festival brings together filmmakers from Asia, the Pacific Rim, and North America to view feature films, documentaries, and shorts. The films are shown at the Holiday Theaters in the Ka'ahumanu Center and at selected resort hotels, where related activities also take place. To find out about specific films and dates, phone the International Film Festival Office (☎ 808/528–3456) in Honolulu.

Lū'au and Revues

Drums of the Pacific. The Hyatt presents a fine Polynesian revue on the hotel's Sunset Terrace. The all-you-can-eat-and-drink buffet dinner includes such fare as fresh fish, kālua pig, chicken, coconut beef, and other Polynesian treats. Afterward, the show features an exciting Samoan fire dance as well as other traditional dances and chants from such island locales as Hawai'i, Tahiti, and New Zealand. ⊠ *Hyatt Regency Maui, Kā'anapali,* ☎ *808/661–1234, ext. 4420.* ⚏ *$62 .* ⊘ *Dinner nightly at 4:45, show at 7.*

Marriott Lū'au. Learn to make Hawaiian crafts and play authentic early Hawaiian games before you sit down to one of the best lū'au's in the Islands. This traditional presentation, which includes an imu ceremony, fire dancing, nonstop mai tais, and a delicious buffet dinner, has been featured on NBC's "Today Show." ⊠ *Maui Marriott, Kā'anapali,* ☎ *808/667–1200, ext. 380.* ⚏ *$60.* ⊘ *Nightly at 5.*

Nāpili Kai Beach Club Keiki Hula Show. Expect to be charmed as well as entertained when 30 children ages 7–16 take you on a dance tour of Hawai'i, New Zealand, Tahiti, Samoa, and other Polynesian islands. The talented youngsters make their own ti-leaf skirts and fresh flower leis that they give to the audience at the end of the show. This is a nonprofessional but delightfully engaging review, and the 80-seat, oceanfront room is usually sold out. ⊠ *Nāpili Kai Beach Club, 5900 Honoapi'ilani Hwy., Nāpili,* ☎ *808/669–6271.* ⚏ *$35.* ⊘ *Dinner Fri. at 6, show at 7:30.*

Old Lahaina Lū'au. Some consider this the best lū'au you'll find on Maui—it's small, personal, and authentic. Its new home is an outdoor theater designed specifically for traditional Hawaiian entertainment; it feels like an old seaside village. In addition to fresh fish and grilled steak and chicken, you'll get all-you-can-eat traditional lū'au fare: kālua pig, chicken long rice, *lomilomi* salmon (massaged until tender and served with minced onions and tomatoes), *haupia* (coconut pudding), and other treats. You'll also get all you can drink. Guests sit either on tatami mats or at tables. Then there's the entertainment, featuring a musical journey from Old Hawai'i to the present with hula, chanting, and singing. ⊠ *1287 Front St., Lahaina (makai of the Lahaina Cannery Mall),* ☎ *808/667–1998.* ⚏ *$62.* ⊘ *Nightly 5:30–8:30.*

Wailea's Finest Lū'au. The Aston Wailea Resort's oceanfront lawn is certainly a beautiful spot to hold a lū'au. The traditional feast begins with a lei greeting and imu ceremony, and the evening includes a world champion fire-knife dancer and colorful Hawaiian hula show. ⊠ *Aston Wailea Resort, Wailea,* ☎ *808/879–1922.* ⚏ *$52.* ⊘ *Tues., Thurs., and Fri. at 5.*

Wailea Sunset Lū'au. The Rennaisance Wailea Beach Resort puts on its excellent Hawaiian lū'au three times a week. It features an open bar, an imu ceremony, a lū'au buffet, music by a Hawaiian band, and a Polynesian show with dancers performing pieces from around the Pacific—including one wielding a fire knife. ⊠ *Renaissance Wailea Beach Resort, 3550 Wailea Alanui Dr.,* ☎ *808/879–4900. Reservations essential.* ⚏ *$57.* ⊘ *Tues., Thurs., and Sat. 5:30–8:30.*

Music

Maui Philharmonic Society. The Society has presented such prestigious performers as Ballet Hispanico, the Shostakovich String Quartet, and the New Age pianist-composer Philip Glass. Performances take place in various spots around the island. ⊠ *J. Walter Cameron Center, 95 Mahalani St., Wailuku 96793,* ☎ *808/244–3771.*

Maui Symphony Orchestra (☎ *808/244–5439*). The symphony orchestra usually performs at the **Maui Arts & Cultural Center** (⊠ Maui

Central Park, Kahului, ☎ 808/242–2787, box office 808/242–7469), offering five season concerts and a few special musical sensations as well. The regular season includes a Christmas concert, an opera gala, a classical concert, and two pops concerts outdoors.

Theater

Baldwin Theatre Guild. Dramas, comedies, and musicals are presented by this group about eight times a year. The guild has staged such favorites as *The Glass Menagerie, Brigadoon,* and *The Miser.* Musicals are held in the Community Auditorium, which seats 1,200; all other plays are presented in the Baldwin High School Mini Theatre. ⊠ *1650 Ka'ahumanu Ave., Kahului,* ☎ *808/984–5673.* ▣ *$8.*

Maui Academy of Performing Arts. For a quarter-century this group has offered fine performances as well as dance and drama classes for children and adults. It has presented such plays as *Peter Pan, Jesus Christ Superstar,* and *The Nutcracker.* At this writing, MAPA had just secured a new home in Wailuku at the old National Dollar Store building and had begun to renovate it into a small theater and two dance studios. ⊠ *Main and Market Sts., Wailuku,* ☎ *808/244–8760.* ▣ *$10–$12.*

Maui Community Theatre. Now staging about six plays a year, this is the oldest dramatic group on the island, started in the early 1900s. Each July, the group also holds a fund-raising variety show, which can be a hoot. ⊠ *'Iao Theatre, 68 N. Market St., Wailuku,* ☎ *808/242–6969.* ▣ *Musicals $10–$15, nonmusicals $8–$13.*

Seabury Hall Performance Studio. This college-preparatory school above Makawao town offers a season of often supercharged shows in its satisfying small theater and two dance studios. The school's formula is to mix talented kids with seasoned adults and innovative, even offbeat, concepts. Dance concerts are always a hit. ⊠ *480 Olinda Rd., 1 mi north of Makawao crossroads,* ☎ *808/573–1257.* ▣ *$7–$12.*

OUTDOOR ACTIVITIES AND SPORTS

Participant Sports

Biking

Maui County has designated hundreds of miles of bikeways on Maui's roads, making biking safer and more convenient than in the past. Painted bike lanes make it possible for a rider to travel all the way from Mākena to Kapalua, and you'll see dozens of these hardy souls pedaling under the hot Maui sun. Some visitors rent a bike just to ride around the resort where they're staying. Whatever your preference, you have several rental choices, including **A & B Rental** (⊠ 3481 Lower Honoapi'ilani Hwy., Lahaina, ☎ 808/669–0027), **West Maui Cycles** (⊠ 4310 Lower Honoapi'ilani Hwy., Lahaina, ☎ 808/669–1169), **Hawai'i Sail and Sport**(⊠ 101 N. Kīhei Rd., Kīhei, ☎ 808/879–0178), and **Maui Sports and Cycle** (⊠ Long's Center, Kīhei, ☎ 808/875–8448, and ⊠ Dolphin Plaza, ☎ 808/875–2882). Bikes rent for $10–$20 a day.

Camping and Hiking

Like the other Hawaiian islands, Maui is riddled with ancient paths. These were the roads the Polynesians used to cross from one side of the island to another. Most of these paths are now too difficult to find. But if you happen to stumble upon something that looks like it might have been a trail, chances are good it was used by the ancients. In fact, most trails on Maui are not well marked. Only three areas have clearly marked trailheads. Luckily, these are some of the best hikes on the island. There's also a nature center, which has walks suited for children.

In Maui's center, **Haleakalā Crater** in Haleakalā National Park is an obvious hiking haven, with several trails. As you drive to the top of the 10,023-ft dormant volcano on the Haleakalā Highway, you'll first come to **Hosmer Grove,** less than a mile after you enter the park. This is a lovely forested area, with an hour-long nature trail. You can pick up a map at the trailhead, and park rangers offer guided hikes on a changing schedule. There are six campsites (no permit needed), pit toilets, drinking water, and cooking shelters. There's also **Halemauʻu Trail,** near the 8,000-ft elevation. The walk to the crater rim is a relative stroll, then it's a switchback trail nearly 2 mi to the crater floor. Nearly 4 mi from the trailhead, you'll find **Hōlua Cabin,** which you can reserve—at least three months in advance—through the National Park Service (⊠ Box 369, Makawao 96768, ☎ 808/572–9306). You can pitch a tent, but you'll need a permit that's issued on a first-come, first-serve basis at Haleakalā National Park Headquarters/Visitors Center (⊠ Haleakalā Crater Rd., ☎ 808/572–9306) at the 7,000-ft elevation point on Haleakalā; they're open daily 7:30–4.

If you opt to drive all the way to the top of Haleakalā, you'll find a trail called **Sliding Sands,** which starts at about the 10,000-ft elevation, descending to the crater floor 4 mi away. The scenery is spectacular; it's colorful and somewhat like the moon. You can reach the above-mentioned Hōlua Cabin in about 7 mi if you veer off to the left and head out of the crater on the Halemauʻu Trail. If you continue on the Sliding Sands Trail, however, you'll come to **Kapalaoa Cabin** within about 6 mi, and at about 10 mi you'll hit **Palikū Cabin,** both also available from the park service with at least three months' notice. All three cabins have bunks, firewood, water, and a stove, and are limited to 12 people. They can be reached in less than a day's walk. Palikū Cabin has tent camping nearby with toilets and drinking water. Tent permits, again, are issued at park headquarters on the day you want to use them.

On the southern slope of Haleakalā is **Polipoli Forest,** which will remind you of a Walt Disney movie. It was once heavily forested, until cattle and goats chewed away most of the natural vegetation. Starting in about 1930, the government began a program to reforest the area, and soon cedar, pine, cypress, and even redwoods took hold. Because of the elevation, it's a bit cooler here and sometimes wet and misty.

To reach the forest, drive on Highway 377 past Haleakalā Road to Waipoli Road. Go up the hill until you reach the park. Next to the lot, you'll see a small campground and a cabin you can rent from the Division of State Parks. Write far in advance for the cabin (⊠ Box 1049, Wailuku 96793, ☎ 808/244–4354); for the campground, you can wait until you arrive in Wailuku, then visit the State Parks office (⊠ 54 High St.). Once you're at Polipoli, there are three trails from which to choose.

ʻOheʻo Gulch in East Maui is part of Haleakalā National Park, but it's very different from the crater. That's because it's over on the Hāna side of the park—which actually extends far beyond the mountain you see in the clouds. This is a lush, rainy, tropical area. You can reach ʻOheʻo Gulch by continuing on the Hāna Highway about 10 mi past Hāna. ʻOheʻo Gulch includes the fabled pools, where the two major trails begin. The first trail is **Makahiku Falls,** a ½-mi jaunt from the parking lot to an overlook. You can go around the barrier and get closer to the falls if you want. From here, you can continue on the second trail for an-

In case you want to see the world.

At American Express, we're here to make your journey a smooth one. So we have over 1,700 travel service locations in over 120 countries ready to help. What else would you expect from the world's largest travel agency?

do more ®

http://www.americanexpress.com/travel

Travel

In case you want to be welcomed there.

We're here to see that you're always welcomed at establishments everywhere. That's why millions of people carry the American Express® Card – for peace of mind, confidence, and security, around the world or just around the corner.

do more

Cards

In case you're running low.

We're here to help with more than 118,000 Express Cash locations around the world. In order to enroll, just call American Express before you start your vacation.

do more

Express Cash

And just in case.

We're here with American Express® Travelers Cheques and Cheques *for Two*.® They're the safest way to carry money on your vacation and the surest way to get a refund, practically anywhere, anytime.

Another way we help you...

do more

**Travelers
Cheques**

other 1½ mi to encounter 400-ft **Waimoku Falls.** The trail spans a sensational gorge and leads through a clonking, mystifying forest of giant bamboo. There's camping down at the grassy seacliffs, with no permit required, although you can stay only three nights. Toilets, grills, and tables are available here, but no water.

In ʻĪao Valley, the **Hawaiʻi Nature Center** (⊠ 875 ʻĪao Valley Rd., Wailuku 96793, ☎ 808/244–6500) leads interpretive hikes for children and their families.

Fitness Centers

Most fitness centers on Maui are in hotels. If your hotel does not have a facility, ask if privileges are available at other hotels. Outside the resorts, the most convenient and best-equipped are **Gold's Gym** (⊠ 840 Waineʻe St., Lahaina, ☎ 808/667–7474; ⊠ Lipoa Ctr., 41 E. Lipoa St., Kīhei, ☎ 808/874–2844; ⊠ 850 Kolu St., Wailuku, ☎ 808/242–6851), and **World Gym** (⊠ 300 Ohukai Rd., G-112, Kīhei Commercial Ctr., Kīhei, ☎ 808/879–1326), which all have complete fitness facilities.

Golf

How do you keep your mind on the game in a place like Maui? It's very hard, because you can't ignore the view, but Maui has become one of the world's premier golf-vacation destinations. The island's major resorts all have golf courses, each of them stunning. They're all open to the public, and most lower their greens fees after 2:30 on weekday afternoons.

Kapalua Golf Club has three 18-holers—the Village Course and the Bay Course, designed by Arnold Palmer, and the Plantation Course, designed by Ben Crenshaw. Kapalua is well known among television-sports watchers. ⊠ *300 Kapalua Dr., Kapalua,* ☎ *808/669–8044.* ⛳ *Greens fee $95– $100 guests, $140–$150 nonguests, including cart; club rental $30–$40.*

The lovely **Mākena Golf Course** has two 18-hole courses, North and South, designed by Robert Trent Jones, Jr. Of all the resort courses, this one is the most remote. At one point, golfers must cross a main road, but there are so few cars that this poses no problem. ⊠ *5415 Mākena Alanui Rd., Kīhei,* ☎ *808/879–3344.* ⛳ *Greens fee $80 guests, $140 nonguests; rates include cart.*

Kāʻanapali Golf Courses are two of Maui's most famous. The layout consists of two 18-hole courses: The North Course was designed by Robert Trent Jones, Sr., and the South Course architect was Arthur Jack Snyder. ⊠ *Kāʻanapali Beach Resort, Kāʻanapali,* ☎ *808/661–3691.* ⛳ *Greens fee $100 guests, $120 nonguests, including cart.*

Silversword Golf Course is just up the hill from Kīhei. ⊠ *1345 Piʻilani Hwy., Kīhei,* ☎ *808/874–0777.* ⛳ *Greens fee $70, including cart.*

The **Wailea Golf Club** also has three courses: the Gold and the Blue, which were designed by Arthur Jack Snyder, and the newer Emerald, designed by Robert Trent Jones, Jr. In his design, Snyder incorporated ancient lava-rock walls to create an even more unusual golfing experience. ⊠ *100 Wailea Golf Club Dr., Wailea,* ☎ *808/875–5111.* ⛳ *Greens fee $110 Wailea guests, $140 nonguests, including cart.*

Maui has municipal courses as well, where the fees are lower. Be forewarned, however, that the weather can be cooler and wetter, and the locations may not be convenient. The **Waiehu Municipal Golf Course** is on the northeast coast of Maui a few miles past Wailuku. ⊠ *Off Hwy. 340 in West Maui,* ☎ *808/244–5934.* ⛳ *Greens fee $25 weekdays, $30 weekends; cart $15.*

Hang Gliding

Through a headset, USHGA instructor Armin Engert of **Hang Gliding Maui** (☎ 808/878–3806) will teach you the basics of weight-shift control while you cruise for 45 minutes on the wind currents over Maui in a motorized open-cockpit Ultralight. There's a weight limit of 200 pounds for this trip, which costs $150 plus $30 for each additional 15 minutes. For a tandem glide from the summit of Haleakalā to the beach below is a 35-minute descent, the weight limit is 185 pounds, and the price of $250 includes membership in the U.S. Hang Gliding Association and 24 snapshots of your adventure taken by a wing-mounted camera.

Parasailing

If you have a yen to be floating in the sky like a bird but lack the derring-do of a barnstormer, parasailing is the perfect alternative to skydiving (you gently rise several hundred feet up from the ground instead of leaping out of an aircraft at 10,000 ft) or hang gliding (the safety rope holds you in your flight pattern). This is an easy and fun way to earn your wings: Just strap on a harness attached to a parachute, and a power boat pulls you up and over the ocean from a launching dock or from a boat's platform.

Several companies on Maui will take you for a ride that usually lasts about 10 minutes, and costs $30–$50. For safety reasons, **West Maui Parasailing** (☎ 808/661–4060) requires that passengers weigh more than 100 pounds, or two must be strapped together in tandem. **Lahaina Para-Sail** (☎ 808/661–4887) lays claim to the only parasail vessel on Maui that is Coast Guard certified for 25 passengers and has bathroom facilities on board. They'll be glad to let you experience a "toe dip" or "freefall" if you request it, and their minimum weight to fly alone is 75 pounds.

Tennis

The state's finest tennis facilities are at the **Wailea Tennis Club** (⊠ 131 Wailea Ike Pl., Kīhei, ☎ 808/879–1958 or 800/332–1614), often called "Wimbledon West" because of its two grass courts; there are also 11 Plexipave courts and a pro shop. You'll pay $25 an hour per person for the hard courts. The grass courts are by well-in-advance reservation only. Weekday mornings there are clinics to help you improve your ground strokes, serve, volley, or doubles strategy.

At the Mākena Resort, just south of Wailea, the **Mākena Tennis Club** (⊠ 5400 Mākena Alanui Rd., Kīhei, ☎ 808/879–8777) has six courts. Rates are $16 per court hour for guests, $18 for nonguests. After an hour, if there's space available, there's no charge.

Over on West Maui, the **Royal Lahaina Tennis Ranch** (⊠ 2780 Keka'a Dr., ☎ 808/661–3611, ext. 2296), in the Kā'anapali Beach Resort, offers 11 recently resurfaced courts and a pro shop. Rates are a flat $10 per person per day whether you are a guest or not.

The **Hyatt Regency Maui** (⊠ 200 Nohea Kai Dr., Kā'anapali, ☎ 808/661–1234, ext. 3174) has six courts, with rentals and instruction. All day passes cost $15 for guests, $20 for nonguests.

Kapalua Tennis Garden (⊠ 100 Kapalua Dr., Kapalua, ☎ 808/669–5677) serves the Kapalua Resort with 10 courts and a pro shop. You'll pay $10 an hour if you're a guest, $12 if you're not, and you're welcome to stay longer for free if there is no one waiting.

Maui Beach & Tennis Club (⊠ 100 Nohea Kai Dr., Kā'anapali, ☎ 808/667–1200, ext. 66689) at the Maui Marriott has five Plexipave courts, with three lit for night play, and a pro shop. Daily rates are $10 for guests and $12 for nonguests.

There are other facilities around the island, usually one or two courts in smaller hotels or condos. Most of them, however, are open only to their guests. The best free courts are the five at the **Lahaina Civic Center** (⊠ 1840 Honoapi'ilani Hwy., Lahaina, ☎ 808/661–4685), near Wahikuli State Park; they're available on a first-come, first-serve basis.

Water Sports

Note that, to reduce interference with whales, no "thrill craft"—specifically parasails and Jet Skis—are allowed in Maui waters from December 15 to April 15.

DEEP-SEA FISHING

If fishing is your sport, Maui is the place for it. You'll be able to throw in hook and bait for fish like 'ahi, *aku* (a skipjack tuna), barracuda, bonefish, *kawakawa* (bonito), mahimahi, Pacific blue marlin, *ono* (wahoo), and *ulua* (jack crevalle). On Maui you can fish throughout the year, and you don't need a license.

Plenty of fishing boats run out of Lahaina and Mā'alaea harbors. If you charter a boat by yourself, expect to spend in the neighborhood of $600 a day. But you can share the boat with others who are interested in fishing the same day for about $100. Although there are at least 10 companies running boats on a regular basis, these are the most reliable: **Finest Kind Inc.** (⊠ Slip 7, Box 10481, Lahaina 96767, ☎ 808/ 661–0338), **Hinatea Sportfishing** (⊠ Slip 27/Lahaina Harbor, Lahaina 96761, ☎ 808/667–7548), and **Lucky Strike Charters** (⊠ Box 1502, Lahaina 96767, ☎ 808/661–4606). **Ocean Activities Center** (⊠ 1847 S. Kīhei Rd., Suite 203A, Kīhei 96753, ☎ 808/879–4485 or 800/798– 0652) can arrange fishing charters as well. You're responsible for finding your own transportation to the harbor.

KAYAKING

A sport that's been gaining in popularity recently, kayaking off the coast of Maui can be a leisurely paddle or more of a challenge, depending on weather conditions and location. If this is your first time in one of these banana-shape boats, it's best to go with a guide until you're comfortable with the equipment, have learned a few techniques for coping with ocean swells and waves, and know which parts of Maui's coastline are best suited to your skill level. A guided trip costs $20– $30 per hour, and the longer ones usually include lunch. Kayak rentals run about $25–$35 a day. Wear a sun visor, and count on getting wet.

Leroy, at the Beach Activities Center of the **Maui Marriott** (⊠ 100 Nohea Kai Dr., Kā'anapali, ☎ 808/667–1200, ext. 374) makes you feel at home on the ocean with a short trip to Kā'anapali's Black Rock for possible turtle sightings. The Marriott's kayaks, with back rests and foot-pedal rudder control, will spoil you for lesser equipment, and if your arms get tired, Leroy will tow you and your craft back to port. Two other outfitters that can help you get started are **South Pacific Kayak** (⊠ 2439 S. Kīhei Rd., Kīhei, ☎ 808/875–4848), and **Kelii's Kayak Tours** (☎ 808/879–3957 or 888/874–7652).

SAILING

Because of its proximity to the smaller islands of Moloka'i, Lāna'i, Kaho'olawe, and Molokini, Maui can provide one of Hawai'i's best sailing experiences. Most sailing operations like to combine their tours with a meal, some throw in snorkeling or whale-watching, while others offer a sunset cruise.

One of the best and longest-running operations is **Trilogy Excursions** (⊠ 180 Lahainaluna Rd., Lahaina 96761, ☎ 808/661–4743 or 800/874– 2666). Their full-day, multihull-catamaran cruise to Lāna'i includes a guided van tour of the island, a barbecue lunch, beach volleyball, and a "Snorkeling 101" class, where you can test your skills in the waters of Hulopo'e Marine Preserve (Trilogy has exclusive commercial access). Snorkeling gear is supplied. They also offer a Molokini snorkel cruise.

Other companies offering cruises include **Maui–Moloka'i Sea Cruises** (✉ 831 Eha St., Suite 101, Wailuku 96793, ☎ 808/242–8777), **Sail Hawai'i** (☎ 808/879–2201), *Scotch Mist* **Charters** (☎ 808/661–0386), the Hyatt Regency Maui's *Kiele V* (✉ 200 Nohea Kai Dr., Lahaina, ☎ 808/661–1234), and *Pride* **Charters** (✉ 208 Kenolio Rd., Kīhei 96753, ☎ 808/875–0955), which has a glass-bottom catamaran, hot-water showers, and live entertainment.

SCUBA DIVING

Believe it or not, Maui is just as scenic underwater as it is above. In fact, some of the finest diving spots in Hawai'i lie along the Valley Isle's western and southwestern shores. If you're a certified diver, you can rent gear at any Maui dive shop simply by showing your PADI or NAUI card. Unless you're familiar with the area, however, it's probably best to hook up with a dive shop for an underwater tour. Additionally, the only really decent shore dive is at Honolua Bay, a marine reserve above Kapalua Resort. The water is usually rough during the winter, but there's always a chance you will spot some of Maui's winter visitors—humpback whales (☞ Whale-Watching Tours box at the end of this chapter).

Maui has no lodging facilities tailored to divers, but there are many dive shops that sell and rent equipment and give lessons and certification. Before signing on with any of these outfitters, however, it's a good idea to ask a few pointed questions (☞ Pleasures and Pastimes *in* Chapter 1).

Some popular stores include **Capt. Nemo's Ocean Emporium** (✉ 150 Dickenson St., Lahaina, ☎ 808/661–5555), **Dive Shop** (✉ Kīhei boat ramp, S. Kīhei Rd., ☎ 808/879–2201), **Ed Robinson's Diving Adventures** (☎ 808/879–3584 or 800/635–1273), **Happy Maui Diving and Tours** (✉ 840 Waine'e St., Suite 106, Lahaina, ☎ 808/669–0123), **Lahaina Divers** (✉ 143 Dickenson St., Lahaina, ☎ 808/667–7496), and **Maui Dive Shop** (✉ Lahaina Cannery Mall, ☎ 808/661–5388). All provide equipment with proof of certification, as well as introductory dives for those who aren't certified. Introductory boat dives generally run about $80.

Area dive sites include:

Honolua Bay, in West Maui, is a marine preserve with many varieties of coral and tame tropical fish, including large ulua, *kāhala,* barracuda, and manta rays. With depths of 20 ft–50 ft, this is a popular spot for introductory dives. Dives are generally given only during the summer months.

Molokini Crater, at 'Alalākeiki Channel, is a crescent-shape islet formed by the top of a volcano. This marine preserve's depth range (10 ft–80 ft), combined with the attraction of the numerous tame fish dwelling here that can be fed by hand, make it a popular introductory dive site.

SNORKELING

If you want a personal introduction to Maui's undersea universe, the undisputable authority is marine biologist **Ann Fielding's Snorkel Maui.** She's the Carl Sagan of Hawai'i's reef cosmos—formerly with University of Hawai'i, Waikīkī Aquarium, and the Bishop Museum and the author of several guides to island sealife. She'll not only show you fish; she'll introduce you to *individual* fish. This is a good first experience for dry-behind-the-ears types. ✉ Box 1107, Makawao 96768, ☎ 808/572–8437.

Of course, the same dive companies that take scuba aficionados on tours will take snorkelers as well. One of Maui's most popular snorkeling spots can be reached only by boat: Molokini Crater, that little bowl of land off the coast of the Mākena Resort. For about $55, you can spend half a day at Molokini, with meals provided.

Ocean Activities Center (⊠ 1847 S. Kīhei Rd., Suite 203A, Kīhei, ☎ 808/879–4485) does a great job, although other companies also offer a Molokini snorkel tour.

You can find some good snorkeling spots on your own. If you need gear, **Snorkel Bob's** (⊠ Nāpili Village Hotel, 5425 Lower Honoapi'ilani Rd., Nāpili, ☎ 808/669–9603; ⊠ 34 Keala Pl., Kīhei Town Center, ☎ 808/879–7449; ⊠ 161 Lahainaluna Rd., Lahaina, ☎ 808/661–4421) will rent you a mask, fins, and snorkel, and throw in a carrying bag, map, and snorkel tips for as little as $5 per day.

Secluded **Windmill Beach** (⊠ take Hwy. 30 3½ mi north of Kapalua, then turn onto the dirt road to the left) has a superb reef for snorkeling. A little more than 2 mi south, another dirt road leads to **Honolua Bay;** the coral formations on the right side of the bay are particularly dramatic. You'll find **Nāpili Bay,** one beach south of the Kapalua Resort, also quite good for snorkeling.

Almost the entire coastline from Kā'anapali south to Olowalu offers fine snorkeling. Favorite sites include the area just out from the cemetery north of Wahikuli State Park, near the lava cone called **Black Rock,** on which Kā'anapali's Sheraton Maui Hotel is built (tame fish will take bread from your hand there), and the shallow coral reef south of **Olowalu** General Store.

The coastline from Wailea to Mākena is also generally good for snorkeling. The best is found near the rocky fringes of Wailea's **Mōkapu, Ulua, Wailea,** and **Polo** beaches.

Between Polo Beach and Mākena Beach (turn right on Mākena Road just past Mākena Surf Condo) lies **Five Caves,** where you'll find a maze of underwater grottoes below offshore rocks. This spot is recommended for experienced snorkelers only, since the tides can get rough. At Mākena, the waters around the **Pu'uōla'i** cinder cone provide great snorkeling.

SURFING

Although on land it may not look as if there are seasons on Maui, the tides tell another story. In winter the surf is up on the northern shores of the Hawaiian Islands, while summer brings big swells to the southern side. Near-perfect winter waves on Maui can be found at **Honolua Bay,** on the northern tip of West Maui. To get there, continue 2 mi north of D. T. Fleming Park on Highway 30 and take a left onto the dirt road next to a pineapple field; a path takes you down the cliff to the beach.

Next best for surfing is **Ho'okipa Beach Park** (off Hwy. 36, a short distance east of Pā'ia), where the modern-day sport began on Maui. This is the easiest place to watch surfing, because there are paved parking areas and picnic pavilions in the park. A word of warning: the surfers who come here are pros, and if you're not, they may not take kindly to your getting in their way.

Pushing the envelope of big wave surfing has reached a new level here in the channel waters off Maui, where surfers get pulled out to sea and then whipped into the big waves. At Ho'okipa Beach Park, viewers with a good pair of binoculars might be able to see out past the windsurfers to view an example of tow-in surfing: Jet Ski pilots pull state-of-the-art big wave surfers out to the 1-mi marker, where the waves can average 30 ft–40 ft during winter swells. Amazing grace!

You can rent surfboards and boogie boards at many surf shops, such as **Second Wind** (⊠ 111 Hāna Hwy., Kahului, ☎ 808/877–7467), **Lightning Bolt Maui** (⊠ 55 Ka'ahumanu Ave., Kahului, ☎ 808/877–3484), and **Ole Surfboards** (⊠ 277 Wili Ko Pl., Lahaina, ☎ 808/661–3459).

Maui Surfing School (☎ 808/875–0625) guarantees one two-hour lesson is all it takes to have "anyone who can walk" standing on a surfboard and riding the gentle waves of Lahaina Harbor. Costs are $60 per person (maximum class size of eight), including equipment rental; group discounts are available.

WINDSURFING

It's been more than 15 years since Ho'okipa Bay was discovered by boardsailors, but in those years since 1980, the windy beach 10 mi east of Kahului has become the windsurfing capital of the world. The spot is blessed with optimal wave-sailing wind and sea conditions and, for experienced windsurfers, can offer the ultimate experience. Other locations around Maui are good for windsurfing as well—Honolua Bay, for example—but Ho'okipa is absolutely unrivaled.

Even if you're a windsurfing aficionado, chances are good you didn't bring your equipment. You can rent it—or get lessons—from these shops: **Maui Ocean Activities** (⊠ Lahaina, ☎ 808/667–1964), **Maui Windsurfing Company and Cort Larned Windsurfing School** (⊠ 520 Keolani Pl., Kahului, ☎ 808/877–4816), **Ocean Activities Center** (⊠ 1847 S. Kīhei Rd., Kīhei, ☎ 808/879–4485), and **Maui Windsurfari** (⊠ 425 Koloa St., Kahului, ☎ 808/871–7766). Lessons range from $30 to $60 and can last anywhere from one to three hours. Equipment rental also varies—from no charge with lessons to $20 an hour. For the latest prices and special deals, it's best to call around once you've arrived.

Spectator Sports

Baseball

From mid-October to mid-December the four teams of **Hawai'i Winter Baseball** compete. The teams consist mostly of local players, plus a few promising minor leaguers from the mainland. The **Maui Stingrays** (☎ 808/242–2950) play their home games at War Memorial Stadium in Wailuku. Reserved seats cost $6, general admission is $5.

Golf

Maui has a number of golf tournaments, most of which are of professional caliber and worth watching. Many are also televised nationally. One of those attention-getters is the **Mercedes Championships** (☎ 808/669–2440), formerly called the Lincoln-Mercury Kapalua International, held now in January. This is the first official PGA tour event, held on Kapalua's Plantation Course. The Aloha Section of the Professional Golfers Association of America hosts the **GTE Hawaiian Tel Hall of Fame** (☎ 808/669–8877) championship at the Plantation Course in May, and a clambake feast on the beach tops off the **Kapalua Clambake Pro-Am** (☎ 808/669–8812) in July.

At Kā'anapali, the **EMC Maui Kā'anapali Classic SENIOR PGA Golf Tournament** pits veteran professionals in a battle for a $1 million purse each October.

Over in Wailea, on June's longest day of the year, self-proclaimed "lunatic" golfers start out at first light to play 100 holes of golf in the annual **Ka Lima O Maui,** a fund-raiser for local charities.

Outrigger-Canoe Races

Polynesians first traveled to Hawai'i by outrigger canoe, and racing the traditional craft has always been a favorite pastime in the Islands. Canoes were revered in Old Hawai'i, and no voyage could begin without a blessing, ceremonial chanting, and a hula performance to ensure a safe journey. At Whaler's Village in May, the two-day launch festivities for the **Ho'omana'o Challenge Outrigger Sailing Canoe World Championship** (☎ 808/661–3271) also include a torchlighting ceremony, arts and crafts demonstrations, and a chance to observe how the vessels are rigged—as well as the start of the race.

Polo

Polo is popular with Mauians. From April to June, Haleakalā Ranch, on Highway 377, 1 mi past the summit turnoff (Hwy. 378), hosts the "indoor" contests, which are played outdoors in a field flanked by sideboards. During the outdoor polo season from September through November, matches are held at Olinda Field, 1 mi above the paniolo town of Makawao on Olinda Road. There is a $3 admission charge for most games, which start at 2 PM on Sunday. Two special events to catch if you're in town include Memorial Day's **Champagne Brunch** match and the **High Goal Benefit** game, which is held on the first Sunday in November and features teams from such countries as Argentina, England, and Australia. For information, contact Moani (☎ 808/877–5544).

Rodeos

With dozens of working cattle ranches throughout the Islands, many youngsters learn to ride a horse before they can drive a car. Mauians love their rodeos and put on several for students at local high schools throughout the year. Paniolos get in on the act, too, at three major annual events: the **Oskie Rice Memorial Rodeo,** usually staged the weekend after Labor Day; the **Cancer Benefit Rodeo** in April, held at an arena 3 mi east of Pā'ia; and Maui's biggest event, drawing competitors from all islands as well as the U.S. mainland, the **4th of July Rodeo,** which comes with a full-on parade and other festivities that last for days. Spectator admission fees to the competitions vary from free to $7. Cowboys are a tough bunch to tie down to a phone, but you can try calling the **Maui Roping Club** (☎ 808/572–2076) for information.

Surfing and Windsurfing

Not many places can lay claim to as many windsurfing tournaments as Maui. The Valley Isle is generally thought to be the world's preeminent windsurfing location, and draws boardsailing experts from around the globe who want to compete on its waves. In March the **Hawaiian Pro Am Windsurfing** competition gets under way. In April the **Da Kine Hawaiian Pro Am** lures top windsurfers, and the **Aloha Classic World Wave Sailing Championships** takes place in October. All are held at Ho'okipa Bay, right outside the town of Pā'ia, near Kahului. For competitions featuring amateurs as well as professionals, check out the **Maui Race Series** (☎ 808/877–2111), six events held at Kanahā beach in Kahului in summer when winds are the strongest and lack of big waves makes conditions excellent for the slalom (speed racing) course. Competitors maneuver their boards close to shore, and the huge beach provides plenty of seating and viewing space. Ho'okipa Bay's large waves are also prime territory for surfers. The **Local Motion Surfing** competition heats up the action in May, and in January the **Maui Rusty Pro,** held jointly at Honolua Bay, invites professionals to compete for a $40,000 purse.

Tennis

At the **Kapalua Jr. Vet/Sr. Tennis Championships** in May, where the minimum age is 30, players have been competing in singles and doubles events since 1979. On Labor Day, the **Wilson Kapalua Open Tennis Tournament,** Maui's grand prix of tennis, calls Hawai'i's hottest hitters to volley for a $12,000 purse at Kapalua's Tennis Garden and Village Tennis Center. Also at the Tennis Center, Women's International Tennis Association professionals rally with avid amateurs in a week of pro-am and pro-doubles competition during the **Kapalua Betsy Nagelsen Tennis Invitational** in December. All events are put on by the **Kapalua Tennis Club** (☎ 808/669–5677).

In East Maui, 1999 marks the 15th year for the **Wailea Open Tennis Championship,** held in July on the Plexipave courts at the **Wailea Tennis Club** (☎ 808/879–1958).

SHOPPING

Whether you head for one of the malls (☞ *below*) or opt for the boutiques hidden around the Valley Isle, one thing you should have no problem finding is clothing made in Hawai'i. The Hawaiian garment industry is now the state's third-largest economic sector, after tourism and agriculture.

Maui has an abundance of locally made art and crafts in a range of prices. In fact, a group that calls itself Made on Maui exists solely to promote the products of its members—items that range from pottery and paintings to Hawaiian teas and macadamia caramel corn. You can identify the group by its distinctive Haleakalā logo.

Business hours for individual shops on the island are usually 9–5, seven days a week. Shopping centers tend to stay open later (until 9 or 10 at least one night of the week).

Art

Maui has more art per square mile than any other Hawaiian island—maybe more than any other U.S. county. There are artists' guilds and co-ops, as well as galleries galore, all over the island. Art shows are held throughout the year at the Maui Arts & Cultural Center. Marine sculptors and painters showcase their work during **Celebration of Whales** at the Four Seasons Resort Wailea in January. The Lahaina Arts Society presents **Art in the Park** under the town's historic banyan tree every Friday and Saturday from 9–5. Moreover, the town of Lahaina hosts **Art Night** every Friday from 7–10; galleries open their doors (some serve refreshments), and musicians stroll the streets.

Hui No'eau Visual Arts Center (✉ 2841 Baldwin Ave., Makawao, ☎ 808/572–6560) presents juried and nonjuried exhibits by local artists.

Lahaina Galleries has two locations in West Maui (✉ 728 Front St., Lahaina, ☎ 808/667–2152 and ✉ Kapalua Resort, ☎ 808/669–0202).

Martin Lawrence Galleries (✉ Lahaina Market Place, Front St. and Lahainaluna Rd., Lahaina, ☎ 808/661–1788) represents noted mainland artists, including Andy Warhol and Keith Haring, in a bright and friendly gallery opened in 1991.

One of the most interesting galleries on Maui is the **Maui Crafts Guild** (✉ 43 Hāna Hwy., Pā'ia, ☎ 808/579–9697). Set in a two-story wooden building alongside the highway, the Guild is crammed with work by local artists; the best pieces are the pottery and sculpture. Upstairs, antique kimonos, hand-painted silks, and batik fabric are on display.

Maui Hands (✉ 3620 Baldwin Ave., Makawao, ☎ 808/572–5194; ✉ Ka'ahumanu Center, Kahului, ☎ 808/877–0368) has work by dozens of local artists, including paniolo-theme lithographs by Sharon Shigekawa, who knows whereof she paints: She rides each year in the Kaupō Roundup. The shop is in the town's old theater.

Viewpoints (✉ 3620 Baldwin Ave., Makawao, ☎ 808/572–5979) calls itself Maui's only fine-arts collective; it is a cooperative venture of about two dozen Maui painters and sculptors, representing a wide variety of styles.

Village Gallery has two locations—one in Lahaina (✉ 120 Dickenson St., ☎ 808/661–4402) and one in the Ritz-Carlton, Kapalua (✉ 1 Ritz-Carlton Dr., ☎ 808/669–1800)—featuring such popular local artists as Betty Hay Freeland, Wailehua Gray, Margaret Bedell, George Allen, Joyce Clark, Pamela Andelin, Stephen Burr, and Macario Pascual.

Wyland Galleries (✉ 697 Front St., Lahaina, ☎ 808/661–7099; ✉ 711 Front St., Lahaina, ☎ 808/667–2285; ✉ 136 Dickenson St., Lahaina, ☎ 808/661–0590) is the only Maui shop to sell the work of Wyland, the marine artist whose giant airbrushed whales adorn the exterior walls of buildings across the United States. The gallery also sells paintings and sculptures by other marine artists.

Clothing

Island Wear

Hilo Hattie (✉ Lahaina Center, Lahaina, ☎ 808/661–8457), Hawai'i's largest manufacturer of aloha shirts and mu'umu'u, also carries brightly colored blouses, skirts, and children's clothing.

Liberty House has the kind of Island wear—colorful shirts and mu'umu'u, as well as other graceful styles—worn by people who live year-round on Maui. The store has several branches on the island, including shops in the Westin Maui, Hyatt Regency, Four Seasons Wailea, and Embassy Vacation Resort; and in Azeka Place Shopping Center in Kīhei, Lahaina Center, and Ka'ahumanu Center in Kahului. The largest Liberty House store is the one at Ka'ahumanu Center (☎ 808/877–3361).

Panama Jack's (✉ Lahaina Cannery Mall, Lahaina, ☎ 808/661–3344) carries everything a man needs for a complete Hawaiian wardrobe: aloha shirts, beachwear, swimsuits, sunglasses, sandals, and accessories.

Pineapple Bay Clothing (✉ Lahaina Cannery Mall, Lahaina, ☎ 808/667–0402) has Hawaiian prints, cool and comfortable linens and cottons, and the ever versatile sarong.

Reyn's (✉ Kapalua Bay Hotel, Kapalua, ☎ 808/669–5260; ✉ Lahaina Cannery Mall, Lahaina, ☎ 808/661–5356; ✉ Hyatt Regency Maui, Kā'anapali, ☎ 808/661–0215; ✉ Whalers Village, Kā'anapali, ☎ 808/661–9032) has high-quality aloha shirts in the subtler shadings local men favor for business attire.

Ukulele Clothing Co. (✉ Ka'ahumanu Center, Kahului, ☎ 808/871–7290; ✉ 834 Front St., Lahaina, ☎ 808/667–2521) has terrific casual wear in subtle prints and solids.

Resort Wear

Not all Maui's casual clothing is floral. You can find island-worthy sportswear in shops all over the Valley Isle, including most of the stores that sell Island wear, as well as these:

Honolua Surf Company (✉ 845 Front St., Lahaina, ☎ 808/661–8848; ✉ Whalers Village, Kā'anapali, ☎ 808/661–5455; ✉ Lahaina Cannery Mall, Lahaina, ☎ 808/661–5777) sells casual clothing and sportswear for young women.

Kramer's Men's Wear (⊠ Lahaina Cannery Mall, Lahaina, ☎ 808/661–5377) has a good selection of men's clothing in large sizes.

Paradise Clothing (⊠ Whalers Village, Kā'anapali, ☎ 808/661–4638) carries Speedo brand swimwear for men, women, and children.

SGT Leisure (⊠ 701 Front St., Lahaina, ☎ 808/667–0661; ⊠ Whalers Village, Kā'anapali, ☎ 808/667–9433) has resortwear by Tori Richards and other designers. **SGT Leisure Cabana** (⊠ Wailea Shopping Center, Wailea, ☎ 808/874–5647) is the company's first men's store on Maui, but ladies, too, shop here for the '40s and '50s vintage silk shirts by Avanti. Also at the Wailea Shopping Center, another SGT Leisure (☎ 808/879–5186), referred to as the logo shop, sells silk-screened and embroidered apparel designed by the company's owners. The stores also carry bags, hats, and other accessories.

At **Tropical Tantrum Outlet Store** (⊠ 395 Dairy Rd., Kahului, ☎ 808/871–9558) you'll find a wide selection of stylish resort wear, as well as aloha shirts and mu'umu'u, for 50% less than the company's retail store prices. This well-known outfitter has four retail stores on Maui (⊠ Azeka Place Shopping Center, Kīhei, ☎ 808/874–3835; ⊠ Ka'ahumanu Center, Kahului, ☎ 808/871–8088; ⊠ Kama'ole Shopping Center, Kīhei, ☎ 808/875–4433; and ⊠ 275 Ka'ahumanu Ave., Kahului, ☎ 808/877–0441).

Flea Market

The **Maui Swap Meet** flea market is the biggest bargain on Maui, with crafts, gifts, souvenirs, fruit, flowers, jewelry, antiques, art, shells, and lots more. ⊠ *Kahului Fairgrounds, Hwy. 350, off S. Pu'unēnē Ave., Kahului.* 🎫 *50¢.* ⏰ *Sat. 5:30–noon.*

Food

Many visitors to Hawai'i opt to take home some of the local produce: pineapples, papayas, coconut, or Maui onions. You can find jams and jellies—some of them "Made on Maui" products—in a wide variety of tropical flavors. Cook Kwee's Maui Cookies have gained quite a following, as have Maui Potato Chips. Both are available in most Valley Isle grocery stores. Coffee sellers now have Maui-grown and -roasted beans alongside the better-known Kona varieties.

Remember that fresh fruit must be inspected by the U.S. Department of Agriculture before it can leave the state, so it's safer to buy a box that has already passed muster.

Airport Flower & Fruit Co. (☎ 808/243–9367 or 800/922–9352) sells ready-to-ship pineapples, Maui onions, papayas, and fresh coconuts.

Take Home Maui (⊠ 121 Dickenson St., Lahaina, ☎ 808/661–8067 or 800/545–6284) will supply, pack, and deliver produce free to the airport or your hotel.

Gifts

Dan's Green House (⊠ 133 Prison St., Lahaina, ☎ 808/661–8412) has some truly unusual offerings—adorable baby animals: pigs, goats, birds, and cotton-eared marmoset or golden-handed tamarin monkeys that go for $2,000 a pair.

Lahaina Printsellers Ltd. has Hawai'i's largest selection of original antique maps and prints pertaining to Hawai'i and the Pacific. They also sell museum-quality reproductions and original oil paintings from the Pacific Artists Guild.

Maui's Best (✉ Ka'ahumanu Center, Kahului, ☎ 808/877–7959; ✉ Wailea Shopping Village, Wailea, ☎ 808/879–4734; ✉ Azeka Place Shopping Center, ☎ 808/874–9216) has a wide selection of gifts from Maui and around the world.

Ola's Makawao (✉ 1156 Makawao Ave., Makawao, ☎ 808/573–1334) contains a delightful assortment of whimsical gifts and affordable, contemporary, functional art made by artists from Hawai'i and the U.S. mainland. They are also the exclusive western-U.S. distributors for chocolates by JoMart Candies.

Hawaiian Crafts

Some visiting shoppers are determined to buy only what they can't get anywhere else. The arts and crafts native to Hawai'i can be just the thing. Such woods as koa and milo grow only in certain parts of the world, and because of their increasing scarcity, prices are rising. In Hawai'i, artisans turn the woods into bowls, trays, and jewelry boxes that will last for years. Look for them in galleries and museum shops as well as the places listed below.

The **Hāna Cultural Center** (✉ Ukea St., Hāna, ☎ 808/248–8622) sells distinctive island quilts and other Hawaiian crafts.

Island Christmas (✉ Kama'ole Shopping Center, 2463 S. Kīhei Rd., Kīhei, ☎ 808/874–1076; ✉ Wailea Shopping Center, Wailea, ☎ 808/875–7418) specializes in locally crafted tree ornaments, Santas, angels, and other holiday-season goodies with a Hawaiian design.

John of Maui & Sons (✉ 810 Ha'ikū Rd., B-6, Ha'ikū, ☎ 808/575–7402) turns out some of the most exacting wood products in the Islands.

A fun place to investigate is the **Kīhei Kalama Village Marketplace** (✉ 1941 S. Kīhei Rd., Kīhei, ☎ 808/879–6610), a shaded collection of outdoor stalls selling everything from printed and hand-painted T-shirts and sundresses to jewelry, pottery, wood carvings, fruit, and gaudily painted coconut husks—all made by local craftspeople.

Quilters Corner (✉ 283 Wili Ko Pl., Lahaina, ☎ 808/661–0944) has a huge selection of Hawaiian quilts and needlepoint, as well as plenty of tropical-print fabrics, silver jewelry, and other local craft and gift items.

Jewelry

Haimoff & Haimoff Creations in Gold (☎ 808/669–5213), at the Kapalua Resort, features the original work of several jewelry designers including the award-winning Harry Haimoff.

Jessica's Gems (✉ Whalers Village, Kā'anapali, ☎ 808/661–4223) has a good selection of Hawaiian heirloom jewelry, and their **Lahaina** store (✉ 858 Front St., ☎ 808/661–9200) specializes in black pearls.

You can buy brooches, rings, pendants, cuff links, tie tacks, and collectors items adorned with this intricately carved sailors' art from **Lahaina Scrimshaw** (✉ 845A Front St., Lahaina, ☎ 808/661–8820; ✉ Whalers Village, Kā'anapali, ☎ 808/661–4034).

Original Maui Divers (✉ 640 Front St., Lahaina, ☎ 808/661–0988) is a company that has been crafting gold and coral into jewelry for more than 20 years.

Shopping Centers

Maui now has five major shopping centers: the Ka'ahumanu Center and Maui Marketplace in Kahului, Whalers Village in Kā'anapali, and the Lahaina Cannery Mall and Lahaina Center in Lahaina.

A $55 million expansion has turned **Ka'ahumanu Center** (⊠ 275 Ka'ahumanu Ave., Kahului, ☎ 808/877–3369), Maui's largest mall, into a showplace with more than 75 stores and a gorgeous glass-enclosed atrium entrance topped by an umbrella-shaded food court. Stop at **Camellia Seed Shop** for what the locals call "crack seed," a delicacy made from dried fruits, nuts, and sugar. Other interesting places to shop here include **Shirokiya**, a popular Japanese retailer; **Maui Hands**, purveyor of prints, paintings, woodwork, and jewelry by some of the island's finest artists; and such American standards as **Foot Locker, Mrs. Field's Cookies,** and **Kinney Shoes.**

A sure sign that Maui has come of age is the opening of the 20-acre **Maui Marketplace** (⊠ 270 Dairy Rd., Kahului, ☎ 808/873–0400), where several outlet stores and big retailers, such as **Eagle Hardware, Sports Authority, OfficeMax,** and **Borders Books & Music,** have made their first expansion to a Neighbor Island. The center couldn't have a better location to entice visitors as well as residents—it's at the busy intersection of Hāna Highway and Dairy Road, close to Kahului Airport.

Chic and trendy, **Whalers Village** (⊠ 2435 Kā'anapali Pkwy., Kā'anapali, ☎ 808/661–4567) has grown into a major West Maui shopping center, with a whaling museum and more than 50 restaurants and shops, including such upscale haunts as **Louis Vuitton, Prada, Ferragamo, Hunting World,** and **Chanel Boutique.** The recently expanded complex offers some interesting diversions: Hawaiian artisans display their crafts daily, hula dancers perform on an outdoor stage weeknights from 7 PM to 8 PM, and a free slide show spotlighting whales and other marine life takes place at the **Whale Center of the Pacific** on Tuesday and Thursday at 7 PM.

Lahaina Cannery Mall (⊠ 1221 Honoapi'ilani Hwy., Lahaina, ☎ 808/661–5304) is set in a building reminiscent of an old pineapple cannery. Unlike many shopping centers in Hawai'i, the Lahaina Cannery isn't open-air; it is air-conditioned. The center has 50 shops, including **Hawaiian Island Gems,** featuring striking Hawaiian heirloom jewelry and pearls; **Superwhale,** with a good selection of children's tropical wear; and **Kite Fantasy,** one of the best kite shops on Maui.

Lahaina Center (⊠ 900 Front St., Lahaina, ☎ 808/667–9216) has added to its roster of shops and to its attractiveness as a "shopping event." **World Cafe** and the **Hard Rock Cafe** are great for eats, while **Arabesque Maui, Banana Republic,** and **Waterwear** offer new clothing venues. Island department stores **Hilo Hattie** and **Liberty House** still anchor the center, which puts on a free hula show at 2 PM every Wednesday and Friday. An additional 10,000 square ft of parking lot space here have been transformed into an ancient Hawaiian village complete with three full-size thatch huts built with 10,000 linear ft of 'ōhi'a wood from the Big Island, 20 tons of *pili* grass, and more than 4 mi of handwoven coconut *senit* (twine). Indoor entertainment is found at the four-screen cinema.

In East Maui, Kīhei offers the large and bustling **Azeka Place Shopping Center** (⊠ 1280 S. Kīhei Rd.). Maui residents favor the locally owned shops at the small **Kama'ole Shopping Center** (⊠ 2463 S. Kīhei Rd.). Another place to rub elbows with Kīhei locals is **Rainbow Mall**

($\boxtimes$ 2439 S. Kīhei Rd.). South of Kīhei, the Wailea Resort has the **Wailea Shopping Village** ($\boxtimes$ Wailea Alanui Dr., Wailea), with 25 gift shops, boutiques, restaurants, and a general store.

MAUI A TO Z

Arriving and Departing

By Plane

Kahului Airport ($\circledR$ 808/872–3894 and 808/872–3830) is efficient and remarkably easy to navigate. Its main disadvantage is its distance from the major resort destinations in West Maui. It will take you about an hour, with traffic in your favor, to get to a hotel in Kapalua or Kā'ana-pali, but only 20–30 minutes to go to Kīhei or Wailea. However, Kahu-lui is the only airport on Maui that has direct service from the mainland.

If you're staying in West Maui, you might be better off flying into the **Kapalua–West Maui Airport** ($\circledR$ 808/669–0623). The only way to get to the Kapalua–West Maui Airport is on an interisland flight from Honolulu, however, since the short runway accommodates only small planes. The little airport is set in the midst of a pineapple field with a terrific view of the ocean far below and provides one of the most pleasant ways to arrive on the Valley Isle. Three rental-car companies have courtesy phones inside the terminal. Shuttles also run between the airport and the Kā'anapali and Kapalua resorts.

Hāna Airport ($\circledR$ 808/248–8208) isn't much more than a landing strip. Only commuter **Aloha IslandAir** flies there, landing twice a day from Honolulu (via Moloka'i and Kahului) and departing 10 minutes later; the morning flight originates in Princeville, Kaua'i. When there is no flight, the tiny terminal usually stands eerily empty, with no gate agents, ticket takers, or other people in sight. If you are staying at the Hotel Hāna-Maui, your flight will be met; if you have reserved a rental car, the agent will usually know your arrival time and meet you. Otherwise you can call **Dollar Rent A Car** ($\circledR$ 808/248–8237) to pick you up.

FLIGHTS FROM THE MAINLAND UNITED STATES
United Airlines ($\circledR$ 800/241–6522) flies nonstop to Kahului from Los Angeles and San Francisco. **American Airlines** ($\circledR$ 800/433–7300) also flies into Kahului, with one stop in Honolulu, from Dallas and Chicago, and nonstop from Los Angeles. **Delta** ($\circledR$ 800/221–1212) has through service to Maui daily from Salt Lake City, Atlanta, and Los Angeles, and one nonstop daily from Los Angeles.

Maui is part of the world's most isolated chains of islands, so even if you fly directly to the Valley Isle, be prepared for a lengthy flight. From the West Coast, Maui is about five hours; from the Midwest, expect about an eight-hour flight; and coming from the East Coast will take about 10 hours. If you have to connect with an interisland flight in Honolulu, add at least another hour.

FLIGHTS FROM HONOLULU
Continental ($\circledR$ 800/525–0280), **Hawaiian** ($\circledR$ 800/882–8811), **North-west** ($\circledR$ 800/225–2525), and **TWA** ($\circledR$ 800/221–2000) fly from the mainland to Honolulu, where Maui-bound passengers can connect with a 40-minute interisland flight. Interisland flights generally run about $50 one-way between Honolulu and Maui and are available from **Hawaiian Airlines** ($\circledR$ 808/871–6132 or 800/367–5320), **Aloha Airlines** ($\circledR$ 808/244–9071 or, from the U.S. mainland, 800/367–5250), and **Island Air** ($\circledR$ 800/652–6541). In fact, Maui is the most visited of the Neighbor Islands and therefore the easiest to connect to on an inter-

island flight. Honolulu–Kahului is one of the most heavily traveled air routes in the nation.

By Car. The best way to get from the airport to your destination —and to see the island itself—is in your own rental car. If you're going to need it for the rest of the trip, you might as well get it right away. Most major car-rental companies have desks or courtesy phones at each airport (☞ Car Rentals, *below*). They also can provide a map and directions to your hotel from the airport.

By Shuttle. If you're staying at the Kā'anapali Beach Resort and fly into the Kapalua–West Maui Airport, you can take advantage of the resort's free shuttle and go back to the airport later to pick up your car. During daylight hours, the shuttle passes through the airport at regular intervals.

The **TransHawaiian Airporter Shuttle** (☎ 808/877–7308) runs between Kahului Airport and the West Maui hotels daily 8 AM–4 PM; one-way fare for adults is $13. You should call 24 hours prior to departure.

By Taxi. Maui has more than two dozen taxi companies, and they make frequent passes through the airport. If you don't see a cab, you can call **Yellow Cab of Maui** (☎ 808/877–7000) or **La Bella Taxi** (☎ 808/242–8011) for islandwide service from the airport. Call **Kīhei Taxi** (☎ 808/879–3000) if you're staying in the Kīhei, Wailea, or Mākena areas. Charges from Kahului Airport to Kā'anapali run about $49; to Wailea, about $31; and to Lahaina, about $42.

By Ship

Approaching the Valley Isle on the deck of a ship is an unforgettable experience. Watching the land loom ever larger conjures up the same kinds of feelings the early Polynesians probably had on their first voyage—except they didn't get the kind of lavish treatment those on board a luxury cruise ship routinely receive. If this is an option that appeals to you, you can book passage through **American Hawai'i Cruises** (✉ 2 North Riverside Plaza, Chicago, IL 60606, ☎ 312/466–6000 or 800/765–7000), which offers seven-day interisland cruises departing from Honolulu on the SS *Constitution* and the SS *Independence*. Or ask about the company's seven-day cruise-resort combination packages.

Getting Around

By Bus

Although Maui has no public transit system, a private company, **TransHawaiian Services** (☎ 808/877–7308) transports visitors around the West Maui area. One-way, round-trip, and all-day passes are available.

By Car

Maui, the second-largest island in the state of Hawai'i, with 729 square mi, has some 120 mi of coastline, not all of which is accessible. Less than one-quarter of its land mass is inhabited. To see the island, your best bet is a car. (☞ Car Rentals, *below*.)

Most of the roads on the island have two lanes. If you're going to attempt the partially paved, patched, and bumpy, and partially dirt-and-gravel road between Hāna and 'Ulupalakua, you'll be better off with a four-wheel-drive vehicle, but be forewarned: Rental-car companies prohibit travel on roads they've determined might damage the car, so if you break down, you're on your own for repairs. There are two other difficult roads on Maui: one is Highway 36, or the Hāna Highway, which runs 56 mi between Kahului and Hāna and includes more twists and turns than a person can count. The other is an 8-mi scenic stretch

of one-lane highway between Kapalua and Wailuku on the north side
of the West Maui mountains.

By Limousine
Arthur's Limousine Service (✉ 283-H Lalo St., Kahului 96732, ☎ 808/
871–5555 or 800/345–4667) offers a chauffeured superstretch Lincoln
complete with bar and two TVs for $88 per hour. Arthur's fleet also
includes less grandiose Lincoln Town Cars for $65 per hour with a two-
hour minimum.

By Moped
Mopeds from **A&B Moped Rental** (✉ 3481 Lower Honoapi'ilani Hwy.,
Lahaina, ☎ 808/669–0027) range from $13 to $24 for two to eight
hours, and are for local use only. Be especially careful navigating roads
where there are no designated bicycle lanes. Note that helmets are optional on Maui, but eye protection is not.

By Shuttle
If you're staying in the right hotel or condo, there are a few shuttles
that can get you around the area. The double-decker **West Maui Shopping Express** ferries passengers to and from Kā'anapali, Kapalua,
Honokōwai (Embassy Vacation Resort area), and Lahaina from 8 AM
to 10 PM. The fare is $1 per person each way, and schedules are avail-
able at most hotels.

The **Kā'anapali Trolley Shuttle** runs within the resort between 9 AM
and 11 PM and stops automatically at all hotels and at condos when
requested. It's free. All Kā'anapali hotels have copies of schedules, or
you can call the Kā'anapali Operation Association (☎ 808/661–7370).

The **Wailea Shuttle** and the **Kapalua Shuttle** run within their respective
resorts and are free; schedules are available throughout each resort.

By Taxi
For short hops between hotels and restaurants, this can be a convenient way to go, but you'll have to call ahead. Even busy West Maui
doesn't have curbside taxi service. **West Maui Taxi** (✉ 761 Kumukahi
St., Lahaina, ☎ 808/667–2605) and **Yellow Cab of Maui** (✉ Kahului
Airport, ☎ 808/877–7000) both service the entire island, but you'd
be smart to consider using them just for the areas where they're located. **Ali'i Cab** (4✉ 75 Kū'ai Pl., Lahaina, ☎ 808/661–3688) specializes
in West Maui, and **Kīhei Taxi** (✉ Kīhei, ☎ 808/879–3000) serves Central Maui.

Contacts and Resources

Bed-and-Breakfast Reservation Services
Bed & Breakfast Honolulu (✉ 3242 Kā'ohinani Dr., Honolulu 96817,
☎ 808/595–7533 or 800/288–4666) has statewide listings, with about
50 B&Bs on Maui. **Bed & Breakfast Maui-Style**(✉ 2825 Kauhale St.,
Kīhei 96784, ☎ 808/879–7865, FAX 808/874–0831) has listings for about
50 B&Bs on Maui. **Island Bed & Breakfast** (✉ Box 449, Kapa'a, Kaua'i
96746, ☎ 808/822–7771 or 800/733–1632), headquartered on Kaua'i,
has listings throughout the state and handles about 35 B&Bs on Maui.
A directory is available for $12.95.

Car Rentals
During peak seasons—summer and Christmas through Easter—be
sure to reserve your car well ahead of time if you haven't booked a
room-car package with your hotel. Expect to pay about $35 a day for
a compact car from one of the major companies. You can get a more
inexpensive deal from one of the locally owned budget companies. For
these, you'll probably have to call for a shuttle from the airport since

most don't have rental desks there. There is a $2 daily road tax on all rental cars in Hawai'i.

Budget (☎ 800/527–0700, or, in Canada, 800/268–8900), **Dollar** (☎ 800/800–4000), and **National** (☎ 800/227–7368) have courtesy phones at the Kapalua–West Maui Airport; **Hertz** (☎ 800/654–3131, or in Canada, 800/263–0600) and **Alamo** (☎ 800/327–9633) are nearby. All the above, plus **Avis** (☎ 800/331–1212 or, in Canada, 800/879–2847), have desks at or near Maui's major airport in Kahului. **Roberts Tours** (☎ 808/523–9323) offers car rentals through package tours. Quite a few locally owned companies rent cars on Maui, including **Rent-A-Jeep** (☎ 808/877–6626), which will pick you up at Kahului Airport.

Doctors

Doctors on Call (✉ Hyatt Regency Maui, Nāpili Tower, Suite 100, Kā'anapali, ☎ 808/667–7676) are doctors serving West Maui.

A walk-in clinic at Whalers Village, **West Maui Health Care Center** was created by two doctors in 1980 to treat visitors to West Maui. ✉ *2435 Kā'anapali Pkwy., Suite H-7, Kā'anapali,* ☎ *808/667–9721.* ☉ *Daily 8 AM–10 PM.*

Kīhei Clinic Medical Services (✉ 2349 S. Kīhei Rd., Suite D, Kīhei, ☎ 808/879–1440) is in the central part of the Valley Isle and geared toward working with visitors in Kīhei and Wailea.

HOSPITALS
Hāna Medical Center (✉ Hāna Hwy., Hāna, ☎ 808/248–8294). **Kula Hospital** (✉ 204 Kula Hwy., Kula, ☎ 808/878–1221). **Maui Memorial Hospital** (✉ 221 Mahalani, Wailuku, ☎ 808/244–9056).

Emergencies

Police, fire, or ambulance (☎ 911). **Coast Guard Rescue Center** (☎ 800/552–6458). **Suicide and Crisis Center Help Line** (☎ 808/244–7407).

Grocers

Safeway has two stores on the island open 24 hours daily. One in Lahaina serves West Maui (✉ Lahaina Cannery Mall, Honoapi'ilani Hwy., Lahaina, ☎ 808/667–4392). The other location (✉ 170 E. Kamehameha Ave., Kahului, ☎ 808/877–3377) provides a convenient stop for visitors who are shopping at Ka'ahumanu Center or touring the historic sites of Central Maui before returning to Wailea lodgings.

Foodland (✉ 1881 S. Kīhei Rd., Kīhei, ☎ 808/879–9350), in the Kīhei Town Center, is the most convenient supermarket for visitors staying in Wailea. It's open around the clock. The **Lahaina Square Shopping Center Foodland** (✉ 840 Waine'e St., Lahaina, ☎ 808/661–0975) serves West Maui and is open daily from 6 AM to midnight.

Guided Tours

AERIAL TOURS
Flightseeing excursions are available by helicopter to Hāna and the Haleakalā Crater or for circle island tours with such fancy names as Ultimate Experience or Circle Island Deluxe. Some trips last two hours or more. Prices run from about $100 for a half-hour rain-forest tour to $250 for a two-hour, champagne-landing mega-experience.

It takes about 90 minutes to travel inside the volcano, then down to the village of Hāna. Some companies stop in secluded areas for refreshments. Helicopter-tour operators throughout the state come under sharp scrutiny for passenger safety and equipment maintenance. Noise levels are a concern as well; residents have become pretty vocal about regulating this kind of pollution. Don't be afraid to ask about a company's safety record, flight paths, age of equipment, and level of operator experience.

Blue Hawaiian Helicopters (✉ Kahului Heliport, Hanger 105, Kahului 96732, ☎ 808/871–8844) has been providing aerial adventures in Hawai'i since 1985. Its ASTAR helicopters are air-conditioned and have noise-canceling headsets for all passengers.

Hawai'i Helicopters (✉ Kahului Heliport, Hangar 106, Kahului 96732, ☎ 808/877–3900, 800/994–9099, or 800/367–7095) is one of the most experienced operators on Maui.

Air Maui (✉ Kahului Heliport, Hangar 110, Kahului 96732, ☎ 808/ 877–7005) is another company with experienced pilots.

If you'd rather stay on the ground while viewing the wonders of Maui from the air—at a much lower cost, **Incredible Journeys** (✉ Hyatt Regency Maui lobby, 200 Nohea Kai Dr., Kā'anapali, ☎ 808/661–0092) will take you on board a flight simulator—a mock-up model of an actual helicopter facing a surround-view screen. The experience is surprisingly realistic, but make sure they have a fairly new film in the projector or the thrill will be marred by scratches and blurred focus.

GROUND TOURS

This is a big island to see in one day, so tour companies combine various sections of it—either Haleakalā, 'Iao Needle, and Central Maui, or West Maui and its environs in various tour packages to appeal to every visitor. Contact the companies listed here for a brochure of their current offerings, or call them when you're on the island. Very often your hotel has a tour desk to facilitate arrangements.

A tour of **Haleakalā** and **Upcountry** is usually a half-day excursion; this tour is offered in several versions by different companies. The trip often includes stops at a protea farm and at Tedeschi Vineyards and Winery, the only place in Hawai'i where wine is made. The cost is about $55. A Haleakalā sunrise tour starts before dawn so that visitors get to the top of the dormant volcano before the sun peeks over the horizon. Some companies throw in champagne to greet the sunrise. Cost of the six-hour tour starts at about $50.

A tour of **Hāna** is almost always done in a van, as the winding road to Hāna just doesn't provide a comfortable ride in bigger buses. Of late, Hāna has so many of these one-day tours that it seems as if there are more vans than cars on the road. Still, it's a more relaxing way to do the drive than behind the wheel of your own car. Guides decide where you stop for photos. Tour costs run $70–$120.

Ground tour companies are usually statewide and have a whole fleet of vehicles. Some use air-conditioned buses, while others prefer smaller vans. Then you've got your minivans, your microbuses, and your mini-coaches. The key is how many passengers each will hold. Be sure to ask how many stops you'll get on your tour, or you may be disappointed to find that all your sightseeing is done through a window.

Most of the tour guides have been in the business for years; some were born in the Islands and have taken special classes to learn more about their culture and lore. They expect a tip ($1 per person at least), but they're just as cordial without one.

Polynesian Adventure Tours (✉ 400 Hāna Hwy., Kahului 96732, ☎ 808/877–4242 or 800/622–3011) has guides that keep up an amusing patter. The talk can get annoying, however, if you're more interested in the serious stuff.

Roberts Hawai'i Tours (⊠ Box 247, Kahului 96732, ☎ 808/871–6226 or 800/767–7551) is one of the largest tour companies in the state, and can arrange tours with bilingual guides if asked ahead of time.

TransHawaiian Services (⊠ 720 Iwilei Rd., Suite 101, Honolulu 96817, ☎ 800/533–8765), one of the larger tour operators, nevertheless manages to keep its tours personal.

HIKING TOURS

Hike Maui (⊠ Box 330969, Kahului 96733, ☎ 808/879–5270) is the oldest hiking company in the Islands, and its rain forest, mountain ridge, crater, coastline, and archaeological/snorkel hikes are led by such knowledgeable folk as ethnobotanists and marine biologists. Prices range from $75 to $115 for hikes of five hours and up, including lunch; Hike Maui supplies waterproof day packs, rain ponchos, first-aid gear, and water bottles.

HORSEBACK TOURS

Several companies on Maui offer horseback riding that's far more appealing than the typical hour-long trudge over a boring trail with 50 other horses.

Mauian Frank Levinson started **Adventures on Horseback** in the '80s with five-hour outings into secluded parts of Maui. The tours traverse ocean cliffs on Maui's north shore, follow the slopes of Haleakalā, and pass along streams, through rain forests, and near waterfalls, where riders can stop for a dip in a freshwater pool. ⊠ *Box 1771, Makawao 96768*, ☎ *808/242–7445.* 💲 *$175 including breakfast, lunch, and refreshments.*

Charley's Trail Rides & Pack Trips requires a stout physical nature—but not a stout physique: riders must weigh under 200 pounds. Charley's overnighters go from Kaupō—a *tiny* village nearly 20 mi past Hāna—up the slopes of Haleakalā to the crater. ⊠ *c/o Kaupō Ranch, Kaupō 96713*, ☎ *808/248–8209.* 💲 *$250 per person for parties of 4–6, including meals and cabin or campsite equipment; higher charge for fewer people.*

PERSONAL GUIDES

Rent-a-Local. This is *the* best way to see Maui—through the eyes of the locals. Started by Laurie Robello, who is part Hawaiian, the company now has excellent guides who will drive your car on a tour tailored to your specific interests. ⊠ *333 Dairy Rd., Kahului 96732*, ☎ *808/877–4042 or 800/228–6284.* 💲 *$195 per day for 2–6 people.*

Temptation Tours offer something extra. Company president Dave Campbell has targeted members of the affluent older crowd (though almost anyone would enjoy these tours) who don't want to be herded into a crowded bus. He provides exclusive tours in his plush, six-passenger limovan and specializes in full-day tours to Haleakalā and Hāna. Dave's "Ultimate" Hāna tour includes lunch at Hotel Hāna-Maui. ⊠ *211 'Āhinahina Pl., Kula 96790*, ☎ *808/877–8888.* 💲 *$110–$249.*

SPECIAL-INTEREST TOURS

Once you have your bearings, you may want a tour that's a bit more specialized. For example, you might want to bike down a volcano, ride a mule, or immerse yourself in art. Here are some options:

Art Tours. A free guided tour of the **Hyatt Regency Maui's art collection and gardens** (⊠ 200 Nokea Kai Dr., Kā'anapali, ☎ 808/661–1234) starts at 11 AM on Monday, Wednesday, and Friday. It takes you through the Hyatt's public spaces, where a multimillion-dollar collection of Asian and Pacific art is constantly changing. Among the treasures to be found are Chinese cloisonné; Japanese dragon pots; Thai elephant bells; Hawaiian quilts; battle shields and masks from Papua, New Guinea; and such contemporary work as *The Acrobats,* a bronze sculpture by Australian artist John Robinson. If you're not fond of group tours, just pick up a copy of the hotel's "Art Guide" for a fascinating do-it-yourself experience.

Exploring the spectacular $30-million art collection housed on the grounds of the **Grand Wailea Resort** (⊠ 3850 Wailea Alanui Dr., Wailea, ☎ 808/875–1234) is like entering an international art museum. Sculptures, artifacts, stained-glass windows, a 200,000-piece ceramic tile mosaic, paintings, and assorted works by Fernand Léger, Andy Warhol, Picasso, Fernando Botero, and noted Hawaiian artists, make this excursion a must for art lovers. The tour leaves from the resort's Napua Art Gallery at 10 AM every Tuesday and Friday, and is free for guests of the resort. Nonguests pay $6.

Crater Bound Tours. Groups assemble at a Haleakalā ranger station at 7:30 AM, then walk 4–10 mi to where Craig Moore (☎ 808/878–1743) and his crew have unpacked the horses, set up the campsite, and organized a social hour. A second day is spent exploring the crater; the third day is a hike back out of the crater. Gourmet breakfasts and dinners are served. A basic three-day, two-night package is $500 per person, or talk to Moore about special arrangements and interests, including shorter treks, hikes, van tours, and his Haleakalā crater mule rides.

Maui Downhill Bicycle Safaris offers your basic Haleakalā Downhill: after instruction in safety fundamentals, you don a helmet, get on a bicycle atop the volcano, and coast down. Lunch or breakfast is included, depending on what time you start. ⊠ *199 Dairy Rd., Kahului 96732,* ☎ *808/871–2155 or 800/535–2453.* ⊡ *$95–$115.*

Maui Mountain Cruisers will put you on a bicycle at the top of Haleakalā and let you coast down. Safety precautions are top priority, so riders wear helmets. Meals are provided. ☎ *808/871–6014.* ⊡ *$86–$99, van riders $55.*

Maui Pineapple Plantation Tour takes you right into the fields in a company van. The 2½-hour experience gives you firsthand experience of the operation and its history, some incredible views of the island, and the chance to pick a fresh pineapple for yourself. Tours go out morning and afternoon, weekdays, from the Kapalua Logo Shop. ⊠ *Kapalua Resort Activity Desk,* ☎ *808/669–8088.* ⊡ *$19.*

WALKING TOURS

The **Lahaina Restoration Foundation** (⊠ Baldwin Home, 696 Front St., Lahaina, ☎ 808/661–3262) has published a walking-tour map for interested visitors. The map will guide you to the most historic sites of Lahaina, some renovated and some not. Highlights of the walk include the Jodo Mission, the Brig *Carthaginian II,* the Baldwin Home, and the Old Court House. These are all sights you could find yourself, but the map is free and full of historical tidbits, and it makes the walk easier.

Rental Agents

Besides the condos listed in Lodging (which operate like hotels and offer hotel-like amenities), Maui has condos you can rent through central booking agents. Most agents represent more than one condo complex (some handle single-family homes as well), so be specific about what kind of price, space, facilities, and amenities you want. The following are multiproperty agents.

Ameri Resort Management, Inc. (⊠ 5500 Honoapiʻilani Rd., Kapalua, Maui 96761, ☎ 808/669–5635 or 800/786–7387). **Aston Hotels & Re-**

WHALE-WATCHING

APPEALING TO BOTH children and adults, whale-watching is one of the most exciting activities in the United States. During the right time of year on Maui—between November and April—you can see whales breaching and blowing just offshore. The humpback whales' attraction to Maui is legendary. More than half the North Pacific's humpback population winters in Hawai'i, as they've been doing for years. At one time there were thousands of the huge mammals, but the world population has dwindled to about 1,500. In 1966 they were put on the endangered species list, which restricts boats and airplanes from getting too close.

Experts believe the humpbacks keep returning to Hawaiian waters because of the warmth. Winter is calving time for the behemoths, and the young whales, born with little blubber, probably couldn't survive in the frigid Alaskan waters. No one has ever seen a whale give birth, but the experts studying whales off Maui know that calving is their main winter activity, since the 1- and 2-ton youngsters sud-denly appear while the whales are in residence.

Quite a few operations run whale-watching excursions off the coast of Maui, with many boats departing from the wharves at Lahaina and Ma'alaea each day. **Pacific Whale Foundation** (✉ Kealia Beach Plaza, 101 N. Kīhei Rd., Kīhei 96753, ☎ 808/879–8811) pioneered whale-watching back in 1979 and now runs four boats, plus sea kayaks and special trips to encounter turtles and dolphins. During humpback season (Dec. 15–May 1) PWF has a marine naturalist stationed at McGregor Point Lookout (on the *pali* or cliffs heading into Lahaina) and also weekdays at 12:15 on the observation deck of their Kīhei office.

Also offering whale-watching in season are **Ocean Activities Center** (✉ 1847 S. Kīhei Rd., Suite 203, Kīhei 96753, ☎ 808/879–4485); **Island Marine** (✉ 113 Prison St., Lahaina 96761, ☎ 808/661–8397); and **Pride Charters** (✉ 208 Kenolio Rd., Kīhei, ☎ 808/874–8835), whose two-hour whale-watch cruise is narrated by a naturalist from Whales Alive and Keiko (Free Willie) Foundation. Ticket prices average $22–$35.

sorts (✉ 2255 Kūhiō Ave., 18th floor, Honolulu 96815, ☎ 800/342–1551). **Destination Resorts** (✉ 3750 Wailea Alanui Dr., Wailea, Maui 96753, ☎ 800/367–5246). **Hawaiian Apartment Leasing Enterprises** (✉ 479 Ocean Ave., Laguna Beach, CA 92651, ☎ 714/497–4253 or 800/854–8843). **Hawaiian Resorts, Inc.** (✉ 1270 Ala Moana Blvd., Honolulu 96814, ☎ 800/367–7040 or, in Canada, 800/877–7331). **Kīhei Maui Vacations** (✉ Box 1055, Kīhei 96753, ☎ 800/542–6284). **Marc Resorts Hawai'i** (✉ 2155 Kalakaua Ave., Suite 706, Honolulu 96815, ☎ 800/535–0085). **Vacation Locations Hawai'i** (✉ Box 1689, Kīhei, Maui 96753, ☎ 808/874–0077 or 800/522–2757).

Road Service
For emergency road service, AAA members may call 800/222–4357. A Honolulu-based dispatcher will send a tow truck, but you will need to tell the driver where to take your car. Don't forget to carry your membership card with you.

Visitor Information
Maui Visitors Bureau (✉ 1727 Wili Pā Loop, Wailuku 96793, ☎ 808/244–3530, FAX 808/244–1337, www.visitmaui.com). **Aunty Aloha's Breakfast Lū'au** (✉ Kā'anapali Beach Hotel, Kā'anapali, ☎ 808/242–8437 or 800/993–8338) is a fun and tasty way to learn about exciting and often unpublicized things to do on Maui. The orientation includes live Hawaiian music, a hula show, a comical slide show, and an all-you-can-eat, Island-style breakfast, and runs weekdays at 8:15 AM. The cost is $13.95, and visitors can get two tickets for the price of one if they attend on their first morning in Maui. **Visitor Channel Seven** televises visitor information 24 hours a day, including video tours, restaurant previews, and activities information.

Weather
Haleakalā Weather Forecast (☎ 808/871–5054). **National Weather Service/Maui Forecast** (☎ 808/877–5111).

4 The Big Island of Hawai`i

The Volcano Isle

The Big Island offers visitors unmatched South Seas scenic diversity. You can hike into volcanic craters, fish for marlin, explore paniolo *(cowboy) country, tour orchid farms, or sunbathe on 266 mi of coastline with black-lava, white-coral, and green-olivine beaches.*

By Betty
Fullard-Leo

NEARLY TWICE AS LARGE AS ALL THE OTHER Hawaiian Islands combined, this youngest island of the chain is still growing, with lava having added black-sand beaches and more than 70 acres of land on its southeast side in the last decade alone. As a matter of fact, the Big Island has the world's most active volcano: The east rift zone below Halema'uma'u on Kīlauea has been spewing lava intermittently since January 3, 1983.

The Big Island is used to setting records. If you measure Mauna Kea from its origins 32,000 ft beneath the ocean's surface to its lofty 13,796-ft peak, it is the tallest mountain in the world. The Big Island's southern tip extends farther south than any other state in the United States. In fact, to the southeast, far beneath the ocean's surface, Lōihi, a sea mount bubbling lava, is slowly building another Hawaiian island, due to emerge in about 10,000 years. Far above the sea floor, at Keck Observatory on the summit of Mauna Loa, the world's most powerful telescope searches the universe from the clearest place on earth for peering into the heavens.

With its diverse climate and terrain, the Big Island offers skiing (but only for experts) in winter and year-round sunshine on its southern and western shores, where the temperature averages 69°–84°F in July and 53°–75°F in January. Yet there is so much rain near Hilo, its major city, that its only zoo is right in the middle of a rain forest, whereas land along the Kona–Kohala Coast is generally dry, with uninhabited stretches of lava.

In earlier times, Hawai'i's kings and queens lived and played along the Kona–Kohala Coast. King Kamehameha I was born close to its northern shores, near the 500-year-old Mo'okini Heiau (a sacred stone platform for the worship of the gods). All along the water's edge are reminders of earlier inhabitants. At Kawaihae, two heiaus, Pu'ukōholā and Mailekini, mark the site of Kamehameha's final victory in 1810 in his battle to unite the Hawaiian Islands.

Most developers are aware of the reverence the Hawaiian people feel for their *'āina* (land), and they attempt to preserve and restore the bits and pieces of Hawaiian history that come to light when a bulldozer rakes the land. Such modern resorts as the Royal Waikoloan and Kona Village conduct tours of petroglyph fields on their grounds. The Royal Waikoloan at 'Anaeho'omalu Bay, the Fours Seasons Resort Hualālai, and the Mauna Lani Resort have restored the fishponds that once supplied the tables of Hawaiian royalty; historic markers make a stroll around the beachfront ponds an interesting and informative experience.

In the calm tranquillity of the Kohala Mountains to the north, where the paniolo ride the range, or at the windswept isolation of South Point—thought to have been populated as early as AD 750—you can reflect on the lives of the early Hawaiians who crossed this land on foot. Did they bring their gods and goddesses from their ancient homeland in Tahiti and the Marquesas? Or was the goddess Pele conceived as an explanation for some violent volcanic eruption?

Five volcanoes formed the Big Island perhaps a half-million years ago: Kohala, Hualālai, Mauna Kea (white mountain), Mauna Loa (long mountain), and Kīlauea, which is currently active. Early Hawaiians believed that Pele lived in whichever crater was erupting. Even today, eerie stories are repeated as fact; they tell of a woman hitchhiker who dresses in red and wanders the volcano area accompanied by a small white dog. "My neighbor gave her a ride, but when he looked in the mirror

The Big Island of Hawai'i *(Boxes Refer to Detail Maps)*

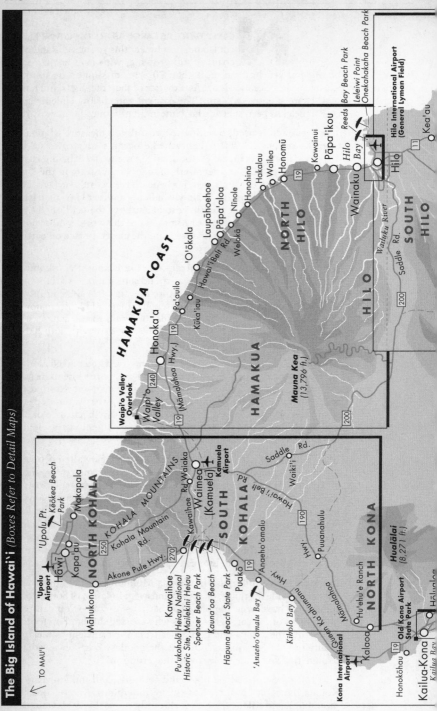

← TO MAUI

'Upolu Pt.

Kēōkea Beach Park

'Upolu Airport

Hāwī

Kapa'au

Makapala

NORTH KOHALA

Māhukona

KOHALA MOUNTAINS

Kohala Mountain Rd.

Akone Pule Hwy.

250

270

Kawaihae

Pu'ukoholā Heiau National Historic Site, Mailekini Heiau

Spencer Beach Park

Kauna'oa Beach

Hāpuna Beach State Park

Puakō

'Anaeho'omalu

'Anaeho'omalu Bay

Kailua-Kona

Kailua Bay

Honokōhau

Kona International Airport

Kalaoa

Old Kona Airport State Park

19

Kīholo Bay

Kawaihae Rd.

Waimea (Kamuela)

Kamuela Airport

SOUTH KOHALA

Mamalahoa Hwy.

190

Hu'ehu'e Ranch

Puuanahulu

NORTH KONA

Queen Ka'ahumanu Hwy.

Hualālai (8,271 ft.)

Hālualoa

Waika

Saddle Rd.

Waiki'i

Hawai'i Belt Rd.

HAMAKUA

Mauna Kea (13,796 ft.)

200

240

Waipi'o Valley Overlook

Waipi'o Valley

19 (Mamalahoa Hwy.)

Honoka'a

Pa'auilo

Kūka'iau

'O'ōkala

Laupāhoehoe

Pā'pa'aloa

Nīnole

Honohina

Honomū

Wailea

Hakalau

Kawainui

Pāpa'ikou

Hilo Bay

Wainaku

Hilo

HAMAKUA COAST

Hawai'i Belt Rd.

Wailuku River

NORTH HILO

SOUTH HILO

Saddle Rd.

200

19

Welokā

11

Kea'au

Reeds Bay Beach Park

Leleiwi Point

Onekahakaha Beach Park

Hilo International Airport (General Lyman Field)

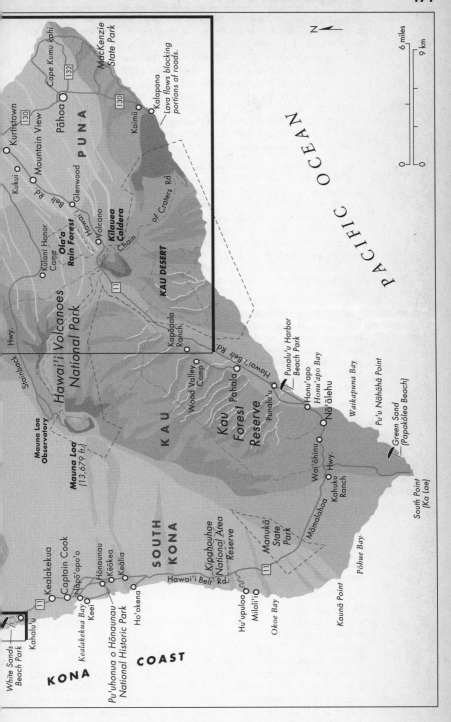

White Sands
Beach Park

KONA
COAST

Kahalu'u

Kealakekua

Captain Cook
Nāpo'opo'o

Kealakekua Bay
Keei

Hōnaunau
Kēōkea
Keālia

Pu'uhonua o Hōnaunau
National Historic Park

Ho'okena

Hu'upuloa
Miloli'i

Okoe Bay

Hawai'i Bell Rd.

Kipahoehoe
National Area
Reserve

**SOUTH
KONA**

Manukā
State Park

Kaunā Point

Pōhue Bay

KAU

Mauna Loa
(13,679 ft.)

Mauna Loa
Observatory

Stainback Hwy.

**Hawai'i Volcanoes
National Park**

Kau
Forest
Reserve

Wood Valley
Camp

Pāhala

Punalu'u

Punalu'u Harbor
Beach Park

Honu'apo
Honu'apo Bay

Nā'ālehu

Wai'ōhinu

Kahuku
Ranch

Hwy.

Māmalahoa

Waikapuna Bay

Pu'u Nāhāhā Point

Green Sand
(Papakōlea Beach)

South Point
(Ka Lae)

Kapōāpala
Ranch

KAU DESERT

Chain of Craters Rd.

Kilani Honor
Camp

**Ola'a
Rain Forest**

Volcano
**Kilauea
Caldera**

Hawai'i Belt Rd.

Hawai'i Belt Rd.

Bell Rd.

Glenwood

Mountain View

Kukui

Kurtistown

Pāhoa

PUNA

Cape Kumukahi

MacKenzie
State Park

Kalapana

Kaimū

Lava flows blocking
portions of roads.

130

130

132

11

11

PACIFIC OCEAN

N

6 miles
9 km

she was gone!" is how one oft-repeated tale goes. As far as volcanic eruptions go, those Pele has caused in recent years have been relatively nondestructive, flowing from rift zones through `ohi`a forests on Kilauea's gentle slopes. Lava has flowed repeatedly through Kalapana and the remote Royal Gardens subdivision since 1983, however, destroying nearly 200 housing units and blocking Chain of Craters Road; but no lives have been lost. You can drive almost to the end of Chain of Craters Road, leave your car, and walk to where molten lava flows into the ocean. Helicopters carry sightseers over the 2½-mi lava lake called Kupaianaha, an 800-ft cinder cone, to view steam clouds rising from the ocean as the hot lava meets the sea.

The drive along the Hāmākua Coast to Hilo, the island's county seat and the fourth-largest city in the state, calls attention to modern development on the island. Few fields of sugarcane still wave in the breeze, as most have been replaced by orchards of macadamia nut trees and other specialty crops raised for chefs who prepare Hawai`i Regional cuisine. With such major companies as C. Brewer turning to macadamias, the nuts have become big business on the Big Island, supplying 90% of the state's yield. Kona coffee, anthuriums and orchids, and *pakalōlō* (marijuana—at one time said to be the state's biggest income-producing, though illegal, crop) are adding a new chapter to the agricultural history of the state.

The Big Island of Hawai`i—with all the diversity and activities it offers—is just beginning to attract hordes of visitors. In the past, hotel occupancy has often dropped to only 50%. Perhaps there's confusion over its name. Sometimes it's called the Orchid Isle or the Volcano Isle (both apt descriptions, by the way), but residents always say "the Big Island of Hawai`i," since the entire chain—Kaua`i, O`ahu, Moloka`i, Lāna`i, Maui, Hawai`i, Kaho`olawe, and Ni`ihau—is called Hawai`i as well. Perhaps it's because nightlife is a little low key or on account of the silly rumor that good beaches are scarce here. But, in fact, the Big Island excites the senses and inspires the adventurer: you can hike into a crater; catch marlin weighing hundreds of pounds; discover another universe from the top of Mauna Kea; and outstare a shark from the safety of a submarine porthole.

Pleasures and Pastimes

Dining
Choosing a place to eat in the western part of the Big Island is difficult—there are so many good, established restaurants and a variety of ethnic eateries to try. All along Ali`i Drive in Kailua-Kona, sunny little restaurants and cafés with indoor-outdoor seating offer Thai, Greek, Chinese, Japanese, Mexican and regular American/Hawai`i Regional menus.

Hotels along the Kohala Coast invariably employ cutting-edge chefs who cook with the freshest local produce, fish, and herbs creating intriguing blends of flavors that reflect the island's varied ethnic background. Little Waimea also has an array of restaurants. With the Kohala Coast resorts established, more and more visitors are willing to make the 40-minute drive inland for a change from hotel dining. Hilo's dining scene generally caters to down-home tastes. Hilo's restaurants are often lower-priced family places where good substantial food makes up for any lack of atmosphere. Fast-food restaurants can be found along Hilo's Kīlauea Avenue, while near Kailua-Kona, McDonald's golden arches are beside Kuakini Highway 11 and a Burger King is on Palani Road (Hwy. 190).

Fishing

A big lure for visiting fishing enthusiasts is deep-sea trolling for marlin, especially off the shores of the Big Island. Each morning an entire fleet of sportfishing boats leaves Kona in search of the elusive game fish. If the marlin aren't biting, reels are often whining with catches of local 'ahi (tuna) and ōpakapaka (snapper).

Golf

Not to be outdone when it comes to scenic golf, many of the Big Island's courses are emerald oases in the midst of black, barren lava fields. Towering over this picture is snow-capped, 13,796-ft Mauna Kea, home of Poli'ahu, the Hawaiian snow goddess. The Big Island has nearly 20 golf courses that range from mountainside meccas to green seaside havens. The challenging courses at Mauna Lani have hosted the Senior Skins tournaments for more than a decade, while the newest course at Hualālai is home to the Senior MasterCard Tournament.

Hiking

The ancient Hawaiians blazed a wide variety of trails across their archipelago domains, and many of these paths can still be hiked today. Part of the King's Trail at 'Anaiho'omalu, on the Big Island, winds through a field of lava rocks covered with prehistoric carvings meant to communicate stories of births, deaths, marriages and other family events. Another option on the Big Island is hiking atop an active volcano at Hawai'i Volcanoes National Park. Here you can take an easy 20-minute walk into a lava tube or around a *kipuka* (verdant island surrounded by lava), where rare Hawaiian honeycreepers trill in the leafy trees overhead, or spend an entire day tramping into a crater where puffs of steam still warm the lava beneath your feet.

Horseback Riding

With its paniolo heritage, the Big Island is a mecca for equestrians who want to get out on the open range. Riders can gallop through green up-country pastures, ride to Kealakekua Bay to see the Captain Cook monument, or saunter into Waipi'o Valley for a taste of old Hawai'i.

Lodging

Accommodations on the Big Island vary tremendously: from hot and sunny resorts to condominiums on cool mountaintops and bed-and-breakfasts in damp, beautifully green little towns geared more toward fishing and farming than vacationing. This is the beauty of a trip to this island: You can sample that elusive thing called "the real Hawai'i" and also have time to stay at a resort designed for fun and fantasy—or, if you're limited for time, opt only for the fantasy and never leave your "total destination resort."

Many visitors are beginning to seek out bed-and-breakfast lodgings for less-expensive yet comfortable accommodations, and B&B hosts (usually outside the resort areas) are opening their doors to guests. You'll need a car if you choose to stay overnight in most of the bed-and-breakfast units or small inns and lodges out of Kailua-Kona, with the possible exception of Kailua Plantation House B&B. Such accommodations are generally small, family-run affairs that provide a cozier, more intimate vacation experience than big hotels. For more information about B&Bs, *see* B&B Information and Reservation Services *in* Contacts and Resources, at the end of this chapter.

Scuba Diving

There are many opportunities for diving on the Big Island. Aquarium, in Kealakekua Bay, is a state underwater park with depths from 15 ft to 110 ft and a popular place for introductory boat dives. A variety of tame fish that can be fed by hand hang around here. Pine Trees, in North

Kona, is an area that includes such sites as Carpenter's House, Golden Arches, and Pyramid Pinnacles—two underwater lava towers with tubes, arches, and large schools of butterfly fish and false moorish idols. Depths run from 10 ft to 50 ft. Plane Wreck Point, off Keahole Point, is for expert divers only. A Twin Beechcraft airplane lies broken in half on a sand bottom 115 ft down. Damselfish, fantail, and filefish hover around in the shadows. Red Hill, south of the Kona Surf Hotel, encompasses six different sites of large caverns and lava tubes. Sites include Boat Wreck Reef, Long Lava Tube, and Fantasy Reef. Sea life in the area includes encrusting sponges, octopus, shells, sleeping reef sharks, and abundant tropical fishes. Depths range from 25 ft to 70 ft.

Shopping

An inordinate number of talented artists seek out the solitude and beauty of the Big Island.

ARTWORK

Galleries abound in Kailua-Kona, Waimea, Holualoa, Volcano, Hilo, and even in such-out-of the way burgs as Kukuihaele, where you can purchase wonderful original artworks, fine woodwork, and other hand made crafts.

KONA COFFEE

The nation's only commercial coffee plantations are on the western slopes of the Big Island (and on Kaua'i, Maui, and Moloka'i). If you want the strongest java go for pure Kona coffee. Kona coffee has a long-standing reputation as a gourmet grind and retails for perhaps twice as much as regular brands. Blends need only contain 10% Kona coffee to bear the prestigious label.

MACADAMIA NUTS

Grown on the Big Island, these nuts are among the richest and most delicious foodstuffs in Hawai'i. You'll find them everywhere and treated in every way—from chocolate-covered to chopped for cookie filling.

Skiing

Believe it or not, you can ski in Hawai'i—atop the Big Island's Mauna Kea volcano. Because of the fickleness of the snowfall, guide companies melt away faster than a snowball in Kailua-Kona. As soon as one operator fades from the scene, however, another makes a shot at running what has to be one of the world's most unusual ski areas. Warning: It's for hardy souls only. There are no lifts, and after schussing down, skiers must herringbone their way back up the slope. The months of December through February are your best bets for skiing Hawaiian-style.

Tennis

Resort courses on the southwestern shore of the island are beautifully appointed; Mauna Kea Beach Hotel's tennis park has the best view and the widest selection of tennis togs in its pro shop. Free public courts are harder to come by but do exist in Hilo at the University of Hawai'i campus and at playgrounds in Kailua-Kona and Waimea. A tennis stadium at Hōlua is headquarters for exhibition tennis.

EXPLORING THE BIG ISLAND

The first secret to enjoying the Big Island to the max is: Rent a car! The second, stay more than three days, or return again and again until you've seen all the facets of this fascinating place. With 266 mi of coastline made up of white-coral, black-lava, and a dusting of green-olivine beaches, and with its cliffs of lava and emerald gorges slashing into jutting mountains, the Big Island is so large and so varied that it is easiest to split your stay and your sightseeing into excursions from Hilo and excursions from Kona when planning a visit.

If your schedule allows a week or 10 days on the island, you might want to spend a night or two in the county seat of Hilo, a night at a bed-and-breakfast after exploring Hawai'i Volcanoes National Park, and another in Waimea before finishing up your vacation at a resort on the sunny side of the island. It's best to follow this east coast–to–west coast order for accommodations so you won't go home with memories of Hilo's often gray skies. If you are short of time, give Hilo a once-over-lightly look, then see Volcanoes National Park on your first day, traveling the Hāmākua Coast route and making your new base in Kailua-Kona that night.

For this guide, the island is divided into an exploration of Hilo, a car trip from Hilo to the volcano area; a tour of the Hāmākua Coast; a walking tour of Kailua-Kona; and a trip around the northwest section, including Waimea and the Kohala Mountains. Later in this chapter, we've included a section on the beaches you won't want to just drive past (☞ Beaches, *below*). Before starting out by car you might want to look over the "Drive Guides" furnished by car-rental agencies; they are marked with major sightseeing stops.

Directions on the island are often referred to as *mauka* (toward the mountains) and *makai* (toward the ocean). You'll find these terms used in this chapter.

Numbers in the text correspond to numbers in the margin and on the Hilo Vicinity, Hawai'i Volcanoes National Park and Puna, Hāmākua Coast, Kailua-Kona, and Kohala District maps.

IF YOU HAVE 1 DAY

If you just have one day for the Big Island, fly directly to Hilo and rent a car or take a pre-arranged tour and concentrate on seeing **Hawai'i Volcanoes National Park** ⑱. At the Kīlauea Visitor Center, watch the film on Kīlauea's eruptions, and find out about the possibility of seeing the lava flow by driving down Chain of Craters Road. Ask about area hikes, then enjoy your day exploring Halema'uma'u Crater, Thurston Lava Tube, fern forests, Devastation Trail, the Sulphur Banks, and other natural phenomena.

IF YOU HAVE 3 DAYS

Three days will give you barely enough time to sample a few of the Big Island's myriad pleasures. Rather than wasting time moving from one hotel to another, it might be best to fly into Kailua-Kona and settle in a hotel, a condominium, or one of the elegant resorts on this, the sunniest side of the island.

Start in **Kailua-Kona** ㊳–㊻, learning about Big Island history by taking in Hulihe'e Palace, Moku'aikaua Church, and Ahu'ena Heiau. Then spend the afternoon at a lovely beach, such as 'Anaeho'omalu, Hapuna, or Kauan'oa on the Kohala Coast. Indulge yourself that first evening with mai tais by the sea and a leisurely dinner, but hit the sack early so you can take off at high speed in the morning.

On day two, head for Hawai'i Volcanoes National Park early, so you'll have time to sightsee along the way. Take Queen Ka'ahumanu Highway (known more informally as the Queen's Highway), turning inland to Waimea on Hwy. 19. Stop at a Gallery of Great Things or Cook's Discoveries (which houses Maha's Café) to see truly beautiful Hawaiian-made crafts. Then continue on with a side trip to the **Waipi'o Valley Overlook** ㊲. Finally, zip through **Hilo** ①–⑮—unless it's a Wednesday or Saturday morning when you might want to stop to absorb a little local color at the Hilo Public Market. From Hilo, it's about half an hour's drive to **Hawai'i Volcanoes National Park** ⑱ (☞ If You Have 1 Day, *above*). The best time to see the lava flow is after sunset when the red hot molten lava paints a vivid line down the side of the mountain. Return via the same route, as the drive around South Point takes forever.

If you've had enough sightseeing and simply want to hang loose on your third day, opt for a morning snorkel cruise to Kealakekua Bay, south of Kailua-Kona; this is a real joy and gives you the opportunity to see where Captain Cook was killed in 1779. If you would prefer to sightsee, consider a drive to the end of the road toward North Kohala, which offers a variety of interesting stops along the way. Head out Queen's Highway again, turning into Mauna Lani Hotel and Bungalows to find the **Puakō Petroglyph Park** (☞ Holoholokai Beach Park *in* Beaches, *below*). Take along a bottle of water to make the 20-minute hike to the petroglyph fields bearable. Return to you car and continue to Kawaihae, stopping just before the intersection at **Pu'ukoholā Visitor Center** ㊼ to take in the Pu'uko'holā Heiau and marvel at King Kamehameha's feats. At Kawaihae, Café Pesto is a great place for lunch, or if you're just in the mood for ice cream, you'll find local flavors at the ice cream shop. You'll enjoy the bucolic scenery on the way to **Hāwī** ㊺, where several little shops, galleries, and the Bamboo Restaurant are worth investigating. A few miles beyond at Kapa'au, pause to snap a photo of **King Kamehameha's statue** ㊿ and then continue directly to the **Pololū Valley** ㊱ overlook. Save some film for this fabulous view, then head for home.

IF YOU HAVE 8 DAYS

With this much time, you might consider splitting your stay into three hotels. Stay the first night in **Hilo** ①–⑮ and spend your first day investigating this old plantation town. Visit the Hilo Public Market if it's going on, shop on Keawe Street, wander through Lyman Mission House and Museum and drive up to **Rainbow Falls** ⑭ and **Pe'epe'e Falls** ⑮, also known as Boiling Pots. Plant lovers will want to visit either **Hawai'i Tropical Botanical Garden** ㉙ for it's misty, rain-forest appeal, or **Nani Mau Gardens** with its more manicured patches of tropical flowers accessible by tram.

Rise early on the morning of the second day to check out the **Suisan Fish Market** ④. Have breakfast, pack for your move to new accommodations around the volcano, but on the way spend much of your day on a leisurely side trip to **Pāhoa** ㉖ and Puna. Splurge on dinner at Kīlauea Lodge. Reserve your third day for a thorough exploration of **Hawai'i Volcanoes National Park** ⑱, including the drive down Chain of Craters Road at dusk to see the lava flow.

On day four, move on to a hotel on the Big Island's southwestern shore. Drive back through Hilo to enjoy sightseeing—**'Akaka Falls State Park** ㉛, **Honoka'a** ㉟, **Waipi'o Valley Overlook** ㊲—along the Hamakua Coast. Make day five primarily a beach day adding only a snorkel cruise or a little run into **Kailua-Kona** ㊳–㊻ for lunch, a visit to Hulihe'e Palace, and some souvenir shopping. Save the morning of day six to discover North Kohala. If you're a hiker, biker, or horseback rider, you might want to book an activity that takes place in this area. For more sedate types, a tour into **Waipi'o Valley**(☞ Guided Tours *in* Contacts and Resources *in* Big Island A to Z, *below*) is a memorable experience. After your morning adventure, the galleries and lunch spots in the little towns of Kapa'au and **Hāwī** ㊺ are alluring, while on the return drive to your hotel, history comes alive at **Mo'okini Heiau** ㊿, **Lapakahi State Historical Park** ㊾, and the **Pu'ukoholā Visitor Center** ㊼ for the Pu'ukoholā Heiau.

On day seven, take the high road through coffee country and head south from Kailua-Kona via the artists' colony of Hōlualoa to Captain Cook, Kealakekua, and Honaunau. Spend an hour or so at **Puʻuhonua o Hōnaunau,** and while you're in the area, check out the Painted Church as well. For those who are truly intent on not missing anything, the drive to **South Point** is long and affords endless impressive views of lava. Kalalea Heiau at South Point leaves you with an eerie feeling of the isolation those first Hawaiian explorers must have experienced on landing at this remote outpost. Day eight, departure day, should be one of rest and relaxation—a leisurely breakfast, a trip to the beach, golf, and last-minute shopping in the morning with departure scheduled for the afternoon.

When to Tour the Big Island

Touring the Big Island is appealing at any time of year, because there are seldom traffic jams, and basically the weather remains stable year round. It's a rare day when Kailua-Kona and the Kohala Coast are not sunny and warm; however, deluges can occur in January and February. It's difficult to predict weather in Hilo. Suffice it to say, if you are traveling in winter you are apt to get wet in Hilo. The volcano area is always cooler because of the higher elevation; you'll want a sweater or light jacket, especially in winter.

Hilo

Hilo is a town of both modern and rustic buildings, stretching from the banks of the Wailuku River to Hilo Bay, where a few major hotels rim stately Banyan Drive. Nearby, the 31-acre Liliʻuokalani Garden, a Japanese-style park with arched bridges and waterways, was established as a safety zone after a devastating tidal wave swept away businesses and homes on May 22, 1960, killing 60 people. Residents don't worry much about a tidal wave recurring, but they haven't built anything except hotels, the park, and a golf course in that area, either.

Though the center of government and commerce for the island, Hilo is primarily a residential town; its perfectly kept yards of lush tropical foliage and tree ferns surround older wooden houses with rusty red and green corrugated roofs. Bring your umbrella—the rainfall averages 139 inches per year—but do plan to spend a day absorbing the charm of Hilo. It's a friendly community, populated primarily by descendants of the contract laborers—Japanese, Chinese, and Portuguese—brought in to work the sugarcane fields during the 1800s.

When the sun shines and the snow glistens on Mauna Kea, 25 mi in the distance, Hilo is truly beautiful. In the rain the town takes on the look of an impressionist painting—brilliant greenery muted alongside weather-worn brown, red, and blue buildings. In the last few years these buildings have been the focus of a refurbishment to revitalize the downtown area and attract more businesses and visitors. The whole town has only 1,200 hotel rooms, most of them strung along Banyan Drive right on Hilo Bay. By contrast, a single hotel on the west coast, the Hilton Waikoloa Village, has 1,241 rooms.

Nonetheless, Hilo (with a population of 40,000) is the fourth-largest city in the state and home to a branch of the University of Hawaiʻi. Often the rain blows away by noon and a colorful arch appears in the sky; one of Hilo's nicknames is the "City of Rainbows."

A Good Drive

Begin this excursion driving southwest from the cluster of hotels along **Banyan Drive** ①, which loops around a peninsula jutting into Hilo Bay. On the right, **Liliʻuokalani Gardens** ② has Oriental gardens and an arched footbridge to **Coconut Island** ③. At the western end of Banyan Drive, early risers who want to see a little local color gravitate to **Suisan Fish Market** ④ at about 7:30 AM. The fish auction is a great place to hang out, "talk story" (chat), and listen to the almost unintelligible bidding that takes place in pidgin English. Continue driving, take a taxi, or hop a Hilo *Sampan* (an old open-side touring car), to **Wailoa Visitor Center** ⑤ and take in the current art show or view a pictorial history of the 1960 tsunami that swept through Hilo.

After another short drive across town to the Hilo Public Library on Waiānuenue Avenue, leave your car and proceed on foot to explore greater downtown Hilo. In front of the library are the ponderous **Naha and Pinao stones** ⑥, which legend says King Kamehameha I was able to lift as a teenager, thus foretelling that someday he would be a powerful king. Stroll southeast along Kapi'olani Street, then turn right on Haili Street for a visit to the historic **Lyman Mission House and Museum** ⑦. The restored and furnished house was built in 1839 by missionaries who came from Boston to run a school for boys. Returning on Haili Street, you'll come across historic **Haili Church** ⑧, where Protestant sermons and hymns are rendered in both Hawaiian and English every Sunday. Farther down Haili, stop at the **Hawai'i Visitors and Convention Bureau** ⑨ for maps and brochures about Big Island attractions.

If you're in the mood for a quick pick-me-up, return northwest along **Keawe Street** ⑩, inspecting the plantation-style architecture along the way; then relax over a good cup of Kona coffee at Bear's. By the time you reach Kalākaua Avenue the benches in **Kalākaua Park** ⑪ will seem a perfect respite. A sundial and statue in the park honor the popular 19th-century king whose nickname is the Merrie Monarch.

Continue makai on Kalākaua Avenue, to amble along the waterfront shops of Kamehameha Avenue. After three blocks you'll come across the **New S. Hata Building** ⑫, which houses additional shops and restaurants, and just next door, on either side of Mamo Street, **Hilo Public Market** ⑬ sets up tarps and tables every Wednesday and Saturday. Individual entrepreneurs hawk a profusion of trinkets and tropical flowers at this colorful market.

If you've left your rental car by the library, now's the time to retrieve it to visit two other popular sights only a couple of miles west of town. Drive up Waiānuenue Avenue about a mile angling to the right when the road forks to reach **Rainbow Falls** ⑭, which, after a good Hilo downpour, thunders into Wailuku River Gorge. Two miles or so farther up the road, also on the right, you'll see a green sign for **Pe'epe'e Falls** ⑮. The turbulent action of the water in potholes at the base of the falls is called Boiling Pots.

TIMING

Hilo has a well-deserved reputation for rainy weather, so strollers might face less of a chance of getting wet if they time a visit for spring, summer, or fall, rather than January, February, or March. Allow a full day to explore Hilo if you try to take in all the sights mentioned, less if you skip Lyman Museum and have little interest in shopping. Depending on your tolerance for extended browsing through Hilo's Public Market, art galleries, and boutiques—and on your curiosity about the ethnic and natural history displays at Lyman Museum—you may want to return more than once to peel away the many layers of this leisurely little town. It's worth timing a visit for a Wednesday or Saturday when the Public Market is in full swing; on Sunday the market is trimmed down to flower vendors and an occasional greengrocer who didn't sell everything the day before.

BONUS MILES MAKE GREAT SOUVENIRS.

Earn Miles With Your MCI Card.

Take the MCI Card along on this trip and start earning miles for the next one. You'll earn frequent flyer miles on all your calls and save with the low rates you've come to expect from MCI. Before you know it, you'll be on your way to some other international destination.

Sign up for MCI by calling 1-800-FLY-FREE

Is this a great time, or what? :-)

Earn Frequent Flyer Miles.

You've read the book. Now book the trip.

© 1998 Preview Travel Inc. CST #2022036-40

For all the best deals on flights, hotels, rental cars, and vacation packages, book them online at www.previewtravel.com. Then click on our Destination Guides featuring content from Fodor's and more. You'll find hotels, restaurants, attractions, and things to do around the globe. There are even interactive maps, videos, and weather forecasts. You'll have everything you need to make your vacation exactly what you want it to be. All it takes is a trip online.

Travel on Your Terms™
www.previewtravel.com
aol keyword: previewtravel

preview travel ℠

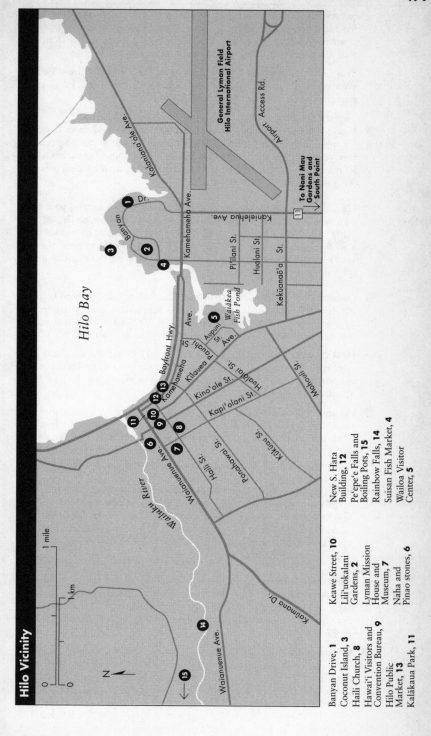

Hilo Vicinity

Hilo Bay

General Lyman Field
Hilo International Airport

Airport Access Rd.

To Nani Mau Gardens and South Point

Banyan Dr.
Kaláaniana'ole Ave.
Kamehameha Ave.
Kanialehua Ave.
Pi'ilani St.
Hualani St.
Kekúanaó'a St.
Waiákea Fish Pond
Aupuni St.
Bayfront Hwy.
Kamehameha Ave.
Pauahi St.
Kílauea Ave.
Hualani St.
Kino'ole St.
Mohouli St.
Kapi'olani St.
Kíkau St.
Ponahawai St.
Haili St.
Waiánuenue Ave.
Wailuku River
Kaúmana Dr.

Banyan Drive, **1**
Coconut Island, **3**
Haili Church, **8**
Hawai'i Visitors and Convention Bureau, **9**
Hilo Public Market, **13**
Kalákaua Park, **11**

Keawe Street, **10**
Lili'uokalani Gardens, **2**
Lyman Mission House and Museum, **7**
Naha and Pinao stones, **6**

New S. Hata Building, **12**
Pe'epe'e Falls and Boiling Pots, **15**
Rainbow Falls, **14**
Suisan Fish Market, **4**
Wailoa Visitor Center, **5**

Remember that morning hours are generally cooler for walking the streets than late afternoon, when the humidity can soar. An umbrella might come in handy at any time, but don't let it hide the beautiful rainbows that are sure to follow a sudden Hilo downpour.

You can easily include Boiling Pots or Pe'epe'e and Rainbow Falls in your day tour; it takes only a few minutes to drive the 2 mi to each. Parking is easy and roads are well maintained.

Sights to See

❶ Banyan Drive. The big, leafy banyan trees with aerial roots dangling from the limbs were planted along here in the '30s by visiting celebrities; you will find such names as Amelia Earhart and Franklin Delano Roosevelt on plaques on the trees. ⊠ *Begin at Hawai'i Naniloa Hotel, 93 Banyan Dr.,* ☎ *808/969–3333.*

NEED A BREAK? For a quick cup of coffee or an early breakfast before starting your day, try Queen's Court at the **Hilo Hawaiian Hotel** (⊠ 71 Banyan Dr., ☎ 808/935–9361). Both the window seats and the raised booths set back from the windows have good views of Hilo Bay. Hilo hosts most of the island's intrastate business travelers, so prices here are not exorbitant for a hotel restaurant.

---

❸ Coconut Island. Just offshore from Lili'uokalani Gardens and across a footbridge, this small (approximately 1 acre) island is easy to explore. Meander over to watch children play in the tidal pools while fishermen try their luck. ⊠ *Lili'uokalani Gardens, Banyan Dr.*

❽ Haili Church. Originally constructed in 1859 by New England missionaries, this church was rebuilt in 1979 following a fire. Haili Church is known for its choir, which sings hymns in Hawaiian. ⊠ *211 Haili St.,* ☎ *808/935–4847.*

❾ Hawai'i Visitors and Convention Bureau. Marked by a red-and-white Hawaiian-warrior sign, the visitors bureau is worth a visit, especially if you are just beginning your stay on the Big Island and don't have every detail of your itinerary nailed down. Brochures, maps, and advice are dispensed with friendly aloha spirit. ⊠ *250 Keawe St.,* ☎ *808/961–5797.*

NEED A BREAK? Sit back and enjoy a cool drink or an interesting and healthy snack from the take-out counter at tables indoors and out at **Broke the Mouth** (⊠ 374 Kino'ole St., ☎ 808/934–7670). Farmer-proprietor Tip Davis grows his own fresh herbs and produce, and whips up special tropical treats and no-fat herbal dressings made with Island flavors. He's closed on Sunday and Monday.

⓭ Hilo Public Market. This splendidly colorful market is open two days a week. Flowers—yellow, purple, and white orchids; orange birds-of-paradise; and red and pink anthuriums—plus tropical fruit provide a riot of color for camera buffs. ⊠ *Mamo and Kamehameha Sts.* ☉ *Wed. and Sat.*

⓫ Kalākaua Park. The park is named for the king who revived the hula after early missionaries had banned it; Hilo's annual celebration of hula, the Merrie Monarch Festival, also honors King Kalākaua. You'll find a sundial in the park inscribed "This sundial was erected in the Fourth Year of the reign of King Kalākaua, AD, Hilo, Hawai'i." A bronze statue, sculpted in 1988, depicts the king with a taro leaf in his left hand to signify the Hawaiian peoples' bond with the land. In his right hand, the king holds an *ipu*, a symbol of Hawaiian culture, chants, and hula. ⊠ *Kalākaua and Kino'ole Sts.*

HULA, THE DANCE OF HAWAI'I

LEGENDS IMMORTALIZE LAKA as the goddess of hula, a gentle deity who journeyed from island to island, sharing the dance with all who were willing to learn. Laka's graceful movements, spiritual and layered with meaning, brought to life the history, the traditions, and the genealogy of the islanders. Ultimately taught by parents to children and by *kumu* (teachers) to students, the hula preserved without a written language the culture of these ancient peoples.

Some legends trace the origins of hula to Moloka'i, where a family named La'ila'i was said to have established the dance at Ka'ana. Eventually the youngest sister of the fifth generation of La'ila'i was given the name Laka, and she carried the dance to all the islands in the Hawaiian chain.

Another legend credits Hi'iaka, the volcano goddess Pele's youngest sister, as having danced the first hula in the hala groves of Puna on the Big Island. Hi'iaka and possibly even Pele were thought to have learned the dance from Hōpoe, a mortal and a poet also credited as the originator of the dance.

In any case, hula thrived until the arrival of puritanical New England missionaries, who with the support of Queen Ka'ahumanu, an early Christian convert, attempted to ban the dance as an immoral activity throughout the 19th century.

Though hula may not have been publicly performed, it remained a spiritual and poetic art form, as well as a lively celebration of life presented during special celebrations in many Hawaiian homes. David Kalakaua, the popular "Merrie Monarch" who was king from 1874 to 1891, revived the hula. Dancers were called to perform at official functions. In 1906, Nathaniel Emerson wrote, "Its (hula's) view of life was idyllic, and it gave itself to the

celebration of those mythical times when gods and goddesses moved on earth as men and women, and when men and women were as gods."

Gradually, ancient hula, called *kahiko*, was replaced with a lively, updated form of dance called *'auana*. Modern costumes of fresh ti-leaf or raffia skirts replaced the voluminous *pa'u* skirts made of *kapa* (cloth made of beaten bark), and the music became more melodic, as opposed to earlier chanted routines accompanied by *pahu* (drums), *'ili 'ili* (rocks used as castanets), and other percussion instruments. Such tunes as "Lovely Hula Hands," "Little Grass Shack," and the "Hawaiian Wedding Song" are considered hula *'auana*. Dancers might wear graceful *holomu'u* with short trains, or ti leaf skirts with coconut bra tops.

In 1963, the Merrie Monarch festival was established in Hilo on the Big Island, and has since become the most prestigious hula competition in the state. Staged annually the weekend after Easter, contestants of various *halau* (hula schools) from Hawai'i and the mainland compete in the categories of Miss Aloha Hula, hula kahiko, and hula 'auana (modern). For more information, contact the **Merrie Monarch Hula Festival** (✉ Hawai'i Naniloa Hotel, 93 Banyan Dr., Hilo, HI 96720, ☎ 808/935–9168).

Moloka'i stages its own Ka Hula Piko festival to celebrate the birth of hula every May. Singers, musicians, and dancers perform in a shaded glen at Papohaku Beach State Park and nearby, Islanders sell food and Hawaiian crafts. During the week preceding the festival, John Kaimikaua, the founder, and his halau present hula demonstrations, lectures, and storytelling at various Moloka'i sites. For more information, contact the **Moloka'i Visitors Association** (✉ Box 960, Kaunakakai, HI 96748, ☎ 808/553–3876 or 800/800–6367).

⑩ Keawe Street. Buildings here have been restored and repainted in original 1920s and '30s plantation styles.

We guarantee that a few sips of fresh-brewed Kona coffee at **Bear's Coffee Shop** (⊠ 110 Keawe St., ☎ 808/935–0708) will revive the tired shopper.

❷ Lili'uokalani Gardens. The wide green expanse on either side of Banyan Drive was home to Hilo businesses until a tsunami in 1960 swept them away and took the lives of 60 people in the process. Today Lili'uokalani Gardens is a public park with fish-stocked streams and half-moon bridges, pagodas, and a ceremonial teahouse. It's a favorite Sunday destination for residents. Just offshore across a footbridge is **Coconut Island.** ⊠ *Banyan Dr.*

★ **❼ Lyman Mission House and Museum.** Of particular interest to history buffs, Lyman House was built in 1839 by David and Sarah Lyman, Congregationalist missionaries from Boston who came to the Islands to run a school for boys. It's the oldest frame building on the island. The adjacent museum, dedicated in 1973, houses the museum's unique acquisitions, such as wooden cuspidors carved by Hawaiians and historical dress representing Hawai'i's various ethnic groups. A walking-tour map of old Hilo Town, explaining the significance of historic sites and buildings, is available in the museum's gift shop for $1.50. ⊠ *276 Haili St.,* ☎ *808/ 935–5021.* ⊡ *$5 including guided tour.* ☉ *Mon.–Sat. 9–4:30.*

❻ Naha and Pinao stones. In front of the public library are two large oblong stones, the legendary Naha and Pinao stones. The Pinao stone is reportedly an entrance pillar of an ancient temple that stood on this site. Legend decreed that the person who could move the 5,000-pound Naha stone would become king of all the Islands. Kamehameha I, who united the Hawaiian Islands, is said to have moved the Naha stone when he was still in his teens. ⊠ *300 Waiānuenue Ave.*

NANI MAU GARDENS – About 4 mi from the center of Hilo on Hwy. 11 is a nature lover's tropical wonderland. Nani Mau Gardens has 100 varieties of tropical fruit trees and 2,000 varieties of ginger, orchids, and anthuriums. The 20-acre gardens include a Hawaiian cultural garden, a botanical museum, waterways, and waterfalls, as well as palm and orchid gardens. A guided tour by tram is available for groups of five or more. The light and airy Nani Mau Gardens restaurant is open daily for lunch. The garden can be used for catered affairs. ⊠ *421 Makalika St., Hilo,* ☎ *808/959–3541.* ⊡ *$7.50, guided tour via tram $5.* ☉ *Daily 8–5.*

⑫ New S. Hata Building. This restored structure houses an art gallery, two restaurants, and offices. The building was erected as a general store in 1912 by the Hata family; the "S." stands for the first name of the original builder, Sadanosuke. During World War II the Hatas were interned and the building confiscated by the U.S. government; when the war was over, a daughter repurchased it for $100,000. The current owner restored the building with materials used in the early 1900s and painted it to resemble the original structure. With its arched windows and decorative moldings, it is a fine example of Renaissance Revival architecture. It won an award of merit from the state for authentic restoration. ⊠ *308 Kamehameha Ave. and Mamo St.*

⑮ Pe'epe'e Falls. The falls drop in four streams of water into a series of circular pools, and the resultant turbulent action (best seen after a good rain when the water is high) has earned them the name **Boiling Pots.**

✉ *3 mi west of Hilo on Waiānuenue Ave., keep to right when road splits and look for green sign for Pe'epe'e Falls.*

⓮ **Rainbow Falls.** After a Hilo rain, these falls thunder into Wailuku River Gorge. If the sun peeks out in the morning hours, a rainbow forms above the mist. This quiet area surrounded by tropical vegetation is a good spot for taking photos, especially when the sun is shining! ✉ *Follow Waiānuenue Ave., 1 mi west of town; when road forks, remain on Waiānuenue Ave. to right; Hawaiian-warrior sign marks Rainbow Falls (from 7:15 AM to 8 AM Waiānuenue Ave. is one-way entering Hilo).*

OFF THE
BEATEN PATH

SOUTH POINT – The southernmost point of land in the United States, Ka Lae is easily accessible for a self-guided excursion by car, but unless you have ample time for exploring all aspects of the Big Island, it is one destination you might choose to pass up. If you do take the 3½-hour, 126-mi Highway 11 route from Hilo to Kona, Ka Lae is slightly farther than midway. The turn to South Point is just beyond Nā'ālehu, the southernmost U.S. town; you go 12 mi down a narrow road to treeless, windswept Ka Lae, where you'll find the small Kalalea Heiau and abandoned structures once used to lower cattle and produce to ships anchored below the cliffs. Old canoe-mooring holes were carved through the rocks, possibly by settlers from Tahiti as early as AD 750.

If you're determined to get even farther into the outback and lucky enough to be driving a four-wheel-drive vehicle, follow the road 3 mi along the shoreline to **Mahana**, or Green Sand Beach. The beach is at the base of a low sea cliff. There are no facilities, and the rip current is dangerous. The beach has a distinct green tint from the glassy olivine formed by the minerals that combine when hot 'a'a (chunky, cinder-type lava) hits the sea.

④ **Suisan Fish Market.** The liveliest action in town takes place at this fish auction mornings from about 7:30 or 8, Monday through Saturday. A fishing fleet arrives sometime in the wee hours with its catch to be sold to retailers. Take your camera (and a flash) to get pictures of the bright red *'aweoweo, aku, 'ahi,* marlin, and other fish as buyers and sellers do their thing, generally in unintelligible pidgin. ✉ *85 Lihiwai St. (Banyan Dr. turns left onto Lihiwai St.),* ☎ *808/935–8051.*

⑤ **Wailoa Visitor Center.** Park and walk through Wailoa State Park to the Wailoa Visitor Center, where changing exhibits of artwork by local artists are displayed upstairs, while downstairs, a photographic exhibit shows the aftermath of the 1960 tidal wave. ✉ *Pi'opi'o St.,* ☎ *808/933–0416.* ☺ *Mon., Tues., Thurs., and Fri. 8–4:30; Wed. noon–4:30.*

Hawai'i Volcanoes National Park and Puna

The most popular attraction on the Big Island, Hawai'i Volcanoes National Park is home to Kīlauea Volcano. If you're lucky enough to be visiting when lava is flowing from Kīlauea, you'll want to make the park your top-priority destination.

Even if you don't witness a fiery display, you'll have plenty to see in the park, which also includes the summit caldera and gently sloping northeast flank of 13,680-ft Mauna Loa volcano. The lush greenery of tree ferns and other tropical plants, lava tubes, cinder cones, odd mineral formations, steam vents, and the vast barren craters along Chain of Craters Road make this the ultimate ecotour. Don't forget to take a sweater (or a jacket in winter), as temperatures can get nippy at the park's 3,700-ft elevation. Also take a flashlight if you plan to visit the shoreline lava flow after sunset.

A Good Drive

Start from Hilo's Banyan Drive and continue out Highway 11, Kanoelehua Avenue, which takes you directly to the park, 30 mi to the southeast. On Highway 11 keep your eyes peeled for Hawaiian-warrior markers, distinctive red-and-white signs (installed by the Hawai'i Visitors and Convention Bureau) that designate visitor attractions. To the right of the road you'll see a sign for **Pana'ewa Rain Forest Zoo** ⑯. Turn right and follow Stainback Highway for five minutes to see this quiet little zoo's colorful peacocks, lively monkeys, and solemn nēnē (the state bird).

About 5 mi south of Hilo on the left of Highway 11 is the marker for **Mauna Loa Plantations** ⑰. The entry road wanders miles through macadamia trees to a macadamia-nut processing plant with large viewing windows and a videotape that describes the harvesting and preparation of the nuts.

Return to Highway 11 and continue to the sign marking the entrance to **Hawai'i Volcanoes National Park** ⑱. The 344-square-mi park, established in 1916, remains a vast showcase of nature's powerful beauty. Beyond the entry booth at the Kīlauea Visitor Center you'll find the latest information on volcanic activity posted. From here walk over to **Volcano Art Center** ⑲ to see the work of Big Island artists. Across the street from the art center is **Volcano House** ⑳, a charming lodge dating from 1941 with a huge stone fireplace, a dining room, and 37 rooms for rent. Walk through the snack bar to the edge of Kīlauea Caldera and peer into the steaming fire pit, called Halema'uma'u Crater, at its center. Currently, the volcano is not erupting from here but from a rift zone on the flanks of Kīlauea. Visitors can fly over that area (☞ Guided Tours *in* The Big Island A to Z, *below*). From the lodge you can hike around or into the crater; then return to your car for an 11-mi drive around the crater's circumference on Crater Rim Road.

Scenic stops along the way include the yellow, acrid-smelling sulfur banks, steam vents, and the park's Thomas A. Jaggar Museum, on the edge of Kīlauea Caldera. As you drive around the crater, you can take several easy walks: a 10-minute stroll to the Halema'uma'u Overlook, a 30-minute jaunt along Devastation Trail, and a 20-minute walk through a fern forest and into Thurston Lava Tube.

Next, if you still have the time and the stamina, drive from the center of the park down **Chain of Craters Road** ㉑—you'll understand how it got its name when you see all the huge depressions. The road offers breathtaking ocean views and the historic lava flows are awesome to behold. A sign on the left as you drive down Chain of Craters Road marks a trail across the lava to **Pu'u Loa petroglyphs** ㉒, a field of etchings in the lava left by early Hawaiians, about a 25-minute walk.

Approximately 28 mi from Kīlauea Visitor Center on the makai side of Chain of Craters Road is the site where the Waha'ula Visitor Center was demolished by lava in June 1989. In 1997 the adjacent, 13th-century sacrificial Waha'ula Heiau was also covered with lava. Just beyond the area, lava has overflowed the road repeatedly since 1984; it's now closed.

At road's end, rangers direct parking, and you can walk (1–5 mi, depending on where you park) to where lava spills into the ocean. Bring drinking water: It's hot, you have to walk back to your car, and there are no facilities.

Return via Chain of Craters Road to exit the park; turn right onto Highway 11 if you are ready to go back to Hilo, and left if you are game for some more sightseeing. At the first crossroad turn right toward the Volcano Golf and Country Club; less than a mile beyond it you'll find **Volcano Winery** ㉓ with its gift shop and tasting room.

Back on Highway 11, drive in a southwesterly direction to the next right, and turn onto Mauna Loa Road. A sign marks Tree Molds, chimneylike formations that were created when molten lava hardened around a tree, burning it away in the process. Farther on is a little park with picnic tables, and at the end of the road you can take a self-guided mile-long walk around **Kīpuka Puaulu** ㉔ to search for native plants and birds, such as the 'apapane or the 'elepaio.

Head back toward Hilo via the Old Volcano Highway, which runs parallel to Highway 11. Pause at **Volcano Store** ㉕ for excellent bargains in cut flowers. On the road again, notice the yellow and white ginger (the aromatic flower prized for lei) and tiny, purple wild orchids that grow in profusion along the sides of the road. Nobody minds if you stop to pick a blossom or two, or you might prefer to stop at any of the anthurium nurseries along the road to see how the bright red, pink, white, and varicolored "little boy" flowers (notice the stamen at the flower's center) grow. You'll see round wooden water tanks beside weathered houses until you draw nearer to Mountain View and Kurtistown, where the city supplies water.

If you've spent a night at Volcano, you might have enough extra time to take a side trip to Puna, the vast verdant plain where farmers grow everything from flowers to bananas, papayas, and pakalōlō. Turn right onto Highway 130 at Kea'au and drive 11 mi to **Pāhoa** ㉖. With its wooden boardwalks and rickety, old wooden buildings, this tired town is reminiscent of the Wild West. It has hole-in-the-wall restaurants, trinket shops, the island's oldest (Akebono) theater, and an assortment of long-haired characters that look as if they came out of the '60s.

From Pāhoa, angle left onto Highway 132 and continue to **Lava Tree State Park** ㉗, where some of the cylindrical black tree molds rise 6 ft in the cool air. Eventually you'll reach the coast beyond Kapoho—a now nonexistent town where two roads cross. In 1960 the entire town was covered with lava. Luckily, everyone was safely evacuated. After 2 mi on an unpaved road, you'll come across lonely-looking **Cape Kumukahi Lighthouse** ㉘, completely surrounded by black lava. Returning to the Kapoho crossroads, turn left to follow Highway 137 along the coast, stopping at either Isaac Hale Beach Park or MacKenzie State Recreation Area to use the facilities or enjoy a picnic lunch (☞ Beaches, *below*).

The Puna district has many black-sand beaches, formed when hot 'a'a hits cold ocean water, to burst into tiny black granules that are broken down even further by wave action. The most famous of the black-sand beaches in this area, Kaimū, was covered by lava in 1990. Since 1977, beaches and nearly 200 Puna homes have been destroyed or moved as a result of the longest lava eruption in recorded history. Get back onto Highway 130 for the hour or so drive back to Hilo.

TIMING

To see Hawai'i Volcanoes National Park properly could take a lifetime. Winter temperatures can dip below the cotton-shirt comfort level and misty weather might not please hikers in search of clear skies and balmy afternoons, but the park is worth visiting at any time of the year and any day of the week. Its attractions are open daily. This is a national park, frequented by families, so it tends to be busier during the summer months, Christmas holidays, and weekends. For travelers who have limited days of vacation, an outing can be structured for ¾ of a day,

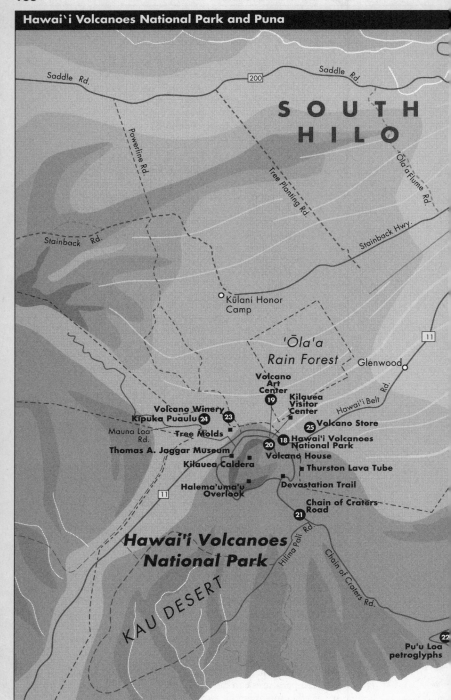

HILO

Pua'inako St.

Kanoelehua Ave.

✈ **Hilo International**
■ **Prince Kuhio Plaza**
■ **Hirose Nursery**

PACIFIC OCEAN

Pana'ewa Rain Forest Zoo 16

11

Macadamia Rd.

Mauna Loa Plantations 17

Kea'au

Kaloli Point

Kurtistown

Kaloli Rd.

Kukui

Kīlani Rd.

130

Mountain View

Cape Kumukahi Lighthouse

Kahakai Blvd.

Lava Tree State Park 27

Kapoho

28

Pāhoa 26

132

P U N A

Pahoa Pohoiki Rd.

Puna

Isaac Hale Beach Park

MacKenzie State Park

137

130

Kaimū

Kalapana

Lava flows blocking portions of roads.

130

Waha'ula Heiau (former site)

N

0   5 miles
0   5 km

or for an overnight stay if you wish to see the lava flow after dark and to take in the Puna District as a side trip on your return. For an easy day-trip, the distance from Hilo to the park can be covered in a quick 45-minute drive along the smooth divided highway, and stops can be limited to sights along the 11-mi drive around the crater's circumference, including visits to Kīlauea Visitor Center, Volcano Art Center, Thomas A. Jaggar Museum, Halema`uma`u overlook, and Thurston Lava Tube. Add a short drive to Volcano Winery, a stop at the Tree Molds, and a half-hour bird-watching walk around Kīpuka Puaulu, and the outing will take most of the day.

If you want to see real flowing lava hitting the ocean in giant billowing clouds of steam, it will take about two hours round-trip to drive 24 mi down the Chain of Craters Road to the Kalapana coastal district of the park. In your planning, include an hour to hike to the edge of the flow and back. An overnight stay at any of dozens of charming B&Bs tucked into the fern forest can add immeasurably to a volcano area experience by allowing you two days for leisurely exploring.

Sights to See

㉘ Cape Kumukahi Lighthouse. This lonely lighthouse stands encircled by lava that stopped 6 ft from its base and tumbled into the sea on either side, as if the quixotic goddess Pele had suddenly changed her mind about its destruction. ⊠ *Hwy. 132, near coast beyond crossroads marked Kapoho on many maps.*

㉑ Chain of Craters Road. No food or gasoline is available along this road that descends 3,700 ft in 24 mi to the Kalapana Coast, so be sure to top off both the tank and your appetite before you go. At road's end, you can walk to where the lava flows into the ocean. ⊠ *Begin in Hawai`i Volcanoes National Park.*

★ ⑱ Hawai`i Volcanoes National Park. The 344-sq-mi park, established in 1916, provides an unmatched volcanic experience. The park and Chain of Craters Road are open 24 hours a day, but visitors must obtain a backcountry hiker's permit to remain in the park area overnight. **Kīlauea Visitor Center** (☎ 808/967–7184; ⊙ Daily 7:45–5) lies just beyond the park's entry booth. It houses displays of park wildlife and vegetation and screens a movie showing past eruptions. If you can't see the real thing, don't miss the hourly movie shown from 9 to 4. The center posts the latest news on volcanic activity, and hikers can obtain trail information as well as information about ranger-escorted scenic walks.

Within the park, **Halema`uma`u Crater** is the steaming pit within gaping **Kīlauea Caldera.** You can hike around or into the crater; then return to your car for the 11-mi drive around the crater's circumference to **Halema`uma`u Overlook** for another view. The smaller Kīlauea Iki Crater (*iki* means little) is adjacent to the big Kīlauea Caldera. If you are in the park for a full day or more, an exhilarating hike into Kīlau Iki Crater can be accomplished in less than half a day. Hiking information and maps are available at the Kīlauea Visitor Center.

Ⓒ Children will enjoy the hands-on fun at the **Thomas A. Jaggar Museum** at the edge of Kīlauea Caldera; seismographs that measure the earth's movement will also record a child's footfall. You can also see fascinating filmstrips of current and previous eruptions.

Nearby **Devastation Trail** was created after a 1959 eruption, when fiery lava from the smaller, adjacent **Kīlauea Iki Crater** burned the surrounding `ōhi`a forest. The 30-minute walk off **Crater Rim Road** is self-guided. A jaunt through a fern forest connects with a boardwalk that leads through an eerie, barren landscape that may make you feel you're on another planet. A 20-minute walk will take you through **Thurston Lava Tube,** a natural tunnel about 10 ft high that formed when the cooling top and sides of a lava flow hardened and the lava inside drained away. You can walk 450 ft into the tube.

Yellow, acrid-smelling sulfur banks and gaping vents emitting warm steam are found throughout the cool environs of the park. Pregnant women and anyone with heart or respiratory problems should avoid both the sulfur banks and the fumes emitted from the center of Halemaʻumaʻu Crater. ⊠ *Highway Belt Rd. (Hwy. 11), Box 52, Hawaiʻi Volcanoes National Park 96718,* ☎ *808/985–6000,* ☞ *$10 per car, $5 on foot or bike, $20 annual pass Thomas A. Jaggar Museum,*☎ *808/967–7643;* ☞ *free;* ⊙ *Daily 8:30–5.*

❷ **Kīpuka Puaulu.** A *kīpuka* is a green, forested island surrounded by a sea of lava; this site is also known as Bird Park. Let the children identify a koa tree and search for native birds, such as the *ʻapapane* or the *ʻelepaio.* A written guide with numbers that correspond to sites along the kīpuka's trail is available at Kīlauea Visitor Center. ⊠ *Mauna Loa Rd., Hawaiʻi Volcanoes National Park.*

❷ **Lava Tree State Park.** Tree molds that rise like blackened smokestacks formed here in 1790 when a lava flow swept through the ʻōhiʻa forest. ⊠ *Hwy. 132, Puna District.* ☞ *Free.* ⊙ *Daily.*

❶ **Mauna Loa Plantations.** You'll see acres of macadamia trees and a processing plant with viewing windows; a videotape describes the harvesting and preparation of the nuts. Children can run off their energy on the nature trail, and there's a place to buy snacks or enjoy your own picnic lunch. ⊠ *Macadamia Rd. on Hwy. 11 south of Hilo,* ☎ *808/966–8612.* ☞ *Orchard tram tour $5; self-guided tour free.* ⊙ *Daily 8:30–5.*

❷ **Pāhoa.** This little town has wooden boardwalks and rickety buildings reminiscent of the Wild West. Restaurants, antiques shops, secondhand stores, natural fiber and tie-dyed clothing boutiques, and art galleries in quaint old buildings are fun to wander through. ⊠ *Turn southeast onto Hwy. 130 at Keaʻau, drive 11 mi to right turn marked Pāhoa.*

🐚 ❶ **Panaʻewa Rain Forest Zoo.** Children enjoy the monkeys and tigers in this quiet, often wet, low-key zoo. Trails have been paved, but take an umbrella for protection from the frequent showers. ⊠ *Stainback Hwy. off Hwy. 11,* ☎ *808/959–7224.* ☞ *Free.* ⊙ *Daily 9–4.*

❷ **Puʻu Loa petroglyphs.** Midway down Chain of Craters Road, a sign on the left marks Puʻu Loa petroglyphs; a 25-minute walk across the lava to where etchings of people, boats, and animals made by early Hawaiians are spread over a vast area of black lava. The round depressions are thought to be *piko* holes, where umbilical cords of newborns were burned. ⊠ *Chain of Craters Rd., Hawaiʻi Volcanoes National Park.*

❶ **Volcano Art Center.** The present building was constructed as a Volcano House, or lodge, in 1877. The first Volcano House was actually a thatch-roof hut built in 1846. The art center features the work of Big Island photographers, artists, and craftspeople. Be sure to take a look at the block prints depicting Hawaiian legends by Dietrich Varez and the unusual hand-painted T-shirts. ⊠ *Hawaiʻi Volcanoes National Park,* ☎ *808/967–7511.* ⊙ *Daily 9–5.*

❷ **Volcano House.** This charming old lodge with its huge stone fireplace, 37 rooms for rent, the Ka ʻŌhelo Dining Room, and a snack bar, dates from 1941. The Ka ʻŌhelo Dining Room is busy with tour groups at lunch time, but dinner can be a quieter experience. ⊠ *Hawaiʻi Volcanoes National Park,* ☎ *808/967–7321.*

㉕ **Volcano Store.** The old stone store has excellent bargains in cut flowers and is one of the few places you can buy liliko'i and butter sauce, a delicious passion-fruit topping made by Tropical Butters. ✉ *Old Volcano Hwy.,* ☎ *808/967–7210.*

NEED A
BREAK?

The **Steam Vent Café** (✉ behind Volcano Store at Volcano Village, ☎ 808/985–8744) is a lifesaver in more ways than one. In addition to serving lattes and distributing leaflets on accommodations and activities, it has the only ATM machine between Hilo and South Point. Drop by for coffee, pastries, sandwiches, a last-minute gift, or some simple good cheer. If you're looking for something a bit more substantial in a place that has tablecloths and an exhibition kitchen, **Surt's** (✉ Haunani St. and Old Volcano Hwy., by Volcano Store, ☎ 808/967–8511) serves a spicy blend of European/Thai dishes for lunch and dinner.

㉓ **Volcano Winery.** There's a gift shop and tasting room at this local winery. A pleasant white table wine made from Symphony grapes grown nearby, plus Lehua Honey, Guava Chablis, Macadamia Nut Honey, and Volcano Blush are available. ✉ *35 Pi'imauna Dr. (Box 843), Volcano,* ☎ *808/967–7772.* ⊙ *Daily 10–5.*

NEED A
BREAK?

Coffee and a steaming bowl of saimin at **Volcano Country Club Restaurant** (✉ Volcano Golf and Country Club, 35 Pi'imauna Dr., Box 46, Volcano, ☎ 808/967–8228) can be a soul-saving snack on a cool wet day. The restaurant, which is not open for dinner, has big plate-glass windows that afford a view of mist-shrouded golf greens, rare golden-blossom lehua trees, and an occasional nēnē goose.

Hāmākua Coast

The Hāmākua Coast is a series of green cliffs and gorges, jungle vegetation, open emerald fields, and stunning ocean scenery along Highway 19, which runs north northwest from Hilo. The 47-mi drive winds through little plantation towns, Pāpa'ikou, Honomū, Laupāhoehoe, and Honoka'a, to the end of the road at the Waipi'o Valley Overlook. The lush valley floor is like a living museum of old Hawai'i, with taro patches, wild horses, and isolated little houses that can be reached only by hiking or by four-wheel-drive vehicles. (For companies that offer escorted tours, wagon rides, and horseback rides, *see* Special Interest Tours *in* The Big Island A to Z, *below.*) If you continue to Kailua-Kona, it is a total of 95 mi via this shorter of the two coastal routes from Hilo.

A Good Drive

Seven miles north of Hilo, turn right off Highway 19 onto a 4-mi scenic drive to reach **Hawai'i Tropical Botanical Garden** ㉙, a 17-acre rain forest preserve showcasing 2,000 species of plants and a profusion of flowers beside Onomea Bay. After the scenic drive rejoins Highway 19, turn left toward **Honomū** ㉚ to travel 4 mi inland to **'Akaka Falls State Park** ㉛. An interesting wayside stop along the way, Honomū's boardwalks and wooden buildings reflect a plantation past quickly being replaced by tourism-geared businesses: an inn, art galleries, restaurants, and a tiny, commercialized flea market. At the park, two falls, 'Akaka and Kahuna, are even more breathtaking after you've walked the hilly 20-minute trail to see them.

Enjoy the ride through sleepy little villages with music in their names: Honohina, Ni'nole, Pāpa'aloa. If you say every letter and pronounce *i* as "ee" and *e* as in "hey," you'll come close to the correct pronunciation. You'll come across three parks, **Kolekole Beach Park** ㉜, with

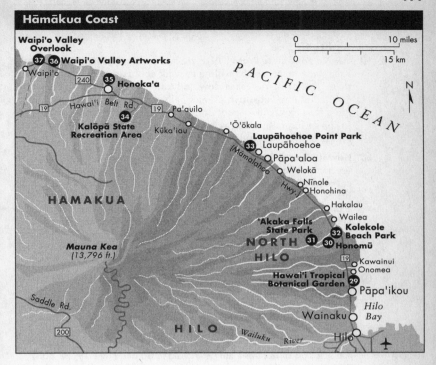

Hāmākua Coast

changing rooms and picnic facilities; **Laupāhoehoe Point Park** ㉝, for fishing; and the inland **Kalōpā State Recreation Area** ㉞, for hiking.

In 1995 the Honoka'a Sugar Company discontinued operations on this coast, and today you'll see more macadamia orchards than waving fields of cane as you near **Honoka'a** ㉟, hailed as the macadamia capital of the world. Along either side of Honoka'a's main street, secondhand and antiques stores fairly burst with dusty dishes, books, baskets, carved wooden bowls, and more.

Just before the road ends, 8 mi beyond Honoka'a, a sign directs travelers to the right to Kukuihaele, on a loop with no street name, where you'll find **Waipi'o Valley Artworks** ㊱. Besides finely crafted wooden bowls, *ipus* (gourds), art by local artists, jewelry, and stitchery items for sale, you can make arrangements here or at **Waipi'o Valley Overlook** ㊲ for a tour (☞ Special-Interest Tours *in* The Big Island A to Z, *below*) to the floor of the valley. At the end of the road, the valley is a tropical Eden bounded by 2,000-ft cliffs, more peaceful today than it was a hundred years ago when it was heavily populated.

TIMING

If you've stopped to explore the quiet little villages with wooden boardwalks and dogs dozing in backyards, or if you've spent several hours in Waipi'o Valley, night will undoubtedly be falling by the time you complete this journey. Don't worry, the return to Hilo via Highway 19 takes only about an hour, or you can continue on the same road to Waimea (20 minutes) and then to the Kohala Coast resorts (another 25 minutes).

Highways might be more heavily traveled during the weekends, but basically this is open country—easy to navigate any time of the week or year. You'll see a few more rainbows from January to March; hopping in and out of the car during these cooler months can be more comfortable than in the heat of the summer.

Sights to See

★ ③ **'Akaka Falls State Park.** There are two falls at the park, 'Akaka and Kahuna; you have to be willing to walk about 20 minutes total to see them. Following the easier downhill trail to your right, you'll pass the 100-ft Kahuna Falls first. 'Akaka Falls drops more than 420 ft, tumbling far below into a pool drained by Kolekole Stream amid a profusion of fragrant white, yellow, and red torch ginger. ⊠ *4 mi inland off Hwy. 19, near Honomū.* ☒ *Free.* ☉ *Daily.*

② **Hawai'i Tropical Botanical Garden.** Seven miles outside of Hilo, lush vegetation and flowers and stunning coastline views appear around each curve of the 4-mi scenic drive that accesses the privately owned, nonprofit, 17-acre nature preserve beside Onomea Bay. Pathways lead past 2,000 species of plants and flowers, including palms, bromeliads, ginger, heliconia, orchids, and ornamentals. You'll see waterfalls and, in the lily lake, the fish called koi that are prized by many Japanese collectors. ⊠ *Pāpa'ikou (call for driving instructions),* ☎ *808/964–5233.* ☒ *$15, family membership $35.* ☉ *Weekdays 9–4.*

③ **Honoka'a** marks the place where the first macadamia nut trees were planted in Hawai'i in 1881 by an Australian named William Purvis. Honoka'a is still called the macadamia capital of the world, though nuts are grown throughout several islands, and Honoka'a is now better known for its secondhand and antiques stores. ⊠ *Hwy. 240.*

NEED A BREAK?

A quick stop at **Tex Drive Inn** (⊠ Pakalana St. and Hwy. 19, ☎ 808/ 775–0598), in the same complex as Makana Aloha, a lovely gift gallery, will give you a chance to taste the snack it is famous for: *malassada,* a puffy, doughy Portuguese doughnut (sans hole), deep-fried and rolled in sugar and best eaten while it's hot. For a soda or a local-style lunch in Honoka'a, **Jolene's** (⊠ Mamane St., ☎ 808/775–9498) is a lace-curtain café where the *kaukau* (food) plates are piled high with *kalbi* (short ribs) and rice, grilled mahimahi, teriyaki beef, and shrimp tempura.

---

③ **Honomū.** A plantation past is reflected in the wooden boardwalks and tin-roof buildings of this small town. It's fun to poke through the collections in such shops as Glass from the Past (filled with old bottles), the 'Akaka Falls Inn and Gift Gallery, Woodshop Gallery/Café (koa furniture, bowls, and jewelry boxes), 'Akaka Falls Flea Market, and Hawai'i's Artist 'Ohana Gallery and Restaurant. The restaurant serves tasty sandwiches while the gallery showcases fine local art. ⊠ *2 mi inland from Hwy. 19 en route to 'Akaka Falls State Park.*

③ **Kalōpā State Recreation Area.** This state recreation area, past the old plantation town of Pa'auilo, is a cool, lush, forested area with picnic tables, rest rooms, and cabins. Some nature trails are bordered with plants identified by small signs. ⊠ *12 mi north of Laupāhoehoe and 2 mi inland off Hwy. 19,* ☎ *808/775–7114.* ☒ *Free.* ☉ *Daily 7–7.*

③ **Kolekole Beach Park.** At the mouth of the Kolekole River, this beach is not safe for inexperienced swimmers or surfers. Leave the local boys surfing offshore and hike 4 mi up the river to a waterfall and pond for a chilly, refreshing dip. Facilities at the park include changing rooms, barbecue pits, and covered picnic areas. ⊠ *Off Hwy. 19.* ☒ *Free.*

③ **Laupāhoehoe Point Park.** This is not a safe place for swimming—surf pounds the jagged black rocks at the base of stunning Laupāhoehoe Point, which is dotted with ironwood trees. Still vivid in the minds of longtime Hilo residents is the April 1, 1946, tragedy during which 20 schoolchildren and four teachers were swept to sea by a tidal wave. In 1988 the state constructed **Laupāhoehoe Harbor,** adding bathrooms, showers, picnic tables (open and covered), and stone barbecue pits. ⊠ *On northeast coastline, makai side of Hwy. 19, north of Laupāhoehoe.* 🎫 *Free.* ◷ *Daily 7 AM–sunset.*

㊱ Waipiʻo Valley Artworks. Finely crafted wooden bowls; oils, pastels, and watercolors by local artists; jewelry; and stitchery items are sold at this remote gallery. Make arrangements here or at the **Waipiʻo Valley Overlook** for a valley tour. ⊠ *Off Hwy. 240, Kukuihaele,* ☎ *808/ 775–0958.*

㊲ Waipiʻo Valley Overlook. Bounded by 2,000-ft cliffs and nicknamed "Valley of the Kings," Waipiʻo was once a favorite retreat of Hawaiian royalty. Waterfalls drop 1,200 ft from the Kohala Mountains to the valley floor, which was the location for parts of the 1995 film *Waterworld.* A tidal wave destroyed the former town on April 1, 1946, but a few residents still cultivate taro farms in the pastoral valley, and horses roam among the flowers and fruit, lotus ponds, and freshwater rivers. ⊠ *Follow Hwy. 240 8 mi northwest of Honokaʻa.*

OFF THE
BEATEN PATH

WAIPIʻO VALLEY – In 1823, the first white visitors found 1,500 people living in this Edenlike environment amid wild fruit trees, banana patches, taro fields, and fishponds. Once a vacation spot for Hawaiian royalty, the area today is home to only a handful of families. Here, in 1780, Kamehameha I was singled out as a future ruler by reigning chiefs. In 1791 he fought Kahekili in his first naval battle at the mouth of the valley. Now, as then, waterfalls frame the landscape.

The no-name hotel (no electricity or private baths, either)—although sometimes it's called the Waipiʻo Hotel—is the only hotel-like accommodation for overnighters. Arrangements for the hotel must be made in advance. Hikers or outdoor types need to pack their own food and bring mosquito repellent and mosquito coils (locally called "punks"). You can walk into the valley or arrange to be dropped off by one of the four-wheel-drive tours that run daily. ⊠ *For hotel, write to Tom Araki, 25 Malana Pl., Hilo 96720,* ☎ *808/775–0368. 5 rooms. No credit cards.*

Kailua-Kona

The touristy seaside village of Kailua-Kona has many historic sites tucked between the open-air shops and restaurants that line Aliʻi Drive, its main oceanfront street. At the base of the 8,271-ft Mt. Hualālai, Kailua-Kona is where King Kamehameha I died in 1819. It was here that his successor, Liholiho, broke the *kapu* (taboo) system, a rigid set of laws that had provided the framework for Hawaiian government. The following year, on April 4, 1820, the first Christian missionaries from New England came ashore at Kailua-Kona.

For visitors who are driving, the easiest place to park (a fee is charged) is at King Kamehameha's Kona Beach Hotel, but free parking is available if you enter Kailua via Palani Road, or Highway 190. Turn left onto Kuakini Highway; in half a block turn right and then immediately left into the parking lot. Walk makai on Likana Lane half a block to Aliʻi Drive.

A Good Walk

Begin the ½-mi walk at **King Kamehameha's Kona Beach Hotel** ㊳ at the northern end of town, where artifacts and pictures of early kings are displayed in the lobby. The hotel offers free tours of **Ahu'ena Heaiu** ㊴ or you can wander around the two stone platforms at the ocean's edge to view a reconstructed grass hut on your own. Next, investigate **Kailua Pier** ㊵ and the seawall where fishermen cast their lines in the afternoon and weavers make bowls and hats of coconut fronds; a submarine ride departs from the pier (☞ Guided Tours *in* Contacts and Resources, *below*). Then take in **Hulihe'e Palace** ㊶, one of only three royal palaces in the United States, and **Moku'aikaua Church** ㊷, built in 1836 of black stone and white coral mortar, before tackling a plethora of shops filled with tropical clothing, souvenir T-shirts, jewelry, and local crafts in the block-long, oceanfront **Kona Inn Shopping Village** ㊸. Much of the shopping area is converted from the old Kona Inn, a once-prestigious hotel now fondly remembered as a symbol of a more gracious era; Kona Inn Restaurant is still a popular gathering place for cocktails at sunset. At the southern end of Ali'i Drive, **Hale Hālāwai Pavilion** ㊹ or the **Waterfront Row** ㊺ restaurant complex furnish welcome respites. You can shop for tropical flowers and fruit in the colorful Kailua Village Market, which is in a public parking lot on Ali'i Drive. End your walk a few steps to the south at **St. Michael's Church** ㊻, next to the site of the first Catholic church built in Kona in the 1840s.

Ali'i Drive continues for 6 mi along the oceanfront, past Disappearing Sands Beach, the tiny blue-and-white St. Peter's Catholic Church, the ruins of a heiau, and Kahalu'u Beach Park. Elegant condos with beautifully landscaped grounds, the golf course of the Kona Country Club, and the Keauhou Shopping Center are all part of the scenery before the road ends just beyond the Kona Surf Resort at Keauhou.

TIMING

You can walk the whole ½-mi length of "downtown" Kailua-Kona and back again in 45 minutes, or else spend an entire day here, taking time to browse in the shops, do the historical tours, have lunch, and simply breathe in the atmosphere.

The village enjoys year-round sunshine—except for the rare deluge in winter. Mornings offer cooler weather, smaller crowds, and more birds singing in the banyan trees, but afternoon outings are good to view the action or stop for a cool drink overlooking the ocean.

Sights to See

39 **Ahu'ena Heiau.** This has been restored with thatched houses, so be sure you have your camera ready. Beside the lagoon on Kamakahonu Beach, just outside King Kamehameha's Kona Beach Hotel, this is the area where King Kamehameha I lived between 1813 and 1819. Built by early Hawaiians, the stone platforms of heiaus often had grass huts on top. Many heiaus can be found in the Islands; only a few have been restored. Free tours start from King Kamehameha's Kona Beach Hotel. ✉ *75-5660 Palani Rd.,* ☎ *808/329–2911.* *Free.* ⏲ *Tours weekdays, 1:30.*

OFF THE BEATEN PATH

ASTRONAUT ELLISON S. ONIZUKA SPACE CENTER – This facility 7 mi north of Kailua-Kona, at the airport, was opened in 1991 as a tribute to Hawai'i's first astronaut, who was killed in the 1986 *Challenger* disaster. The space center has computer-interactive exhibits. Visitors can launch a miniature rocket and rendezvous with an object in space, feel the effects of gyroscopic stabilization, and view educational films in the 20-seat theater. ✉ *Kona International Airport, Kailua-Kona,* ☎ *808/329–3441.* *$3.* ⏲ *Daily 8:30–4:30.*

44 **Hale Hālāwai Pavilion.** Benches under the trees at the ocean's edge are a perfect place to soak up the view and enjoy a calm respite from shopping in town. ✉ *Southern end of Ali'i Dr.*

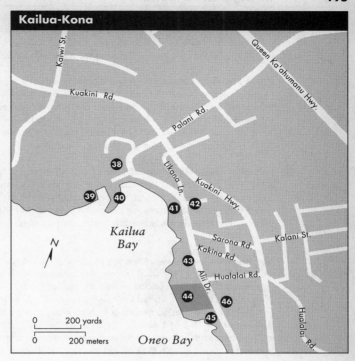

Kailua-Kona

★ ④¹ **Huliheʻe Palace.** Fronted by a wrought-iron gate decorated with the royal crest, Huliheʻe Palace is one of only three royal palaces in America. The two-story residence was built of lava, coral, koa wood, and ʻōhiʻa timbers in 1838 by the island's governor, John Adams Kuakini, a year after he completed Mokuʻaikaua Church. During the 1880s it served as King David Kalākaua's summer palace. Tour guides at the restored palace can fill you in on the royal lifestyle here, but the oversize doors and koa-wood furniture will more graphically illustrate how huge some of the Hawaiian people were—chiefs and kings alike. During weekday afternoons hula *hālau* (schools) rehearse on the grounds. ⊠ *75-5718 Aliʻi Dr.,* ☎ *808/329–1877.* 🎟 *$5.* ☉ *Weekdays 9–4, weekends 10–4.*

④⁰ **Kailua Pier.** Built in 1918, Kailua Pier is the hub of ocean activity. Outrigger canoe teams practice, snorkeling and fishing tours depart, and fishing boats come in at dusk to weigh their catches. Though big game fish are now often weighed at Honokohau Harbor, north of Kailua-Kona, pier activity is intense during marlin tournament season in August and September. Each October 1,400 international athletes swim 2½ mi from the pier to begin the grueling Ironman Triathlon competition that includes a 112-mi bike race and a marathon.

Along the **seawall** fishermen and children daily cast their lines. For youngsters, a bamboo pole and hook are easy to come by in the village, and plenty of locals are willing to give pointers. ⊠ *Next to King Kamehameha Kona Beach Hotel; seawall is between Kailua Pier and Huliheʻe Palace on Aliʻi Dr.*

③⁸ **King Kamehameha's Kona Beach Hotel.** Stroll through the high-ceiling lobby, reminiscent of a covered shopping mall, to view museum-quality displays of Hawaiian artifacts and mounted marlin and trophies from past Hawaiian International Billfish Tournaments. The 1986 winner of the Hawaiian Billfish Tournament, a marlin that weighed in at 1,062 pounds, hangs on one wall; the 1,166-pound 1993 record-setter is a floor display. Lobby shops in this hotel are some of the nicest in town. ⊠ *75-5660 Palani Rd., Kailua-Kona,* ☎ *808/329–2911.*

OFF THE
BEATEN PATH

KONA BREWING COMPANY – A few blocks mauka of King Kamehameha's Kona Beach Hotel, Kona Brewing Company offers thirst-quenching tours and tastings. Its wheat ale, flavored with liliko'i, is a staple of the company's pub, which opened on site in 1998. ⊠ *North Kona Shopping Center, 75-5629 Kuakini Hwy., Kailua-Kona,* ☎ *808/ 334–1133.* ☒ *Free.* ☺ *Weekdays 9–5, Sat. 10–4.*

43 Kona Inn Shopping Village. Much of this shopping arcade was once Kona Inn, a hotel built in 1929 that was a longtime landmark. Prior to the construction of the inn, the personal heiau of King Liholiho was on this shore. Broad lawns on the ocean side are lovely for afternoon picnics. The boardwalk is bordered with shops and restaurants. ⊠ *75-5744 Ali'i Dr.*

NEED A
BREAK?

Mrs. Barry's Kona Cookies (⊠ Kona Inn Shopping Village, 75-5744 Ali'i Dr., ☎ 808/324–6055) is the only place you can buy Mrs. Barry's prize-winning Mac Nut (macadamia nut) cookies (or 10 other varieties). Next door is the Kona Coffee Café, which serves 100% Kona coffee. For cocktails at sunset go next door to Mrs. Barry's to the **Kona Inn Restaurant** (⊠ 75-5744 Ali'i Dr., ☎ 808/329–4455), a traditional favorite. Some visitors bring lawn chairs and stretch out with a good book in the afternoon beneath the coconut trees on the lawn between the restaurant and the ocean.

★ **42 Moku'aikaua Church.** Also known as the Church of the Chimes—they sound on the hour—the present church was built in 1836, though the original was founded in 1820 by Hawai'i's first missionaries and was the earliest Christian church in the Islands. Moku'aikaua Church is built of black stone from an abandoned heiau, which was mortared with white coral and topped by an impressive steeple. Inside are pews, balconies, and at the back, a panel of gleaming koa wood, behind which is a model of the brig *Thaddeus.* There are no tour guides, but church employees are happy to tell you about the artifacts. ⊠ *75–5713 Ali'i Dr.,* ☎ *808/329–0655.*

OFF THE
BEATEN PATH

PU'UHONUA O HŌNAUNAU – Far off the beaten path, about 20 mi south of Kailua-Kona, this 180-acre national historic park is perfect for a painless dose of history. In early times, kapu breakers, criminals, and prisoners of war who escaped and reached this place of refuge were allowed to live and to escape punishment upon purification by the priests who lived within its walls. Hale-o-Keawe Heiau, built in 1650, has been restored, and wood images of Hawaiian gods have been replaced within and along its outer boundaries. With a self-guided tour map you can proceed at your own pace. Demonstrations of Hawaiian skills, games, poi pounding, canoe making, and more are frequently scheduled. Tidal pools and a picnic area with bathrooms are part of the complex. ⊠ *Follow Hwy. 11 south of Kailua-Kona to Kēōkea, turn right and follow Hwy. 160 3½ mi to Pu'uhonua o Hōnaunau,* ☎ *808/328–2326.* ☒ *$2.* ☺ *Daily 7:30–5:30.*

46 St. Michael's Church. The site of the first Catholic church built in Kona, in 1840, is marked by a small thatch structure to the left of the present pink church at the entrance to a poorly maintained graveyard.

In front of the church a grotto shrine constructed of coral holds a statue of the Virgin Mary. ⊠ *75-5769 Ali'i Dr.,* ☎ *808/326–7771.*

NEED A
BREAK?

Lava Java (⊠ 75-5799 Ali'i Dr., ☎ 808/327–2161) is a dandy place to while away an early morning hour or take a sunset break with a cappuccino, a mocha java accompanied by fresh-baked cinnamon rolls, or a scoop of Tropical Dreams ice cream.

45 **Waterfront Row.** Built in the early 1990s, this wooden complex houses several restaurants, including the popular Chart House, reliable for steak and seafood. A view tower and benches are in the two-level complex for those who want to enjoy the ocean vista. ⊠ *75-5770 Ali'i Dr.*

The Kohala District

Along the roadside brightly colored bougainvillea and white-coral rocks—carefully arranged by local youths to spell out names and messages—stand out in relief against the chunky black lava landscape that stretches far as the eye can see. Most of the lava flows, spreading from the mountain to the sea, are from the last eruptions of Mt. Hualālai in 1800–1801; they are interrupted only by the green oases of irrigated golf courses surrounding the glamorous luxury resorts rising along the Kona–Kohala Coast. On clear mornings the mountain looms in the distance; later in the day it is often shrouded in mist. The landscape along this long stretch of coastline changes considerably from the cool 2,500-ft altitude of the cowboy-cute town of Waimea to the incredibly green rolling fields that comprise much of North Kohala. On the coast you'll see ancient stone heiau and the remains of a fishing village, moving legacies of the Hawaiian people who still inhabit the area.

A Good Drive

If you're staying in Kona or at Kohala Coast resorts, begin this tour early in the morning by driving north on Queen Ka'ahumanu Highway 19 along the base of Mt. Hualālai. When you get to the split in the road 33 mi from Kailua-Kona, turn left on Highway 270 toward Kawaihae and stop at **Pu'ukōhōla Visitor Center** ㊼. The park service ranger at this National Historic Site tells the history of three heiau (stone temples), two large ones on land and a third submerged just offshore, that King Kamehameha I had his men rebuild from 1790 to 1791. You can get a good photo of the two heiau by driving a bit farther down the road and turning into Samuel M. Spencer Beach Park.

Retrace your route and continue east, climbing on Highway 19 through Parker Ranch land toward Waimea. (Note: You may find this town referred to as Waimea-Kamuela, as well. Technically, the name of the Waimea post office is Kamuela, the name of the town is Waimea. The post office is named either in honor of a former postmaster, or for the son of the founder of Parker Ranch, depending on your source.) Where the road divides and Kohala Mountain Road (Hwy. 250) makes a sharp left, you'll find **Kamuela Museum** ㊽, with an impressive number of Hawaiian artifacts.

In Waimea you'll want to take some time to poke around and shop at **Parker Square** ㊾, distinctive red buildings with white trim to the right of Kawaihae Road as you enter town. Gallery of Great Things and Waimea General Store stock high-quality artwork and gifts to take home. On the far side of town, at Parker Ranch Shopping Center, a long-established visitor attraction is **Parker Ranch Visitor Center and Museum** ㊿. Mānā, the original koa-wood residence of the ranch founder, and the century-old Smart family home, Pu'u'ōpelu, which contains an extensive private art collection, are on the outskirts of town.

The Kohala District

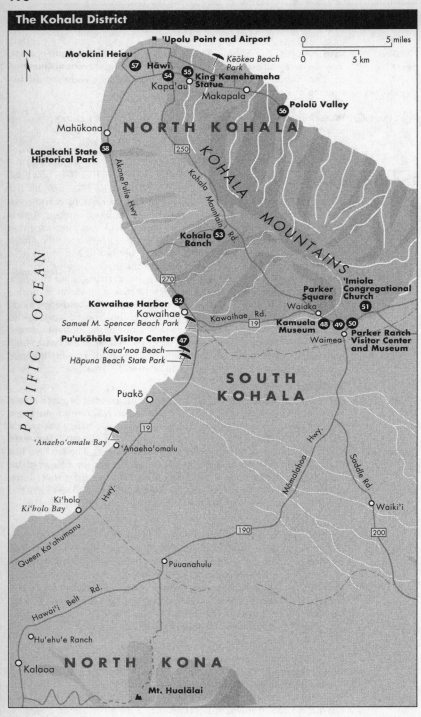

■ 'Upolu Point and Airport

Mo'okini Heiau

Kēōkea Beach Park

57 Hāwī

54 55 King Kamehameha Statue

Kapa'au

Makapala

56 Pololū Valley

NORTH KOHALA

Mahūkona

Lapakahi State Historical Park 58

250

KOHALA

Akone Pulie Hwy.

Kohala Mountain Rd.

MOUNTAINS

Kohala Ranch 53

270

'Imiola Congregational Church

Parker Square

Kawaihae Harbor 52

Kawaihae

Waiaka

51

Samuel M. Spencer Beach Park

Kawaihae Rd.

19

Kamuela Museum 48 49 50

Pu'ukōhōla Visitor Center 47

Waimea

Parker Ranch Visitor Center and Museum

Kaua'noa Beach

Hāpuna Beach State Park

PACIFIC OCEAN

SOUTH KOHALA

Puakō

19

'Anaeho'omalu Bay

'Anaeho'omalu

Māmalahoa Hwy.

Saddle Rd.

Ki'holo
Ki'holo Bay

Waiki'i

Queen Ka'ahumanu Hwy.

190

200

Puuanahulu

Hawai'i Belt Rd.

Hu'ehu'e Ranch

NORTH KONA

Kalaoa

▲ Mt. Hualālai

0   5 miles
0   5 km

N

From Parker Ranch Visitor Center drive northeast on Highway 19 to pass the Keck Control Center on the left (it is the headquarters for the Keck Observatory, containing the world's largest mirrored telescope, at the top of Mauna Kea). Then drive by the first church on the left, but stop to peek into the cream-color **'Imiola Congregational Church** (51) to view its unique koa-wood interior and wooden calabashes that hang from the ceiling.

Return through town and turn right on Kohala Mountain Road (Hwy. 250) for a scenic ride through the mountains to Hāwī. An overlook affords a view of the entire coastline, including the protective breakwater at **Kawaihae Harbor** (52) directly below. Farther on, through ironwood trees that act as windbreaks along the road, you'll see an exclusive country-home subdivision called **Kohala Ranch** (53), where cowboys and gentlemen horsemen often can be found galloping around the Polo Arena on weekends. Just up the road, Paniolo Riding Adventures guides horseback rides through the countryside (☞ Outdoor Activities and Sports, *below*).

The road rises and then drops gradually from 3,564 ft; after about 20 mi it rejoins Highway 270 at the dilapidated old sugar plantation village of **Hāwī** (54). Turn right to Kapa'au to visit the original **King Kamehameha Statue** (55).

The road ends at an overlook with a stunning view of **Pololū Valley** (56). A hiking trail for the very hardy leads into the valley and over several ridges beyond, eventually reaching Waipi'o Valley. Drive back toward Hāwī to complete the loop via Highway 270, past Kapa'a Beach Park and Mahūkona Beach Park. Feel free to pass up the two parks if you're short of time, as they do not have particularly enticing swimming beaches.

We recommend you turn off to 'Upolu Point and the 'Upolu Airport if you have a four-wheel-drive vehicle and are truly intent on not missing anything historically important. At the remote airport a rough lane leads left to **Mo'okini Heiau** (57), an impressively huge sacrificial heaiu built about AD 480. If it's not too late in the afternoon, make a final stop at **Lapakahi State Historical Park** (58), a hillside beach park that closes at 4 PM. You might want to take only part of the trail through the reconstructed ancient fishing village, unless, of course, you are driving the Kohala Loop in the opposite direction and are ready for some fine snorkeling and a bit of feasting on a picnic lunch. Return to Kona via Highway 270.

TIMING

This is an all-day excursion covering a lot of miles over ground that ranges from lava-covered flatlands with glorious seaside views to lush mountain pastures. If you're short on time, head straight for Waimea to shop, dine, and visit the Parker Ranch museum and homes, skipping the loop out to Hāwi' entirely. Allow half a day or more for the abbreviated trip depending on how long you dally in shops and over lunch.

If you're lucky enough to be in Waimea on a Saturday or Sunday before 11:30 AM, drop by the neighborhood swap meet across from the public school to pick up cookies, cut flowers, or any number of secondhand finds that residents offer for sale. Up-country Waimea can get cool and misty in the winter, but that's often a welcome relief after the incessant sunshine of the Big Island's southern coast.

Sights to See

54 **Hāwī.** The road drops gradually from 3,564 ft, and after about 20 mi it rejoins Highway 270 at this old plantation village, now home to some interesting shops, boutiques, and galleries. ✉ *Kohala Mt. Rd. off Hwy. 270.*

NEED A
BREAK?
The **Bamboo Restaurant and Bar** (⊠ Hāwī, ☎ 808/889–5555) is like a set from *South Pacific,* complete with Bloody Mary for a waitress. Sip a cool drink, or sample a tasty Caesar salad just to see the place and explore the adjacent art gallery. If dessert is more to your taste, a few miles up the road at Kapa'u, **Tropical Dreams** (☎ 808/882–1891) dishes out freshly made ice cream with such Island flavors as mango, guava, and liliko'i.

🟢**51** **'Imiola Congregational Church.** Be careful not to walk in while a service is in progress, as the front entry of this cream-color church, which was established in 1832 and rebuilt in 1857, is behind the pulpit. Note the dark, all-koa interior and the unusual wooden calabashes hanging from the ceiling. ⊠ *Off Hwy. 19, Waimea,* ☎ 808/885–4987.

🟢**48** **Kamuela Museum.** Parker descendant Harriet Solomon and her husband, Albert, have amassed fascinating artifacts from Hawai'i and around the world in this privately owned museum. The Solomons have an eclectic collection including a satiny-smooth koa table that once graced 'Iolani Palace and a stuffed black bear from British Columbia. ⊠ *Hwys. 19 and 250, Kamuela,* ☎ 808/885–4724. 🎟 *$5.* ◷ *Daily 8–5.*

🟢**52** **Kawaihae Harbor.** Of Big Island harbors, this one near the Kawaihae Shopping Center is second in size only to Hilo Harbor on the east coast. King Kamehameha I and his men launched their canoes from here when he set out to conquer the Island chain. More recently, sets for the film *Waterworld* were anchored here until sunk offshore to create an artificial reef. ⊠ *Hwy. 270, Kawaihae.*

🟢**55** **King Kamehameha Statue.** This is the original of the statue in front of the Judiciary Building on King Street in Honolulu. This statue was cast in Florence in 1880, but lost at sea when the German ship transporting it sank near the Falkland Islands. A replica was shipped to Honolulu. Two years later an American sea captain found the original in a Port Stanley (Falkland Islands) junkyard and brought it to the Big Island. The legislature voted to erect it near Kamehameha's birthplace. ⊠ *Hwy. 270, Kap'au.*

🟢**53** **Kohala Ranch.** White-board fences extend across emerald pastures dividing the land into 3-, 5-, and 10-acre lots in this exclusive country-home subdivision. An impressive **Polo Arena and Equestrian Center** (☞ Outdoor Activities and Sports, *below*) sets the stage for weekend exhibition polo matches; visitors are welcome to attend. ⊠ *Off Hwy. 250, Kohala Mountain Rd.*

🟢**58** **Lapakahi State Historical Park.** It's a healthy walk down an arid hillside to take a self-guided tour through the ruins of an ancient fishing village. Displays illustrate early Hawaiian fishing, salt gathering, legends, games, shelters, and crops. A tour guide hands out maps marked with sites and walking distances. There's good snorkeling offshore at Koale Cove State Underwater Park at the northern edge of Lapakahi Park. ⊠ *Makai side of Hwy. 270, midway between Kawahae and Māhukona in North Kohala,* ☎ 808/889–7133. 🎟 *Free.* ◷ *Daily 8–4.*

🟢**57** **Mo'okini Heiau.** Few people seek out this isolated luakine (sacrificial) heiau, but it is so impressive in size it will give you "chicken skin" (goose bumps), especially when you think that it was built about AD 480. A nearby sign marks the place where Kamehameha I was born. If you have a four-wheel-drive vehicle, take the turnoff to 'Upolu Airport on 'Upolu Point. A rough lane to the left of the airport leads to Mo'okini Heiau. ⊠ *Turn off Hwy. 270 at sign for 'Upolu Airport, near Hāwī.*

★ ⑤ **Parker Ranch Visitor Center and Museum.** The center chronicles the life of John Palmer Parker (and his descendants), who founded Parker Ranch in 1847, when King Kamehameha I gave each newcomer 2 acres of land. The museum uses life-size dioramas and a 22-minute video to detail the growth of the ranch. A couple of miles south of town, **Mānā**, the original koa-wood family residence, is open, as is **Puʻuʻōpelu**, the century-old residence of the late Richard Smart, a former ranch owner and a sixth-generation Parker. Smart was an avid art collector: Venetian glass, antique Chinese vases, bronze sculptures, and oils by a variety of artists, including Utrillo and Renoir, are on view at Puʻuʻōpelu. Tickets for all attractions can be purchased at the Parker Ranch Shopping Center, at the junction of Highways 19 and 190. ⊠ *67-1185 Māmalahoa Hwy., Kamuela,* ☎ *808/885–7655.* ⊡ *Museum $5, homes $7.50, combined admission $10.* ☼ *Museum daily 9–5, homes daily 10–5.*

⑭ **Parker Square.** This classy little shopping mall yields fine art, Oriental antiques, Japanese kimonos, kitchen items, and nifty gifts to take home. Just down the street is a shopping opportunity of a different sort. On weekends before 11:30 AM, drop by the tiny swap meet (flea market) behind nearby St. James's Episcopal Church. ⊠ *Kawaihae Rd., Waimea,* ☎ *808/885–7178.*

NEED A BREAK? At **Aioli's** (⊠ ʻOpelo Plaza, Hwy. 19 and ʻOpelo Rd., ☎ 808/885–6325) you can pick up ready-to-go gourmet box lunches or opt for a custom-made sandwich. In the evening, bistro-style dinners are served from 5 to 8, while special weekend menus might include herb-crusted prime rib, roasted turkey, or roast pork loin. If you've got a sweet tooth or want a pastry for breakfast, check out **Leilani Bakery** (⊠ Waimea Shopping Center, Hwy. 19, ☎ 808/885–2772), where you can pick up guava Danish or a loaf of cinnamon bread; it's a few blocks away.

㊅ **Pololū Valley.** A hiking trail for the very hardy leads into the valley and over several ridges beyond. The trail eventually reaches Waipiʻo Valley. ⊠ *End of Hwy. 270.*

★ ㊼ **Puʻukōhōla Visitor Center.** In 1790, a prophet told King Kamehameha I to build **Puʻukōhōla Heiau,** just above Mailekini Heiau (constructed about 1550), and dedicate it to the war god Kūkāʻilimoku by sacrificing his principal Big Island rival, Keoua Kuahuʻula. After doing so, the king would achieve his goal of conquering the Hawaiian Islands. The sacrifice was made, and the prophecy was finally fulfilled in 1810. Weather permitting (the trail is closed on windy days at this National Historic Site), it is a short, downhill walk over arid landscape from the visitor center to Puʻukōhōla Heiau and then across the road to the smaller **Mailekini Heiau** for a snapshot that will include both of the stone structures. You can get another photo of the two heiau by driving a bit farther down the road and turning into **Samuel M. Spencer Beach Park** (⊠ Hwy. 270, uphill from Kawaihae Harbor, ☎ 808/882–7094), which is safe for children and has extensive facilities. ⊠ *Hwy. 270, Kawaihae,* ☎ *808/882–7218.* ⊡ *Free.* ☼ *Daily 7:30–4.*

BEACHES

Don't believe it if anyone tells you the Big Island lacks beaches. It actually has 80 or more, and new ones appear—and disappear—regularly. In 1989 a new black-sand beach, Kamoamoa, formed when molten lava shattered as it hit cold ocean waters. Kamoamoa was the largest of the black-sand beaches, more than ½ mi long and 25 yd wide, until it was closed by new lava flows in 1992. Some beaches are just a little hard to get to—several are hidden behind elaborate hotels or down unmarked roads for which you'll want a four-wheel-drive vehicle or dauntless hiking spirit (or both)—and others have dangerous undertow and should be used for sunning and fishing rather than swimming. In 1990, two of the Big Island's most popular beach parks—Harry K. Brown and Kaimū—were covered by lava flows from Kīlauea. In Kailua-Kona and even in Keauhou, it's true, there are no broad expanses of coral sand. The most beautiful, swimmable white-sand beaches stretch along the Kohala coastline. The surf tends to get rough in winter; to be safe, swim only when you see local people swimming in the area. The tropical sun can be deceptive. Even on a cloudy day, it's wise to take along a sunscreen with an SPF of 15 or more and reapply it often, as saltwater and perspiration reduce its effectiveness. Public transportation to beaches does not exist. Few public beaches have lifeguards or staffed beach centers. Beaches are listed in a counterclockwise direction around the island, starting from the northern tip.

Keōkea Beach Park. Driving back from the end of Highway 270 at the Pololū overlook to the north, you'll see a curvy road angle off to the right. Follow it for a mile, pass the cemetery with the weathered old stones, and you'll come upon the green lawns and large picnic pavilion of Keōkea Beach Park. The black-boulder beach is suited for fishing and snorkeling in the calm summer months, but heavy surf in the winter makes this a hazardous swimming beach. A shallow, protected cove on the northeastern side of the bay is great for children. Some of the picnic tables are under cover, others are in the open; rest rooms, showers, drinking water, electricity, and a campsite make this a popular weekend destination for local folks. ⊠ *Off Hwy. 270 near Pololū overlook.*

Mahūkona Beach Park. Next to the abandoned Port of Mahūkona, in the Kohala District, where sugar was once shipped by rail to be loaded on boats, Mahūkona Beach's old docks and buildings are a photographer's treat. Divers and snorkelers can view both marine life and remnants of shipping machinery in the clear water. Heavy surf makes water activities off-limits in the winter, however. Boats can be launched with the chain hoist and winch on the old dock. It's a pleasant picnicking spot, with rest rooms, showers, and a camping area, but no sandy beach. ⊠ *Off Hwy. 270, Mahūkona.*

Samuel M. Spencer Beach Park. This spot is popular with local families because of its reef-protected, gently sloping white-sand beach, and it is safe for swimming year-round. There are cooking and camping facilities, showers, tennis courts, and a large covered pavilion with electrical outlets. Mynah birds and sparrows make their homes in large shade trees on the grounds here. You can walk to see the Pu`ukōhola and Mailekini heiau, midway between the park and Kawaihae Harbor, which is a mile to the north. ⊠ *Entry road off Hwy. 270, uphill from Kawaihae Harbor,* ☎ *808/882-7094.*

**Kauna`oa Beach at Mauna Kea Beach Resort.** It's a toss-up whether this or neighboring Hāpuna is the most beautiful beach on the island. Kauna`oa is long and white, and it slopes very gradually. In winter, when the surf is high, swimmers should consult beach attendants before taking a dip, as the powerful waves can be dangerous. Hotel guests generally congregate near the hotel's beach facilities. Near the public-access end, there's plenty of shady and sunny beach if you prefer to stay away from the action. Amenities are hotel-owned; there are 30 public parking spaces. ⊠ *Entry through gate to Mauna Kea Beach Resort, off Hwy. 19.*

Hāpuna State Recreation Area. This beach is a ½-mi crescent of glistening sand guarded by rocky points at either end. The surf can be hazardous in winter, but in summer the gradual slope of the beach can stretch as wide as 200 ft into a perfectly blue ocean—ideal for swimming, snorkeling, and scuba diving. Children enjoy the shallow cove with tidal pools at the north end, while at the southern end, adventuresome swimmers like to jump from the sea cliffs into the ocean. Signs restrict the use of surfboards and similar beach equipment. State cabins and public facilities are available nearby, and there is a conveniently located snack bar. There are no lifeguards to rescue swimmers from rough seas in winter, so keep out of the water at that time. ⊠ *Between Mauna Kea Beach and Mauna Lani resorts, off Hwy. 19,* ☎ *808/882–7995.*

Holoholokai Beach Park. A rocky beach of black-lava formations and white coral clinkers is fine for surfers and snorkelers, while a small grassy area is available to sunbathers. Bathrooms, picnic tables, and barbecue grills are nicely maintained. Just before the beach park, you can explore historic **Puakō Petroglyph Park.** Malama Trail meanders ⁷⁄₁₀ mi through brush and kiawe trees to an area of lava covered with the ancient etchings of Hawaiian figures and animals. ⊠ *Off Hwy. 19 at Mauna Lani Hotel and Bungalows.*

'Anaeho'omalu Beach, at the Royal Waikoloan Resort. This expansive beach on the west coast is perfect for swimming, windsurfing, snorkeling, sailing, and scuba diving. Equipment rental and instruction can be arranged at the north end. Be sure to wander around the ancient fishponds and petroglyph fields that the hotel has preserved. ⊠ *Follow Waikoloa Beach Dr. to Royal Waikoloan Resort, then signs to park and beach right-of-way to south.*

Ki'holo Bay. Access here via an unmarked road requires a four-wheel-drive; the road seems to disappear into nowhere across the lava, but it actually leads to homes built along the oceanfront and to Ki'holo Bay. The huge, spring-fed **Luahinewai Pond** anchors the south end of the bay, while the three black-pebble beaches are fine for swimming in calm weather. At the northern end, **Wainānāli'i Pond** (a 5-acre lagoon) is a feeding site for green sea turtles. Kamehameha I had a well-stocked fishpond here that was destroyed by lava in 1859. The two ponds are off-limits to swimmers. Secluded areas of the 2-mi bay are sometimes sought out by nude sunbathers, although nudity is officially illegal on all Big Island beaches. You'll find good swimming, fishing, and hiking here, but no facilities. ⊠ *Unmarked road, makai side of Hwy. 19.*

Kona Coast Beach Park. Kona Coast was a popular local swimming area before the state officially declared it a beach park a few years ago. In a primitive setting, the sandy white beach is in a bay area with gentle surf. It has a limited number of picnic tables shaded by coconut trees, but no drinking water. Portable toilets are the only additional facilities. ⊠ *Sign about 1 mi north of Kona International Airport, off Hwy. 19, marks rough 1½-mi road to beach.*

Honokōhau and 'Alula. These two beaches are down the road to Honokōhau Harbor: 'Alula is a slip of white sand a short walk over the lava to the left of the harbor entrance; Honokōhau Beach is north of the harbor (turn right at Gentry Marina and go past the boat-loading dock). Follow the trail to the right through the bush until you come upon the ¾-mi beach and the ruins of ancient fishponds. The center portion of the beach is comparatively rock-free, though a shelf of lava along the water's edge lines most of the shore. The **'Aimakapā fishpond** is directly inland. At the north end of the beach a trail leads mauka across the lava to a freshwater pool. The only public facilities are at the boat harbor. ⊠ *Off Hwy. 19, 1 mi north of Kailua-Kona.*

Old Kona Airport Recreation Area. The unused runway is still visible above this beach at Kailua Park, which has picnic tables, showers, bathroom facilities, and palm trees strung out along the shore. The beach has a sheltered, sandy inlet for children, but for adults it's better for snorkeling and scuba than it is for swimming. An offshore surfing break known as Old Airport is popular with Kona surfers. ⊠ *Follow Hwy. 11 north to its end outside Kailua,* ☎ 808/329–6727.

White Sands, Magic Sands, or Disappearing Sands Beach Park. Now you see it, now you don't. Overnight, winter waves wash away this small white-sand beach on Ali'i Drive just south of Kailua-Kona. In summer, you'll know you've found it when you see the body- and board-surfers. Rest rooms, showers, a lifeguard tower, and a coconut grove create a favorite and convenient summer hangout, but this isn't a great beach for swimming. ⊠ *South on Ali'i Dr., 1 mi past Royal Kona Hotel in Kailua-Kona; beach is before St. Peter's Catholic Church.*

Kahalu'u Beach Park. This spot was a favorite of King Kalākaua, whose summer cottage is on the grounds of the Keauhou Beach Hotel next door. Kahalu'u is popular with commoners, too, and on weekends there are just too many people. A strong rip current during high surf pulls swimmers away from shore. Facilities include a pavilion, rest rooms, showers, a lifeguard tower, and limited parking. ⊠ *Beside Ali'i Dr., between Kailua-Kona and Keauhou.*

Ho'okena Beach Park. You'll feel like an adventurer when you come upon Ho'okena, at the northern corner of Kauhako Bay. When Mark Twain visited, 2,500 people populated the busy seaport village. You can still find gas lampposts dating from the 1900s. Good swimming, bodysurfing, fishing, and hiking can be had here, but there's no drinking water at this dark gray coral-and-lava-sand beach. Rest rooms, showers, and picnic tables are available at the park. The access road is narrow and bumpy. ⊠ *2-mi drive down road bordered by ruins of stone wall off Hwy. 11, 23 mi south of Kailua-Kona.*

Nāpō'opo'o Beach Park. The best way to see this black-sand beach and marine preserve is to take a snorkel, scuba, or glass-bottom boat tour from Keauhou Bay. A 27-ft white obelisk indicates where Captain James Cook was killed in 1779. This 6-acre beach park has a picnic pavilion, tables, showers, rest rooms, and a basketball court. ⊠ *Kealakekua Bay.*

Green Sand (Papakōlea) Beach. You need a four-wheel-drive vehicle to get to this beach, whose greenish tint is caused by an accumulation of the olivine that forms in volcanic eruptions. You can get to South Point (where you'll find ruins of a heiau and the winches once used to load cattle and produce onto boats from the cliffs) in a regular car, but it's a few rugged road miles to where the beach lies at the base of Pu'u o Mahana, a cinder cone formed during an early eruption of Mauna Loa. Swimming can be hazardous when the surf is up in this windy, remote area. There are no facilities and no shade trees. ⊠ *2½ mi northeast of South Point, off Hwy. 11.*

Punalu'u Beach Park. Turtles swim in the bay (you can watch them surface and submerge), nest, and lay their eggs in the black sand of this beautiful beach. Fishponds are just inland, and you can find the ruins of a heiau and a flat sacrificial stone at the northern end of the beach near the boat ramp. Sugar was shipped by rail to this former port town, and in 1941 Army troops were stationed here. The tidal wave of 1946 destroyed the Army buildings. Offshore currents here can be dangerous, though you'll see a few local surfers riding the waves. There are rest rooms across the road. Inland from the ponds, among buildings that once held a visitor center and restaurant, is a memorial to Henry Opukaha'ia. In 1809, when he was 17, Opukaha'ia swam out to a fur-trading ship in the harbor and asked to sail as a cabin boy. When he reached New England, he entered the Foreign Mission School in Connecticut, but he died of typhoid fever in 1818. His dream of bringing Christianity to the Islands inspired the American Board of Missionaries in 1820 to send the first Protestant missionaries to Hawai'i. ✉ *Hwy. 11, 27 mi beyond Volcanoes National Park.*

Pū'āla'a Park. This 3-acre beach park with a ½-acre pond opened in 1993 to replace earlier beach parks that were lost to lava flows. The pond here is good for swimming, but the nearby ocean is rough. Drinking water and a few tables are available for picnicking. Improvements are planned, but for now there are portable rest rooms. ✉ *On Kapoho Coast southeast of Pāhoa Town, 2½ mi south of junction of Hwys. 132 and 137, Puna District.*

MacKenzie State Recreation Area. This spacious 13-acre park, shaded by ironwoods, is good for picnicking and camping. You can't swim here, but there are rest rooms, fresh water, and plenty of free parking. ✉ *In Puna district between Hwy. 137 and sea cliff.*

Isaac Hale Beach Park. Oceanfront park facilities include rest rooms and picnic areas. It's a good place for an afternoon nap. ✉ *In Puna district between Hwy. 137 and sea cliff.*

Onekahakaha Beach Park. A protected, white-sand beach makes this a favorite for Hilo families with small children. Lifeguards are on duty year-round. The park has picnic pavilions, rest rooms, and showers. ✉ *Follow Kalaniana'ole Ave. east along the water about 3 mi south of Hilo.*

Leleiwi Beach Park and Richardson Ocean Park. Near Hilo, these two beaches are adjacent to each other. Richardson's tiny beach, just beyond the seawall, allows entry to the water for good snorkeling, swimming, bodysurfing, board surfing, and net fishing. Showers, rest rooms, paved walkways, covered picnic pavilions, and lifeguard service are available. ✉ *2349 Kalaniana'ole Ave.; follow Kalaniana'ole Ave. east along the water about 4 mi south of Hilo.*

Reeds Bay Beach Park. Rest rooms, showers, drinking water, calm and safe swimming, and proximity to downtown Hilo are the enticements of this cove. Most swimmers take a dip in the **Ice Pond** adjoining the head of Reeds Bay. Cold freshwater springs seep from the bottom of the pond and rise in the saltwater. ✉ *Banyan Dr. and Kalaniana'ole Ave., Hilo.*

DINING

For price category explanations, *see* On the Road with Fodor's at the beginning of the book.

Hilo

American

$$ ✕ **Harrington's.** A popular and reliable steak and seafood restaurant
★ with 27 tables right on Reeds Bay, Harrington's has a dining lānai that extends over the water. The fresh ono or mahimahi meunière, served with browned butter, lemon, and parsley, and the Slavic steak, thinly sliced and slathered with garlic butter, are two outstanding dishes. Daily specials might include lobster or rack of lamb. ✉ *135 Kalaniana'ole St.,* ☎ *808/961–4966. MC, V.*

206

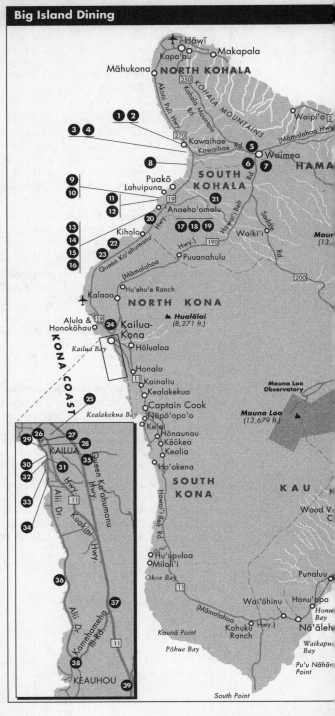

Big Island Dining

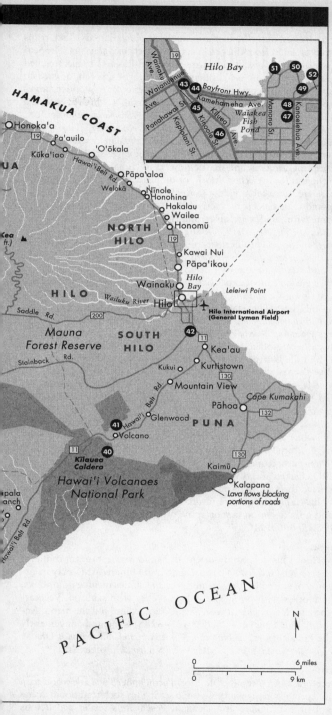

$–$$ ✕ **Seaside.** In a family home that sits on the edge of 50-acre Lake Loko-Waka, this is Hilo's most unusual dinner restaurant. Most of the fish served are raised in the lake or are caught in Hawaiian-style fish traps when they swim in from the ocean via a connecting waterway. The Seaside is one of the few restaurants that serves fried āhole, or mullet steamed in ti leaves, or combination dinners of mullet, trout, perch, or catfish. Steaks and vegetable pasta are also on the menu. Bare wooden tables overlook great water views on the patio or from a window-enclosed room. Beer, wine, and sake are available. ✉ *1790 Kalanianaole Ave.,* ☎ *808/935–8825. DC, MC, V. Closed Mon. No lunch.*

$–$$ ✕ **Uncle Billy's Restaurant.** The decor is pure Hawaiian kitsch—right out of 1930s Hollywood, but the thatch roofs, tinkling capiz-shell wind chimes, Tahitian print curtains, and plastic flowers in lauhala-covered planters add to the fun for breakfast, lunch, or dinner. Choose fish presented in meunière sauce, macadamia nut sauce, admiral sauce (with shallots), or shrimp-and-wine sauce; or try teriyaki beef or shrimp *Orientale*. Full dinners come with salad, vegetables, and rice pilaf. A wine list is available. ✉ *87 Banyan Dr.,* ☎ *808/935–0861. AE, D, DC, MC, V.*

$ ✕ **Fiasco's.** Booths with floor-to-ceiling dividers provide complete privacy in this cheerful restaurant with something for everyone, from tasty fajitas and snacks to a garden-fresh fruit and salad bar. Prime rib at $15.95 is Fiasco's most expensive item. Margarita specials and 23 varieties of domestic and imported beer enliven the menu—not to mention the imbibers. There is live entertainment Friday and Saturday nights. ✉ *200 Kanoelehua Ave.,* ☎ *808/935–7666. AE, D, DC, MC, V.*

$ ✕ **Ken's House of Pancakes.** For years, this 24-hour coffee shop has been a gathering place for Hilo residents for breakfast. Between the airport and the Banyan Drive hotels, Ken's serves good pancakes and omelets—they're cheap, too. Local favorites, such as hot and cold sandwiches, steaks, and fish, round out the lunch and dinner menus. ✉ *1730 Kamehameha Ave.,* ☎ *808/935–8711. Reservations not accepted. AE, D, DC, MC, V.*

$ ✕ **Scruffles.** This spotless, modern coffee shop is a cool retreat decorated in white and pastel turquoise, rose, and lavender—and it's inexpensive. Ethnic dishes range from Chinese chicken salad, Japanese shrimp tempura, Korean Teri steak, Mexican taco salad, and an American BBQ chicken and ribs combo. There are hamburgers, sandwiches, and a drive-through take-out window, too. The connecting Paradise Bakery has tables in a more intimate setting. It's a great place for a latte and a flaky lemon tart or apple turnover. ✉ *1438 Kīlauea Ave.,* ☎ *808/935–6664. MC, V.*

Chinese

$–$$$ ✕ **Ting Hao.** This is a family-oriented, Mandarin restaurant that emphasizes fresh Island fish. The Szechuan and Hunan dishes may be ordered mild or spicy hot; the scrumptious specialties include dumplings, stir-fry noodles with pork, and spicy noodles with seafood. Vegetarian dishes, such as eggplant with garlic sauce, round out the menu. Another branch of Ting Hao (☎ 808/959–6288) is located conveniently near the Hilo airport. ✉ *Hawai`i Naniloa Hotel, 93 Banyan Dr.,* ☎ *808/935–8888. AE, D, DC, MC, V. ⊙ No lunch weekends.*

Italian

$$ ✕ **Pescatore's.** An intimate Old World atmosphere of dark wood trim and lace curtains on the windows is the setting for such traditional dishes as eggplant parmigiana and lasagna. Pescatore's serves a delicious seafood *fra diavolo* (shrimp, clams, and fish in a spicy marinara sauce aromatic with garlic and basil). Dinners are a little pricey for Hilo, but lunches are reasonable. ✉ *235 Keawe St. at Haili St.,* ☎ *808/969–9090. DC, MC, V.*

Thai

$ ✕ **Royal Siam.** Mild, medium, or hot-and-spicy are the choices for more than 50 Thai dishes based on chicken, beef, seafood, pork, and vegetables. Appetizers, daily specials, and delicious curries round out the menu at this small dining spot. ⊠ *70 Mamo St.,* ☎ *808/961–6100. AE, D, DC, MC, V. Closed Sun.*

Kohala-Kona–Keauhou

American

$$$–$$$$ ✕ **The Grill and Lounge at the Orchid at Mauna Lani.** Rich koa-wood
★ paneling and a long koa bar give this restaurant the feeling of an established club, and the food gives it a top-notch reputation. A traditional grill menu includes fresh local seafood, meats, and produce. Signature items are pan-roasted loin of lamb and beef tenderloin with lobster. There's nightly entertainment and a dance floor. ⊠ *Orchid at Mauna Lani, 1 N. Kanikū Dr., Kohala Coast,* ☎ *808/885–2000. AE, D, DC, MC, V.*

$$–$$$$ ✕ **Kamuela Provision Company at the Hilton Waikoloa Village.** You'll have a spectacular view of the Kona–Kohala coastline as you sample excellent salad selections, broiled and grilled steak, or seafood. Tables along the lānai open to sea breezes, while ceiling fans cool the rest of the dining room, which seats 192 people. Before or after dinner, sip cocktails on the lānai overlooking the resort's impressive waterfall and swimming pool. The fresh-fish menu includes all the Hawaiian favorites: Order your *'ōpakapaka* (pink snapper), *ono, onaga,* or *'ahi,* sautéed, grilled, poached, or blackened. ⊠ *425 Waikoloa Beach Dr., Kamuela,* ☎ *808/886–1234. AE, D, DC, MC, V.*

$$–$$$ ✕ **Big Island Steak House.** The walls here are adorned with Hawaiian kitsch memorabilia dating from the '30s, '40s, and '50s—'ukuleles, steamer trunks, a zany grass-skirted gorilla, and the like. Try baby back ribs, Ke'ahole lobster, beef kabobs, or coconut prawns, and for dessert, liliko'i cheesecake for a delicious change. A second-floor loft holds the Merry Wahine Bar and a dance floor where a DJ plays music ranging from '50s nostalgia to country-western. ⊠ *King's Shops, Waikoloa Resort, Waikoloa Beach Dr., across from Royal Waikoloan Hotel, Waikoloa,* ☎ *808/885–8805. AE, D, DC, MC, V. ♥ No lunch.*

$$–$$$ ✕ **Chart House at Waterfront Row.** This attractive two-story restaurant in the shopping and dining complex on Ali'i Drive overlooks the ocean. Koa-wood booths, and floral arrangements complement the fine artwork displayed in the restaurant. Dinners of thickly sliced prime rib, fresh local fish, and Alaskan king crab come with squaw and sourdough bread. ⊠ *75-5770 Ali'i Dr., Kailua-Kona,* ☎ *808/329–2451. AE, D, DC, MC, V. ♥ No lunch.*

$$–$$$ ✕ **Jameson's by the Sea.** Sit outside next to the ocean or just inside the picture windows for glorious sunset views over Magic Sands Beach. The chef and co-owner serves three or four island fish specials daily, plus a tasty baked shrimp stuffed with crab and garnished with hollandaise sauce. ⊠ *77-6452 Ali'i Dr., Kailua-Kona,* ☎ *808/329–3195. AE, D, DC, MC, V. ♥ No lunch weekends.*

$$–$$$ ✕ **Kona Inn Restaurant.** This open-air restaurant, which faces a wide lawn with the ocean beyond, has been a longtime favorite for cocktails at sunset. Fresh fish—*'ahi* (tuna) and *'ōpakapaka* (snapper)—and chicken entrées are consistently delectable. Burgers at lunch are generously sized and reasonably priced, while the most expensive dinner item is steak and lobster. ⊠ *75-5744 Ali'i Dr., Kailua-Kona,* ☎ *808/ 329–4455. AE, MC, V.*

$$ ✕ **Kona Ranch House.** This reliable dining spot is known in the area for its big portions and pleasant service. The Kona Ranch House has

two sections; the Plantation Lānai offers more of a fine-dining experience with its turn-of-the-century Hawaiian wicker furniture, tablecloths, and candles. The adjoining Paniolo Room serves food from the same kitchen, but the decor is simple café-style, with booths and no tablecloths. The fresh local fish and big barbecue platters warrant the short walk up the hill from King Kamehameha's Kona Beach Hotel for breakfast, lunch, or dinner. ⊠ *75-5653 Olioli St., Kailua-Kona,* ☎ *808/329–7061. AE, D, DC, MC, V.*

$–$$ ✕ **Jolly Roger.** This restaurant with a nautical theme and pink-and-gray decor is right at the ocean's edge, although some of the 100 tables are set back from the water. Jolly Roger is better for a leisurely breakfast or an afternoon mai tai than for dinner. Try the 4-ounce steak and a half order of eggs Benedict with a papaya wedge. Smaller appetites can opt for the bargain-price breakfast special described on the signboard out front. ⊠ *75-5776 Ali'i Dr., Kailua-Kona,* ☎ *808/329– 1344. Reservations not accepted. AE, D, DC, MC, V.*

$–$$ ✕ **Kona Beach Restaurant at King Kamehameha's Kona Beach Hotel.** At this centrally located major hotel in the Kailua-Kona area, the tables look out on a torch-lit lawn; beyond is the beach, with outrigger canoes and a thatch house built on a restored heiau. Some of the tantalizing entrées served here are kiawe wood–grilled prime rib, fresh local catch, and Maine lobster. Sunday champagne brunch is served from 9 to 1. ⊠ *75-5660 Palani Rd., Kailua-Kona,* ☎ *808/329–2911. AE, D, DC, MC, V.*

$ ✕ **Ocean View Inn.** To those on a tight budget, this local hangout with an ocean view has been a lifesaver for breakfast, lunch, and dinner since the 1920s. Chinese and American food are on the plate-lunch menu, and you can get Hawaiian specialties à la carte. Although there's no atmosphere, the servings are ample. ⊠ *75-5683 Ali'i Dr., Kailua-Kona,* ☎ *808/329–9998. No credit cards. Closed Mon.*

Chinese

$–$$$ ✕ **Grand Palace Chinese Restaurant.** A reasonable alternative in a land of high-priced hotel dining, this popular Chinese restaurant was instantly successful when it opened in 1995. Nicely decorated with rosewood chairs, green marble-top tables, a floral carpet, and etched-glass panels, the restaurant seats 102, but you may have to wait. An extensive menu offers the regular Chinese items, such as egg foo young, wonton soup, chicken with snow peas, and beef with broccoli, but also boasts local sautéed seafood in a taro nest and sizzling scallops with pepper black bean sauce. ⊠ *King's Shops, Waikoloa Resort, Waikoloa Beach Dr., Waikoloa,* ☎ *808/885–6668. AE, DC, MC, V.*

French

$$–$$$ ✕ **La Bourgogne.** A genial husband-and-wife team owns this relaxing, country-style French restaurant with dark-wood walls and blue-velvet booths; it's just 4 mi out of town. Classic French cooking at its best keeps the 10 tables filled six nights a week. Chef Ron Gallaher is particularly proud of his sweetbreads of veal with Madeira sauce, rack of lamb with mustard sauce, and Lāna'i venison with currants and pomegranate glaze. ⊠ *Kuakini Plaza S on Hwy. 11, 77-6400 Nālani St., Kailua-Kona,* ☎ *808/329–6711. AE, D, DC, MC, V. No smoking. Closed Sun. No lunch.*

Greek

$$ ✕ **Cassandra's Greek Taverna.** Clean and bright in the blue and white colors of the Greek flag, Cassandra's offers plenty of selections to suit every appetite. Greek and Caesar salads, a gyro plate of ground beef and lamb, *dolmades* (grape leaves stuffed with meat and rice), moussaka, and a variety of souvlaki (beef, pork, chicken, shrimp) keep dinners interesting. For dessert, the *Ek Mek* has a crunchy cinnamon–cracker crust, a vanilla pudding filling, and a frothy whipped topping sprinkled with almonds. A full bar includes Greek retsinas and other wines. ⊠ *75-5719 W. Ali'i Dr., Kailua-Kona,* ☎ *808/334–1066. AE, D, DC, MC, V.* ☉ *No lunch Sun.*

Hawai'i Regional/Pacific Rim

$$$–$$$$ ✕ **Batik Restaurant at Mauna Kea Beach Hotel.** This is Mauna Kea's fine dining restaurant dressed in an understated decor hinting of exotic India, with bulbous pillars, subtle gray carpeting, and an ornate, canopied *howdah* (elephant seat). Beautiful presentation of entrées—fresh Hawaiian snapper with lobster mushroom ragoût, rack of lamb with eggplant or venison loin with chestnut purée—add to dining enjoyment. Liliko'i soufflé and baklava of apples with macadamia nut ice cream give desserts a local flair. ⊠ *62-100 Mauna Kea Beach Dr., Kamuela,* ☎ *808/882–7222. Jacket required. AE, D, DC, MC, V.* ☉ *No lunch.*

$$–$$$$ ✕ **CanoeHouse at the Mauna Lani Bay Hotel and Bungalows.** This open-
★ air beachfront restaurant, surrounded by fishponds, is widely hailed as one of Hawai'i's premier restaurants. An enormous koa canoe is the focal point of this restaurant serving Pacific Rim cuisine; imaginative entrées include seared scallop skewers with vegetable couscous in a Malaysian curry sauce, and grilled chili-rubbed filet mignon with a mango-cabernet sauce. ⊠ *68-1400 Mauna Lani Dr., Kohala Coast,* ☎ *808/885–6622. AE, D, DC, MC, V.*

$$–$$$$ ✕ **Coast Grille at Hāpuna Beach Prince Hotel.** This spacious, high-ceiling restaurant has lānai seating overlooking the ocean—a great place to sit when the nights are balmy, but take a sweater when the trade winds are up. Oyster lovers should head to the fresh-oyster bar, the only one on the Big Island, while those with hearty appetites might consider the peppercorn-crusted lamb rack with star anise sauce. Pastas and entrées of Island fish—*shutome* (swordfish), *opah* (moon fish), 'ōpakapaka, and more—are prepared with a nori or pistachio crust, or sometimes in ti leaves. The signature dessert, sugar-crusted ginger crème brûlée in a crispy, caramelized basket with seasonal fruits, is delicious. ⊠ *62-100 Kauna'oa Dr., Kamuela,* ☎ *808/880–1111. AE, D, DC, MC, V.*

$$–$$$$ ✕ **Pavilion Restaurant at Mauna Kea Beach Hotel.** Sit on the lānai overlooking the white sands of Kauna'oa Beach to savor a meal that makes you appreciate Hawai'i. This family-oriented restaurant serves pastas and grilled items as well as such treats as garlic-crusted salmon, veal scallopini, and herb-coated rack of lamb served with garlic-mashed potatoes. ⊠ *62-100 Mauna Kea Beach Dr., Kamuela,* ☎ *808/882–7222. AE, D, DC, MC, V.*

$$–$$$ ✕ **Café Tiare at the Royal Waikoloan Resort.** This beautiful restaurant is decorated with etched-glass panels, crystal, and fresh orchids for a romantic atmosphere. You can order the fresh catch sesame-crusted with spicy coconut sauce, basted with herbs and broiled, sautéed in white wine, or seared with lemongrass and chili oil. Big Island beef and lamb; pastas; a good selection of appetizers with a local touch, such as crab cakes, Thai beef, and seafood *laulau* (morsels wrapped with taro leaves); and new specials nightly round out this tasty menu. ⊠ *62-275 Waikoloa Beach Dr., Kamuela,* ☎ *808/885–6789. AE, D, DC, MC, V. Closed Wed. and Sun. No lunch.*

$$–$$$ ✕ **Gallery Restaurant and Knicker's Bar and Lounge at Mauna Lani Resort.** Set apart from the hotel overlooking the Francis H. I'i Brown Golf Course, the Gallery has mahogany paneling, highlighted by a massive koa bar, which creates a comfortable clubhouse atmosphere. The chef is continuing a tradition of using fresh Island ingredients in new

and creative ways, and you can make personal requests as well. An appealing menu includes such tasty appetizers as shrimp in phyllo with lemon butter and tomato concasse, and such entrées as lobster, shrimp, and clams in a basil shellfish broth with garlic mashed potatoes, and roasted rack of lamb with sweet potato puree and thyme jus. ✉ *68-1400 Mauna Lani Dr., Kohala Coast,* ☎ *808/885–7777. AE, D, DC, MC, V. Closed Sun. and Mon.*

$$–$$$ ✕ **Huggo's.** Open windows look out over the rocks at the ocean's edge, so you can actually feed the fish, if you wish. Fresh local seafood (sesame-crusted mahimahi, shrimp scampi) is the safest bet on the menu, though the prime rib is also recommended in this fine dining establishment with a casual atmosphere. ✉ *75-5828 Kahakai Rd., Kailua-Kona,* ☎ *808/329–1493. D, DC, MC, V.* ☾ *No lunch weekends.*

$$–$$$ ✕ **Sam Choy's Restaurant.** In the Koloko Industrial Park near Kona International Airport, Sam's attracts workers in the surrounding area for hearty, local-style breakfasts and lunches—saimin, stew omelets, and Hawaiian burritos. Wednesday through Saturday nights, the chef-owner puts out white tablecloths, and customers bring their own wine and settle in for some of the finest Hawai'i Regional cuisine. The dinner menu changes weekly, but might include such fresh fish as 'ōpaka-paka, crisp fried *'ōpelu* (mackerel scad) or *akule* (big-eyed scad) served with soy lemon-butter sauce and fresh cilantro, or seafood lau lau (steamed in ti leaves). ✉ *73-5576 Kauhola St., Bay 1, Koloko Industrial Park, Kailua-Kona,* ☎ *808/326–1545. Reservations required. MC, V. BYOB.*

$$ ★ ✕ **Roy's at the King's Shops.** Roy Yamaguchi designs his restaurants as places to have fun, so the noise level is sometimes high. This one, with green carpets, green marble bar, an exhibition kitchen, and window tables that overlook a golf-course lake, is the nicest yet. You can sample several appetizers: spicy Korean chicken mandoo, grilled Szechuan-style baby back ribs, or Thai noodle peanut chicken salad. With the extensive wine list, it's no problem matching a wine to such entrées as imu-roasted pork lau lau, pizza, bamboo-skewered lemongrass shrimp, or cornmeal-crusted pork loin. ✉ *King's Shops, Waikoloa Resort, Waikoloa,* ☎ *808/885–4321. AE, D, DC, MC, V.*

$$ ✕ **Tropics at Royal Kona Resort.** Within walking distance of central Kailua-Kona, this open-air dining room overlooks Kailua Bay. At dusk, when the sun outlines the boats bobbing offshore, you'll have a lovely, peaceful view. Jumbo prawns, fresh fish, and scallops are all winning choices. Big eaters can go for the seafood and prime rib buffet every Friday and Sunday. ✉ *75-5852 Ali'i Dr., Kailua,* ☎ *808/329–3111. AE, D, DC, MC, V.*

Italian

$$–$$$ ✕ **Donatoni's at the Hilton Waikoloa Village.** Lighter cuisine, shellfish, and the more subtle sauces of Italy, as well as specialty pizzas made to suit your taste, are served in this romantic restaurant. Reminiscent of an Italian villa and overlooking a lagoon, Donatoni's seats 158 on various levels and a wide lānai, so no view is obstructed. Prices on the extensive Italian wine and champagne list range from $14 to $39. ✉ *425 Waikoloa Beach Dr., Kamuela,* ☎ *808/886–1234. AE, D, DC, MC, V.* ☾ *No lunch.*

$–$$$ ✕ **Café Pesto.** Even people who don't like pizza like the pizza made here. The chef uses fresh Island ingredients in his version of nouvelle cuisine. Sample pizza al pesto, with sundried tomatoes, eggplant, and fresh-basil pesto, or the popular seafood risotto made with sweet Thai chili, Hawaiian spiny lobster, jumbo scallops, and tiger prawns. Thirty tables seat 100 at this harborside restaurant with a contemporary art deco decor. ✉ *Wharf Rd. and Mahūkona Hwy., Kawaihae Center, 1st* *floor, Kawaihae,* ☎ *808/882–1071;* ✉ *308 Kamehameha Ave., Hilo,* ☎ *808/969–6640. AE, D, DC, MC, V.*

Japanese

$$–$$$ ✕ **Imari at the Hilton Waikoloa Village.** This elegant Japanese restaurant, complete with waterfalls and a teahouse, serves teriyakis and tempuras aimed to please mainland tastes. Beyond the display of Imari porcelain at the entrance, you'll find beef and chicken cooked at your table, complete *teppan* (grilled) dinners, and an outstanding sushi bar. Impeccable service by kimono-clad waitresses adds to your dining pleasure. The restaurant seats 149. ✉ *425 Waikoloa Beach Dr., Kamuela,* ☎ *808/886–1234. AE, D, DC, MC, V.* ☯ *No lunch.*

$–$$ ✕ **Teshima's.** The local lawyers and doctors show up at Teshima's whenever they're in the mood for Big Island Japanese-American cooking. Teshima's is on the dark side with well-worn decor and clattering dishes. Service is so-so, but residents come for the sashimi, sukiyaki, and puffy shrimp tempura. You might also want to try a *teishoku* (tray) of assorted Japanese delicacies. The teriyaki steak is under $12. ✉ *15 mins from Kailua-Kona on Māmalahoa Hwy., Honalo,* ☎ *808/322–9140. No credit cards.*

Mexican

$–$$ ✕ **Très Hombres Beach Grill.** Lānai dining overlooks the fishing fleet at Kawaihae Harbor at this cute, clean, and casual Mexican restaurant offering a less expensive lunch and dinner alternative to those staying at Kohala Coast resorts. Mexican beer and specialty drinks (some are nonalcoholic) promote conviviality in the lounge, which has a '50s Surf City look. Burgers, sandwiches, and huevos rancheros are served at lunch. Dinner items include Tex-Mex combinations, fresh fish, salads, steaks, and gazpacho. A "fit for life" menu offers black bean tacos and other low-fat entrées. ✉ *Wharf Rd. and Mahūkona Hwy., Kawaihae Center,* ☎ *808/882–1031. MC, V.*

Mixed Menu

$$$–$$$$ ✕ **Hale Samoa at Kona Village Resort.** Ferns, tapa screens, and hurricane lamps bathed in the glow of sunset set a magical mood at this Kona Village signature restaurant, which has 18 tables. The escargots and artichokes, baked in Boursin cream and garlic sauce, are heavenly. Boneless lamb loin stuffed with mushrooms and spinach, baked in pastry and served with a Maui-onion sauce is the chef's favorite. Asian, French, and Hawaiian cuisines are featured and the prix-fixe dinners are a great value. The entry road to Kona Village is 6 mi out Highway 19 from Kailua. ✉ *Queen Ka'ahumanu Hwy., Kailua-Kona,* ☎ *808/ 325–5555. Reservations essential. AE, DC, MC, V. Closed Wed., Fri., and 1 wk in Dec. No lunch.*

$$–$$$$ ✕ **Pahu i'a at Four Seasons Resort Hualālai.** This restaurant appears
★ to be closer to the rhythmic ocean surf than any other. Outdoor deck seating is romantic even at breakfast, but indoors, a 9-ft by 4-ft aquarium casts a dreamy light in the polished wood interior as well. Meals are imaginative and beautifully presented: Lobster crepe with Swiss cheese and spinach for breakfast, hoisin duck pizza for lunch, or Asian and American (with a touch of the southwest) entrées for dinner. Thai curry with shrimp and scallops, and pan-seared 'ōpakapaka with saffron risotto are delicious. ✉ *Four Seasons Resort Hualālai, Kailua-Kona,* ☎ *808/ 325–8000. AE, D, DC, MC, V.*

$$–$$$ ✕ **Edward's at Kanaloa.** This intimate but hard-to-find restaurant is a local favorite; the food is delicious, and dinner prices are within reason. Open-air seating is pool and oceanside. Chef Edward Frady is proud of his medallions of pork with prunes and white wine; his *bastya,* a Moroccan pie of Cornish hen in phyllo pastry; and his fresh fish with

Provençale sauce of garlic, fresh tomatoes, green olives, and butter. Desserts are made fresh and vary daily. ⊠ *Kanaloa at Kona, 78-261 Manukai St., Kailua-Kona,* ☎ *808/322–1434 or 808/322–9625. AE, DC, MC, V.*

$$–$$$ ✕ **Orchid Court at The Orchid at Mauna Lani.** You can be cool and comfortable dining inside under elegant chandeliers or on the terrace at glass-top tables. *Farfel* (egg noodles) with smoked duck breast; wild mushrooms and asparagus in roasted garlic sauce; salads and sandwiches; pizzas topped with goat cheese and smoked shrimp; and fresh fish that might be sesame wok-seared or served with ginger butter, suit the light fresh ambience. Tropical fruits and berries over coconut flan, warm apple cobbler, and sorbets satisfy any sweet tooth. ⊠ *The Orchid at Mauna Lani, 1 N. Kanikū Dr., Kohala Coast,* ☎ *808/885–2000. AE, D, DC, MC, V.* ☉ *No lunch.*

$$–$$$ ✕ **Palm Terrace at the Hilton Waikoloa Village.** This open-air restaurant sits next to a cascading waterfall and a pond with swans floating by. It's open for breakfast and lunch (American-style omelets, etc.) and offers theme buffet dinners, such as a Polynesian spread that includes curried veal, *kālua* (roasted) pork, teriyaki beef, and seafood. ⊠ *425 Waikoloa Beach Dr., Kamuela,* ☎ *808/885–1234. AE, D, DC, MC, V.* ☉ *No lunch.*

$–$$ ✕ **Oodles of Noodles.** This is a cheerful, modern place to drop by for quality food at a reasonable price. Indoors colorful prints, Hawaiian woods—mango, ohia, koa—in a wood-topped counter, and orchids complement vivid blue, green and yellow walls. Sidewalk-seating is at wrought-iron tables. Besides noodles of all types—pasta primavera, Kona-style tuna noodle casserole, Pho Vietnamese beef noodle soup, seafood green curry cake noodle—you can order smoked pork rolls, salads, and such desserts as mango, chunky ginger, haupia ice cream and Asian-style shave ice. ⊠ *Crossroads Shopping Center, 75–1129 Henry St., Kailua-Kona,* ☎ *808/329–9222. D, DC, MC, V. Closed Sun.*

Thai

$–$$ ✕ **Thai Rin Restaurant.** A black-and-white tile floor, white tablecloths, blue napkins, and orchids on the tables make this an attractive spot for lunch or dinner. Thai spring rolls, chicken *satay* (marinated and skewered, served with peanut sauce) and cucumber salad, fried noodles Thai style, and Thai garlic shrimp or squid are favorites. ⊠ *75-5799 Ali'i Dr., Kailua-Kona,* ☎ *808/329–2929. AE, D, DC, MC, V.*

Volcano

American

$$–$$$ ✕ **Ka 'Ōhelo Room.** Perched right at the edge of Kīlauea Crater in a mountain-lodge setting, this restaurant serves up breakfast and luncheon buffets primarily for tour groups during the day. But at night it's quiet, yet cheerful, with white tablecloths; you can't go wrong with the fresh catch of the day or the prime rib at dinner. ⊠ *Volcano House, Hawai'i Volcanoes National Park,* ☎ *808/967–7321. AE, D, DC, MC, V.*

$$–$$$ ✕ **Kīlauea Lodge.** Even Hiloans make the half-hour drive to the volcano area for dinner at Kīlauea Lodge. Built in 1938 as a scouting retreat, the restaurant still has the original stone "Friendship Fireplace" embedded with coins from around the world. Owner-chef Albert Jeyte is known for such entrées as venison, duck à l'orange, *paupiettes* of beef (sliced prime rib roll stuffed with mushrooms, herbs, and cheese), and seafood Mauna Kea (seafood and mushrooms in a crème fraîche sauce on fettuccine). For an Old World dessert try bread pudding made with a special Portuguese sweet bread, or the Grand Marnier custard. ⊠ *Old Volcano Rd., Volcano Village,* ☎ *808/967–7366. AE, MC, V.* ☉ *No lunch.*

Waikoloa Village

Mixed Menu

$$ ✕ **Roussel's.** Hilo's best restaurant before moving to Waikoloa, Roussel's still serves Creole entrées but bows to golfers' demands for burgers, club sandwiches, and chicken wings during much of the day. At lunch, shrimp or soft-shell po'boy sandwiches and spicy Creole pasta go well with peaceful golf-course views through big, white-frame windows that open to the trade winds. The chef-owner prepares fresh-baked bread and beignets, tortes, mousse, and other desserts. Recommended for dinner are shrimp Creole, with a piquant tomato sauce, and *supreme* of trout (a boneless fillet smothered in creamy crabmeat sauce). ⊠ *68-1792 Melia St., Waikoloa Village Golf Club, Waikoloa,* ☎ *808/883–9644. AE, DC, MC, V.* ☽ *No dinner Sun. and Mon.*

Waimea

Continental

$$ ✕ **Edelweiss.** Faithful local diners and visitors alike flock to this relaxed family-oriented restaurant with rustic redwood furnishings. The chef's rack of lamb is always excellent. A varied menu includes 14 daily specials (such as a sausage platter), many with a European flavor. Go early—5:30–6:30—to avoid a long wait for one of the 15 tables. ⊠ *Hwy. 19, entering Waimea,* ☎ *808/885–6800. Reservations not accepted. MC, V. Closed Sun. and Mon. No lunch.*

Hawai`i Regional

$$–$$$ ✕ **Merriman's.** It's worth the 20-minute drive from the Kohala Coast
★   hotels to cowboy country in Waimea to sample Peter Merriman's imaginative cuisine. The menu includes vegetarian selections along with lamb and veal dishes named for local ranches. Wok-charred 'ahi is a favorite entrée, usually served with Pāhoa corn and black-and-white Thai rice. Decorated in bright colors, for a Hawaiian art deco feeling, Merriman's brings to mind the steamship days in Hawai'i. ⊠ *'Opelo Plaza II, Hwy. 19 and 'Opelo Rd., Waimea,* ☎ *808/885–6822. AE, MC, V.*

Mediterranean

$$–$$$ ✕ **Bree Garden Restaurant.** An enormous window wall opens the view to a graceful old banyan tree springing from a cactus garden at this attractive restaurant. Rose tablecloths and soft aqua carpeting in the two-level dining area create a soothing backdrop to enjoy chef-owner Bernard Bree's fresh *agnello alla Martinese* (rack of lamb with burgundy-garlic sauce), or *bacca* (veal stuffed with cheese, ham, and chanterelles). For dessert, sorbets and ice creams have tropical fruit flavors. ⊠ *64-5188 Kinohou St., Waimea,* ☎ *808/885–8849. MC, V. Closed Sun.*

LODGING

Generally, you'll always be able to find a room on the Big Island; however, you might not get your first choice if you wait until the last minute. Make your plans early if you're visiting during the winter season, which runs from December 15 through April 15. Amazingly enough, you will not be able to find a room in Hilo during the first week in April, when the Merrie Monarch Festival (☞ Nightlife and the Arts, *below*) is in full swing. Kailua-Kona bursts at the seams in mid-October: athletes and their support teams fill the hotels during the Ironman World Triathlon Championships. An even bigger problem than finding a room at these times is finding a rental car. Be sure to make reservations well in advance—six months to a year—if your stay coincides with the festival, the triathlon, or any major holiday.

Hotel, room, and car package deals are often available in all price categories; a reputable travel agent should be able to furnish up-to-date information. Some of the older hotels do not have air-conditioning, but they will almost always have fans, which should be adequate except during the hot summer and early fall seasons. All rooms have a TV and phone unless otherwise indicated.

If you choose a bed-and-breakfast, inn, or an out-of-the-way hotel, explain your expectations fully and ask plenty of questions before booking. Be clear about your travel and location needs. Many B&Bs close to Hawai'i Volcanoes National Park, for example, are not the perfect locations for beach and sun worshipers. Some require stays of two or three days. When booking, ask about car-rental arrangements, as many B&B networks can offer discounted rates. For B&B referrals, *see* B&B Reservation Services *in* Contacts and Resources, *below*. For price category explanations, *see* On the Road with Fodor's at the beginning of the book.

Hilo

$$-$$$$ 🏨 **Hawai'i Naniloa Hotel.** Ask for a room with an ocean or bay view when you book here. Recent refurbishing in 1997 included new carpeting and a fresh paint job; rooms are done in rose with dark blue rugs. The deluxe rooms on the ninth floor are especially nice. The 10- and 12-story towers are connected by an open, modern lobby area with shops, and on the lower level are the Sandalwood dining room, a health club, and a beauty salon. An executive golf course, the Naniloa Country Club, is just across Banyan Drive. ⊠ *93 Banyan Dr., Hilo 96720,* ☎ *808/969–3333 or 800/367–5360,* 𝖥𝖠𝖷 *808/969–6622. 306 rooms, 19 suites. 2 restaurants, bar, refrigerators, beauty salon, massage, health club, dance club. AE, DC, MC, V.*

$$$ 🏨 **Shipman House Bed & Breakfast Inn.** Possibly Hilo's most pho-
★ tographed mansion, the Shipman House is on the national and state registers of historic places. Restored by W. H. Shipman's great-granddaughter Barbara Ann and her husband, Gary Andersen, in 1997, the 100 year-old turreted "castle" has three gracious B&B rooms in the house and two in a separate cottage, each with a private entrance. The house is furnished with antique koa and period pieces, some dating from the days when Queen Lili'uokalani came to tea, and it sits on 5½ acres of lush grounds on Reed's Island. A nice touch are the kimonos for guest use. ⊠ *131 Ka'iulani St., Hilo 96720,* ☎ *808/934– 8002 or 800/627–8447,* 𝖥𝖠𝖷 *808/934–8002. 3 rooms in house, 2 cottage units. Fans, refrigerators, library. CP. AE, MC, V.*

$$-$$$ 🏨 **Hilo Hawaiian Hotel.** One of the most pleasant lodgings on Hilo Bay has large bayfront rooms with spectacular views of Mauna Kea and Coconut Island. Streetside rooms overlook the golf course. Beige carpets and rattan furniture enliven the decor, and most accommodations have private lānai. Kitchenettes are available with one-bedroom suites. Views of the bay are showcased in the Queen's Court dining room, while Wai'oli Lounge has entertainment daily. ⊠ *71 Banyan Dr., Hilo 96720,* ☎ *808/ 935–9361 or 800/367–5004,* 𝖥𝖠𝖷 *808/961–9642. 279 rooms, 6 suites. Restaurant, bar, pool, 18-hole golf course, meeting rooms. AE, D, DC, MC, V.*

$$ 🏨 **Hale Kai Bjornen Bed & Breakfast.** On a bluff above Hilo Bay, just 2 mi from downtown Hilo, this large modern home has four rooms and a suite—all with grand ocean views and within earshot of lapping waves. Units have private baths and access to a pool, hot tub, and patio; four have private entrances. The hosts, Evonne and Paul Bjornen, serve a hearty breakfast—macadamia nut waffles, Portuguese sausage, fruits, breads, and special egg dishes—on an outdoor deck or in the kitchen's bay-window dining area. ⊠ *111 Honoli'i Pali St., Hilo 96720,* ☎ *808/935–6330,* FAX *808/935–8439. 4 rooms, 1 suite. Fans, pool, hot tub, coin laundry. Full breakfast. No credit cards.*

$$ 🏨 **Hilo Bay Hotel, Uncle Billy's.** This is a popular stopover for Neighbor Islanders, who enjoy proprietor Uncle Billy Kimi's Hawaiian hospitality. A nightly hula show and entertainment during dinner are part of the fun. ⊠ *87 Banyan Dr., Hilo 96720,* ☎ *808/935–0861 or 800/367–5102,* FAX *808/935–7903. 120 rooms, 25 suites. Bar, kitchenettes, refrigerators, pool, meeting rooms. AE, D, DC, MC, V.*

$$ 🏨 **Hilo Seaside Hotel.** The most pleasant rooms here have private lānai and overlook the koi-filled lagoon or are situated around the pool. Lots of foliage along the walkways and friendly personnel create a very Hawaiian ambience. This is a peaceful place, except when planes take off and land, as the hotel is near the airport's flight path. ⊠ *126 Banyan Dr., Hilo 96720,* ☎ *808/935–0821 or 800/367–7000,* FAX *808/ 969–9195. 136 rooms. Restaurant, bar, kitchenettes, fans, pool, meeting rooms. AE, D, DC, MC, V.*

$–$$ 🏨 **Dolphin Bay Hotel.** All units have kitchens in this clean, homey hotel in a lovely, green Hawaiian garden setting four blocks from Hilo Bay. The rooms do not have phones, but a pay phone is in the lobby. Desk fans stir the air in each room. Guests of the hotel, which is away from the beach in a residential area called Pu'ue'o, return repeatedly. ⊠ *333 'Iliahi St., Hilo 96720,* ☎ *808/935–1466,* FAX *808/935–1523. 13 rooms, 4 1-bedroom units, 1 2-bedroom unit. MC, V.*

$ 🏨 **Arnott's Lodge.** Designed as a budget lodge for backpackers, bicyclists, and other active visitors, it affords dormitory-style accommodations for up to four people per room. There are also semiprivate rooms, suites, and a shared kitchen and TV/video room. Though it's minutes from the airport, the setting is a lush wilderness. An international clientele takes advantage of guided hikes and barbecues offered by the lodge. ⊠ *98 'Apapane Rd., Hilo 96720,* ☎ *808/969–7097,* FAX *808/ 961–9638. 6 1- and 2-bedroom units, 36 bunks. Camping, coin laundry, travel services, airport shuttle. DC, MC, V.*

$ 🏨 **Wild Ginger Inn Bed & Breakfast.** This one-of-a-kind, 28-room inn is reminiscent of '40s Hawai'i plantation-style accommodations. Three levels of clean, simple rooms with blue-green carpets and eyelet curtains are in an old wooden building. A big lawn and a jungle garden run along a stream bank. Most rooms have double and twin beds. A complimentary buffet breakfast is served on the lānai lobby. There is no air-conditioning, but it's seldom needed with Hilo's cool trade winds. ⊠ *100 Pu'u'eo St., Hilo 96720,* ☎ *808/935–5556 or 800/882– 1887. 26 rooms, 2 suites. Refrigerators, coin laundry. CP. D, MC, V.*

Puna

$$–$$$ 🏨 **Kalani Honua Eco-Resort.** This out-of-the-way, back-to-nature retreat is a mile from Puna beach. A nonprofit organization, Kalani Honua offers healthful cuisine, nearby thermal springs, and a variety of programs on Hawaiian culture, physical and spiritual wellness, and ecology. Generator power means lights out at 10:30 PM. Accommodations include campsites, shared rooms with shared bath, cottage units, and lodge rooms with private or shared bath. Bathing suits are optional at the Olympic-size pool in the evening. ⊠ *RR 2, Hwy. 137 (Box 4500), Kehena Beach 96778,* ☎ *808/965–7828 or 800/800–6886. 24 rooms, 7 cottages, guest house. Fans, pool, sauna, camping, coin laundry. AE, MC, V.*

Volcano/South Point

$$$–$$$$ 🏨 **Chalet Kīlauea–The Inn at Volcano.** This romantically luxurious haven comprises two theme rooms and four suites, each with whirlpool tubs

218

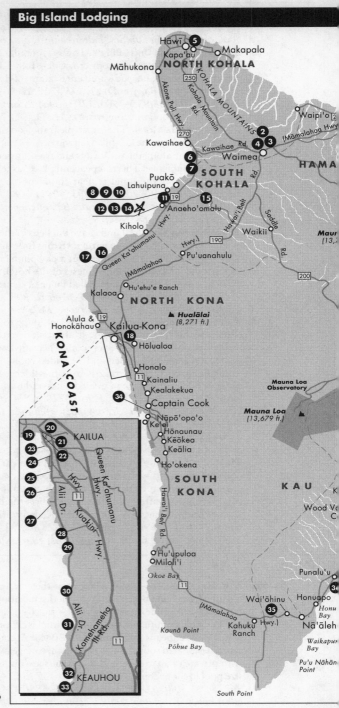

Big Island Lodging

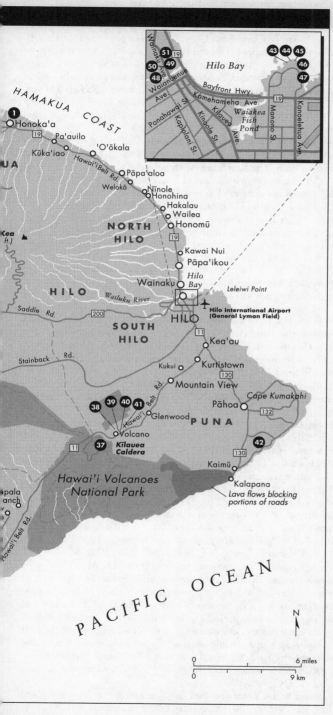

My Island Bed and
Breakfast, **41**

Orchid at Mauna Lani
Resort, **10**

Royal Kona Resort, **23**

Royal Waikoloan, **12**

Shipman House
Bed and Breakfast
Inn, **50**

Shirakawa Motel, **35**

Volcano House, **37**

Waikoloa Villas at
Waikoloa Village, **15**

Waimea Country
Lodge, **4**

Waimea Gardens
Cottage Bed and
Breakfast, **3**

Wild Ginger Inn
Bed and Breakfast, **49**

and marble bathrooms, some with fireplaces. The second-story Tree-House bedroom, with wraparound windows, gives the impression of floating on the tops of tree ferns. Guests share a large sitting room where afternoon tea/light supper is served before a fireplace. A gourmet candlelit breakfast under a glittering chandelier is hosted by proprietors Lisha and Brian Crawford. Separate hideaway homes are also available elsewhere on the island. ⊠ *Wright Rd., ¾ mi off Hwy 11(Box 998), Volcano Village 96785,* ☎ *808/967–7786 or 800/937–7786,* FAX *800/577–1849 or 808/967–8660. 2 rooms, 4 suites. Hot tub, massage, laundry service. AE, D, DC, MC, V.*

$$$ 🏠 **Mountain House and Hydrangea Cottage.** About a mile from Volcanoes National Park, Mountain House has three bedrooms, each with its own bath. The Koa Suite (with antique furnishings) is next to a smaller den/bedroom with a double bed, convenient for families. On the other side of the gourmet kitchen, the Obake Room looks out onto giant tree ferns. Behind the estate home, Hydrangea Cottage is a private retreat with a wraparound covered deck, modern kitchen, living room, bedroom, and bath. All units have a kitchen, washer, and dryer as well as fixings for a self-prepared breakfast. ⊠ *Pacific Islands Reservations, 571 Pauku St., Kailua 96734,* ☎ *808/262–8133 or 808/261–3584,* FAX *808/262–5030. 3 rooms, 1 cottage. No credit cards.*

$$–$$$ 🏠 **Colony One Sea Mountain.** Avid golfers and seekers of seclusion will enjoy the spacious Colony One condominiums, bordered by the ocean and fairways and near Hawai'i Volcanoes National Park. Units are not plush but have a country feel, with comfortable wicker and rattan furnishings and complete kitchens. The property includes the Punalu'u Conference Center, available for meetings of up to 100. There's weekly maid service and a two-day minimum stay. ⊠ *95–789 Ninole Loop Rd., Punalu'u (Box 460), Pahala 96777,* ☎ *808/928–6200 or 800/344–7675,* FAX *808/928–8075. 6 rooms, 18 1-bedroom units, 6 2-bedrooms units. Kitchens, pool, 18-hole golf course, 4 tennis courts, meeting rooms. MC, V.*

$$–$$$ 🏠 **Kīlauea Lodge.** A mile from the Volcanoes National Park entrance, this is possibly the most convenient place to stay in the area. The rooms, several with fireplaces, are slickly decorated to reflect an Oriental or Hawaiian theme. Set amid tree ferns and forests, the lodge offers cool mountain air and opportunities for brisk walks along the peaceful back roads of Volcano. The country-style restaurant has earned a reputation for good food. A big breakfast is included in the price of the room, and one room is accessible to guests with disabilities. Tutu's Place, a 1929 remodeled cottage with two bedrooms, is also available. ⊠ *Old Volcano Hwy., about 1 mi northeast of Volcano Store (Box 116), Volcano Village 96785,* ☎ *808/967–7366,* FAX *808/967–7367. 12 rooms, 1 cottage. Restaurant. Full breakfast. AE, MC, V.*

$$–$$$ 🏠 **Volcano House.** The charm of the Volcano House is its location at the edge of Kīlauea Caldera, so if you choose to stay, plan on paying a bit extra to book one of the rooms with a crater view. The clean and comfortable rooms have period koa furniture. Dinner at the Ka 'Ōhelo Room can stir romance, as can a walk in the cool, crisp air, topped off with a nightcap sipped while nestling by an ohia-wood fire in the lobby's stone fireplace. ⊠ *Box 53, Hawai'i Volcanoes National Park 96718-0053,* ☎ *808/967–7321,* FAX *808/967–8429. 42 rooms. Restaurant. AE, D, DC, MC, V.*

$–$$ 🏠 **My Island Bed & Breakfast Inn.** Gordon and Joann Morse opened their historic, century-old, three-story house to visitors in 1985. Surrounded by 6 acres of lawns and gardens, the house is the oldest in Volcano, built in 1886 by the Lyman missionary family (Hilo has the Lyman Museum). Three rooms are available in the house (one sleeps up to five), and you will definitely want a guided tour from your genial hosts. If you seek privacy and an uncluttered haven, choose the studio apartment with a kitchenette or one of the garden apartments separate from the house. Vacation houses are also available. ⊠ *19–3896 Old Volcano Rd., Volcano Village 96785 (Box 100, Volcano 96785),* ☎ *808/967–7216,* ℻ *808/967–7719. 6 rooms, 5 with private bath. Full breakfast. No credit cards.*

$ ⛤ **Shirakawa Motel.** In the remote Ka'ū District, midway between Kona and Hilo near Nā'ālehu, the southernmost town in the United States, this bare, basic, and clean motel has been run by the same family since 1921. Families can get connecting units with cooking facilities, though there are places to eat nearby in town. ⊠ *95–6040 Māmalahoa Hwy. 11, Wai'ōhinu 96772 (Box 467, Na'alehu 96772),* ☎ *808/929–7462. 12 rooms. No credit cards.*

Up-Country Kona District

$$$ ⛤ **Hōlualoa Inn.** Two suites and four rooms, each with private bath, are available in this cedar estate home. In up-country Kona amid the coffee trees and bucolic fields 4 mi above Kailua Bay, the artsy town of Hōlualoa is steps away. Guest rooms are named after their decor: Polynesian and Balinese suites, Pineapple, Orchid Isle, Oriental, and Hibiscus Rooms. There's also a rooftop gazebo. ⊠ *76–5932 Māmalahoa Hwy. (Box 222, Hōlualoa 96725),* ☎ *808/324–1121 or 800/392–1812,* ℻ *808/322–2472. 4 rooms, 2 suites. Pool, hot tub, billiards. Full breakfast. AE, DC, MC, V.*

$ ⛤ **Manago Hotel.** You'll get a great view high above the Kona Coast in the newer wing of this family-run hostelry. The rooms are reminiscent of a mainland motel, except for one—a Japanese-style room with tatami (sleeping mats) instead of beds and a *furo* (deep bathtub), which the proprietor has kept in remembrance of his grandparents, who built the main hotel in 1917. ⊠ *81–6155 Māmalahoa Hwy. (Box 145, Captain Cook 96704),* ☎ *808/323–2642,* ℻ *808/323–3451. 65 rooms, 42 with bath. Restaurant. D, MC, V.*

Kailua-Kona and Keauhou

$$$$ ⛤ **Aston Kona by the Sea.** Complete modern kitchens and tile lānai can be found in every suite in this comfortable oceanfront condo complex. An open-air lobby and a helpful reception desk add to the friendly atmosphere. There's no sandy beach, but the pool is next to the ocean. ⊠ *75-6106 Ali'i Dr., Kailua-Kona 96740,* ☎ *808/327–2300 or 800/367–5124,* ℻ *808/327–2333. 36 1-bedroom condominiums, 37 2-bedroom condominiums. Pool. AE, D, DC, MC, V.*

$$$$ ⛤ **Kanaloa at Kona.** The 13-acre grounds provide a verdant setting for
★   this low-rise condominium complex bordering the Keauhou-Kona Country Club. Large one- and two-bedroom apartments have wall-to-wall carpeting, koa-wood cabinetwork, and tile and marble surfaces. Oceanfront suites have private hot tubs, the bathroom showers are big enough for two, and laundry service is free. Edward's at the Terrace restaurant has a romantically tropical atmosphere, in addition to serving reasonable and good American cuisine with local flavor. ⊠ *78-261 Manukai St., Kailua-Kona 96740,* ☎ *808/322–9625, 808/322–2272 or 800/688–7444,* ℻ *808/322–3818. 79 1- and 2-bedroom condominiums. Restaurant, fans, kitchenettes, 3 outdoor pools, 2 tennis courts, laundry service. AE, D, DC, MC, V.*

$$$–$$$$ ⛤ **Aston Royal Sea Cliff Resort.** This is a Mediterranean-style condominium resort on 7 coastal acres with pleasant tree-shaded grounds. Plushly furnished one- and two-bedroom apartments, decorated in soft, tropical colors, have large lānai and kitchen/dining areas, and in-room washers and dryers. ⊠ *75-6040 Ali'i Dr., Kailua-Kona 96740,* ☎ *808/329–8021 or 800/922–7866,* ℻ *808/326–1887. 37 1-bed-*

room, 100 2-bedroom condominiums, 5 2-bedroom villas. 2 pools, hot tub, sauna, tennis court. AE, D, DC, MC, V.

$$$–$$$$ 🏠 **Kailua Plantation House B&B.** At the ocean's edge just outside Kailua-Kona, this immaculate two-story house was built in 1990 as a B&B, with four rooms upstairs (two overlooking the ocean) and one oceanfront suite downstairs. Rooms with private lānai are done in a unique range of styles, with names that reflect their decor—Pilialoha (Friendship Room) or Ali'i Wikolia (Queen Victoria Room) for example. An extensive display of local art and vines draped along the second-story stairwell maintain the tropical ambience throughout the house. ✉ 75-5948 Ali'i Dr., Kailua-Kona 96740, ☎ 808/329–3727, FAX 808/326–7323. 5 rooms. Refrigerators. Full breakfast. AE, MC, V.

$$$–$$$$ 🏠 **Kona Bali Kai.** These older, family-style units midway between Kailua-Kona and Keauhou Country Club all have kitchen-dining areas; only some units have air-conditioning. The property is divided, so ask for a place makai rather than mauka of the road. ✉ 76-6246 Ali'i Dr., Kailua-Kona 96740, ☎ 808/329–9381 or 888/329–6500, FAX 808/326–6056. 14 rooms, 156 condominiums (26 1-bedroom rentals, 22 2-bedroom rentals). Pool, coin laundry. AE, D, DC, MC, V.

$$$ 🏠 **Royal Kona Resort.** Of the major hotels, the Royal Kona Resort is nearest to Kailua on the south side of town. It has a distinctive profile (built to resemble an early Hawaiian *holua* slide dropping toward the sea) that is easy to pick out from downtown. Corner rooms in the Beach Building are the best because they have huge lānai that overlook the ocean. ✉ 75-5852 Ali'i Dr., Kailua-Kona 96740, ☎ 808/329–3111 or 800/774–5662, FAX 808/329–7230 or 808/329–9532. 434 rooms, 18 suites. Restaurant, bar, coffee shop, in-room safes, refrigerators, pool, 4 tennis courts, meeting rooms. AE, D, DC, MC, V.

$$–$$$ 🏠 **King Kamehameha's Kona Beach Hotel.** The most conveniently lo-
★ cated of the major hotels, it is right next to Kailua Pier. Rooms are not particularly special (fifth- and sixth-floor oceanfront rooms are best), but it rates a star because it is the only central Kailua-Kona hotel with a white-sand beach—plus there's a shopping mall in the lobby. Free tours explore the grounds and Ahu'ena Heiau, which King Kamehameha I had reconstructed in the early 1800s. ✉ 75-566 0 Palani Rd., Kailua-Kona 96740, ☎ 808/329–2911 or 800/367–6060, FAX 808/329–4602. 460 rooms, 6 suites. 2 restaurants, 2 bars, pool, sauna, 4 tennis courts, beach. AE, D, DC, MC, V.

$$ 🏠 **Hale Kona Kai.** This small vacation condominium on the ocean's edge, next door to the Royal Kona Resort, requires a three-day minimum stay. These privately owned units are all furnished differently; the corner units with wraparound lānai have the best views. It is within walking distance of restaurants and shopping. ✉ 75-5870 Kahakai Rd., Kailua-Kona 96740, ☎ 808/329–2155 or 800/421–3696, FAX 808/329–2155. 25 condominiums. Pool. AE, MC, V.

$$ 🏠 **Keauhou Beach Hotel.** Light and airy color schemes brighten rooms in the ocean wing of this oceanfront hotel. At the Kuakini Terrace restaurant, nightly buffets are popular, as is local entertainment in the open-air Makai Bar. The hotel's real plus is its location: adjacent to Kahalu'u, one of the Big Island's best snorkeling beaches, and 5 mi to Kailua. There's a heiau on the grounds. ✉ 78-6740 Ali'i Dr., Kailua-Kona 96740, ☎ 808/322–3441 or 800/367–6025, FAX 808/322–6586. 304 rooms, 6 suites. Restaurant, bar, refrigerators, 2 pools, sauna, 6 tennis courts, exercise room, meeting room. AE, D, DC, MC, V.

$$ 🏠 **Kona Bay Hotel, Uncle Billy's.** These two- and four-story motel-type units are right in the center of town, across the street from the ocean. The place is owned and managed by the same local family that owns the Hilo Bay Hotel. The atmosphere is friendly and fun-loving; open-air dining around the pool is casual. Some rooms have kitchenettes.

⊠ *75-5739 Ali'i Dr., Kailua-Kona 96740,* ☎ *808/329–1393, 800/367–5102, or 800/423–8733, ext. 220,* ℻ *808/329–9210. 146 rooms. 2 restaurants, bar, pool. AE, D, DC, MC, V.*

$$ 🏨 **Kona Magic Sands.** This condo complex is near Magic Sands Beach, which is a plus for swimmers and sunbathers in summer (the sand washes away in winter). Units vary, because they are individually owned, but all are oceanfront; some have enclosed lānai. Maid service is available on request for an additional fee. ⊠ *77-6452 Ali'i Dr., Kailua-Kona 96740,* ☎ *808/329–9393 or 800/553–5035,* ℻ *808/326–4137. 15 rooms. Restaurant, bar, kitchenettes, pool. D, MC, V.*

$$ 🏨 **Kona Surf Resort.** Catering to Japanese tour groups, this large, easy-to-get-confused-in hotel is the last property at the end of the road in Keauhou. Some rooms have a beige-and-green color scheme with white rattan furniture; many are in need of updating. A charming copper-roof wedding chapel beside peaceful koi ponds is available for visitors who want to tie the knot during their vacation. Paths and open spaces allow strolls along the cliff edge with the waves crashing below. ⊠ *78-128 Ehukai St., Kailua-Kona 96740,* ☎ *808/322–3411 or 800/367–8011,* ℻ *808/322–3245. 522 rooms, 8 suites. Restaurant, 3 bars, refrigerators, 2 pools (1 saltwater), 18-hole golf course, 3 tennis courts, meeting rooms. AE, D, DC, MC, V.*

$–$$ 🏨 **Kona Islander Inn.** Its close-to-the-village location and turn-of-the-century plantation-style architecture in a setting of palms and torch-lit paths make this pleasant but older apartment-style hotel a good value. Studios, with queen and twin beds, are across the street from Waterfront Row. ⊠ *75-5776 Kuakini Hwy., Kailua-Kona 96740,* ☎ *808/329–3181 or 800/535–0085,* ℻ *808/326–4137. 145 condominiums (40 rentals). Pool. AE, D, DC, MC, V.*

$–$$ 🏨 **Kona Seaside Hotel.** The old Hukilau Hotel and the adjoining Kona Seaside have been combined and renovated, with rooms in four price categories (according to size and location). This hotel has a great central location across the street from Kailua Bay. Rooms nearest the main street are built around a pool. The small rooms have tiny bathrooms and showers but are completely adequate for the budget traveler. ⊠ *75-5646 Palani Rd., Kailua-Kona 96740,* ☎ *808/329–2455 or 800/367–7000,* ℻ *808/329–6157. 224 rooms, 1 suite. Restaurant, bar, 2 pools, meeting rooms. AE, D, DC, MC, V.*

$ 🏨 **Kona Tiki Hotel.** The best thing about this simple, older three-story walk-up hotel about a mile south of Kailua-Kona is that all the units have lānai right next to the ocean. The rooms are simple, clean, and pleasantly decorated. Guests can sunbathe by the seaside pool. There are no in-room TVs or phones. ⊠ *75-5968 Ali'i Dr., Kailua-Kona 96745,* ☎ *808/329–1425,* ℻ *808/327–9402. 15 rooms. Fans, refrigerators, grill, pool. CP. No credit cards.*

Kohala Coast and Waikoloa

$$$$ 🏨 **Aston The Shores at Waikoloa.** These red-tile-roof villas are set amid
★ landscaped lagoons and waterfalls at the edge of the championship Waikoloa Golf Course. The spacious one-bedroom/one-bath and two-bedroom/two-bath condo units are decorated in such muted shades as rose and light green; sliding glass doors open onto large lānai. Oversize tubs and large separate glassed-in showers add to the luxury. ⊠ *69-1035 Keana Pl., Waikoloa 96743,* ☎ *808/885–5001 or 800/922–7866,* ℻ *808/885–8414. 120 1- and 2-bedroom villas. Fans, kitchenettes, room service, pool, hot tub, 2 tennis courts. AE, D, DC, MC, V.*

$$$$ 🏨 **Four Seasons Resort Hualālai.** Bungalows house six or eight rooms
★ each in this romantic oceanfront hotel built in 1996. Sisal carpeting, natural slate floors, Hawaiian artwork, and louvered sliding doors of

dark wood create a peaceful haven. Six suites have outdoor garden showers. Three main pools (including a lap pool), plus a children's pool and natural historic anchialine ponds, dot the property. Anchialine ponds are brackish water pools located near the ocean with no visible connection, yet they rise and fall with the tide. They were used for aquaculture by early Hawaiians. The Hawaiian Cultural Center and Sports Club and Spa create other diversions. The resort's golf course annually hosts the SENIOR PGA Tournament of Champions. ⊠ *100 Ka'ūpūlehu Dr., Ka'ūpūlehu/Kona 96740 (Box 1269, Kailua-Kona 96745), ☎ 808/325–8000 or 800/332–3442, ℻ 808/325–8100. 222 rooms, 21 suites. 3 restaurants, 4 pools, 8 tennis courts, beach, children's programs, concierge, meeting rooms, airport shuttle. AE, DC, MC, V.*

$$$$ 🏨 **Hāpuna Beach Prince Hotel.** This Kohala Coast luxury hotel fronts
★ the beach, which has been named the best in the nation. The hotel is a glitzy beauty with 350 rooms decorated in cool sand and soft-green tones with sculpted bilevel sand-color carpeting and marble bathrooms. All rooms face the ocean and have lānai. The showpiece is an 8,000-square-ft four-bedroom suite with its own swimming pool. ⊠ *62-100 Kauna'oa Dr., Kohala Coast 96743, ☎ 808/880–1111 or 800/882–6060, ℻ 808/880–3142. 350 rooms, 36 suites. 5 restaurants, pool, hot tub, 18-hole golf course, 13 tennis courts, exercise room, meeting rooms. AE, D, DC, MC, V.*

$$$$ 🏨 **Hilton Waikoloa Village.** This 62-acre property on a rocky stretch
★ of coast is elaborately landscaped, with shaded pathways—punctuated with items from a multimillion-dollar Pacific Island art collection—that connect three tower buildings. The swimming pool is nearly an acre in size with a 175-ft water slide; a meandering river that connects smaller pools; and a sandy, man-made beach bordering a 4-acre lagoon. Rooms are large and have their own lānai. You can have an encounter with the resort's dolphins through a special lottery for adults, or by reservation for youngsters. The Kohala Spa has the finest fitness facilities on the island. ⊠ *425 Waikoloa Beach Dr., Kamuela 96743, ☎ 808/885–1234 or 800/445–8667, ℻ 808/885–2900. 1,233 rooms, 8 suites. 6 restaurants, 6 bars, 3 pools, 2 18-hole golf courses, 8 tennis courts, children's programs. AE, D, DC, MC, V.*

$$$$ 🏨 **Islands at Mauna Lani.** Surrounded by saltwater ponds, streams, and waterfalls, the individual two- and three-bedroom, duplex condominium town houses have cathedral windows that look out over Mauna Lani's Francis H. I'i Brown Golf Course. Each unit has a private drive and a private lānai with a wet bar. Spacious kitchens are stocked with a generous supply of groceries and guests have access to the workout room and tennis courts at the nearby racquet club, as well as a variety of dining options throughout the resort. ⊠ *Classic Resorts, 68–1310 Mauna Lani Dr., Suite 101, Kohala Coast 96743, ☎ 808/885–5022 or 800/642–6284. 16 2-bedroom units, 5 3-bedroom condominium units. Pool, hot tub, 2 18-hole golf courses, coin laundry. AE, DC, MC, V.*

$$$$ 🏨 **Kona Village Resort.** Without phones, TVs, or radios, it's easy to
★ feel you are part of an extended Polynesian *ohana* (family), with your own thatch-roof *hale* near the resort's sandy beach. Extra-large rooms are cooled by ceiling fans and decorated in neutral shades. Rates include meals, tennis, sailing, kayaking, snorkeling, volleyball, and rides in the resort's glass-bottom boat. ⊠ *Queen Ka'ahumanu Hwy., Kaupulehu–Kona 96740 (Box 1299, Kailua-Kona 96745), ☎ 808/325–5555 or 800/367–5290, ℻ 808/325–5124. 92 1-bedroom bungalows, 33 2-bedroom bungalows. 2 restaurants, 3 bars, 2 pools, 2 hot tubs, health club, 3 tennis courts, beach, children's programs, meeting rooms, airport shuttle. AP. AE, DC, MC, V.*

$$$$ ★ ☆ **Mauna Kea Beach Hotel.** This world-class resort hotel was developed by Laurence S. Rockefeller in 1965 on one of the Islands' finest white-sand beaches. Rooms have a fresh look with beige tiles and area carpets and a rose-and-green color scheme. At the large Pavilion restaurant, diners can sit outdoors overlooking the ocean. Shuttle service and reciprocal charging privileges with the adjacent Hāpuna Beach Prince Hotel allow the easy use of facilities at both stellar hotels. ✉ *62-100 Mauna Kea Beach Dr., Kohala Coast 96743,* ☎ *808/882–7222 or 800/882–6060,* FAX *808/882–5700. 310 rooms. 4 restaurants, in-room safes, pool, 2 18-hole golf courses, 13 tennis courts, beach. AE, D, DC, MC, V.*

$$$$ ★ ☆ **Mauna Lani Bay Hotel and Bungalows.** Almost all the spacious rooms in this modern hotel have ocean views and all have a large lānai. Comfortable furnishings and marble coffee tables grace rooms decorated with white natural fabrics and teak. The resort is known for its two spectacular golf courses. Pacific Rim cuisine can be enjoyed at the oceanfront CanoeHouse (☞ Dining, *above*); lighter eaters can graze on appetizers, and enjoy live entertainment in the Honu Bar. Gourmands will want to visit during the annual Cuisines of the Sun celebration in July. ✉ *68-1400 Mauna Lani Dr., Kohala Coast 96743,* ☎ *808/885–6622 or 800/367–2323,* FAX *808/885–6183. 350 rooms, 12 suites, 5 bungalows. 5 restaurants, 5 bars, refrigerators, in-room safes, in-room VCRs, pool, 2 golf courses, 10 tennis courts, children's programs. AE, D, DC, MC, V.*

$$$$ ☆ **Mauna Lani Point Condominiums.** These elegant and roomy suites are set off by themselves on one of the world's most beautiful oceanside golf courses, a few steps away from the Mauna Lani Bay Hotel. Rooms have a modern tropical decor in soft pink and eggshell colors. Guests may use the golf and tennis facilities of the adjacent Mauna Lani Bay Hotel. Each suite has its own washer-dryer. ✉ *68-1310 Mauna Lani Dr., Kohala Coast 96743,* ☎ *808/885–5022 or 800/642–6284,* FAX *808/885–5015. 24 1-bedroom, 37 2-bedroom, 1 3-bedroom condominiums. Kitchenettes, room service, pool, hot tub, sauna, 2 golf courses, 10 tennis courts. AE, DC, MC, V.*

$$$$ ★ ☆ **The Orchid at Mauna Lani.** This ITT Sheraton hotel sits on 32 beachfront acres. Rooms are handsome and traditional, with marble-top tables, massive highboys, and marble bathrooms. Sailing, snorkeling, and scuba are options, and there's a protected swimming lagoon. For landlubbers, tennis, golf, or pampering at the health club can fill the day. Restaurants include the Grill, the Orchid Court, and the poolside Brown's Beach House. The hotel hosts Big Island Bounty, a celebration of food and wine that's usually held over Memorial Day weekend. ✉ *1 N. Kanikū Dr., Kohala Coast 96743,* ☎ *808/885–2000 or 800/845–9905,* FAX *808/885–1064. 539 rooms, 54 suites. 3 restaurants, 4 bars, pool, sauna, 2 golf courses, 10 tennis courts, health club, beach, snorkeling, boating, children's programs. AE, D, DC, MC, V.*

$$$–$$$$ ☆ **Royal Waikoloan.** The emphasis here is on Hawaiiana with demonstrations of Hawaiian quilting and other crafts in the lobby. The majority of rooms have an ocean view; all have private lānai. An additional 17 plush cabanas are near the ocean. The resort is on 16 acres bordered by royal fishponds, next to a white-sand beach and ʻAnaehoʻomalu Bay—perfect for windsurfing and snorkeling. Lūʻau are twice a week. An optional all-inclusive package includes meals and activities. ✉ *69-275 Waikoloa Beach Dr., Kamuela 96743,* ☎ *808/886–6789 or 800/462–6262,* FAX *808/885–7852. 547 rooms, 17 cabanas. 3 restaurants, 3 bars, pool, hot tub, sauna, 2 18-hole golf courses, 6 tennis courts, exercise room, beach, children's programs, coin laundry, meeting rooms. AE, D, DC, MC, V.*

$$$–$$$$ ☆ **Waikoloa Villas at Waikoloa Village.** This is about the only moderately priced Waikoloa-area accommodation, although it's 6 mi inland. Individually owned condominium units are all decorated differently, but they each meet standards set by the rental agency. Two-night minimum stays are required. The wide-open spaces of cowboy country attract golfers and the horsey set. ⊠ *68-3840 Lua Kua St. (Box 38-5134), Waikoloa 96738, ☎ 808/883–9144 or 800/535–0085,* FAX *808/883–8740. 5 1-bedroom, 10 2-bedroom, 3 3-bedroom condominiums. 2 pools, 18-hole golf course, 2 tennis courts, horseback riding. AE, MC, V.*

$–$$ 🏨 **Kohala Village Inn.** This simple, clean little hotel is the only one in the country town of Hāwī. Cable TV and friendly proprietors make this inn, built around a courtyard, an adequate place to stay. Guests get a 15% discount at breakfast in the restaurant next door. Bathrooms have showers but not tubs. ⊠ *55-514 Hāwī Rd., Hāwī 96719, ☎ 808/889–0105 or 808/889–0419,* FAX *808/889–0419. 17 rooms, 1 suite. MC, V.*

Waimea/Hamakua Coast

$$$ 🏨 **Waimea Gardens Cottage B&B.** These two charming country stream-side cottages have kitchens stocked with your choice of breakfast items, French doors, lace curtains, decorative antique accents, and window boxes spilling over with flowers. One cottage has an extra-deep Grecian tub with jets that opens onto its own private garden. You can awake in the cool, up-country mornings to collect your own eggs from the hen's nest outside. Hosts Charles and Barbara Campbell provide warm robes. ⊠ *Reservations: Hawai'i's Best Bed and Breakfasts,* ⊠ *Box 563, Kamuela 96743, ☎ 808/885–4550 or 800/262–9912,* FAX *808/885–0559. 2 cottages. CP. D.*

$$ 🏨 **Waimea Country Lodge.** Formerly the Parker Ranch Lodge, in cool upcountry surroundings, this lodge has rooms that look out onto green pastures. New paint, beds, drapes, light-color carpets, and Hawaiian print bedspreads added in 1998 have made the lodge far more appealing than it was. ⊠ *65–1210 Lindsey Rd. (Box 2559, Kamuela 96743), ☎ 808/885–4100,* FAX *808/885–6711. 21 rooms. Kitchenettes. AE, D, DC, MC, V.*

$–$$ 🏨 **Kamuela Inn B&B.** You might choose to spend a night in Waimea just to stay at this nicely decorated country inn. Every room is attractively designed; a penthouse suite sleeps six and has a sunset lānai and full kitchen. Continental breakfast is served at the cheery breakfast lānai. The inn has a peaceful, lush, country setting, yet it's near shops, a theater, restaurants, and a museum. ⊠ *65–1300 Kawaihae Rd. (Box 1994, Kamuela 96743), ☎ 808/885–4243,* FAX *808/885–8857. 31 rooms, 3 suites. CP. AE, D, DC, MC, V.*

$ 🏨 **Hotel Honoka'a Club.** This bargain hotel, built in 1908, is rustic yet inviting. Every room has its own decor, with old-fashioned dressers and different color schemes. Rooms range from lower-level hostel units with three or four beds and an adjoining shower per room, to upper-story units with queen-size beds, showers, TVs, and views of kukui, mango, African tulip, and avocado trees and of the distant ocean. Collectors will enjoy poking through the secondhand stores in the country town of Honoka'a. ⊠ *45–3480 Māmane St. (Box 247, Honoka'a 96727), ☎ 808/775–0678 or 800/808–0678. 11 rooms, 2 suites, 4 hostel rooms. Restaurant, meeting rooms. MC, V.*

NIGHTLIFE AND THE ARTS

Clubs and Cabarets

If you're the kind of person who doesn't come alive until after dark, you're going to be pretty lonely on the Big Island. In Hilo, the streets roll up at dusk. There is live music at **Fiascos** (⊠ 200 Kanoelehua Ave., ☎ 808/935–7666) on Friday and Saturday nights.

Even on the visitor-oriented Kona–Kohala Coast, there's not a lot doing after dark. Blame it on the plantation heritage—people did their cane-raising in the morning. The hottest place, actually half an hour out of town, is the **Second Floor,** a disco with a DJ, at the Hilton Waikola Village (⊠ 425 Waikoloa Beach Dr., off Queen Ka'ahumanu Hwy., ☎ 808/886–1234, ext. 2891). This is a high-energy, Toulouse-Lautrec–theme club for the young at heart. Tuesday through Saturday, you also might be able to find some easy listening jazz at the **Honu Bar** at the Mauna Lani Bay Hotel and Bungalows (⊠ 68-1400 Mauna Lani Dr., Kohala Coast, ☎ 808/885–6622). Cocktail tables and cozy booths, a dance floor, a game room with two pool tables, sushi and sashimi prepared "au table," as well as other appetizers and libations have made this a popular gathering spot.

In Kailua the **Eclipse Restaurant** (⊠ 75-5711 Kuakini Hwy., ☎ 808/329–4686) boasts a DJ and disco music from 10 PM, Wednesday through Saturday. Sunday features a big-band sound.

Dinner Cruise

Captain Beans' Polynesian Dinner Cruise is the ever-popular standby in sunset dinner cruises. You can't miss it. As the sun sets in Kailua, look out over the water and you'll see a big, gaudy, orange-and-brown boat with distinctive orange sails. This cruise is corny, and you would get a better full-course dinner in a restaurant for less, but it's an experience, for adults only. ⊠ *73-4800 Kanalani St., Suite 200, Kailua-Kona ,* ☎ *808/329–2955 or 800/831–5541.* ▣ *$49, including dinner, entertainment, and open bar.* ☉ *Sails daily 5:15.*

Film

Hilo
Films are shown regularly at **Prince Kūhiō Theaters 1 and 2** (⊠ Prince Kūhiō Plaza, 111 E. Puainako Ave., ☎ 808/959–4595); **Kress Cinemas, Wallace Theaters Four-Plex** (⊠ 174 Kamehameha Ave., ☎ 808/961–3456); and at **Waiākea Theaters 1, 2, and 3** (⊠ Waiākea Kai Shopping Plaza, 88 Kanoelehua Ave., ☎ 808/935–9747).

Kailua-Kona
Hualālai Theaters 1, 2, and 3 (⊠ Hualālai Center, Kuakini Hwy. and Hualālai St., ☎ 808/329–6641) has regular showings. **Kona Marketplace Cinemas** (⊠ Kona Marketplace, 75-5719 Ali'i Dr., ☎ 808/329–4488) shows current movies.

Around the Island
Akebono Theater and Playhouse (⊠ Hwy. 130, Pāhoa, ☎ 808/965–9943) sometimes shows special-engagement movies, such as surfing films; and also occasionally is the setting for plays by the fledgling **Hawai'i Island Theater.**

Kahei Theaer (⊠ Hawi, ☎ 808/889–6831) shows first-run movies Friday, Saturday, and Sunday evenings.

Honoka'a Peoples Theater (⊠ Manane St., Honoka'a, ☎ 808/775–0000) shows commercial movies on weekends.

Na'alehu Theater (⊠ Hawai'i Belt Rd., Hwy. 11, Na'alehu, ☎ 808/929–9133) shows movies Friday, Saturday, and Sunday evenings.

Hula

For dance lovers, the biggest wingding of the year is the **Merrie Monarch Festival** (✉ Hawai'i Naniloa Hotel, 93 Banyan Dr., Hilo 96720, ☎ 808/935–9168) staged in Hilo during the first week following Easter Sunday. Hula hālau converge on the town to honor King David Kalākaua, Hawai'i's last king. The dance competition names the best male, female, group, and so on. For accommodations you need to book rooms as much as a year in advance.

Lū'au and Polynesian Revues

Three lū'au are recommended in the Kohala Coast and Waikoloa area:

The **Hilton Waikoloa Village** seats 650 outdoors at the Kamehameha Court for its "Legends of the Pacific" show. A buffet dinner provides samplings of Hawaiian food, as well as fish, beef, and chicken to appeal to all tastes, and two cocktails. ✉ *425 Waikoloa Beach Dr., Waikoloa,* ☎ *808/885–1234.* ✍ *$55.* ⊙ *Fri. from 6:30 PM.*

Everybody knows **Kona Village Resort** has the best lū'au of the Big Island resorts, if you are judging by authenticity, atmosphere, and attitude—and they don't even use too much salt in the seasoning. Mainland taste buds might reject some items, such as 'opihi (a limpet, considered a chewy delicacy in Hawai'i, it sells for about $24 a pound), but don't worry, there's plenty to appeal to everyone. A Polynesian show on a stage over a lagoon is magical. ✉ *6 mi north of Kona International Airport, off Queen Ka'ahumanu Hwy., Box 1299, Kailua-Kona,* ☎ *808/325–5555.* ✍ *$66.50.* ⊙ *Fri. walking tour 5:30, imu ceremony 6:15 PM, dinner 7, show 8.*

The **Royal Waikoloan** does a nice job with its Sunday- and Wednesday-night lū'au at the Lū'au Grounds, where the Polynesian revue showcases the well-known Tihati presenting the entertainment. ✉ *69-275 Waikoloa Beach Dr., Kamuela,* ☎ *808/885–6789.* ✍ *$52.50.* ⊙ *Wed. and Sun. 5:30–8:30.*

In Kailua, two lū'au fill the bill, with Polynesian entertainment, an *imu* ceremony (placing and removing the pig from the underground oven), pageantry, and an open bar.

King Kamehameha's Kona Beach Hotel's Island Breeze Lūa'u. After enjoying the evening's entertainment and a 22-course buffet, stroll through the hotel's lobby to view educational Hawaiiana displays and fishing trophies. ✉ *75-5660 Palani Rd., Kailua-Kona,* ☎ *808/326–4969.* ✍ *$52.* ⊙ *Tues., Wed., Thurs., Sun. at 5:30.*

The **Royal Kona** lights lū'au torches for the Drums of Polynesia show three times a week in an oceanfront setting. ✉ *75-5852 Ali'i Dr., Kailua-Kona,* ☎ *808/329–3111, Ext. 4.* ✍ *$49.* ⊙ *Mon., Fri., Sat. at 6.*

Theater

Hilo Community Players (✉ 141 Kalākaua Ave., Hilo, ☎ 808/935–9155) stages plays on an occasional basis.

Nearer Kailua-Kona, if you're dying to see a play, check with the **Aloha Performing Arts Center** (✉ Aloha Theatre Café, Hwy. 11, Kainaliu, ☎ 808/322–9924) for its next production.

For legitimate theater, the little town of Waimea is your best bet. The **Kahilu Theater Foundation** (☎ 808/885–6017) produces plays and imports entertainment on a fairly regular basis.

OUTDOOR ACTIVITIES AND SPORTS

Participant Sports

The Big Island attracts active people. You'll see them running, bicycling, hiking, sailing, and even skiing. In general, water-sports activities center on the Kailua-Kona area because of its calmer waters.

Biking

Although pedalers should be fairly physically fit for extended bicycling tours, there seems to be no typical rider—everyone from college students to retirees has completed tours of a week or longer. How much you ride is up to you, as generally the support van that carries gear will also stop to pick up tired riders. Helmets are strongly recommended, and some operators require them. Also, sheepskin seat covers and bicycle shorts add greatly to personal comfort on long trips.

Backroads Bicycle Touring (✉ 801 Cedar St., Berkeley, CA 94710-1740, ☎ 510/527–1555 or 800/462–2848) has been pushing pedaling in Hawai'i since 1985. They sponsor eight-day, 320-mi circle-island biking and walking trips, overnighting in hotels. Hotel accommodations and meals are included, but the bicycle and airfare are extra.

Bicycle Adventures, Inc. (✉ Box 11219, Olympia, WA 98508, ☎ 360/786–0989 or 800/443–6060). Six and eight-day winter bicycle tours of the Big Island cover 40–50 mi a day. Pedalers enjoy beach time, snorkeling, hiking excursions, comfortable accommodations and fine dining, in addition to visits to Kīlauea Volcano and Pu'uhonua o Hōnaunau. The cost of rental bicycles are in addition to the $1,500–$2,000 rates.

Chris' Adventures Bike or Hike (✉ Box 869, Kula, ☎ 808/326–4600) has half- and full-day biking excursions ranging from easy down-the-volcano tours to challenging off-road treks. Morning tours include breakfast and lunch; afternoon tours include a light snack.

BIKE RENTAL

If you want to strike out on your own, consider renting a bicycle in Kailua at **B&L Bike and Sports** (✉ 75–5699 Kopiko Pl., Kailua-Kona, ☎ 808/329–3309). In Kailua-Kona, **Hawaiian Pedals Bicycle Rentals** (✉ Kona Inn Shopping Village, 75–5744 Ali'i Dr., Kailua-Kona, ☎ 808/329–2294) has mountain-, road-, and full suspension–bicycles for rent.

Fitness Centers

In Hilo, exercise addicts might try **Spencer Health and Fitness Center** (✉ 197 Keawe St., ☎ 808/969–1511). The **Hawai'i Naniloa Hotel** (✉ 93 Banyan Dr., ☎ 808/969–3333 or 800/367–5360) has a spa and fitness center available to nonguests for $15, with such extra services as herbal wraps and massages available.

In Kona, the **Club** (✉ 75–5699 Kopiko Rd., Kona Center, ☎ 808/326–2582) has high-tech fitness facilities at a daily rate of $10.

Two major hotels, the **Hilton Waikoloa Village** (Kohala Spa, $20 daily for nonguests) and the **Hāpuna Beach Prince** ($10 daily, $20 weekly for nonguests) have spa facilities that may be used by nonguests.

Golf

If there is one thing the Big Island is known for, it's the beautiful golf courses that appear like green oases in the black, arid landscape of lava rock fields. Three of the Big Island's golf courses, the Mauna Kea Beach Resort course and, at Mauna Lani Resort, the Francis H. I'i Brown golf courses (North and South), are repeatedly chosen by golfing magazines as the best, the most spectacular, and the favorite of businesspeople and others. Costs are very reasonable at the municipal golf courses.

At **Discovery Harbor Golf and Country Club** you can play 18 holes, par 72, at this public course designed by Robert Trent Jones, Sr. ⊠ *Kamaoa Rd. off Hwy. 11, Nā'ālehu,* ☎ *808/929–7353.* 🖼 *Greens fee: $28; cart included.*

At the Big Island's newest course, an 18-hole Jack Nicklaus–designed beauty at **Four Seasons Resort Hualālai,** players can see the ocean from four tee boxes at every hole. Play here is a treat reserved for Four Seasons guests and resort residents, so the course is seldom crowded. ⊠ *100 Ka'ūpūlehu Dr., Ka'ūpūlehu–Kona 96740 (Box 1119), Kailua-Kona, 10 min north of Kona International Airport,* ☎ *808/325–8480.* 🖼 *Greens fee: $125, cart included.*

The **Francis H. I'i Brown Golf Course at the Mauna Lani Resort** was re-designed in 1991 by Nelson Wright Haworth into two 18-hole courses (North and South). The men's tee at the 15th hole of the Mauna Lani's Francis H. I'i Brown South Course is famous among golfers because they must carry their tee shot over a stretch of open ocean to reach the green. ⊠ *68-1400 Mauna Lani Dr., Suite 102, Kohala Coast,* ☎ *808/ 885–6655.* 🖼 *Greens fee: either North or South courses, guests $90, nonguests $175, twilight $55; cart included.*

Hāmākua Country Club is a nine-hole private course open to the public weekdays only, with greens fees deposited into a drop box on the honor system. ⊠ *41 mi north of Hilo on ocean side of Hwy. 19, Honoka'a,* ☎ *808/775–7244.* 🖼 *Greens fee: $10; no carts available.*

Hāpuna Golf Course is called "environmentally sensitive" because it's landscaped with indigenous plants, trees, and grasses. The par-72 course, designed by Arnold Palmer and Ed Seay, has both the first and 18th holes within easy walking distance of Mauna Kea Resort hotels. ⊠ *62-100 Kauna'oa Dr., Kamuela,* ☎ *808/880–3000.* 🖼 *Greens fee: guests $85, nonguests $135; cart included.*

Hilo Municipal Golf Course on the east side of the island, is an 18-hole, flat, Hilo-green course with four sets of tees; it's near the airport. ⊠ *340 Haihai St., Hilo,* ☎ *808/959–7711.* 🖼 *Greens fee: nonresidents, weekdays $20, weekends $25; cart $14.50.*

The **King's Course,** a par-72 Tom Weiskopf/Jay Morrish–designed course featuring four large lakes, is adjacent to the Hilton Waikoloa Village. ⊠ *600 Waikoloa Beach Dr., Waikoloa,* ☎ *808/885–4647.* 🖼 *Greens fee: $98, cart included.*

On the west coast, golf is a bit more expensive at the **Kona Country Club,** but free shuttle service is available from Keauhou hotels and condos to Kona's two 18-hole courses. The greens fee varies with the season and time of day. ⊠ *78-7000 Ali'i Dr., Keauhou,* ☎ *808/322–2595.* 🖼 *Greens fee: $60–$125; cart included.*

Mākālei Country Club has 18 holes with four sets of tees. Set at 2,500 ft, the cool elevation is home to peacocks, wild turkeys, and pheasants that wander across the bent-grass greens. ⊠ *7 mi from Kona International Airport, 72-3890 Māmalaoha Hwy., Kailua-Kona,* ☎ *808/ 325–6625 or 800/303–7416.* 🖼 *Greens fee: $110; cart included.*

Off Highway 19, a gem that receives award after award from golf magazines is the **Mauna Kea Beach Resort's** par-72, 18-hole course, designed by Robert Trent Jones, Sr. ⊠ *62-100 Mauna Kea Beach Dr., Kamuela,* ☎ *808/882–5400.* 🖼 *Greens fee: $175; cart included.*

Naniloa Country Club Golf Course is a nine-hole course most convenient to Hilo's major hotels. ⊠ *120 Banyan Dr., Hilo,* ☎ *808/935–3000.* ☑ *Greens fee: guests of Hawai'i Naniloa Hotel $20, nonguests $30; cart $7.*

Sea Mountain Golf Course is about 30 mi south of Volcano Village. The 18-hole, par-72 course stretches from the Pacific Coast up the slopes of Mauna Loa. ⊠ *Hwy. 22, Ninoli Loop Rd., Punalu'u,* ☎ *808/928–6222.* ☑ *Greens fee: $40; cart included.*

At **Volcano Golf and Country Club,** an 18-hole, par-72 course is comfortably cool and countrified, though sometimes a bit soggy in winter. ⊠ *Box 46, Hawai'i Volcanoes National Park,* ☎ *808/967–7331.* ☑ *Greens fee: $60; cart included.*

The **Waikoloa Beach Golf Course,** designed by Robert Trent Jones, Jr., in 1981, is affiliated with the Royal Waikoloan Resort and the Hilton Waikoloa Village on the Kohala Coast. An 18-hole, par 70 course with three sets of tees, this course wends through incredible lava formations and has beautiful ocean views as well. ⊠ *1020 Keana Pl., Waikoloa,* ☎ *808/885–6060.* ☑ *Greens fee: $120 non guests, $87 guests; shared cart included.*

The **Waikoloa Village Golf Course,** the second of the two Robert Trent Jones, Jr.–designed Waikoloa courses, is inland in South Kohala. You may walk the course after 11 AM. ⊠ *68-1792 Melia St., Waikoloa Village,* ☎ *808/883–9621.* ☑ *Greens fee: $75 before 1 PM, $40 after 1 PM; cart included.*

Waimea Country Club opened as an 18-hole, par-72 course in the cool, misty highlands on the Hilo side of Waimea in May 1994. ⊠ *47-5220 Māmalahoa Hwy., Kamuela,* ☎ *808/885–8777.* ☑ *Greens fee: $48; cart included.*

Hiking and Camping

For the hardy and fit adventurer, hiking is a great way to explore the Big Island's natural beauty. In addition to hiking on Mauna Kea and into Kīlauea Iki Crater (☞ Hawai'i Volcanoes National Park *in* Exploring, *above*), a little-known trek to the top of 13,680-ft **Mauna Loa,** with overnight stops at two cabins, one at 10,000 ft and the other at the summit, can be arranged. The cabins are free but must be reserved well in advance. ⊠ *Write: Superintendent, Hawai'i Volcanoes National Park, Volcano 96743.*

Nāakani Paio Cabins, at the 4,000-ft level, 3 mi beyond the Volcano House, are managed by Volcano House, a concession of the National Park Service. Each cabin has a double bed, two bunk beds, and electric lights. Guests should bring extra blankets, because it gets cold. ⊠ *Write: Volcano House, Hawai'i Volcanoes National Park, Box 53, Volcano 96718-0053,* ☎ *808/967–7321,* FAX *808/967–8429.* ☑ *Single or double $32, $15 refundable deposit allows guests to pick up bedding and keys (for cabins and separate bath facilities) at Volcano House.*

For information on cabins at state parks, including Hāpuna Beach Park and the three campgrounds at Kīlauea, write to the **Department of Parks and Recreation** (⊠ 25 Aupuni St., Hilo 96740, ☎ 808/961–8311).

Horseback Riding

Some resorts, such as **Mauna Kea Resort** (⊠ 62-100 Mauna Kea Beach Dr., Kohala Coast, ☎ 808/882–4288), maintain stables while others offer transportation to commercial stables. Ask at your hotel activities desk.

King's Trail Rides O'Kona, Inc. (✉ Box 1366, Kealakekua, ☎ 808/323–2388 or 808/323–2890), 20 minutes from Kailua-Kona at the 111-mi marker on Highway 11, offers riders with some experience 4½-hour rides to Captain Cook monument in Kealakekua Bay. This excursion includes snorkeling and lunch for $95. Custom rides can be arranged.

Paniolo Riding Adventures (✉ Box 363, Honoka`a , ☎ 808/889–5354) gears trail rides for beginners to buckaroos through lush Kohala ranch land. Never nose-to-tail, 2½-hour rides are $88.40; a four-hour Paniolo Picnic Adventure (bring your own lunch) is $130. Overnight camping trips can also be arranged.

Waipi`o Na`alapa Trail Rides leads horseback rides twice daily, except Sunday, in Waipi`o for $78. ✉ *Box 992, Honoka`a,* ☎ *808/775–0419.*

Skiing

Skiing on Mauna Kea is for intermediate and experienced skiers only. Currently the ski area has no lodge or lifts. Christopher Langan of Mauna Kea Ski Corporation runs **Ski Guides Hawai`i** (✉ Box 1954, Kamuela, in ski season, ☎ 808/885–4188), which is licensed to furnish transportation, guide services, and ski equipment on Mauna Kea. Snow can fall from Thanksgiving through June, but the most likely months are February and March. For an eight-hour day trip for up to six people, Langen charges $250 per person, including refreshments and a mountain-top lunch, equipment, guide service, transportation from Waimea and four-wheel-drive shuttle back up the mountain after each ski run.

Tennis

School and park courts are free and open to anyone who wishes to play, though students have first priority during school hours at high-school courts. In Hilo you will find courts at the **University of Hawai`i–Hilo campus** (✉ 333 W. Lanikāula St.), and there are four free, lighted courts at **Lincoln Park** (✉ Kino`ole and Ponahawai Sts.). The eight courts (three lighted for night play) at **Hilo Tennis Stadium** (✉ Pi`ilani and Kalanikoa Sts.) charge a small fee. **Waiākea Racket Club** (✉ 400 Hualani St., ☎ 808/961–5499) is also open to the public for a reasonable fee.

Across the island the Keauhou-Kona resorts have become renowned for their beautiful tennis courts. **Hōlua Stadium** is a headquarters for exhibition tennis. One of the few courts where not-so-heavy hitters can play free is at **Kailua Playground**—the wait may be long, however. Nonguests can play for a fee at the **Kona Surf Hotel's Racquet Club** and on the four courts at the **Royal Kona Resort** (☞ Lodging, *above*). At **King Kamehameha's Kona Beach Hotel** (☞ Lodging, *above*) nonguests may purchase memberships to play. Farther afield, there are two free, lighted courts at **Waimea Park** (on Hwy. 19) in Waimea. Courts at the **Royal Waikoloan, Hilton Waikoloa Village** (two of their eight courts are clay), and **Sea Mountain at Punalu`u** (☞ Lodging, *above*) are open at an hourly charge. The **Orchid at Mauna Lani** (☞ Lodging, *above)* has 10 courts (including one exhibition court). **Mauna Kea Resort**'s (☞ Lodging, *above*) 13 courts are in a beautiful 12-acre oceanside tennis park. The pro shop carries the most complete line of tennis wear on the Kohala Coast.

Triathlon

The highly popular **Ironman Triathlon** is not for the faint of heart. The Ironman is limited to 1,500 competitors, who do a 2.4-mi open-water swim, bicycle 112 mi, and run a marathon, and most entrants must qualify by doing well in other international competitions, though a few slots are awarded by lottery. The annual competition begins with a swim from Kailua Pier at 7 AM on a Saturday in October. Spectators cheer on their favorite contestants from vantage points along Ali`i Drive and the

Queen Ka'ahumanu Highway. The course closes at midnight. ✉ *75-127 Lunapule Rd., Suite 11, Kailua-Kona 96740,* ☎ *808/329–0063.*

Water Sports

DEEP-SEA FISHING

In Kona the game-fishing excitement hits its peak during July, August, and September, when a number of tournaments are held, but charter fishing goes on year-round. You don't have to be in a tournament to experience the thrill of landing a big Pacific blue marlin or a mahimahi, tuna, wahoo, or other game fish. More than 50 charter boats, averaging 36–42 ft, are available for hire, most of them out of **Honokōhau Harbor,** just north of Kailua. Prices for a full day of fishing average $550, though there are a few larger, luxury boats in the $600–$800 range. Half-day charters are also available in the $200–$400 range and might be preferable if you've never experienced the hypnotic effect of sun, wind, and waves on a small boat. Tackle is furnished. Most boats do not allow you to keep your entire catch, although if you ask, many captains will send you home with a few fish fillets. Ask your hotel to pack a box lunch or purchase one at the **Kona Marlin Center** at Honokōhau Harbor. If you want to bring stronger refreshments, most boats allow beer or liquor on board.

Make arrangements for deep-sea fishing at your hotel activities desk or call the **Kona Charters Skippers Association** (☎ 808/329–3600) or **Kona Activities Center** (☎ 808/329–3171 or 800/367–5288) for information. At Honokōhau Harbor, book charters or get information on tournaments from **Charter Services Hawai'i** (✉ Box 5234, Kailua-Kona, ☎ 808/334–1881 or 800/567–5662).

The biggest of the fishing tournaments is the **Hawaiian International Billfish Tournament** at the beginning of August, which attracts teams from around the world. During the HIBT, the Richard Boone Award is given by participating anglers. Tournament participants rate boats' cleanliness, crew, equipment, etc., so the listing can serve as a helpful guide in choosing which boat to charter. In addition, be sure to describe your expectations when you book your charter so the booking agent can match you with a captain and a boat you will like.

Tournament catches are often weighed in at the pier adjacent to the King Kamehameha's Kona Beach Hotel in Kailua-Kona, which, because of its central location, is a popular headquarters for tournament participants and viewers. Both old and young head for either the Kailua Pier or Honokōhau Harbor's Fuel Dock between 4 PM and 5 PM to watch the weigh-in of the day's catch.

PARASAILING AND WINDSURFING

These are two of the newer water sports, and both are generally considered quite safe. Parasailers sit in a harness attached to a parachute that lifts off from the boat deck and sails aloft. Call **UFO Parasail** (✉ Across the street from the King Kamehameha Kona Beach Hotel, Kailua-Kona, ☎ 808/325–5836) to make arrangements for parasailing.

One of the best windsurfing locations on the Big Island is at 'Anaeho'omalu Bay, on the beach in front **Royal Waikoloan Resort** (✉ Waikoloa Rd., Waikoloa, ☎ 808/885–5555). You can arrange for lessons or rent equipment right at the resort's beach services desk.

SCUBA DIVING

Two-tank dives should cost from $65 to $75, depending on whether they are in one or two locations and if they are dives from a boat or from the shore. Many dive outfits have underwater cameras for rent, in case you're lucky enough to glimpse humpback whales and their calves during the winter months or simply want to capture colorful reef fish on film. Instruction with PADI certification in three to five days is $450–$500. The Kona Coast has calm waters for diving, and dive operators there are helpful about suggesting dive sites.

Reputable scuba charters to consider in Kailua-Kona are **Big Island Divers** (⊠ 75-5467 Kaiwi St., ☎ 808/329–6068 or 800/488-6068) and **Sandwich Isle Divers** (⊠ 75-5729–I Ali'i Dr., ☎ 808/329–9188, FAX 808/326-5652). Both outfitters offer classes and night and shore dives; both take only six divers at a time.

At Anaeho'omalu Bay at Waikoloa Resort in Waikoloa and the Hāpuna Beach Prince Hotel on the Kohala Coast, the friendly operators at **Red Sail Sports** (⊠ 1 Waikoloa Beach Dr., Waikoloa, ☎ 808/885–2876) organize scuba dives from the 38-ft *Lanikai*. **Body Glove Cruises'** (⊠ 75–5629 Kuankini Hwy., Suite P, Kailua-Kona, ☎ 808/329–4807 or 800/551–8911) 55-ft catamaran sets off from the Kailua Pier daily for a 4½-hour dive and snorkel cruise that includes a Continental breakfast and a buffet lunch.

SNORKELING

Colorful tropical fish frequent the lava outcroppings along many Big Island shorelines, so it's easy to arrange a do-it-yourself snorkeling tour by simply renting masks and snorkels from **Snorkel Bob's** (⊠ 75-5831 Kahakai St., Kailua-Kona, ☎ 808/329–0770). Prices start at $9 a week and go up for finer equipment and prescription masks. If you're island hopping and want to drop off the equipment on O'ahu, Maui, or Kaua'i, there is no extra charge.

Many snorkel and scuba cruises are available. Shop for prices, ask about the size of the boat, and make sure you know what is included and how much the extras (e.g., underwater cameras) cost.

Among the Big Island's wet and wild offerings is the **Captain Zodiac Raft Expedition** (⊠ 74–425 Kealakehe Parkway #16, Kailua-Kona, ☎ 808/329–3199, FAX 808/329–7590) along the Kona Coast. The four-hour trip begins at Honokōhau Harbor, pokes into gaping lava-tube caves, and drifts through Kealakekua Bay, where passengers can snorkel and eat a light lunch. January through April you might see the humpback whales. If you love water and crave adventure, sit at the front edge of the inflatable raft for an exciting, wind-in-your-hair ride. Wear a bathing suit (you'll get a chance to snorkel) and take a towel, sunscreen, and camera. Captain Zodiac furnishes a plastic bag to keep your possessions dry.

The family-owned and -operated **Fair Wind Snorkeling and Diving Adventures** sails from Keauhou Bay for 4½-hour morning and 3½-hour afternoon excursions. The afternoon sail includes snacks and juice. The 63-ft catamaran supplies inner tubes and snorkel gear. Morning sails include Continental breakfast and barbecue lunch. Ask about scuba, snuba, and videos available at an additional fee. ⊠ 78-7130 Kalei-o-Papa St., Kailua-Kona, ☎ 808/322–2788. 🖾 Morning sail $72, afternoon $46.

Spectator Sports

Baseball

Hilo Stars. When on home turf, the Hilo Stars play at Doctor Francis Wong Stadium in the Ho'olulu Park Sports Complex, Hilo. The Hawai'i season for these professional players, who are top prospects from major league baseball clubs on the mainland United States, Japan, and Korea, runs from mid-October to mid-December. ⊠ 421 Kalanikoa St. #4, Hilo, ☎ 808/969–9033, FAX 808/961–6053.

Golf

Ample opportunities for celebrity-spotting exist at a growing number of golf tournaments held at resort golf courses in the Kohala area. The biggest and best attended is the **Senior Skins Game** at Mauna Lani Resort, which attracts competitors the caliber of Arnold Palmer, Jack Nicklaus, and Lee Trevino, all competing for their share of the $540,000 purse. This tournament kicks off the year in January, always on Super Bowl weekend. ☎ *808/885–6655.*

In January the Four Seasons Resort Hualālai hosts the **MasterCard Championship, A SENIOR PGA TOUR event.** ☎ *800/417–2770,* FAX *808/661–1875.*

Polo

Games sponsored by Mauna Kea Polo Club are scheduled every Sunday, September through December. ⊠ *Waiki'i Ranch, off Saddle Rd., 6½ mi from Māmalahoa Hwy.,* ☎ *808/322–3880.*

Polo matches are held weekends from the end of September through mid-December at the impressive **Polo Arena and Equestrian Center.** ⊠ *Kohala Ranch, off Hwy. 250, Kohala Mountain Rd.,* ☎ *808/322–3880.*

SHOPPING

Residents like to complain that there isn't much to shop for on the Big Island, but unless you're searching for career clothes or a formal ball gown you'll find plenty to deplete your pocketbook. Kailua-Kona has a range of souvenirs from far-flung corners of the globe. Resorts along the Kohala coast have quality goods. The **Mauna Lani Bay Hotel and Bungalows** (☞ Lodging, *above*), for example, has **Collections**, an exclusive apparel shop that is a subsidiary of Liberty House.

In general, major stores and shopping centers on the Big Island open at 9 or 9:30 and close by 4:30 or 5. Hilo's **Prince Kūhiō Shopping Plaza** (☞ *below*) stays open until 9 on Thursday and Friday. In Kona, most of the stores at the **Kona Coast Shopping Center** (☞ *below*) are open daily 9–9, though the **KTA Super Stores** outlet (a supermarket) is open from 6 AM to midnight. Many small grocery stores also maintain longer hours, as do the shops along Kona's main Ali'i Drive, which are geared toward tourists.

Hawaiian Art and Crafts

At **Ackerman Gallery** (Hwy. 270, between Kapa'au from Hāwī, ☎ 808/889–5971) painter Gary Ackerman and his wife, Yesan, have a fine collection of local gifts, handmade jewelry, and artifacts for sale. It's across the street from the King Kamehameha Statue.

At the **Kona Arts and Crafts Gallery** (⊠ 75–5699 Ali'i Dr., Kailua-Kona ☎ 808/329–5590), absolutely everything is handcrafted in Hawai'i; you'll find iridescent volcano-glass necklaces, pictures made of banana bark, bowls and ornaments made of native woods, Hawaiian dolls, and *'opihi*-shell jewelry.

At Keauhou Shopping Village stop in at **Alapaki's Hawaiian Gifts** (⊠ 78–6831 Ali'i Dr., ☎ 808/322–2007), for fine original art, Hawaiian hula instruments, feather leis, genuine kukui nut jewelry, and wooden *kōnane* game boards (a Hawaiian board game reminiscent of checkers, played with white and black stones).

In Hilo you can go through the workshop of **Dan DeLuz's Woods, Inc.** (⊠ Hwy. 11, 12-mile marker, Mountain View, ☎ 808/935–5587; ⊠ 64–1013 Mamalahoa Hwy., Waimea, ☎ 808/885–5856), where master bowl-turner Dan DeLuz creates works of art from 50 types of exotic wood grown on the Big Island; his wares are sold in the adjoining shop.

If you're driving around the Big Island via the South Point route, stop at the **Woodworks** (☎ 808/328–9667, closed Wed. and Sun.) next to the Manago Hotel in Captain Cook for nicely finished wooden pens, books, boxes, and picture frames that are generally less expensive than at major malls.

Within Hawai'i Volcanoes National Park, the **Volcano Art Center** (☎ 808/967–7511) remains a favorite with everyone. The Art Center represents more Hawai'i Island artists than any other gallery, and it carries a selection of fine art prints and oils as well.

Two hamlets are especially noted for their art communities: Hōlualoa and Waimea. Just up-country of Kailua, the little town of Hōlualoa, on Highway 180, is a nest of artists, possibly because years ago a California couple, Bob and Carol Rogers, moved to town and opened the **Kona Arts Center** (☎ 808/322–2307). Carol still gives classes, and the center's doors are open to curious drop-in visitors or aspiring students. Classes at the Kona Arts Center were what originally encouraged Hiroki Morinoue, who then studied in California and Japan and returned to Hōlualoa to open his own gallery, **Studio 7** (☎ 808/324–1335), a half block from the Kona Arts Center. In the same building, you'll want to investigate **Hōlualoa's Koa T** for woodcrafted articles. Also wonderful for browsing are **Hale O Kula Goldsmith Gallery** (☎ 808/324–1688), **White Garden Gallery** (☎ 808/322–7733), and **Hōlualoa Gallery** (☎ 808/322–8484), for stunning raku pottery. Most shops in Hōlualoa close at 4 PM and are closed all day on Sunday and Monday.

The other creative hamlet, Waimea, is home to the **Waimea Arts Council** (⊠ Box 1818, Kamuela 96743, ☎ 808/885–7671), dedicated to promoting the arts in the towns of Waimea, Hāmākua, Kohala, and Waikoloa. The council sponsors free *kaha ki'is* (one-person shows) at the **Firehouse Gallery**, in the old fire station near the main stoplight in Waimea. The gallery is open Tuesday through Thursday, and Saturday 10–2.

Also in Waimea, at **Parker Square** (⊠ Kawaihae Rd., ☎ 808/885–7178), in the **Gallery of Great Things** (☎ 808/885–7706), you'll drool over the Ni'ihau shell leis ($200–$4,000) and bowls by Jack Straka ($300–$700), but there are attractive mirrors and wooden earrings for much less.

Cook's Discoveries (⊠ Waimea Center, Spencer House, Waimea, ☎ 808/885–3633) also houses **Maha's Café** for light snacks and lunches at tables set among displays of handcrafted treasures by local artisans: silver and clay jewelry, feather leis, and wooden boxes.

Menswear

Virtually every golf course has a logo shop; even the casual **Volcano Golf Course** (☎ 808/967–7331) has a monogrammed line of golf shirts, shorts, and visors.

For those men who need a little top-level protection from the tropical sun, the old-time, family-run **Kimura Lauhala Shop** (⊠ 77–996 Hualālae Rd., Hwy. 182, ☎ 808/324–0053) in the up-country town of Hōlualoa has authentic made-in-Hawai'i lau hala hats.

Resort Wear

Hotel shops generally offer the most attractive and original resort wear. **Kona Inn Shopping Village** (⊠ 75–5744 Ali'i Dr.), that long boardwalk on the ocean side of Aliʻi Drive, is stuffed with intriguing shops. Searching for beach sandals or perhaps a Panama hat? Try **Big Island Hat Company** (☎ 808/328–3332).

Up-country in the one-street town of Kainaliu, **Paradise Found** (✉ Māmalahoa Hwy. 11, ☎ 808/322–2111) has contemporary silk and rayon clothing. If you'd like to take home some of Hawaiʻi's splashy material, on Kainaliu's main street is **Kimura's Fabrics** (✉ Māmalahoa Hwy. 11, ☎ 808/322–3771).

Across the island in Hilo, **Sig Zane** (✉ 122 Kamehameha Ave., ☎ 808/935–7077), a popular designer, sells his distinctive Island wearables, bedding, and gifts. Also in Hilo, **Kristina Lilleeng** (✉ 140 Keawe St., ☎ 808/961–0838) sells contemporary designer wear, such as pants and vests of natural fiber fabrics or handpainted silk.

In recent years, **Hilo Hattie** (✉ 111 E. Puainako St., Bldg. G, Hilo, ☎ 808/961–3077; ✉ 75-5597A Palani Rd., Kailua-Kona, ☎ 808/329–7200 for free transportation from selected hotels), an old standby, has gone beyond matching his-and-her aloha wear to carry a huge selection of casual clothes, slippers, jewelry, and souvenirs.

Shopping Centers

In Hilo the most comprehensive mall, similar to mainland malls, is **Prince Kūhiō Shopping Plaza** (✉ 111 E. Puainako, at Hwy. 11). Here you'll find **Liberty House** and **Sears** for fashion, **House of Adler** and the **Diamond Company** for jewelry, **Safeway** for food, and **Longs Drugs** for just about everything else. There is a one-hour photo store, in case you want to send home a current photo.

The older **Hilo Shopping Center** (✉ 70 Kekuanaoa St., at Kīlauea Ave.) has more than 40 air-conditioned shops and restaurants and plenty of free parking. The centrally located **Kaikoʻo Mall** (✉ 777 Kīlauea Ave., Hilo) has 27 shops, including JCPenney, Singer's, and Kinney Shoe Store.

On the western side of the island, **Keauhou Shopping Village** (✉ 78-6831 Aliʻi Dr.) has an attractive steak-and-seafood restaurant, **Drysdale's Two,** and upscale boutiques, plus **Showcase Gallery** for works by Hawaiian artists and imaginative feather jewelry, and a post office where you can drop a card and make the folks back home envious. A **Liberty House Penthouse,** a discounted branch of Hawaiʻi's leading department store, stocks contemporary clothing and home fashions. For golfers who want to take home a truly special souvenir, **Keauhou Golf Shop** specializes in custom club making.

Shopping in Kailua-Kona has begun to go the way of mainland cities with **Wal-Mart,** a huge **Safeway,** and **Borders Books and Music** at **Crossroads Shopping Center** (✉ 75-1000 Henry St., ☎ 808/331–1668), which opened in 1997 on Queen Kaʻahumanu Highway. Right in Kailua-Kona, however, there are so many small shopping malls along Aliʻi Drive that they tend to blend into one another. Virtually all of them offer merchandise to appeal to visitors. On the makai side of Aliʻi Drive, extending an entire block, is **Kona Inn Shopping Village** (✉ 75-5744 Aliʻi Dr., ☎ 808/329–6573). Here the **Big Island Hat Company** (☎ 808/329–3332) has great tropical toppers and sandals, and **Honolua Surf Company** (☎ 808/329–1001) is filled with ocean-going necessities, including surfboards. **Alleygeckos** (☎ 808/326–1134) has nifty gifts from around the world.

Kona Marketplace (✉ 75-5729 Aliʻi Dr., Kailua-Kona), across the street from Kona Inn Shopping Village, is a valuable find simply for the fact that public rest rooms are upstairs, and for visitors looking for a little evening entertainment, the movie theater, **Kona Marketplace Cinemas** shows current movies.

A block off Ali`i Drive, **Lanihau Center** (⊠ 75–5595 Palani Rd.) houses Long's Drug Store and 21 other stores. In **King Kamehameha's Kona Beach Hotel** (⊠ 75–5660 Palani Rd., Kailua-Kona), **Liberty House** department store, **Jafar** clothing boutique, **Ali`i Artworks** (for hand-painted silks and cottons), **Mele O Polynesian,** the **Shellery,** and **Kona Village Artists** offer interesting browsing.

King's Shops (⊠ 250 Waikoloa Beach Dr., ☎ 808/885–8811) houses **Under the Koa Tree** and **Pacific Rim Collections,** which both carry gift items by artisans, as well as **Liberty House, Crazy Shirts,** and **Noa Noa** for quality clothing, a food pavilion, the **Big Island Steak House,** and an attractive Chinese restaurant called the **Grand Palace.**

The harborside **Kawaihae Center** (⊠ Mahūkona Hwy.) houses restaurants, art galleries, and the **Nui Nui Ice Cream Shop** (for locally made white chocolate–ginger ice cream and mango sorbet). In Waimea, **Parker Ranch Shopping Center** (⊠ Junction of Hwys. 19 and 190) houses 35 shops and the **Parker Ranch Visitor Center.** The red-and-white buildings of **Parker Square** (⊠ Kawaihae Rd., Waimea, ☎ 808/885–7178) house the **Gallery of Great Things,** the place to find beautifully crafted milo- and koa-wood sculptures, bowls, and boxes. **Waimea Woolcraft, Waimea Coffee Company,** and **Waimea General Store** are fun to browse here as well for quality gift items. **Waimea Center** (⊠ Hwy. 19), with the area's first **McDonald's,** was completed in 1990. **Cook's Discoveries** at the **Historic Spencer House,** in the center, is chock-full of exquisite Hawai`i-made clothing, jewelry, books, crafts, food items, and gifts.

Tropical Flowers and Produce

About 22 mi from Hilo, check out **Akatsuka Orchid Gardens.** You can buy tropical blooms here and have them shipped home. ⊠ *Hwy. 11, Glenwood,* ☎ *808/967–8234.* ☉ *Daily 8:30–5.*

Fuku-Bonsai Cultural Center. In addition to selling and shipping miniature brassaia lava plantings and other bonsai plants, this nursery on the way to Volcano has free educational exhibits of different ethnic styles of pruning. ⊠ *Ola`a Rd., Kurtistown,* ☎ *808/982–9880.* ☉ *Mon.– Sat. 8–4.*

Hilo Farmers' Market. Individual entrepreneurs hawk a profusion of tropical flowers, produce and trinkets at this colorful, open-air market. ⊠ *Kamehameha Ave. and Mamo St.* ☉ *Wed., Sat. 6–3.*

Kailua Village Market. You'll see the stalls, some shaded with blue tarps, set up in the open-air parking lot of the Kona Inn Shopping Village. This is a low-key farmers' market filled with colorful tropical flowers and locally grown produce, including macadamia nuts and coffee. ⊠ *75-7544 Ali`i Dr.* ☉ *Wed, Fri., and weekends 6:30–2:30.*

THE BIG ISLAND A TO Z

Arriving and Departing

By Plane

The Big Island has two main airports. Visitors whose accommodations are on the west side of the island, at Keauhou, Kailua-Kona, or the Kohala Coast, normally fly into **Kona International Airport** (☎ 808/329–2484 or, for visitor information, 808/329–3423), 7 mi from Kailua. Those staying on the eastern side, in Hilo or near the town of Volcano, fly into **Hilo International Airport** (☎ 808/934–5801 or, for visitor information, 808/934–5840), just 2 mi from Hilo's Banyan Drive hotels.

In addition, one O'ahu-based airline, **Trans Air** (☎ 808/885–5134 or 800/634–2094), has a schedule of regular flights into **Waimea-Kohala Airport** (☎ 808/885–4520), called Kamuela Airport by residents. Midway between Hilo and Kailua-Kona, Kamuela Airport is used primarily by residents of Waimea to commute between islands. Another airstrip, at 'Upolu Point, services small private planes only.

FLIGHTS FROM THE MAINLAND UNITED STATES

United Airlines (☎ 800/241–6522) is the only carrier that flies daily from the mainland to the Big Island. United flies to Kona International Airport from San Francisco. **Hawaiian Airlines** (☎ 800/367–5320) flies from San Francisco, Portland, and Seattle to Honolulu Airport, where a transfer is necessary to continue to the Big Island. Flying time from the West Coast to Honolulu is about 4½–5 hours.

FLIGHTS FROM HONOLULU

Between the Neighbor Islands, both **Aloha Airlines** (☎ 800/367–5250) and **Hawaiian Airlines** (☎ 800/367–5320) offer jet flights, which take about 45 minutes from Honolulu to Hilo International Airport and 34 minutes from Honolulu to Kona. Fares are approximately $75, though both Aloha and Hawaiian discount their first (6 AM) and last (8 PM or 9 PM, depending on the airplane) flights of each day.

BETWEEN THE AIRPORT AND HOTELS

By Car. The distance from Kona International Airport to Kailua, the resort area on the western side of the Big Island, is 7 mi, or a 10-minute drive, while the Keauhou resort area stretches another 6 mi to the south beyond Kailua. Visitors staying at the upscale resorts along the Kona–Kohala Coast north of Kona International Airport should allow 30–45 minutes driving time to reach their hotels.

On the eastern side of the island, Hilo International Airport is just 2 mi, or a five-minute drive, from Hilo's Banyan Drive hotels. If you've chosen Volcano Lodge or a B&B near the little mountain town of Volcano, plan on a half-hour drive from Hilo International Airport.

If you have booked out-of-the-way accommodations near Waimea, you might want to fly into Kamuela Airport, but be sure to arrange your rental car in advance (☞ Car Rentals, *below*), as few car-rental companies service that airport.

Unfortunately, no buses operate from the airports.

By Limousine. Limousine service with a chauffeur who will act as your personal guide is $70–$75 an hour, with a two-hour minimum. **Luana's** (☎ 808/326–5466) in Kona provides all the extras—TV, bar, and narrated tours, plus Japanese-speaking guides. **Roberts** offers service in both Kailua-Kona (✉ 73-4800 Kanalani St., Suite 200, ☎ 808/329–1688) and Hilo (✉ Shipman Industrial Park, ☎ 808/966–5483).

By Shuttle. There is no regularly scheduled shuttle service from either main airport, although private service is offered by four major Kohala-coast resorts to the north of Kona International Airport. Mauna Kea, Mauna Lani, the Hilton Waikoloa Village, and the Royal Waikoloan offer lei greetings and transportation to their hotels for about half the cost of a taxi. The rates vary depending on the distance each resort is from the airport. Arriving guests must simply check in at the **Kohala Coast Resort Association** counters at the Aloha and Hawaiian airlines arrival areas.

By Taxi. Taxis are generally on hand for plane arrivals at both major airports. Some services from Hilo's Airport include **Bob's Taxi** (☎ 808/959–4800), **Ace One** (☎ 808/935–8303), and **Hilo Harry's** (☎ 808/935–7091). Taxis from Hilo International Airport to Hilo charge about $9 for the 2-mi ride to the Banyan Drive hotels. Often drivers will charge an extra $1 for large bags.

A number of taxis service Kona International Airport. The following also offer guided tours: **Aloha Transporation Company** (☎ 808/325–5448) and **Marina Taxi** (☎ 808/329–2481). From the airport to King Kamehameha's Kona Beach Hotel, taxi fares are about $18; to the Kona Surf in Keauhou, the cost is about $33. Taxis to South Kohala from the airport are even more expensive: approximately $40 to the Royal Waikoloan and $56 to the Mauna Kea Beach Hotel.

Guests staying in Kailua or at the Keauhou resort area to the south of the airport should check with their individual hotels upon booking to see if shuttle service is available.

By Ship

FROM HONOLULU

American Hawai'i Cruises runs seven-day excursions departing Honolulu Harbor every Saturday on the SS *Independence*. You have the option of choosing a four-day cruise and disembarking on the Big Island, where special rates can be arranged at the Kona Surf, Aston Shores at Waikoloa, or Aston Royal Sea Cliff resorts. Pre- and postcruise hotel packages are offered at a variety of rates. ✉ *American Hawai'i Cruises, 1380 Port of New Orleans Pl., New Orleans, LA 70130–1890,* ☎ *800/765–7000.*

Getting Around

By Bus and Shuttle

A locally sponsored **Hele-On Bus** (☎ 808/961–8744) operates Monday–Saturday between Hilo and Kailua-Kona. (*Hele* translates roughly as "go.") The bus goes from Kailua-Kona to Hilo and back again, at $6 each way. For luggage and backpacks that do not fit under the seat, an additional $1 is charged per piece. Hele-On departs from Moku'aikaua Church, on Ali'i Drive in Kailua-Kona, at 6:43 AM arriving in Hilo at 9:45 AM. It leaves from the Mo'oheau Bus Terminal, between Kamehameha Avenue and Bayfront Highway in Hilo, at 1:30 PM to arrive in Kailua-Kona at 4:30 PM.

In Hilo, a Hele-On operates between downtown and the shopping malls for 75¢ (exact fare required). **Hilo Sampans** (☎ 808/959–7864) provides transportation in open-side jitneys between downtown Hilo hotels and various tourist destinations. The Hilo Sampans follow a circular route that takes about an hour. The historic downtown route goes along Banyan Drive to the Kress Building, Lyman Museum, Ka'iko Mall, Nani Mau Gardens, Prince Kuhio Plaza, Hilo Hattie's and Wal-Mart. The $2 fare, called a one-way fare, allows you to ride nearly the whole way, as long as you get off at least one stop before your point of origin; it's a $4 fare to ride the whole route and $7 for a daily unlimited pass.

Within Keauhou, a **free shuttle** (☎ 808/322–3500 or 808/322–3000) runs from hotels and condos to Keauhou Shopping Village and the Kona Country Club golf course.

By Car

An automobile is necessary to see the sights of the Big Island in any reasonable amount of time. Even if you're solely interested in relaxing at your self-contained megaresort, you may still want to rent a car, simply to travel to Kailua-Kona or Waimea for their restaurants.

Though there are perhaps two-dozen car-rental companies to choose from, cars can be scarce during holiday weekends and peak seasons— from mid-December through mid-March and sometimes during August. It's best to book well in advance (☞ Car Rentals, *below*).

By Motorcycle
Scooters and motorcycles can be rented in Kailua-Kona from **DJ's Rentals** (☎ 808/329–1700), across from King Kamehameha's Kona Beach Hotel. Some words of warning: Big Island roads often have narrow shoulders, and the drafts from oversize tour buses swooping by can double the excitement of a simple Sunday ride. Helmets are advised but not mandatory in Hawai'i.

By Plane
Big Island Air (☎ 808/329–4868 or 800/303–8868) offers charter flightseeing from Kona International Airport in nine-passenger aircraft at a basic hourly rate of $550. "Wait time" (for example, if you fly to Waimea for lunch and the plane sits on the ground for several hours while you dine) is negotiable.

By Taxi
Several companies advertise guided tours by taxi, but it is an expensive way to travel, with a trip around the island totaling about $350. Meters automatically register $2 on pickup, and most click off another $2 with each passing mile. If you've got the urge to splurge, in Hilo call **Ace One Taxi** (☎ 808/935–8303) or **Hilo Harry's** (☎ 808/935–7091). In Kona, try **Aloha Transportation Company** (☎ 808/325–5448) or **Marina Taxi** (☎ 808/329–2481).

Contacts and Resources

B&B Information and Reservation Services
Members of the Big Island–based Hawai'i Island Bed and Breakfast Association are listed with phone numbers and rates in a leaflet available from **The Hawai'i Island B&B Association** (✉ Box 1890, Honoka'a 96727). These Big Island–based networks will help you find a B&B to meet your needs and make reservations for you: **Hawai'i's Best B&B's** (✉ Box 563, Kamuela 96743, ☎ 808/885–4550 or 800/262–9912, FAX 808/885–0559), **Go Native Hawai'i** (✉ 65 Haulaulani Pl., Box 11418, Hilo 96721, ☎ 808/935–4178 or 800/662–8483), and **Volcano Reservations–Select Statewide Accommodations** (✉ Box 998, Volcano Village 96785, ☎ 808/967–7244 or 800/736–7140, FAX 800/577–1849).

Car Rentals
If you pick up an auto at either airport and drop it off at the other, be aware that it could cost you as much as $50 extra. If you decide to return a car to the original pickup point, allow 2¼ hours to drive the 96-mi Hāmākua Coast route. To get the best rate on a rental car—and surprisingly, Hawai'i's rates are often better than mainland rates—book it in conjunction with a round-trip interisland Hawaiian or Aloha airlines flight, or ask your travel agent to check out room-and-car packages for you.

The national car-rental firms represented on the Big Island are: **Alamo** (☎ 800/327–9633), **Avis** (☎ 800/831–8000), **Budget** (☎ 800/527–7000), **Dollar** (☎ 800/800–4000), **Hertz** (☎ 800/654–3131), and **National** (☎ 800/227–7368).

Harper's Car Rental (✉ 1690 Kamehameha Ave., Hilo 96720, ☎ 808/969–1478), a Hawai'i-based company at Hilo International Airport only, is the only agency with a rental contract that allows its four-wheel-drive vehicles to be taken on Saddle Road, although a number of other agencies have four-wheel-drives in their fleets. Driving on Saddle Road is restricted by most car-rental companies, because it twists and turns and has no gas stations or emergency phones from Waimea to Hilo. (You'll need a four-wheel-drive to reach some rugged shoreline sites.) Use of its $100-a-day Isuzu Rodeos, Trooper IIs, and Toyota Four-runners are restricted to those 25 years and older.

Emergencies
Ambulance or fire (☎ 911). **Police** (☎ 808/935–3311 or 911). **Help Line Crisis Center** (☎ 808/935–3393). **Poison Control Center** (☎ 800/362–3585). **Volcano watchers** (☎ 808/985–6000 for 24-hr recorded information).

Doctors and Dentists
Hilo Medical Center (✉ 1190 Waiānuenue Ave., ☎ 808/974–4700). **Dentist.** Ask personnel at Hilo Hospital to call a dentist who will take emergency patients.

Kona Community Hospital (✉ Hwy. 11 at Hau Kapila St., Kealakekua 96750, ☎ 808/322–9311). **Dentist.** Kona Community Hospital can refer you to a dentist.

Guided Tours
AERIAL TOURS
Hovering over a waterfall that drops a couple of thousand feet into multiple pools is absolutely breathtaking—never mind the noise. You can fly above the lava lake on Kīlauea, then follow the flow to the ocean, where huge clouds of steam billow into the air. (Currently the flow is mostly underground through a lava tube, but that can change, so ask exactly what you'll see when you book your flight.)

Volcano Heli-Tours (✉ Box 626, Volcano 96785, ☎ 808/967–7578) is the only helicopter that departs from the Volcano area (right near the golf course), and since flying time over the lava lake and to the ocean is minimized, the 45-minute flights are somewhat cheaper than other helicopter tours. You must make reservations in advance, however, as the flights are well booked.

Mauna Kea Helicopters (☎ 808/885–6400 or 800/400–4354) pilots have plenty of experience and offer flights that take off from the Waikoloa Helipad, Kamuela Airport, and Hilo International Airport.

From both Hilo International Airport and the Waikoloa Helipad, **Blue Hawaiian** (☎ 808/961–5600 or 800/786–2583) is reputable and will film a video of your flight if you wish to purchase one. Blue Hawaiian flies over Kīlauea and Hawai'i Volcanoes National Park, as well as over waterfalls from either point of origin.

Big Island Air (☎ 808/329–4868 or 800/303–8868) flies two-hour circle-island tours in nine-passenger planes for $170 per person. Flights depart daily from Kona International Airport at 8, 11, 2, and 4. Weight is critical on these smaller planes, so be prepared to divulge your true body weight.

Hawai'i Island Hoppers (✉ Gate 29, Hilo International Airport, Hilo 96720, ☎ 808/969–2000 or 800/538–7590) offers a one-hour flight-seeing tour over the volcano and a waterfall on three-passenger planes. Everyone gets a window seat and a headset to talk to the pilot. The cost is $79 for adults; children fly half-price, and those under five fly free with their parents. Two longer, more expensive flights—a 2½-hour circle island tour and a 2-hour volcano tour—also depart from Kona.

ASTRONOMY TOURS

Mauna Kea. The clearest place in the world for viewing the heavens is reputedly the summit of 13,796-ft Mauna Kea. The trick is getting there. It takes a four-wheel-drive vehicle to reach the top, and you must traverse Saddle Road on the way. If you decide to strike out on your own, follow the access road off Highway 20 between Hilo and West Hawai'i to reach the **Onizuka Center for International Astronomy,** about 34 mi from Hilo.

For those 16 and older, a caravan of four-wheel-drive vehicles makes free tours to the Mauna Kea observatories on weekends. Departure is from **Onizuka Visitor Center** at 1 PM. To reach this visitor center from Hilo, take Highway 200, Saddle Road, turning right at the 28-mi marker onto the Summit Access Road. The center is about 6 mi from the intersection on the right side of the road. Reservations are not required, but for detailed information call **Mauna Kea Support Services** (☎ 808/961–2180).

Freezing temperatures are common at the summit, even when the heat is high at the seashore, so you must take along warm parkas. Weekends at 6 PM stargazing programs (for gazers of all ages) are offered at the **Visitor Information Station** (☎ 808/961–2180), which can be reached in a standard automobile via the access road off Highway 20 out of Hilo.

Three companies take all the worry out of a trip to the top. You may book a day or evening van tour with knowledgeable Pat Wright of **Paradise Safaris** (✉ Box 9027, Kailua 96745, ☎ 808/322–2366 or 888/322–2366). He supplies lunch or dinner and warm parkas for the excursion as well as pickup at three locations. **Waipi'o Valley Shuttle** (✉ Box 5128, Kukuihaele 96727, ☎ 808/775–7121) conducts Mauna Kea summit tours that leave from Parker Ranch Shopping Center in Waimea for a minimum of four passengers. **Waipi'o on Horseback** (✉ Box 183, Honoka'a 96727, ☎ 808/775–7291) furnishes transportation up Mauna Kea by four-wheel-drive van for a minimum of six passengers. Prices among the various companies are $50–$85.

COFFEE TOURS

The Big Island coffee industry has experienced a renaissance ever since the mainland became enamored of gourmet coffees. Kona Coffee Living History Farm, more commonly known as the **Uchida Coffee Farm** was an actual working farm where coffee was grown by the Uchida family. The house and mill, built in 1925, are being restored by the Kona Historical Society. Visitors can see the old farmhouse surrounded by coffee trees, a Japanese bath house, coffee processing mill, drying platforms and outbuildings. The farm is open by tour only. ✉ *For location, inquire at Kona Historical Society, 81–6551 Māmalahoa Hwy., Kealakekua, ☎ 808/323–2005.* ▭ *$15.* ☯ *Tours Tues., Thurs. 9 AM.*

In sharp contrast is **Greenwell Farms,** with its modern coffee mill, even though many of the trees are more than 90 years old. Coffee and macadamia nuts from the estate are sold here and several kinds of coffee are available to sample. ✉ *81–6581 Māmalaloa Hwy. 11, Kealakekua, ☎ 808/323–2862.* ☯ *Mon.–Sat. 8–3.*

If you prefer to fashion your own self-guided tour, drop by the conveniently located **Royal Kona Coffee Museum and Visitor Center** (✉ 83–5427 Mamalahoa Hwy. 11, next to the treehouse in Honaunau, ☎ 808/328–2511), with displays of coffee trees and photos, plus a three-minute video detailing the history and processing of coffee.

Visitors to the **Holualoa-Kona Coffee Company** tour its mill and roasting establishment, seeing coffee processing from green beans to roasting to packaging. ⊠ 77-6261 Old Māmalahoa Hwy., Hwy. 180, Hōlualoa, ☎ 808/322–9937 or 800/334–0348. ☜ Free. ☉ Weekdays 8–4.

Visitors are encouraged to stop by coffee farms, mills, and co-ops along the up-country coffee belt from Holualoa to Honaunau, including **Kahauloa Coffee Company Plantation** (⊠ 83-5799 Māmalahoa Hwy. 11, near Mile Marker 109, Captain Cook, ☎ 808/328–9555) and **Bayview Farm** (⊠ ½-mile north of St. Benedict's Painted Church on Painted Church Rd., Hōnaunau, ☎ 808/328–9658) to sample coffee and see how it is farmed and milled.

FOUR-WHEEL DRIVE TOURS

Besides four-wheel-drive van tours to Mauna Kea, to Volcanoes National Park and through historic Kohala, geologist Lee Meyerson and his wife Betty of **Hawaiian Eyes Tours** (⊠ 74–5196 Kanai Pl., Kailua-Kona 96740, ☎ 808/937–2530, FAX 808/326–5661) may be the only Big Islanders who conduct four-wheel-drive van tours to the volcanic landscapes at the 11,000-ft level of Mauna Loa. Informal "talk story" sessions along the way, furnish insights into Hawai'i's geology and culture. Day and evening outings to Volcanoes National Park include lunch or no-host dinner. Prices range from $79 to $109 each for a minimum of two or a maximum of six.

GARDEN TOURS

Amy B. H. Greenwell Ethnobotanical Garden is landscaped to showcase 250 plants on 12 acres that were typical in an early Hawaiian ahupua'a, a pie-shape land division that ran from the mountains to the sea. ⊠ 82-6188 Māalahoa Hwy., Captain Cook, ☎ 808/323–3318. ☜ Free weekdays to walk-in visitors; donations welcome; suggested donation $2 for tour. ☉ Guided tour 2nd Sat. of each month at 10.

ORIENTATION TOURS

Roberts Hawai'i (⊠ 680 Iwilei Rd., Honolulu, ☎ 808/523–7750 or 800/767–7551) conducts a Hilo-Volcano-Kalapana tour out of Hilo for about $52 and a circle-island tour, which takes eight hours. From Kona the tour costs about $60.

SUBMARINE TOURS

***Atlantis* Submarine.** A boat shuttles passengers from Kailua Pier to the 65-ft *Atlantis IV* submarine, which, with its clean plastic seats, feels more like an amusement park ride than the real thing. A large glass dome in the bow and 13 viewing ports on the sides allow up to 48 passengers clear views of the watery world outside. A scuba diver feeds fish along a coral reef, keeping the viewing ports filled with the colorful finned creatures. Children must be at least 3 ft tall. Sign up across from King Kamehameha's Kona Beach Hotel. ⊠ 75-5669 Ali'i Dr., Kailua-Kona, ☎ 808/329–6626. ☜ $79.

WAIPI'O VALLEY TOURS

This Edenlike refuge in the north of the island, once the vacation spot for Hawaiian royalty, is accessible via a number of means. **Waipi'o on Horseback** (⊠ Box 183, Honoka'a 96727, ☎ 808/775–7291) hosts horseback rides and van trips into Waipi'o Valley with pickup at the Last Chance Store in Kukuihaele. **Waipi'o Valley Shuttle** (⊠ Box 5128, Kukuihaele 96727, ☎ 808/775–7121) leaves Waipi'o Valley Artworks daily on 1½-hour tours; tours cost about $35. **Waipi'o Valley Wagon Tours** (⊠ Box 1340, Honoka'a 96727, ☎ 808/775–9518) has tours departing from the Last Chance Store for 1½-hour excursions at a cost of $40.

WALKING AND HIKING TOURS

You can take a self-guided walking tour of downtown Hilo with the help of a **"Discover Downtown Hilo"** map from the Lyman House Memorial Museum. Points of interest are indicated at Kalākaua Park and at 15 historic buildings. ✉ *276 Haili St., Hilo,* ☎ *808/935–5021.* ⌨ *Map $1.50.* ☉ *Mon.–Sat. 9–5, Sun. 1–4.*

Docents from the **Kona Historical Society** lead 1½-hour walking tours of Kailua-Kona starting at the King Kamehameha Kona Beach Hotel to Hale Hālāwai Pavilion at the opposite end of town, covering history about Ahuʻena Heiau, Huliheʻe Palace, Mokuʻaikaua Church, and Kona Inn, the town's first hotel. ✉ *Box 398, Captain Cook 96704,* ☎ *808/323–3222.* ⌨ *$10.* ☉ *Tues.–Sat. 9:30, Fri. also 1:30.*

The following companies specialize in Big Island hikes. Since 1984, Hugh Montgomery of **Hawaiian Walkways** (✉ Box 2193, Kamuela, ☎ 808/885–7759 or 800/457–7759) has been custom-designing hikes to suit the individual's skill level and choice of scenery. A full-day hike averages $110 per person. The personable founder of **Hawaiʻi Forest and Trails** (✉ Box 2975, Kailua-Kona, ☎ 808/322–8881 or 800/464–1993), Rob Pacheko, leads nature hikes on a valley hike to 300-ft Kalopa Falls, through normally inaccessible areas of Hawaiʻi Volcanoes National Park, to Hakalau Wildlife Refuge, and to the Puʻu ʻŌʻō rain forest. **Chris' Adventures Bike or Hike** (✉ Box 869, Kula, ☎ 808/326–4600) provides a chance to explore the Big Island through Waipiʻo Valley, Pololū Valley, along the Kohala Coast and over other secluded trails. Morning tours include breakfast and lunch; afternoon tours include a light snack.

WATER-SPORTS TOURS

Youngsters (5 and older) love floating through the pitch-black, eerie tunnels of the Kohala Ditch, emerging now and then to pristine rain forests; grandparents find the history of these irrigation ditches, built between 1905 and 1906 by Japanese plantation workers in North Kohala, fascinating. And at the end of the 22½-mi **Kohala Mountain Kayak Cruise** in inflatable double-hulled kayaks, there's a chance to swim in a mountain pool—if the waterfall that fills it is pumping out enough water. ✉ *Box 660, Sakamoto Building, Hwy. 270, Kapaʻau,* ☎ *808/889–6922,* ⅢX *808/889–6944.* ⌨ *$75.*

Eye of the Whale Marine and Wilderness Adventures (✉ Box 1269, Kapaʻau 96755, ☎ 808/889–0227 or 800/659–3544) offers a six-day inn-to-inn, hike/swim/sail excursion for $1,025 on the Big Island. A similar 10-day, three-island package for $1,675 includes the Big Island, Kauaʻi, and Maui.

WHALE-WATCHING

Although most Hawaiian whale-watching cruises focus on the migratory humpbacks that are seen here only from December through April, Captain Dan McSweeney offers 3½-hour trips year-round to find six other species of whales that rarely stray far from the Kona coast, as well as the seasonal humpback. He's spent 20 years researching these local creatures, and his cruises offer a close-up and informative look at all Hawaiʻi's whales. McSweeney's 40-ft double-decked boat is specially equipped for listening to the whales while they're underwater. A sighting is guaranteed, or you cruise again for free. ✉ *Dan McSweeney's Year-Round Whale Watching Adventures, Box 139, Hōlualoa,* ☎ *808/322–0028 or 888/942–5376,* ⅢX *808/322–2732.* ⌨ *$44.50.*

Visitor Information

Information and brochures are dispensed at the **Hawaiʻi Visitors & Convention Bureau** (HVCB) booths at Big Island airports and at HVCB offices in Hilo and Kailua-Kona. ⊠ *250 Keawe St., Hilo,* ☎ *808/961–5797,* FAX *808/961–2126;* ⊠ *75-5719 Ali'i Dr., Kailua-Kona,* ☎ *808/329–7787,* FAX *808/326–7563.*

For detailed street maps, **Basically Books** (⊠ 160 Kamehameha Ave., Hilo, ☎ 808/961–0144) is a complete map shop. Good maps are also available at the **Middle Earth Bookshoppe** (⊠ 75-5719 Ali'i Dr., Kailua-Kona, ☎ 808/329–2123) and **Borders Books and Music** (⊠ 75-1000 Henry St.,☎ 808/331–1668). If you rent a car, be sure to get a **"Drive Guide."** These handy booklets have all the maps you'll probably need to navigate the island.

Another helpful source of information is the **Kohala Coast Resort Association** (⊠ HC02, Box 5300, Waikoloa 96743, ☎ 808/885–4915), a group of resorts and luxury hotels cooperating to promote the Kohala Coast as a resort destination. For information about Kona Coast attractions, contact **Destination Kona Coast** (⊠ Box 2850, Kailua-Kona 96745, ☎ 808/322–6809). For questions about east Hawai'i, write to: **Destination Hilo** (⊠ Box 1391, Hilo 96721 (☎ 808/935–5294). For general information about the entire island, write **Big Island Group** (⊠ HCO 2, Box 5900, Kamuela 96743, ☎ 808/885–5900 or 800/648–2441).

Weather: For daily reports call (☎ 808/961–5582).

5 Kaua'i

The Garden Isle

Greenest and most tropical of all, Kaua'i is the only Hawaiian island with sizable rivers. Polynesians first chose to settle here on the banks of the bubbling Wailua, on the east coast. The lushness of the misty, magical north shore is a startling contrast to the west coast's Waimea Canyon—the "Grand Canyon of the Pacific"—with its rich, vivid coloration of copper, rust, and gold.

NICKNAMED THE GARDEN ISLE, Kaua'i is Eden epitomized. In the mountains of Kōke'e, lush swamps ring with the songs of rare birds, while the heady aroma of ginger blossoms sweetens the cool rain forests of Hā'ena. Time and nature carved the elegant spires along the remote northwestern shore known as the Nā Pali (the cliffs) Coast as seven coursing rivers gave life to the valleys where ancient Hawaiians once dwelled. Today visitors can explore this South Seas paradise by land, sea, and air—hiking along the Kalalau Trail, kayaking up the Hanalei River, or hovering in a helicopter high above 5,148-ft Wai'ale'ale, the wettest spot on earth.

Updated by
Betty Fullard-
Leo

Though devastating hurricanes are rare in Hawai'i, in September 1992 Hurricane 'Iniki swept right across the island and caused hundreds of millions of dollars' worth of damage. The people of Kaua'i were quick to rebuild and revitalize their communities, and today Kaua'i looks better than ever thanks to extensive renovations and improvements—although several hotels have yet to reopen.

The Garden Isle is a laid-back, restful retreat—an island of unmatched physical beauty that easily rewards those who love the great outdoors. You can take a boat trip up Nā Pali Coast to snorkel in azure waters, ride a horse-drawn coach around a plantation-era sugar estate, or play golf on the world-class greens of Princeville Resort, where a majestic mountain peak, nicknamed Bali Hai, rises just beyond the fairways. Then again, you might just want to saddle up and go horseback riding into Waimea Canyon and see why these steep ridges and ravines are often called the "Grand Canyon of the Pacific."

One road runs almost all the way around the island, but dead-ends on either side of a 15-mi stretch of the rugged Nā Pali Coast. Driving from one end to the other takes you past lustrous green stands of sugarcane, which are gradually being replaced with coffee and macadamia nut orchards. Sugar had been a key economic force on the island from the 1990s dating back to 1836, when Hawai'i's first sugar mill was built in Kōloa. Patches of taro are found around Hanalei Valley; this longtime staple of the Hawaiian diet is grown for its root (to make *poi*, a puddinglike accompaniment for fish and meat) as well as its leaves (used to wrap and cook food). Traveling around the island you'll see such movie settings as the Hulē'ia River, where Indiana Jones made his daring escape at the beginning of *Raiders of the Lost Ark*. Other locations on the island were used in filming *Honeymoon in Vegas, Jurassic Park,* and *Six Days, Seven Nights,* starring Harrison Ford and Anne Heche.

Kaua'i, the fourth-largest island in the Hawaiian chain, has its capital in Līhu'e, a town whose government buildings resemble a small New England village. Līhu'e is the island's commercial center, yet its collection of businesses—a pair of banks, a library, a school, a museum, some family-run restaurants, and hotels—is small enough to keep the pace unhurried.

On the south coast the sunny beaches and clear skies around Po'ipū have spawned a crop of classy condos and resort hotels. The area has also come into its own as a golf destination, and several fine restaurants have found a home here as well. Head west, beneath the slopes of the Hoary Head Mountains, to encounter such storybook plantation villages as Hanapēpē, Kalāheo, and Waimea—where Captain James Cook first landed back in 1778. Beyond Waimea lies Polihale Beach, an idyllic stretch of golden sand sprawled beneath the cool highlands of Kōke'e State Park.

From the southwestern part of Kaua'i you can see the island of Ni'ihau 17 mi off the coast. Until 1987 no uninvited guests were allowed to visit this family-owned island. Most people who live in Hawai'i still consider Ni'ihau off-limits, but its mysteries can now be breached by helicopter—Kaua'i-based tours touch down each weekday for three-hour visits.

North of Līhu'e the climate turns cooler and wetter, and everything sparkles in luxuriant shades of green. In Wailua and Kapa'a several resort complexes huddle along a picturesque shoreline called the Royal Coconut Coast for its abundant array of palms. As you head farther north to Anahola, Kīlauea, Princeville, and Hanalei, a dense web of vines and flowers takes over. At the end of the road, in Hā'ena, you'll encounter a misty otherworldliness conjuring up the legends of the ancients.

More myths are attached to the natural landscape of Kaua'i than to any other Hawaiian island. A favorite among locals is the legend of the Menehune, a community of diminutive yet industrious workers said to have lived on Kaua'i before the Polynesians. Few people actually saw the Menehune because they worked in privacy at night—practicing, it seems, their impressive stoneworking skills. There are bridges, walls, fishponds, and other solid constructions attributed to the engineering skill of these mysterious mythical stonemasons.

The oldest of the Hawaiian Islands, Kaua'i's 550 square mi are rich in natural history and the resonance of past cultures. A sense of relaxation and unaffected natural beauty calmly welcomes all who step off the plane at the Līhu'e Airport and wraps them in a lei of traditional Hawaiian hospitality. The people in the tourism and hospitality industry here work hard to keep visitors and guests satisfied, and the aloha spirit reigns everywhere. In fact, many feel that Kaua'i's people are the friendliest in all the Islands, and that this splendid jewel of an island harbors all that nature allows from a tropical paradise.

Pleasures and Pastimes

Beaches

As the oldest of the Hawaiian Islands, Kaua'i has had more time to develop—and perfect—its beaches. The Garden Isle is embraced by stretches of magnificent ivory sands, many with breathtaking mountain backdrops. Po'ipū, on the south shore, has the sandiest, most consistently sunny beaches for water lovers. Here is some of the island's best swimming, snorkeling, and bodysurfing in waters that are generally safe year-round. You do need to look out for occasional patches of coral, which can leave a nasty cut on your foot when stepped on.

The north shore is a different story altogether. Although some of Kaua'i's most scenic beaches can be found here, they are treacherous in winter. In summer, however, they are safe for swimming. No matter what time of year it is, be sure to exercise caution, because only a few of these beaches have lifeguards.

The beaches that front the hotels and condominiums along the eastern shore are conducive to seaside strolling but less favorable for swimming. The strong surf and rip currents of the winter months are unpredictable, and it's often windy. If you want beaches with plenty of wide open spaces, drive to the west coast beyond Waimea. This is where many locals go to fish and swim, and you'll catch the best sunsets from this vantage point. Waimea has a black-sand beach where sunsets are dramatic, while the Kekaha and Barking Sands beaches are a dazzling white-sand continuation of the beach that starts beneath the cliffs at Polihale.

HAWAIIAN MYTHS AND LEGENDS

THE MOST WELL-KNOWN DEITY in Hawaiian lore is Pele, the volcano goddess. Although visitors are warned not to remove lava rocks from Pele's domain without her permission, some do and find themselves dogged by bad luck until they return the stolen items. The Hawai'i Volcanoes National Park Service often receives packages containing chunks of lava along with letters describing years of misfortune.

Tales of Pele's fiery temper are legion. She battled Poli'ahu, ruler of snow-capped Mauna Ke'a on the Big Island, in a fit of jealousy over the snow goddess's extraordinary beauty. She picked fights with her peace-loving sister, Hi'iaka, turning the younger goddess's friends into pillars of stone. And her recurring lava-flinging spats with suitor Kamapua'a, a demigod who could change his appearance at will, finally drove him into the sea where he turned into a fish to escape from her wrath.

But Pele can be kind if the mood suits her. It is said that before every major eruption, she appears in human form as a wrinkled old woman walking along isolated back roads. Those who pass her by find their homes devastated by molten lava. Those who offer her a ride home return home to find a river of boiling magma abruptly halted inches from their property or diverted around their houses. Many hula *hālau* (schools) still make pilgrimages to the rim of Kīlauea—Pele's home—where they honor the fickle goddess with prayers, chants, and offerings of gin and flower leis.

A less volatile but equally intriguing figure in Hawaiian lore is Māui, a demigod who is credited with pulling the Hawaiian Islands up from the bottom of the sea with a magic fishhook, pushing the sky away from the tree-tops because it had flattened all the leaves, and his most prestigious feat—lassoing the sun as it came up over the top of Haleakalā and demanding that it move more slowly across the sky in summer so that Māui's mother would have longer daylight hours to dry her *kapa* (cloth made from bark).

In addition to battling the elements and each other, gods were thought to have intervened in the daily lives of early Hawaiians. Storms that destroyed homes and crops, a fisherman's poor catch, or a loss in battle were blamed on the wrath of angry gods. And, according to legend, an industrious race of diminutive people called *menehune* built aqueducts, fishponds, and other constructs requiring advanced engineering knowledge unavailable to early Hawaiians. Living in remote hills and valleys, these secretive workers toiled only in darkness and completed complex projects in a single night. Their handiwork can still be seen on all the islands.

Also at night, during certain lunar periods, a traveler might inadvertently come across the Night Marchers—armies of dead warriors, chiefs, and ancestral spirits whose feet never touch the ground as they tread the ancient highways, chanting and beating their drums, and pausing only to claim the spirits of their brethren who died that night. It was believed that such an encounter would mean certain death unless a relative among the marchers pleaded for the victim's life.

The moral? Leave the lava rocks as they are and pick up any elderly hitchikers you might come across. Straightforward enough. But I'd still hightail it in the other direction if I heard mysterious chanting or drum beating.

Beaches along the northwest shore are inaccessible except to those who hike the rugged Nā Pali trail from the opposite end of the road at Haena, or who book a boat tour along the north shore. Some tour operators, such as Captain Zodiac Raft Expeditions (☞ Guided Tours *in* Kauaʻi A to Z, *below*) offer a hiker/camper drop-off service from May through September, transporting passengers one way so they can enjoy a secluded beach, then hike back on their own.

Dining

The sugar plantations of 19th-century Kauaʻi brought together a universe of cultures, as workers from other countries sought new jobs in Hawaiʻi. With them came an international array of foods, reflected in the cuisines found today on Kauaʻi. You can choose from among Hawaiian Regional restaurants or those preparing Chinese, Japanese, Thai, Mexican, Italian, and French specialties, mixed with a heavy dose of traditional Hawaiian food, available in just about any town on the island.

When it's time for a snack, look for the carryout wagons that are often parked at major beaches. They serve local foods, such as the "plate lunch"—two scoops of rice served with such entrées as teriyaki beef or chicken, veal cutlet, or luncheon meat. Another standard component is a mound of either macaroni salad or potato salad, with a few token greens thrown in for show. The "mixed plate" is a plate lunch with two or sometimes three entrée selections.

Lodging

Part of the appeal of the Garden Isle is its range of hotel properties—from swanky and pricey resorts to rustic mountain-top cabins to bare-bones lodgings whose main appeal is a rock-bottom price. Sunshine seekers often head south to the shores of Poʻipū, where three- and four-story condos line the coast and the gentle surf offers ideal swimming. Poʻipū has more condos than hotels, with prices in the $$–$$$$ range, although several oceanfront cottages are in demand with budget travelers. Guests interested in the history of the islands often stay on the east coast near the Wailua River, home to Kauaʻi's first inhabitants. Many of the hotels here place an emphasis on the legends and lore of the area. Shops and restaurants are within walking distance of most accommodations. The beaches are so-so for swimming, but nice for sunbathing.

Farther north are the swanky hotels and condominiums of the Princeville Resort. You can't go wrong here, because just about any accommodation offers views of the bay or the chiseled mountain peaks of Hanalei. Golfers find the courses here a duffer's paradise.

Bed-and-breakfasts are an attractive option if you're looking for a more settled-in and residential experience. There are a range of private homes scattered around the island; a good booking service (☞ B&B Reservation Services *in* Contacts and Resources *in* Kauaʻi A to Z, *below*) can help you locate one.

Outdoor Activities and Sports

GOLF

Princeville Resort's stunning Robert Trent Jones–designed Prince Course is rated the second most difficult course in Hawaiʻi. The resort's (and Jones's) neighboring Makai Course is also beautiful, with the so-called Zen bunker (a boulder in the middle of a huge sand trap) and an eighth hole played across an ocean chasm. Jack Nicklaus's Kiele course has many greens positioned diagonally to the fairway. Nicklaus' adjacent Lagoons course is less dramatic and wider. As you play the four closing holes of Jones's Poipu Bay course you will hear the crashing surf on your left. Endangered wildlife, such as the nēnē goose, monk seal, and sea turtle can often be spotted—the geese in ponds on the back nine, and the seals and turtles on the beach or in the water below. Kiahuna Plantation is Jones's fourth course on Kaua'i. It's a challenging inland course that winds over streams, through woods, and past lava formations.

HIKING

Best known for the challenging North Shore Kalalau Trail, Kaua'i is also a mecca for hikers searching for an easy day walk. Trails at Kōke'e State Park range from easy to difficult; they overlook the green ramparts of the Nā Pali coastline or showcase views of the painted wonders of Waimea Canyon. Easy excursions through Keāhua Forestry Arboretum, Limahuli Garden, and other tropical gardens appeal to all ages.

HORSEBACK RIDING

Kaua'i offers possibly the broadest selection of equestrian outings of all the Islands. You can saddle up to ride along the rim of Waimea Canyon, to a secluded waterfall, along the edge of a moonlit beach, or through the greenest of mountain pastures.

WATER SPORTS

Safe yet exciting water adventures are possible through a vast number of companies. Kayaks can be rented for do-it-yourself or guided excursions. This is the only island where you have the choice of kayaking on rivers, ancient fishponds, or in the ocean. Fishing, scuba, and snorkel guides are quick to locate the spots where the biggest and most colorful array of fish hang out, and surfing and windsurfing instructors can help you soar like a tropical bird across the cresting waves of the ocean.

There are three great dive sites on Kaua'i. Cannon's Reef, on the north shore, drops quickly from the shoreline forming a long ledge permeated with lava tubes. Plate coral is found here, and turtles are a common sight. You may come across white tip sharks sleeping in caverns or patroling the ledge. Depths range from 30 ft to 60 ft, and you can only dive here in summer.

General Store, at Kukui'ula, is the site of a 19th-century shipwreck. The horseshoe-shape ledge and two caverns teem with schools of lemon butterfly fish that follow divers around. There are also green moray eels and black coral at this site, which runs to depths of 65 ft–80 ft.

Sheraton Caverns, off Po'ipū, are formed by three immense, parallel lava tubes. There's a lobster nursery in one cavern, sea turtles swim in all three, and the occasional white tip shark cruises by. Depths range from 35 ft to 60 ft.

EXPLORING KAUA'I

The main road tracing the island's perimeter takes you past a variety of easily explored landscapes and attractions. There are magical mountains, cascading waterfalls, verdant fern grottoes, mist shrouded caves, and a lighthouse designated a National Historic Landmark. All around the island are beautiful overlooks where you can stop to take a breath and soak up the fragrant beauty of the scenic South Seas.

Mauka means on the mountain side of the road, and *makai* means on the ocean side. These terms will be used in this section as they are used all over the island.

Numbers in the text correspond to numbers in the margin and on the Kaua'i map.

Great Itineraries

With Līhu'e as your point of departure, it's easy to explore the island by traveling to sights along its eastern and northern coasts, then visiting attractions around Līhu'e itself, and finally striking out toward the southern and western coasts. Each of these routes can easily fill a day of sightseeing. Allow one day for the north and east sections of the island and another day for sights to the south and west. To fully enjoy the sunning, surfing, hiking, golfing, and other activities and adventures on Kaua'i, plan on spending at least five or six days.

IF YOU HAVE 2 DAYS

In two full days you can barely scratch the surface of Kaua'i's idyllic beauty. Plan to stay along the southeast shoreline, anywhere from Po'ipū to Kapa'a, and then spend one day exploring in either direction. Beginning your trek in **Līhu'e** ⑮, drive around **Nāwiliwili** ⑰ Harbor and drive past the harbor and head up the hill to the lookout for an encompassing view of **Menehune Fishpond** ⑱, connecting with Highway 50 until a left turn on Highway 520 takes you through the **Tunnel of Trees** to **Kōloa** ㉑ for shopping and **Po'ipū** ㉓ for sightseeing. Follow the signs to **Spouting Horn** ㉕ for a quick look at this natural waterspout and then continue on through Po'ipū for a beach break at Brennecke's. Head back to Hwy. 50, stopping at the ruins of **Ft. Elisabeth** ㉜ for a glimpse of Russia's influence on this island, then proceed directly to **Waimea Canyon** ㉟ to revel in colorful vistas and fresh, cool air. It's a 36-mi return to Līhu'e.

On your second day, make your goal the end of the road at Ha'ena, 40 mi north of Līhu'e. On the way, stretch your legs at the the **Kīlauea Lighthouse and Kīlauea Point National Wildlife Refuge** ⑧. Check out the orchard and have some juice at **Guava Kai Plantation,** pause at the **Maniniholo Dry Cave** ⑪ and at **Waikapala'e and Waikanaloa Wet Caves** ⑬, turn around and eat lunch in Hanalei, and spend the afternoon at the beach before heading back.

IF YOU HAVE 4 DAYS

Basically you'll want to cover the same ground as you would in two days, but you'll have more leisure time to enjoy beach and shopping breaks. Spend day one exploring **Līhu'e** ⑮ more thoroughly. Get a feeling for Kaua'i's history at the **Kaua'i Museum** ⑯, then drive south to **Po'ipū** ㉓ for some leisurely shopping in **Kōloa** ㉑, and then have lunch and sun on the beach in Po'ipū before calling it a day.

A drive directly to Kōke'e on day two will allow time for longer hikes and perhaps a stop at a west side beach as well as a trek around the ruins of **Ft. Elisabeth** ㉜ on the return leg.

Make day three a full-day's exploration of Kaua'i's north shore. Take in **Kīlauea Lighthouse and Kīlauea Point National Wildlife Refuge** ⑧, examine **Maniniholo Dry Cave** ⑪ and **Waikapala'e and Waikanaloa Wet Caves** ⑬, and amble through **Limahuli Garden** ⑫, then stop in Hanalei for lunch before stretching out on Ke'e Beach in the afternoon sun.

On your fourth day stick close to Kapa'a. In the morning, make the **Fern Grotto** your destination, either aboard on of the Wailua river boats, or rent a kayak and ask directions before paddling off on the river. On your return, pick up a plate lunch or a few picnic supplies, then drive up Mā'alo Road to see the **Pōhaku-ho'ohānau and Pōhaku Piko** ④ (royal birthing stones) and **'Ōpaeka'a Falls** ⑤. If you follow the road nearly to its end you'll come upon the Keāhua Forestry Arboretum, where picnic tables and a freshwater pool offer a soothing respite before returning to Kapa'a for some last-minute shopping at the Coconut Marketplace.

With six days, you might want to split your vacation nights into two hotels, spending the first two nights on the south side and the last three at Princeville on the north shore. On day one, explore the **Waimea Canyon** ㉟ area, also stopping at **Ft. Elisabeth** ㉜ and perhaps walking the main street (one block off the highway) of **Hanapēpē** ㉚, a quiet town with an extraordinary number of art galleries for its size. Spend the morning of day two in **Līhu'e** ⑮, touring **Grove Farm Homestead** ⑲ (with prior reservations) and/or the **Kaua'i Museum** ⑯. In the afternoon take time to explore the main street of **Kōloa** ㉑ and see **Spouting Horn** ㉕ in Po'ipū; then relax during the late afternoon at the beach.

Pack and get away early on day three, so you can take in the **Fern Grotto,** the **Pōhaku-ho'ohānau and Pōhaku Piko** ④, and **'Ōpaeka'a Falls** ⑤, with a little time for lunch or shopping in Kapa'a on your way to your new north shore location.

On day four you might simply want to revel in the beauty of your new surroundings: play golf, visit the spa, paddle a kayak up Hanalei River, or soak in the sun at the pool. For hikers, day five could involve a long hike along the Kalalau Trail to Hanakāpi'ai Beach and inland to the falls, or if you prefer a less strenuous stroll, investigate the grounds at **Limahuli Garden** ⑫, which are a peaceful retreat with archaeological sites and plants identified by signage. In any case, this fifth day is the time to drive to the end of the road at Ha'ena, visiting **Maniniholo Dry Cave** ⑪ and **Waikapala'e and Waikanaloa Wet Caves** ⑬ along the way and reserving time for lunch at one of the casual little restaurants in Hanalei.

Reserve your sixth and final day to accomplish activities and see sights you missed along the northeast shore. You might discover Secret Beach (officially called Kauapea Beach), which is just to the left of **Kīlauea Lighthouse and Kīlauea Point National Wildlife Refuge** ⑧; shop at Kong Lung store in Ki'lauea; seek out a farmer's market; or explore a side road to 'Anini Beach. Of course, if you've had enough sightseeing, day six could be a repeat of day four—a day to relax and to dream about repeating day four endlessly.

When to Tour Kaua'i

Kaua'i is beautiful in every season, however if it's hot beach weather you prefer, you might schedule your visit from June through October when rainfall is at its lightest. The northern coast of Kaua'i generally receives more rainfall than the rest of the island, particularly during the December to February span. To avoid family crowds, time a visit for pre- and postschool months, May or October, for example, when the weather is generally fine and plenty of rooms are available.

The Heavenly Northeast

Traveling north from Līhu'e you'll encounter green pastureland, lush valleys, and untamed tropical wilderness. An area rich in history and legend, it was one of the first communities of the Polynesians who settled here more than 1,000 years ago. As the road turns west, tracing the island's north shore, you'll time-travel through historic plantation towns and the definitely here-and-now resort of Princeville, winding up in the mist-shrouded primeval wilds around Ke'e Beach and Nā Pali Coast State Park.

A Good Drive

Highway 56 traces the eastern and northern coasts of Kaua'i and forms the main artery for a tour of the region. Head north out of Līhu'e on Highway 56. For an early scenic side-trip turn left on Mā'alo Road (Hwy. 583) at the bottom of the hill in Kapaia, then drive 4 mi to **Wailua**

Falls ①, one of the Aloha State's most beautiful cascades. Backtrack 4 mi to Highway 56 and continue north to the historic town of **Wailua** ②, the island's early capital.

Before you reach Wailua, a short drive makai at Kaua'i Resort will take you to a former "city of refuge," **Lydgate State Park** ③. Today the park's community-built Kamalani Playground offers a present-day refuge to parents with active kids in the car. On the mauka side of Highway 56, follow the sign directing you to Wailua Marina, where cruise boats depart for the **Fern Grotto.** Past the mouth of the Wailua, turn left off Highway 56 onto Kuamo'o Road (Hwy. 580). Just beyond Wailua River State Park on your left is one of seven revered *heiau* (outdoor shrines) and the royal birthing stones, **Pōhaku-ho'ohānau and Pōhaku Piko** ④. Farther up Kuamo'o Road, you'll reach the most intact of the stone temples, Poli'ahu, complete with story boards. On clear days you can see Wai'ale'ale, the misty peak that is the source of the Wailua River. Across the road is the spectacular **'Ōpaeka'a Falls** ⑤. For a look at this beautiful cascade, return to Kuamo'o Road and drive 1 mi to the lookout on the right.

Adventurers can follow Kuamo'o Road another 7 or 8 mi to its end in Keāhua Forestry Arboretum for a picnic amid aromatic yellow ginger. A huge, shady mango tree on a river bank in the arboretum comes equipped with a dangling rope—so take your bathing suit, because the spirit of Tarzan is sure to surface when you see the inviting pool below.

Head back to Highway 56 and drive north toward the historic village of Waipouli, now famous for its Coconut Marketplace(☞ Shopping, *below*), a low-rise shopping complex with storefronts that open invitingly onto a large central mall. On your left you'll pass a mountain ridge resembling a mythical **Sleeping Giant** ⑥; it's thought to be the body of a sleeping warrior. Follow the meandering highway along the eastern coast to Kapa'a, Kaua'i's largest town; its quaint storefronts and buildings house boutiques and eateries.

To the north you'll pass Keālia and the turn-off to Anahola Beach Park; 7 mi farther is **Kīlauea** ⑦, another former plantation town worth a brief stop if only to check out Kong Lung, a one-of-a-kind boutique filled with Hawaiiana and other fine treasures, or to buy pastries or a loaf of fresh-baked bread from Kīlauea Bakery and Pizza. Turn right on Kolo Road when you see the post office, next to which is Christ Memorial Episcopal Church. Take the first left off Kolo Road, onto Kīlauea Road, and follow it to the end where you'll find **Kīlauea Lighthouse and Kīlauea Point National Wildlife Refuge** ⑧.

When you reach the 25-mi marker of Highway 56, you'll be at Kalihi Wai Valley Overlook, a splendid point for photographing the valley and the glimmering waterfall across the road. There's room on the right side of the road to pull over safely. As you drive farther along you'll pass Princeville Airport (on the mauka side of the road) before you reach **Hanalei Valley Overlook** ⑨, across the street from the Princeville Shopping Center. From here you can look out across vast acres of taro fields in the valley below.

The road descends and switches back to cross a rustic, arched one-lane bridge dating from 1912, then switches back again into the town of Hanalei, home to the 19th-century **Wai'oli Mission House** ⑩.

West of Hanalei the highway (now labeled 560 on street signs) winds its way between the mountains and the sea and crosses a series of old one-lane bridges. As the road rises and curves left, look for the marker to Lumaha'i Beach (☞ Beaches, *below*). You can park on the makai

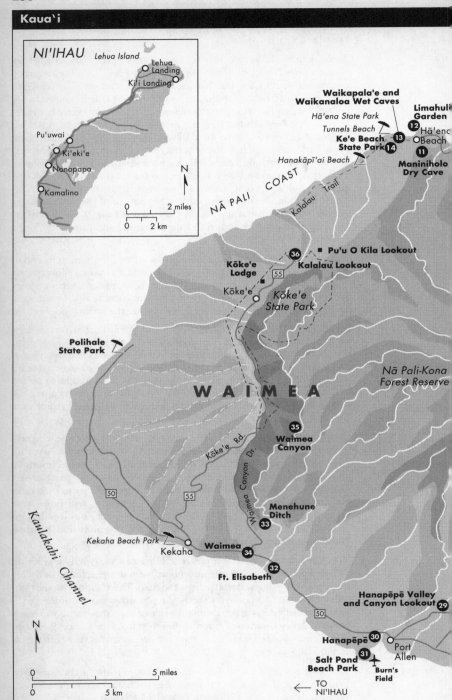

NI'IHAU

Lehua Island

Lehua Landing

Ki'i Landing

Pu'uwai

Ki'eki'e

Nonopapa

Kamalino

N

0   2 miles

0   2 km

Waikapala'e and
Waikanaloa Wet Caves

Hā'ena State Park

Tunnels Beach

Ke'e Beach
State Park

Hanakāpī'ai Beach

Limahuli
Garden

12

Hā'ena
Beach

13

14

11

Maniniholo
Dry Cave

NĀ PALI COAST

Kalalau Trail

Kōke'e
Lodge

36

Kalalau Lookout

Pu'u O Kila Lookout

Kōke'e

Kōke'e
State Park

Polihale
State Park

Nā Pali-Kona
Forest Reserve

W A I M E A

Kōke'e Rd.

Waimea Canyon Dr.

35

Waimea
Canyon

50

55

Menehune
Ditch

33

Kekaha Beach Park

Kekaha

Waimea

34

32

Ft. Elisabeth

Kaulakahi Channel

N

0   5 miles

0   5 km

Hanapēpē Valley
and Canyon Lookout

29

50

Hanapēpē

30

Port
Allen

Salt Pond
Beach Park

31

Burn's
Field

← TO
NI'IHAU

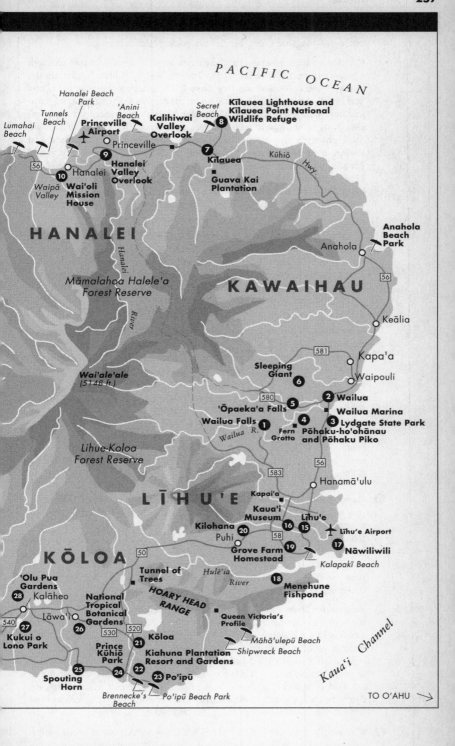

PACIFIC OCEAN

Lumahai
Beach

Tunnels
Beach

Hanalei Beach
Park

'Anini
Beach

Secret
Beach

Kīlauea Lighthouse and
Kīlauea Point National
Wildlife Refuge

8

**Princeville
Airport**

Princeville

Kalihiwai
Valley
Overlook

7

56

9

**Hanalei
Valley
Overlook**

Kīlauea

Kūhiō

Hwy.

10 Hanalei

Waipā
Valley

**Wai'oli
Mission
House**

**Guava Kai
Plantation**

**Anahola
Beach
Park**

H A N A L E I

*Māmalahoa Halele'a
Forest Reserve*

K A W A I H A U

Anahola

56

Keālia

Hanalei
River

Wai'ale'ale
(5148 ft.)

*Lihue-Koloa
Forest Reserve*

**Sleeping
Giant**

6

581

Kapa'a

Waipouli

580

5

2 Wailua

'Ōpaeka'a Falls

Wailua Marina

Wailua Falls 1

4

3 **Lydgate State Park**

Wailua R.

**Fern
Grotto**

**Pōhaku-ho'ohānau
and Pōhaku Piko**

56

583

Hanamā'ulu

L Ī H U 'E

Kapai'a

**Kaua'i
Museum**

16 **15**

Līhu'e

Līhu'e Airport

Kilohana

Puhi

20

58

19

17 **Nāwiliwili**

K Ō L O A

50

**Grove Farm
Homestead**

Kalapakī Beach

'Olu Pua
Gardens

28 Kalāheo

**Tunnel of
Trees**

Hule'ia

River

**HOARY HEAD
RANGE**

18

**Menehune
Fishpond**

540

Lāwa'i

**National
Tropical
Botanical
Gardens**

26

520

530

27

**Kukui o
Lono Park**

21

Kōloa

Queen Victoria's
Profile

**Prince
Kūhiō
Park**

**Kiahuna Plantation
Resort and Gardens**

Māhā'ulepū Beach

Shipwreck Beach

25

24

22

23 **Po'ipū**

**Spouting
Horn**

*Brennecke's
Beach*

Po'ipū Beach Park

Kaua'i Channel

TO O'AHU →

side of the road and walk down the steep (and sometimes muddy) path to where some scenes in *South Pacific* were filmed amid a spectacular setting of majestic cliffs, black lava rocks, and hala trees.

Continuing west, just past the 8-mi marker, you'll see a right turn through a grove of trees. This takes you to Tunnels Beach. A little farther, on the mauka side, is **Maniniholo Dry Cave** ⑪. Just across the way is Hā'ena State Park. A few miles farther, also on the mauka side, is a national tropical botanical garden, **Limahuli Garden** ⑫, with its ancient taro *loi* (terraces), stone walls, and well-marked, peaceful paths. Less than ½ mi up the highway, a five-minute uphill walk takes you to **Waikapala'e and Waikanaloa Wet Caves** ⑬. When you reach the end of Highway 560 in Hā'ena, you'll be at the Kalalau trailhead near **Ke'e Beach State Park** ⑭. Here, where an ancient stone hula platform is still intact, Laka, Hawaiian goddess of the hula, did most of her dancing. You might still be able to catch her spirit here . . . then come away with a sway in your hips!

TIMING

Without stopping, you can drive the 40 mi from Līhu'e to Hā'ena in under 90 minutes. You'll probably want to allow a full day, however, including meal breaks, to stop and explore at least some of the sights along the way, take a short hike around Hā'ena's caves, and pause for some photos. The northeast is green year-round, but profusions of unusual wildflowers are a sure sign of spring.

Sights to See

Fern Grotto. A 3-mi boat ride up the Wailua River culminates at a yawning lava tube covered with enormous fishtail ferns. You can rent a kayak, hire a boat and captain, or take one of the popular boat tours (☞ Guided Tours *in* Kaua'i A to Z, *below*) to this site, which is only approachable via the river.

OFF THE BEATEN PATH

GUAVA KAI PLANTATION – Try a free sample of juice and jelly at the visitor center, then stretch your legs with a nature walk through a 480-acre guava orchard with displays of medicinal plants beside a heart-shape fishpond. The nearest site is Kīlauea (☞ below). ⊠ *Hwy. 56, 34 mi north of Līhu'e; turn mauka onto Kuawa Rd. off Hwy. 56, near turnoff to Kīlauea, and follow signs.* ☎ *Free.*

❾ Hanalei Valley Overlook. One of the state's red-caped Hawaiian-warrior site markers identifies this spot. In the 1850s Robert Wyllie attempted to establish a coffee plantation here. After that failed the Chinese farmed rice in the valley until the early 1900s. Now the valley floor is a patchwork of taro, a staple of the traditional Hawaiian diet. From this panoramic overlook you can see more than ½ mi of taro, plus the 900 acres that comprise a National Wildlife Refuge for endangered waterfowl. ⊠ *Hwy. 56, Princeville.*

★ ⑭ **Ke'e Beach State Park.** You can view the spectacular Nā Pali coastline from this idyllic beach. This is also where you'll find the start of the difficult 11-mi **Kalalau Trail** (☞ Hiking *in* Outdoor Activities and Sports, *below*). Another path leads from the beach to an open, grassy meadow with a stone altar called **Lohi'au's Hula Platform.** Treat this beautiful site with reverence, for it is full of historical and spiritual mana (power). It's said that Laka, goddess of the hula, did most of her dancing on this very spot; today's hula practitioners sometimes leave offerings here for her. ⊠ *Western end of Hwy. 56, Hā'ena.*

❼ Kīlauea. This former plantation town is known today for its aquacultural successes, especially with prawns. It has also distinguished itself as the guava capital of the world. One of Kīlauea's most notable buildings,

Christ Memorial Episcopal Church (✉ 2518 Kolo Rd.), dates from 1941. The church is constructed of native lava rock, and its stained-glass windows came from England. ✉ *Hwy. 56, 25 mi north of Līhu'e.*

★ ❽ **Kīlauea Lighthouse and Kīlauea Point National Wildlife Refuge.** A beacon for passing air and sea traffic since it was built in 1913, the lighthouse, a National Historic Landmark, still has the largest clamshell lens of any lighthouse in the world, but it has laid its traffic responsibilities aside. It is surrounded by the Kīlauea Wildlife Refuge, home to eight species of seabirds, some of them endangered. ✉ *Kīlauea Rd., Kīlauea,* ☎ *808/828–1413.* ✇ *$2.* ☉ *Daily 10–4.*

NEED A
BREAK?

Banana Joe's Tropical Fruit Farm (✉ 5–2719 Kūhiō Hwy., Kīlauea, ☎ 808/828–1092) occupies a rustic yellow shelter with a distinctly Polynesian look to it on the mauka side of Highway 56, just past the turn-off to Kīlauea. Sample the native Kaua'i-grown fruit here (fresh or dehydrated, or in smoothies and salads)—it's the perfect tropical energy booster. Banana Joe also sells fresh corn and other vegetables in season.

⑫ **Limahuli Garden.** This lovely, natural garden is one of five gardens and three preserves known as the National Tropical Botanical Garden. Limahuli's sometimes steep ¾-mi trail passes ancient taro loi, labeled plants and trees, and mountain streams. You'll picnic with pleasure here, surrounded by views of the ocean and the peak known as Bali Hai. Reservations are required for guided tours. ✉ *Hwy. 56, Hā'ena,* ☎ *808/ 826–1053.* ✇ *Self-guided tour $10, guided tour $15.* ☉ *Tues.–Fri. and Sun. 9:30–4.*

☞ ❸ **Lydgate State Park.** Named for the Rev. J. M. Lydgate, founder of the Līhu'e English Union Church, the park houses a children's playground and the remains of a heiau. In pre–Captain Cook days, the area was a city of refuge for Hawaiians who had violated one of the religious *kapu* (taboos). If they made their way to this beachfront haven, they could escape banishment or death by remaining until their families arranged for their forgiveness. ✉ *Near the mouth of Wailua River, turn makai off Hwy. 56 onto Lehu Dr. and left onto Nalu Rd.*

⑪ **Maniniholo Dry Cave.** An eerie grotto said to have been dug by a Menehune chief searching for an evil spirit, this cave was a site of ancient worship. Walk 75 yards into it—if you dare—but don't be spooked; some or another Hawaiian goddess removed the traces of evil that lurked here long ago, most likely Laka and her hula followers. Across the highway from Maniniholo Dry Cave is **Hā'ena State Park,** a fine beach for swimming when there's no current. The well-protected **Tunnels Beach** adjoins Hā'ena State Park. A lunch wagon stands ready to feed hungry surfers and sightseers. ✉ *Hwy. 56, Hā'ena.*

★ ❺ **'Ōpaeka'a Falls.** This dramatic waterfall plunges hundreds of feet to the pools below. 'Ōpaeka'a means "rolling shrimp," which refers to the little creatures that are said to have been so abundant at one time that they could be seen tumbling in the falls to the pool below. ✉ *Hwy. 580 (Kuamo'o Rd.), Wailua.*

❹ **Pōhaku-ho'ohānau and Pōhaku Piko.** These two rocks make Wailua one of the most sacred sites in all Hawai'i, as it was here that all the royal births of Kaua'i took place. An expectant royal mother supported her back against the birthing stone Pōhaku-ho'ohānau. After the newborn's umbilical cord fell off, it was wrapped in kapa and deposited in the crevices of the Pōhaku Piko for safekeeping. Just up the road is Poli'ahu Heiau, where story boards tell about the heiau, the Wailua River area, and its former inhabitants. ✉ *Hwy. 580 (Kuamo'o Rd.), Wailua.*

⑥ Sleeping Giant. This formation on Mount Nounou is said to be the mythical giant, Puni. Sleeping face-down, his back outlining the mountain ridge, he has dozed here undisturbed since hungry villagers fed him stones after he ate all their taro and fish. ⊠ *Hwy. 56, about 1 mi north of Wailua River.*

♨ Smith's Tropical Paradise. Right next to Wailua Marina on the east side of the island, Smith's Tropical Paradise is 30 acres of family fun, with orchards, jungle paths, exotic foliage, tropical birds, ethnic village settings, and tranquil lagoons. A lū'au banquet and live show are offered Monday, Wednesday, and Friday from 5 to 9, and there is free shuttle service from Wailua. Reservations are essential for the lū'au, shuttle, and show. ⊠ *174 Wailua Rd., Kapa'a,* ☎ *808/821–6895.* ☞ *$5, lū'au and show $52.* ۞ *Daily 8:30–4.*

OFF THE BEATEN PATH

SUNSHINE MARKETS – If you want to rub elbows with the locals and get an eyeful of home-grown produce and flowers, head for one of these County of Kaua'i–sponsored outdoor markets, held once a week at five locations around the island, including sessions in Kapa'a and Kīlauea. Hours and locations change frequently; call County of Kaua'i (☎ 808/ 241-6303) for a current schedule.

⑬ Waikapala'e and Waikanaloa Wet Caves. Said to have been dug by Pele, goddess of fire, these watering holes used to be clear, clean, and great for swimming. Now stagnant, they're nevertheless a photogenic example of the many haunting natural landmarks of Kaua'i's north shore. Across the road from a small parking area, a five-minute uphill walk leads to Waikapala'e. Waikanaloa is visible right beside the highway. ⊠ *Western end of Hwy. 56, Hā'ena.*

❷ Wailua. Kaua'i's first communities were built along the Wailua River. Among Wailua's historic treasures, tucked away along the riverbanks, are remnants of important heiau. The town itself was the island's early capital, its name means "two waters" in Hawaiian. ⊠ *Hwy. 56, 7 mi north of Līhu'e.*

NEED A BREAK?

Every be-bopper who remembers the '50s fondly will love **Beezers** (⊠ 1378 Kuhio Hwy., Kapa'a, ☎ 808/822–4411), just a few miles north of Wailua. Its jukebox plays tunes you can sing to, the walls are decked with pictures of Marilyn and Elvis, and the counter has red leatherette stools that spin around so you can talk to your neighbors. Malts, root-beer floats, and a Mustang Sally (chocolate brownie topped with ice cream and smothered in hot fudge, whipped cream, and chopped nuts) make this a great haven on hot days.

❶ Wailua Falls. You may recognize this impressive cascade from the opening sequences of the "Fantasy Island" television series. Kaua'i has plenty of picturesque waterfalls, but this one surpasses most. ⊠ *End of Hwy. 583, Ma'alo Rd., 4 mi from Hwy. 56.*

⑩ Wai'oli Mission House. This 1837 mission was once the home of missionary teachers Lucy and Abner Wilcox. Its prim and proper koa-wood and other furnishings are straight out of missionary Hawai'i, and its tidy architecture feels like it belongs back in New England. Half-hour guided tours are available. ⊠ *Kūhiō Hwy., Hanalei,* ☎ *808/245–3202.* ☞ *Donations accepted.* ۞ *Tues., Thurs., and Sat. 9–3.*

NEED A BREAK?

Bubba's (⊠ Hanalei Center, Hanalei, ☎ 808/826–7839) is where you can find the "Slopper" (open-face burger with chili) or a "Hubba Bubba" (burger, hot dog, chili, and rice). Burgers range in size from ⅙ pound to the three-patty Big Bubba, and there are chicken burgers, fish burgers, corn dogs, and fish-and-chips, too. Orders, filled quickly and with just the irreverent humor you'd expect at a place called Bubba's, may be eaten at the four picnic tables on the lawn right out front.

Līhu'e and Southward

As you follow the main road south from Līhu'e the air seems gradually to become warmer and drier. This is one way to tell you're nearing the region called Po'ipū, named after the south-shore resort town that is its unofficial center. The sun shines steadily on the populated, friendly beaches here. A string of condominiums and hotels lines the sparkling coastline, and an impressive variety of water sports is available.

A Good Drive

Begin in **Līhu'e** ⑮, the commercial and political center of Kaua'i, and visit the **Kaua'i Museum** ⑯, where displays and an exciting aerial movie provide an overview of this tropical isle. Head south on Rice Street, the town's main road, until it dead-ends, then turn right onto Wa'apā Road, which takes you to **Nāwiliwili** ⑰, Kaua'i's major port. From Wa'apā Road, turn right onto Hulemalu Road and follow the Hulē'ia River to view **Menehune Fishpond** ⑱.

Return to Nāwiliwili, take a left on Nāwiliwili Road (Hwy. 58), and begin to look on your right for **Grove Farm Homestead** ⑲. This 80-acre plantation estate and living museum affords a wonderful look at 19th-century agricultural life on the island. At the intersection of Nāwiliwili Road and Highway 50, turn left and head west on Highway 50. Two miles farther on your right you'll find the entrance to **Kilohana** ⑳, another attraction with shops and galleries that will enrich your experience of earlier plantation days.

Continuing west on Highway 50 you'll pass the majestic slopes of the Hoary Head Mountains. On the top of the range to your right is a formation called Queen Victoria's Profile, indicated by a Hawaiian-warrior marker. Some folks see a resemblance between the monarch and the mountain. When you get to the intersection of Highways 50 and 520, you have reached Kōloa Gap, which is the natural pass between Mt. Wai'ale'ale on your right and the Hoary Heads on your left. Turn left on Highway 520 (Maluhia Rd.), also known as the Tunnel of Trees because of a long stretch of eucalyptus trees that borders the road to form a canopy overhead.

Highway 520 takes you to **Kōloa** ㉑, site of Kauai'i's first sugar mill, dating from 1835. Kōloa's main street is lined with old buildings that have been preserved to house shops, art galleries, and restaurants. Head south on Highway 520, which here is also called Po'ipū Road. At the fork, stay to the left and look for a sign on the right to **Kiahuna Plantation Resort and Gardens** ㉒. You can easily amble around its lavish gardens and lava-rock pools before heading back onto Po'ipū Road.

From here turn right onto Honowili Road, which takes you through the heart of sunny **Po'ipū** ㉓, the major resort area of Kaua'i's south shore. On the makai side of the road are Po'ipū Beach Park and Brennecke's Beach, prime spots for sunbathers and bodysurfers (☞ Beaches, *below*). Return to Po'ipū Road and follow it past the stunning Hyatt Regency Kaua'i, which fronts Shipwreck Beach. The road abruptly turns to dirt, but 3 mi farther awaits beautiful Māhā'ulepū Beach. To reach it, follow the road to the T intersection, turn right, stop at the gates to sign in (this is private property), and park at the end of the dirt road to walk to the beach. When you head back on Po'ipū Road, instead of turning to Kōloa, go left onto Lāwa'i Road just after you cross the bridge over Waikomo Stream. This takes you past **Prince Kūhiō Park** ㉔, honoring the birthplace of one of Hawai'i's most beloved members of Congress. At the end of this beachfront road is **Spouting Horn** ㉕, a waterspout that shoots up out of an ancient lava tube. Its rising plume signals your drive's end.

TIMING

From Līhu'e to Po'ipū it's only 14 mi, but there is plenty to see and do along the way, and you can easily devote a day or two to this itinerary. If you have only half a day, try to make it an afternoon, so you can watch the sunset from Brennecke's Beach. The bodysurfers on this legendary beach are something to see, especially if it's big-wave season—summer.

Sights to See

⑲ **Grove Farm Homestead.** One of Kaua'i's oldest plantation estates, founded in 1864 by George Wilcox, today offers a look at 19th-century life on Kaua'i. On the 80 acres comprising this living museum are the original family mansion (filled with turn-of-the-century memorabilia), workers' quarters, and elaborate gardens of tropical flowers and tall palm trees. Tours are limited to six people, and reservations are essential. ⊠ *Hwy. 58, ½ mi south of Nāwiliwili Rd., Līhu'e,* ☎ *808/ 245–3202.* ⊡ *$5.* ☉ *Tour Mon., Wed., and Thurs. at 10 and 1.*

⑯ **Kaua'i Museum.** A permanent display, "The Story of Kaua'i," provides an overview of the Garden Isle and traces its mythology and its geological and cultural history; it's highlighted by a 20-minute aerial movie. Works by local artists are on display in the Mezzanine Gallery, and the gift shop offers a good selection of books and souvenirs. ⊠ *4428 Rice St., Līhu'e,* ☎ *808/245–6931.* ⊡ *$5.* ☉ *Weekdays 9–4:30, Sat. 10–4.*

㉒ **Kiahuna Plantation Resort and Gardens.** This resort condominium estate, known for its lava-rock pools and 4,000 varieties of plants, has earned a listing in the book *Great Gardens of America.* You can amble through on your own, or take a free tour, which also takes in a Hawaiian garden, to learn how herbs and plants were used by early settlers. ⊠ *2253 Po'ipū Rd., Po'ipū,* ☎ *808/742–6411.* ⊡ *Free.* ☉ *Grounds open 24 hrs.; tours Tues. at 9, Thurs. at 4.*

★ ⑳ **Kilohana.** Dating from 1935, this is the site of the old Wilcox sugar plantation, which has been transformed into a 35-acre visitor attraction. The estate is a beautiful showpiece from plantation days, with agricultural exhibits, local arts and crafts, horse-and-carriage rides, specialty shops, and a garden courtyard restaurant called Gaylord's, which is pleasant for breakfast or Sunday brunch. ⊠ *3–2087 Kaumuali'i Hwy. (Hwy. 50), Līhu'e,* ☎ *808/245–5608.* ⊡ *Free.* ☉ *Mon.–Sat. 9:30–9:30, Sun. 9:30–5.*

㉑ **Kōloa.** Kaua'i's first sugar mill began operating here in 1835. You can see the remains of its old stone smokestack on the right side of the road. A sculpture depicting the various ethnic groups that made their mark on the sugar industry on Kaua'i sits on a small green nearby. The main street of Kōloa is lined with old buildings that have been preserved to house expensive boutiques, an old general store, and a selection of restaurants. Placards outside each building describe its original tenants and tell something about how life was lived in the old mill town. ⊠ *Hwy. 520.*

NEED A   An open-air establishment called **Kōloa Broiler** (⊠ Old Kōloa Rd.,
BREAK?   Kōloa, ☎ 808/742–9122), concocts the best mai tai cocktail on the is-

land. The left side of the restaurant is the bar, a rustic wood-panel room. Sit by one of the huge open windows if you can, and watch the world go by as you recap the day's events. When you're ready for dinner, you can cook your own top sirloin, fresh fish, ribs, or chicken on the open grill in the adjacent dining room.

★ ⓐ **Līhu'e.** The commercial and political center of Kaua'i County, which includes the islands of Kaua'i and Ni'ihau, Līhu'e is the home of the island's major airport and harbor. Its main thoroughfare, Rice Street, offers a short pleasant stroll from the War Memorial and Convention Hall (Rice and Hardy Sts.), past government offices, to the Līhu'e Shopping Center (Rice St. and Hwy. 50). ✉ *Hwys. 56 and 50.*

NEED A BREAK? If you're looking for a down-home Kaua'i-style meal or a filling snack, stop by **Hamura Saimin** (✉ 2956 Kress St., Līhu'e, ☎ 808/245–3271), a ramshackle diner with booths and counter seating. Each day the Hiraoka family serves about 1,000 orders of saimin, which is a steaming bowl of broth and noodles with varying garnishes (fish cake, wonton, slices of scrambled egg, and roast pork are the most popular). This little landmark also turns out tasty chicken and beef grilled on barbecue sticks, as well as *liliko'i* (passion fruit) chiffon pie.

⓲ **Menehune Fishpond.** Secretive little workers are said to have built these intricate walls, 4 ft thick and 5 ft high, for a princess and prince. Today the walls of this ancient aquaculture structure, also known as *'alekoko,* still contain placid waters where mullet thrive and kayakers enjoy blissful serenity. ✉ *Hulemalu Rd., Niumalu.*

⓱ **Nāwiliwili.** At Kaua'i's major port, a host of fishing and recreational boats come and go, as well as tour boats that offer snorkeling and sightseeing adventures along the coast. This is a port of call for container ships, U.S. Navy vessels, and the American Hawai'i Cruise line. Nearby there's protected swimming and sunbathing at **Kalapakī Beach** (☞ Beaches, *below*). ✉ *Makai end of Wa'apā Rd., Līhu'e.*

⓽ **Po'ipū.** The major resort town of the south shore remains irrepressibly sunny despite the shadowy hulk of an empty hotel looming eerily on the beach. Although the Stouffer Waiohai resort has not reopened since Hurricane Iniki blew through in 1992, the Sheraton Kaua'i Resort and a half dozen condominiums, including Kiahuna Plantation, rim the beach's golden sands. Boogie-boarders, swimmers, and families enjoy the good-time atmosphere. ✉ *Hwy. 520.*

⓴ **Prince Kūhiō Park.** The park behind the Prince Kūhiō condominium honors the birthplace of one of Hawai'i's most beloved congressional representatives, Prince Jonah Kūhiō Kalaniana'ole, a man who might have become Hawai'i's king if Queen Lili'uokalani had not been overthrown in 1893. ✉ *Lāwa'i Rd., Po'ipū.*

★ ㉕ **Spouting Horn.** Kaua'i's natural wonders never cease. This one is a waterspout that shoots up like Old Faithful out of an ancient lava tube. Follow the paved walkways around this area, because the rocks are slippery and people have been known to fall in. Vendors display their wares under the shade of canopied kiosks at Spouting Horn. Aside from inexpensive souvenirs and costume jewelry, you'll find one of the best selections of rare and treasured Ni'ihau shell necklaces. When purchasing a Ni'ihau shell lei, ask for a certificate of authenticity and an address in case you need to reorder or repair your purchase at a later date. ✉ *Lāwa'i Bay, Po'ipū.*

The Western Route and Kōke'e

Heading west along Kaua'i's south shore, you'll pass through one former plantation town after the next, each with its own story to tell: Hanapēpē, whose salt ponds have been harvested since ancient times; Ft. Elisabeth, from which an enterprising Russian tried to take over the island in the early 1800s; and Waimea, home of the Menehune Ditch, supposedly built by the legendary race of little people.

From Waimea you can drive up along the rim of magnificent Waimea Canyon to reach the crisp, cool climate of Kōke'e, 3,000 ft above sea level. Here you'll discover another facet of this ancient island: Sequoia forests and swamp lands provide a home to remarkable indigenous birds and plants, while a mountain lodge welcomes guests with old-style warmth and hospitality.

From the Burns Field airstrip here on the western side of the island, helicopter tours depart for the "Forbidden Isle" of Ni'ihau and snorkeling excursions can be planned from Port Allen harbor. By land, sea, or air, this part of Kaua'i is worth exploring.

A Good Drive

The west side of the island offers a look at the sleepiest—as well as the most dramatic—sections of Kaua'i. Begin this tour by heading west on Highway 50 out of Līhu'e. The first town you come to is called Lāwa'i. This tiny town once housed the Kaua'i Pineapple Cannery. In its wake, Lāwa'i has emerged as a significant producer of tropical fruits and plants. Turn left on Kōloa Road, then take the right fork down Ha'ilima Road to the **National Tropical Botanical Gardens** ㉖, a botanical research center and showcase for a multitude of rare and endangered plant species. The next town along Highway 50 is Kalāheo. Turn left on Pāpālina Road to make the climb to **Kukui O Lono Park** ㉗, where you can bliss out on Japanese gardens and spectacular scenic vistas before you depart.

Just past Kalāheo on Highway 50, look on your right for macadamia nut groves and a Hawaiian-warrior marker indicating **'Olu Pua Gardens** ㉘. This plantation estate is another showplace for exotic tropical flora. Farther along Highway 50 you'll pass acres of shiny-leaf coffee trees; on your right you'll see a sign indicating the **Hanapēpē Valley and Canyon Lookout** ㉙. This dramatic divide holds a place in Hawaiian history as the site of Kaua'i's last battle in 1824.

Hanapēpē ㉚, the "Biggest Little Town on Kaua'i," lies just west of the lookout. At the fork turn right to drive down Hanapēpē's dusty main street, or angle left and follow Highway 50 past the town, then turn makai on Lele Road to reach **Salt Pond Beach Park** ㉛. Early Hawaiians harvested salt here. Nearby is Burns Field, Kaua'i's first airfield and the departure point for flightseeing adventures and helicopter trips to Ni'ihau. It's a taste of a more primitive Hawai'i (☞ Special-Interest Tours *in* Kaua'i A to Z, *below*). Just around the bend and across the bay from the airstrip is Port Allen Harbor, the shipping center for the west side of the island, and home base for snorkeling excursions from September to May (☞ Snorkeling *in* Outdoor Activities and Sports, *below*).

Head west again on Highway 50 and look on the makai side of the road for the Hawaiian-warrior marker to **Ft. Elisabeth** ㉜. The ruins of this stone fort are testament to a time when Imperial Russia had designs on conquering the Islands. Cross the Waimea River Bridge and take your first right on Menehune Road, which leads you 2½ mi up Waimea Valley to **Menehune Ditch** ㉝, a stone aqueduct carved with the mysterious markings of an earlier era. As you enter **Waimea** ㉞ you might spot the statue commemorating Captain Cook's arrival here in 1778. The remains of a missionary church built here in 1846 will hold your interest as well.

Highway 50 meanders through the sugar town of Kekaha. Eventually it passes the Pacific Missile Range Facility. Take the right fork after you pass the missile range and you can follow Highway 50 to where it ends near Polihale State Park. The park is accessible only by a dirt road through sugarcane fields; during or after heavy rain, you might want to skip it. When the road is passable, though, it's worth a visit to this immense stretch of glistening golden sand fringed by dramatic mountains.

As you return to Līhu'e you have two choices for visiting **Waimea Canyon** ㉟, the "Grand Canyon of the Pacific." The main route, Kōke'e Road (Hwy. 550), makes a steep climb from Kekaha. The other, more scenic option is Waimea Canyon Drive, which you pick up near the western edge of Waimea, by the church. It's narrow but well-paved and climbs quickly for immediate views of the town and ocean below. A few miles up, the roads converge and continue the steep ascent; spectacular birds-eye views out over the canyon encompass you. Be sure to stop at the Pu'u-ka-Pele and Pu'u-hinahina lookouts for the most appealing vistas. As the road rises to 4,000 ft, it passes through Kōke'e State Park with its cozy Kōke'e Lodge. The road out of the park leads past the NASA Tracking Station.

Waimea Canyon Drive ends 4 mi above the park at the **Kalalau Lookout** ㊱. This is the beginning of a beautiful hiking trail that passes Pu'u-o-Kila Lookout. Be sure to bring a jacket for the cool weather here.

TIMING

The 36-mi drive from Līhu'e to Waimea Canyon takes about 90 minutes with no stops for botanical gardens, beaches, or quaint little towns. If you want to spend a half day or more hiking in the canyon, you might save south-shore sightseeing for another day. Save at least a half day for your air adventure over to Ni'ihau. In winter be prepared for chilly temperatures in the heights above the canyon, especially in the early morning.

Sights to See

★ ㉜ **Ft. Elisabeth.** The ruins of this stone fort, built in 1816 by an agent of the Imperial Russian government named Anton Scheffer, are reminders of the days when Scheffer tried to conquer the island for his homeland . . . and the czar! King Kaumuali'i eventually chased the foreigner off the island. The crumbling walls of the fort, at the ocean's edge, cover about an acre and are overgrown with brush. ⊠ *Hwy. 50, Waimea.*

㉚ **Hanapēpē.** This quiet farming town on the south coast supplies Kaua'i with much of its produce—and all the Islands with Lappert's ice cream. **Hanapēpē Road** had a featured role (as an Australian town) in the television miniseries *The Thorn Birds*. Today, shops sell koa wood and other crafts; talented artist James Hoyle has his art gallery here. **Burns Field,** Kaua'i's first airfield and now the base of operations for several helicopter companies, is nearby. Just to the east is **Port Allen** harbor, still the shipping center for the west side of Kaua'i and headquarters of the McBryde Company, which has replaced its cane fields with coffee trees. If you want further proof that Hanapēpē was once a power center, check out **'Ele'ele Shopping Center** on Lele Road. It was the first "modern" shopping center built on Kaua'i. ⊠ *Hwy. 50, Hanapēpē.*

NEED A
BREAK?

You can sit at the spiffy black-and-white bar for a quick espresso or relax at one of five tables while you snack on garden burgers, Caesar salads, soup, croissants, or calzone at **Hanapēpē Bookstore Café** (⊠ 3830 Hanapēpē Rd., Hanapēpē, ☎ 808/335–5011). The bookshop is filled with Hawaiian cards, gifts, and publications. There's a vegetarian breakfast and lunch menu, with coffee and pastries served until 3. Dinner, with live music by local guitarists, is served Thursday–Saturday 6–9.

㉙ Hanapēpē Valley and Canyon Lookout. This dramatic divide once housed a thriving Hawaiian community, and some remains of its taro patches still exist. Hanapēpē is a historic canyon; it's the site of Kaua'i's last battle led in 1824 by Humehume, son of the island's King Kaumuali'i. ⊠ *Hwy. 50.*

★ ㊱ **Kalalau Lookout.** Kalalau Lookout, near the end of the road high above Waimea Canyon, is the beginning of a beautiful hiking trail that also passes **Pu'u-o-Kila Lookout.** On a clear day at either lookout you can gaze right down into the gaping valley at sawtooth ridges and waterfalls. But stick around for a few minutes if clouds are obscuring the view—winds are strong up here and just might blow away the clouds so you can snap a photo. If you turn your back to the valley and look to the northwest, you might pick out the shining sands of Kalalau Beach, gleaming like a tiny golden thread against the vast blue Pacific. ⊠ *Waimea Canyon Dr., 4 mi north of Kōke'e State Park.*

㉗ **Kukui o Lono Park.** Translated "light of the god Lono," Kukui o Lono has serene Japanese gardens, and a display of significant Hawaiian stones—an anchor stone and salt pan—collected by Walter McBryde, the sugar plantation heir who founded the estate in the 1900s. Spectacular panoramic views make this one of Kaua'i's most scenic park areas and an ideal picnic spot. There is also a golf course spread across a 9-acre expanse. ⊠ *Pāpālina Rd., Kalāheō.* ⊡ *Free.* ☉ *Daily 6–6.*

㉝ **Menehune Ditch.** Archaeologists claim that this aqueduct was built before the first Hawaiians lived on Kaua'i, and it is therefore attributed to the industrious hands of the tiny Menehune. The way the flanged and fitted cut-stone bricks are stacked and assembled indicates a knowledge of construction that is foreign to Hawai'i, and the ditch is inscribed with mysterious markings. Until someone comes up with a better suggestion, the Menehune retain the credit for this engineering feat. ⊠ *Menehune Rd., Waimea Valley.*

㉖ **National Tropical Botanical Gardens.** A good example of a tropical green thumb can be found at this 186-acre scientific research center (Lawa'i Gardens) and 100-acre estate property (Allerton Gardens) for botany and horticulture. The visitor center showcases 2,600 different plant species, some of them rare and endangered Hawaiian varieties. There's a gift shop, too. The grounds are open only for visitors with reservations for the guided 2½-hour walking tour. ⊠ *Ha'ilima Rd., Lāwa'i; tour departs from far west end of Spouting Horn parking lot, Po'ipū,* ☎ *808/332–7361.* ⊡ *$25.* ☉ *Tours Tues.–Sat. at 9, 11:30, and 2.*

NEED A
BREAK?

Fourteen kinds of hot dogs, burgers made with such fresh fish as mahimahi, and a big condiment bar make **Mustard's Last Stand** (⊠ Corner of Hwy. 50 and Old Kōloa Rd., Lāwa'i, ☎ 808/332–7245) an appropriate, if not essential, snack-time stop while you're touring the south side of the island. After you eat, the kids can play a round on the miniature-golf course, while mom shops for deals in the adjacent Old Hawaiian Trading Company, which sells souvenirs including eel-skin leather items and Ni'ihau shell leis.

㉘ **'Olu Pua Gardens.** One of Kaua'i's fine botanical showcases, 12-acre *'Olu Pua* ("floral serenity") is a 1931 plantation estate. Visiting is only via a guided tour, which meanders down shaded paths past exotic flowers and plants and a pond fashioned in the shape of a hibiscus blossom. ✉ *Hwy. 50, Kalāheo,* ☎ *808/332–8182.* ✍ *$12.* ☉ *Gift shop daily 9–4, guided 1-hr tour 9:30–2:30.*

㉛ **Salt Pond Beach Park.** Here you can see how the Hawaiians harvested salt for almost 200 years. They let the sun evaporate the sea water in mud-lined drying beds, then gathered the salt left behind. This is a safe area for swimming. ✉ *Lele Rd., Hanapēpē.*

㉞ **Waimea.** This is the town that first welcomed Captain James Cook to the Sandwich Islands in 1778. An easy-to-miss monument on the mauka side of the road commemorates his landfall, as does a statue near the entry to town. Waimea was also the place where Kaua'i's King Kaumuali'i ceded his island to the unifying efforts of King Kamehameha. Waimea played host to the first missionaries on the island, and you can still see what's left of their old **Waimea Christian Hawaiian and Foreign Church** on Mākeke Road. Constructed in 1846, the church was made of huge timbers brought down from the mountains 8 mi away, as well as limestone blocks from a nearby quarry. The church suffered severe damage from Hurricane 'Iniki, but the beautiful stonework of its front and side walls is well worth a photo. ✉ *Hwy. 50.*

★ **㉟** **Waimea Canyon.** Created by an ancient fault in the earth's crust, the canyon has been eroding over the centuries due to weather, wind, and the water of its rivers and streams. "The Grand Canyon of the Pacific" is 3,600 ft deep, 2 mi wide, and 10 mi long. Its deep reds, greens, and browns are ever-changing in the light. Be sure to allow time to soak up the views from **Pu'u-ka-Pele** and **Pu'u-hinahina** lookouts.

Kōke'e State Park, at the north end of Waimea Canyon, is 4,000 ft above sea level. Here the air is cool and crisp, and the vegetation turns to evergreens and ferns. This 4,345-acre wilderness park is full of wild fruit, heady flowers, and colorful rare birds that make their home in these forests. A 45-mi network of hiking trails takes you to some of Kaua'i's most remote places. Before you set off, ask about trail conditions. ✉ *Hwy. 550 (contact Division of State Parks, Box 1671, Līhu'e 96766),* ☎ *808/335–5871.*

Kōke'e Natural History Museum in the park holds displays of plants, native birds and other wildlife, as well as a weather exhibit that describes the formation of hurricanes. ✉ *Koke'e State Park, 96766,* ☎ *808/335–9975,* ℻ *808/335–6131.* ✍ *$1 donation.* ☉ *Daily 10–4.*

NEED A BREAK? Treat yourself to a cup of coffee or a sandwich at **Kōke'e Lodge** (✉ Waimea Canyon Dr., Kōke'e State Park, ☎ 808/335–6061), a comfortably rustic mountaintop inn. With temperatures almost always nippy outside, the fireplace is usually going. Peruse the gift shop for T-shirts, postcards, or Kōke'e memorabilia.

BEACHES

The waters that hug the island are clean, clear, and inviting, but be careful to go in only where it's safe. All beaches on Kaua'i are free and open to the public, and none has a phone number. For information about beaches around the island, call the **County Department of Parks and Recreation** (☎ 808/241–6670) and the **State Department of Land and Natural Resources** (☎ 808/241–3446).

The list of beaches below starts from the western end of Highway 50 and goes counterclockwise around the island to the end of the road on the north shore.

Polihale Beach Park. This magnificent stretch of sand, flanked by impressive sea cliffs, stretches from the town of Kekaha to end miles away within 140-acre Polihale Sate Park. The beach is beautiful for sunbathing, beachcombing, and surfcasting, but the rip currents are often too rough for swimming. Locals dune buggy here on the weekends. Polihale has no lifeguards. ⊠ *Drive to end of Hwy. 50 and turn left at Hawaiian-warrior marker onto dirt road, which leads several mi through sugarcane fields; turn left at small national park sign.*

Salt Pond Beach Park. A protected bay here is particularly safe for swimmers, so this is a real family spot. There are picnic tables under covered pavilions, showers, rest rooms, and a large grassy lawn. Camping is allowed. ⊠ *Follow Lele Rd., makai off Hwy. 50 in Hanapēpē.*

Kekaha Beach Park. Stretching for miles along the south shore, this strip of sand brings to mind the long beaches of southern California. Dune buggying is popular here; if you don't like the noise, stay away. There are no lifeguards, rest rooms, or showers. ⊠ *Hwy. 50 west of Kekaha.*

Po'ipū Beach Park. A prime bodysurfing and sunbathing spot, Po'ipū Beach has clean white sand. It's a fun place for a picnic or a barbecue under the palm trees. There are lifeguards, showers, rest rooms, and a take-out deli across the street. A walk on the beach takes strollers past a half dozen condominiums to the Sheraton Kaua'i Resort, which has an inviting cocktail lounge overlooking the beach—a cool respite from the hot sun. ⊠ *Po'ipū Rd. on south shore, opposite Ho'ōne and Pane Rds.*

Brennecke's Beach. A steady stream of small- to medium-size waves makes this a bodysurfer's heaven. Waves are bigger here in summer than in winter. Showers, rest rooms, and lifeguards are on hand, and there are several food stands nearby. ⊠ *Po'ipū Rd. on south shore.*

Keoneloa, or Shipwreck Beach. Nicknamed Shipwreck Beach for an old wooden boat that wrecked on the 2-mi stretch of sand fronting the Hyatt Regency Po'ipū, this beach is popular with surfcasters who fish from Makawehi Point on the east side of the beach. Sea turtles and monk seals like the coves, but strong rip currents and shore break can make swimming dangerous for human water lovers. Showers, rest rooms, and a walkway can be found along the dunes. ⊠ *Turn into Hyatt Regency Po'ipū Resort, drive along the east side of the hotel, turn right and park.*

Kalapakī Beach. This sheltered bay is ideal for swimming, surfing, and windsurfing in the small waves. It fronts the Kaua'i Marriott Resort. There are rest rooms, lifeguards, showers, and food and drink nearby. ⊠ *Nāwiliwili off Wapa'a Rd., which runs from Līhu'e.*

Lydgate State Park. Depending on the wind, this is a good spot for family picnicking and swimming, with a swimming area protected by a rock wall and a covered pavilion. Any time of year it's a nice place for beachcombing and reflecting on the days when this was a Hawaiian city of refuge. Rest rooms and showers are available, and there's a large playground for kids. ⊠ *Before mouth of Wailua River turn makai off Hwy. 56 onto Lehu Dr. and left onto Nalu Rd.*

Anahola Beach Park. This quiet stretch of sand edged by a grassy park on the east shore offers calm waters for swimming and snorkeling. The Makalena Mountains are your backdrop here. There are rest rooms and showers. ⊠ *After 13-mi marker on Hwy. 56 turn makai on Anahola Rd.*

ʻAnini Beach County Park. Safest of the north shore beaches, this 3-mi golden beach lies beside a reef-protected blue lagoon, making it ideal for beginning windsurfers, snorkelers, and swimmers. A beachside park, a polo field, campground, public rest rooms, showers, grills, and picnic tables keep families happy year round. ✉ *Turn makai off Hwy. 56 onto Kalihi Wai Rd. on Hanalei side of Kalihi Wai Bridge; road angles left along beach onto ʻAnini Rd.*

Hanalei Beach Park. With views of Nā Pali Coast and shady trees over picnic tables, this is beach bum heaven. But swimming here can be treacherous, stay near the old pier where the water is a bit calmer. There are rest rooms and showers. ✉ *In Hanalei, turn makai at Aku Rd. and right at dead-end.*

Lumahaʻi Beach. Known for its striking natural beauty, Lumahaʻi is flanked by high mountains and lava rocks. In the movie *South Pacific,* this is where Mitzi Gaynor sang "I'm Gonna Wash That Man Right Outta My Hair." Swimming is good only in summer. There are no lifeguards, showers, or rest rooms. ✉ *On winding section of Hwy. 56 west of Hanalei between Mile Markers 4 and 5; park on makai side of road and walk down a steep path to the beach.*

Tunnels Beach. Kauaʻi's best-protected, big, deep lagoon for swimming and snorkeling is rimmed by a beach shaded with ironwood trees. There are no lifeguards, showers, or rest rooms. ✉ *⅒ mi past Mile Marker 8 on Hwy. 56; turn makai onto dirt road that runs through grove of trees; if parking lot is packed, continue ½ mi to Haʻena Beach Park and walk back.*

Hāʻena Beach Park. This beach on Maniniholo Bay is good for swimming when the surf is down, which means summertime. There are rest rooms, showers, camping facilities, picnic tables, and food wagons. ✉ *On north shore near end of Hwy. 56 across from lava-tube sea caves.*

Keʻe Beach. In summer this is a fine swimming beach, with a reef just made for snorkeling. In winter, big waves wash away the sand, so stay out of the water and enjoy the views of the Nā Pali Coast. This is where the Kalalau Trail begins. Changing facilities are available, as are showers and rest rooms. ✉ *Northern end of Hwy. 56, 7 mi from Hanale.*

Hanakāpīʻai Beach. This crescent of beach changes length and width throughout the year as fierce winter waves rob the shoreline of sand and summer's calm returns it. Be very careful swimming here in summer, and don't even think of going in during the winter swells. Hike an additional 2 mi inland beside the adjacent stream and you'll find Hanakāpīʻai Falls, which splashes into a freshwater pool perfect for shutterbugs or a cool dip. ✉ *Mi 2 of Kalalau Trail, which begins near Keʻe beach, at northern end of Hwy. 56.*

DINING

In addition to preparing all kinds of ethnic dishes, a growing contingent of independent restaurateurs experiments with Hawaiʻi Regional cuisine, using the best produce grown on native soil. On Kauaʻi there is an especially heavy emphasis on the fruits from its extensive groves. Thanks to the abundance of fish in the waters surrounding Kauaʻi, the catch of the day is always well worth trying.

Restaurants are open daily unless otherwise noted. Reservations are rarely required on Kauaʻi, but it's never a mistake to avoid disappointment and call ahead. For an explanation of price categories, *see* On the Road with Fodor's at the beginning of the book.

The East Coast

American

$ ✕ **Eggbert's.** If you are big on breakfasts, try indoor or outdoor dining at Eggbert's, in the Coconut Marketplace. It's a great spot for omelets, banana pancakes, and eggs Benedict—you can even create your own Benedicts, adding mushrooms, spinach, or other meats and veggies as you please. Such kid-size meals as "pigs in a blanket" keep down the costs of family outings here. ⊠ *Coconut Marketplace, Kapa`a,* ☎ *808/ 822–3787. MC, V.*

Japanese

$$ ✕ **Restaurant Kintaro.** This pretty restaurant with sliding shoji-screen doors and Asian prints on the walls serves complete sukiyaki dinners in an iron pot and tempura combinations that use fresh local fish. *Teppan* (grilled) dinners include tender hibachi shrimp sautéed in lemon butter and served with bean sprouts and steamed rice. Dinners come with chilled buckwheat noodles, miso soup, rice, Japanese pickles, and tea. A sushi bar is also on hand. ⊠ *4-370 Kūhiō Hwy., Kapa`a,* ☎ *808/ 822–3341. AE, D, DC, MC, V. Closed Sun. No lunch.*

Natural Foods

$ ✕ **Papaya's.** Courtyard dining is the draw at this tidy natural foods restaurant under the whale tower at Kaua`i Village. Sit beneath a pretty blue umbrella and enjoy grilled fish, a vegetarian burger, pasta with pesto, or Thai and Mexican fare. Take-out is also available. ⊠ *Kaua`i Village Shopping Center, Hwy. 56, Kapa`a,* ☎ *808/823–0190. MC, V. Closed Sun.*

Pacific Rim

$$$ ✕ **A Pacific Cafe.** With its East-meets-West atmosphere and cutting-
★ edge cuisine, chef Jean-Marie Josselin's restaurant has won high acclaim and numerous awards: He combines a love of Asian cooking with a commitment to fresh, homegrown ingredients. The menu changes daily. In true nouvelle fashion he might present grilled moonfish with black-olive polenta, sundried tomatoes, pancetta, and shiitake mushrooms; or lamb with a cabernet-hoisin sauce and fried grated potatoes. The macadamia nut torte comes topped with toasted coconut and the crème brûlée, a huge portion served in a pastry shell, is deliciously creamy. ⊠ *Kaua`i Village Shopping Center, Hwy. 56, Kapa`a,* ☎ *808/822–0013. AE, D, DC, MC, V.* ◷ *No lunch.*

$$ ✕ **Postcards Cafe.** In what was once an old house in the rice fields, this "Old Hawai`i" restaurant is decorated with vintage photos and postcards to capture the mood of an earlier era, but the food is deliciously up-to-date. Smoothies and salads made with organic fruits and vegetables, vegan dishes, Thai coconut curry, taro fritters, and fish tacos highlight a varied menu that emphasizes local seafood. Desserts, often made with macadamia nuts and in-season fruits, have an island flavor. Brunch is great but service can be slow. ⊠ *5-5075A Kuhiō Hwy.,* ☎ *808/826–1191. AE, MC, V.*

Steak and Seafood

$$ ✕ **Kapa`a Fish & Chowder House.** The gray-and-blue color scheme of this open-air restaurant is punctuated by thick hanging ferns and nautical memorabilia. Fish selections offered daily are served sautéed or broiled with a variety of sauces. Try a pot of steamed Pacific shrimp served with drawn butter or the baked tiger prawns stuffed with shrimp and crab; the seafood fettuccine is also recommended. Ask for a table in the Garden Room, a veritable Eden. ⊠ *4-1639 Kūhiō Hwy., Kapa`a,* ☎ *808/822–7488. AE, D, MC, V.* ◷ *No lunch.*

$–$$ ✕ **Bull Shed.** The A-frame design of this popular restaurant imparts a distinctly rustic feel, but the interior is brightened with light-color walls and unobstructed ocean views. Although it is known especially for prime rib, teriyaki sirloin, and fresh fish, the pasta and Alaskan king crab dishes are also good. Entrées come with salad from a rather basic salad bar and bread, but in true local style, plates are light on vegetables. ✉ *796 Kūhiō Ave., Kapa'a,* ☎ *808/822–3791. AE, D, DC, MC, V.* ◷ *No lunch.*

$–$$ ✕ **Wailua Marina Restaurant.** Dockside views of boats chugging along the Wailua River make this an ideal stop before or after a trip to the Fern Grotto. An open-air dining lānai is perched right on the water, next to shores where ancient Hawaiian communities once stood. For the large number of people it serves, the restaurant has a surprisingly thoughtful menu. For instance, baked stuffed chicken is cooked in plum sauce and served with a lobster salad. The menu includes a good choice of steak and fresh seafood dishes. Complimentary transportation is available from Wailua-area hotels and condos in the evenings. ✉ *Wailua River State Park, Wailua Rd., Wailua,* ☎ *808/822–4311. AE, DC, MC, V. Closed Mon.*

Thai

$–$$ ✕ **Mema, Thai Chinese Cuisine.** Such menu items as broccoli with oyster sauce and cashew chicken reveal their Chinese origins, but the emphasis in this attractive restaurant is on Thai dishes. A host of curries—red, green, yellow, and house—made with coconut milk and kaffir lime leaves run from mild to mayhem in spiciness. You have a choice of chicken, beef, pork, or shrimp with several side dishes, such as stir-fried eggplant with fresh basil. Orchids, torch ginger, and Asian memorabilia highlight a pretty-in-peach interior. ✉ *Wailua Shopping Plaza, 4-361 Kuhio Hwy., Kapa'a,* ☎ *808/823–0899. AE, D, DC, MC, V.*

$ ✕ **King and I.** Delicate sprays of purple orchids, colorful paintings, and Asian artifacts decorate this cozy Thai restaurant. Spring rolls come with a tangy sauce and garnishes of mint, cucumbers, and peanuts. For a sweet-spicy treat try the green papaya salad. If you want to taste several dishes, order dinner for two; it comes with spring rolls, green papaya salad, broccoli beef, yellow curry chicken, rice, tea, and dessert. A vegetarian menu is available, and everything tastes even better when accompanied by Thai beer. ✉ *Waipouli Plaza, 4-901 Kūhiō Hwy., Kapa'a,* ☎ *808/822–1642. AE, D, DC, MC, V.* ◷ *No lunch weekends.*

The North Coast

American

$–$$ ✕ **Zelos Beach House.** Call the menu eclectic with its American-Italian-Thai-Creole leanings—unlike the strictly South Pacific decor in this "beach blanket bingo goes to the South Seas" kind of place. A bamboo bar, *lau hala* (pandanus leaf) mats on the walls, a kayak overhead, and Tahitian-print bar stools add to the fun—and the food is good. Burgers, burritos, and jambalaya are served on an open-air deck. For dinner, large salads, fresh fish, pasta, steaks, and chicken pesto tortellini fill the bill. ✉ *5-5156 Kūhiō Hwy., Hanalei,* ☎ *808/826–9700. MC, V.*

$ ✕ **Hanalei Gourmet.** A casual north-shore atmosphere has made this a popular hangout. There's bar and table seating and big open windows. The TV over the bar is usually tuned to sports and music programs, but the clientele is generally too busy eating and talking to watch. Breakfasts include lox and bagels with cream cheese, and *huevos Santa Cruz* (scrambled eggs with diced tomatoes, chilies, cheese, and enchilada sauce on a flour tortilla). Lunch and dinner menus feature hot sandwiches, burgers, salads, and big *pūpū* (appetizer) platters. There's live music of one sort or another every night. ✉ *5-5161 Kūhiō Hwy., across from Ching Young Center, Hanalei,* ☎ *808/826–2524. D, MC, V.*

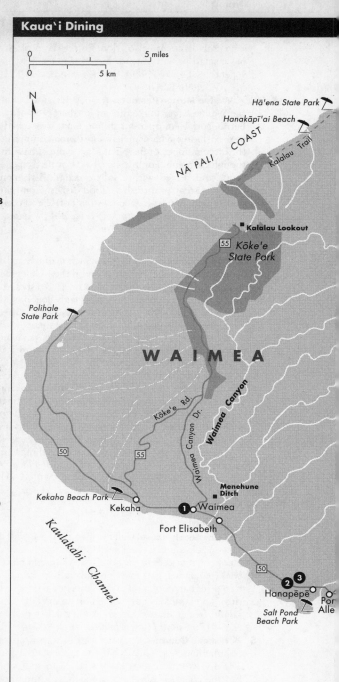

Kaua'i Dining

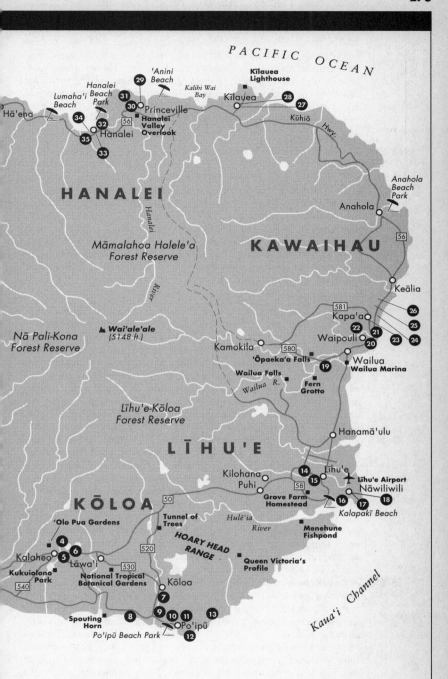

PACIFIC OCEAN

'Anini Beach

Kīlauea Lighthouse

Lumaha'i Beach

Hanalei Beach Park

Kalihi Wai Bay

Kīlauea

Hā'ena

Princeville

Hanalei Valley Overlook

Hanalei

56

Kūhiō Hwy.

Anahola Beach Park

Anahola

HANALEI

Hanalei River

KAWAIHAU

56

Māmalahoa Hale'ea Forest Reserve

Keālia

Nā Pali-Kona Forest Reserve

▲ Wai'ale'ale (5148 ft.)

Kamokila

581

Kapa'a

Waipouli

580

'Ōpaeka'a Falls

Wailua

Wailua Marina

Wailua Falls

Fern Grotto

Wailua R.

Līhu'e-Kōloa Forest Reserve

Hanamā'ulu

LĪHU'E

Kilohana

Puhi

Līhu'e

Līhu'e Airport

Nāwiliwili

'Olo Pua Gardens

Grove Farm Homestead

Kalapakī Beach

KŌLOA

50

Tunnel of Trees

Hule'ia River

Menehune Fishpond

Kalaheo

Lāwa'i

520

HOARY HEAD RANGE

Queen Victoria's Profile

Kukuiolono Park

540

530

National Tropical Botanical Gardens

Kōloa

Spouting Horn

Po'ipū

Po'ipū Beach Park

Kaua'i Channel

$ ✕ **Old Hanalei Coffee Company.** In a restored 1920s home, this green-and-white emporium provides a wake-up call with its specialty coffees. Also on hand are light meals—spinach and basil quiche, salad with orange-basil dressing, and granola with yogurt. Pastries include German chocolate cake, and the fresh fruit smoothie of the day is reliably yummy. Visits here can be habit-forming; there's almost nothing on the menu for more than $5. Relax on the pretty white porch, sip your cappuccino, and watch the Hanalei scene drift by. ✉ *5-5183 Kūhiō Hwy., across from Ching Young Center, Hanalei,* ☎ *808/826–6717. No credit cards.*

Continental

$$–$$$ ✕ **Cafe Hanalei and Terrace.** Indoor and outdoor tables take full advantage of glorious views of Hanalei Bay and the peak popularly
★ known as Bali Hai. The Sunday brunch and daily breakfast buffet are a feast of to-order omelets, crepes, and fresh fruit, but the vanilla Belgian waffles and smoked peppered salmon with cream cheese, capers, and bagels are equally tasty. Luncheon selections include Japanese specialties in addition to lobster bisque, Cobb salad, and super sandwiches. For dinner try steamed '*ōpakapaka* (snapper) with ginger, cilantro, and mushrooms, or sample Friday night's seafood buffet. ✉ *Princeville Hotel, Princeville Resort,* ☎ *808/826–9644. Reservations essential. AE, D, DC, MC, V.*

Italian

$$$ ✕ **La Cascata.** Terra-cotta floors, hand-painted murals, and trompe l'oeil paintings give La Cascata an Italian villa flair and picture windows offer dazzling views of Hanalei Bay. The menu emphasizes light sauces; plenty of pastas; plus fresh seafood, beef, and lamb. Begin with a potato-crusted crab cake with red pepper aioli, then try cioppino with lobster, shrimp, and scallops in a spicy fennel tomato broth, or grilled island tuna with risotto-fried capellini pasta. Top it off with tiramisu, an airy coffee-flavor mascarpone pudding with ladyfingers, or savor the day's sorbet selection. ✉ *Princeville Hotel, Princeville Resort,* ☎ *808/826–9644. Reservations essential. AE, D, DC, MC, V.* ☺ *No lunch.*

$$–$$$ ✕ **Café Luna.** In a historic schoolhouse converted into shops and restaurants, Café Luna has indoor and outdoor garden patio dining, an exhibition kitchen, and a good wine selection. For lunch or dinner, individual pizzas from the wood-burning oven come with toppings ranging from tried-and-true pepperoni and black olives to smoked fish, caramelized onion, capers, and béchamel. Polenta with shrimp and '*ahi* (tuna), *ono* (wahoo), and crab bisque are all flavorful starters, and for entrées the seared fresh fish on organic greens with wasabi vinaigrette or shrimp pasta with porcini mushrooms are recommended. Mocha mousse or tiramisu are rich and satisfying desserts. ✉ *Hanalei Center, 5-5161 Kūhiō Hwy., Hanalei,* ☎ *808/826–1177. AE, MC, V.*

$$–$$$ ✕ **Casa di Amici.** Casa di Amici means "house of friends," and with windows that open wide to the balmy air, it feels that way. The menu is broader than Italian/Mediterranean, including French, Thai, Japanese, and Vietnamese touches, but you'll find traditional antipasti (starters), *zuppe* (soup), pasta, *insalata* (salads), and *pietanza maggiore* (main courses). You can mix your favorite pasta with your choice of sauce, including pesto and *salsa arrabiatta* (a spicy tomato sauce with sautéed pancetta and crushed chili pepper), or savor the house scampi. Most entrées can be ordered in "light" or regular portions. There's live piano music Thursday through Saturday evenings. ✉ *2484 Keneke St., at Lighthouse Rd., Kīlauea,* ☎ *808/828–1555. Reservations essential. AE, D, DC, MC, V.*

Mexican

$–$$ ✕ **Roadrunner Bakery and Café.** Casual with a capital "C," the Roadrunner has a counter where you can order fresh-baked taro rolls or bread, in addition to your breakfast, lunch, or dinner. Their huevos rancheros are poached eggs on corn tortillas with tomatillo sauce, beans, cheese, salsa, and guacamole and come with rice and tortillas. Burritos are huge; the filling for the "black dog" is pork, grilled taro, and black beans. Mexican scenes painted on the walls, hanging plants, and ceiling fans, add to the "let-it-all-hang-out" atmosphere. ✉ *2430 Oka St., Kīlauea,* ☎ *808/828–8226. MC, V.*

Steak and Seafood

$$–$$$ ✕ **Bali Hai.** Views of the bay are as memorable as the cuisine at this open-air, tropical restaurant, richly appointed with natural wood. Fresh seafood is particularly good, such as baked mahimahi with a crab-meat crust. Another specialty is Kaua'i onion soup topped with melted provolone cheese and croutons. Lamb, filet mignon, and vegetarian offerings are also on the menu. For breakfast, there are poi pancakes, fried taro, eggs, and griddle fare. In the adjacent Happy Talk Lounge, there's nightly entertainment. ✉ *Hanalei Bay Resort, 5380 Honoiki Rd., Princeville,* ☎ *808/826–6522. AE, D, DC, MC, V.*

$$ ✕ **Chuck's Steak House.** A *paniolo* (cowboy) feeling permeates this split-level eatery, right down to the saddles and blankets that hang from the open-beam ceiling. Barbecue pork ribs, lobster, chicken, and Alaskan king crab are all good, but steak is what Chuck's is known for. Can't make up your mind? They can put steak alongside almost any other entrée on a combination platter for you; salad bar comes with any entrée. If you saved room for dessert, Chuck's special mud pie is a winner, made with coffee ice cream and a chocolate and walnut crust, topped with fudge sauce and whipped cream. ✉ *Princeville Shopping Center, Princeville,* ☎ *808/826–6211. AE, D, DC, MC, V. Closed weekends.*

Līhu'e and Vicinity

American

$–$$ ✕ **JJ's Broiler.** Easy to find, with dining on an open-deck overlooking Kalapakī Bay, this is a nautically and natty place to stop for lunch or dinner. The Caesar salad could use a little spicing up, but thick, crispy French fries, potato skins, burgers, and pastrami and Swiss and club sandwiches are reliable favorites. Dinners—herbed seafood linguini, coconut shrimp—are fancier and come with a salad bar rolled to your table. The house specialty is Slavonic steak, a broiled sliced tenderloin dipped in a buttery wine sauce. There's a shuttle bus from the harbor to take you here—a nice touch for those arriving by sea. ✉ *Anchor Cove, Nāwiliwili,* ☎ *808/246–4422. D, MC, V.*

$ ✕ **Jean-Marie's Pacific Bakery and Grill.** In an old building restored to look like something straight out of Kaua'i's plantation past—shuttered windows, ceiling fans, cement floors—the dining areas on two levels are painted in warm southwestern colors: ochre, clay, and sienna. Go early before the chocolate croissants sell out or you may have to get really decadent with eggs Benedict with smoked ham, herb scones, and orange hollandaise. For lunch chicken Caesar salad, grilled eggplant pasta with basil and tomato sauce, or a four cheese pizza from the wood-burning oven are healthier choices. ✉ *4479 Rice Street, Līhu'e,* ☎ *808/246–0999. MC, V. ☉ No dinner Sun.–Wed.*

Italian

$$ ✕ **Café Portofino.** Dining here affords patrons a panoramic view of mountain, sea, and sky across from Kalapakī Bay. Hint: Tables out on the lānai offer the best views. A northern Italian cuisine includes such fresh pasta dishes as fettuccine in tomato, mushroom, garlic, and herbs. Specialties include rabbit with white wine, black olives, and herbs, and sweetbreads in a cream sauce on a bed of linguine. Italian gelati is made fresh daily. Entertainment is offered Thursday through Saturday evenings. ⊠ *Pacific Ocean Plaza, 3501 Rice St., Nāwiliwili,* ☎ *808/245–2121. AE, D, DC, MC, V.* ☽ *No lunch weekends.*

Mixed Menu

$$–$$$ ✕ **Kukui's Poolside Restaurant and Bar.** An imaginative marriage of Asian, Hawaiian, Mexican, and Continental tastes characterizes the menu at this comfortable restaurant. Open-air tables face the hotel's sprawling pool—a perfect spot to enjoy a lunch or an afternoon snack of *kālua* (roasted) pork quesadillas or Thai chicken pizza. A more formal atmosphere prevails at dinner when the menu features selections with a Pacific Rim twist. Try braised duck breast with hibiscus demiglace and citron marmalade, or a barbecued, frenched rack of lamb with shiitake risotto. At breakfast the temptations are two-fold: a buffet or a full à la carte menu. ⊠ *Kaua'i Marriott Hotel, Līhu'e,* ☎ *808/246–5171. AE, D, DC, MC, V.*

$ ✕ **Dani's Restaurant.** Kaua'i residents frequent this big and bare local eatery, near the Līhu'e Fire Station. Owners Tsutao and Harriet Morioka have created a friendly "come as you are" ambience for breakfast or lunch. Dani's is a good place to try lu'au food without commercial lu'au prices. For instance, you can order Hawaiian-style *laulau* (pork wrapped in ti leaves and steamed) or *kalua* (roasted) pig and rice. Other island-style dishes include Japanese-prepared *tonkatsu* (pork cutlet) and teriyaki beef, or an all-American New York steak. ⊠ *4201 Rice St., Līhu'e,* ☎ *808/245–4991. No credit cards. Closed Sun. No dinner.*

Seafood

$$–$$$ ✕ **Duke's Canoe Club.** This popular club is a feast of beautiful native woods, greenery, and Duke Kahanamoku memorabilia, enhanced by the liquid sounds of a waterfall running alongside the staircase that leads from the upstairs dining room to the beachside Barefoot Bar. Prime ribs, seafood coconut curry, smoked marlin, and pasta primavera are available if you like, but the essence of delicious here is in trying the fresh catch of the day—prepared as you like it, from broiled plain, to baked in fresh ginger, orange zest, and macadamia nuts. Hula pie is the star of the dessert menu—with strolling musicians as an accompaniment. Bar menu and lunch available. ⊠ *Kalapakī Beach, Līhu'e,* ☎ *808/246–9599. AE, D, DC, MC, V.*

The South and West Coasts

American

$–$$ ✕ **Camp House Grill.** A simple plantation-style camp house has been transformed into a quaint little restaurant with creaky wooden floors on the road to Waimea Canyon. The food is equally down-home, with hamburgers, cheeseburgers, chicken, pork ribs, and fresh fish aimed to please families. Barbecued specialties include chicken and ribs, and huge sandwiches at lunchtime. Home-style breakfasts are served, and pies are baked fresh daily. As you enter Kalāheo heading west, look for the blue building on the right. ⊠ *Kaumuali'i Hwy. (Hwy. 50), Kalāheo,* ☎ *808/332–9755. MC, V.*

$–$$ ✕ **Tomkats Grille.** This casual drop-in eatery keeps the kids in the family happy during lunch or early dinner hours with tropical ponds and a little waterfall, plus a child's section of the menu geared to young tastes. Adults might pass up the PB&J for chicken marinara, barbecue pork ribs, a burger, or a Reuben accompanied by a glass of wine or a choice of 35 ales, stouts, ports, and lagers. Plenty of Tomkats' Nibblers—buffalo wings, stuffed mushrooms, jalapeño poppers—enliven happy hour from 4 to 6. ⊠ *5402 Kōloa Rd., Kōloa,* ☎ *808/742–8887. DC, MC, V.*

Italian

$$–$$$ ✕ **Dondero's at the Hyatt Regency Kaua'i.** Inlaid marble floors, or- nate green tile work, and ivy and Italianate murals make it difficult to choose between indoor and outdoor dining in this elegant restaurant. Porcini mushroom crepes with Parmesan sauce, a perfectly seasoned Caesar salad, and *spiedini* (skewered lobster, scallops, and shrimp sus- pended over tender pasta pillows of gnocchi) might have sprung from an artist's palate. Flourless chocolate cake or sinfully rich crème brûlée are decadent indulgences to close the meal. ✉ *Hyatt Regency Kaua'i Resort and Spa, 1571 Po'ipu Rd., Kōloa,* ☎ *808/742–1234. AE, D, DC, MC, V.* ☾ *No lunch.*

$$–$$$ ✕ **Pomodoro.** This intimate, family-run restaurant is brightened with pink linens, rattan chairs, and two walls of windows. Begin with prosciutto and melon, then proceed directly to the lasagna (a chef's fa- vorite). Other menu highlights include eggplant or veal parmigiana and scampi in a garlic, caper, and white wine sauce. Freshly baked garlic bread and seasonal vegetables come with each meal. ✉ *Upstairs at Rain- bow Plaza, Kaumuali'i Hwy. (Hwy. 50), Kalāheo,* ☎ *808/332–5945. AE, DC, MC, V.* ☾ *No lunch.*

$$ ✕ **Piatti.** This historic home, once the residence of a plantation manager, now offers Italian food served in a Polynesian atmosphere—a tripartite mix you'll find only in Alohaland. Gardens with torchlit paths, rock work, rich wood interiors, and verandah dining will spark romance. Fresh herbs come from the manager's garden and the island fish might have been caught only hours before reaching your table. Flavors in such dishes as marinated grilled eggplant filled with goat cheese and sun-dried toma- toes, pizza with portobello mushrooms, pancetta and fontana cheese baked in the wood-burning oven, or the tenderest osso bucco served with saf- fron risotto melt on your tongue. ✉ *2253 Po'ipū Rd., Kiahuna Planta- tion, Kōloa,* ☎ *808/742–2216. AE, D, DC, MC, V.* ☾ *No lunch.*

Mexican

$–$$ ✕ **Sinaloa.** Boasting that it serves "the best authentic Mexican food on Kaua'i," Sinaloa is run by *Mexicanos* who know their stuff. Inside the turquoise building, the aqua, yellow, and pink motif is a playful counterpart to simple concrete floors. A fancier dinner room has jun- gle scenes and animals painted on the walls. Starters include a fiesta platter of nachos, quesadilla, guacamole, and sour cream. Headlining the traditional plates are *chili verde* (lean pork sautéed in a tomatillo and chili jalapeño sauce) and *burrito supremo* (giant tortilla filled with rice, beans, cabbage, salsa, sour cream, and guacamole). You can choose Mexican beers or margaritas, and take home a bottle of salsa from the gift shop. ✉ *1-3959 Kaumuali'i Hwy. (Hwy. 50), Hanapēpē,* ☎ *808/335–0006. DC, MC, V.*

Mixed Menu

$$–$$$ ✕ **Roy's Po'ipū Bar & Grill.** Hawai'i's culinary superstar Roy Yamaguchi
★ opened his sleek Kaua'i restaurant in 1994, and it quickly became a mecca for fans of his Euro-Asian Pacific cuisine. Who but Roy would turn smoked duck into *gyoza* (Japanese dumplings) and serve the ap- petizer with star-fruit passion sauce, or team fresh seared *'ōpakapaka* (snapper) with orange shrimp butter and Chinese black bean sauce? There are 15–20 or more specials nightly. Dark chocolate soufflé and volcanic puffed pastry are regulars on the dessert menu. ✉ *Po'ipū Shop- ping Village, 2360 Kiahuna Plantation Dr., Po'ipū Beach,* ☎ *808/ 742–5000. AE, D, DC, MC, V.* ☾ *No lunch.*

$–$$ ✕ **Green Garden.** Hanging and standing plants throughout characterize this aptly named family-run restaurant, a favorite dining spot for Kaua'i residents and visitors since 1948. The Green Garden is very low- key, and the waitresses treat you like longtime friends. The food is no-frills local fare; come here for the atmosphere first and the meals second. Dinner includes some 30 items of local, Asian, and American influence. The seafood special is breaded mahimahi fillet, scallops, oysters, and deep-fried shrimp. The homemade desserts are the best part of a meal here, particularly the liliko'i chiffon pie. ⊠ *Hwy. 50, Hanapēpē,* ☎ *808/335–5422. AE, MC, V. Closed Tues.*

Pacific Rim

$$–$$$ ✕ **The Beach House.** This may be the best ocean view from any restau-
★   rant on the south shore. It's equally possible to get swept away by the cuisine, now that Chef Jean-Marie Josselin (owner of the highly acclaimed A Pacific Café on Kaua'i, Maui, and O'ahu) oversees the kitchen, with chef Linda Yamada on site. The menu changes more often than the artwork on the walls by local artists, but you might find grilled salmon with spinach wonton and shrimp tomato broth; wok-charred, sesame-crusted mahimahi with a ginger-lime beurre blanc; or grilled Black Angus fillet with tumbleweed shrimp and a port-Gorgonzola sauce. ⊠ *5022 Lawai Rd., Kōloa,* ☎ *808/742–1424. AE, D, DC, MC, V.* ✆ *No lunch.*

Pizza

$–$$ ✕ **Pizz 'n Café.** A friendly place in Po'ipū Shopping Village, with red tablecloths and a black-and-white floor, Pizz 'n Café offers sit-down, take-out, and delivery service for lunch and dinner. You can order pizza local-style with Portuguese sausage, nouvelle-style with chicken and shiitake mushrooms, southwestern-style with steak and onions, or topped with "the works." Besides pizza, there's always something on the menu that's sure to suit anyone's taste—from bay shrimp salad, to meatball sandwiches, to penne pasta, to desserts of warm apple calzone with ice cream—and everything is delicious. Wine and beer are served. ⊠ *Po'ipū Shopping Village, 2360 Kiahuna Plantation Dr., Kōloa,* ☎ *808/742–7373. AE, D, MC, V.*

Steak and Seafood

$$–$$$ ✕ **House of Seafood.** Tropical vines wrap themselves around the handsome exposed beams and climb in this restaurant overlooking the Po'ipū Resort tennis courts. Under this establishment's soaring ceilings try island seafood, from 'ahi to *weke* (goatfish). Preparations for nine types of island fish vary nightly. A variety of shellfish is available, including lobster. Caesar salad is made fresh at your table, and all entrées come with fresh vegetables, almond rice pilaf, and freshly baked rolls. Delicious kiwi crepes flambées and bananas Foster garner rave reviews for dessert. ⊠ *Po'ipū Kai Resort, 1941 Po'ipū Rd., Po'ipū,* ☎ *808/742–6433. AE, D, DC, MC, V.* ✆ *No lunch.*

$$–$$$ ✕ **Tidepools.** The Hyatt Regency Kaua'i has three superb restaurants, but this one delivers the most tropical atmosphere. Dine in one of the grass-thatched huts that float on a koi-filled pond, and enjoy views of the romantic torchlit grounds and starry Po'ipū skies. A major advocate of Hawai'i Regional cuisine, which utilizes Kaua'i-grown products, the chef seasons fresh-caught mahimahi with Kaua'i herb butter and bakes it on a slab of Kekaha *kiawe* (mesquite) wood. The chicken breast with mango-papaya relish is a winner, as are the charred 'ahi sashimi, prime rib, lobster, beef satay, and pan-seared swordfish. ⊠ *Hyatt Regency Kaua'i, 1571 Po'ipū Rd., Kōloa,* ☎ *808/742–6260. AE, D, DC, MC, V.* ✆ *No lunch.*

$–$$$ ✕ **Brennecke's Beach Broiler.** Right across from Po'ipū Beach Park, this place has been around for years, and happily so. Large picture windows look out onto palm trees and the ocean, and pretty window boxes filled with petunias further brighten the scene. The restaurant specializes in kiawe-broiled foods—New York steak covered with mushrooms and beef ribs smothered in barbecue sauce. Brennecke's also serves fresh clams, catch of the day, Hawaiian spiny lobster, and gourmet burgers. The well-stocked all-you-can-eat salad bar with bread and chowder is a good deal. ⊠ *Ho'one Rd., Po'ipū,* ☎ *808/742–7588. AE, MC, V.*

$$ ✕ **Kalāheo Steak House.** It's the huge cut of prime rib, the tender top sirloin, the Cornish game hen in spicy herb and citrus marinade, and the succulent Alaskan king crab legs that make locals seek out this restaurant. Ceiling fans stir the air through open wooden louvers in the dark wood-paneled interior of this old building. Dinners are served with salad, rolls, and a choice of rice or baked potato. Rum cake, baked fresh daily, comes with Lappert's ice cream (made at a factory just up the road). Wines range from $8 to $25 a bottle. Children up to 11 can order from a separate low-priced menu. ⊠ *4444 Papalina Rd., Kalāheo, Kaua'i,* ☎ *808/332–9780. D, MC, V. ☺ No lunch.*

$–$$ ✕ **Keoki's Paradise.** Seafood stars at this Po'ipū favorite, styled to resemble a dockside boathouse. Though it sits in a corner of the inland Po'ipū Shopping Village, tinkling streams, lush foliage, and thatched roofs over the bar create an outdoor Polynesian atmosphere. Even the appetizers have an ocean flavor—from sashimi to fisherman's chowder. There is a sampling of beef and pork entrées for committed carnivores, but the day's fresh catch is what brings patrons to Keoki's; choose from a half-dozen preparation styles and sauces, and save room for the hula pie (Oreo cookie crust with ice cream). ⊠ *Po'ipū Shopping Village, Po'ipū Beach,* ☎ *808/742–7534. AE, D, DC, MC, V.*

$–$$ ✕ **Wrangler's Steakhouse.** Wrangler's seems right out of the Wild West with wooden floors and tables, denim upholstered seating, and saddles and a stagecoach on display. Steak—sizzling and prepared with either garlic, capers, peppers, or teriyaki—can be ordered in a he-man 16-ounce size, but if meat is not your thing, opt for the fresh catch, scampi, or one of the Mexican entrées. Local folks love the kau kau tin lunch: soup, rice, beef teriyaki, and shrimp tempura served in a three-tiered tin lunch pail (the kind that sugar plantation workers once carried). A gift shop features local crafts (and sometimes a craftsperson), a deck out back allows open-air dining, and the adjoining Pacific Pizza and Deli (with some of the most imaginative pizzas around) is part of the same family-run complex. ⊠ *98-52 Kaumuali'i Hwy., Waimea,* ☎ *808/338–1218, AE, MC, V. Closed Sun.*

LODGING

Whether you choose to stay at a plush Po'ipū resort or condo, where you can bask all day in the sun; at the posh Princeville Resort, where you can enjoy world-class golfing; or at a Coconut Coast guest house, where you can take advantage of an abundance of nearby shops and restaurants; plan to make advance reservations. Peak months are February and August. When booking your accommodations, ask about such extras as special tennis, golf, honeymoon, and room-and-car packages. For explanations of price categories, *see* On the Road with Fodor's at the beginning of the book.

The East and North Coasts

$$$$ ▣ **Princeville Hotel.** As you walk through the enormous, grand lobby
★ you can't miss the sweeping views across Hanalei Bay and the majestic backdrop of Bali Hai's mountain peaks; you feel as if you've truly arrived in the Land of the Lotus Eaters. Almost all guest rooms take advantage of this jaw-dropping vista; all have marble bathrooms, gold-plated fixtures, handsome appointments, and a bathroom feature called a privacy window, which can be opaque or, with a flip of a switch, clear so you can see through the bedroom to the view outside while in the

shower. A drink at sunset at the Living Room, the lobby bar, is an event, complete with a traditional Hawaiian ceremony; there's often entertainment, such as a jazz trio, here in the evening. There are two top-ranked 18-hole golf courses, one of which was voted one of the 10 best in country in 1998 by *Golf Digest*. There's an exercise room in the hotel and a health club that can be reached by the hotel shuttle. The pool area, with several hot tubs and a swim-up bar, is stunning. The hotel has a wonderful check-in procedure: The valet parking attendant has your room key, and the bellman who delivers your bags checks you in. ⊠ *5520 Ka Haku Rd. (Box 3069), Princeville 96722,* ☎ *808/826–9644 or 800/826–4400,* FAX *808/826–1166. 201 rooms, 51 suites. 3 restaurants, 2 bars, pool, massage, 2 18-hole golf courses, 8 tennis courts, exercise rooms, health club, beach, shops, laundry service, dry cleaning, concierge, business services, meeting rooms, children's programs, travel services, cinema, free parking. AE, D, DC, MC, V.*

$$$$ 🏨 **Secret Beach Hideaway.** You could start a romance or write the great American novel—anything seems possible at this sumptuous, very private retreat. The one-bedroom, one-bath cottage and kitchen with an indoor-outdoor garden shower has marble and granite touches. Picture windows in the living room frame 11 acres of landscaped grounds—with a natural waterfall—that slope to Secret Beach; few find these hidden sands, a haven for families and privacy-seekers. There's a one-time cleaning fee of $100. ⊠ *Box 781, Kīlauea 96754,* ☎ *808/828–2862 or 970/ 925–7445,* FAX *808/828–2863. 1 cottage. Fans, hot tub.*

$$$–$$$$ 🏨 **Hanalei Bay Resort.** The clifftop location of these 16 low-rise buildings overlooks Hanalei Bay and the north shore. Units are extremely spacious, some as large as 2,000 square ft. They have high, sloping ceilings and large private lānai with mountain or bay views. Rattan furniture and Hawaiian art add a casual feeling to rooms that come with kitchens. Studios, which have kitchenettes that are not meant for serious cooking, have rattan furniture and forest green decor. There's a lava-rock waterfall by the hot tub. ⊠ *5380 Honoiki Rd., Princeville 96722,* ☎ *808/826–6522 or 800/367–5004,* FAX *808/826–6680. 161 rooms, 75 suites. Restaurant, lobby lounge, pool, hot tub, 18-hole golf course, 4 tennis courts, coin laundry. AE, D, DC, MC, V.*

$$$–$$$$ 🏨 **Hanalei Colony Resort.** This 5-acre beachfront property has an ideal location near the mysterious and verdant north end of the island. It sits on the road heading north, with magnificent mountains on one side and the ocean on the other. Each two-bedroom unit has a private lānai and kitchen, but no TVs or phones will interrupt the peaceful splendor of your visit. Free weekly workshops teach guests about Hawaiian culture and art, from stringing lei to weaving lau hala mats. A barbecue gazebo is a welcome addition. ⊠ *Box 206, 5–7130 Kūhiō Hwy., Hā'ena 96714,* ☎ *808/826–6235 or 800/628–3004,* FAX *808/826– 9893. 52 suites. Kitchens, pool, hot tub, coin laundry. AE, MC, V.*

$$$–$$$$ 🏨 **Holiday Inn SunSpree Resort.** Renovations ushered in a fresh look in 1997–98, as well as a name change from the former Wailua Bay Resort. A bubbling waterfall and exotic flowers enhance the lobby, and rooms have pastel colors, rattan furnishings, and large windows. A complimentary children's program and such adult activities as shuffleboard, tennis, and beach volleyball are part of the package, as are free local phone calls and in-room coffee. ⊠ *3–5920 Kūhiō Hwy., Kapa'a 96746,* ☎ *808/246–6976 or 888/823-5111,* FAX *808/823–6666. 188 rooms, 2 suites, 26 cabana suites. Restaurant, deli, lobby lounge, 2 pools, hot tub, exercise room, 2 tennis courts, children's programs. AE , DC, MC, V.*

$$$–$$$$ 🏨 **Lae nani.** Ruling Hawaiian chiefs once returned from ocean voyages to this spot, now host to condominiums comfortable enough for minor royalty. An oceanside heiau and hotel-sponsored Hawaiiana programs, with a booklet for self-guided historical tours, are a special plus.

Units are all decorated differently, with full kitchens and expansive lānai. Your view of landscaped grounds is interrupted only by a large pool before ending at a sandy ocean beach. A barbecue and picnic area is on-site as well. ✉ *410 Papaloa Rd., Kapa'a 96746,* ☎ *808/822–4938 or 800/367–7052,* FAX *510/939–6644. 84 condominiums (70 rentals). Picnic area, kitchens, pool, tennis court, beach. AE, MC, V.*

$$$ 🏨 **Plantation Hale Resort.** Across from the beach and near Coconut Marketplace, these attractive units have kitchens, garden lānai, and a homey feel. Rooms are clean and pretty with rose carpets, white rattan furnishings, and pastel colors. You couldn't ask for a more convenient location for dining, shopping, and sightseeing on either end of the island. Ask for a unit on the makai side, away from Kūhiō Highway. ✉ *484 Kūhiō Hwy., Kapa'a 96746,* ☎ *808/822–4941 or 800/775–4253,* FAX *808/822–5599. 160 condominiums (146 rentals). Air conditioning, in-room safes, kitchens, 3 pools, hot tub, putting green. AE, D, DC, MC, V.*

$$–$$$ 🏨 **Aston Kaua'i Beachboy.** Eight miles north of Līhu'e Airport, this hotel is well situated for east- and north-shore sightseeing. It's also a five-minute drive from the Wailua Golf Course and within walking distance of the Coconut Marketplace. The three-building, three-story hotel is set along an uncrowded stretch of Waipouli Beach. Rooms have large sliding screen doors as well as white louvered doors, which open onto private lānai. Bold Hawaiian-print bedspreads and scenes of Kaua'i contrast with the white walls. ✉ *4-484 Kūhiō Hwy., Kapa'a 96746,* ☎ *808/822–3441 or 800/922–7866,* FAX *808/822–0843. 233 rooms, 10 suites. Restaurant, lobby lounge, refrigerators, 2 pools, tennis court. AE, D, DC, MC, V.*

$$–$$$ 🏨 **Islander on the Beach.** The eight, three-story buildings of this pleasant 6-acre beachfront property, have a low-key Hawai'i plantation look. Rooms have showers, but not tubs; dark carpeting is brightened by open-air lānai and lovely green lawns outside. A free-form pool is right next to a golden sand beach, and you can take the lounge chairs to the ocean's edge. Shops, restaurants, and a cinema are at the adjacent Coconut Marketplace. ✉ *484 Kūhiō Hwy., Kapa'a 96746,* ☎ *808/822–7417 or 800/ 847–7417,* FAX *808/822–1947. 194 rooms, 2 suites. Restaurant, bar, pool, hot tub, tennis court, volleyball, shop, meeting room. AE, D, DC, MC, V.*

$$–$$$ 🏨 **Kaua'i Sands.** For money-saving beachfront accommodations this establishment might serve you well. The green-and-blue decor of the rooms and dark carpets may seem sadly outdated, but with the ocean right outside and your need to get wet and tan primary . . . who cares? Wide lawns to the beach look inviting for play or unwinding, and for shade you'll find a restaurant and lounge up-close to sunswept seas and ocean vistas. Units in the two two-story buildings are air-conditioned; those with kitchenettes cost a few extra dollars. ✉ *420 Papaloa Rd., Kapa'a 96746,* ☎ *808/822–4951 or 800/367–7000,* FAX *808/922–0052. 198 rooms, 2 suites. Restaurant, kitchens, lobby lounge, pool. AE, D, DC, MC, V.*

$$ 🏨 **Kapa'a Sands.** With only 24 condominiums, the Kapa'a Sands is an intimate gem. At seaside on the eastern coast, it's on the site of an old Japanese Shinto temple—an old rock etched with Japanese characters is a remnant of its presence. Small rooms furnished in rustic wood and equipped with ceiling fans, appropriate for beachside bungalows, have full kitchens, some with dishwashers and garbage disposals. Ask for an oceanfront room to get an open-air lānai. The landscaping around the eight two-story buildings includes meandering pathways lined with palms, gingers, and other tropical flora. ✉ *380 Papaloa Rd., Kapa'a 96746,* ☎ *808/822–4901 or 800/222–4901,* FAX *808/822–1556. 24 condominiums. Fans, pool. AE, D, DC, MC, V.*

282

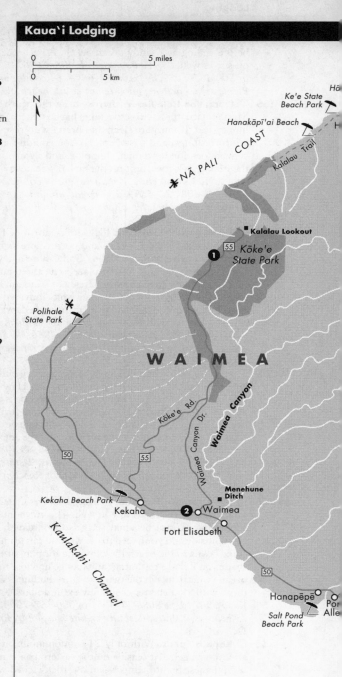

Kaua'i Lodging

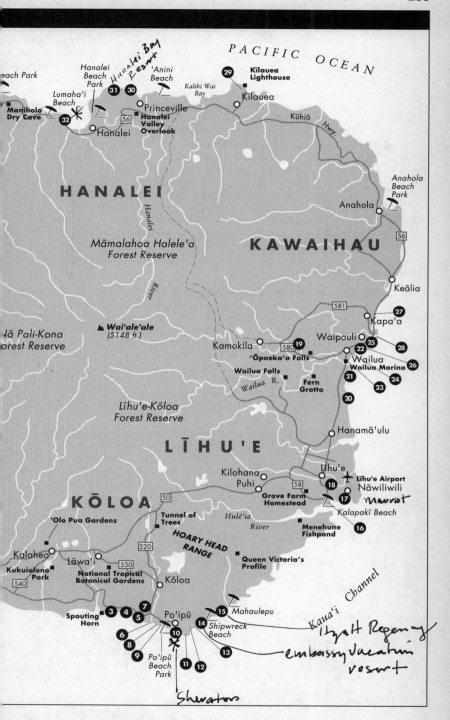

PACIFIC OCEAN

each Park

Hanalei Bay Resort

Hanalei
Beach
Park

'Anini
Beach

29 **Kīlauea
Lighthouse**

*Kalihi Wai
Bay*

Kīlauea

Lumaha'i
Beach

31 30

**Maniholo
Dry Cave**

32

Princeville

56 **Hanalei
Valley
Overlook**

Hanalei

Kūhiō

Hwy.

*Anahola
Beach
Park*

Anahola

56

HANALEI

Hanalei

*Māmalahoa Halele'a
Forest Reserve*

KAWAIHAU

River

Keālia

Jā Pali-Kona
orest Reserve

▲ **Wai'ale'ale**
(5148 ft.)

581 27

Kapa'a

Kamokila

580 19 Waipouli 22 25 28

'**Ōpaeka'a Falls**

**Wailua
Wailua Marina** 26

Wailua Falls

Wailua R. Fern
Grotto

21 23 24

*Līhu'e-Kōloa
Forest Reserve*

20

Hanamā'ulu

LĪHU'E

Kilohana

Līhu'e

18 **Līhu'e Airport**
Nāwiliwili *Marriott*

Puhi

58 17

KŌLOA

'Olo Pua Gardens

50 **Grove Farm
Homestead**

Kalapakī Beach

**Menehune
Fishpond**

16

Tunnel of
Trees

Hulē'ia River

Kalaheo

Lāwa'i

520 **HOARY HEAD
RANGE**

**Queen Victoria's
Profile**

Kaua'i Channel

**Kukuiolono
Park**

540 530 **National Tropical
Botanical Gardens**

Kōloa

Hyatt Regency

3 4 7

15 *Mahaulepu*

**Spouting
Horn**

5

Po'ipū

14 **Shipwreck
Beach**

*embassy vacation
resort*

6

10

8

9 **Po'ipū
Beach
Park**

11 12

13

Sheraton

$–$$ ▦ **Hotel Coral Reef.** This older, well-maintained hotel is right on the sand's edge, although the swimming in front of the hotel is not as good as at public beaches nearby. Colorful bedspreads liven up the bare-minimum furnishings. Upper units have carpeting; ground-level rooms are done in terrazzo tile with patios that lead directly to the beach, where there are barbecue grills. Oceanfront accommodations have private lānai and refrigerators. The property is ideally situated, near shopping, dining, and sightseeing, and the rates are attractive. ⊠ *1516 Kūhiō Hwy., Kapa'a 96746,* ☎ *808/822–4481 or 800/843–4659,* ℻ *808/822–7705. 22 rooms, 2 suites. Kitchenettes, coin laundry. MC, V.*

$–$$ ▦ **Kay Barker's Bed & Breakfast.** Run by longtime Kaua'i resident Gor-
★ don Barker and named after his late mother, this unpretentious B&B is a great choice for visitors on a budget who don't need to be in the center of things. A cottage and four rooms each have their own bath or shower, and there's a pleasant common room, with a TV, for relaxing. Each morning Gordon cooks up a tasty breakfast for his guests. Try the macadamia nut hotcakes and other homemade pastries. ⊠ *5921 Ki'inani Pl. (Box 740), Kapa'a 96746,* ☎ *808/822–3073 or 800/835–2845. 4 rooms, 1 cottage. Library. AE, D, MC, V.*

Līhu'e and Vicinity

$$$$ ▦ **Kaua'i Marriott Resort & Beach Club.** Public areas here impart a sense
★ of grandeur, carried out by an elaborate tropical garden, luxuriant plantings, and waterfalls right off the lobby, plus there's a huge, cinematic pool worthy of Xanadu. Poolside dining makes use of this two-tier, templelike extravaganza. The hotel nestles in the 800-acre, independently owned, Kaua'i Lagoons Resort. There's a lovely beach and lagoon to rest beside as well. ⊠ *3610 Rice St., Kalapakī Beach, Līhu'e 96766,* ☎ *808/245–5050 or 800/220–2925,* ℻ *808/245–5049. 356 rooms, 11 suites. 2 restaurants, lobby lounge, pool, 5 outdoor hot tubs, spa, 2 18-hole golf courses, 7 tennis courts, fitness center, beach, shops, children's programs. AE, D, DC, MC, V.*

$$$ ▦ **Outrigger Kaua'i Beach Hotel.** Designed with sensitivity to the history of the nearby Wailua River area, this low-rise, horseshoe-shape hotel surrounds a pool complex designed with rock-sculpted slopes, waterfalls, tropical flowers, and a cave resembling the Fern Grotto. Each night at sunset, staff in native dress light 100 tiki torches around the pools. Guest rooms are decorated in muted tones of peach, mauve, teal, and off-white, with a lānai and views of mountains, gardens, or the sea. ⊠ *4331 Kaua'i Beach Dr., Līhu'e 96766,* ☎ *808/245–1955 or 800/688–7444,* ℻ *808/ 246–9085. 341 rooms, 5 suites. 2 restaurants, 2 lobby lounges, 18-hole golf course, 3 pools, hot tub, 4 tennis courts. AE, D, DC, MC, V.*

$–$$ ▦ **Garden Island Inn.** This handy three-story inn, across the road from Nāwiliwili harbor and Anchor Cove shopping center, is a bargain. The facilities and fantasy of the elegant Kaua'i Marriott are just down the beach. Orchid suites on the top floor and tropical rooms on the second have lānai and glimpses of the ocean. Budget rooms are on the ground floor. Rooms have linoleum tile and queen beds or two twins. Innkeepers Steve and Susan Layne loan boogie boards and snorkeling and golf equipment and give away fruit from their trees. ⊠ *3445 Wilcox Rd., Kalapaki Bay 96766,* ☎ *808/245–7227 or 800/648–0154,* ℻ *808/245–7603. 20 room, 1 suite. Ceiling fans, kitchenettes, microwaves. AE, DC, MC, V.*

$ ▦ **Hale Līhu'e Motel.** Nearly all the sights of the north, south, and west portions of the island are within an easy hour's drive of this well-situated Līhu'e motel. And the price can't be beat. From the outside the low-rise building looks run-down, but the inside is clean. Budget backpackers, bicyclists, and other travelers will find small, depressing rooms with dark indoor-outdoor carpet, cinder-block walls, and utilitarian furnishings. Kitchenettes are available. Ask in advance for one of the air-conditioned rooms. ⊠ *2931 Kalena St., Līhu'e 96766,* ☎ *808/ 245–2751. 18 rooms. No credit cards.*

The South Coast

$$$$ ★ 🏨 **Embassy Vacation Resort Po'ipū Point.** Kaua'i's most luxurious condominium complex combines hotel services with such condo-style amenities as kitchens and washer-dryers. Large suites have plush carpeting, European-style cabinetry, and granite kitchen countertops. The 22-acre grounds include lily ponds, reflecting pools, and a swimming pool surrounded by sand. Complimentary buffet breakfast and evening cocktail reception are hosted in the club room. ⊠ *1613 Pe'e Rd., Kōloa 96756,* ☎ *808/742–1888 or 800/426–3350,* FAX *808/742–1924. 210 2-bedroom suites. Air conditioning, pool, 2 hot tubs, health club, concierge. AE, D, DC, MC, V.*

$$$$ ★ 🏨 **Hyatt Regency Kaua'i.** This superbly designed, dramatically handsome, classic Hawaiian low-rise hotel has airy courtyards and gardens. Rooms, two-thirds with ocean views, further the plantation theme with bamboo and wicker furnishings and Island art. Five acres of meandering fresh and saltwater swimming lagoons are beautifully set amid landscaped grounds. The Anara Spa and Fitness Center, with food bar, lap pool, hot tub, and massage rooms, covers 25,000 square ft. ⊠ *1571 Po'ipū Rd., Kōloa 96756,* ☎ *808/742–1234 or 800/233–1234,* FAX *808/742–6229. 600 rooms, 41 suites. 4 restaurants, 2 bars, 3 lobby lounges, 3 pools (1 saltwater), spa, 18-hole golf course, 4 tennis courts, health club, beach, nightclub. AE, D, DC, MC, V.*

$$$$ 🏨 **Po'ipū Shores.** These three low-rise buildings with a pool in front of the middle one sit right on a rocky point above pounding surf, perfect for whale or turtle watching. Weddings are staged on a little lawn beside the ocean. A sandy swimming beach is a 10-minute walk away. Units are all decorated differently by individual owners. Two share a sundeck, the rest have lānai, but all have full-length view windows and three of them have bedrooms on the ocean side. Kitchens have microwaves, washers, and dryers; there are two barbecue areas on the property. ⊠ *1775 Pe'e Rd., Kōloa 96756,* ☎ *808/742–7700 or 800/367–5004,* FAX *808/ 742–7700. 33 condominium suites. Kitchens, fans, pool. AE, MC, V.*

$$$$ 🏨 **Sheraton Kaua'i Resort.** Returning guests will recognize a few touches from the old Sheraton Kaua'i—which was reopened late in 1997 after rebuilding due to Hurricane 'Iniki. The lobby opens onto a central courtyard surrounded by shops and an area under a banyan tree where Hawaiian artisans stage demonstrations. Four-story guest wings are right on the beach or in a garden cluster. Beachfront rooms in muted sand and eggshell colors are highlighted with tapa dividers, while garden rooms have a brighter palette. A wedding gazebo has an ocean backdrop. There's a children's pool and children's programs are free in summer. ⊠ *2440 Ho'onani Rd., Po'ipū Beach, Kōloa 96756,* ☎ *808/ 742–1661, 800/921–4063,* FAX *808/742–0777. 399 rooms, 14 suites. 4 restaurants, bar, 4 pools, massage, 3 tennis courts, exercise room, beach, water slide, nightclub, children's programs, meeting rooms. AE, D, DC, MC, V.*

$$$$ 🏨 **Whalers Cove.** All 38 one- and two-bedroom condos in two low-rise buildings face the water and share a swimming pool, which is almost near enough to the surf to cast out a fishing line. The rocky beach is good for snorkeling, but a short drive or brisk walk will get you to a sandy stretch. A handsome koa-bedecked reception area offers full services for the plush units. The grandest bathrooms have whirlpool tubs on a raised platform, separate showers, and twin sinks. Big picture windows, spacious living rooms, and lānai and modern kitchens with washer/dryers make this a place to leave home for. ⊠ *2640 Pu'uholo Rd., Kōloa 96756,* ☎ *808/742–7571 or 800/225–2683,* ℻ *808/742–1185. 38 1 and 2-bedroom condominiums. Fans, pool, hot tub. AE, MC, V.*

$$$–$$$$ 🔲 **Kiahuna Plantation.** This 35-acre oceanfront resort's expansive lawns hold 42 plantation-style low-rise buildings. These one- and two-bedroom units have pastel color schemes and rattan furnishings. The administrative office and an excellent Italian restaurant, Piatti, are in a lovely sugar plantation manor house dating from the early 1900s. Free tours around lily ponds and cacti and Hawaiian gardens are offered weekly. ⊠ *2253 Po'ipū Rd., Kōloa 96756,* ☎ *808/742–2200 or 800/367–5004,* ℻ *808/939–6644. 333 condominiums. Restaurant, kitchenettes, pool, 18-hole golf course, 6 tennis courts. AE, D, DC, MC, V.*

$$$–$$$$ 🔲 **Makahuena at Po'ipū.** These extra large, tastefully decorated suites with white tile and sand-color carpets are housed in two- and three-story white wooden buildings with blue trim surrounded by well-kept lawns. Suites have kitchens and washer-dryers; there's a barbecue area on the property. Situated near the center of Po'ipū on a rocky point over the ocean, Shipwreck Beach is several blocks to the east and Po'ipū Beach is also close by. ⊠ *1661 Pe'e Rd., Po'ipū 96756,* ☎ *808/742–2482 or 800/356–5004,* ℻ *808/742–2379. 79 2- and 3-bedroom suites. Tennis court. AE, MC, V.*

$$$ 🔲 **Garden Isle Cottages.** The theme of each of these reasonably priced oceanside accommodations is Hawaiian, and tropical flower gardens surround the cottages for an exotic touch. The spacious rooms have no telephones. Some do include kitchens, so ask in advance if you wish to reserve one. It's a five-minute walk to the restaurants of nearby Po'ipū. The owners also rent another cottage, Hale Waipahu, which sits on the highest point in Po'ipū for a 360-degree ocean vista near Brennecke's Beach. Here, a studio and a two-bedroom unit share a lap pool. Six units have kitchens with microwaves, ceiling fans, a washer and dryer. There's also a barbecue area. ⊠ *2666 Pu'uholo Rd., Kōloa 96756,* ☎ *808/742–6717 or 800/742–6711. 9 cottages. Fans. No credit cards.*

$$$ 🔲 **Gloria's Spouting Horn Bed & Breakfast.** The classiest ocean-front
★   bed-and-breakfast on Kaua'i, this cedar home was built by owners Gloria and Bob Merkle specifically to house guests. Breakfast, snacks, and a chilled beverage are available in the comfortable common room with its soaring A-frame ceiling and ocean-immediate deck. Waves dash the black rocks below, while just above the ocean's edge a man-made sand beach invites sunbathers. All three bedrooms have four-poster beds with romantic canopies, oceanside lānai, deep soaking tubs, and separate showers. ⊠ *4464 Lawai Rd., Po'ipū,* ☎ *808/742–6995. 3 rooms. Refrigerators, in-room VCRs, lap pool. No credit cards.*

$$$ 🔲 **Po'ipū Kapili.** Ultraspacious one- and two-bedroom units, minutes from Po'ipū restaurants, enjoy garden and across-the-street ocean views combined with privacy. Architects managed to give a plantation look to the two-story white-frame exteriors and double-pitched roofs that complement the tropical landscaping. Decorator-designed interiors include full kitchens and entertainment centers. Guests can choose to mingle at a weekly morning coffee hour held beside the ocean-view pool, in the herb garden, or perhaps in the on-site library, stocked with videos and books. ⊠ *2221 Kapili Rd., Kōloa 96756,* ☎ *808/742–6449 or 800/443–7714,* ℻ *808/742–9162. 60 condominiums. In-room VCRs, pool, 2 tennis courts. AE, D, DC, MC, V.*

$$$ 🔲 **Suite Paradise Po'ipū Kaī.** Luxuriously appointed apartments, many with cathedral ceilings and light-color carpets, all with big windows surrounded by spreading lawns, give this property the feeling of a spacious, quiet retreat inside and out. Big furnished lānai have views to the ocean and across the 110-acre landscaped grounds. Some units are two-level, some have sleeping lofts, all are furnished with modern kitchens; there's barbecue facilities as well. House of Seafood Restaurant is a few blocks away. ✉ *1941 Po'ipū Rd., Kōloa 96756,* ☎ *808/ 742–6464 or 800/777–1700,* FAX *808/742–7865. 130 condominiums. Fans, in-room safes, in-room VCRs, 2 pools, hot tub, 9 tennis courts. AE, D, DC, MC, V.*

$$ ⊞ **Kūhiō Shores.** Every unit in this four-story waterfront condo has an ocean view, with large windows and spacious lānai to help you enjoy it whenever you can tear yourself away from the surfing and snorkeling activity right outside. Accommodations are large—a sure sign that individual owners enjoy vacationing here themselves—with tropic-tone rattan furniture and kitchens. ✉ *5050 Lāwa'i Beach Rd., Kōloa 96756,* ☎ *808/742–7555 or 800/367–8022,* FAX *808/742–1559. 75 condominium suites. Restaurant, beach, coin laundry. MC, V.*

$–$$ ⊞ **Kōloa Landing Cottages.** Guests are treated like family here by the helpful owners, who came to Hawai'i from Holland. Kōloa Landing has five cottages including a studio situated about a 10-minute walk from a swimming beach. Open-beam ceilings, fans, and light-color decor keep the interiors cool. Book well in advance for these in-demand, comfortably spacious, but not overly fancy accommodations with kitchens and phones; barbecue grills are available as well. ✉ *2704-B Ho'onani Rd., Kōloa 96756,* ☎ *808/742–1470 or 800/779–8773,* FAX *808/332–9584. 5 cottages. Laundry room. No credit cards.*

The West Side

$$$ ⊞ **Waimea Plantation Cottages.** Tucked into a coconut grove, these reconstructed sugar-plantation cottages, near the stunning Waimea Canyon and many beautiful beaches, make for a laid-back vacation experience. The one- to five-bedroom cottages are unpretentious to the point of being a bit rough around the edges, but they're spacious and all have porches. Wooden floors, ceiling fans (no air-conditioning), rattan furniture, and claw-foot bathtubs are mixed with modern kitchens and cable TVs; barbecue grills, hammocks, and porch swings are on the property. Cottages are steps away from a black-sand beach with equally murky water. ✉ *9400 Kaumuali'i Hwy., Box 367, Waimea 96796,* ☎ *808/338–1625 or 800/992–4632,* FAX *808/338–2338. 48 cottages. Pool, tennis court, horseshoes, beach. AE, D, DC, MC, V.*

$ ⊞ **Kōke'e Lodge.** Outdoors-oriented visitors can experience Kaua'i's
★   mountain wilderness at this lodge—a little different than the usual beachfront property one expects on a tropical isle. Twelve rustic cabins have wood-burning stoves (wood is a few dollars extra) to ward off any chill from the mountain air. Eight older wooden cabins cost less than four newer, cedar structures, but both styles are bargains for Kaua'i. The Lodge serves breakfast and lunch. Many residents head for Kōke'e for the weekend, so make your reservations in advance. Advance payment is required. ✉ *Box 819, Kōke'e State Park, Waimea 96796,* ☎ *808/ 335–6061. 12 cabins. Restaurant. Credit cards accepted for bookings 10 days in advance; otherwise, personal checks are preferred.*

NIGHTLIFE AND THE ARTS

People on Kaua'i take great pride in their culture, and enjoy sharing their unique traditions with those who come to call. As a result, on the Garden Isle you will find more traditional Hawaiiana and less razzmatazz and glitz than on neighboring O'ahu.

Most of the island's dinner and lū'au shows take place within a hotel or resort; major credit cards are accepted. Hotel lounges and restaurant bars offer live music with no cover charge.

Check the local newspaper, the *Garden Island Times,* for listings of weekly happenings. Free publications like *Kaua'i Gold, This Week on Kaua'i,* and *Kaua'i Magazine* also list entertainment events. You can pick them up at the Hawai'i Visitors Bureau and at Līhu'e Airport.

Bars and Clubs

For the most part, discos never fit into the serenity of Kaua'i, and the bar scene is extremely limited. The major resorts generally host their own live entertainment and happy hours. The drinking age in Hawai'i is 21, and if you look younger than that, you may be asked to show some identification. All bars and clubs that serve alcohol must close at 2 AM, except for those with a cabaret license, which close at 4 AM.

The following establishments present dance music on a regular basis.

Duke's Barefoot Bar. Contemporary Hawaiian music is performed in the beachside bar on weekends, while upstairs a traditional Hawaiian trio plays nightly for diners. ⊠ *Kalapakī Beach, Līhu'e,* ☎ *808/246–9599.* ◷ *Barefoot Bar Fri.–Sun. 10–12:30.*

Gilligan's. At the Outrigger Kaua'i Beach near Wailua, Gilligan's has varying entertainment (call ahead to confirm), and in the hotel's lobby lounge a duo presents live Hawaiian music Monday and Wednesday–Saturday 7:30–10. ⊠ *Outrigger Kaua'i Beach Hotel, 4331 Kaua'i Beach Dr., Līhu'e,* ☎ *808/245–1955.* ◷ *Line dancing Thurs. 8–midnight, line dancing and karaoke Fri. 8–midnight, DJ music Sat. 9:30–1.*

Hanalei Gourmet. The sleepy north shore comes alive each evening in this small, convivial setting. The emphasis here is on local jazz, rock, and folk music. ⊠ *5-5161 Kūhiō Hwy., Hanalei Center, Hanalei,* ☎ *808/826–2524.* ◷ *Mon.–Sat. 8–10:30, Sun. 4–9.*

Kūhiō's Nightclub. This is the south shore's most popular hot spot. High-energy entertainment and late-night dancing are the drawing cards in this very '90s nightclub. ⊠ *Hyatt Regency Kaua'i, Po'ipū,* ☎ *808/742–1234.* ◷ *Music Fri. and Sat. 9–2.*

Side Out Bar & Grill. A sports bar on the weekends, this funky hangout presents live Island-style music two nights a week. ⊠ *4–1330 Kūhiō Hwy., at Kauwila St., Kapa'a,* ☎ *808/822–7330.* ◷ *Music Mon. and Wed., 6–10.*

Lū'au

Drums of Paradise Lū'au. More than just music and dance, this hotel lū'au features displays of Hawaiian artwork, as well as a traditional and contemporary menu to suit all tastes and the dances of Polynesia. ⊠ *Hyatt Regency Kaua'i Resort and Spa, 1571 Po'ipū Rd., Kōloa,* ☎ *808/742–1234.* ▨ *$57.* ◷ *Thurs. and Sun. 5–8.*

Kaua'i Coconut Beach Resort Lū'au. The music, dance, and food of Polynesia come together at this hotel-based lū'au, regarded by many as the island's best. It takes place in a lovely setting of flaming tiki torches. ⊠ *Coconut Plantation, Kapa'a,* ☎ *808/822–3455, Ext. 651.* ▨ *$52.* ◷ *Nightly 6–9.*

Pa'ina o Hanalei. The blowing of the conch calls guests to the beach at Hanalei Bay for a Hawaiian feast and "A Show of Splendor by the Sea" with local entertainer Nani Marsten. ⊠ *Princeville Hotel, Princeville Resort,* ☎ *808/826–9644.* ▨ *$52.* ◷ *Thurs. 6–9.*

Smith's Tropical Paradise Lū'au. Amid 30 acres of tropical flora and fauna, this lū'au begins with the traditional blowing of the conch shell and *imu* (underground oven) ceremony, followed by cocktails, an Island feast, and an international show in the Lagoon Amphitheater. ⊠ *174 Wailua Rd., Kapa'a,* ☎ *808/821–6895.* ▨ *$52.* ◷ *Mon., Wed., and Fri. 5–9:15.*

Tahiti Nui Lūʻau. This venerable institution is a welcome change from the standard commercial lūʻau, because it's smaller, for about 40 guests, and put on by a family that really knows how to party. The all-you-can-eat buffet includes kālua pig that has been slow-roasted in an imu; the show features plenty of dancing, music, and laughs. ✉ *Kūhiō Hwy., Hanalei,* ☎ *808/826–6277.* 🎫 *$40.* ⊘ *Wed. at 6.*

Music

Very little classical arts activity takes place on laid-back Kauaʻi. The island doesn't have its own symphony, but the **Honolulu Symphony Orchestra** (☎ 808/537–6191) does perform on the Garden Isle from time to time. For a specific schedule, call the **Kauaʻi Concert Association** (☎ 808/245–7464). **Kauaʻi Community College Performing Arts Center** (✉ 3-1901 Kaumualiʻi Hwy., Līhuʻe, ☎ 808/245–8311) provides a venue for Hawaiian music and dance as well as visiting performers. Call to find out what's on the bill.

In Līhuʻe, the **Līhuʻe Public Library** (✉ 4344 Hardy St., ☎ 808/241–3222) often plays host to films, storytelling, musical presentations, and arts and crafts events.

Theater

The **Kauaʻi Community Players** (✉ Līhuʻe Parish Hall, 4340 Nāwiliwili Rd., Līhuʻe, ☎ 808/245–7700) is a talented local group that presents a variety of plays throughout the year.

OUTDOOR ACTIVITIES AND SPORTS

Participant Sports

Biking

You can coast for four hours starting at dawn (Continental breakfast is included), for 12 scenic mi—all downhill—from the Waimea Canyon Rim with **Kauaʻi Coasters** (✉ Box 3038, Līhuʻe 96766, ☎ 808/639–2412).

Outfitters Kauaʻi rents bikes and provides information on how to do a self-guided tour of Kōkeʻe State Park and Waimea Canyon. They also lead coasting tours from Waimea Canyon to the island's west-side beaches. ✉ *2827-A Poʻipū Rd., Poʻipū 96756,* ☎ *808/742–9667.*

Pedal ʻnʻ Paddle (✉ Ching Young Village, Hanalei, ☎ 808/826–9069) rents bicycles for $20 a day. Hourly and weekly rates are also available.

Ray's Rentals and Activities (✉ 4-1345 Kūhiō Hwy., ☎ 808/822–5700) sometimes offers a two-for-one bike rental deal for $75 a week.

MOUNTAIN BIKING

Tri-athletes need to train to conquer the 12-mi Power Line Trail, which begins in the mountains above Wailua in Keāhua Arboretum—you'll see the poles heading across the mountains—and ends mauka of Princeville Resort. You're sure to be covered in red clay mud from head to toe by the time you're halfway into the ride, but you'll have views of Waiʻaleʻale that are usually seen only from the air. Be sure your mountain bike is in top condition, take plenty of water and high energy bars, and let someone know when and where you are going. If you rent a mountain bike (☞ Bicycling, *above*) explain what you've got in mind and heed any advice offered by the experts.

Fitness Centers

The centrally located **Kaua'i Athletic Club** (✉ 4370 Kukui Grove, Līhu'e, ☎ 808/245–5381) has saunas, racquetball, aerobic classes, swimming, cardio-fitness instruction, and a hot tub.

Princeville Health Club & Spa (✉ 53-900 Kūhiō Hwy., Princeville, ☎ 808/826–5030) has state-of-the-art equipment in a workout room surrounded by inspiring views of mountains, sea, and sky. A variety of massage treatments induces total relaxation.

Spa and Tennis Club at the Kaua'i Lagoons (✉ 3351 Ho'olaulea Way, Līhu'e, ☎ 808/246–2414) has coed facilities; the weight room, sauna, steam room, and hot tub are in elegant pink marble surroundings.

One hotel in the resort area of Po'ipū, the **Hyatt Regency Kaua'i** (✉ 1571 Po'ipū Rd., Po'ipū, ☎ 808/742–1234), opens its **Anara Spa** to visitors. For $20 per day you'll have use of the weight room, lap pool, steam, sauna, and hot tub in this deluxe 25,000-square-ft facility.

Golf

Kaua'i's newest course, **Grove Farm Golf Course** at Puakea, opened in December 1997. A nine-hole beauty, it made *Sports Illustrated*'s list of Top 10 nine-hole courses in the country. ✉ *4315 Kalepa St., Līhu'e,* ☎ *808/245–8756.* ✎ *$35 for 10 holes, $60 for 20 holes; includes cart.*

Two Jack Nicklaus–designed par-72 courses at the **Kaua'i Lagoons Golf Club** adjoin the Kaua'i Marriott Resort & Beach Club. The championship Kiele course challenges golfers of all levels; the links-style Lagoons course promises a satisfying round for everyone. Forty acres of tropical lagoons provide breathtaking views. ✉ *3351 Ho'olaulea Way, Līhu'e,* ☎ *808/241–6000.* ✎ *Greens fee Kiele $145, Lagoons $100; includes shared cart, spa admission, and same-day use of practice facility.*

In the southern part of the island is the **Kiahuna Golf Club.** Robert Trent Jones, Jr., designed the 18-hole course, and there's a pro shop, rentals, a snack bar, and a bar. ✉ *2545 Kiahuna Plantation Dr., Kōloa,* ☎ *808/742–9595.* ✎ *Greens fee: nonresidents $35 after 1:30; includes shared cart.*

At the **Kukui-o-lono Golf Course** you can play nine holes or a full round in a peaceful wooded hilltop setting with spectacular views of Kaua'i's eastern shore. ✉ *Box 1031, Kalāheo 96741,* ☎ *808/332–9151.* ✎ *Greens fee $7; cart $6 for 9 holes, $14 for 18 holes.*

Next to the Hyatt Regency Kaua'i, **Po'ipū Bay Resort Golf Course** is an 18-hole links-style course, the site of the MasterCard PGA Grand Slam for many years. ✉ *2250 'Ainakō St., Kōloa,* ☎ *808/742–8711.* ✎ *Greens fee $95 Hyatt Regency guests, $140 nonguests; includes shared cart.*

Kaua'i's best-known golf facility is the **Princeville Resort Makai Course.** Designed by Robert Trent Jones, Jr., it features a pro shop, a driving range, a practice area, lessons, club rental and storage, instruction, and a snack bar. This course has been the setting for the LPGA Women's Kemper Open, including the Helene Curtis Pro-Am. ✉ *Hwy. 56, Princeville,* ☎ *808/826–3580.* ✎ *Greens fee $95 guests, $115 nonguests; includes shared cart.*

The 18-hole **Princeville Resort Prince Course** has spectacular ocean and mountain views. It is also rated Kaua'i's toughest course. A restaurant and bar are open for breakfast and lunch. ✉ *Off Hwy. 56, Princeville,* ☎ *808/826–5000.* ✎ *Greens fee $100 guests, $150 nonguests; includes cart.*

Wailua Municipal Golf Course sits next to the Wailua River and beach. Its 18 holes have hosted national tournaments, and there's a pro shop, a driving range, and a restaurant. ⊠ *3-5351 Kūhiō Hwy., Wailua,* ☎ *808/241–6666.* 🏌 *Greens fee $25 weekdays, $35 weekends; carts are $14.*

Hiking

Before planning any hike on Kaua'i, contact the **Department of Land and Natural Resources** (⊠ State Parks Division, Box 1671, Līhu'e 96766, ☎ 808/274–3444) for information on which trails are open and what condition they are in. For your safety, wear sturdy shoes, bring plenty of water, never hike alone, stay on the trail, and avoid hiking when it's wet and slippery. All hiking trails on Kaua'i are free.

Kaua'i's prize hiking venue is the **Kalalau Trail,** which begins at the western end of Highway 56 and proceeds 11 mi to Kalalau Beach. With hairpin turns, sometimes very muddy conditions, and constant ups and downs, this hike is a true test of endurance and can't be tackled roundtrip in one day. For a good taste of it, hike just the first 2 mi to Hanakāpī'ai Beach (☞ Beaches, *above*). For the best trail and weather conditions, hike Kalalau between May and September.

Kōke'e State Park is a glorious 45-mi network of hiking trails of varying difficulty, all worth the walk. Its acres of native forests, home to many species of birds, are a wonder to behold. The Kukui Trail takes hikers right down the side of Waimea Canyon. Awa'awapuhi Trail leads 4 mi down to a spectacular overlook into the canyons of the north shore. All hikers should register at Kōke'e Park headquarters, which offers trail maps and information. ⊠ *Kōke'e Rd. 20 mi north from Hwy. 50 in Kekaha,* ☎ *808/335–5871.*

Horseback Riding

Kaua'i's scenic mountain pastures and shorelines can be explored on escorted rides along panoramic oceanside cliffs and beaches.

CJM Country Stables (☎ 808/742–6096) charges $60–$100 for three guided rides: a two-hour ranch ride with ocean scenery, a three-hour hidden-valley beach breakfast ride, and a 3½-hour swim and picnic ride. **Esprit de Corps** (☎ 808/822-4688) offers private lessons, pony parties for children, and half-day horse camps, as well as trail rides that range from two-hour jaunts, for $79, to four-hour excursions, for $99. Or for $179 you can have an all-day adventure with lunch served by a stream where you can swim. Longer rides require some experience as they traverse ridge lines and canyons. Private custom rides at sunset are available.

Princeville Ranch Stables (☎ 808/826–6777) leads guided horseback tours into the less-explored reaches of the island. A 90-minute country ride is $55 per person; a scenic three-hour bluff ride is $100 and includes a snack; a four-hour waterfall picnic ride is $110, including lunch. This is a very professional operation.

At **Silver Falls Ranch** (☎ 808/828–6718) you can take an individual excursion or private lesson or take a two-hour Hawaiian Discovery ride with refreshments, for $73, or a three-hour Silver Falls ride, for $98, which includes picnicking by a waterfall and a swim in a secluded freshwater pool.

Tennis

Kaua'i has 20 lighted public tennis courts and more than 70 private courts at the hotels.

Hanalei Bay Resort (☎ 808/826–6522) has eight courts. Guests play free; nonguests pay $30 per day.

Hyatt Regency Kaua'i (⊠ 1571 Po'ipū Rd., Kōloa, ☎ 808/742–1234) has four tennis courts, a pro shop, and a tennis pro. The cost is $20 per hour.

Kaua'i Coconut Beach Resort (☎ 808/822–3455) offers three courts. Guests pay $5 per hour, nonguests $7.

Princeville Tennis Center (☎ 808/826–9823) has six courts. The cost is $10 for 90 minutes.

Spa & Tennis Club at the Kaua'i Lagoons (⊠ 3351 Ho'olaulea Way, Līhu'e, ☎ 808/246–2414) has the island's only tennis stadium and seven courts for mere mortals. Unlimited court time costs $20 per day, private lessons are $45 per hour, lessons for two are $55 per hour, and a 75-minute daily clinic is $15.

Water Sports

FISHING

For freshwater fishing, head for the bass- and trout-filled streams near Kōke'e and Waimea Canyon. A 30-day visitor license for freshwater fishing, costing $3.75, must be obtained from the **Department of Land and Natural Resources** (⊠ 1151 Punchbowl St., Room 131, Honolulu 96815, ☎ 808/587–0077).

No matter which company you choose for ocean fishing, plan to spend $125–$150 for a full day of charter fishing on a shared basis, $85–$90 for a half day on a shared basis, $600–$700 for an exclusive full day, and $400–$450 for an exclusive half day.

The following are reliable enterprises:

'Anini Fishing Charters (⊠ Box 594, Kīlauea 96754, ☎ 808/828–1285) has a 33-ft sport cruiser, *Sea Breeze V,* that skipper Bob Kutkowski completed himself for sport or bottom-fishing charters.

Gent-Lee Fishing (⊠ Box 1691, Līhu'e 96766, ☎ 808/245–7504) has 32- and 36-ft, six-passenger custom sportfishers; spectators can join the ride for half price.

Sportfishing Kaua'i (⊠ Box 1195, Kōloa 96756, ☎ 808/742–7013 or 808/639–0013) runs a 28-ft, six-passenger custom sportfisher.

True Blue (⊠ Box 1722, Kalapakī Beach, Līhu'e 96766, ☎ 808/246–6333) offers charters on a roomy 55-ft Delta certified to carry 33, but fishing trips are limited to eight anglers; four-hour share charters run $90 per person; a four-hour exclusive charter is $600; a ¾-day charter $700.

KAYAKING

Kayak Kaua'i rents kayaks to individuals and offers half- and full-day guided, open-cockpit kayak tours along the Nā Pali Coast and up the Hanalei River with snorkeling included. (☞ Guided Tours *in* Kaua'i A to Z, *below*). ☎ *808/826–9844 or 800/437–3507.* ⚅ *$48–$130.*

Outfitters Kaua'i offers guided kayak excursions for novices, as well as longer Nā Pali Coast and jungle stream paddles. Experienced paddlers can rent a kayak, grab a plastic coated map, and discover a romantic waterfall on their own. ⊠ *2827-A Po'ipū Rd., Po'ipū 96756,* ☎ *808/742–9667.*

Paradise Outdoor Adventures provides topographical maps, motorboat rental, and free delivery of kayaks to Wailua River. A full-day guided Wailua Jungle-River Safari includes a hike to a waterfall and lunch for $65.⊠ *Across from Kaua'i Community College, Kaumuali'i Hwy., Līhu'e,* ☎ *808/822–1112 or 800/626–2628.* ⚅ *2-person kayak $50 per day.*

SCUBA DIVING

Dive Kaua'i (⊠ 976 Kūhiō Hwy., #C, Kapa'a 96746, ☎ 808/822–0452 or 800/828–3483) offers an introductory half-day scuba excursion for $85. One-tank shore dives for certified divers cost $90, a refresher course is $80, and a five-day PADI (scuba-diving certification) course is $395. A boat dive with two tanks costs $100, including equipment.

Ocean Odyssey (⊠ Outrigger Kaua'i Beach Hotel, 4331 Kaua'i Beach Dr., Līhu'e 96766, ☎ 808/245–8681) will arrange lessons, shore dives, even night dives and underwater videotaping for you. Packages range from a simple one-tank shore dive starting at $60 for certified divers to a more expensive three- to five-day PADI certification course.

Seasport Divers (⊠ 2827 Po'ipū Rd., Kōloa 96756, ☎ 808/742–9303 or 800/685-5889) has a full-service PADI, NAUI, and SSI scuba training facility and a full range of dive options, from beginner lessons and introductory dives to private charters, plus equipment rental and repair service.

SNORKELING

The following experts operate entertaining and well-run snorkeling cruises. Several companies depart from the north shore for snorkeling trips along the scenic Nā Pali Coast. Schedules vary with the weather; call in advance for details.

Blue Water Sailing (☎ 808/828–1142) ferries snorkelers to south shore sites on a 12-passenger, 42-ft, luxury Pearson sailing yacht, the *Lady Leanne II.* A fun excursion for all ages and the only monohull sailing charter on Kaua'i, this four-hour snorkeling voyage off the island's southern shores includes gear, instruction, swimming, fishing, a gourmet picnic lunch, snacks, and beverages. In winter you might catch glimpses of whales. Trips leave from Port Allen mid-September–mid-May and from Hanalei Bay during the rest of year. The cost is $85. A two-hour sunset sail that carries 15 is $50.

Captain Andy's Sailing Adventures (☎ 808/822–7833) takes up to 49 passengers on its 55-ft catamaran, the *Spirit of Kaua'i;* cruises depart from Kukui'ula Harbor in Po'ipū. The rate for the four-hour morning "ultimate adventure" is $75, including gear and lunch. Whale-watching excursions are run during the winter months. Seasonal Nā Pali Coast tours are offered that include Continental breakfast, lunch, snorkeling gear, and instruction for $95.

Catamaran Kahanu (☎ 808/826–4596) has two-hour and four-hour Nā Pali Coast cruises on its 36-ft power catamaran that includes snorkeling, dolphin watching, and a bit of Hawaiian history and culture. Prices are $65 and $85.

Hanalei Watersports (☎ 808/826–7509) offers SCUBA and surfing lessons and tours, and guided kayak and snorkel tours. These accommodating guides are willing to craft a full day's land and sea adventure to suit your every whim. They also offer an idyllic sunset cruise from the Princeville Resort aboard a Hawaiian outrigger canoe rigged with a traditional sail. Prices run the gamut, but are in the $50 bracket for simple dives.

Hanalei Sea Tours (☎ 808/826–7254 or 800/733–7997) runs "eco" tours, including snorkeling, on Power Cats and Zodiac rafts. Narrated sightseeing trips range from $55 to $110 and take from two hours to a full day. Longer cruises include snorkeling gear, lunch, and cold drinks.

Nā Pali Adventures (☎ 808/826–6804 or 800/659–6804) takes groups on four-hour snorkeling and snack excursions or two-hour sightseeing trips along the north shore in power catamarans that hold 18, or 28 people. Rates range from $55 to $90.

SURFING AND WINDSURFING

'Anini Beach Windsurfing (☎ 808/826–9463) stands ready to help you get started as a windsurfer. An introductory group lesson and certification lesson include equipment; each of three one-hour sessions is $65.

Private lessons are available, and sailboard rentals are $25 per hour, $50 per day.

Margo Oberg Surfing Lessons (⊠ Nukumoi Surf Shop, Po'ipū Beach, next to Brennecke's Restaurant, ☎ 808/742–8019). Here seven-time world surfing champion Margo Oberg furnishes surfboards and she and her staff give dry-land and wave instruction to beginning surfers. Lessons are $45 for 1½ hours.

SHOPPING

Kaua'i may not have the myriad shopping alternatives of its cosmopolitan neighbor, O'ahu, but what it does have is character. Along with a few major shopping malls, Kaua'i has some of the most delightful mom-and-pop shops and family-run boutiques imaginable.

Kaua'i also offers one-of-a-kind options for souvenirs. For instance, the famous shell jewelry from nearby Ni'ihau is sometimes sold on Kaua'i for less than it is on other islands. The Garden Isle is also known for its regular outdoor markets, where you find bargain prices on various souvenirs and produce and get a chance to mingle with island residents.

Kaua'i's major shopping centers are open daily from 9 or 10 to 5, although some stay open until 9. Stores are basically clustered around the major resort areas and Līhu'e.

Books

Several fine books have been written about Kaua'i, and many more about Hawai'i. **Border's Books & Music** (⊠ 4303 Nāwiliwili Rd., Līhu'e,☎ 808/246–0862) has a healthy section of books focused on Hawai'i, plus plenty of magazines for beach reading.

One of the cutest of the island's bookshops is the **Hanapēpē Bookstore** (⊠ 3830 Hanapēpē Rd., Hanapēpē, ☎ 808/335–5011), which emphasizes Hawai'i-oriented publications.

The gift shop in Līhu'e's **Kaua'i Museum** (⊠ 4428 Rice St., ☎ 808/ 245–6931) sells some fascinating books, maps, and prints.

Clothing

Crazy Shirts (⊠ Po'ipū Shopping Village, 2360 Kiahuna Plantation Dr., ☎ 808/742–9000; ⊠ Anchor Cove, 3416 Rice St., Līhu'e, ☎ 808/245–7073; ⊠ Kōloa, ☎ 808/742–7161) has a wide variety of shirts, from classy to crazy designs. It's a good place for active wear.

Liberty House (⊠ Kukui Grove Center, 3-2600 Kaumuali'i Hwy., ☎ 808/245–7751) carries high-quality designer labels as well as nice resort wear.

M. Miura Store (⊠ 4-1419 Kūhiō Hwy., Kapa'a, ☎ 808/822–4401) has a great assortment of clothes for the outdoor fanatic, including tank tops, visors, swimwear, and Kaua'i-style T-shirts.

Paradise Sportswear (⊠ Kaumuali'i Hwy., Kalāheo, ☎ 808/335–5670), the retail outlet of the folks who invented Kaua'i's popular "red dirt" shirts, offers styles and sizes from infants up to 5X. Do let the salesperson tell you the charming story behind these shirts.

Sears (⊠ Kukui Grove Center, 3-2600 Kaumuali'i Hwy., ☎ 808/245–3325) features reliably handsome men's and women's clothing in mainland and some tropical stylings.

Resort Wear

Art to Wear (⊠ Kaua'i Village Shopping Center, 4-831 Kūhiō Hwy., ☎ 808/822–7511) offers hand-painted, hand-sewn originals decorated with flowers, seascapes, and animal motifs.

Hilo Hattie Fashion Factory (⊠ 3252 Kūhiō Hwy., Līhu'e, ☎ 808/245–3404) is the big name in inexpensive aloha wear for tourists throughout the Isles. You can visit the factory, a mile from Līhu'e Airport, to pick up cool, comfortable aloha shirts and mu'umu'u in bright floral prints, and other souvenirs.

Tropical Shirts (⊠ Coconut Marketplace, 4-484 Kūhiō Hwy., ☎ 808/822–0203; ⊠ Po'ipū Shopping Village, ☎ 808/742–6691; ⊠ Po'ipū Shopping Village, ☎ 808/742–6691) captures the beauty of Kaua'i with clothing embroidered or hand-screened by local artists. There is also a selection of the island's unique "red dirt" T-shirts, dyed and printed with the characteristic local soil.

Department Stores

Kmart (⊠ Kukui Grove Center, 3-2600 Kaumuali'i Hwy., ☎ 808/245–7742) opened on Kaua'i in 1995 with the same merchandise you can buy back home.

Sears (⊠ Kukui Grove Center, 3-2600 Kaumuali'i Hwy., ☎ 808/245–3325) has moderately priced merchandise—everything from clothing to cookware.

Wal-Mart (⊠ 3-3300 Kūhiō Hwy., ☎ 808/246–1599) carries the same huge jumble found in mainland Wal-Marts, with slightly more emphasis on rubber slippers and tropical clothing.

Flowers

Petal Pushers (⊠ Princeville Center, 5-4280 Kūhiō Hwy., ☎ 808/826–7420) can help you ship leis, corsages, and flower arrangements to friends and family back home.

Kaua'i Tropicals (⊠ Box 449, Lāwa'i, ☎ 808/332–9071 or 800/303–4385) ships heliconia, anthuriums, ginger, and other tropicals directly from the flower farm in 5-ft boxes.

Food

Kaua'i has its own yummy specialties that you won't be able to resist while on the island. The **Kaua'i Products Council** (☎ 808/823–8714) will tell you the best places to find Kaua'i Kookies, taro chips, Kaua'i boiled peanuts, salad dressings, and jams and jellies made from locally grown fruit. Kaua'i now produces more coffee than any other island in the state, and the local product, somewhat milder than the Big Island's better-known Kona coffee, makes a worthy souvenir.

Near Līhu'e, you can buy fresh pineapple, sugarcane, ginger, coconuts, local jams, jellies, and honey, plus Kaua'i-grown papayas, bananas, and mangos in season—all at **Kaua'i Fruit and Flower Company** (⊠ 3-4684 Kūhiō Hwy., ☎ 808/245–1814). Special gift packs are available, inspected and certified for shipment out of the state.

Don't forget to try a big scoop of **Lappert's Ice Cream** (⊠ 1-3555 Kaumuali'i Hwy., ☎ 808/335–6121; ⊠ Coconut Marketplace, 4-484 Kūhiō Hwy., ☎ 808/822–0744; ⊠ Kōloa, ☎ 808/742–1272; or ⊠ Princeville Center, ☎ 808/335–3153), created by Walter Lappert in Hanapēpē in 1983 and now a favorite all over Hawai'i. The Lappert shops also sell locally produced gourmet coffees, which are easier to ship home than the ice cream.

Nutcracker Sweet (✉ Coconut Marketplace, 4-484 Kūhiō Hwy., ☎ 808/822–4811) has a delicious assortment of chocolates, preserves, fudges, and gift packs to carry or to mail.

Some of the best prices on Hawai'i's famous macadamia nuts are available at **Star Market** (✉ Kukui Grove Center, 3-2600 Kaumuali'i Hwy., ☎ 808/245–7777).

Gifts

If you've neglected shopping for take-home gifts while you were sightseeing, hiking, and diving, **Hilo Hattie Fashion Factory** (✉ 3252 Kūhiō Hwy., Līhu'e, ☎ 808/245–3404) is the place where you can buy all the hats, baskets, inexpensive shell jewelry, rubber slippers, golf towels, and other trinkets you need to carry home to friends and family. The location is perfect for a last-minute stop en route to Līhu'e airport.

Kong Lung Co. (✉ 2490 Keneke St., Kīlauea, ☎ 808/828–1822), an elegant gift shop sometimes called the Gump's of Kaua'i, combines clothing, glassware, books, and artwork in a unique way, housed in a beautiful 1892 stone structure in out-of-the-way Kīauea.

Eelskin is popular in the Islands, and you can buy it wholesale at **Lee Sands' Eelskin** (✉ Hwy. 50 at Kōloa Rd. in Lāwa'i, ☎ 808/332–8664), an unusual store with such skin lines as sea snake, chicken feet, and frog skin. A lizard card case is available for about $12.

How about a fun beach towel for the folks back home? That's just one of the gifts you can find in the **Village Variety Store** (✉ Ching Young Village, Kūhiō Hwy., Hanalei, ☎ 808/826–6077). It also has shell leis, Kaua'i T-shirts, macadamia nuts, and other great Island souvenirs at low prices.

Hawaiian Arts and Crafts

The **Art Shop** (✉ 3173 'Akahi St., ☎ 808/245–3810) in Līhu'e is an intimate gallery that sells original oils, photos, and sculptures.

You can purchase the works of many local artists—including seascapes by George Sumner and Roy Tabora—at **Kahn Galleries** (✉ Coconut Marketplace, 4-484 Kūhiō Hwy., Kapa'a, ☎ 808/822–3636; ✉ Kilohana Plantation, Līhu'e, ☎ 808/246–4454; and ✉ Kaua'i Village shopping center, Kapa'a, ☎ 808/822–4277).

Kapaia Stitchery (✉ Kūhiō Hwy., in a red building ½ mi north of Līhu'e, ☎ 808/245–2281) features quilting and other fabric arts, plus kits for trying your own hand at various crafts; the kits are great gifts for crafters.

Kaua'i Images Gallery (✉ 4-939D Kūhiō Hwy., ☎ 808/822–1950), in Kapa'a, features original artwork by many of Hawai'i's finest artists. Among the treats are hand-painted photographs by Diane Ferry, whose work has won numerous awards in Kaua'i art shows. Kaua'i Images also offers a large variety of quality frames, some in koa, the rare and highly prized island wood.

Wyland Galleries (✉ Kaua'i Village, 4-831 Kūhiō Hwy., Kapa'a, ☎ 808/822–9855; ✉ Po'ipū Shopping Village, Po'ipū, ☎ 808/742–6030) showcases the work of Wyland, a famed artist of marine life. You can buy his original works, lithographs, prints, and sculptures, plus pieces by other Island artists. Wyland is known for his massive wall murals, and you can see an example of his work on Kūhiō Highway, on the side of a building fronting Kaua'i Village.

Kaua'i artist Peter Kinney specializes in scrimshaw pocket and army knives, available at **Ye Olde Ship Store & Port of Kaua'i** (⊠ Coconut Marketplace, 4-484 Kūhiō Hwy., ☎ 808/822–1401).

Jewelry

Jim Saylor Jewelers (⊠ 1318 Kūhiō Hwy., Kapa'a, ☎ 808/822–3591) showcases a good selection of gems from around the world, with black pearls, diamonds, and unique settings. Jim Saylor has been designing these pretty keepsakes for more than 20 years on Kaua'i.

Kaua'i Gold (⊠ Coconut Marketplace, 4-484 Kūhiō Hwy., ☎ 808/822–9361) presents a wonderful selection of rare Ni'ihau shell leis, strung by women from the Forbidden Isle and ranging from $20 to $200 and up. Take time to ask about these remarkable necklaces before you buy; you'll appreciate the craftsmanship, understand the sometimes high prices, and learn to care for and preserve their fragile beauty. The store also has a selection of 14K gold jewelry.

Remember Kaua'i (⊠ Outrigger Kaua'i Beach Hotel, 4331 Kaua'i Beach Dr., Līhu'e, ☎ 808/245–6650), which also stocks a booth at Po'ipū Spouting Horn, offers mementos of your trip in the form of fashion jewelry, gifts, and Ni'ihau shell necklaces.

Shopping Centers

Ching Young Village (⊠ Kūhiō Hwy., in the heart of Hanalei) draws people to its **Village Variety Store**, with cheap prices on beach towels, macadamia nuts, film and processing, wet suits—you name it. Ching Young Village also has the well-stocked **Hanalei Natural Foods** store, a few steps away from the streetside **Evolve Love Artists Gallery**, where you can find work by local artisans.

In Waipouli, the **Coconut Marketplace** (⊠ 4-484 Kūhiō Hwy.) is part of a larger complex of resort hotels and restaurants, with more than 70 shops selling everything from snacks and slippers to scrimshaw. **Ye Olde Ship Store** sponsors an annual contest for scrimshaw artists and carries pocket knives, boxes, and ivory and bone works of art decorated with intricate designs and scenes.

Kaua'i's west side has a scattering of stores, including those at the no-frills **'Ele'ele Shopping Center** (⊠ Hwy. 50 near Hanapēpē), a good place to rub elbows with local folk.

Hanalei Center (⊠ 5-5016 Kūhiō Hwy., ☎ 808/826–7677) is situated in the old Hanalei School, a building listed on the Historic Register, that has been refurbished and rented out to boutiques and restaurants. After you dig through a wonderful collection of '40s and '50s vintage clothing and memorabilia in the **Yellow Fish Trading Company** or search for that unusual gift at **Sand People,** you can grab a shaved ice and relax on the front deck or lawn, or go Italian for lunch at a charming courtyard restaurant called **Luna Café**.

In Kapa'a, the buildings at **Kaua'i Village** (⊠ 4-831 Kūhiō Hwy., Kapa'a) re-create the style of 19th-century plantation towns. Its **ABC Discount Store** sells sundries, **Safeway** sells groceries and alcoholic beverages, **Wyland Gallery** sells Island art, and **Kaua'i One-Hour Photo** provides speedy film processing.

Kilohana Plantation (⊠ 3-2087 Kaumuali'i Hwy., 1 mi west of Līhu'e) offers a unique collection of plantation-style shops and galleries sprinkled throughout both levels of the main house as well as in quaint guest cottages. Here you'll find an emphasis on handcrafted goods of the Islands; for example, the **Artisans Room,** in the plantation's guest bedroom, sells paintings by Rosalie Rupp Prussing, carvings by Russ Graff, and collages by Cece Rodriguez, as well as limited-edition prints, ceramics, and glass; the **Hawaiian Collection Room,** in the restored cloak room, focuses on unusual crafts, with Ni'ihau shell leis and scrimshaw.

On Kūhiō Highway in Kapa'a is **Kinipopo Shopping Village** (⊠ 4-356 Kūhiō Hwy., across from Sizzler restaurant), which has created a tropical garden setting for casual shopping. Here you'll find the **Goldsmith's Gallery,** which sells handcrafted Hawaiian-style gold jewelry. You can also rent water skis and beach paraphernalia at **Kaua'i Water Ski & Surf Co.** here.

Old **Kōloa** is not a shopping center, but its main street, **Old Kōloa Road,** concentrates several boutiques and eateries in one handy location. Favorites are **Kōloa Ice House and Deli,** which sells shave ice fantasies laced with tropical syrups, **Koloa Fish Market,** for a take-out taste of poke or sashimi, and **Progressive Expressions,** which offers surfing and windsurfing accessories, swimwear, and beachwear.

Kaua'i's largest assemblage of shops is **Kukui Grove Center** (⊠ 3-2600 Kaumuali'i Hwy. on Hwy. 50, just west of Līhu'e). Besides the island's major department stores, it offers a **Longs Drugs,** for personal needs, and **Star Market,** for groceries. You'll find Island-inspired garb at **Hawaiian Islands Creations,** Kaua'i-made gifts at **Kaua'i Products Store,** and athletic footwear at **Foot Locker.**

Po'ipū Shopping Village (⊠ 2360 Kiahuna Plantation Dr., Po'ipū) caters mainly to guests in nearby hotels and condos. Its two dozen shops and half-a-dozen restaurants offer resort wear, gifts, souvenirs, sundries, jewelry, and art.

Princeville Center (⊠ 5-4280 Kūhiō Hwy., Princeville) is an upscale little gathering of such trendy shops as **Kaua'i Kite and Hobby Shop, Pretty Woman,** and **JM's Jewels.** If you're vacationing in a nearby condo and want to shop for dinner, you'll also find a **Foodland,** where you can pick up not only dinner, but a bottle of wine to sip at sunset.

The little town of Kekaha is proud of its tidy **Waimea Canyon Plaza** (⊠ Kōke'e Rd. at Hwy. 50), with shops offering local foods, souvenirs, and gifts.

On the east coast of the island is **Waipouli Town Center** (⊠ 4-901 Kūhiō Hwy.) in Kapa'a, a modest collection of 10 shops where you can buy a T-shirt at **Waipouli Variety** and then grab a good-value plate lunch or sample other local food at **Waipouli Restaurant.**

KAUA'I A TO Z

Arriving and Departing

By Plane

The **Līhu'e Airport** (☎ 808/246–1400) handles most of the air traffic in and out of Kaua'i. Three miles east of the town of Līhu'e, the terminal is spacious and contemporary; it easily accommodates the growing number of visitors to the Garden Isle. Once you arrive, if you have any immediate questions, stop by the **Līhu'e Airport Visitor Information Center** (☎ 808/246–1440), outside each baggage claim area. It's open daily.

North of Līhu'e is **Princeville Airport,** a tiny strip in the middle of rolling ranch lands and sugarcane fields today used primarily by private planes. Princeville Airport is just a five-minute drive from the Princeville development area, which plays home to condos and a luxurious accommodation called the Princeville Hotel. The airport is also about a 10-minute drive from the shops and accommodations of sleepy Hanalei.

FLIGHTS FROM HONOLULU

Carriers flying from Honolulu International Airport to Līhu'e Airport include **Aloha Airlines** (☎ 808/484–1111 or 800/367–5250) and **Hawaiian Airlines** (☎ 808/838–1555 or 800/367–5320). The rates go up and down depending on which airline is trying to outdo the other, ranging from about $61 to $90 one way. Aloha offers more than 20 round-trip flights a day between Honolulu and Līhu'e, while Hawaiian has 14 round-trips. It's a 30- to 40-minute flight between Honolulu and Līhu'e, depending on the aircraft.

BETWEEN THE AIRPORT AND HOTELS

The driving time from Līhu'e Airport to the town of Līhu'e is a mere five minutes. If you're staying in Wailua or Kapa'a, your driving time from Līhu'e is 15 minutes, and to Princeville and Hanalei it takes about 45 minutes behind the wheel. If you're staying in Hanalei, flying into Princeville Airport can save you some driving time.

To the south, it's a 30-minute drive from Līhu'e to Po'ipū, the major resort area. To Waimea it takes one hour, and if you choose the rustic accommodations in the hills of Kōke'e, allow a good hour and a half of driving time from Līhu'e.

Check with your hotel or condo to see if it offers free shuttle service from the airport.

By Car. Car-rental companies have offices at both airports. They'll also provide you with driving directions to your hotel or condo (☞ Car Rentals, *below*).

By Limousine. For luxurious transportation between the airport and your accommodations, contact **Custom Limousine Service** (✉ Box 3267, Līhu'e 96766, ☎ 808/246–6318). Rates are $73.50 per hour, with a two-hour minimum. Also providing more comfortable pre-arranged airport pickup is **Al's Kōloa-Po'ipū VIP Taxi** (✉ Box 374, Po'ipū 96756, ☎ 808/742–1390). **North Shore Limousine** (✉ Box 757, Hanalei 96714, ☎ 808/826–6189) can pick you up at Princeville Airport.

By Taxi. Fares around the island are $2 at the meter drop plus $2 per mile. That means a taxicab from Līhu'e Airport to Līhu'e town runs about $6, and to Po'ipū, about $32, excluding tip.

Two taxi companies that will take you to Līhu'e and Po'ipū are **South Shore Taxi and Tour** (☎ 808/742–1525) and **Kaua'i Cab** (☎ 808/246–9554). Cabs are also available from **ABC Taxi** (☎ 808/822–7641) and **Scotty Taxi** (☎ 808/245–7888).

From the Princeville Airport to Hanalei, you'll pay about $12 when you ride with the **North Shore Cab Company** (☎ 808/826–6189), which serves only the northeast portion of the island.

By Ship

A romantic way to visit Kaua'i for a short time is to book passage on an interisland cruise ship. The massive white "love boat," the *SS Independence,* leaves Honolulu each Saturday and stops at Kaua'i, as well as Maui and Hilo and Kona on the Big Island. At each port of call, you may get off the ship for sightseeing and shore excursions. At Kaua'i, the ship docks at Nāwiliwili on the east coast. Optional extension packages allow you to add a hotel stay before or after the cruise in the port of your choice. **American Hawai'i Cruises** (✉ 1380 Port of New Orleans Pl., New Orleans, LA 70130-1890, ☎ 800/765–7000) has been presenting these successful excursions for years, and the ship was refurbished in 1997. A three-day cruise sampler begins at $624 per person, double occupancy, with weekly rates beginning at $1,145, including meals activities and entertainment on board.

Getting Around

By Bike

A two-wheeler is an exciting way to cruise around the Garden Isle. Its country roads are generally uncrowded, so you can ride along at your own pace and enjoy the views. This is a safe island to explore by bicycle, as long as you exercise caution on the busier thoroughfares. Guests can rent bikes from the activities desks of certain hotels around the island. Check with your concierge or front desk. ☞ Biking *in* Outdoor Activities and Sports, *above,* for information on where to rent bikes.

By Bus

Excursion buses take visitors to such specific commercial attractions as the Fern Grotto, Waimea Canyon, Spouting Horn, Ft. Elisabeth, 'Ōpaeka'a Falls, and Menehune Fishpond (☞ Guided Tours, *below*).

By Car

Although Kaua'i is relatively small, its sights reach from one end of the island to the other. You can walk to the stores and restaurants in your resort area, but the important attractions of the island are generally not within walking distance of each other. As a result, you'll probably want to rent a car, unless you plan to do all your sightseeing with tour companies (☞ Car Rentals, *below*).

It's easy to get around on Kaua'i, for it has one major road that almost encircles the island. Your rental-car company will supply you with a map with enlargements of each area of the island. The traffic on Kaua'i is pretty light most of the time, except in the Līhu'e area during rush hour (6:30 AM–8:30 AM and 3:30 PM–5:30 PM). Major attractions are indicated by a Hawaiian-warrior marker on the side of the road.

As is the case throughout Hawai'i, a seat-belt law is enforced on Kaua'i for front-seat passengers. Children under the age of three must be in a car seat, which you can get from your car-rental company. Although Kaua'i looks like paradise, it has its fair share of crime. Play it safe and lock your car whenever you park it. Don't leave valuables in the car, and pay attention to parking signs, particularly in Līhu'e.

By Limousine

One doesn't see many limousines cruising the country roads of Kaua'i, but if the idea intrigues you, contact **Custom Limo** (✉ Box 3267, Līhu'e 96766, ☎ 808/246–6318). Among its options are airport service, touring, wedding packages, lei greetings, and complete ground handling. Another option for luxury travel is **Al's Kōloa-Po'ipū VIP Taxi** (✉ Box 374, Po'ipū 96756, ☎ 808/742–1390). **North Shore Limousine** (✉ Box 757, Hanalei 96714, ☎ 808/826–6189) specializes in service in the Hanalei and Princeville areas.

By Taxi

A taxicab will take you all around the island, but you'll pay dearly for the service. The cost for each mile is $2, after a $2 meter drop, so from Līhu'e to Po'ipū the price is $32; from Līhu'e to Princeville, $50, excluding tip. Your best bet is to call a cab for short distances only (to a restaurant, for instance). A 5-mi cab ride will run you about $12 plus tip. The drivers are often from Kaua'i, which means they'll give you information about the island.

Two reliable cab companies on the island are **City Cab** (☎ 808/245–3227) and **Kaua'i Cab** (☎ 808/246–9554). Based in Princeville is the **North Shore**

Cab Company (☎ 808/826–6189), which provides complete ground handling services for the north and east sections of the island.

Contacts and Resources

B&B Reservation Services

The following are two Kauai-based services: **Bed and Breakfast Kaua'i** (✉ 6436 Kalama Rd., Kapa'a, 96746,☎ 808/822–1177 or 800/822–1176, ℻ 808/822–5757) and **Bed and Breakfast Hawa'ii** (✉ Box 449, Kapa'a 96746, ☎ 808/822–7771 or 800/733–1632).

Island-wide reservations services include the following: **All Islands Bed and Breakfast** (✉ 463 Iliwahi Loop, Kailua 96734, ☎ 808/263–2342 or 800/542–0344, ℻ 808/263–0308), **Bed and Breakfast Honolulu** (✉ 3242 Kā'ohinani Dr., Honolulu 96817, ☎ 808/595–7533 or 800/288–4666, ℻ 808/595–2030), and **Hawaiian Islands Bed and Breakfasts and Vacation Rentals** (✉ 1277 Mokulua Dr., Kailua 96734,☎ 808/261–7895 or 800/258–7895).

Car Rentals

Unless you plan to do all of your sightseeing as part of guided van tours, you will want a rental car on Kaua'i. The vast beauty of the island begs to be explored, and its attractions are sprinkled from one end to the other. It is advisable to reserve your vehicle before you arrive, especially if you will be on Kaua'i during the peak seasons of summer, the Christmas holidays, and February.

Right across from the baggage claim area at Līhu'e Airport you'll find several rental-car firms, as well as vans that will shuttle you to offices nearby. Rental companies also have desks at Princeville Airport. There are also several lesser-known and local companies that offer slightly lower rates. Daily prices for a car from the major-name companies begin at $25. A fly-drive deal can sometimes reduce that cost to $22, and many hotels and even some condos offer packages that include rental cars. There is a $2 daily surcharge on all rentals.

Car-rental companies with offices at or near Līhu'e Airport are **Alamo** (☎ 800/462–5266), **Avis** (☎ 800/831–8000), **Budget** (☎ 800/527–0700), **Dollar** (☎ 800/342–7398 or, from outside HI, 800/800–4000), **Hertz** (☎ 800/654–3011), and **National** (☎ 800/227–7368).

Companies with Princeville Airport offices are **Avis** and **Hertz.** Several companies also operate reservation desks at the major hotels on the island. These include **Avis** (✉ Hyatt Regency Kaua'i, ☎ 808/742–1627).

You can get some good deals on a car if you book with one of Kaua'i's budget or used-car rental companies. These include the reliable **Westside U-Drive** (☎ 808/332–8644), which rents cars from $19.95 and jeeps from $59.95. They keep their vehicles in good shape, and they offer free delivery and pickup of your car at your hotel or condo.

Doctors

The **Kaua'i Medical Clinic** (KMC) has staff with 32 different specialties, so they can handle all medical problems. It has lab and X-ray facilities, physical therapy, optometry, and emergency rooms. The **main clinic** (✉ 3420-B Kūhiō Hwy., Līhu'e, ☎ 808/245–1500) is in Līhu'e. Other KMC clinics are in Kīlauea (North Shore Clinic; ☎ 808/828–1418), Kukui Grove (☎ 808/246–0051), Kōloa (☎ 808/742–1621), and Kapa'a (☎ 808/822–3431). Physicians are on call 24 hours (☎ 808/245–1831).

Emergencies

Police, ambulance, or **fire department** (☎ 911).

Wilcox Memorial Hospital (⊠ 3420 Kūhiō Hwy., Līhu'e, ☎ 808/245–1100). **Kaua'i Veterans Memorial Hospital** (⊠ 4643 Waimea Canyon Dr., Waimea, ☎ 808/338–9431).

Guided Tours

There are three major methods for getting a good guided look at the Garden Isle: by land, by sea, and by air. You can book these tours through the travel desk of your hotel or call directly.

Kayak Kaua'i. Hawai'i's forests and marshes are the home of rare and exceptional flora and fauna, which often go unseen. In addition to kayak rentals and half-day tours for intrepid explorers that traverse mountains, rivers, and ocean, Kayak Kaua'i also offers a Discovery Tour of Kaua'i, a seven-day paddling and hiking adventure with six nights spent in out-of-the-way inns and cottages. ⊠ *Box 508, Hanalei 96714,* ☎ *808/826–9844.* ⊠ *$1,350, including accommodations, transportation, boats, and meals.*

Kaua'i Mountain Tours. You'll get *way* off the beaten track on this four-wheel-drive van excursion through Nā Pali–Kona Forest Preserve and the rugged side of Waimea Canyon. The price includes picnic lunch and hotel pickup. ⊠ *Box 3069, Līhu'e 96766,* ☎ *808/245–7224 or 800/452–1113.* ⊠ *$88.*

Kaua'i from the air is mind-boggling. In an hour you can see waterfalls, craters, and places that are inaccessible even by hiking trails. Expect to pay $125 or more per person for the longest, most comprehensive tours, but call around for itineraries; a shorter, less expensive flight might suit your needs. Don't be afraid to ask about the pilot's experience and safety record. The companies use top-of-the-line equipment and the operators listed below each have reliable flight experience.

Bali Hai Helicopters (☎ 808/335–3166 or 800/325–8687) offers a round-island, photographer's delight aboard a Bell 206-B Jet Ranger on Kaua'i's west side.

Hawai'i Helicopters (☎ 808/826–6591 or 800/367–7095) flies out of Princeville on the north shore and offers three tours ranging from 30 minutes to 60 minutes and from $99 to $179.

South Sea Tour Co. (☎ 808/245–2222 or 800/367–2914) has a choice of tours available from Līhu'e.

Will Squyres Helicopter Tours (☎ 808/245–8881) has group rates and charters from Līhu'e.

Sometimes called the **Wailua River/Waimea Canyon Tour,** this is a good overview of the island, because you get to see all the sights, including Ft. Elisabeth, 'Ōpaeka'a Falls, and Menehune Fishpond. Guests are transported in air-conditioned 17-passenger minivans. The trip includes a boat ride up the Wailua River to Fern Grotto, then a drive around the island to scenic views above Waimea Canyon. The tour stops at a casual restaurant for lunch (not included in tour price). Companies offering round-the-island ground tours include Polynesian Adventure Tours and Roberts Hawai'i Tours (☞ Tour Companies, *below*).

Best of Kaua'i Tour. This whirlwind daylong tour, sponsored by the North Shore Cab Company, focuses on the highlights of the east and north shores. It includes a visit to **Kilohana**, a refurbished plantation mansion in Līhu'e, followed by a boat ride to the **Fern Grotto**. Later, you take a tour of **Kīlauea Lighthouse** and end with a helicopter tour out of Līhu'e Airport. Ground transportation is in 15-passenger, air-conditioned vans. North Shore Cab will pick you up at Līhu'e Airport or at your hotel if it's on the north or east side of the island. ⊠ *Box 757, Hanalei 96714,* ☎ *808/826–6189.* 🚐 *$129 per person with minimum 12 people.*

SPECIAL-INTEREST TOURS

Fern Grotto. Cruise boats depart Wailua Marina at the mouth of the Wailua River for the **Fern Grotto.** Round-trip excursions, on 150-passenger flat-bottom riverboats, take an hour and a half, including time to walk around the grotto and environs. During the boat ride, guitar and 'ukulele players regale you with Hawaiian melodies, and tell the history of the river. The 3-mi upriver trip culminates at a yawning lava tube that is covered with enormous fishtail ferns. Two companies offer several trips daily to Fern Grotto: **Wai'ale'ale Boat Tours** (⊠ Wailua Marina, Kapa'a, ☎ 808/822–4908) and **Smith's Motor Boat Service** (⊠ 174 Wailua Rd., Kapa'a, ☎ 808/821–6892). Both charge $15 for the trip.

Ni'ihau Tours. Once it was called the Forbidden Isle. Now it takes only 12 minutes to fly from Kaua'i to an island that few outsiders have set foot on since Elizabeth Sinclair bought it from King Kamehameha V in 1864. This 72-square-mi island just 17 mi from Kaua'i is now run by the Robinson family, who raise cattle and sheep on the barren, arid land. The Robinsons continue to preserve Ni'ihau as a last refuge of primitive Hawai'i. Island residents speak Hawaiian and do not use electricity, plumbing, or telephones; they ride bikes and horses to get around. Bruce Robinson initiated Ni'ihau Helicopters in 1987 in order to boost the struggling island economy. Tours avoid the western coastline, where Pu'uwai village—home to the island's 200 residents—is located. Flights depart from and return to Kaua'i's **Burns Field,** near Hanapēpē, and are conducted in an Agusta 109 twin-engine, seven-passenger, single-pilot helicopter. The first touchdown on the two-stop tour is near the sunken crater of Lehua. The second takes you to a cliff overlooking the beach coves of Keanahaki Bay. It's the perfect tour for those with a yen to explore untrammeled territory. There is a four-passenger minimum for each flight, and reservations are essential. Ground transportation is not available. ⊠ *Ni'ihau Helicopters, Box 370, Makaweli 96769,* ☎ *808/335–3500.* 🚁 *3-hr tour with 2 stops $280.*

SUNSET CRUISES

Blue Water Sailing. Up to 12 passengers can board a 42-ft luxury Pearson sailing yacht in Port Allen for a two-hour sunset cruise in the turquoise waters of the southern shore. Juice, sodas, and snacks are included in the $45 cost. ⊠ *Box 250, 'Ele'ele 96705,* ☎ *808/822–0525.*

Captain Andy's Sailing Adventures. The 55-ft catamaran *Spirit of Kaua'i* takes passengers on a two-hour sunset sail along the south shore. Hors d'oeuvres and beverages are included in the $45 cost. Captain Andy also offers a four-hour snorkeling excursion with snacks for $75 and a five-hour Nā Pali cruise from Port Allen with breakfast and lunch for $95. ⊠ *Box 1291, Kōloa 96756,* ☎ *808/822–7833.*

TOUR COMPANIES

The companies that take you on guided ground tours of Kaua'i use big air-conditioned buses and stretch limousines as well as smaller vans. The latter seem to fit in more with the countrified atmosphere of Kaua'i. Whether you choose a bus or van tour, the equipment will be in excellent shape, because each of these companies wants your business. When you make your reservations, ask what kind of vehicle you'll be riding in and which tours let you get off and look around. The guides are friendly and generally know their island inside out. It's customary to tip them $2 or more per person for their efforts.

If you're interested in a north-shore sea excursion, be forewarned that big winter waves often cause trips to be cancelled, so call first to find out if the company you're interested in is operating. The best-known and most reliable land, sea, and air tour companies on Kaua'i are the following:

Captain Zodiac Raft Expeditions (⊠ Box 456, Hanalei 96714, ☎ 808/826–9371 or 800/422–7824) has long been known for its three-, four-, and five-hour boat trips along the Nā Pali Coast.

Kaua'i Island Tours (⊠ Box 1645, Līhu'e 96766, ☎ 808/245–4777 or 800/733–4777) takes you around Kaua'i in 11-, 21-, 45-, and 57-passenger vans and six-passenger Lincoln Town Cars.

Liko Kaua'i Cruises (⊠ Box 18, Waimea 96796, ☎ 808/338–0333 or 888/732–5456) tour the northern coastline in a 38-ft cabin cruiser while captains share Hawaiian history and legends. Boats depart for 4 ½-hour tours from Kīkīaola Harbor in Waimea.

Nā Pali Explorer (⊠ 'Ele'ele Shopping Center, 9600 Kaumuali'i Hwy., Waiema 96796, ☎ 808/335–9909) departs at 8:30 from Port Allen (convenient to South and East Shore visitors), to tour the southern coast or the Nā Pali Coast (weather permitting) in a 48-ft adventure craft with an onboard toilet and shade canopy. During the winter months, whale watching can get up close and personal, as the boat gets you down close to the water. Trips include Continental breakfast, snacks and/or picnic lunch, snorkel gear, and a Hawaiian cultural specialist to answer questions at rates that range from $62.50 to $122.92 depending on length and type of excursion. Charters are available.

Polynesian Adventure Tours (⊠ 3113-B Oihana St., Līhu'e 96766, ☎ 808/246–0122 or 800/622–3011) specializes in full- and half-day mini-coach tours of Waimea Canyon, Wailua River, and Kaua'i's north shore.

Roberts Hawai'i Tours (⊠ Box 3389, Līhu'e 96766, ☎ 808/245–9558) has top-of-the-line air-conditioned vehicles.

South Sea Tours (⊠ 2901 Mokulele Loop, Box 32, Līhu'e 96766, ☎ 808/245–2222 or 800/367–2914) offers one-hour tours and a 4½-hour around-the-island tour on *Thunder,* a 38-ft Fountain Speedboat that seats six, as well as a number of helicopter tours.

Trans Hawaiian Services (⊠ 1770 Haleukana St., Puhi 96766, ☎ 808/245–5108 or 800/533–8765) offers multilingual tours of Waimea Cayon and Hanaei.

Pharmacies

Except for Long's Drug Store most pharmacies close about 5 PM on Kau'i. The **Kaua'i Medical Clinic** (⊠ 3420-B Kūhiō Hwy., Līhu'e 96766, ☎ 808/245–1500) has well-stocked pharmacies at its several locations (☞ Doctors, *above*). In Līhu'e, try **Longs Drug Store** (⊠ Kukui Grove Center, Hwy. 50, ☎ 808/245–7771); in Kapa'a, try **Shoreview Pharmacy** (⊠ 4-1177 Kūhiō Hwy., Suite 113, ☎ 808/822–1447); and in Hanapēpē, **Westside Pharmacy** (⊠ 1-3845 Kaumuali'i Hwy., ☎ 808/335–5342).

Visitor Information

The **Hawai'i Visitors and Convention Bureau** (⊠ 3016 'Umi St., Līhu'e Plaza, Suite 207, Līhu'e 96766, ☎ 808/245–3971, ꜰᴀx 808/246–9235) is easy to find. 'Umi Street runs off Rice Street, Līhu'e's main thor-

oughfare, right near the Kaua'i Museum. The bureau has a good selection of brochures and other visitor's literature, including such free
weekly visitor's magazines as *Spotlight Kaua'i* and *This Week on
Kaua'i,* and the quarterly *Menu* magazine.

Po'ipū Resort Association (✉ Box 730, Koloa 96756, ☎ 808/742–7444,
FAX 808/742–7887) is the central source of information about the south
shore. Maps and brochures are sent on request.

The **Kaua'i Visitor Center** (✉ Kaua'i Village, Kapa'a, ☎ 808/639–
6175, FAX 808/332–8676) is another good source of information about
the Garden Isle. It handles reservations for a variety of activities and
has current brochures and schedules on hand.

Several activity centers will help visitors book tours, arrange sporting
excursions, rent cars, reserve rooms in hotels and condos, and even plan
weddings. These centers include **Ray's Rentals and Activities** (✉ 4558
Kukui St., Kapa'a, ☎ 808/822–5700), **Hawaiian Fantasy Activities** (✉
4331 Kaua'i Beach Dr., Līhu'e, ☎ 808/246–0111), and the **Chopper
Shop** (✉ Po'ipū Shopping Village, 2360 Kiahuna Plantation Dr., Po'ipū,
☎ 808/742–7000 or 800/829–5999).

6 Moloka'i

Something about this island makes it stand out from its neighbors. You can see it in the way the sun hits the water of ancient fishponds, or hear it as the waves break on Pāpōhaku Beach. There's a mysterious sensuality here that springs from the island's history and inspires its present.

NICKNAMES FOR MOLOKA'I have come and gone. In ancient times it was called "Moloka'i of the Potent Prayers," for its powerful *kahuna* (priests) who worshiped in solitude. During the late 1800s it was dubbed the "Forbidden Isle," because Hawai'i's lepers were banished here to a remote peninsula on the northern shore called Kalaupapa. Only in the last few decades has it worn the nickname, "Friendly Isle."

By Marty
Wentzel

Updated by
Betty Fullard-
Leo

Today those who visit the Friendly Isles' shores quickly become aware of its down-to-earth charm. As its neighboring islands become crowded with high-rise hotels, Moloka'i greets its guests modestly with a handful of basic accommodations and unusual sightseeing alternatives.

The Friendly Isle seduces visitors to explore its enveloping tropical outdoors. You can ride a mule or hike a switchback trail down a steep mountain to Kalaupapa, the historic colony once reserved for sufferers of Hansen's disease (leprosy). Tours of the settlement begin at the base of towering sea cliffs. To the east, a horse-drawn wagon tour takes you to Hawai'i's largest *heiau* (outdoor shrine) and through enormous mango and coconut groves. In the island's highest reaches you can explore the Kamakou Preserve atop Mt. Kamakou, the 2,774-acre refuge for endangered birds, plants, and wildlife.

Moloka'i also appeals to visitors who enjoy adventure at a personal pace. Plenty of opportunities are available for snorkeling, swimming, hiking, and sunbathing, but there are fewer facilities for organized sports such as fishing, horseback riding, tennis, and golf. The more creative you are, the more you will enjoy your stay.

A major plus of the Friendly Isle is that it is uncluttered. You can drive your rental car down any road and take your time looking around without fear of someone honking at you to maintain the speed limit. Sometimes yours is the only car on the road. There are no buildings higher than three stories, no elevators, no traffic jams, and no stoplights. The fanciest hotels are bungalow-style low rises.

Moloka'i has miles and miles of undeveloped countryside, like the picturesque farmlands of Moloka'i Ranch (the island's largest local landholder) and the acres of abandoned pineapple fields. Pineapples—seemingly synonymous with Hawai'i in the popular imagination—were once big business for the Dole and Del Monte companies, but the crop's significance to the island's economy has sharply diminished in the face of foreign competition.

At night from beaches on the western shore, you can see the twinkling lights of O'ahu 25 mi across the channel. In spirit, however, Moloka'i is much, much farther away from its highly developed neighbor. With its slow pace and simple beauty, Moloka'i drowses in another era, and, if its 6,861 proud people have their way, it's likely to continue to.

Pleasures and Pastimes

Dining

The choice of restaurants on Moloka'i is limited. During a week's stay, you might easily hit all the dining spots worth a visit, then return to your favorites for a second round. The dining scene is fun, nevertheless, because it is a microcosm of Hawai'i's diverse cultures. You'll find locally grown vegetarian foods, spicy Filipino cuisine, and Hawaiian-style fish—such as ahi or aku (types of tuna), mullet or moon fish, grilled, sautéed, or sliced and mixed with seaweed and eaten raw as poke—all on Ala Malama Street in Kaunakakai, with pizza, pasta, and ribs only a block away. What's more, the price is right at Kaunakakai's eateries—most of them fall into our least expensive ($) category. For something a bit fancier (but casual just the same), try dinner at Kaluako'i Hotel and Golf Club's Ohia Lodge.

Festivals and Seasonal Events

The island has several events around which you might want to plan a trip. For more information, *see* Festivals and Seasonal Events *in* Chapter 1. Translated, **Moloka'i Ka Hula Piko** means "A Celebration of the Birth of Hula on Moloka'i." The annual day-long event in May brings performances by some of the state's best hula troupes, musicians, singers, lecturers, and storytellers. It's all in tribute to Kā'ana, on the slopes of Maunaloa Mountain, which is reputed to be the birthplace of the hula. The **Moloka'i-to-Oahu Canoe Race** is the world's major long-course outrigger canoeing event. The best in the field turn up to participate. It begins on the southwest coast near the harbors of Haleolono. After paddling across the rough Kaiwi Channel, participants finish at Ft. DeRussy Beach in Waikīkī. The event takes place each September (women) and October (men). The **Moloka'i Mule Drag** is based on the principle that when you pull a mule, the mule pulls back. Teams of draggers do whatever it takes to move their mules 200 yards to the finish line as spectators cheer them on. It all takes place on Kaunakakai's main street at the end of September. The **Moloka'i Ranch Rodeo** draws cowpokes from around the state, who vie for a $25,000 cash purse and prizes in contests ranging from bull riding to barrel racing. It takes place over Thanksgiving Day weekend.

Lodging

Moloka'i appeals less to travelers who like impeccable furnishings and swanky amenities than to those who appreciate genuine Hawaiian hospitality in no-frills, down-home surroundings. Because much of the island is still undeveloped, hotel and condominium properties range from adequate to funky. Kaluako'i Hotel and Golf Club has the best hotel, while Kaunakakai's accommodations lend themselves to visitors on a tight budget and to those who want a central location. There's also a handful of bed-and-breakfasts, as well as the luxury campsites at Moloka'i Ranch, where you can stay in a bungalow-size tent, complete with a queen-size bed and a private bathroom.

Your interest in sports might influence your lodging choice. Moloka'i Ranch is the place to stay for people who want to be active: horseback riding, mountain biking, snorkeling, kayaking, and other activities are included in the lodging price and are available only to guests. Ke Nani Kai and Wavecrest have tennis courts available only to guests.

Outdoor Activities and Sports

Moloka'i's unspoiled beauty, sunny skies, and fragrant winds constantly beckon outdoors lovers. See Lodging, *above,* for tips on choosing your accommodations based on your interests in different sports. Moloka'i's leading adventure, by far, is a mule ride down a narrow 1,664-foot cliff over a 2.9-mi 26-switchback trail to Kalaupapa National Historical Park (☞ Central Molokai, *below*). You can also take a guided trek through Kamakou Preserve (☞ Central Molokai, *below*), a Hawai'i Nature Conservancy rain-forest preserve for endangered plants and birds, but arrangements must be made in advance.

GOLF

Hitting that little dimpled ball becomes a challenge when the wind is up on the beachfront course designed by Ted Robinson at Kaulako'i Hotel and Golf Club. Moloka'i's only other golf course, the public Ironwood Hills Golf Course, is a cool alternative at a reasonable price for nine holes of play, and you can get a discount if you go around the course a second time.

WATER SPORTS

Kayakers and hikers can head out on their own or try a guided excursion. At Kaunakakai Wharf, you can arrange a fishing charter, a sailing-snorkeling-scuba outing or book a whale-watching cruise. Divers should try Mokuho'oniki Island, at the east end of the island. It was once a military bombing target, and artifacts from World War II are scattered throughout its many pinnacles and drop-offs. The area is home to barracuda and gray reef sharks; black coral is also found here. Depths range from 30 ft to 100 ft.

EXPLORING MOLOKA'I

Moloka'i is long and shaped like a slipper with the "heel" facing west and the "toe" pointing to the east. The imaginary dividing line is the town of Kaunakakai, which is right in the center of the island's southern shore. West, Central, and East Moloka'i are used as natural divisions in this chapter.

You'll have the most fun if you explore at your own pace in a rental car. Most of the highlights are natural landmarks—waterfalls, valleys, overlooks, and the like—and it's nice to get out and wander around an area at your leisure without worrying that you'll miss the tour bus.

Directions on Moloka'i are often referred to as *mauka* (toward the mountains) and *makai* (toward the ocean). You'll find these terms used in this chapter.

Numbers in the text correspond to numbers in the margin and on the Moloka'i map.

Great Itineraries

Moloka'i is small enough that you can travel it end to end in a rental car in a single day. There are no traffic jams to hold you up—unless you get behind a horseback rider or couple of friendly locals who have stopped their vehicles in the middle of the road to chat. The essence of Moloka'i is the "hang loose" attitude, so to experience the island properly, pace yourself—focus on just a few sights per day rather than trying to cram it all in at once.

IF YOU HAVE 1 DAY

Book a **Moloka'i Mule Ride** ④ and a tour of **Kalaupapa** ⑥ prior to leaving home. Fly into Ho'olehua Airport and drive to to Ka La'e where the steep, 26-switchback trail begins. The tour of the former leper colony, where 68 people live with the now manageable disease now known as Hansen's disease, is the most emotionally moving experience on Moloka'i, and if you ask nicely, you might be able to convince your driver to stop at **Pālā'au State Park** ⑧ for a photo of the Phallic Rock before you head back to the airport in the afternoon. For less adventurous souls, flights directly to Kalaupapa can be arranged, thereby eliminating the grueling mule ride.

IF YOU HAVE TWO DAYS

Maunaloa ③ on West Moloka'i makes a good starting point, particularly because many visitors stay in the hotel or condominiums at **Kalu-ako'i Hotel and Golf Club** ①, or in Moloka'i Ranch's luxurious camping facilities. Spend a little time poking through the jumble of treasures at the Plantation Gallery and the adjacent Big Wind Kite Factory, then explore the rest of the town. Stop for lunch at the Village Grill. On Moloka'i, one of the first orders of business for any vacation ought to be to relax, so by afternoon you'll want to head for the nearest beach—this could be Kaluako'i Hotel and Golf Club's own Kawākiu Beach or, if you prefer privacy, **Pāpōhaku Beach** ② a few miles southwest of the hotel. When the lengthening rays of the sun signal dinner time, the resort's Ohia Lodge is a natural choice. Reserve day two for the **Moloka'i Mule Ride** ④ and a tour of **Kalaupapa** ⑥, taking in **Pālā'au State Park** ⑤ and the Phallic Rock afterward. If you've got the stamina after the ride, stop by **Coffees of Hawai'i** ⑧, **R.W. Meyer Sugar Mill** ⑦, and **Purdy's Macadamia Nut Farm** ⑨. If not, pause for chocolate macadamia nut cheesecake at the Kualapu'u Cookhouse before heading back to your resort to pack for a late flight.

IF YOU HAVE FOUR DAYS

Follow the itinerary above for your first two days, then visit **Kaunakaka'i** ⑫ on your third day to pick up souvenir T-shirts, sample ethnic foods, and stop at the Kanemitsu Bakery for the basis of a picnic later in the day; try the *lavosh,* a Kanemitsu specialty flavored with sesame, Maui onion, parmesan cheese, or jalapeño; or a round Moloka'i bread—a sweet, pan-style white loaf. Check out **Kaunakakai Wharf** ⑬ (you might rent a kayak to take along, or set out on a fishing or scuba excursion from here). Otherwise, continue on a leisurely drive to Moloka'i's east end. Along the way, you'll find such sightseeing points as **Kaloko'eli Fishpond** ⑭, Saint Joseph's Church near **Kamalō** ⑮, and **'Ili'ili'ōpae Heiau,** turning around for the return drive when you reach **Hālawa Valley** ⑱. Your final day on Moloka'i should be reserved for your own pleasures—perhaps a morning game of golf, an easy hike, a return to the pleasures of the beach, or an easy drive to see anything you might have missed.

When to Tour Moloka'i

Moloka'i's weather is good year round, and you'll seldom encounter big crowds either in-season or out. At any time of year the west end of the island is relatively dry and free of rain—hence its arid landscape. The island gets crowded during special events and festivals, but for a real taste of old Hawai'i you might want to visit during these weekends anyway. Just be sure you make reservations well in advance if you schedule a trip during the Moloka'i Ka Hula Piko in May, Moloka'i Ranch's Rodeo Days over Thanksgiving weekend, or the Moloka'i Mule Drag at the end of September.

West Moloka'i

Much drier than the east, the western region of the island is largely made up of Moloka'i Ranch, a 53,000-acre tract. Its rolling pastures and farmlands are presided over by Maunaloa, a sleepy little plantation town with a dormant volcano of the same name. West Moloka'i has two additional claims to fame: Kaluako'i Hotel and Golf Club and Pāpōhaku, the island's best beach.

A Good Drive

This driving tour focuses on two of Moloka'i's only areas of "civilization." If you're approaching the west end from Kaunakakai on Highway 460 (also called the Kamehameha V Highway), turn right down Kaluako'i Road and right again at the sign for **Kaluako'i Hotel and Golf Club** ①. Park in one of the many small public lots in front of the resort, then stroll the grounds past the swimming pool, golf course, tennis courts, and restaurant. Stop on the hillside above the beach for gorgeous ocean views, particularly at sunset. If you need information about touring the island, ask at the activities desk in the lobby.

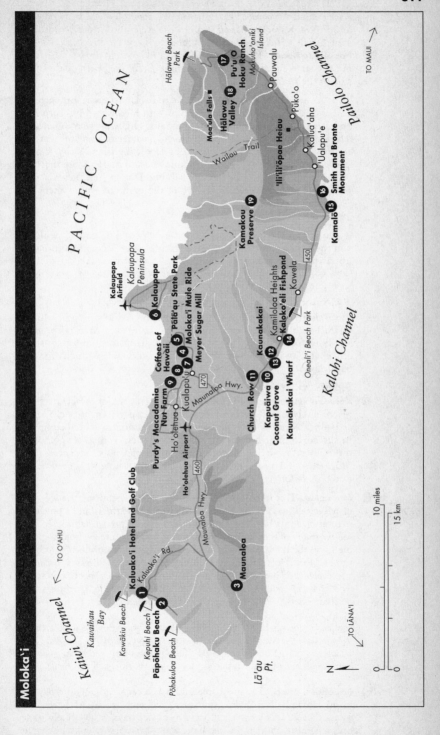

Moloka'i

PACIFIC OCEAN

Kaiwi Channel

TO O'AHU

Kauaibau Bay

Kawākiu Beach

Kepuhi Beach

Pāpōhaku Beach

Pōhakuloa Beach

Lā'au Pt.

TO LĀNA'I

N

0   10 miles
0   15 km

Kaluako'i Hotel and Golf Club **1**

Pāpōhaku Beach **2**

Kaluako'i Rd.

Maunaloa **3**

Maunaloa Hwy.

Maunaloa Hwy.

Ho'olehua

Ho'olehua Airport

460

Purdy's Macadamia Nut Farm

Coffees of Hawaii

Kaunakakai Wharf

Kapuāiwa Coconut Grove

Church Row **11**

Kualapu'u

470

Meyer Sugar Mill

Moloka'i Mule Ride **4**

Pālā'au State Park **5**

Kalaupapa **6**

Kalaupapa Airfield

Kalaupapa Peninsula

9 Purdy's Macadamia Nut Farm

8 **7**

10 Kapuāiwa Coconut Grove

13 **12** Kaunakakai

Kamiloloa Heights

14 Kaloko'eli Fishpond

Kawela

450

Onealí'i Beach Park

Kalohi Channel

Kamakou Preserve **19**

'Ili'ili'ōpae Heiau

16 Smith and Bronte Monument

15 Kamalō

Kalua'e

'Ualapu'e

Kalua'aha

Pūko'o

Pauwalu

Pu'u O Hoku Ranch **17**

Hālawa Valley **18**

Mo'oula Falls

Hālawa Beach Park

Wailau Trail

Mokuho'oniki Island

Pailolo Channel

TO MAUI

Back behind the wheel, turn right out of Kaluako'i Hotel and Golf Club and follow Kaluako'i Road 2 mi to the west until it dead-ends. This shoreline drive takes you past a number of lovely beach parks, including **Pāpōhaku Beach** ②, the largest white-sand beach in the Islands. To get out and stroll in the sand, look for a big sign for the beach on the makai side of the road.

Turn around and follow Kaluako'i Road back past the resort entrance, and continue uphill to its intersection with Highway 460. Turn right and drive 2 mi on Highway 460 (Maunaloa Highway) to **Maunaloa** ③, a former plantation town with a colorful past, a charming present, and controversial plans for the future. In 1997, the island's first cinema opened by Moloka'i Ranch in Maunaloa, and in 1998 the first fast-food restaurant—a KFC—started serving. Due in June 1999 is a 60-room lodge. All these changes are in the name of employment and economic opportunity.

TIMING

If you follow this excursion at a leisurely Moloka'i pace, it will take you the better part of a day, particularly if your accommodations are not on the west end of the island. A walk around Kaluako'i Hotel and Golf Club, with stops in its shops, can take an hour or more. Most stores are open 9–5.

Another hour can fly by at Pāpōhaku Beach, as you dig your toes in its sands and picnic on its shady grassy area. Avoid sitting or walking on the beach between 11 AM and 1 PM when the sun is at its peak. Allow one hour for exploring Maunaloa's main street to shop for souvenirs and chat with local shop owners. Do your shopping Monday through Saturday or you will likely find a CLOSED sign on the door.

Sights to See

❶ **Kaluako'i Hotel and Golf Club.** Moloka'i's only major resort covers approximately 6,700 acres of beachfront property including 5 mi of coastline. Developed in 1968, it looks tame and manicured compared to the surrounding wilds of Moloka'i Ranch. Kaluako'i comprises three bungalow-style condominiums and a hotel, plus residences, ranch properties, a 10-acre beach park, and an 18-hole golf course. (☞ Lodging, *below*.)

★ ❸ **Maunaloa.** This blink-and-you'll-miss-it town anchoring the west end of Moloka'i was established in 1923 to support the island's pineapple plantation in its heyday. Although the fields of golden fruit have gone fallow, many of the workers' dwellings still stand and new homes springing up at the far end of town evoke an earlier plantation-style architecture. Colorful local characters run the half-dozen businesses (including a kite shop and a classic old market) along the town's short main street. This is also headquarters for Moloka'i Ranch, with its Outfitters Center and rodeo arena. ⊠ *Western end of Maunaloa Hwy. (Hwy. 460).*

NEED A
BREAK?

Maunaloa town's best—albeit only—place for a sit-down snack is **The Village Grill** (⊠ Mauka side of Maunaloa Hwy. , ☎ 808/552–0012), which has an antique wooden bar. Stop in for just a cold soda or something more substantial—a burger, salad, pasta, ribs, or fresh fish.

❷ **Pāpōhaku Beach.** The most splendid beach on Moloka'i, and perhaps in all Hawai'i, Pāpōhaku, the state's biggest beach, stretches 3 mi along the island's western shore. On busier days you're likely to see only a handful of other people. If the waves are up, stay out of the water. Instead, sunbathe, relax in the shade of its grassy area, or take a walk along the sand. ⊠ *Kaluako'i Rd., 2 mi from Kaluako'i Resort.*

Central Moloka'i

The center of the island is where the action is, relatively speaking. If you opt to do the Moloka'i Mule Ride in the morning and still feel up to exploring afterwards, you can make quick stops at the places along the drive that follows. Central Moloka'i has the shops and eateries of Kaunakakai, the water sports based at Kaunakakai Wharf, and the attractions and natural beauty of the central highlands.

A Good Drive

Driving from the Kaluko'i Resort in West Moloka'i toward the center of the island, you can see how the island is laid out: two dormant volcanoes connected by a vast plain. If you have reserved the **Moloka'i Mule Ride** ④, go directly to Kae Lae. Head mauka on Highway 460 and north on Highway 470 to reach the ride. The highway ends at **Pālā'au State Park** ⑤, where you can admire knockout views of **Kalaupapa** ⑥ and the Kalaupapa Peninsula. Bring along a light jacket for your time outdoors here.

On the way back down the hill on Highway 470, stop at the **R.W. Meyer Sugar Mill** ⑦ to see photos and machinery from earlier times. Then turn right on Farrington Highway to visit the miniscule town of Kualapu'u, where **Coffees of Hawai'i** ⑧ has a plantation store and espresso bar, and offers tours of its coffee fields and processing plant. A five-minute drive west takes you to **Purdy's Macadamia Nut Farm** ⑨ in Ho'olehua.

Head back on Farrington Highway, then take a right onto Highway 470; take it down the rest of the hill and turn left on Highway 460. Near the ocean on Highway 460 are two stops of note—and they're practically right across the road from each other: **Kapuāiwa Coconut Grove** ⑩ and **Church Row** ⑪.

Follow Highway 460 east to reach **Kaunakakai** ⑫, Moloka'i's "big city." Folks who love the ocean will want to locate the **Kaunakakai Wharf** ⑬, the home base for deep-sea fishing excursions and other adventures.

TIMING

If you save the Moloka'i Mule Ride for another day, there's no need to rush; otherwise many shops in Kaunakakai may be closed by the time you get there. Allow at least a day to explore this part of the island. If you like big breakfasts, reserve an hour for the Kualapu'u Cookhouse. During your tour of the highlands, take an hour to visit the sugar museum and another hour or more for the macadamia nut farm and plantation store. Enjoy these activities Monday through Saturday, since they're closed on Sunday. Once you hit Kaunakakai, indulge yourself: take an hour or two to stroll around town and "talk story" with the locals. Be sure to save a half hour for snacks at the Kanemitsu Bakery, a local institution.

Sights to See

⑪ **Church Row.** Standing cheek by jowl along the highway are several houses of worship with primarily native Hawaiian congregations. Notice the unadorned, boxlike style of architecture so familiar to missionary homes. ⊠ *Mauka side of Hwy. 460, 5½ mi southwest of airport.*

⑧ **Coffees of Hawai'i.** Tour 500 acres of shiny-leafed coffee trees in a mule-drawn wagon, then move indoors for an illuminating tour of the coffee processing plant. ⊠ *Farrington Hwy., off Hwy. 470, Kualapu'u,* ☎ *808/567–9023.* ☞ *$14.* ☉ *Tour weekdays 10 and 1.*

NEED A
BREAK?

In a green plantation-style country store with a big front lānai and fields of coffee trees across the road is **Coffees of Hawai'i Espresso Bar and Gift Shop** (⊠ Farrington Hwy., Kualapu'u, ☎ 808/567–9023), where you can sample the two coffee varieties grown on 450 acres of central Molokaʻi land. Try a mango biscotti and wash it down with an espresso or cappuccino.

6 **Kalaupapa.** Kalaupapa is the name of a peninsula, a town, and a park. Views of the peninsula from Kalaupapa Lookout in Pālāʻau State Park are a standout. Founded in the 1860s and now a National Historical Park, the town of Kalaupapa was once a community of about 1,000 victims of Hansen's disease (leprosy), banished from other parts of Hawaiʻi. A Belgian man named Joseph de Veuster, ordained in Hawaiʻi in 1864 and known as Father Damien, committed himself to the care of the afflicted until he died here of the same disease in 1889. At press time, there were 68 patients still living in Kalaupapa—now by choice, as the disease is controlled by drugs and patients are no longer carriers. Visitors will most likely not see any patients other than perhaps the tour guide, who might be a bit disfigured, with missing fingers or something unusual about the face. The history of the community is fascinating and heart wrenching. The settlement is accessible via the Molokaʻi Mule Ride (☞ *below*) in Kualapuʻu or by guided tour (☞ Damien Tours *in* Guided Tours *in* Molokai A to Z, *below* and Hiking *in* Outdoor Activities and Sports, *below*). ⊠ *North end of Hwy. 470.*

10 **Kapuāiwa Coconut Grove.** At first glance this looks like a sea of coconut trees. Close-up you'll see that the tall, stately palms are planted in long elegant rows leading down to the sea. This is one of the last surviving royal groves planted by Prince Lot, who ruled Hawaiʻi as King Kamehameha V from 1863 to 1872, the year of his death. ⊠ *Hwy. 460, 5½ mi south of airport.*

★ **12** **Kaunakakai.** Molokaʻi's commercial hub is a quiet center—not as much commercial commotion as the other links in this island chain. What Kaunakakai does have is personality: It looks like an Old West movie set. Along its one-block main drag is a cultural grab bag of restaurants and shops. People are friendly and willing to supply directions, and no one dresses in anything fancier than a muʻumuʻu or aloha shirt; more often, the preferred dress is shorts and a tank top. ⊠ *Hwy. 460, about 3 blocks north of Kaunakakai Wharf.*

NEED A BREAK?

Stop by **Kanemitsu Bakery and Restaurant** (⊠ Ala Malama St., ☎ 808/ 553–5855) for a taste of its lavosh or its round Molokaʻi bread, which makes excellent French or cinnamon toast. There's also a calorie-laden assortment of rolls, buns, doughnuts, pies, and cakes. You can sit right at the counter and have a diner-style breakfast or lunch.

13 **Kaunakakai Wharf.** The docks, once bustling with watercraft exporting pineapples, now ship out potatoes, tomatoes, baby corn, herbs, and other produce. The wharf is also the starting point for various excursions, including deep-sea fishing, sailing, snorkeling, whale watching, and scuba diving. ⊠ *Hwy. 450 and Ala Malama St., drive makai on Kaunakakai Pl., which dead-ends at the wharf.*

4 **Molokaʻi Mule Ride.** To reach the town of Kalaupapa, do it on the back of a sure-footed, stubborn steed. Mount a friendly mule and wind your way along a 2.9-mi, 26-switchback trail built in 1886 as a supply route to the settlement below. Once in Kalaupapa, you'll get a guided tour of the town and a picnic lunch. No one under the age of 16 is allowed to visit Kalaupapa; and everyone—even those who walk down—must be part of a tour. The trail is very steep, down some of the highest sea cliffs in the world. It's narrow and has no rails so if it's muddy, the ride is cancelled. Only those in good shape should attempt the ride, as two hours each way on a mule can take its toll. The entire tour takes seven hours. ⊠ *100 Kala'e Hwy./Hwy. 470, Kualapu'u,* ☎ *808/567–6088.* ☞ *$135, including picnic lunch and souvenirs.* ⊙ *Tour Mon.–Sat. 8:30–3:30.*

★ ⑧ **Pālā'au State Park.** One of the island's few formal recreation areas, this cool retreat commands 233 acres at a 1,000-ft elevation. A short path through a heady pine forest leads to **Kalaupapa Lookout,** a magnificent overlook with views of the town of Kalaupapa and the 1,664-ft-high sea cliffs protecting it. Informative plaques have been set up at the lookout with facts about leprosy, Father Damien, and the colony itself.

The park is also the site of **Phallic Rock,** known as Kauleonānāhoa to the ancient Hawaiians. It is said that if women sit by this large rock formation they will become more fertile. The park, open daily, is well maintained with camping facilities, washrooms, and picnic tables. ⊠ *Hwy. 460 west from Kaunakakai, then mauka on Hwy. 470, which dead-ends at the park.*

⑨ **Purdy's Macadamia Nut Farm.** Moloka'i's only working macadamia nut farm is open for tours. A family business on Hawaiian homestead land in Ho'olehua, it takes up 1½ acres with a flourishing grove of some 50 trees more than 70 years old. Taste a fresh, delicious nut right out of its shell, then try the farm's fresh macadamia blossom honey. Look for Purdy's sign behind Moloka'i High School. ⊠ *Lihipali Ave., Ho'olehua,* ☎ *808/567–6495.* ☞ *Free.* ⊙ *Weekdays 9:30–3:30, Sat. 10–2.*

⑦ **R.W. Meyer Sugar Mill.** Built in 1877, this old mill has been reconstructed to signify Moloka'i's agricultural history. The old equipment is still in working order, including a mule-driven cane crusher, redwood evaporating pans, some copper clarifiers, and a steam engine. There is also a museum with exhibits on the island's early history and a gift shop on the grounds. ⊠ *Rte. 470, Kala'e, 2 mi southwest of Pālā'au State Park,* ☎ *808/567–6436.* ☞ *$3.50.* ⊙ *Mon.–Sat. 10–2.*

East Moloka'i

On the beautifully undeveloped eastern end of Moloka'i, you'll find ancient fishponds, a magnificent coastline, splendid ocean views, and a gaping valley that's been inhabited for centuries. The east is flanked by Mt. Kamakou, the island's highest point at 4,961 ft and home to the Nature Conservancy's Kamakou Preserve. There are miles of rain forests burgeoning with tropical fruit, misty valleys with waterfalls, and ancient lava cliffs jutting out from the sea.

A Good Drive

The road from Kaunakakai east on Highway 450 is 30 mi long, and much of it runs next to the ocean. The farther east you drive, the wilder the coastline, changing from white sandy beaches to rocky shores. Be forewarned that the road, which hugs the shore as it twists and turns, is wrought with bumps and potholes. However, there are several bays beside which you can stop and take a breather. Keep your eyes open for mile markers along the side of the road; at times, they'll be your only references for locating the sights of the east side.

Six miles east of Kaunakakai, look offshore to see **Kaloko'eli Fishpond** ⑭, surrounded by the most picturesque of Moloka'i's historic rock walls. After another 5 mi you reach the natural harbor of **Kamalō** ⑮, followed a mile later by the easy-to-miss **Smith and Bronte Monument** ⑯, dedicated to a pair of transpacific pilots. At Mile 15, a hidden trail leads to the enormous **'Ili'ili'ōpae Heiau.** Close to Mile 20 the road climbs and winds through **Pu'u O Hoku Ranch** ⑰, a vast up-country expanse with sparkling ocean panoramas.

The road east dead-ends at **Hālawa Valley** ⑱, a lush destination beckoning you to explore its inner reaches on foot. Please don't. Although there is a gorgeous 3-mi trail to the back of the valley, landowners here are known to chase away unsuspecting hikers. You're better off heading for the luscious, tropical **Kamakou Preserve** ⑲; hiking tours can be arranged in advance.

TIMING

Give yourself a full day for this meandering drive, especially if you want to break it up with a picnic at one of the beach parks along the way. From Kaunakakai, you can complete the tour in a half day. If you're going to tour the Kamakou Preserve, allow for a full-day's excursion. The sights on the east of the island are natural, so opening and closing hours don't apply. You might want to save this excursion for a weekend and visit the shops and attractions of east and central Moloka'i during the week, when they're open.

Sights to See

⑱ **Hālawa Valley.** As far back as AD 650, a busy community lived in this valley, the oldest recorded habitation on Moloka'i. They grew fruit and taro and fished here until 1946, when a fierce tidal wave struck. Now, much of the valley is overrun with lush vegetation, though you can still see the remains of house platforms and garden walls.

At the base of the road into Hālawa Valley is the beginning of a 3-mi trail, which leads back to **Moa'ula Falls,** a 250-ft cascade. Exploring the trail is not recommended, as the valley landowners are not hiker-friendly. ⊠ *Eastern end of Hwy. 450.*

OFF THE
BEATEN PATH

'ILI'ILI'ŌPAE HEIAU – This impressive heiau, listed on the National Register of Historic Places, is hard to find. As long as a football field, it is a well-preserved example of Hawai'i's ancient outdoor shrines. This revered site is said to hold great power to this day; please act with respect by speaking in a soft voice. Human sacrifices took place here. This practice was introduced by Tahitian immigrants who came between AD 1090 and 1240, but the heiau could have existed before then—as early as AD 650, the time of the first Island habitation. The old religion, which included human sacrifice, was no longer practiced as of 1819. Don't wander off the designated trail; the whole area is private property (but the owners don't object to people simply visiting the heiau). ⊠ *15 mi east of Kaunakakai and ½ mi inland of Hwy. 450; park at side of road, look for Wailau Trail sign, and walk about 10 mins mauka until you see sign on left for heiau.*

★ ⑭ **Kaloko'eli Fishpond.** With its narrow rock walls connecting two points of the shore, Kaloko'eli is typical of the numerous fishponds that define southern Moloka'i. Many of them were built around the 13th century. This early type of aquaculture, which is unique to Hawai'i, exemplifies the ingenuity of precontact Hawaiians. Fishpond walls were built of lava rocks or coral or both. You can see the tops of the dark circular stone walls a foot or two above the surface of the water all along the coast, ringing off little bays of water. Usually they were built on fringing reefs. One or more openings were left in the wall, where gates with grills (wooden slats side by side) called *makaha* were installed. These gates could be opened and closed. They allowed sea water and tiny fish to enter the enclosed pond, kept larger predators out, and allowed water to circulate so the pond didn't get stagnant. The ponds were stocked with fish too big to escape through the slats, but tiny fish that entered and were not eaten by bigger ones, often grew too big to get out, as well. When fish were needed, they were harvested by throw net or by surrounding them with a longer net. At one time there were 62 fishponds around Moloka'i's coast. ⊠ *Hwy. 450 about 6 mi east of Kaunakakai.*

★ ⑲ **Kamakou Preserve.** Tucked away on the slopes of Mt. Kamakou, Moloka'i's highest peak, is a Nature Conservancy of Hawai'i property affording a safe haven for endangered birds and plants. With its 2,774 lush acres, the preserve is a dazzling wonderland full of wet 'ohi'a (also called lehua, hardwood trees of the myrtle family, with red flowers) forests, rare bogs, and native trees and wildlife. Guided hikes can be arranged with the Conservancy in advance; hikers are picked up at Ho'olehua Airport (even if you're staying on the island, you meet at the airport) at 8:30 and returned by 4. About 12 hikes, limited to eight people, are held each year on Saturdays; reservations in writing are required well in advance. You can visit the park without the tour, but you need a four-wheel-drive vehicle, and the Nature Conservancy requests that you sign in with them first and get directions at the following address. ⊠ *Nature Conservancy, 23 Pueo Place (Box 220), Kualapu'u 96757,* ☎ *808/553–5236.* ☞ *Free; $25 nonmembers for guided hike.*

⑮ **Kamalō.** A natural harbor for small cargo ships during the 19th century, this is also the site of **St. Joseph's,** a tiny white church built by Father Damien (☞ Kalaupapa *in* Central Molokai, *above*) in the 1880s. ⊠ *Hwy. 450 about 11 mi east of Kaunakakai, on makai side.*

⑰ **Pu'u O Hoku Ranch.** A 14,000-acre private spread in the highlands of East Moloka'i, Pu'u O Hoku was developed in the '30s by wealthy industrialist Paul Fagan. Highway 450 cuts right through this rural gem with its green pastures and grazing horses and cattle. As you drive along enjoy the splendid views of Maui and Lāna'i. The small island you can see just off the coast is **Mokuho'oniki,** where the United States military practiced its bombing techniques during World War II. ⊠ *Hwy. 450 about 20 mi east of Kaunakakai.*

⑯ **Smith and Bronte Monument.** This humble sight tucked away in a grove of trees and bushes is dedicated to Ernest Smith and Emory Bronte, Americans who crash-landed here in 1927. They were the first civilians to complete a transpacific flight from California, a noteworthy feat even if it did have a bumpy ending. They ran out of fuel over Moloka'i and ended up in a grove of kiawe trees, both wings having been sheared off the airplane and the fuselage broken in two. Amazingly, the aviators walked away with only scratches from the trees. ⊠ *Hwy. 450, 12 mi east of Kaunakakai, makai side.*

NEED A BREAK? The best place to grab a snack or stock up on picnic supplies is the **Neighborhood Store 'N Counter** (⊠ Hwy. 450, 12 mi east of Kaunakakai, Puko'o, ☎ 808/558–8498). It's the last store on your drive heading east from Kaunakakai on Highway 450.

BEACHES

Moloka'i has numerous beaches, many of them quite remote and undisturbed, so don't be surprised if you're the only person sunbathing for miles. The largest and most beautiful beaches are along the west coast, but steer clear of their high winter waves. Beaches fronting the Kaunakakai hotels and condominiums are narrow and less appealing, yet the shallow waters are almost always calm for wading. At the extreme east end of the island is the beach fronting Hālawa Valley, a nice place to relax after the long drive it takes to get there.

All of the beaches are free and open to the public. None have telephones; to find out more about them, contact the **Department of Parks, Land and Natural Resources** (⊠ Box 153, Kaunakakai 96746, ☎ 808/567–6083).

West Moloka'i

Kawākiu Beach. One of the best swimming beaches on Moloka'i, Kawākiu is part of the Kaluako'i Hotel and Golf Club. It has also been set aside as a beach park in honor of its archaeological sites, including house platforms and structures from an ancient Hawaiian settlement. Outdoor showers are available at the resort. ⊠ *Kaluako'i Rd., northern end of bay in front of Kaluako'i Hotel and Golf Club.*

Kepuhi Beach. Ideal for strolling, sunbathing, and watching the sunset, this white-sand beach stretches about ½ mi in front of Kaluako'i Resort. However, it is fairly windy here all year long, which makes the swimming somewhat dangerous during high tide. There are outdoor showers at the resort, but no lifeguards. ⊠ *Kaluako'i Hotel and Golf Club, Kaluako'i Rd.*

Pāpōhaku Beach. Perhaps the most sensational beach in Hawai'i, Pāpōhaku is a 3-mi-long strip of white-sand, the longest of its kind in the state. It's also quite wide, so you can sunbathe at a comfortable distance from your neighbor. Some places are too rocky for swimming; look carefully before entering the water, and go in only when the waves are small (generally in summer). Between the parking lot and the beach are outdoor showers, picnicking facilities, and a rest room. There are no lifeguards. ⊠ *Kaluako'i Rd., 2 mi beyond Kaluako'i Hotel and Golf Club, look for sign on makai side of road.*

Pōhakuloa Beach. Parents like to bring their children here because a protective cove makes the water calm and safe for swimming most of the year. As a result, it can get pretty busy with families on weekends. There's an outdoor shower but no lifeguards. ⊠ *Drive about 1½ mi beyond Pāpōhaku Beach to end of coastal road on northwest end of island; sign on makai side of road points to parking lot.*

Central Moloka'i

Oneali'i Beach Park. From this spot there are smashing views of Maui and Lāna'i across the Pailolo Channel. It's also the only decent beach park on the island's south-central shore. A narrow and long beach, Oneali'i has adequate swimming in calm waters year-round, along with rest rooms, outdoor showers, and tree-shaded picnic tables. There are no lifeguards. ⊠ *Hwy. 450 east of Hotel Moloka'i.*

East Moloka'i

Hālawa Beach Park. The long drive to Hālawa Valley is worth it, in part because it culminates in this pretty, curving beach flanked by cliffs. Swimming is safe only during the summer; watch out for the hazardous currents and high surf in winter. A small pavilion with grassy areas on either side is popular with locals for family picnics. An outdoor shower is available, but there aren't any lifeguards. ⊠ *Drive east on Hwy. 450 until it dead-ends at beach.*

DINING

Moloka'i is not the dining hub of the Islands. For example, East Moloka'i only has one dining establishment, which is listed in Exploring as a Need a Break? spot. Restaurants listed are open daily unless otherwise noted. For an explanation of price categories, *see* On the Road with Fodor's at the beginning of the book.

West Moloka'i

$$ ✗ **Ohia Lodge.** Although it's the most formal restaurant on Moloka'i, this '70s-style hotel dining room is pretty casual. High ceilings and dark wood are offset by bright ocean vistas during the day. Ask for a table on the lower level, close to the picture windows. The menu is American with island overtones—*kalua* pork, potstickers, tempura, and Portuguese bean soup with Moloka'i bread. Fresh catch of the day is either sautéed with soy sauce and butter or broiled with lemon and tartar sauce. ⊠ *Kaluako'i Hotel and Golf Club, Kepuhi Beach, Maunaloa,* ☎ *808/552–2555. Reservations essential. AE, D, DC, MC, V.* ☾ *No lunch.*

Central Moloka'i

$–$$ ✗ **Banyan Tree Terrace.** The Pau Hana Inn's dining room opens onto a terrace with views of the ocean and a 100-year-old banyan tree. Such tasty American dishes as honey-dipped chicken, roast pork, fresh fish, and barbecued-beef short ribs rule the menu. Evenings, locals party into the wee hours out on the terrace; live bands provide pulsating music for dancing on weekends. ⊠ *Pau Hana Inn, Seaside Pl. off Oki Pl., Kaunakakai,* ☎ *808/553–5342. AE, DC, MC, V.*

$–$$ ✗ **Kualapu'u Cookhouse.** Known for its excellent homemade pies, ★ this Moloka'i culinary gem is cozy and casual. In a small plantation house next to the old run-down Kualapu'u Market and post office, it's the *only* eatery in rural Kualapu'u, so it usually draws a crowd. Grab a seat at a table or in one of the booths and try the mix of cuisines, such as teriyaki plates, honey-dipped chicken, stir-fry chicken, or tropical chili. For breakfast, don't overlook the smoky, spicy Portuguese sausage with eggs and rice. Save room for the rich and creamy chocolate macadamia nut cheesecake. ⊠ *Farrington Ave., 1 block west of Hwy. 470, Kualapu'u,* ☎ *808/567–6185. Reservations not accepted. No credit cards. Closed Sun.*

$–$$ ✗ **Moloka'i Pizza Cafe.** This cheerful, air conditioned, order-at-the-counter restaurant is a popular gathering spot with visitors and locals. Pizza, sandwiches, salads, pasta, frozen yogurt, and fresh fish are simply prepared and tasty. ⊠ *Kaunakakai Pl. on the Wharf Rd.,* ☎ *808/ 553–3288. Reservations not accepted. No credit cards. Closed Mon.*

$ ✗ **Moloka'i Drive Inn.** Open since 1960, this simple eatery in the heart of Kaunakakai is Moloka'i's answer to McDonald's. You'll find the usual take-out staples—hot dogs, fries, floats, and sundaes. But locals come here for the food they grew up on, like *manapua* (Chinese dumplings stuffed with pork), *wonton min* (chicken soup with wontons), shave ice (snow cone with flavored syrup), and the beloved *loco moco* (rice topped with a hamburger and fried egg, covered in gravy). ⊠ *Ala Malama St., Kaunakakai,* ☎ *808/553–5655. No credit cards.*

$ ✗ **Outpost Natural Foods.** Vegetarian cuisine has made its way to Kaunakakai in the form of this unpretentious natural foods store and carry-out. Just off Ala Malama Street, it stocks good salads (taco, chef's, and fruit), as well as vegetarian burritos, tempeh burgers, and a daily special hot entrée, such as curried vegetables over brown rice. Their fruit smoothies are delicious, and they sell fresh produce. ⊠ *Makaena St., Kaunakakai,* ☎ *808/553–3377. Reservations not accepted. No credit cards. Closed Sat.*

$ ✗ **Oviedo's.** As Moloka'i's commercial center, Kaunakakai may seem lacking in many ways, but it does have two authentic Filipino diners, Oviedo's and Rabangs. Oviedo's, where the waitresses treat you like family, is the better of the two. It specializes in *adobos* (stews) with traditional Filipino spices and sauces. Try the tripe, pork, or beef adobo for a real taste of tradition. A mixed plate comes with vegetables and rice. You can eat in or take out. ⊠ *145 Ala Malama St., Kaunakakai* ☎ *808/553–5014. Reservations not accepted. No credit cards.*

LODGING

Several of the lodging establishments listed in this chapter arrange outdoor excursions and have sports facilities that aren't accessible to nonguests and are hard to find elsewhere. Check each review to find the accommodation that best suits your needs. Some properties also offer free shuttle transportation from the airport—ask when you book your room. For an explanation of price categories, *see* On the Road with Fodor's at the beginning of the book.

West Moloka'i

$$$$ 🔥 **Moloka'i Ranch.** Comfortable camping is the name of the game at these one- and two-unit tents managed by Moloka'i Ranch. Canvas and yurt tents are grouped in three distinctly different locations. Upcountry near Maunaloa and the rodeo arena—with views of Cookpines, grassy pasturelands, and the ocean—is Paniolo Camp, which is the most economical; Kolo Cliffs Camp, on a bluff overlooking the ocean and a short distance from the beach, is good for couples; and Kaupoa Beach Camp has all double units (good for families or couples traveling in groups) right on the beach. Mounted on wooden platforms, tents have solar-powered running water and lights and self-composting flush toilets. Three meals are served family-style each day in an open-air pavilion; box lunches are also available. Meals and most outdoor activities are included in the price. ⊠ *Maunaloa Hwy. (Box 259), Maunaloa 96770,* ☎ *808/552–2741 or 800/254–8871. 100 tents. Hiking, horseback riding, mountain bikes, beach, airport shuttle. AE, MC, V.*

$$–$$$ 🏨 **Paniolo Hale.** Perched high on a ledge overlooking the beach, Pa-
    ★   niolo Hale is one of Moloka'i's best condominium properties. Some units have spectacular ocean views. Guests can choose from among studios and one- or two-bedroom units, all with screened lānai and kitchens; some have hot tubs for an additional charge. Kitchens are well equipped, and the rooms are tidy and simple. Adjacent to the Kaluako'i Golf Course and a stone's throw from the Kaluako'i Hotel and Golf Club, the property is some nights a playground for wild turkeys and deer. ⊠ *Lio Pl. (Box 190), Maunaloa 96770,* ☎ *808/552–2731 or 800/367–2984,* ℻ *808/552–2288. 77 condominiums (33 rentals). Kitchens, pool, 18-hole golf course, paddle tennis. AE, MC, V.*

$$ 🏨 **Kaluako'i Hotel and Golf Club.** Now managed by its owners, this property does its best to provide a sense of laid-back elegance for its guests, but it's showing signs of wear and tear. Two-level complexes are set on ultragreen lawns shaded by immense palm trees and brightened by bougainvillea bushes. Rooms have high ceilings with exposed-wood beams, rattan furnishings, and bright tropical colors. Some units have kitchenettes and furnished lānai. Golf is free for hotel guests, except for the $15 cart fee. ⊠ *Kaluako'i Rd. (Box 1977), Maunaloa 96770,* ☎ *808/552–2555 or 888/552–2550,* ℻ *808/552–2821. 104 rooms. Restaurant, bar, snack bar, pool, 18-hole golf course, shops. AE, D, DC, MC, V.*

$$ 🏨 **Kaluako'i Villas.** Studios and one-bedroom ocean-view suites are decorated in blue and mauve, with island-style art, rattan furnishings, and private lānai. Units are spread out in 21 two-story buildings covering 29 acres. Guests can take advantage of Kaluako'i Hotel and

Golf Club's many activities, though there are no signing privileges. ✉ *1131 Kaluako'i Rd. (Box 200), Maunaloa 96770,* ☎ *808/552–2721 or 800/367–5004,* FAX *808/552–2201. 2 1-bedroom cottages, 11 suites, 56 rooms. Kitchenettes, in-room VCRs, pool, 18-hole golf course, shops. AE, MC, V.*

$$ 🖼 **Ke Nani Kai.** This well-managed condominium complex is set back from the water. Views are of the gardens and golf course, but the beach is a mere five-minute walk away. Sliding screen doors open onto furnished lānai with flower-laden trellises, and the spacious interiors are decorated with tropical rattans and pastels. Each unit has a washer and dryer and a completely equipped kitchen. ✉ *Kaluakoi Rd., Kaluakoi Resort, (Box 289), Maunaloa 96770,* ☎ *808/552–2761 or 800/ 888–2791,* FAX *808/552–0045. 120 condominiums (37 rentals). Pool, 18-hole golf course, 2 tennis courts. AE, D, DC, MC, V.*

Central Moloka'i

$$$ 🖼 **Moloka'i Shores.** Every room in this oceanfront, three-story property has a view of the water. Guests can stay in either one-bedroom/one-bath units or two-bedroom/two-bath units; all have furnished lānai, which look out on 4 acres of tropical gardens. In addition, picnic tables and barbecue areas are available for outdoor family fun. ✉ *Kamehameha Hwy. #450 (Box 1037), Kaunakakai 96748,* ☎ *808/553–5954 or 800/535–0085,* FAX *800/633–5085. 100 units (28 1-bedroom rentals). Kitchenettes, pool, shuffleboard. AE, D, MC, V.*

$ 🖼 **Hotel Moloka'i.** Although this hotel is run-down, each room is kept clean and neat and the price is appropriately reasonable. It's also right on the beach, but the pool on premises is a better alternative for swimming. Furnishings are rustic, with basket swings on the lānai and wood beams on the ceiling. The hotel often offers overnight deals in conjunction with airlines and rental car companies; ask about this when you make your reservation. Take note that there's no on-site restaurant here, and the closest dining room is 2 mi away at the Pau Hana Inn. ✉ *Box 546, Kaunakakai 96748,* ☎ *808/553–5347 or 800/423–6656,* FAX *808/553–5047. 49 rooms. Pool. MC, V.*

$ 🖼 **Pau Hana Inn.** Choose the somewhat funky accommodations of this good-time hotel if you like to rough it. It's a ramshackle set of cottages with clean but uninspired furnishings reminiscent of motels on the mainland. Count on high noise levels on weekend evenings, when there's live entertainment on the Banyan Tree Terrace. On the plus side, a nice swimming pool makes up for the lack of a nearby swimming beach. ✉ *40 Oke St. (Box 546), Kaunakakai 96748,* ☎ *808/553–5342 or 800/ 423–6656,* FAX *808/553–5047. 40 rooms. Restaurant, lobby lounge, kitchenettes, pool. DC, MC, V.*

East Moloka'i

$$–$$$ 🖼 **Hale Kawaikapu.** A cottage and a house, both fully furnished, are available for weekly or longer rentals on a 10-acre oceanfront site. The house has a large lanai with a queen-size sofa bed and large dining room table. The two bedrooms have Polynesian decor; one has a queen bed, the other two twins. The cottage, which has grass mats on the floor, has two sofa beds in a downstairs living area and a queen bed in an upstairs loft cooled by a ceiling fan. ✉ *532 'Elepaio St., Honolulu 96816,* ☎ *808/521–9202. 2-bedroom home sleeps 6, cottage sleeps 4. No credit cards.*

$$–$$$ 🖼 **Wavecrest.** An oceanfront, south-shore condominium 13 mi east
★   of Kaunakakai, this property is suited to travelers who love the east side of the island and to those who want to explore it for the first time. Wavecrest has one- and two-bedroom condominiums with full kitchens,

rattan furniture, and a pastel color scheme. Each unit has a furnished lānai, some with views of Maui and Lāna'i. The shallow water here is bad for swimming but good for fishing. Car-and-room package rates are sometimes available; ask when you book. ⊠ *Hwy. 450 near Mile Marker 13 (HC 1, Box 541), Kaunakakai 96748,* ☎ *808/558–8103 or 800/535–0085,* FAX *800/633–5085. 126 1- and 2-bedroom condominiums (15 rentals). Kitchens, pool, shuffleboard, 2 tennis courts. AE, D, MC, V.*

$$ ⊞ **Honomuni House.** A tropical garden setting, complete with waterfalls and a freshwater stream, awaits you 17 mi east of Kaunakakai. Inside, there's a furnished kitchen, one bath, and a large living/dining room. ⊠ *17½ mi east of Kaaunakakai on Hwy. 450 (HC 1, Box 700), Kaunakakai 96748,* ☎ *808/558–8383. 1-bedroom; pullout couch sleeps 4. No credit cards.*

$$ ⊞ **Pu'u O Hoku Ranch.** At the east end of Moloka'i, near the 25-mi marker, are two ocean-view accommodations in isolated surroundings. The draws here are the views and the peaceful surroundings. The cottage has basic wicker furnishings and lau hula matting on the floors. The lodge, which has seven rooms opening off a main hallway, is similarly decorated. The owners maintain living quarters in the lodge. ⊠ *HC 1 (Box 900), Kaunakakai 96748,* ☎ *808/558–8100,* FAX *808/558–8109. 2-bedroom cottage sleeps 6, 7 rooms in lodge sleep 16. No credit cards.*

$ ⊞ **Kamalo Plantation Bed and Breakfast.** At this tropical paradise 15 minutes east of Kaunakakai, guests can either stay in the cottage or in the guest suite in a separate wing of the main house. The Polynesian-style cottage has a fully equipped kitchen, a living room, a dining room, and a deck. The large, airy suite, accessed by a private entrance, has picture windows, a sitting room, and a deck overlooking the gardens. Its kitchen facilities include a microwave, a refrigerator, and a toaster. Home-grown fruit and fresh-baked bread are provided for breakfast. ⊠ *10½ mi east of Kaunakakai off Hwy. 450, HC1 (Box 300), Kaunakakai 96748,* ☎ FAX *808/558–8236. Cottage sleeps 4, 1 guest suite in main house. No credit cards.*

$ ⊞ **Kumul'eli Farms.** Floor-to-ceiling windows allow a spectacular view of the peaks of Ka'apahu and Kamakou and 8-acre garden surrounding this property. Several pathways lead to old Hawaiian archaeological sites—agricultural terraces and house sites. The room, which is connected to the main house via covered deck, has its own deck, separate entry, an alcove with a kitchenette, and a big shower and separate tub with a 6-ft window that opens onto the garden deck. Dorothe and David Curtis have decorated the high-ceiling room with white wicker furniture. ⊠ *10½ mi east of Kaunakakai off Hwy. 450 (Box 1829), Kaunakakai 96748,* ☎ *808/558–8284, 808/558–8281,* FAX *808/558–8284. 1 room. Lap pool, fan, in-room VCR, refrigerator, kitchenette. Full breakfast. No credit cards.*

NIGHTLIFE AND THE ARTS

Moloka'i doesn't have much of a nightlife in the traditional sense. Locals enjoy simply sitting around with friends and family, sipping a few cold ones, strumming 'ukulele and guitars, singing old songs, and "talking story" (chatting). Still, opportunities are available to kick up your heels for a festive night out. Go into Kaunakakai, pick up a copy of the weekly *Moloka'i Dispatch,* and see if there's a church supper or square dance taking place where you can mix and mingle. A walk on the beach under the evening stars is always an option.

Bars and Clubs

Ohia Lodge Lounge. A few steps away from the Ohia Lodge dining room, this laid-back lounge delivers mellow island music by Moloka'i's own. The pūpū menu is strictly local, from potstickers to spring rolls. ⊠ *Kaluako'i Hotel and Golf Club,* ☎ *808/552–2555.* ☾ *Live music Fri. and Sat. 8–11.*

Pau Hana Inn. The outdoor terrace at this hotel is the island's liveliest forum for local music. The regulars can get pretty rowdy here on the weekends, but visitors are more than welcome to join in the fun. ⊠ *Seaside Pl. off Oki Pl., Kaunakakai,* ☎ *808/553–5342.* ⊠ *Happy hour 4–6, dance music Fri. and Sat. 9–1.*

Film

Maunaloa Town Cinemas (⊠ Maunaloa Town, ☎ 808/552–2707), opened in 1997, draws folks from all around Moloka'i nightly for current blockbusters.

OUTDOOR ACTIVITIES AND SPORTS

Participant Sports

Golf

Compared with the more commercialized Neighbor Islands, Moloka'i has a relatively mellow golf scene. The best option is the **Kaluako'i Golf Course** at the Kaluako'i Hotel and Golf Club. Its 18-hole, 6,564-yard course was designed by Ted Robinson, and its 160 manicured acres include five holes next to the beach. ⊠ *Kaluako'i Hotel and Golf Club, Kaluako'i Rd. 3½ mi from intersection with Hwy. 460,* ☎ *808/552–2739.* ⊠ *Greens fee: $80; cart included (free for hotel guests, except for $15 cart rental).*

The **Ironwood Hills Golf Club** is in up-country Kala'e. ⊠ *Turn off Hwy. 460 onto 470 and go north uphill 3.7 mi; the dirt road to the golf course is on the left side of the road; Kualapu'u,* ☎ *808/567–6000.* ⊠ *Greens fee: $14; cart $14.*

Hiking

You can make a day of hiking to Kalaupapa and back along the 2.9-mi, 26-switchback trail that is also used for the Moloka'i Mule Ride. The trail is well-maintained by the National Park Service. You will need a permit to hike the trail, as well as a confirmed reservation with **Damien Tours** (☞ Guided Tours *in* Molokai A to Z, *below*) to tour Kalaupapa. For further information contact the **National Park Service** (⊠ Box 2222, Kalaupapa 96742, ☎ 808/567–6802).

Halawa Falls and Cultural Hike is a guided hike through private property on the east end of Moloka'i in the lush and lovely Halawa Valey. Along the way the guide points out a heiau, old rock walls, house sites, and native fruit trees. At Halawa Falls you can swim in the pool and eat food you've brought yourself. Hikers meet at 8 AM, begin hiking by 9:45, and return to their cars by 2. ⊠ *Meet at Neighborhood Store, beyond Mile Marker 15 on Hwy. 450,* ☎ *808/553–4355 after 5.* ⊠ *$25.*

Horseback Riding

Molokai'i Horse and Wagon Ride is a 1½-hr ride that takes in a heiau, a mountain lookout to search for whales in the ocean below, a mango grove, and a beach. ⊠ *15 mi east of Kaunakakai off Hwy. 450 (Box 1528), Kaunakakai,* ☎ *808/558–8380.* ⊠ *$40.* ☾ *10–2.*

Water Sports

FISHING

Based at Kaunakakai Wharf, the four-passenger, 31-ft twin-diesel cruiser **Alyce C.** (✉ Kaunakakai, ☎ 808/558–8377) runs excellent sportfishing excursions. Shared cost is about $200 a day, or $150 a half day. On an exclusive basis, the full-day cost runs approximately $400, and $300 for a half day.

SAILING

The 42-ft Cascade sloop *Satan's Doll* is your craft when you sign up with **Moloka'i Charters** (✉ Box 1207, Kaunakakai 96748, ☎ 808/553–5852). The company arranges two-hour sails for $30 per person. Half-day sailing trips cost $40 per person, including soft drinks and snacks. A minimum of four people is required, but shared charters can be arranged. **Fun Hogs Hawai'i** (✉ Box 424, Ho'olehua 96729, ☎ 808/552–0017 or 808/552–2791) coordinates sailing excursions off the south and west shores of the island for $50. They also offer afternoon whale-watching, fishing, boogie boarding, and surfing expeditions on a rotating basis. These two-hour guided experiences cost $50. In June, July, and August, Fun Hogs offers two-hour morning snorkeling sessions from a catamaran for $50, including equipment.

SNORKELING AND SCUBA DIVING

Moloka'i Charters (✉ Box 1207, Kaunakakai 96748, ☎ 808/553–5852) takes people via sailboat on full-day snorkeling excursions to the island of Lāna'i for $75 per person; soft drinks and a picnic lunch are included. **Bill Kapuni's Snorkel & Dive** (✉ Box 1962, Kaunakakai 96748, ☎ 808/553–9867) leaves Kaunakakai Wharf daily for two-hour snorkeling excursions. Prices vary, depending on the length of dive and number of people involved. You can rent your own equipment or book a snorkeling excursion with **Fun Hogs Hawai'i** (✉ Box 424, Ho'olehua 96729, ☎ 808/552–0017 or 808/552–2791). Jim Brocker, owner of **Moloka'i Fish and Dive** (☞ Sporting Goods *in* Shopping, *below*) in Kaunakakai, can fill you in on how to find the best snorkel sites and can rent you the gear you'll need for your trip.

SHOPPING

Moloka'i has two major commercial drags: Maunaloa Road in Maunaloa and Ala Malama Street in Kaunakakai. Happily, there are no department stores or shopping malls, and the fanciest clothes you'll find are pretty mu'umu'u and aloha shirts—but now that you've gone totally "native," could you ask for anything more?

Each tiny hamlet has emporiums with flair and diversity; the best bargains are locally made artwork and jewelry. Kaluako'i Hotel and Golf Club shops are higher-priced and more tourist-oriented than the family-run shops in other parts of the island.

Most stores in Kaunakakai are open Monday through Saturday between 9 and 6; a few open their doors on Sunday. In Maunaloa most shops close by 4 in the afternoon and all day Sunday. Call ahead to confirm hours.

West Moloka'i

There's a handful of family-run businesses along the main drag of Maunaloa, a rural plantation town. Shop proprietors always extend the aloha spirit to visitors.

Arts and Crafts

Plantation Gallery (⊠ 120 Maunaloa Hwy., ☎ 808/552–2364) is Maunaloa's best arts-and-crafts emporium, crammed with everything from clothes to sculpture to musical instruments.

Clothing

Liberty House (☎ 808/552–2344), at Kaluako'i Hotel and Golf Club, sells resort wear with tropical prints.

Grocery Store

Victuals and travel essentials are available at the **Maunaloa General Store.** It's convenient for guests staying at the nearby condos of Kaluako'i Hotel and Golf Club, who shop here for meat, produce, dry goods, and the fixings for their holiday libations. ⊠ *200 Maunaloa Hwy.,* ☎ *808/552–2346.* ⊙ *Mon.–Sat. 8–6.*

Kites

The **Big Wind Kite Factory,** a fixture of the Maunaloa community, has custom-made, appliquéd kites you can fly or display. Designs range from hula girls to tropical fish. Also in stock is a wide variety of kite kits, paper kites, minikites, and wind socks. Ask to go on the factory tour, then take a free kite-flying lesson. ⊠ *120 Maunaloa Hwy.,* ☎ *808/552–2364.*

Central Moloka'i

You can walk from one end of Kaunakakai's main street (Ala Malama) to the other in about five minutes—unless you like to peruse, of course; Ho'olehua has just one must-shop stop, the Plantation Store, next to Coffees of Hawaii.

Clothing

Casual, knockabout island wear is available at the **Imports Gift Shop** (⊠ 82 Ala Malama St., Kaunakakai,☎ 808/553–5734), across from Kanemitsu Bakery.

Moloka'i Island Creations (⊠ 63 Ala Malama St., Kaunakakai, ☎ 808/ 553–5926) carries exclusive swimwear, beach cover-ups, sun hats, and tank tops.

Moloka'i Surf (⊠ 93C Ala Malama St., Kaunakakai, ☎ 808/553–5093) is known for its wide selection of Moloka'i T-shirts, swimwear, and sports clothing. Look for it under the "Wear in There" sign.

Grocery Stores

Friendly Market Center in Kaunakakai is the best-stocked supermarket on the island. Its slogan—"Your family store on Moloka'i"—is truly credible: Hats, T-shirts, and sun-and-surf essentials keep company with fresh produce, meat, groceries, liquor, and sundries. ⊠ *93 Ala Malama St., Kaunakakai,* ☎ *808/553–5595.* ⊙ *Weekdays 8:30–8:30, Sat. 8:30–6:30.*

Misaki's Inc. is a grocery with authentic island allure—it's been in business since 1922. Pick up dry goods, housewares, and beverages here, as well as your food staples. ⊠ *78 Ala Malama St., Kaunakakai,* ☎ *808/553–5505.* ⊙ *Mon.–Sat. 8:30–8:30, Sun. 9–noon.*

Don't let the name **Moloka'i Wines 'n' Spirits** fool you. Along with a surprisingly good selection of fine wines and liquors, it also carries gourmet foods and snacks. ⊠ *77 Ala Malalma St., Kaunakakai,* ☎ *808/ 553–5009.* ⊙ *Sun.–Thurs. 9 AM–10 PM, Fri. and Sat. 9 AM–10:30 PM.*

Island Goods

The Plantation Store, next to Coffees of Hawai'i, is the only shop of interest in Kualapu'u. Once inside you'll find the most complete range of Moloka'i-made products on the island. In the market for seed bracelets, or perhaps some jewelry made from coconut shells and wiliwili seeds? This is your place. You'll also find local artwork, homemade jellies and jams, island soaps, pen-and-ink drawings of Moloka'i landscapes, and handcrafted pottery. ⊠ *Kualapu'u Base Yard, Farrington Hwy.,* ☎ *808/567–9023.* ⊙ *Daily 10–3.*

Jewelry

Along with casual clothing, the **Imports Gift Shop** (⊠ 82 Ala Malama St., Kauanakai☎ 808/553–5734) has a decent collection of 14-karat-gold chains, rings, earrings, and bracelets, plus freshwater pearl jewelry. It also carries Hawaiian Heirloom Jewelry, unique replicas of popular Victorian pieces. These stunning gold pieces are made to order with your Hawaiian name inscribed on them.

Moloka'i Island Creations (⊠ 82 Ala Malama St., Kaunakakai, ☎ 808/553–5926) carries its own unique line of jewelry, including sea opal, coral, and sterling silver.

Leis

Pali & Sons of Moloka'i (⊠ Kualapu'u, ☎ 808/567–6769) creates leis from such island flowers as ginger and pīkake, an Asian vine with fragrant white flowers. The company does a beautiful job with the traditional circular *haku* lei, which is worn on the head.

Sporting Goods

Moloka'i Fish and Dive is a main source for sporting needs, from snorkeling rentals to free and friendly advice. Owner Jim Brocker knows the island inside out and can recommend the best spots for fishing and diving. Ask to see his original-design Moloka'i T-shirts, and check out his parrots. ⊠ *61 Ala Malama St., Kaunakakai,* ☎ *808/553–5926.* ⊙ *Weekdays 8:30–6, Sat. 8–6, Sun. 8–2.*

Video Equipment

When you're ready to document your island adventures, **Moloka'i Sight and Sound** (⊠ Kaunakakai, ☎ 808/553–3600) can restock you with tape and batteries, or even rent you a camcorder.

MOLOKA'I A TO Z

Arriving and Departing

By Plane

Moloka'i's transportation hub is **Ho'olehua Airport** (☎ 808/567–6140), a tiny airstrip 8 mi west of Kaunakakai and about 15 mi east of Kaluako'i Hotel and Golf Club. If you're flying in from the mainland United States, you must first make a stop in Honolulu; from there, it's a 25-minute trip to the Friendly Isle.

Hawaiian Airlines (☎ 800/367–5320) flies its DC-9 jet aircraft daily between O'ahu and Moloka'i. A round-trip ticket can cost up to $164 per person. **Island Air** (☎ 800/323–3345) provides daily flights on its 18-passenger deHaviland Dash-6 Twin Otters.

An even smaller airstrip serves the little community of Kalaupapa (☎ 808/567–6331), on the north shore. **Island Air** flies here directly from Honolulu for $164 round-trip, and for $136 round-trip from Ho'olehua Airport. However, you must first have a land-tour confirmation for Kalaupapa. Your arrival should coincide with one of the authorized ground tours of the area (☞ Guided Tours, *below*), otherwise you'll be asked to leave.

BETWEEN THE AIRPORT AND HOTELS

From Ho'olehua Airport, it takes about 10 minutes to reach Kaunakakai and 25 minutes to reach the hotels and condominiums of Kaluako'i Hotel and Golf Club by car. Since there's no rush hour on the
Friendly Isle, traffic won't be a problem. There is no public bus transport on the island.

By Car. From the Ho'olehua Airport, it's easy to find your way on the
island's roads. Turn right on the main road, Highway 460 (also called
Maunaloa Highway) to reach Kaluako'i Hotel and Golf Club, and left
if you're staying in Kaunakakai. **Budget** and **Dollar** are the two rental
companies with offices at Ho'olehua Airport (☞ Car Rentals, *below*).

By Taxi. For taxi service call **Moloka'i Off-Road Tours and Taxi** (☎ 808/
553–3369) or **Kukui Tours and Limousines** (☎ 808/553–5133). There's
an initial charge of $1.40, plus $1.40 for each additional mile and 25¢
for each piece of luggage. Drivers are on call 24 hours a day. It costs
two people about $16 from Ho'olehua Airport to Kaunakakai, and about
$14 to Kaluako'i Hotel and Golf Club.

Getting Around

By Car

If you want to explore Moloka'i from one end to the other, it's best to
rent a car (☞ Car Rentals, *below*).

With just a few main roads to choose from, it's a snap to drive on
Moloka'i. You'll find gas stations in Kaunakakai and Maunaloa. If you
park your car somewhere, be sure to lock it. Even on the Friendly Isle,
theft has been known to occur. Drivers must wear seat belts or risk a
$15 fine. Children under three must ride in a federally approved child
passenger restraint device, easily leased at the rental agency. Ask your
rental agent for a free *Moloka'i Drive Guide*.

By Taxi

Kukui Tours and Limousines (☎ 808/553–5133) coordinates exclusive
tours (from 2½ hours to a full day) to various points of interest in seven-
passenger vehicles, in addition to its basic meter rates (☞ *above*).
Moloka'i Off-Road Tours and Taxi (☎ 808/553–3369) provides personalized service to any point on the island.

Contacts and Resources

Car Rentals

Both **Budget** (☎ 800/350–0540) and **Dollar** (☎ 800/367–7006), the
only car-rental agencies on the island, have offices at Ho'olehua Airport. Expect to pay between $30 and $48 per day for a standard compact, and from $36 to $53 for a midsize car. Rates are seasonal and
may run higher during the peak winter months. It's best to make rental
arrangements in advance. If you're flying on Island Air or Hawaiian
Airlines, see whether fly-drive package deals are available—you might
luck out on a less-expensive rate.

Doctors

Round-the-clock medical attention is available at **Moloka'i General Hospital** (✉ 280A Puali St., Kaunakakai 96748, ☎ 808/553–5331).

Emergencies

Ambulance (☎ 808/553–5331). **Coast Guard** (☎ 808/244–5256). **Fire**
(☎ 808/553–5601 in Kaunakakai, ☎ 808/567–6525 at Ho'olehua Airport). **General emergencies** (☎ 911). **Police** (☎ 808/553–5355).

Guided Tours

Moloka'i Action Adventures. Walter Naki is a friendly, knowledgeable guide who custom-designs tours to Moloka'i's outdoors attractions. One of his most popular excursions is a north shore cruise aboard a 21-ft Boston whaler. Prices vary. ⊠ *Box 12269, Kaunakakai 96748,*☎ *808/558–8184.*

Moloka'i Off-Road Tours and Taxi. Visit Hālawa Valley, Kalaupapa Lookout, Maunaloa town, and other points of interest in the comfort of an air-conditioned Jeep Cherokee or Ford Ranger pickup. Pat and Alex Pua'a are your personal guides; they'll even help you mail a coconut back home. ☎ *808/553–3369.* ⌦ *$50.* ☉ *Daily; generally, pickup at 9, return at 2:30, but other arrangements are possbile.*

Moloka'i Wagon Ride. Island residents Junior and Nani Rawlins take folks on a scenic and informative amble in a horse-drawn wagon. First stop is 'Ili'ili'ōpae Heiau, the largest outdoor shrine in Hawai'i. Next, tour the largest mango grove in the world before hitting the beach for coconut husking, a barbecue, and fishing. ☎ *808/558–8132.* ⌦ *$35.* ☉ *Daily.*

Damien Tours is operated by longtime residents of Kalaupapa who are well-versed in its history. The four-hour van tour begins and ends at Kalaupapa Airport if you arrive by air, or at the foot of the 2.9-mi trail if you hike down the mountain. Departing at 10:15 AM, the tour gives you a thorough look at this historic site. No one under age 16 is allowed. Bring your own lunch. ☎ *808/567–6171.* ⌦ *$30.*

Visitor Information

You can pick up free brochures and tourist information in kiosks and stands at the airport in Ho'olehua. Car-rental agencies distribute the free *Moloka'i Drive Guide* along with maps and other up-to-date information.

Moloka'i Visitors Association (⊠ Box 960, Kaunakakai 96748, ☎ 808/553–3876 or 800/800–6367) and **Maui Visitors Bureau** (⊠ Box 580, Wailuku, Maui 96793, ☎ 808/244–3530) can offer advice on accommodations and tours and provide other visitor information.

7 Lāna'i

Lāna'i's only population center is Lāna'i City, smack in the middle of the island. The town is surrounded by natural wonders: Garden of the Gods, strewn with colorful boulders, to the northwest; breathtaking Hulopo'e Beach to the south; and Lāna'ihale, the highest point on the island, to the east.

By Marty
Wentzel

FOR DECADES, LĀNA'I WAS KNOWN as the Pineapple Island, with hundreds of acres of fields filled with the golden fruit. Today this 140-square-mi island has been renamed "Hawai'i's Private Island," as developers replace its pineapple fields with sophisticated hotels in an effort to boost tourism. Once rarely visited, Lāna'i has joined most of its sister islands in the tourism business. Since 1990, Dole Foods Inc., which owns 98% of the island, has opened the luxurious 102-room Lodge at Kō'ele and the 250-room Mānele Bay Hotel, plus two championship golf courses. Despite these new additions, Lāna'i—the third smallest of the islands— still remains the most remote and intimate visitor destination in Hawai'i.

Most of the island's population is centered in Lāna'i City, an old plantation town of 2,700 residents, whose tiny houses have colorful facades, tin roofs, and tidy gardens. Although the weather across much of the island is hot and dry, the Norfolk Island pines that line Lāna'i City's streets create a cool refuge. Here, you'll encounter some of the people who came from the Philippines in the 1920s to work in Lāna'i's pineapple fields. You'll also notice the many other nationalities of Hawai'i, from Korean, Chinese, and Japanese to transplanted mainland *haole* (Caucasians). Though Lāna'i City has a few family-run shops and stores, its options are limited. You'll find a couple of diner-style eateries, a restored theater, and the comfy old Hotel Lāna'i, an 11-room hostelry that serves as a gathering place for locals and tourists.

With its well-planned grid of paved roads with small businesses, the town adds a hint of civilization to a mostly wild island. However, Lāna'i City is not the primary reason for coming to Lāna'i. Among the island's unique outdoor attractions is the Garden of the Gods, where rocks and boulders are scattered across a crimson landscape as if some divine being had placed them there as a sculpture garden. The waters at Hulopo'e Beach are so clear that within a minute of snorkeling you can see fish the colors of turquoise and jade. And you can drive or hike to the top of Lāna'ihale, a 3,370-ft-high, windswept perch from which you can see nearly every inhabited Hawai'ian island.

Although today it is an island that welcomes visitors with its friendly, rustic charm, Lāna'i has not always been so amiable. The earliest Polynesians believed it to be haunted by evil ghosts who gobbled up unsuspecting visitors. In 1836 a pair of missionaries named Dwight Baldwin and William Richards came and went after failing to convert the locals to their Christian beliefs. In 1854 a group of Mormons tried to create the City of Joseph here, but they were forced to abandon their mission after a drought in 1857.

One of Lāna'i's more successful visitors was a man named Jim Dole (1877–1958). In 1922 Dole bought the island for $1.1 million and began to grow pineapples on it. He built Lāna'i City on the flatlands, where the crater floor is flanked by volcanic slopes. Then he planned the harbor at Kaumālapa'u, from which pineapples would be shipped. Four years later, as he watched the first harvest sail away to Honolulu, this enterprising businessman could safely say that Lāna'i's Dole Plantation was a success. Over the past decade, however, pineapples have ceased to be a profitable crop in Hawai'i because of global competition; thus the new thrust toward tourism.

A visit to Lāna'i can be either simple or elegant. Solitude is easily acquired, though you may encounter the occasional deer on the hillsides, the spirits that linger in the ancient fishing village of Kaunolū, and the playful dolphins of Mānele Bay. On the other hand, you can rub elbows with sophisticated travelers during a game of croquet at the Lodge at Kō'ele or a round of golf at one of the island's two championship courses. Bring casual clothes, because many of your activities will be laid-back, whether you're riding the unpaved roads in a four-wheel-drive vehicle or having a drink on the front porch of the Hotel Lāna'i. Come, take your time, and enjoy yourself before the island changes too much more.

Pleasures and Pastimes

Dining
Some call it Lāna'i Regional Cuisine. Others call it Private Island Palate. Either way, the menus at Lāna'i's two resorts reflect the fresh-flavored products provided by local farmers, hunters, and fishermen—everything from Mānele ahi (yellowfin tuna) to Lāna'i liliko'i (passion fruit). Lāna'i City's eclectic fare ranges from grilled cheese to eggplant creole. Pricing is straightforward: Hotel dining rooms are expensive, while family-run eateries are much more affordable. Picnic lunches are the best option for visitors on the go. Some outfitters include them in their packages, or you can head to either of the two grocery stores in Lāna'i City and concoct your own afternoon treat.

Hiking
Treks are distinctive, from a self-guided walk through Hawai'i's largest native dryland forest, to an 8-mi adventure over Lāna'ihale with ocean and island views from here to eternity. Before you go, fill a water bottle and arm yourself with provisions, in case you get a little off track. Also, look at Craig Chisholm's paperback, *Hawaiian Hiking Trails* (Touchstone Press, 1977), and Robert Smith's *Hawai'i's Best Hiking Trails* (Wilderness Press, 1987).

Lodging
Lāna'i offers a mixed bag of lodging options, though the number of properties is limited due to the island's small size. You'll pay top dollar for upscale digs at The Lodge at Kō'ele and Mānele Bay Hotel. If you're on a tight budget, seek out a bed-and-breakfast spot (the ones we've mentioned have particularly friendly hosts). House rentals are expensive, but they do give you a taste of what it's actually like to live on such a remote isle.

Snorkeling and Scuba Diving
With Cathedrals (pinnacle formations) for a dive site and marine life like angelfish, it's no wonder that snorkeling and scuba-diving buffs call the waters off Lāna'i a religious experience. For the best underwater viewing, try the south shore's Hulopo'e Beach, a marine-life conservation area, or go on a snorkeling/diving excursion with Trilogy Ocean Sports (☞ Outdoor Activities and Sports, *below*).

EXPLORING LĀNA'I

Most of Lāna'i's sights are out of the way; that is, you won't find them in Lāna'i City or along paved roads. You'll have to look to find them, but the search is worth it. Ask your hotel's concierge for a road and site map; it's a good resource. Bring along a cooler with drinks and snacks for your explorations, because there are no places to stop for refreshments along the way. Admission to all sights mentioned in this chapter is free.

Numbers in the text correspond to numbers in the margin and on the Lāna'i map.

Great Itineraries

Lāna'i is small enough to explore in a couple of days of leisurely travel, depending on how you want to experience it. Be selective with your time, for it goes by fast here.

IF YOU HAVE 1 DAY

If you can only tear yourself away from your lounge chair for one day of exploring, rent a four-wheel-drive vehicle and get to know the back-roads of Lāna'i, where the power of the landscape is overwhelming. If you're staying at the Lodge at Kō'ele or Hotel Lāna'i, allow yourself enough time to see the **Garden of the Gods** ⑦ in the morning. After lunch in Lāna'i City, drive down to **Lu'ahiwa Petroglyphs** ② and **Kaunolū** ③, followed by a late-afternoon swim at **Hulopo'e Beach** ⑥. Guests of the Mānele Bay Hotel should reverse the itinerary, with the beach, petroglyphs, and Kaunolū in the morning and Garden of the Gods in the afternoon.

IF YOU HAVE 3 DAYS

Follow the one-day itinerary. Then on day two, take an adventurous tour of the undeveloped north and east shores. Start the day with a drive to **Shipwreck Beach** ⑨ for a morning walk and some sunbathing. Then drive along the bumpy coastal road to **Keōmuku** ⑩, **Kahe'a Heiau** ⑪, **Naha** ⑫, and Lōpā Beach, where you can eat that picnic you packed. After retracing your route and returning your rental vehicle, relive the day's adventures over tropical drinks at your hotel's lounge. Start your third day with a cool morning hike atop Lāna'ihale, stopping mid-way for a picnic. In the afternoon, relax those tired muscles with an after-noon spa treatment or some time in the swimming pool and hot tub.

IF YOU HAVE 5 DAYS

Follow the three-day itinerary then dedicate day four to the sport of choice, be it golf on one of the island's two championship courses, ten-nis at Mānele or Kō'ele, horseback riding from Kō'ele Stables, or sport-ing clays in the highlands; or sign up for a lesson and learn a new sport. On day five, see the island from the sea by going on a half-day fishing trip or snorkeling/scuba diving expedition. In the afternoon, stroll around Lāna'i City, chat with the residents and shop owners, and pick up some island souvenirs, like Lāna'i T-shirts and hand-carved pine bowls.

When to Tour Lāna'i

The weather on Lāna'i is warm and clear throughout the year. It's sun-niest at sea level, while in upcountry Lāna'i City, the nights and morn-ings can feel chilly and the fog can settle in on the tops of the pine trees. As in all of Hawai'i, winter weather is cooler and less predictable. For a taste of local arts, crafts, and entertainment, time your trip with an island event such as autumn's Aloha Festivals.

South and West Lāna'i

Pineapples once blanketed the Pālāwai Basin, the flat area south of Lāna'i City. Today it is used primarily for agriculture and grazing, but it does hold historic and natural treasures worth exploring.

In the Islands, the directions *mauka* (toward the mountains) and *makai* (toward the ocean) are often used. We've included them in the text here as well.

A Good Drive

From Lāna'i City, drive south on Highway 440 a few blocks until you reach a major intersection. Go straight, following the highway west to **Kaumālapa'u Harbor** ①, the island's main seaport. Backtrack to the in-tersection, turn right, and take Highway 440 south (also called Mānele

Lāna'i

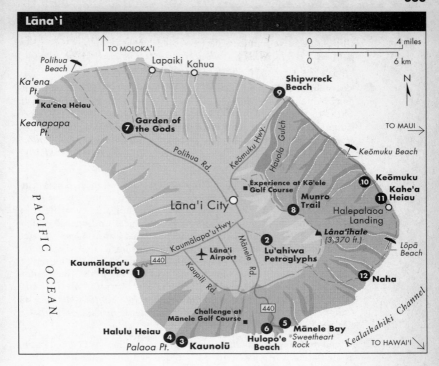

Road). After about a mile you'll see a dirt road on your left, which will lead you to **Lu'ahiwa Petroglyphs** ② and its ancient rock carvings.

Return to Highway 440 and drive another 2 mi south until the road veers left. Here, go straight on bumpy and unpaved Kaupili Road, then take the fourth left onto another unnamed dirt road. All of this four-wheeling pays off when you reach your destination: the well-preserved archaeological sites of **Kaunolū** ③ and **Halulu Heiau** ④.

Back on Highway 440, drive down the long steep hill. At the bottom awaits **Mānele Bay** ⑤, with its boat harbor. Take a look at **Sweetheart Rock** and its sheer 50-ft-high cliffs. The road ends at the island's only true swimming area, **Hulopo'e Beach** ⑥ (☞ Beaches, *below*).

TIMING

Although it's a small area, south and west Lāna'i deserves a full day of exploration. If you're a fan of water sports, you'll want to spend half the day at Hulopo'e Beach and use the rest for visiting the other attractions. The south is almost always sunny, clear, and warm, so wear sunscreen and head for shade in the middle of the day.

Sights to See

④ **Halulu Heiau.** The carefully excavated remains of an impressive stone *heiau* (outdoor shrine) attest to the sacred history of this spot, which was actively used as a place of worship by the earliest residents of Lāna'i. As late as 1810, this hilltop sight was also considered a place of refuge for wayward islanders. ✉ *From Lāna'i City, follow Hwy. 440 (Mānele Rd.) south; when road makes sharp left, continue straight on Kaupili Rd., which leads you through pineapple fields; turn onto 4th dirt road in makai direction.*

⑥ **Hulopo'e Beach.** Lāna'i's only swimming beach, Hulopo'e beckons with its perennially clear waters, great snorkeling reefs, and views of spinner dolphins at play. Shady trees and grassy expanses make it a good picnic spot, and there are showers, rest rooms, and changing facilities. It's a five-minute walk from the Mānele Bay Hotel via a short path. ⊠ *From Lāna'i City, follow Hwy. 440 (Mānele Rd.) south to bottom of hill; road dead-ends at beach's parking lot.*

❶ **Kaumālapa'u Harbor.** Built in 1926 by the Hawaiian Pineapple Company (which later became Dole), this is the principal seaport for Lāna'i. The cliffs flanking the western shore are as much as 1,000 ft tall. Since Kaumālapa'u is actively used for shipping, no swimming, snorkeling, or other water activities are allowed here. ⊠ *From Lāna'i City, follow Hwy. 440 (Kaumālapa'u Hwy.) west as far as it goes; turn left and drive about 7 mi to ocean.*

❸ **Kaunolū.** Set atop the island's highest sea cliffs, Kaunolū was a fishing village in precontact times. A team from Honolulu's prestigious Bishop Museum (☞ Exploring O'ahu *in* Chapter 2) excavated the ruins of this important Hawaiian archaeological find, including terraces, stone floors, and platforms where 86 houses and 35 shelters once stood. You'll also see petroglyphs, a series of intricate rock carvings that have been preserved in tribute to the once-thriving community. Kaunolū has additional significance because Hawai'i's King Kamehameha I sometimes lived here. ⊠ *From Lāna'i City, follow Hwy. 440 (Mānele Rd.) south; when road makes sharp left, continue straight on Kaupili Rd., which leads you through pineapple fields; turn onto 4th dirt road, in makai direction.*

❷ **Lu'ahiwa Petroglyphs.** On a steep slope overlooking the Pālāwai Basin, in the flatlands of Lāna'i, are 34 boulders with ancient rock carvings inscribed on them. Drawn in a mixture of ancient and historic styles by the Hawaiians of the early 19th century, the simple stick-figure drawings represent humans, nature, and life on Lāna'i. ⊠ *From Lāna'i City, follow Hwy. 440 (Mānele Rd.) south for 1 mi until you see an unmarked dirt road that leads left through pineapple fields; at end of that road, walk up unmarked trail to petroglyphs.*

❺ **Mānele Bay.** Flanked by lava cliffs that are hundreds of feet high, Mānele Bay is the only public boat harbor on Lāna'i, and it was the location of most post-contact shipping until Kaumālapa'u Harbor was built in 1926. Today it hosts a regular influx of small boats whose owners are generally from other Neighbor Islands. The ferry to and from Maui also pulls in here. To the right of the harbor are the foundations of some old Hawaiian houses; in fact, this was the site of ancient Hawaiian villages dating back to AD 900.

Just offshore you can catch a glimpse of **Sweetheart Rock.** Called Pu'u Pehe in Hawaiian, the rock is an isolated 50-ft-high formation that carries a sad Hawaiian legend—to make a long story short, a man hid his sweetheart there, and later she drowned. ⊠ *From Lāna'i City, follow Hwy. 440 (Mānele Rd.) south to bottom of hill, and look for harbor on your left.*

North and East Lāna'i

With a ghost town and heiau to its credit, the north and east sections of Lāna'i are wild and untamed. The best way to explore the area's distinctive beauty is by hiking or four-wheel driving, since most of its attractions are accessible only by rugged dirt roads.

A Good Drive

From Lāna'i City, take Keōmuku Highway north. Turn left on the road that runs between the Kō'ele Stables and tennis courts. This leads you to a dirt road, which cuts through hay fields for a couple of miles. At the crossroad, turn right. This road heads upward through an ironwood forest and, 1½ mi beyond, to the **Garden of the Gods** ⑦. Red and black lava rocks are scattered across this unique landscape; beyond is a crystal-blue seascape.

Return to Keōmuku Highway, turn left, and drive toward the top of the hill. Make a right onto the only major dirt road in sight, and you're on your way to the **Munro Trail** ⑧, an 8-mi route that runs over the top of Lāna'ihale, the mountain that rises above Lāna'i City.

Keōmuku Highway makes its long descent down Lāna'ihale and then heads north to **Shipwreck Beach** ⑨ (☞ Beaches, *below*), an 8-mi expanse of sand where you can stretch your legs and look for glass balls (used as flotation devices for fishing nets) and other washed-up treasures.

There's more excitement if you feel adventurous. A word of caution: Do not continue unless you have a four-wheel-drive vehicle. The going is rough and often muddy.

From the end of the paved road (Keōmuku Hwy., which dead ends at Shipwreck Beach), head southeast (the opposite direction from Shipwreck Beach) along the very bumpy dirt road. Five miles later you will see dozens of tall coconut trees and an old, run-down church. This is **Keōmuku** ⑩, an abandoned town where 2,000 people once lived.

A mile and a half farther down the road, you can see the ruins of a shrine called **Kahe'a Heiau** ⑪. The road ends 3 mi later at the remnants of an old Hawaiian fishpond at **Naha** ⑫ and the often-deserted Lōpā Beach. To get back to Keōmuku Highway, retrace your route.

TIMING

Give yourself a day to tour the north and east reaches of the island. You can visit all of the following sights any day of the year, but keep your eye on the sky; it's more apt to rain in the highlands than in Lāna'i City. If you're a hiker, you'll want a day just to enjoy the splendors of Lāna'ihale. Bring a jacket; it gets cool up there. A walk along Shipwreck Beach makes a nice morning outing, with stops for shell-collecting, picture-taking, and picnicking.

Since most of the driving is on rugged roads, it takes more time to reach such places as the Garden of the Gods and Keōmuku than it does to actually experience them. Relax; on Lāna'i, getting there is half the fun.

Sights to See

❼ **Garden of the Gods.** This heavily eroded landscape is scattered with boulders of different sizes, shapes, and colors that seem to have been placed here for some divine purpose. Stop and enjoy this inspiring scenery for a while, for its lunar appearance is unmatched in Hawai'i. Anyone who's a geology buff will want to photograph the area, which presents magnificent views of the Pacific Ocean, Moloka'i, and on clear days, O'ahu. Stand quietly and you might spot a deer here. ⊠ *From Kō'ele Stables, follow dirt road that cuts through hay fields; 2 mi later, turn right at crossroads and head through ironwood forest for 1½ mi.*

⓫ **Kahe'a Heiau.** This ancient temple was once a place of worship for the people of Lāna'i. Today you must look hard to find its stone platforms and walls, for they have succumbed to an overgrowth of weeds and bushes. ⊠ *6½ mi southeast from where Keomuku Hwy. dead ends at Shipwreck Beach, on dirt road running along island's north shore.*

⓾ **Keōmuku.** During the late 19th century, this busy Lāna'i community of some 2,000 residents served as the headquarters of the Maunalei Sugar Company. When the sugar company failed, Keōmuku shut down in 1901. For a while the land was used for cattle and sheep ranching, but by 1954 the area was abandoned. You can still go into its ramshackle church, the oldest on the island. There's an eerie beauty about Keōmuku, with its once-stately homes now reduced to weed-infested ruins and crumbling stone walls. There are dozens of tall coconut trees. ⊠ *5 mi along unpaved road southeast of Shipwreck Beach.*

★ ⑧ **Munro Trail.** This 8-mi path winds through a lush tropical rain forest. It was named after George Munro, ranch manager of the Lāna'i Ranch Co., who began a reforestation program in the 1950s. Use caution if it has been raining, as the roads get very muddy.

The trail winds over the top of **Lāna'ihale.** This is the highest point of the island, at 3,370 ft. Its peak delivers spectacular views of nearly all the Hawaiian Islands. From here, you can see 2,000 ft down into Lāna'i's deepest canyon, Hauola Gulch. ⊠ *From Lodge at Kō'ele head north on Keōmuku Hwy. for about 1¼ mi, then turn right onto tree-lined dirt road; trailhead is ½ mi past cemetery on right.*

⑫ **Naha.** An ancient rock-walled fishpond can be seen clearly here at low tide, where the sandy shorelines end and the cliffs begin their rise along the south, west, and north shores of the island. Local fishermen come here to fish, but the treacherous tide and currents make this a dangerous place for swimming. ⊠ *East side of Lāna'i, at end of dirt road that runs from the end of Keomuku Hwy. along the eastern shore.*

★ ⑨ **Shipwreck Beach.** Beachcombers come for its shells and washed-up treasures, photographers love the spectacular view of Moloka'i across the channel, and walkers enjoy ambling along this broad stretch of sand—in all a beach with great allure. It's not for swimmers, however. Have a look at the tanker rusting offshore and you'll see that these are not friendly waters. ⊠ *End of Keōmuku Hwy. heading north.*

BEACHES

Only a few beaches on Lāna'i are worth seeking out, and only one of them has good swimming in protected waters. None has a phone number, so if you need more information, try **Destination Lāna'i** (⊠ Box 700, Lāna'i City 96763, ☎ 808/565–7600) or ask at your hotel desk. The beaches below are listed clockwise from the south.

Hulopo'e Beach. A sparkling crescent, this marine-life conservation area is also Lāna'i's only easily accessed white-sand beach. One of the best beaches in all of Hawai'i, it's an ideal spot for a picnic lunch, a dip in the water, and a nap under the trees. The waves are gentle enough for beginning bodysurfers, and the waters are full of fish that are easily visible to snorkelers. There are no lifeguards. ⊠ *Mānele Rd., south shore of Lāna'i, 10 mi south of Lāna'i City.*

Polihua Beach. Due to its more obscure location and frequent high winds, this beach is often deserted, except for the turtles that nest here. That makes it all the more spectacular, with its long white-sand beach and glorious views of Moloka'i. Because of strong currents, swimming is dangerous here. To find it, you need four-wheel drive—and a map. ⊠ *Northwest shore, 11 mi from Lāna'i City, past Garden of the Gods.*

Shipwreck Beach. A nice beach for walking, but not swimming, Shipwreck is an 8-mi stretch of sand on the Kalohi Channel between Lāna'i and Moloka'i. The beach has no lifeguards, no changing rooms, and no outdoor showers. ⊠ *North shore, 10 mi north of Lāna'i City at end of Keōmuku Hwy.*

DINING

Although Lāna'i's restaurant choices are limited, the menus are wide-ranging. If you dine at the Lodge at Kō'ele or Mānele Bay Hotel, you'll be treated to unique preparations of ingredients harvested or caught locally and served in upscale surroundings. Dining in Lāna'i City is a different story; its restaurants have simple fare, homey atmospheres, and nondescript service.For an explanation of price categories, *see* On the Road with Fodor's in the beginning of the book.

South and West Lāna'i

$$$–$$$$ ✕ **'Ihilani.** The Mānele Bay Hotel's specialty dining room shimmers with crystal and silver and lace-trim tables. The executive chef uses fresh local ingredients to create a cuisine called "Mediterranean French Gourmet." Menus change nightly and include such dishes as sautéed fresh-caught prawns atop local greens, and fillet of sea bass in saffron sauce. There are 14 desserts, including concoctions made from Hawai'i-grown cocoa beans. ⊠ *Mānele Bay Hotel,* ☎ *808/565–7700. Reservations essential. AE, DC, MC, V.* ☾ *No lunch.*

North and East Lāna'i

$$$–$$$$ ✕ **Formal Dining Room.** Reflecting the elegant country atmosphere of the Lodge at Kō'ele, the hotel's main restaurant has hefty wood beams, gleaming crystal, a roaring fireplace, and hand-stenciled walls. Inventive Island cuisine is created by a chef who works closely with local farmers and fishermen to keep the ingredients fresh. Try the Lāna'i venison carpaccio with shaved reggiano cheese or the smoked salmon with potato salad for an appetizer. Entrées include grilled mahimahi (dolphinfish) with rock shrimp succotash and buttermilk mashed potatoes. ⊠ *Lodge at Kō'ele,* ☎ *808/565–7300. Reservations essential. Jacket required. AE, DC, MC, V.* ☾ *No lunch.*

$$–$$$ ✕ **Henry Clay's Rotisserie.** Don't overlook this charming, popular spot at the Hotel Lāna'i. You'll find much to choose from, including Cajun-style spit-roasted meats and fish, gourmet pizzas, and salads. Chef Henry Clay Richardson calls his menu "American Country," and spices it up with such fresh local ingredients as axis deer, Hawaiian-caught seafood, and island produce. Late-night snacks are served at the bar. ⊠ *828 Lāna'i Ave.,* ☎ *808/565–7211. AE, MC, V.*

$ ✕ **Blue Ginger Cafe.** This small, no-frills eatery may look run-down, but the menu is diverse. There's even some art on the walls. At breakfast enjoy a three-egg omelet with rice or a big plate of French toast. The only bakery in town, Blue Ginger also has fresh pastries each morning. Lunchtime selections include burgers, chef's salad, pizza, and *saimin* (noodle soup). Try the stir-fry fish for dinner. There are no waiters here: You simply order at the counter and dine with mismatched silverware on Formica tables. ⊠ *409 7th Ave.,* ☎ *808/565–6363. Reservations not accepted. No credit cards.*

$ ✕ **Pele's Other Garden.** Call it a juice bar, a deli, or a pizza parlor. By any name, this white building with the blue trim adds a healthy twist to the Lanai City dining scene, with its mile-high sandwiches, vegetarian dishes, and fresh-baked pastries. The 16-inch whole wheat–crust pizza with four types of cheese, organic tomatoes, and garlic is a great reward after an arduous hike. Though it's cramped, there are two tables if you want to eat inside. It's better to have a seat on the porch or carry out. ⊠ *811 Houston St.,* ☎ *808/565–9628. Reservations not accepted. No credit cards.*

LODGING

In years past the only accommodation on the island was the no-frills Hotel Lāna'i in Lāna'i City. Today you can choose among two classy resorts, pleasant bed-and-breakfasts, and a few house rentals. Let your tastes and your budget determine which place you choose. For an explanation of price categories, *see* On the Road with Fodor's in the beginning of the book.

South and West Lāna'i

$$$$ ⊞ **Mānele Bay Hotel.** Rooms with views of Hulopo'e Bay, the coastline, and the island of Maui attract daydreamers to this elaborate beachfront property. Its design is reminiscent of traditional Hawaiian architecture, with lots of open-air lānai. Three two-story buildings overlook a courtyard; a reception building houses the lobby and specialty boutiques. ⊠ *Box 310, Lāna'i City 96763,* ☎ *808/565–7700 or 800/321–4666,* ℻ *808/565–3868. 222 rooms, 28 suites. 3 restaurants, bar, pool, spa, 18-hole golf course, 6 tennis courts, health club, shops. AE, DC, MC, V.*

North and East Lāna'i

$$$$ ⊞ **Captain's Retreat.** Single-room bookings are not available, but split between four couples, this two-story private home turns out to be a reasonably priced lodging alternative. Within walking distance of town, it's the ultimate group getaway, with 3,000 square ft, four bedrooms, a redwood deck, an outside shower, and a roomy kitchen. ⊠ *Okamoto Realty, 730 Lāna'i Ave., Lāna'i City 96763,* ☎ *808/565–7519. No credit cards.*

$$$$ ⊞ **Lodge at Kō'ele.** The feeling here—on 21 acres in the highlands on
★ the edge of Lāna'i City—is of a luxurious private mountain retreat: The temperature is cool and the pine trees are plentiful. There's a generous porch with a relaxing view; interiors have high beam ceilings, natural stone fireplaces, and island artwork. More than 1½ mi of pathways wind through the property's orchid gardens and palms. Don't be surprised to see wild turkeys strolling across the back lawn. ⊠ *Box 310, Lāna'i City 96763,* ☎ *808/565–7300 or 800/321–4666,* ℻ *808/565–3868. 92 rooms, 10 suites. 2 restaurants, bar, lobby lounge, pool, 18-hole golf course, 3 tennis courts, croquet, exercise room, horseback riding, shops. AE, DC, MC, V.*

$$$ ⊞ **Jasmine Garden.** The Hunters, who run the Dreams Come True B&B (☞ *below*), also rent out a three-bedroom house. In the older section of Lāna'i City, it sleeps six, so three couples can share it for a relatively low price. ⊠ *547 12th St., Lāna'i City 96763,* ☎ *808/565–6961,* ℻ *808/565–7056. No credit cards.*

$$–$$$ ⊞ **Hotel Lāna'i.** Built in 1923 to house visiting plantation executives, this quaint 11-room inn was once the only accommodation on the island. Today, even though two luxury hotels may tempt you, you shouldn't overlook this Lāna'i institution. The old front porch with the big wicker chairs has long been a meeting place for residents and locals, who gather to read the paper, order a drink, and "talk story" (chat). The rooms, simple with single or twin beds and flowered wallpaper, make you feel like you're in a great-aunt's country home. ⊠ *Box 520, Lāna'i City 96763,* ☎ *808/565–7211 or 800/795–7211,* ℻ *808/565–6450. 11 rooms. Restaurant. CP. AE, MC, V.*

$$ ⊞ **Blue Ginger Bed and Breakfast.** Georgia Abilay of Blue Ginger Cafe (☞ Dining, *above*) fame invites guests into her home, in a newer neighborhood of Lāna'i City. Grounds are landscaped with tropical plants and roses and room decor is modern and light-colored but not distinctive. One of the bedrooms has a double bed, the other has twin beds, and the living room's overstuffed couch converts to a bed. ⊠ *421 Lama St., Lāna'i City 96763,* ☎ *808/565–6363 or 808/565–7016. 2 rooms. Full breakfast. No credit cards.*

$$ 🖬 **Dreams Come True.** Michael and Susan Hunter's bed-and-breakfast in the heart of Lāna'i City has canopy beds, antique furnishings, and memorabilia from their many years in Asia and on Lāna'i. Fresh fruit from their own trees enhances the big morning meal. A trained massage therapist, Susan provides in-house massage for $35 an hour. Vehicle rental is available. ⊠ *547 12th St., Lāna'i City 96763,* ☎ *808/ 565–6961,* FAX *808/565–7056. 3 rooms, 2 with bath. Full breakfast. No credit cards.*

NIGHTLIFE AND THE ARTS

Locals entertain themselves by gathering on the front porch of the **Hotel Lāna'i** (☎ 808/565–7211) for drinks and conversation. Each evening the classy billiards room at the **Mānele Bay Hotel** (☎ 808/565–7700) attracts a young crowd in search of some friendly competition. The cozy cocktail lounge at the **Lodge at Kō'ele** (☎ 808/565–7300) stays open until 11 PM. The lodge also features music in its Great Hall. Entertainment is offered by Lāna'i residents who share songs, dances, and chants of the island. In addition, there are occasionally outside entertainers in the Music Room.

The 153-seat **Lāna'i Theater and Playhouse** (☎ 808/565–7500), a '30s landmark, presents first-run movies, occasional plays, and special events.

Lāna'i's **Visiting Artist Program** brings world-renowned authors and musicians to the island once a month for free, informal presentations. Past visitors have included humorist Garrison Keillor, author William Styron, and pianist Awadagin Pratt. These events take place at either the Lodge at Kō'ele or Mānele Bay Hotel.

OUTDOOR ACTIVITIES AND SPORTS

Golf

Cavendish Golf Course is a 9-hole course in the pines. Though it's free to the public, a donation for upkeep is requested. Call the Lodge at Kō'ele concierge (☎ 808/565–7300) for information and directions. Bring your own clubs.

The **Challenge at Mānele** is an 18-hole course designed by Jack Nicklaus. ⊠ *Mānele Bay Hotel,* ☎ *808/565–2222 or 800/321–4666.* 🖼 *Greens fee $125 guests of the Lodge at Kō'ele or Mānele Bay Hotel, $175 nonguests, including cart.*

Experience at Kō'ele is an 18-hole championship course designed by Greg Norman, with Ted Robinson as architect. The lodge also has an 18-hole executive putting course, free for guests but not accessible to nonguests.⊠ *Lodge at Kō'ele,* ☎ *808/565–4653.* 🖼 *Greens fee $125 guests, $175 nonguests, including cart.*

Hiking

The most popular Lāna'i hike is the **Munro Trail,** a strenuous 8-mi trek that takes about eight hours. There is an elevation gain of 1,400 ft, leading you to the lookout at Lāna'i's highest point, Lāna'ihale. No permission is necessary to hike this route.

Horseback Riding

The **Stables at Kō'ele** (☎ 808/565–4424) takes you to scenic high-country trails. They have a corral full of well-groomed horses for riders of all ages and skill levels. Rides cost $35 for one hour, $65 for two hours, and $90 for one that includes lunch. Need a lesson? This is your place.

Mountain Biking

Lāna'i City Service (☎ 808/565–7227) rents sturdy mountain bikes for $20 a day. The **Lodge at Kō'ele** (☎ 808/565–7300) rents mountain bikes only to guests of the lodge and of the Mānele Bay Hotel for $8 per hour.

Sporting Clays

Take aim on your target-shooting skills at **Lāna'i Pine Sporting Clays Range,** the only resort course of its kind in Hawai'i. The rustic 14-station course is in a pine-wooded valley overlooking the sea. A single shooter can complete the course in an hour. Cost is $125 for 100 targets and $65 for 50 targets. There's no phone at the sporting clays headquarters. Instead, you may arrange to play the course through the concierge of your hotel.

Water Sports

SCUBA DIVING

Trilogy Ocean Sports (☎ 808/667–7721) offers introductory and one-tank dives. There's a free diving session for novices at the **Mānele Bay Hotel pool**; you can book any of their offerings through the hotel concierge (☎ 808/565–7700). The intro dive costs $130; breakfast, lunch, and gear are included. The one-tank dive costs $120. Scuba diving is also available on Trilogy's daily snorkel/sail (☞ Snorkeling, *below*).

What follows are two dive sites. **Cathedrals,** off the south shore, gets its name from the numerous pinnacles that rise from depths of 60 ft to just below the water's surface. Its spacious caverns create a cathedral effect. In these beautiful chambers live friendly spotted moray eels, lobster, and ghost shrimp. **Sergeant Major Reef,** on the south shore, is made up of three parallel lava ridges, a cave, and an archway, with rippled sand valleys between the ridges. Several large schools of sergeant major fish that live here give the site its name. Depths range from 15 ft to 50 ft. Other nearby sites include Lobster Rock; Menpachi Cave; Grand Canyon; Sharkfin Rock; and Monolith, home to Stretch, a 5-ft-long moray eel.

SNORKELING

Trilogy Ocean Sports (☎ 808/667–7721) presents a daily five-hour morning snorkel/sail on a 51-ft sailing catamaran for $85. Continental breakfast, lessons, equipment, and lunch are included. You can make arrangements with the concierge at the Mānele Bay Hotel (☎ 808/565–7700). The boat leaves at 9 AM

Hulopo'e Beach is one of the most outstanding snorkeling destinations in all of Hawai'i. It attracts brilliantly colored fish to its protected cove, in which you can also marvel at underwater coral and lava formations. Ask your hotel's concierge about renting equipment.

SHOPPING

Except for the boutiques at the Lodge at Kō'ele and Mānele Bay Hotel, Lāna'i City is the island's only place to buy what you need. Its main streets, 7th and 8th avenues, have a small scattering of shops straight out of the '20s. In the most literal sense, the main businesses in town are what you would call general stores. They do offer personal service and congenial charm.

Stores open their doors Monday through Saturday between 8 and 9 and close between 5 and 6. Some shops are closed on Sunday and between noon and 1:30 on weekdays.

General Stores

You can get everything from cosmetics to canned vegetables at **Pine Isle Market** (⊠ 356 8th Ave., ☎ 808/565–6488), one of Lāna'i City's two supermarkets. It's a great place to buy fresh fish.

In 1946, Richard Tamashiro founded **Richard's Shopping Center** (⊠ 434 8th Ave., ☎ 808/565–6047), and the Tamashiro clan continues to run the place. Along with groceries, the store has a fun selection of Lāna'i T-shirts, which make great souvenirs.

You may not find everything the name implies at **International Food and Clothing Center** (⊠ 833 'Ilima Ave., ☎ 808/565–6433). However, this old-fashioned emporium, founded in 1952, does stock many items for your everyday needs.

Lāna'i City Service (⊠ 1036 Lāna'i Ave., ☎ 808/565–7227) is more than a gas station and car-rental operation. It also sells microwave pizzas and burritos, sodas, sundries, paperbacks, T-shirts, and island crafts. It even rents cellular phones.

Specialty Stores

Crafts

Akamai Trading & Gifts (⊠ 408 8th Ave., ☎ 808/565–6587) sells such unique Lāna'i crafts as pine-tree bowls and flower-dyed gourds alongside its Lāna'i posters, T-shirts, and tropical jellies and jams.

At **Heart of Lāna'i** (⊠ 363 7th Ave., ☎ 808/565–6678) you'll find local crafts like Norfolk pine bowls, fiber-woven mats, quilts, and jewelry.

Lāna'i Art Studio (⊠ 339 7th Ave., ☎ 808/565–7503) is the home of the Lāna'i Art Program, which offers art classes to residents and visitors. Its gift shop sells unique Lāna'i handicrafts, from painted silk scarves to beaded jewelry.

Hotel Shops

The **Lodge at Kō'ele** (☎ 808/565–7300) and **Mānele Bay Hotel** (☎ 808/565–7700) have sundries shops that are handy for guests who need to stock up on suntan lotion, aspirin, and other vacation necessities. They also carry classy logo wear, resort clothing, books, and jewelry.

LĀNA'I A TO Z

Arriving and Departing

By Plane

The small **Lāna'i Airport** (☎ 808/565–6757) is centrally located in the southwest area of the island. There's a gift shop, food concession, plenty of parking, and a federal agricultural inspection station so that departing guests can check luggage directly to the mainland.

In order to reach Lāna'i from the mainland United States, you must first stop at O'ahu's Honolulu International Airport; from there it takes about a half hour to fly to Lāna'i. **Hawaiian Airlines** (☎ 800/367–5320) offers two round-trip flights daily between Honolulu and Lāna'i. A round-trip on one of its DC-9 jets costs $162. **Island Air** (☎ 800/323–3345) has 12 round-trip flights daily on its 18-passenger Twin Otters and its Dornier 228s, at a cost of $164.

BETWEEN THE AIRPORT AND HOTELS

Lāna'i Airport is a 10-minute drive from Lāna'i City. If you're staying at the Hotel Lāna'i, the Lodge at Kō'ele, or the Mānele Bay Hotel, you will be met by a complimentary shuttle. Don't expect to see any public buses at the airport, because there aren't any on the island.

By Car. There is a distinct advantage to renting your own vehicle on Lāna'i: Public transportation is virtually nonexistent and attractions are far apart. Make your car- or four-wheel-drive-rental reservation way in advance of your trip, because Lāna'i is small and its fleet of vehicles limited (☞ Car and Four-Wheel-Drive Rentals, *below*).

By Taxi. Taxi transfers between Lāna'i City and the airport are handled by **Lāna'i City Service** (☎ 808/565–7227 or 800/533–7808). One-way charges are $5 per person.

Getting Around

Private transportation is advised on Lāna'i, unless you plan to stay in one place during your entire visit. Avoid that urge, because the island has natural splendors from one end to the other.

By Bike
☞ Mountain Biking *in* Outdoor Activities and Sports, *above*.

By Car
Driving around Lāna'i isn't as easy as on other islands—most roads aren't marked. But renting a car can be fun (☞ Car and Four-Wheel-Drive Rentals, *below*). From town, the streets extend outward as paved roads with two-way traffic. Keōmuku Highway runs north to Shipwreck Beach, while Highway 440 leads south down to Mānele Bay and Hulopo'e Beach and west to Kaumālapa'u Harbor. The rest of your driving takes place on bumpy and muddy dirt roads, best navigated by a four-wheel-drive vehicle or van.

The island doesn't have traffic lights, and you'll never find yourself in a traffic jam. However, heed these words of caution: before heading out on your explorations, ask at your hotel desk for a road and site map, and ask them to confirm that you're headed in the right direction. Some of the major attractions don't have signs, and it's easy to get lost.

By Moped
Lāna'i City Service (☎ 808/565–7227 or 800/533–7808) will set you up with a moped for $30 a day. Pay $5 extra and they'll give you lunch to take along on your explorations.

By Taxi
It costs about $5 per person for a cab ride from Lāna'i City to almost any point on the paved roads of the island. Call **Lāna'i City Service** (☎ 808/565–7227 or 800/533–7808).

Contacts and Resources

Car and Four-Wheel-Drive Rentals
Two companies on Lāna'i rent vehicles to visitors. **Lāna'i City Service** (✉ Box N, Lāna'i City, ☎ 808/565–7227 or 800/533–7808) is the Dollar Rent-a-Car affiliate on the island. You'll pay $60 a day for a compact car, from $129 a day for a seven-passenger minivan, and from $119 to $129 a day for a four-wheel-drive Jeep Wrangler. The company offers complimentary airport pickup and drop-off.

Red Rover (✉ Lāna'i Ave. at 15th St., Lāna'i City, ☎ 808/565–7722) specializes in Land Rovers. Their fleet ranges from a two-passenger softtop for $139 a day to a nine-person African safari vehicle for $159 a day. You get a CB radio for emergencies, and cell phones and cassette tapes are available. Snorkeling masks, fins, and boogeyboards are gratis, and a staff member will meet you at the airport with your vehicle.

Emergencies

Police, fire, or **ambulance** (☎ 911).

The **Lāna'i Community Hospital** (✉ 628 7th Ave., Lāna'i City, ☎ 808/ 565–6411) is the health-care center for the island. It has 24-hour ambulance service and a pharmacy.

Guided Tours

A trained docent from the **Nature Conservancy of Hawai'i** (☎ 808/ 537–4508) leads a free hike once a month through Kānepu'u, a 590-acre preserve northwest of Lāna'i City, on the island's western plateau. Kānepu'u contains the state's largest remnant of native dryland forest, hosting 48 plant species unique to Hawai'i, such as *'iliahi* (sandalwood). Call for reservations. You can also go on a self-guided hike here by following the interpretive signs.

For an old-fashioned way to tour the town, take a horse-drawn carriage ride around Lāna'i City courtesy of the **Stables at Kō'ele** (☎ 808/ 565–4424). A one-hour ride costs $75 for two people.

Many sites are accessible only from the island's unpaved back roads. On a tour you can leave the navigation to a driver, while you simply hang on and enjoy the ride in a Geo Tracker. Along the way you will see petroglyphs, the Garden of the Gods, Shipwreck Beach, and the Munro Trail. Tours are about five hours long, require a minimum of four people, and cost $80 per person. **Lāna'i City Service** (☎ 808/565– 7227 or 800/533–7808) offers such tours throughout the week.

Tours of the island's two major hotels are free and open to the public. **Mānele Bay Hotel** (☎ 808/565–7700) offers daily free one-hour tours of the hotels and grounds. Check with the concierge desk for a **Lodge at Kō'ele** tour (☎ 808/565–7300).

Visitor Information

You can write ahead of time to **Destination Lāna'i** (✉ Box 700, Lāna'i City 96763, ☎ 808/565–7600) for brochures and maps; the office is not open to visitors. The **Maui Visitors Bureau** (✉ 1727 Wili Pa Loop, Wailuku, Maui 96793, ☎ 808/244–3530, FAX 808/244–1337) has information about Lāna'i as well as Maui.

Once on the island, the information desks of two major hotels—the Lodge at Kō'ele and the Mānele Bay Hotel—are useful sources for guests of those properties.

8 Portraits of Hawai`i

These Volcanic Isles

The Aloha Shirt: A Colorful Swatch of Island History

Hawaiian History at a Glance: A Chronology

Books and Videos

Hawaiian Glossary

Menu Guide

THESE VOLCANIC ISLES

DAWN AT THE CRATER ON horseback. It's cold at 10,023 ft above the warm Pacific—maybe 45°. The horses' breath condenses into a smoky cloud, and the riders cling against their saddles. It's eerily quiet except for the creak of straining leather and the crunch of volcanic cinders under foot, sounds that are absurdly magnified in the vast empty space that yawns below.

This is Haleakalā, the "house of the sun." It's the crown of east Maui and the largest dormant volcano crater in the world. Every year thousands of visitors shake themselves awake at three in the morning to board vans that take them from their comfortable hotels and up the world's most steeply ascending auto route to the summit of Haleakalā National Park. Sunrise is extraordinary here, colors from the palest pink to the most fiery red slowly spread across the lip of the summit. Mark Twain called it "the sublimest spectacle" he had ever witnessed.

But sunrise is only the beginning. The park encompasses 28,665 acres, and the valley itself is 21 mi in circumference and 19 square mi in area. At its deepest, it measures 3,000 ft from the summit. The two towers of Manhattan's World Trade Center could be placed one atop the other and still not reach the top. While Haleakalā is dormant, the vast, wondrous valley here isn't a single crater created by some devastating explosion. Misnamed by the first European explorers, Haleakalā's huge depression would be more properly called an "erosional valley," the result of eons of wind and rain wearing down what was likely a small crater at the mountain's original summit. The small hills within the valley are volcanic cinder cones, each the site of an eruption.

More than anything, entering Haleakalā is like descending to the moon. Trails for hiking and horseback riding crisscross the crater for some 32 mi. The way is strewn with volcanic rubble, crater cones, frozen lava flows, vents, and lava tubes. The colors you see on your descent are muted yet dramatic—black, yellow,

russet, orange, lavender, browns, and grays, even a pinkish-blue. It seems as if nothing could live here, but in fact this is an ecosystem that sustains, among other, more humble life forms, the sure-footed mountain goat, the rare nēnē goose (no webbing between its toes, the better to negotiate this rugged terrain with), and the strange and delicate silversword. The silversword, a spiny, metallic-leafed plant, once grew abundantly on Haleakalā's slopes. Today it survives in small numbers at Haleakalā and at high elevations on the Big Island of Hawai'i. The plants live up to 20 years, bloom only once, scatter their seeds, and die.

The valley's starkness is overwhelming. Even shadows cast in the thin mountain air are flinty and spare. It's easy to understand why in the early days of this nation's space program, moon-bound astronauts trained in this desolate place.

It is also not difficult to see this place as a bubbling, sulfurous cauldron, a direct connection not to the heavens but to the core of the Earth. Haleakalā's last—and probably final—eruption occurred in 1790, a few years after a Frenchman named La Perouse became the first European to set foot on Maui. That fiery outburst was only one of many in Hawai'i over the millennia, just as Maui and its now-cold crater are just one facet of the volcanic variety of the Aloha State.

Large and small, awake or sleeping, volcanoes are Hawai'i's history and its heritage; behind their beauty is the story of the flames that created this ethereal island chain. The tale began some 25 million years ago, yet it is still unfinished.

The islands in the Hawaiian archipelago are really only the very crests of immense mountains rising from the bottom of the sea. Formed by molten rock known as magma, the islands were slowly pushed up from the Earth's volatile, uneasy mantle, forced through cracks in the thin crust that is the ocean floor. The first ancient eruptions cooled and formed pools on the Pacific bottom. Then, as more and more magma spilled from the vents over millions of years, the pools became ridges and grew into crests; the latter built upon themselves over the eons, until finally, miles high, they at last towered above the surface of the sea.

AS THE ISLANDS COOLED in the Pacific waters, the stark lava slopes slowly bloomed, over centuries, with colorful flora—exotic, jewel-like species endemic only to these islands, with their generous washings of tropical rain and abundant sunshine. Gradually, as seeds, spores, or eggs of living creatures were carried by the winds and currents to these isolated volcanic isles more than 2,000 mi from the closest continental land mass, the bare and rocky atolls became a paradise of greenery.

This type of volcano, with its slowly formed, gently sloping sides, is known as a shield volcano, and each of the Hawaiian isles is composed of them. As long as the underwater vents spew the lifeblood lava out from the Earth's core and into the heart of the mountain, a shield volcano will continue to grow.

The Hawaiian Islands rest on an area called the Pacific Plate, and this vast shelf of land is making its way slowly to the northwest, creeping perhaps 2–3 inches every year. The result is that contact between the submarine vents and the volcanoes' conduits for magma is gradually disrupted and closed off. Slowly, the mountains stop growing, one by one. Surface eruptions slow down and finally halt completely, and these volcanoes ultimately become extinct.

That, at least, is one explanation. Another—centuries older and still revered in Hawaiian art and song—centers upon Pele, the beautiful and tempestuous daughter of Haumea, the Earth Mother, and Wakea, the Sky Father. Pele is the Hawaiian goddess of fire, the maker of mountains, melter of rocks, eater of forests, and burner of land—both creator and destroyer. Legend has it that Pele came to the Islands long ago to flee from her cruel older sister, Na Maka o Kahai, goddess of the sea. Pele ran first to the small island of Ni'ihau, making a crater home there with her digging stick. But Na Maka found her and destroyed her hideaway, so Pele again had to flee. On Kaua'i she delved deeper,

but Na Maka chased her from that home as well. Pele ran on—from O'ahu to Moloka'i, Lana'i to Kaho'olawe, Molokini to Maui—but always and ever Na Maka pursued her.

Pele came at last to Halema'uma'u, the vast firepit crater of Ki'lauea, and there, on the Big Island, she dug deepest of all. There she is said to remain, all-powerful, quick to rage, and often unpredictable; the mountain is her impenetrable fortress and domain—a safe refuge, at least for a time, from Na Maka o Kahai.

Interestingly, the chronology of the old tales of Pele's flight from isle to isle closely matches the reckonings of modern volcanologists regarding the ages of the various craters. Today, the Big Island's Ki'lauea and Mauna Loa retain the closest links with the Earth's superheated core and are active and volatile, though three other volcanoes that shaped the island are not. The remainder of the Hawaiian volcanoes have been carried beyond their magma supply by the movement of the Pacific Plate. Those farthest to the northwest in the island chain are completely extinct. Those at the southeasterly end of the island chain—Haleakalā, Mauna Kea, and Hualālai—are dormant and slipping away, so that the implacable process of volcanic death has begun.

Eventually, experts say, in another age or so, the same cooling and slow demise will overtake all of the burning rocks that are the Hawaiian Islands. Eventually, the sea will claim their bodies and, to Pele's rage, Na Maka o Kahai will win in the end. Or will she? Off the Big Island of Hawai'i a new island is forming. It's still ½ mi below the water's surface. Several thousand years more will be required for it to break into the sunlight. But it already has a name: Loihi.

By far the largest island of the archipelago, the Big Island of Hawai'i rises some 13,796 ft above sea level at the summit of Mauna Kea. Mauna Loa is nearly as high at 13,667 ft. From their bases on the ocean floor, these shield volcanoes are the largest mountain masses on the planet. Geologists believe it required more than 3 million years of steady volcanic activity to raise these peaks up above the waters of the Pacific.

Mauna Loa's little sister, Ki'lauea, at about 4,077 ft, is the most active volcano in the world. Between the two of them, they have covered nearly 200,000 acres of land with their red-hot lava flows over the past 200 years or so. In the process, they have ravished trees, fields, meadows, villages, and more than a few unlucky human witnesses. For generations, Ki'lauea, in a continually eruptive state, has pushed molten lava up from the Earth's magma at 1,800°F and more. But as active as she and Mauna Loa are, their eruptions are comparatively safe and gentle, producing continuous small and especially liquid lava flows rather than dangerous bursts of fire and ash. The exceptions were two violently explosive displays during recorded history—one in 1790, the other in 1924. During these eruptions, Pele came closest to destroying the Big Island's largest city, Hilo. She also gave residents another scare as recently as 1985.

T IS AROUND THESE major volcanoes that the island's Hawai'i Volcanoes National Park was created. A sprawling natural preserve, the park attracts geology experts, volcanologists, and ordinary wide-eyed visitors from all over the world. They come for the park's unparalleled opportunity to view, up close and in person, the visual wonders of Pele's kingdom of fire and fantasy. They come to study and to improve methods for predicting the times and sites of eruptions. They have done so for a century or more.

Thomas Augustus Jaggar, the preeminent volcanologist and student of Ki'lauea, built his home on stilts wedged into cracks in the volcanic rock of the crater rim. Harvard-trained and universally respected, he was the driving force behind the establishment of the Hawaiian Volcano Observatory at Ki'lauea. When he couldn't raise research funds from donations, public and private, he raised pigs to keep the scientific work going. After his death, his wife scattered Jaggar's ashes over the great fiery abyss.

The park is on the Big Island's southeastern flank, about 30 minutes out of Hilo on the aptly named Volcano Highway. Wear sturdy walking shoes and carry a warm sweater. It can be a long hike across the lava flats to see Pele in action, and at 4,000 ft above sea level, temperatures can be brisk, however hot the volcanic activity. So much can be seen at close range along the road that circles the crater that Ki'lauea has been dubbed the "drive-in volcano."

At the park's visitor center sits a large display case. It contains dozens of lava-rock "souvenirs"—removed from Pele's grasp and then returned, accompanied by letters of apology. They are sent back by visitors who say they regret having broken the *kapu* (taboo) against removing even the smallest grain of native volcanic rock from Hawai'i. A typical letter might say: "I never thought Pele would miss just one little rock, but she did, and now I've wrecked two cars . . . I lost my job, my health is poor, and I know it's because I took this stone." The letters can be humorous, or poignant and remorseful, requesting Pele's forgiveness.

It is surprisingly safe at the crater's lip. Unlike Japan's Mount Fuji or Washington State's Mount St. Helens, Hawaii's shield volcanoes spew their lava downhill, along the sides of the mountain. Still, the clouds of sulfur gas and fumes produced during volcanic eruptions are noxious and heady and can make breathing unpleasant, if not difficult. It has been pointed out that the chemistry of volcanoes—sulfur, hydrogen, oxygen, carbon dioxide—closely resembles the chemistry of the egg.

It's an 11-mi drive around the Ki'lauea crater via the Crater Rim Road, and the trip takes about an hour. But it's better to walk a bit. There are at least eight major trails in the park, ranging from short 15-minute strolls to the three-day, 18-mi (one way) Mauna Loa Trail, which is, as you might expect, only for the seasoned hiker. A comfortable walk is Sulfur Banks, with its many vast, steaming vents creating halos of clouds around the rim of Ki'lauea. The route passes through a seemingly enchanted forest of sandalwood, flowers, and ferns.

Just ahead is the main attraction: the center of Pele's power, Halema'uma'u. This yawning pit of flame and burning rock measures some 3,000 ft wide and is a breathtaking sight. When Pele is in full fury, visitors come here in droves, on foot and by helicopter, to see her crimson expulsions coloring the dark earth and smoky sky. Recently, however, Ki'lauea's most violent activity has occurred along vents in the mountain's sides instead of at its summit crater. Known as rift zones, they are lateral conduits that often open in shield volcanoes.

KI'LAUEA HAS TWO RIFT zones, one extending from the summit crater toward the southwest, through Kau, the other to the east–northeast through Puna, past Cape Kumakahi, and into the sea. In the last two decades, repeated eruptions in the east rift zone have blocked off 12 mi of coastal road—some under more than 300 ft of rock—and have covered a total of 10,000 acres with lava. Where the flows entered the ocean, roughly 200 acres have been added to the Big Island.

Farther along the Crater Rim Road (about 4 mi from the visitor center) is the Thurston Lava Tube, an example of a strangely beautiful volcanic phenomenon common on the Islands. Lava tubes form when lava flows rapidly downhill; the sides and top of this river of molten rock cool, while the fluid center flows on. Most formations are short and shallow, but some measure 30 ft–50 ft high and hundreds of yards long. Dark, cavelike places, lava tubes are often used to store remains of the ancient Hawaiian royalty—the *ali'i.* Thurston Lava Tube sits in a beautiful prehistoric fern forest called Fern Jungle.

Throughout the park, new lava formations are continually being created. Starkly beautiful, these volcanic deposits exhibit the different types of lava produced by Hawaii's volcanoes: *'a'ā,* the dark, rough lava that solidifies as cinders of rock; and the more common *pahoehoe,* the smooth, satiny lava that forms the vast plains of black rock in ropy swirls known as lava flats, which in some areas go on for miles. Other terms that help identify what may be seen in the park include *caldera,* which are the open, bowl-like lips of a volcano summit; *ejecta,* the cinders and ash that float through the air around an eruption; and *olivine,* the semiprecious chrysolite (greenish in color) found in volcanic ash.

But it isn't all fire and flash, cinders, and devastation in this volcanic landscape. Hawai'i Volcanoes National Park is also the home of some of the most beautiful of the state's black-sand beaches; humid forest glens full of lacy butterflies and colorful birds like the dainty flycatcher, called the *'elepaio;* and exquisite grottoes sparked with bright wild orchid sprays and crashing waterfalls. Even as the lava cools, still bearing a golden, glassy skin, lush, green native ferns—the *ama'uma'u, kupukupu,* and *'ōkupukupu*—spring up in the midst of Pele's fallout, as if defying her destructiveness or simply confirming the fact that after fire, she brings life.

Some 12 centuries ago, in fact, Pele brought humans to her verdant islands: the fiery explosions that lit Ki'lauea and Mauna Loa like twin beacons in the night probably guided to Pele's side the first stout-hearted explorers to Hawai'i from the Marquesas Islands, some 2,400 mi away across the trackless, treacherous ocean.

Once summoned, they worshiped her from a discreet distance. Great numbers of religious *heiau* (temples) dot the landscapes near the many older and extinct craters scattered throughout Hawai'i, demonstrating the great reverence the native islanders have always held for Pele and her creations. But the ruins of only two heiau are to be found near the very active crater at Halema'uma'u. There, at the center of the capricious Pele's power, native Hawaiians caution one even today to "step lightly, for you are on holy ground."

For all the teeming tourism and bustle that is modern Hawai'i, no one today steps on the ground that Pele may one day claim for her own. In future ages, when mighty Ki'lauea is no more, this area will still be a volcanic isle. Beneath the blue Pacific waters, fiery magma flows, and new mountains form and grow. Just below the surface, Loihi waits.

— Gary Diedrichs

THE ALOHA SHIRT: A COLORFUL SWATCH OF ISLAND HISTORY

ELVIS PRESLEY had an entire wardrobe of them in the '60s films *Blue Hawaii* and *Paradise, Hawaiian Style*. During the '50s, entertainer Arthur Godfrey and bandleader Harry Owens often sported them on television shows. John Wayne loved to lounge around in them. Mick Jagger felt compelled to buy one on a visit to Hawai'i in the 1970s. Dustin Hoffman, Steven Spielberg, and Bill Cosby avidly collect them.

From gaudy to grand, from tawdry to tasteful, aloha shirts are Hawai'i's gift to the world of fashion. It's been more than 50 years since those riotously colored garments made their first appearance as immediately recognizable symbols of the Islands.

The roots of the aloha shirt go back to the early 1930s, when Hawai'i's garment industry was just beginning to develop its own unique style. Although locally made clothes did exist, they were almost exclusively for plantation workers, and were constructed of durable palaka or plain cotton material.

Out of this came the first stirrings of fashion: Beachboys and schoolchildren started having sport shirts made from colorful Japanese kimono fabric. The favored type of cloth was the kind used for children's kimonos—bright pink and orange floral prints for girls; masculine motifs in browns and blues for boys. In Japan, such flamboyant patterns were considered unsuitable for adult clothing, but in the Islands, such rules didn't apply, and it seemed the flashier the shirt, the better—for either sex. Thus, the aloha shirt was born.

It was easy and inexpensive in those days to have garments tailored to order; the next step was moving to mass production and marketing. In June 1935, Honolulu's best-known tailoring establishment, Musa-Shiya, advertised the availability of "Aloha shirts—well tailored, beautiful designs and radiant colors. Ready-made or made

to order . . . 95¢ and up." This is the first known printed use of the term that would soon refer to an entire industry. By the following year, several local manufacturers had begun full-scale production of "aloha wear." One of them, Ellery Chun of King-Smith, registered as local trademarks the terms "Aloha Sportswear" and "Aloha Shirt" in 1936 and 1937, respectively.

These early entrepreneurs were the first to create uniquely Hawaiian designs for fabric as well—splashy patterns that would forever symbolize the Islands. A 1939 *Honolulu Advertiser* story described them as a "delightful confusion (of) tropical fish and palm trees, Diamond Head and the Aloha Tower, surfboards and leis, ukuleles and Waikīkī beach scenes."

The aloha wear of the late 1930s was intended for—and mostly worn by—tourists, and interestingly, a great deal of it was exported to the mainland and even Europe and Australia. By the end of the decade, for example, only 5% of the output of one local firm, the Kamehameha Garment Company, was sold in Hawai'i.

World War II brought this trend to a halt, and during the postwar period, aloha wear really came into its own in Hawai'i itself. A strong push to support local industry gradually nudged Island garb into the workplace, and kamaaina began to wear the clothing that previously had been seen as attire for visitors.

In 1947, for example, male employees of the City and County of Honolulu were first allowed to wear aloha shirts "in plain shades" during the summer months. Later that year, the first observance of Aloha Week started the tradition of "bankers and bellhops . . . mix(ing) colorfully in multihued and tapa-designed Aloha shirts every day," as a local newspaper's Sunday magazine supplement noted in 1948. By the 1960s, "Aloha Friday," set aside specifically for the wearing of aloha attire, had become a tradition. In the following decade, the suit and tie practically

"The Aloha Shirt: A Colorful Swatch of Island History" first appeared in ALOHA Magazine. *Reprinted with permission of Davick Publications.*

disappeared as work attire in Hawai'i, even for executives.

Most of the Hawaiian-theme fabric used in manufacturing aloha wear was designed in the Islands, then printed on the mainland or in Japan. The glowingly vibrant rayons of the late '40s and early '50s (a period now seen as aloha wear's heyday) were at first printed on the East Coast, but manufacturers there usually required such large orders, local firms eventually found it impossible to continue using them. By 1964, 90% of Hawaiian fabric was being manufactured in Japan—a situation that still exists today.

Fashion trends usually move in cycles, and aloha wear is no exception. By the 1960s, the "chop suey print" with its "tired cliches of Diamond Head, Aloha Tower, outrigger canoes (and) stereotyped leis" was seen as corny and garish, according to an article published in the *Honolulu Star-Bulletin*. But it was just that outdated aspect that began to appeal to the younger crowd, who began searching out old-fashioned aloha shirts at the Salvation Army and Goodwill thrift stores.

These shirts were dubbed "silkies," a name by which they're still known, even though most of them were actually made of rayon.

Before long, what had been 50¢ shirts began escalating in price, and a customer who had balked at paying $5 for a shirt that someone had already worn soon found the same item selling for $10—and more. By the late 1970s, aloha wear designers were copying the prints of yesteryear for their new creations.

The days of bargain silkies are now gone. The few choice aloha shirts from decades past that still remain are offered today by specialized dealers for hundreds of dollars apiece, causing many to look back with chagrin to the time when such treasures were foolishly worn to the beach until they fell apart. The best examples of vintage aloha shirts are now rightly seen as art objects, worthy of preservation for the lovely depictions they offer of Hawai'i's colorful and unique scene.

— DeSoto Brown

HAWAIIAN HISTORY AT A GLANCE: A CHRONOLOGY

ca. AD 500 The first human beings to set foot on Hawaiian shores are Polynesians, who travel 2,000 mi in 60- to 80-ft canoes to the islands they name *Havaiki* after their legendary homeland. Researchers today believe they were originally from Southeast Asia, and that they discovered the South Pacific Islands of Tahiti and the Marquesas before ending up in Hawai'i.

ca. 1758 Kamehameha, the Hawaiian chief who unified the Islands, is born.

1778 In January, Captain James Cook, commander of the HMS *Resolution* and the consort vessel HMS *Discovery*, lands on the island of Kaua'i and "discovers" it for the Western world. He names the archipelago the Sandwich Islands after his patron, the Earl of Sandwich. In November, he returns to the Islands for the winter, anchoring at Kealakekua Bay on the Big Island.

1779 In February, Cook is killed in a battle with Hawai'i's indigenous people at Kealakekua.

1785 The isolation of the Islands ends as British, American, French, and Russian fur traders and New England whalers come to Hawai'i. Tales spread of thousands of acres of sugarcane growing wild, and farmers come in droves from the United States and Europe.

1790 Kamehameha begins his rise to power with a series of bloody battles.

1791 Kamehameha builds Pu'ukoholā *Heiau* (temple) and dedicates it by sacrificing a rival chief he has killed.

1795 Using Western arms, Kamehameha wins a decisive confrontation on O'ahu. Except for Kaua'i (which he tries to invade in 1796 and 1804), this completes his military conquest of the Islands.

1810 The chief of Kaua'i acknowledges Kamehameha's rule, giving him suzerainty over Kaua'i and Ni'ihau. Kamehameha becomes known as King Kamehameha I, and he rules the unified Kingdom of Hawai'i with an iron hand.

1819 Kamehameha I dies, and his oldest son, Liholiho, rules briefly as Kamehameha II, with Ka'ahumanu, Kamehameha I's favorite wife, as co-executive. Ka'ahumanu persuades the new king to abandon old religious taboos, including those that forbade women to eat with men or to hold positions of power. The first whaling ships land at Lahaina on Maui.

1820 By the time the first missionaries arrive from Boston, Hawai'i's social order is beginning to break down. First, Ka'ahumanu and then Kamehameha II defy *kapu* (taboo) without attracting divine retribution. Hawaiians, disillusioned with their own gods, are receptive to the ideas of Christianity. The influx of Western visitors also introduces to Hawai'i Western diseases, liquor, and what some view as moral decay.

1824 King Kamehameha II and his favorite wife die of measles during a visit to England. Honolulu missionaries gave both royals a Christian burial outside Kawaiaha'o Church, inspiring many Hawaiians to convert to the Protestant faith. The king's younger brother, Kau'ikea'ōuli, becomes King Kamehameha III, a wise and gentle sovereign who reigns for 30 years with Ka'ahumanu as regent.

1832 Ka'ahumanu is baptized and dies a few months later.

1840 The Wilkes Expedition, sponsored by the U.S. Coast and Geodetic Survey, pinpoints Pearl Harbor as a potential Naval Base.

1845 Kamehameha III and the legislature move Hawai'i's seat of government from Lahaina, on Maui, to Honolulu, on O'ahu.

1849 Kamehameha III turns Hawai'i into a constitutional monarchy, and the United States, France, and Great Britain recognize Hawai'i as an independent country.

1850 The Great Mahele, a land commission, reapportions the land to the crown, the government, chiefs, and commoners, introducing for the first time the Western principle of private ownership. Commoners are now able to buy and sell land, but this great division becomes the great dispossession: by the end of the 19th century, white men own 4 acres for every 1 owned by a native. Some of the commission's distributions continue to be disputed to this day.

1852 As Western diseases depopulate the Islands, a labor shortage occurs in the sugarcane fields. For the next nine decades, a steady stream of foreign labor pours into Hawai'i, beginning with the Chinese. The Japanese begin arriving in 1868, followed by Filipinos, Koreans, Portuguese, and Puerto Ricans.

1872 Kamehameha V, the last descendent of the king who unified the Islands, dies without heirs. A power struggle ensues between the adherents of David Kalākaua and William Lunalilo.

1873 Lunalilo is elected Hawai'i's sixth king in January. The bachelor rules only 13 months before dying of tuberculosis.

1874 Kalākaua vies for the throne with the Dowager Queen Emma, the half-Caucasian widow of Kamehameha IV. Kalākaua is elected by the Hawai'i Legislature, against protests by supporters of Queen Emma. American and British marines are called in to restore order, and Kalākaua begins his reign as the "Merrie Monarch."

1875 The United States and Hawai'i sign a treaty of reciprocity, assuring Hawai'i a duty-free market for sugar in the United States.

1882 King Kalākaua builds 'Iolani Palace, an Italian Renaissance–style structure, on the site of the previous royal palace.

1887 The reciprocity treaty of 1875 is renewed, giving the United States exclusive use of Pearl Harbor as a coaling station. Coincidentally, successful importation of Japanese laborers begins in earnest (after a false start in 1868).

1891 King Kalākaua dies and is succeeded by his sister, Queen Lili'uokalani, the last Hawaiian monarch.

1893 After a brief two-year reign, Lili'uokalani is removed from the throne by American business interests led by Lorrin A. Thurston (grandson of the missionary and newspaper founder Asa Thurston). Lili'uokalani is imprisoned in 'Iolani Palace for nearly eight months.

1894 The provisional government converts Hawai'i into a republic and proclaims Sanford Dole president.

1898 With the outbreak of the Spanish-American War, president William McKinley recognizes Hawai'i's strategic importance in the Pacific and moves to secure the Islands for the United States. On August 12, Hawai'i is officially annexed by a joint resolution of Congress.

1901   Sanford Dole is appointed first governor of the territory of Hawai'i. The first major tourist hotel, the Moana (now called the Sheraton Moana Surfrider), is built on Waikīkī Beach.

1903   James Dole (a cousin of Sanford Dole) produces nearly 2,000 cases of pineapple, marking the beginning of Hawai'i's pineapple industry. Pineapple eventually surpasses sugarcane as Hawai'i's number-one crop.

1907   Fort Shafter Base, headquarters for the U.S. Army, becomes the first permanent military post in the Islands.

1908   Dredging of the channel at Pearl Harbor begins.

1919   Pearl Harbor is formally dedicated by the U.S. Navy. Representing the Territory of Hawai'i in the U.S. House of Representatives, Prince Jonah Kūhiō Kalaniana'ole, the adopted son of Kapi'olani, the wife of Kalākaua, and with his brother one of the designated heirs to the throne of the childless Lili'uokalani, introduces the first bill proposing statehood for Hawai'i.

1927   Army lieutenants Lester Maitland and Albert Hegenberger make the first successful nonstop flight from the mainland to the Islands. Hawai'i begins to increase efforts to promote tourism, the industry that eventually dominates development of the Islands. The Matson Navigation Company builds the Royal Hawaiian Hotel as a destination for its cruise ships.

1929   Hawai'i's commercial interisland air service begins.

1936   Pan American World Airways introduces regular commercial passenger flights to Hawai'i from the mainland.

1941   At Pearl Harbor the U.S. Pacific Fleet is bombed by the Japanese, forcing U.S. entry into World War II. Nearly 4,000 men are killed in the surprise attack.

1942   James Jones, with thousands of others, trains at Schofield Barracks on O'ahu. He later writes about his experience in *From Here to Eternity*.

1959   Congress passes legislation granting Hawai'i statehood. In special elections the new state sends to the U.S. House of Representatives its first American of Japanese ancestry, Daniel Inouye, and to the U.S. Senate its first American of Chinese ancestry, Hiram Fong. Later in the year, the first Boeing 707 jets make the flight from San Francisco in a record five hours. By year's end 243,216 tourists visit Hawai'i, and tourism becomes Hawai'i's major industry.

1986   Hawai'i elects its first native Hawaiian governor, John Waihe'e.

1992   Hurricane Iniki, the most devastating hurricane to hit Hawai'i, tore through Kaua'i on September 11. The island's people, infrastructure, gardens, and tourism industry have happily all since recovered.

1993   After Native Hawaiians commemorate the 100th anniversary of the overthrow of Queen Lili'uokalani with a call for sovereignty, Congress issues an apology to the Hawaiian people for the annexation of the Islands.

BOOKS AND VIDEOS

If you like your history in novel form you'll enjoy James A. Michener's weighty *Hawaii* for its overall perspective; it's also available on audiocassette. *Hawaii: An Uncommon History,* by Edward Joesting, gives a factual behind-the-scenes look at the same events depicted in the Michener book. Captain James Cook's *A Voyage to the Pacific Ocean,* one of the first guidebooks to the Islands, contains many valid insights; *Shoal of Time,* by Gavan Daws, chronicles Hawaiian history from Cook's time to the 1960s. History also comes to life in the pages of *Travels in Hawaii,* by Robert Louis Stevenson; *Stevenson in Hawaii,* by Sister Mary Martha McGaw, tells of the traveling storyteller. *History Makers of Hawaii,* by A. Grove Day, is a biographical dictionary of people who shaped the territory from past to present. To gain familiarity with the gods and goddesses who've also had a hand in this land's development, read *Hawaiian Mythology,* by Martha Beckwith. *Hawai'i's Story by Hawai'i's Queen,* the tale of the overthow of the Hawaiian monarchy in Queen Lili'uokalani's own words, is poignant and thought-provoking.

A whole new genre of Hawaiian writing offers insights into Island lifestyles through the use of pidgin prose and local settings. Paul Wood's essays, collected in *Four Wheels, Five Corners: Facts of Life in Upcountry Maui,* convey a real sense of place. Recent novels that capture the South Seas texture include *Shark's Dialogue,* by Kiana Davenport; the book weaves together multiethnic stories, legends, and ancient beliefs, to create a mystical air. *Wild Meat and the Bully Burgers,* by Lois Ann Yamanaka, is a tale of growing up on the Big Island, told in an authentic native voice.

Those interested in the physical side of the Islands will want to pick up *A Guide to Tropical and Semitropical Flora,* by Loraine Kuck and Richard Tongg. The *Handbook of Hawaiian Fishes,* by W. A. Gosline and Vernon Brock, is great for snorkelers; *Hawaii's Birds,* by the Hawai'i Audubon Society, is perfect for birdwatchers. *Hawaiian Hiking Trails,* by Craig Chisholm, is just the guide for day hikers and backpackers. *Surfing: The Ultimate Pleasure,* by Leonard Lueras, covers everything about the sport from its early history to the music and films of its later subculture.

Preparing your palate for an upcoming visit, or have you returned from the Islands in love with haute Hawaiian cuisine? *The New Cuisine of Hawaii,* by Janice Wald Henderson, is beautifully designed and features recipes from the 12 chefs credited with defining Hawai'i Regional cuisine. Rachel Laudan's *The Foods of Paradise* describes local foods and their histories in addition to providing recipes.

For swaying musicologists, there's *Hula is Life, the Story of Maiki Aiu and Hālau Hulo o Maiki,* by Rita Aryioshi; it's the definitive book on hula's origins and development. *Hawaiian Traditions in Hawaii,* by Joan Clarke, is an illustrated book detailing ethnic celebrations in the Islands. *Nam Mamo, Hawaiian People Today,* by Jay Hartwell furnishes an interesting look at real islanders. Albert J. Schütz's souvenir-worthy paperback, *All About Hawaiian,* is a good introduction to the authentic language of the Islands and recent efforts to preserve it.

ALOHA Magazine (✉ Box 3260, Honolulu 96801, ☎ 808/593–1191), subscription $19.95 for six issues, is an attractive bimonthly magazine devoted to the 50th state. Another bimonthly is *Hawai'i Magazine* (✉ Box 420235, Palm Coast, FL 32142, ☎ 800/365–4421); subscription $17.97 for six issues.

Movie buffs will enjoy *Made in Paradise: Hollywood's Films of Hawaii and the South Seas,* by Luis Reyes; it points out movie locations and pokes gentle fun at some of the misinformation popularized by Tinseltown's version of Island life. Guided tours of Kaua'i locations used in filming are provided by **Hawai'i Movie Tours** (☎ 800/628–8432).

Most people automatically think of Elvis when the words "Hawai'i" and "movie" are mentioned in the same sentence. Elvis Presley's Hawaiian-filmed movies are *Girls! Girls! Girls!* (1962), *Paradise, Hawaiian Style* (1966), and *Blue Hawaii*

(1962), which showcases O'ahu's picturesque Hanauma Bay and Kaua'i's Coco Palms Resort, the site of Elvis' celluloid wedding.

Films such as Shirley Temple's *Curly Top* (1935); *Waikiki Wedding* (1937), with Bing Crosby; and *Gidget Goes Hawaiian* (1962) feature Hawai'i's beaches, palm trees, and hula dancers. The Islands' winter waves have taken center stage in a legion of hang-ten films of which only *North Shore* (1987) is on video.

Military-theme movies filmed in Hawai'i include *Mister Roberts* (1955), starring Henry Fonda, Jack Lemmon, and James Cagney; and *Lt. Robin Crusoe, USN* (1966), with Dick Van Dyke. Some serious military films, often dealing with WW II, with Hawaiian locales often posing as the South Pacific, include *Between Heaven and Hell* (1956) starring Robert Wagner; *The Enemy Below* (1957) with Robert Mitchum; and John Wayne's *Donovan's Reef* (1963). *Tora! Tora! Tora!* (1971) recreated the December 7, 1941 bombing of Pearl Harbor. For *Flight of the Intruder* (1991), director John Milius turned taro farms at the base of Kaua'i's Mount Wai'ale'le into the rice paddies of Southeast Asia.

Hawai'i has repeatedly doubled for other places. Kaua'i's remote valleys and waterfalls and O'ahu's Kualoa Ranch portrayed a Costa Rican dinosaur preserve in Steven Spielberg's *Jurassic Park* (1993). The opening beach scene of that movie's sequel, *The Lost World* (1997), was also filmed on Kaua'i. Spielberg was no stranger to Kaua'i though, having filmed Harrison Ford's escape via seaplane from Kaua'i's Menehune Fishpond in *Raiders of the Lost Ark* (1981). The fluted cliffs and gorges of Kaua'i's rugged Na Pali coastline play the misunderstood beast's island home in *King Kong* (1976) and a jungle dweller of another sort, *George of the Jungle* (1997), frolicked on Kaua'i. Harrison Ford returned to the island for 10 weeks during the filming of *Six Days, Seven Nights* (1998), a romantic adventure set in French Polynesia; this should be out on video by the time this book hits bookstores.

Mitzi Gaynor washed that man right out of her hair on Kaua'i's Lumaha'i Beach in *South Pacific* (1958). And the tempestuous love scene between Burt Lancaster and Deborah Kerr in *From Here to Eternity* (1954) took place on O'ahu's Halona Cove beach.

James Michener's story *Hawaii* (1967) chronicles the lives of the Islands' missionary families. *Picture Bride* (1995) tells the story of a young Japanese girl who arrives on the Islands to face harsh realities as the wife of a sugar plantation laborer she has only seen in a photograph. And in *Race the Sun* (1996), a group of Big Island high school students build a solar-powered car and go on to win an international competition.

Other movies with Hawai'i settings include *Black Widow* (1987), in which journalist Debra Winger travels to the Big Island's lava fields to prevent a murder; *Honeymoon in Vegas* (1992); *Under the Hula Moon* (1995); and *A Very Brady Sequel* (1997).

HAWAIIAN GLOSSARY

Although an understanding of Hawaiian is by no means required on a trip to the Aloha State, a *malihini*, or newcomer, will find plenty of opportunities to pick up a few of the local words and phrases. Traditional names and expressions are widely used in the Islands, thanks in part to legislation enacted in the early '90s to encourage the use of the authentically spelled Hawaiian language. Visitors are likely to read or hear at least a few words each day of their stay. Such exposure enriches a trip to Hawai'i.

With a basic understanding and some uninhibited practice, anyone can have enough command of the local tongue to ask for directions and to order from a restaurant menu. One visitor announced she would not leave until she could pronounce the name of the state fish, the *humuhumunukunukuāpua'a*. Luckily, she had scheduled a nine-day stay.

Simplifying the learning process is the fact that the Hawaiian language contains only eight consonants—H, K, L, M, N, P, W, and the silent *'okina* or glottal stop, written '—plus the five vowels. All syllables, and therefore all words, end in a vowel. Each vowel, with the exception of a few diphthongized double vowels such as *au* (pronounced "ow") or *ai* (pronounced "eye"), is pronounced separately. Thus *'Iolani* is four syllables (ee-oh-la-nee), not three (yo-la-nee). Although some Hawaiian words have only vowels, most also contain some consonants, but consonants are never doubled.

Pronunciation is simple. Pronounce *A* "ah" as father; *E* "ay" as in weigh; *I* "ee" as in marine; *O* "oh" as in no; *U* "oo" as in true.

Consonants mirror their English equivalents, with the exception of *W*. When the letter begins any syllable other than the first one in a word, it is usually pronounced as a *V*. *'Awa*, the Polynesian drink, is pronounced "ava"; *'ewa* is pronounced "eva."

Nearly all long Hawaiian words are combinations of shorter words; they are not difficult to pronounce if you segment them into shorter words. *Kalaniana'ole*, the

highway running east from Honolulu, is easily understood as *Kalani ana 'ole*. Apply the standard pronunciation rules—the stress falls on the next-to-last syllable of most two- or three-syllable Hawaiian words—and Kalaniana'ole Highway is as easy to say as Main Street.

Now about that fish. Try *humu-humu nuku-nuku āpu a'a*.

The other unusual element in Hawaiian language is the *kahakō* or macron, written as a short line (¯) placed over a vowel. Like the accent (´) in Spanish, the kahakō puts emphasis on a syllable that would normally not be stressed. The most familiar example is probably *Waikīkī*. With no macrons, the stress would fall on the middle syllable; with only one macron, on the last syllable, the stress would fall on the first and last syllables. Some words become plural with the addition of a macron, often on a syllable that would have been stressed anyway. No Hawaiian word becomes plural with the addition of an *S* since that letter does not exist in *'ōlelo Hawai'i* (which is Hawaiian for "Hawaiian language").

What follows is a glossary of some of the most commonly used Hawaiian words. Don't be afraid to give them a try. Hawaiian residents appreciate visitors who at least try to pick up the local language.

'a'ā: rough, crumbling lava, contrasting with *pāhoehoe*, which is smooth.

'ae: yes.

akamai: smart, clever, possessing savoir faire.

ala: a road, path, or trail.

ali'i: a Hawaiian chief, a member of the chiefly class.

aloha: love, affection, kindness. Also a salutation meaning both greetings and farewell.

'a'ole: no.

'auwai: a ditch.

auwē: alas, woe is me!

'ehu: a red-haired Hawaiian.

'ewa: in the direction of 'Ewa plantation, west of Honolulu.

hala: the pandanus tree, whose leaves (*lau hala*) are used to make baskets and plaited mats.

hale: a house.

hana: to work.

haole: originally a stranger or foreigner. Since the first foreigners were Caucasian, *haole* now means a Caucasian person.

hapa: a part, sometimes a half; often used as a short form of *hapa haole,* to mean a person who is part-Caucasian; thus, the name of a popular local band, whose members represent a variety of ethnicities.

hauʻoli: to rejoice. *Hauʻoli Makahiki Hou* means Happy New Year. *Hauʻoli lā hānau* means Happy Birthday.

heiau: an outdoor stone platform; an ancient Hawaiian place of worship.

holo: to run.

holoholo: to go for a walk, ride, or sail.

holokū: a long Hawaiian dress, somewhat fitted, with a yoke and a train. Influenced by European fashion, it was worn at court, and at least one local translates the word as "expensive muʻumuʻu."

holomū: a post–World War II cross between a *holokū* and a *muʻumuʻu,* less fitted than the former but less voluminous than the latter, and having no train.

honi: to kiss, a kiss. A phrase that some tourists may find useful, quoted from a popular *hula,* is *Honi Kaʻua Wikiwiki:* Kiss me quick!

hoʻomalimali: flattery, a deceptive "line," bunk, baloney, hooey.

huhū: angry.

hui: a group, club, or assembly. A church may refer to its congregation as a *hui* and a social club may be called a *hui.*

hukilau: a seine; a communal fishing party in which everyone helps to drive the fish into a huge net, pull it in, and divide the catch.

hula: the dance of Hawaiʻi.

iki: little.

ipo: sweetheart.

ka: the. This is the definite article for most singular words; for plural nouns, the definite article is usually *nā.* Since there is no S in Hawaiian, the article may be your only clue that a noun is plural.

kahuna: a priest, doctor, or other trained person of old Hawaiʻi, endowed with special professional skills that often included the gift of prophecy or other supernatural powers; plural: kāhuna.

kai: the sea, saltwater.

kalo: the taro plant from whose root poi is made.

kamaʻāina: literally, a child of the soil, it refers to people who were born in the Islands or have lived there for a long time.

kanaka: originally a man or humanity in general, it is now used to denote a male Hawaiian or part-Hawaiian, but is occasionally taken as a slur when used by non-Hawaiians. *Kanaka maoli,* originally a full-blooded Hawaiian person, is used by some native Hawaiian rights activists to embrace part-Hawaiians as well.

kāne: a man, a husband. If you see this word on a door, it's the men's room. If you see *kane* on a door, it's probably a misspelling; that is the Hawaiian name for the skin fungus, Tinea.

kapa: also called by its Tahitian name, *tapa,* a cloth made of beaten bark and usually dyed and stamped with a repeat design.

kapakahi: crooked, cockeyed, uneven. You've got your hat on *kapakahi.*

kapu: keep out, prohibited. This is the Hawaiian version of the more widely known Tongan word *tabu* (taboo).

keiki: a child; *keikikāne* is a boy, *keikiwahine* a girl.

kona: the leeward side of the Islands, the direction (south) from which the *kona* wind and *kona* rain come.

kuleana: a homestead or small plot of ground on which a family has been installed for some generations without necessarily owning it. By extension, *kuleana* is used to denote any area or department in which one has a special interest or prerogative. You'll hear it used this way: If you want to hire a surfboard, see Moki; that's his *kuleana.* And conversely: I can't help you with that; that's not my *kuleana.*

lamalama: to fish with a torch.

lānai: a porch, a balcony, an outdoor living room. Almost every house in Hawaiʻi has one. Don't confuse this two-syllable word with the three-syllable name of the island, Lānaʻi.

lani: heaven, the sky.

lau hala: the leaf of the *hala* or pandanus tree, widely used in Hawaiian handcrafts.

lei: a garland of flowers.

luna: a plantation overseer or foreman.

mahalo: thank you.

makai: toward the ocean.

malihini: a newcomer to the Islands.

mana: the spiritual power that the Hawaiian believed inhabited all things and creatures.

manuwahi: free, gratis.

mauka: toward the mountains.

mauna: mountain.

mele: a Hawaiian song or chant, often of epic proportions.

Mele Kalikimaka: Merry Christmas (a transliteration from the English phrase).

Menehune: a Hawaiian pixie. The *Menehune* were a legendary race of little people who accomplished prodigious work, such as building fish-ponds and temples in the course of a single night.

moana: the ocean.

mu'umu'u: the voluminous dress in which the missionaries enveloped Hawaiian women. Now made in bright printed cottons and silks, it is an indispensable garment in a Hawaiian woman's wardrobe. Culturally sensitive locals have embraced the Hawaiian spelling, but often shorten the spoken word to "mu'u." Most English dictionaries include the spelling *muumuu*, and that version is a part of many apparel companies' names.

nani: beautiful.

nui: big.

Pākē: Chinese. This *Pākē* carver makes beautiful things.

palapala: document, printed matter.

pali: a cliff, precipice.

pānini: prickly pear cactus.

paniolo: a Hawaiian cowboy, a rough transliteration of *español,* the language of the Islands' earliest cowboys.

pau: finished, done.

pilikia: trouble. The Hawaiian word is much more widely used here than its English equivalent.

puka: a hole.

pupule: crazy, like the celebrated Princess Pupule. This word has replaced its English equivalent in local usage.

wahine: a female, a woman, a wife, and a sign on the ladies' room door; plural: *wāhine.*

wai: fresh water, as opposed to saltwater, which is *kai.*

wikiwiki: to hurry, hurry up. (Since this is a reduplication of *wiki,* quick, neither W is pronounced as a V.)

Note: Pidgin is the unofficial language of Hawai'i. It is a creole language, with its own grammar, evolved from the mixture of English, Hawaiian, Japanese, Portuguese, and other languages spoken in 19th-century Hawai'i, and it is heard everywhere: on ranches, in warehouses, on beaches, and in the hallowed halls (and occasionally in the classrooms) of the University of Hawai'i.

MENU GUIDE

Much of the Hawaiian language encountered during a stay in the Islands will appear on restaurant menus and lists of lū'au fare. Often these menus will also include terms from Japanese, Chinese, and other cultures. Here's a quick primer.

'ahi: locally caught yellowfin tuna.

aku: skipjack, bonito tuna.

'ama'ama: mullet; it's hard to get, but tasty.

bento: a box lunch.

chicken lū'au: a stew made from chicken, taro leaves, and coconut milk.

guava: This tasty fruit is most often used in juice and in jellies. As a juice, it's pink and quenches a thirst like nothing else.

haupia: a light, gelatinlike dessert made from coconut.

imu: the underground ovens in which pigs are roasted for lū'au.

kālua: to bake underground. A *kālua* pig is the pièce de résistance of a Hawaiian feast.

kaukau: food. The word comes from Chinese, but it is widely used in the Islands.

kim chee: pickled Chinese cabbage made with garlic and hot peppers.

Kona coffee: coffee grown in the Kona district of the Big Island; prized for its rich flavor.

laulau: literally, a bundle. In everyday usage, *laulau* are morsels of pork, butterfish, or other ingredients wrapped along with young taro shoots in ti leaves for steaming.

liliko'i: (passion fruit) a tart, seedy yellow fruit that makes delicious desserts, jellies, and sherbet.

lomilomi: to rub or massage; also a massage. Lomilomi salmon is fish that has been rubbed with onions and herbs, commonly served with minced onions and tomatoes.

lū'au: a Hawaiian feast, also the leaf of the taro plant used in preparing such a feast.

lū'au leaves: cooked taro tops with a taste similar to spinach.

macadamia nuts: These little, round, buttery-tasting nuts are mostly grown on the Big Island, but are available throughout the Islands.

mahimahi: mild-flavored dolphin fish, not to be confused with the marine mammal.

mai tai: fruit punch with rum, from the Tahitian word for "good."

malasada: a Portuguese deep-fried doughnut without a hole, dipped in sugar.

manapua: dough wrapped around diced pork.

mango: a juicy sweet fruit, with a yellowish-red smooth skin and a yellow pulpy interior.

manō: shark.

niu: coconut.

'ōkolehao: a liqueur distilled from the ti root.

onaga: pink or red snapper.

ono: (n.) a long, slender mackerel-like fish; also called a wahoo.

'ono: (adj.) delicious; also hungry.

'ōpakapaka: snapper.

'opihi: a tiny shellfish, or mollusk, found on rocks; also called limpets.

papaya: This green or yellow melonlike fruit will grow on you; it's high in vitamin C and is most often eaten at breakfast with a squeeze of lemon or lime.

pāpio: a young ulua or jack fish.

pohā: Cape gooseberry. Tasting a bit like honey, the pohā berry is often used in jams and desserts.

poi: a paste made from pounded taro root, a staple of the Hawaiian diet.

poke: chopped, pickled raw fish and seafood, tossed with herbs and seasonings.

pūpū: Hawaiian hors d'oeuvre.

saimin: long thin noodles and vegetables in a thin broth, often garnished with small pieces of fish cake, scrambled egg, luncheon meat, and green onion.

sashimi: raw fish sliced thin, usually eaten with soy sauce.

sushi: a variety of raw fish, served with vinegared rice and wasabi (Japanese horseradish).

ti leaves: leaves of a member of the agave family, used to wrap food in cooking; they are removed before eating.

uku: deep-sea snapper.

ulua: a member of the jack family that also includes pompano and amberjack. Also called crevalle, jack fish, and jack crevalle and can also refer to the giant trevally.

INDEX

NOTES

NOTES

NOTES

Looking for a different kind of vacation?

Fodor's makes it easy with a full line of guidebooks to suit a variety of interests—from sports and adventure to romance to family fun.

At bookstores everywhere.
www.fodors.com

WHEREVER YOU TRAVEL, *H*ELP IS NEVER FAR AWAY.

From planning your trip to providing travel assistance along the way, American Express® Travel Service Offices are always there to help you do more.

Hawaii

OAHU

American Express Travel Service
Hilton Hawaiian Village
2005 Kalia Road
Honolulu
808-947-2607

American Express Travel Service
Hyatt Regency Waikiki
2424 Kalakaua Avenue
Honolulu
808-926-5441

American Express Travel Service
Commerce Tower, Suite 104
1440 Kapiolani Blvd.
Honolulu
808-946-7741

MAUI

American Express Travel Service
Westin Maui Hotel, Shop #101
2365 Kaanapali Pkwy
Lahaina
808-661-7155

American Express Travel Service
Ritz Carlton Kapalua
1 Ritz Carlton Drive
Lahaina
808-669-6200

American Express Travel Service
Grand Wailea Resort & Spa
3850 Wailea Alanui Drive
Wailea
808-875-4526

do more   AMERICAN EXPRESS

Travel

http://www.americanexpress.com/travel

American Express Travel Service Offices are found in central locations throughout Hawaii.